MEDIA, FEMINISM, CULTURAL STUDIES

*Genius and Loving It! Mel Brooks*
by Thomas Christie

*The Comic Art of Mel Brooks*
by Maurice Yacowar

*Marvelous Names*
by P. Adams Sitney

*The Art of Katsuhiro Otomo*
by Jeremy Mark Robinson

*Akira: The Movie and the Manga*
by Jeremy Mark Robinson

*The Art of Masamune Shirow* (3 vols)
by Jeremy Mark Robinson

*Detonation Britain: Nuclear War in the UK*
by Jeremy Mark Robinson

*Julia Kristeva: Art, Love, Melancholy, Philosophy, Semiotics*
by Kelly Ives

*Luce Irigaray: Lips, Kissing, and the Politics of Sexual Difference*
by Kelly Ives

*Helene Cixous I Love You: The* Jouissance *of Writing*
by Kelly Ives


FORTHCOMING BOOKS

*Legend of the Overfiend*
*Death Note*
*Naruto*
*Bleach*
*Vampire Knight*
*Mushishi*
*One Piece*
*Nausicaä of the Valley of the Wind*
*The Twilight Saga*
*Harry Potter*

# TSUI HARK

## THE DRAGON MASTER
## OF CHINESE CINEMA

# TSUI HARK

## THE DRAGON MASTER
## OF CHINESE CINEMA

## VOLUME 2: FROM 2001

Jeremy Mark Robinson

CRESCENT MOON

Crescent Moon Publishing
P.O. Box 1312
Maidstone, Kent
ME14 5XU, Great Britain
www.crmoon.com

First published 2025.
© Jeremy Mark Robinson 2025.

Set in Helvetica 9 on 12pt.
Designed by Radiance Graphics.

British Library Cataloguing in Publication data available for this title.

I.S.B.N.-13 9781861718778
I.S.B.N.-13 9781861711830

# CONTENTS

**PART THREE**
**TSUI HARK**
**MOVIES AS PRODUCER**

## ACKNOWLEDGEMENTS

To the authors and publishers quoted.
To the copyright holders of the illustrations.


## ABBREVIATIONS

LM *The Cinema of Tsui Hark* by Lisa Morton


## PICTURE CREDITS

Golden Harvest. Shaw Brothers. Paragon. Cinema City. Film Workshop. China Entertainment. Paka Hill. Eastern Production. Win's Entertainment. Star East. Jing Productions. Media Asia. Beijing Polyabana Publishing. United Filmmakers Organization. China Film Co-Production. Big Pictures. China Juli Entertainment Media. Distribution Workshop. Different Digital Design. Huxia Film Distribution. New Classics Pictures.

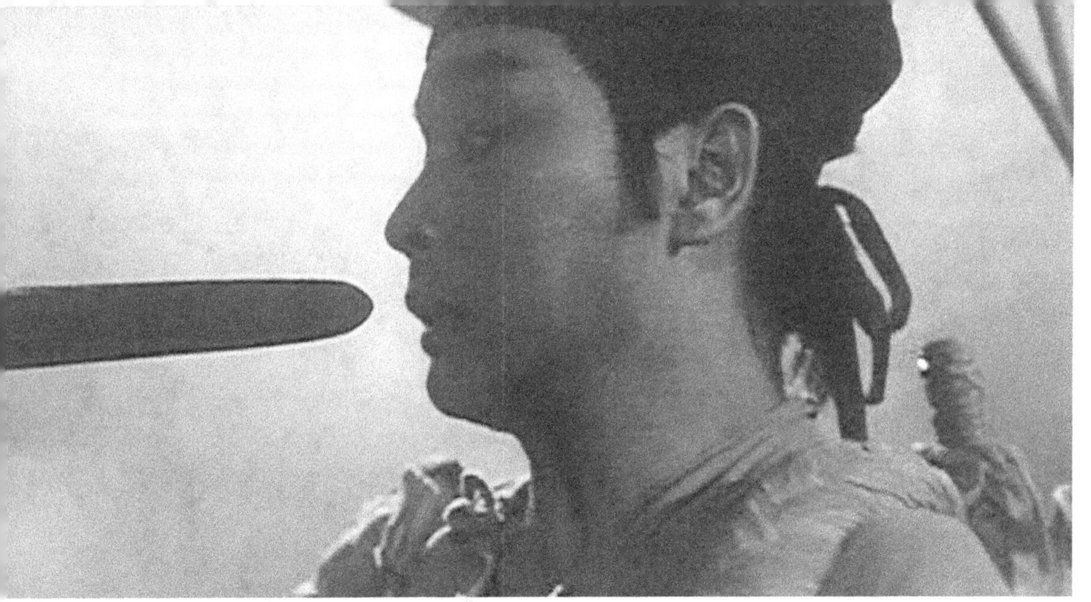

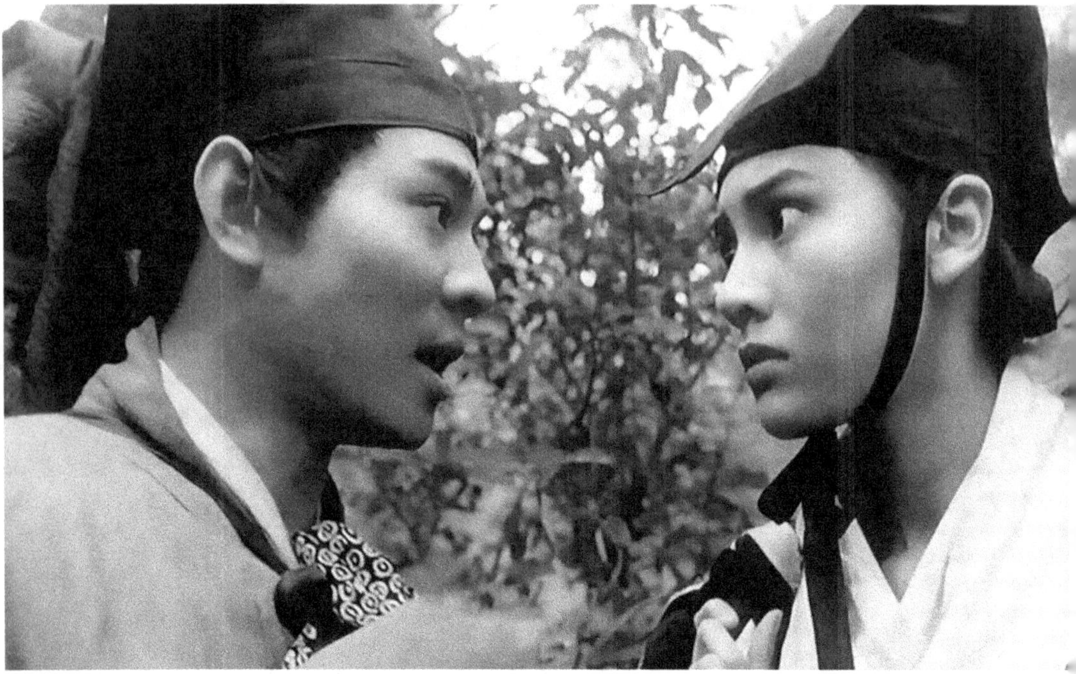

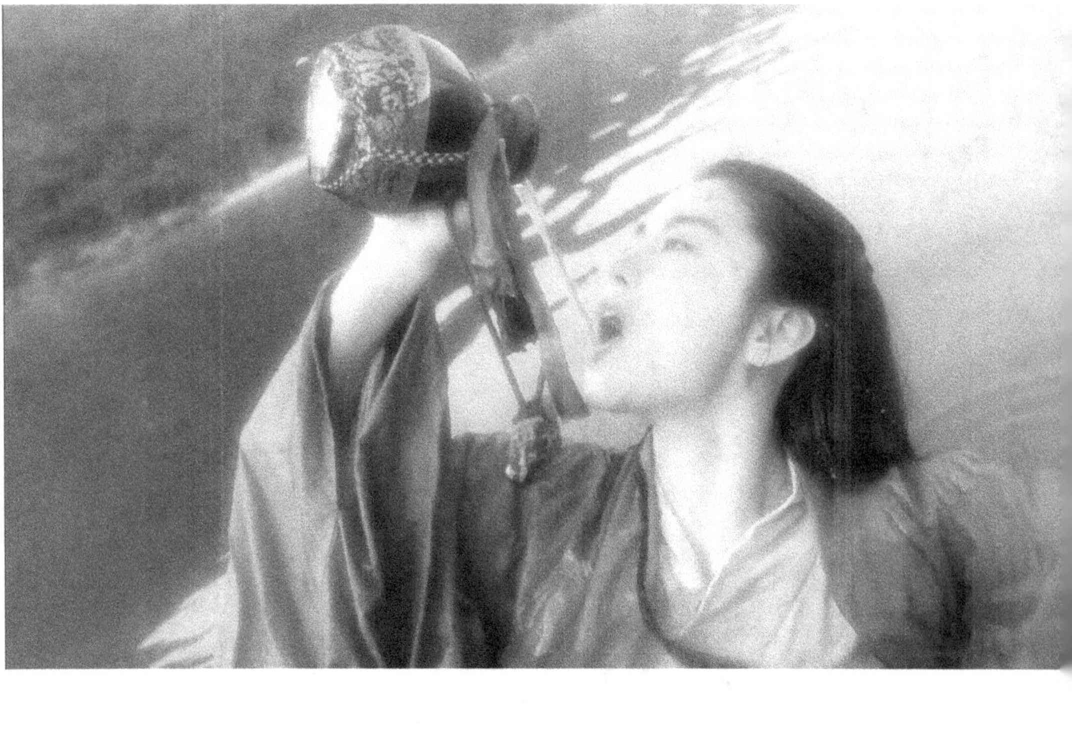

PART ONE

TSUI HARK

BIOGRAPHY

# 1

# TSUI HARK: BIOGRAPHY

Tsui Hark is the dragon master of Chinese cinema (Stephen Teo calls Tsui a 'lion dancer among film directors' [173]). Yes – a master, a lion dancer, a *sifu*, a wizard, a dragon.

Tsui Hark is a one-man film industry – as a glance as his list of credits will show, along with setting up his own film company in 1983, Film Workshop.

Tsui Hark directs movies like a force of nature. The *energy* coming off the screen is stupendous! He is a fearless filmmaker, willing to try *anything* to get a good shot. And I do mean *anything*! That feeling of fear-lessness, and wildness, coupled with imagination and technical brilliance, makes Tsui an incredibly *formidable* filmmaker. There are very few filmmakers on the scene today with those qualities in such abundance.

When you come back to a Tsui Hark picture after looking at other movies for a while, you realize, wow, this guy is *so* passionate about cinema, *so* willing to try anything, to experiment, to push the boundaries of what cinema can do, of what cinema can *be*. I've never felt, for example, that Tsui is a 'director for hire', unengaged with the material, or that he is merely punching through the shots as if he's on a factory floor.

No, this man is *on fire*.

BIOGRAPHY

Tsui Hark was born on January 2, 1951 (or February 15; some sources say 1950), in French Cochin China (Saigon, Vietnam). His name was originally Tsui Man-kong (he has also been known as Mark Yu). In Cantonese, his name is Chui Hak; in Mandarin, it's Xu Ke (Xu2 Ke4). He had sixteen siblings (from three marriages). His father was a pharmacist. Tsui changed his name from 'Tsui Man-kong' to 'Tsui Hark' because he thought it was too soft, and for his 'King Kong' nickname (1997, 136). It's pronounced 'Choy Hawk'. Tsui grew up in Saigon until the family moved to Hong Kong in 1966 (Tsui said he migrated around the age of 13, which makes it 1964; Lisa Morton says he was 14).[1]

Tsui Hark is a truly international filmmaker, as well as being a thoroughly Chinese/ Vietnamese one. After going to Hong Kong, he studied filmmaking in the U.S.A., at Southern Methodist University, Dallas in 1969 (for a year) before transferring to the University of Texas in Austin (Austin is a minor filmmaking centre in North America, with its own film culture, where filmmakers such as Richard Linklater are based). He also travelled around the U.S.A.

Tsui Hark graduated in 1975 (he studied for 2 years in Austin, where he was known as 'King Kong'). Tsui later worked in New York City: his first jobs were in television, not cinema: he gravitated from TV to film, as so many filmmakers have done (and as his fellow Hong Kong New Wave filmmakers did). His first jobs in Gotham were as a reporter for a Chinese TV cable station; he was a Chinese newspaper editor; worked with a community theatre group (New Art Drama Group); and helped to make a documentary about Chinatown (as a DP) called *From Spikes To Spindles* (Christine Choy, 1976). Tsui moved back to Hong Kong in 1976 (when he was 25).

Tsui Hark's film career got off to a roaring start with three outstanding pictures. Tsui's first theatrical movie as a director was *The Butterfly Murders* (1979), which combined martial arts, horror, sci-fi, comedy and romance. This was followed swiftly by *We're Going To Eat You* (1980) and *Dangerous Encounter of the 1st Kind* (1980) – both released in 1980.[2]

Directors often work in contrasts – if they've just done a comedy, they might fancy a drama next. Tsui Hark wanted to do something silly after his first three movies, which were 'very serious and very depressing' (LM, 47). Hence *All the Wrong Clues,* which was his first commercial hit (in 1981). And since then, Tsui had rarely let a year pass without releasing a movie as a director or producer (sometimes two! Sometimes three!). By 2014, Tsui had directed around 43 feature films.

As a producer, Tsui Hark has been responsible for masterpieces including: the *A Better Tomorrow* series, the *Chinese Ghost Story* series, the *Swordsman* series, *New Dragon Gate Inn* and *The Killer,* plus a host of hugely enjoyable films, such as: *Once Upon a Time in China 4, Once Upon*

1 Some accounts have Tsui coming to Hong Kong at the age of thirteen; others at fifteen (Tsui's year of birth is usually given as 1950 or 1951). It was in 1966 that Tsui's family moved to Canton.
2 After *We're Going To Eat You*, Tsui Hark became 'very disappointed in myself', and considered giving up filmmaking.

*a Time In China 6, Vampire Hunters, The Climbers* and *Black Mask.*

Tsui Hark is much more than a film director. Many directors do the job and go home afterwards. That's it. Some offer to produce other people's projects. Some form their own companies to develop and produce items they might direct themselves, or they might bring in colleagues they know. But only a few opt to take on numerous producing jobs, to the point where their career as a producer is as significant as their directing work. Tsui thus is not only a film director, *and* a film producer, he is also a movie mogul. (To do that amount of work, you have to *really* be committed).

In the press interviews for *Detective Dee and the Mystery of the Phantom Flame*, Tsui Hark was described by the cast and crew as brilliant, stern, tough, sweet, a free spirit, a teacher, boundlessly imaginative, and someone who lives in a different world from the rest of us.

Like many film directors, Tsui Hark has also filmed TV commercials (tho' not as many as some directors). They include *China Motion* (1998), for a telecommunications company on the Mainland (which was likened to the 1984 Apple ad); and *Singapore National Day* (1998).

Change and transformation are key elements in survival in the Hong Kong film industry, Tsui Hark asserted: if you don't change rapidly, you won't survive (LM, 22).

> For me, being commercial is very basic because you need the box office record in order to keep the investor surviving in this industry. But then, you need to be different. You need to be outstanding in terms of film. (2011)

Over the course of his film career, Tsui Hark has worked with practically every big star[3] in the Chinese film industry, as well as every action choreographer,[4] every DP and every major player in film production. (The Hong Kong film industry is small – everybody knows everybody else).

Tsui Hark's energy is legendary. Does he ever sleep? Can he survive on two or three hours sleep a night when he's shooting? (according to rumour). It does seem like that (it seems as if the last time that Tsui slept was in 1978). Tsui is one of those filmmakers who doesn't sit down on set, and is running at a high level of intensity as he's filming.

For instance, in more recent times, Tsui Hark has directed an enormous film production each year! *Detective Dee and the Mystery of the Phantom Flame* (2010), *The Flying Swords of Dragon Gate* (2011), *Young Detective Dee: Rise of the Sea Dragon* (2013) and *Taking Tiger Mountain* (2014). Plus directing other movies, such as *Catching Monkey 3-D.*

---

3 As a producer, Tsui Hark has been influential on the careers of Brigitte Lin, John Woo, Chow Yun-fat, Jet Li, Tony Ching Siu-tung, and many others. Jenny Kwok Wah-Lau noted that 'in Hong Kong, most people realize that it is Tsui Hark, the *producer* of *A Better Tomorrow,* who almost single-handedly revised and modernized the action genre and thus directly or indirectly launched the Hollywood careers of John Woo and superstars Chow Yun-Fat (through the same film) and Jet Li (through *Once Upon a Time In China,* which Tsui directed).' (in J. Geiger, 739).
4 Tsui Hark has worked with practically every celebrated action choreographer in the Hong Kong film business: Sammo Hung, Jackie Chan, Yuen Bun, Yuen Woo-ping, Tony Ching Siu-tung, Yuen Wah, Lau Kar-leung, Xiong Xin-xin, etc.

There are times in the writing of this book (starting 2013-14), that I couldn't believe just how much Tsui Hark has achieved. Even compared to other workaholic film directors and producers, Tsui stands out. He really is a one-off. (Sometimes I wonder if 'Tsui Hark' is really a conglomerate of writers, producers, directors and visual effects mavens which uses the person we know and love, Tsui Hark, as their spokesman).

Tsui Hark's films have earned numerous awards. 1992 was one of Tsui's best years for awards – 21 nominations at the Hong Kong Film Awards – for *Once Upon a Time In China 2, New Dragon Gate Inn, The Swordsman 2* and *King of Chess*.

It's usually the same movies from Tsui Hark that feature in top ten lists – *Zu: Warriors From the Magic Mountain, Once Upon a Time In China, A Better Tomorrow, The Killer,* and occasionally the early, angry films: *We're Going To Eat You* and *Dangerous Encounters of the First Kind.* Tsui Hark has 7 films in the Top 100 Hong Kong Films in *Time Out.*

Some observers reckoned that Tsui Hark's film career stalled somewhat in the late 1990s and early 2000s, and that his movies didn't seem to find an audience during that time. Tsui said, yes, he had been trying different things; but he had also been doing the same thing he always did – make movies. It's all relative, tho', and box office success doesn't always match up with critical praise, or what a filmmaker regards as his best work. We all know filmmakers who produced much better movies than the ones that made the most $$$$$. However, commercial success *is* important if you want to produce movies on an ambitious scale (which Tsui often does).

A filmmaker of Tsui Hark's astounding abilities might be expected to go to Hollywood, as some of his Chinese contemporaries have done (notably John Woo, Tony Ching Siu-tung, Jet Li and Yuen Woo-ping). Tsui could've worked in Europe or Hollywood for all of his career following the big success of *Aces Go Places*. But Tsui's career in the U.S.A. has been patchy and somewhat disappointing. For example, instead of being hired by a film studio to helm a historical epic or a contemporary fantasy blockbuster (*Memoirs of a Geisha, X-Men, The Avengers* or *Pirates of the Caribbean*, say – Tsui would be perfect for *Pirates*!),[5] Tsui was hired to direct two Jean-Claude van Damme actioners. While John Woo directed *Mission: Impossible* and *Face-Off*, and Ringo Lam Ling-tung and Ronnie Yu made *Maximum Risk* and *Replicant* (Lam) and *51st State* and *Freddy vs. Jason* (Yu), high budget action movies, Tsui helmed a couple of van Damme movies which nobody has seen (altho' Woo also directed a Muscles From Brussels picture, *Hard Target*, 1993, as did Ringo Lam – *Maximum Risk*. Everyone in Hong Kong, it seemed, worked with van Damme at one time or another).[6]

Altho' the three Hollywood pictures helmed by Tsui Hark – *Knockoff, Double Team* and *Time and Tide* – were fascinating (and *Time and Tide* was as good an action thriller as has ever been made), the first two were still

5 And he delivered his own version in the *Detective Dee* series.
6 The deal seemed to be: you can make an American production, but only if van Damme is the star.

below the potential and talents of a director like Tsui. (All three were pointedly *not* filmed in the United States of America, however, but in Europa and Asia).

The anti-American politics in some of Tsui Hark's movies may have contributed towards his lack of success in the U.S.A (LM, 14), even tho' his movies are steeped in Hollywood/ Western cinema.

Following his uneven spree in Tinseltown, Tsui Hark has remained devoted to *Chinese* subjects – nearly *all* of his movies as director and producer have had Chinese settings, Chinese stories, Chinese themes and Chinese characters.

❀

Tsui Hark has gained a reputation for arguing with his collaborators, for taking over from other directors, or for directing when he should be producing. Or for being 'difficult'. Tsui doesn't understand it himself, but there are too many stories for there to be nothing in it! (Yet when actors meet him, expecting a difficult or irritable guy, they find someone very different).

When Tsui Hark is involved in a production, whether as producer, director, writer or backer, you know it's going to be interpreted as 'a Tsui Hark movie' (the same thing happens with filmmakers such as Steven Spielberg or George Lucas – they are such big, influential names in the movie business). Tsui is like that – he's the gorilla in the room that nobody talks about.

But one look at Tsui Hark's filmography, and you see an *enormous* amount of work, containing quite a few classics, plenty of ambitious works, and also several landmark movies in Chinese film history. Any history of recent cinema will have to include an entry on Tsui.

Tsui Hark is not a martial artist, and doesn't practise martial arts. He is not, as are Steven Spielberg, John Milius, Masamune Shirow and Mamoru Oshii, a gun nut.[7] For him, martial arts and guns are part of creating a fantasy.

Stephen Teo likens Tsui Hark's role in Hong Kong cinema to the Taoist priest in *A Chinese Ghost Story*: 'although he's not the hero, the Doaist plays the role of a *deus ex machina* in putting things right and making sure that the natural order is not disturbed' (1997, 228).

That Tsui Hark is a workaholic goes without saying. Tsui could've retired ages ago, or found a much easier way of making a buck than producing movies. Everybody who works with Tsui attests to his boundless energy. On the set, Tsui seems to wear everyone out with his relentless determination to get what he's after.[8] Tsui may come over in interviews as a slim and affable Asian guy who's happy to discuss any topic, but on the set[9] he must be a tough task-master at times.

When it comes to work, Tsui Hark's philosophy is simple: *if you see an*

7 Tsui Hark doesn't know much about guns, or martial arts, and relies on other people for that. Instead, Tsui says that he's a fantasist, he imagines things that're the opposite of his real life.
8 According to rumours, actors would bring their toothbrushes and pyjamas to the studio, because sometimes filming wended on for 48 or 72 hours.
9 According to onlookers, the mood on a Tsui Hark set is pretty serious; not much goofing around, but getting on with the job.

*opportunity, take it!* It sums up Tsui's incredible drive and ambition: this is a filmmaker with a truly extraordinary level of energy.

Hong Kong filmmakers are not known for their integrity: they have to survive, so, as Tsui Hark noted, 'they will do anything' (LM, 27). So it's the worst, because the filmmakers don't have integrity, but it's also the best because they are always looking for the next thing, for change.

Tsui Hark is happy to be interviewed and there are many interviews available of Tsui. Among the pieces on video and television about Tsui (apart from the usual 'making of' pieces on home releases), I would recommend *Action et Vérité* (2006), about the production of *The Blade*, a short but illuminating interview on *The Butterfly Murders*, *The Incredibly Strange Film Show* (1988-89), and *Yang ± Yin*, a documentary on gender in Chinese cinema directed by Stanley Kwan (1997).

Among Western movies, Tsui Hark has cited Orson Welles (*Citizen Kane*), Francis Coppola, John Ford, Roman Polanski (*Macbeth*), and Frederick Wiseman. The Marx Brothers have certainly influenced Tsui's comical style – not the speedy quips of Groucho, but the surreal bickering, and the silent comedy of Harpo.

You can see Tsui Hark's influence in many places: in movies like *The Stormriders* (Andrew Lau Wai-keung, 1999), *Initial D, He's a Woman, She's a Man, Ashes of Time*, and in filmmakers such as Wong Kar-wai, John Woo, Daniel Lee, Tony Ching, Peter Chan, Andrew Lau, Ang Lee, and Wong Jing. And the many Hong Kong movies which have emulated the Tsui Hark approach are easy to spot.

The *Once Upon a Time In China* series, as Jeff Yang put it, 'single-handedly revived the *kung fu* genre,[10] re-energized the Hong Kong film industry, and launched Mainland *wushu* master Jet Li's career into superstardom throughout Asia, and eventually, the world' (2003, 97). Tsui Hark called Jet Li a 'very special person'.

To make so many movies, as producer and director, means that Tsui Hark must *really* ♥ movies and filmmaking. Hooked on it, perhaps. Obsessive, even. Tsui is simply a natural filmmaker, like Jean-Luc Godard, Ingmar Bergman and Akira Kurosawa, filmmakers who seem to be live and breathe cinema. Tsui seems happiest when he's deep into production on a wild adventure in the archaic *jiangzhu*, or exploring a little-known corner of Chinese history.

Some have dubbed Tsui Hark the 'Asian Steven Spielberg', while others have noted that Spielberg should be so lucky.[11] Because Tsui goes beyond Spielberg in some respects. But they share numerous affinities: they are film buffs, they enshrine cinema of the past, they remake and update old classics,[12] they have taken on a wide variety of genres, they prefer storytelling with music and images above all, they are workaholics, they work very fast on set, they make 'movie-movies', they are both

10 Certainly *Once Upon a Time In China* was a key movie in reviving the *kung fu* and martial arts genre – to the level of an artform.
11 Tsui has remarked: 'I don't know – it's unfair to him, I think. It's unfair to me too: he's so rich' (1997, 136).
12 Altho' Tsui Hark has gone back and remade the movies he enjoyed as a kid, he also knows that sometimes those movies one enshrined turn out to be silly and disappointing (LM, 23).

moguls with their own companies, they have worked as film producers extensively, they adore visual effects and the artificiality of cinema, and they are master showmen.

Tsui Hark is also a movie and television generation filmmaker, like the 'movie brats' of the 'New Hollywood' era, such as Steven Spielberg, Brian de Palma, George Lucas and Jonathan Kaplan. There's no doubt that, like his N. American counterparts, Tsui is also remaking and updating many of the movies and TV shows he enjoyed as a youth. There is certainly a strong baby boomer aspect to Tsui's cinema, and a postmodern reworking of earlier forms and genres.

Stephen Teo calls Tsui Hark 'Hong Kong cinema's one genuine prodigy', a filmmaker who's 'primitive, even brutish', whose movies are too fast and too cluttered for some and remain indigestible. Teo reckons that the super-fast Tsui doesn't really have a counterpart in the West.

Stephen Teo:

Tsui Hark has what Hong Kong critics call a "devil's talent" (*gui cai*), a talent so broad and brilliant that it does not seem human. He is one of the prime movers in the industry and an original New Wave director who pushes his commercial instincts to the limit. (1998, 157)

Lisa Morton summed up Tsui Hark in her 2001 study:

Tsui Hark is unique in world cinema, a prolific filmmaker (Tsui has directed, written, produced and/ or acted in more than 60 feature films since 1979) who is also a master stylist; a political auteur and a populist; an artist with an obsessive private vision who is also commercially successful; and a filmmaker who seems to revel in deconstructing genres even while celebrating their tropes. (6)

Jeff Yang described Tsui Hark as 'one of the most reliable box office breadwinners of the eighties', a conceiver of new trends, a developer of new technologies and new cinematic techniques, a filmmaker who 'has generally beaten a path for the rest of the industry to follow' (2003, 95).

THE FILM CREDITS OF TSUI HARK

MOVIES AS DIRECTOR

*The Butterfly Murders,* 1979
*We're Going To Eat You,* 1980
*Dangerous Encounters of the First Kind,* 1980
*All the Wrong Clues,* 1981
*Zu: Warriors From the Magic Mountain,* 1983

*Search For the Gods*, 1983
*Aces Go Places 3*, 1984
*Shanghai Blues*, 1984
*Working Class*, 1985
*Peking Opera Blues*, 1986
*Spirit Chaser Aisha*, 1986
*The Master*, 1989
*A Better Tomorrow 3*, 1989
*The Swordsman*, 1990
*Once Upon a Time in China*, 1991
*The Banquet*, 1991
*The Raid*, 1991
*Once Upon a Time in China 2*, 1992
*Twin Dragons*, 1992
*Once Upon a Time in China 3*, 1993
*Green Snake*, 1993
*Once Upon a Time in China 5*, 1994
*The Lovers*, 1994
*The Chinese Feast*, 1995
*Love In the Time of Twilight*, 1995
*The Blade*, 1995
*Tristar*, 1996
*Double Team*, 1997
*Knock Off*, 1998
*Time and Tide*, 2000
*The Legend of Zu*, 2001
*Black Mask 2: City of Masks*, 2002
*In the Blue*, 2005
*Seven Swords*, 2005
*Triangle*, 2007
*Missing*, 2008
*All About Women*, 2008
*Detective Dee and the Mystery of the Phantom Flame*, 2010
*The Flying Swords of Dragon Gate*, 2011
*Young Detective Dee: Rise of the Sea Dragon*, 2013
*Catching Monkey 3-D*, 2013
*The Taking of Tiger Mountain*, 2014
*Journey To the West: Conquering the Demons*, 2017
*Detective Dee and the Four Heavenly Kings*, 2018
*The Battle At Lake Changjin*, 2021
*The Battle At Lake Changjin: Water Gate Bridge*, 2022
*The Legend of the Condor Heroes: The Great Hero*, 2025

## MOVIES AS PRODUCER

*All the Wrong Spies*, 1983
*A Better Tomorrow*, 1986
*The Laser Man*, 1986
*A Chinese Ghost Story*, 1987
*A Better Tomorrow 2*, 1987
*The Big Heat*, 1988
*Gunmen*, 1988
*Diary of a Big Man*, 1988
*The King of Chess*, 1988/ 1992
*The Master*, 1989
*A Better Tomorrow 3*, 1989
*The Killer*, 1989
*Just Heroes*, 1989
*The Terracotta Warrior*, 1989
*The Swordsman*, 1990
*A Chinese Ghost Story 2*, 1990
*A Chinese Ghost Story 3*, 1991
*Once Upon a Time in China*, 1991
*New Dragon Gate Inn*, 1992
*The Swordsman 2*, 1992
*The Wicked City*, 1992
*Once Upon a Time in China 2*, 1992
*Once Upon a Time in China 3*, 1993
*Green Snake*, 1993
*The Swordsman 3: The East Is Red*, 1993
*Once Upon a Time in China 4*, 1993
*Once Upon a Time in China 5*, 1994
*The Lovers*, 1994
*Burning Paradise*, 1994
*The Chinese Feast*, 1995
*The Blade*, 1995
*Shanghai Grand*, 1996
*A Chinese Ghost Story: The Tsui Hark Animation*, 1997
*Once Upon a Time in China and America*, 1997
*Time and Tide*, 2000
*The Legend of Zu*, 2001
*Old Master Q*, 2001
*Tsui Hark's Vampire Hunters*, 2002
*Black Mask 2: City of Masks*, 2002
*Xanda*, 2004
*Seven Swords*, 2005
*The Warrior*, 2006
*Triangle*, 2007
*Missing*, 2008
*All About Women*, 2008

*Detective Dee and the Mystery of the Phantom Flame*, 2010
*The Flying Swords of Dragon Gate*, 2011
*Young Detective Dee: Rise of the Sea Dragon*, 2013
*Christmas Rose*, 2013
*The Taking of Tiger Mountain*, 2014
*Sword Master*, 2016
*The Thousand Faces of Dunjia*, 2017
*Journey To the West: Conquering the Demons*, 2017
*Detective Dee and the Four Heavenly Kings*, 2018
*The Climbers*, 2019
*The Battle At Lake Changjin*, 2021
*The Battle At Lake Changjin 2*, 2022

By any standards, that list of film credits is completely remarkable! And it's a selective list, which doesn't include everything that Tsui has done.[13] You have to add writing credits to that list, and entries in anthology films, plus several TV series, as well as plenty of acting and cameos. And design work, editing and visual effects.

Up to 2013, Tsui Hark had writing credits on 36-42 movies,[14] story credits for 10 films, director credits for 43-45 movies, producer credits for 58-62 productions, and actor credits for 26 films.

Tsui Hark has writing credits on most of the movies he's directed, and he has producer credits on most of them, too. Which means that Tsui can properly be regarded as an *auteur*. The key production credit in many respects, in relation to the cinema of Tsui (and most cinema), is *producer*, more even than director or writer. (But Tsui is also more than a producer, director and writer, he is also a movie mogul with his own production company and visual effects company).

Among the movies directed by Tsui Hark, the following are masterpieces: *Once Upon a Time In China 1*, *Once Upon a Time In China 2*, *Once Upon a Time In China 3*, *Seven Swords*, *Detective Dee and the Mystery of the Phantom Flame*, *Young Detective Dee*, *Zu: Warriors From the Magic Mountain*, *The Flying Swords of Dragon Gate*, *The Taking of Tiger Mountain*, *Shanghai Blues*, *Peking Opera Blues* and *The Swordsman*. Many other movies directed by Tsui are fantastically enjoyable cinema: *Green Snake*, *The Blade*, *The Master*, *Detective Dee and the Four Heavenly Kings*, *The Legend of Zu* and *Time and Tide*. Only one or two movies with Tsui at the helm are disappointing: *Triangle* (co-directed with To and Lam), and *All About Women*.

One striking aspect of Tsui Hark's output is that fully half or more of his movies as director and producer have been historical pictures, a much greater ratio than most other filmmakers. Tsui is a specialist in costume films, and most of his masterpieces have also been historical movies. Notice, too, that in the more recent part of his career, the 2000s and

13 *The Legend of Famen Temple* (*Fa Men Si Mi Ma*), another historical fantasy, was rumoured in 2016-2017, based on a novel by Huang Shang Jin-yu, and starring Kenny Lin, Chen Kun, Zitao Huang and Xun Shou.
14 44 films to 2016, at Internet Movie Database.

2010s, Tsui has been focussing on history – going back to the mid-20th century in the war pictures (*Tiger Mountain, Lake Changjin*) or Ancient China (*Detective Dee*). The last feature films set in the contemporary era was in 2008 (*All About Women* and *Missing*).

So for my book on Tsui Hark, which I started in 2013, I decided to work my way through as much of Tsui's work I could obtain (some of it is difficult to source). And it's taken a *long* time! Not only to see all of Tsui's films as a director, but also his films as a producer. (The movies in a series have been grouped together – the *Once Upon a Time In China* series, etc).

The production roles are important, because we know that Tsui Hark is a very hands-on producer. The role of a producer varies widely, from someone way back in a project's history who oversaw one of the numerous script rewrites to a producer who oversees every aspect of the production.

Well, we know that Tsui Hark has performed second unit direction on some movies he's produced, and also co-directed some of them. And when Tsui insists that he *didn't* direct some of the movies (such as those directed by Tony Ching Siu-tung), his influence as writer or co-writer and of course as producer can felt everywhere in those movies.

TSUI HARK AS FILM PRODUCER

The movies that were produced by Tsui Hark can be regarded as part of his *œuvre* to a greater degree than many films which other directors have acted as a producer on – because Tsui is a hands-on producer.

But what is a film producer? Critics don't really know, yet the Western/ Hollywood film industry is a producer-led, producer-based business, and in the Hong Kong industry, too, producers lead the way. Among the many functions a good film producer does is: (1) buying and developing material; (2) hiring writers; (3) putting together deals; (4) approaching investors, and finding backing/ money/ resources; (5) hiring directors and other personnel; (6) over-seeing the all-important pre-production, which includes 100s of elements; (7) casting; (8) over-seeing shooting; (9) over-seeing post-production (again, this involves 100s of ingredients); (10) music, selecting composers; and (11) publicity, marketing, advertizing.

Tsui Hark has performed all of those tasks many times, and there's no doubt that as a film producer he is right in there, selecting and developing projects, and shepherding them to pre-production (that's when a movie is really made). If he's sometimes a dictator, well, he replies, the creative process needs that.[15]

Among Tsui Hark's numerous production credits, apart from acting as the producer on the movies he's directed, are (Tsui also has writing credits on most of these movies):

---

15 Is he a dictator? Yes, he admits, 'But the creative process needs that'.

• *All the Wrong Spies* (Teddy Robin, 1983), a sequel to *All the Wrong Clues* (dir. by Tsui Hark). Written by Raymond Wong Pak-min, it starred George Lam, Teddy Robin, Paul Chun Pui, Brigitte Lin, Shing Fui-on, Joe Junior, Tsui Hark and Anders Nelsson. Tsui and his wife Nansun Shi Nansheng are credited as production designers.

• The two *A Better Tomorrow* movies[16] (1986 and 1987).

• *The Laser Man* (1986), was executive produced by Tsui Hark and Sophie Lo, written, directed and co-produced by Peter Wang, and starred Marc Hiyashi, Peter Wang, Tony Leung and Sally Yeh.

• *Gunmen* (Kirk Wong, 1988),[17] starring Tony Leung, Adam Cheng, Elvis Tsui, Waise Lee and Carrie Ng.

• *The Big Heat* (Johnny To Kei-fung & Andrew Kam, 1988), written by Gordon Chan, starring Waise Lee, Philip Kwok, Paul Chu-kong, Stuart Ong Sai Kit, Michael Chow Man Kin, Ken Boyle and Joey Wong. Tsui Hark appears in some credits as the co-director in this very troubled production.

• *Diary of a Big Man* (1988) was produced by Tsui Hark, directed by Chor Yuen, and starred Chow Yun-fat, Joey Wong, Sally Yeh, Waise Lee and Kent Cheng.

• *A Chinese Ghost Story* (Tony Ching Siu-tung, 1987), starring Leslie Cheung, Joey Wong and Wu Ma.

• *A Chinese Ghost Story 2* (Tony Ching Siu-tung, 1990) starring Leslie Cheung, Joey Wong, Michelle Reiss, Jacky Cheung and Waise Lee.

• *A Chinese Ghost Story 3* (Tony Ching Siu-tung, 1991), starring Tony Leung Chiu-wai, Joey Wong, Jacky Cheung and Nina Le Chi.

• *I Love Maria* (a.k.a. *Roboforce*, 1988), was a Hong Kong version of *RoboCop* (1987), co-produced by Tsui Hark with John Sham, directed by David Chung Chi-man,[18] starring Sally Yeh, Tsui Hark, John Sham and Tony Leung.

• *The Killer* (John Woo, 1989), starring Chow Yun-fat, Danny Lee, Shing Fui-on and Sally Yeh.

• *Deception* (a.k.a. *Web of Deception*, David Chiang, 1989), starring Brigitte Lin, Joey Wong and Pauline Wong.

• *The Terracotta Warrior* (Tony Ching Siu-tung, 1989), starring Zhang Yimou, Gong Li and Yu Rongguang.

• *Just Heroes* (a.k.a. *Tragic Heroes*, 1989) was a benefit movie for the Hong Kong directors' union. It starred a host of names, including David Chiang, Danny Lee, Chen Kuan-tai, Stephen Chow, Lo Lieh, Ti Lung, Cally Kwong, Wu Ma, Shing Fui-on, James Wong Jim, Bill Tung, Zhao Lei and Tien Niu.

• *Spy Games* (David Wu Tai-wai, 1990) was a spy movie spoof directed by Wu, who's edited many of Tsui's movies. It was written by Ng Man-fai, Philip Cheng, Lam Kee-to and Lau Tai-mok, and starred Joey Wong, Kenny Bee, Noriko Izumoto, Waise Lee and Shut Yam.

• *The Raid* (Tony Ching Siu-tung and Tsui Hark, 1991) was a 1930s

---

16 The *Better Tomorrow* movies inevitably inspired cash-ins – such as *Return To Better Tomorrow* (Wong Jing, 1994).
17 Critics have discerned the influence of Tsui Hark in *Gunmen* (which he produced), in the romantic atmosphere, and in the action.
18 Tony Ching Siu-tung was 2nd unit director.

adventure comedy co-written by Tsui Hark and Yuen Kai-chi, and starring Jacky Cheung, Dean Shek, Tony Leung, Paul Chu, Fennie Yuen and Joyce Godenzi.

• *The Swordsman* (King Hu *et al*, 1990), starring Sam Hui, Cecilia Yip, Yuen Wah, Jacky Cheung and Cheung Man.

• *The Swordsman 2* (Tony Ching Siu-tung, 1991), starring Jet Li, Brigitte Lin, Rosamund Kwan, Michelle Reiss and Fennie Yuen.

• *The Swordsman 3: The East Is Red* (Tony Ching Siu-tung & Raymond Lee, 1993), starring Brigitte Lin, Yu Rongguang, Joey Wong and Eddie Ko.

• *Dragon Inn* (a.k.a. *New Dragon Gate Inn*, Raymond Lee, 1992), starring Tony Leung, Brigitte Lin, Maggie Cheung and Donnie Yen.

• *The Wicked City* (*Yiu Sau Do Si*, dir. Peter Mak Tai-kit, 1992), a live-action version of the Japanese *animé* (1987), staring Leon Lai Ming, Jacky Cheung Hak-yow, Michelle Reiss and Tatsuya Nakadai.

• *Iron Monkey* (Yuen Woo-ping, 1993), co-written by Tsui Hark with Tang Pik-yin and Lau Tai-mok, and starring Donnie Yen, Yu Rongguang and Jean Wong.

• *The Magic Crane* (Benny Chan, 1993), co-written by Tsui Hark (with Jobic Chui Daat-Choh), and starring Anita Mui, Tony Leung Chiu-wai, Rosamund Kwan and Damian Lau.

• *Burning Paradise*, a.k.a. *Red Lotus Temple* (Ringo Lam Ling-tung, 1994), starring Willie Chi, Wong Kam-long and Carman Lee.

• *Once Upon a Time In China 4* (Yuen Bun, 1993), co-written by Tsui and Tang Pik-yin, was released only four months after the third *Once Upon a Time In China* movie, and starred Vincent Zhao, Jean Wong, Xiong Xin-xin, Max Mok and Lau Shun.

• *Shanghai Grand* (Poon Man-kit, 1996), was a period gangster tale co-written by Sandy Shaw, Matthew Chow Hoi-kwong and Poon Man-kit. It starred Andy Lau Tak-wah, Leslie Cheung and Lau Shun.

• *Black Mask* (Daniel Lee Yan-kong, 1996) was a wild superhero adventure co-written by Koan Hui-on, Teddy Chan Tak-sum and Joe Ma Wai-ho, and starring Jet Li, Karen Mok, Lau Ching-wan, Francoise Yip, Moses Chan and Anthony Wong.

• *Once Upon a Time in China and America* (Sammo Hung Kam-bo, 1997), was co-written by Roy Szeto Cheuk-hon, Shut Mei-yee, Sharon Hui Sa-long, Philip Kwok and So Man-Sing, and starred Jet Li, Rosamund Kwan, Xiong Xin-xin, Chan Kwok Pong, Richard Ng and Jeff Wolfe.

• *Old Master Q* (2001) was co-written by Tsui Hark with Roy Szeto Cheuk-hon, Herman Yau and Man Choi-lee, exec-prod. by Charles Heung and Tsui Hark, and dir. by Herman Yau.

• *Tsui Hark's Vampire Hunters* (2002) was produced and written by Tsui Hark, and dir. by Wellson Chin Sing-wai.

• *Xanda* (*Sanda*, 2004) was wr. by Kai-Cheung Chung, Derick Lau, Ask Lee, Xiao-Long Lin and Tsui Hark, exec-prod. by Satoru Iseki, Nansun Shi Nan-sheng and Le Qun Song, prod. by Tsui Hark, and directed by Marco Mak Chi-sin.

• *The Warrior* (literal title: *Wong Fei-hung: Brave Into the World*, 2006) was a Wong Fei-hung movie as an animation, directed by Tiger Fu Yin and Chen Yue-Hu and produced by Yang Yong.

• *Sword Master* (Derek Yee, 2016) was a 3-D *wuxia pian* produced by Tsui Hark and co-written by Tsui with Derek Yee and Chun Tin-nam.

Another aspect is immediately obvious: there were years when Tsui Hark was directing not one but two movies! And in some years, even more! In 1995: *The Chinese Feast, Love in the Time of Twilight* and *The Blade*! (In the North American film industry, it's typical for a film director to direct every three years).

TSUI HARK AS WRITER

Among Tsui Hark's writing for cinema credits are: *Di yu wu men, Dangerous Encounters of the First Kind, All the Wrong Clues, A Better Tomorrow 2*,[19] *Tit gaap mou dik maa lei aa, The Master, A Better Tomorrow 3: Love and Death in Saigon, A Chinese Ghost Story, A Chinese Ghost Story 3, Once Upon a Time in China, The Banquet, Twin Dragons, The Swordsman, Once Upon a Time in China 2, New Dragon Gate Inn, Once Upon a Time in China 3, The Swordsman 3: The East Is Red, Once Upon a Time in China 4, Iron Monkey, Ching Se, Yiu sau dou si, The Magic Crane, Once Upon a Time in China 5, The Chinese Feast, Love In the Time of Twilight, The Lovers, The Blade, Da san yuan, Black Mask,* the animated *Chinese Ghost Story, Time and Tide, Old Master Q, The Legend of Zu, Black Mask 2: City of Masks, The Era of Vampires, Xanda, Seven Swords, Missing, All About Women, Flying Swords of Dragon Gate, Young Detective Dee: Rise of the Sea Dragon, Sword Master, Detective Dee and the Four Heavenly Kings, The Thousand Faces of Dunjia* and the two *Battle of Lake Changjin* movies.

Tsui Hark has also worked uncredited as a writer, sometimes helping out pictures that are in trouble. For ex, Tsui contributed (along with Gordon Chan) to *Dr Wai* (Tony Ching Siu-tung, 1996), a Jet Li actioner.

Lisa Morton noted that Tsui Hark has only made one proper sci-fi movie – *I Love Maria* (a.k.a. *Roboforce*). Actually, the two *Black Mask* movies are science fiction. But Tsui has acknowledged that he hasn't done much in sci-fi – he prefers Ancient Chinese fantasy and mythology.

However, Tsui Hark has certainly directed movies which portray savage realms that come across like post-apocalyptic worlds: the brutish martial arts world (*jiangzhu*) of *The Blade*[20] and *Seven Swords* come to mind.

19 *A Better Tomorrow 2* (1987) was written and directed by John Woo, produced by Tsui Hark, with action direction by Tony Ching Siu-tung, and starred Chow Yun-fat, Dean Shek, Ti Lung, Leslie Cheung and Emily Chu.
20 Paul Fonoroff reckoned that 'if movies were judged on visuals alone, *The Blade* would certainly rank as one of the decade's most stunning motion pictures' (527).

Like other filmmakers of the Chinese New Wave cinema, Tsui Hark is a film school graduate: Ann Hui and Yim Ho studied in London; Tsui in Austin, Texas; and Ringo Lam Ling-tung in Toronto (York University). They studied in the West, or in Western-style institutions in Hong Kong. They could speak English with critics, which no doubt helped, because they'd spent time in the West. And they were familiar with the art film traditions of Europe and the U.S.A.

Following film school, they went to work in television. (Hui, Ho and Tsui were part of the first wave of the New Wave, along with Allan Fong, Patrick Tam, Kirk Wong, and Tony Ching Siu-tung); the second wave included Stanley Kwan, Alex Law, Clara Law, Jacob Cheung, Wong Kar-wai, Cheung Yuen-ting, and Eddie Fong.21

The Hong Kong New Wave did not have a unified style or an approach: it took on aspects of youth: 'school, sex, drugs and other travails of growing up in a materialistic society, misunderstood by parents and adults in authority', according to Stephen Teo (1997, 156).

Tsui Hark said that the Hong Kong New Wave wasn't really a *nouvelle vague*, like the French New Wave, and didn't have a philosophy behind it. For some critics, the New Wave of 1979 ended with the crude commercialism of comedies such as *All the Wrong Clues* (1981), directed by Tsui.

It was no surprise that many of the first films of the Hong Kong New Wave were thrillers or crime stories (including Tsui Hark's films) – because they are a staple of Hong Kong cinema, and of cinemas the world over, because they tend to be cheap to make, because the genre was versatile, and because a huge proportion of source material was in the crime or thriller genre.

For Stephen Teo, the two strands of the Hong Kong New Wave cinema – realism and genre conventions – developed towards the latter: the New Wavers started out tackling realism but leant towards genre filmmaking (1997, 149). The forms and conventions of genre were updated for modern audiences in the 1980s. (The first official, Hong Kong New Wave film was *The Extras* (1978), but the unofficial film that launched it, according to Cheuk Pak-tong, was *Jumping Ash* (1976). In 1979, some of the first New Wave films included *The Secrets* (dir. Ann Hui), *The Butterfly Murders* (dir. Tsui Hark), *The System* (dir. Peter Yung) and *Cops and Robbers* (dir. Alex Cheung)).

At the height of the 1990s New Wave, actors and crew were commonly rushing from one movie set to another. Andy Lau Tak-wah slept in his car while filming a movie a month in 1991, and according to rumour making four movies in four locations at the same time. (Chinese filmmakers became geniuses at stretching footage of actors who could only give them a day or so, by using doubles, re-arranging scripts, focussing on reaction shots, etc).

21 According to Jenny Kwok Wah-Lau, 30-40 directors made their debut films in 1979-80 (in J. Jeiger, 740).

You'll see the same actors and directors in the New Wave of Hong Kong and Chinese cinema, continuing up to the present day. The actors include: Jet Li, Jackie Chan, Brigitte Lin, Tony Leung, Leslie Cheung, Michelle Yeoh, Zhao Wei, Donnie Yen, Maggie Cheung, Jacky Cheung, Zhang Ziyi, Yuen Biao, Chow Yun-fat, Josephine Siao, Stephen Chow, Gong Li, Rosamund Kwan, Zhao Wenzhou, Kent Cheng, and Xiong Xin-xin.

And directors such as Tsui Hark, Ronny Yu, Ringo Lam Ling-tung, King Hu, Sammo Hung Kam-bo, Zhang Yimou, Ann Hui, Wong Jing, Yuen Woo-ping, Wong Kar-wai, Peter Chan, Stanley Tong, Tony Ching Siu-tung and John Woo.

## TSUI HARK AND TELEVISION

Television nurtured the New Wave filmmakers in Hong Kong – becoming something like a Shaolin Temple for *cinéastes*, as critic Law Kar put it. They worked at stations such as C.T.V. (Commercial Television), R.T.H.K. (Radio Television Hong Kong) and T.V.B.22 (Hong Kong Television Broadcast, Ltd.). Selina Chow, a TV executive, was instrumental in hiring the 'New Wave' filmmakers in television (LM, 221). They were also a film school generation: the New Wave directors studied at film schools abroad partly because they didn't really exist in Asia (the Chinese State film school, Beijing Film Academy, didn't re-open until 1978). Tsui Hark:

> I went to film school simply because I like to express my feelings on certain issues through film, which was a pretty popular medium during the 1960s. We spent a lot of time in movie theaters. At that time I was already thinking how to make Chinese cinema more interesting.

Tsui Hark first worked in television in the late 1970s; his first TV shows were *Golden Dagger Romance* (1978), made for C.T.V., adapted from a novel by Gu Long (during Tsui's 6 months there) and *Aries, Scorpio, Aquarius* (T.V.B., 1978). Tsui was also one of five directors (Ringo Lam Ling-tung was another) of *The Family* (1978, at T.V.B.), a 104-episode soap opera ('people die, get rich, get divorced', as Tsui summed it up [1997, 133]). Tsui came back to television several times – for the *Wong Fei-hung* and *Seven Swordsmen* TV series, for example.

For Stephen Teo, Tsui Hark's cinema is a vivid embodiment of the maturation of the New Wave, and the postmodernism of commercial cinema:

> Using Tsui as a yardstick, the postmodern phenomena grew from a ragbag of causes and effects: new wave æsthetics mixed with Cinema City-style slapstick, anxiety over 1997 and the China

22 T.V.B. was the television arm of Shaws.

syndrome, the assertion of Hong Kong's own identity as different from China, and a new sexual awakening arising from an increasing awareness of women's human rights and the decriminalisation of homosexuality. (1997, 246)

## CINEMA CITY

Tsui Hark was part of the group of filmmakers at Cinema City (from 1981). A new studio, Cinema City wasn't independent – it was owned by Golden Princess. It had been founded by Raymond Wong Pak-min, Karl Maka (b. 1944) and Dean Shek in 1979 (as the Fun Dao Film Company). The so-called 'Gang of Seven' at Cinema City were Tsui, Maka, Wong, Shek, Teddy Robin Kwan, Eric Tsang and Tsui's wife Nansun Shi Nan-sheng. As Tsui recalled, they would consider everything, go thru scripts at length and discuss them.

*All the Wrong Clues... For the Right Solution* (1981) was Tsui Hark's first Cinema City production: it was produced by Karl Maka and Dean Shek, written by Roy Szeto Cheuk-hon (a regular collaborator with Tsui) and Raymond Wong Pak-min, and starred George Lam, Teddy Robin Kwan, Maka and Wong Tso-sze (for some critics, this movie announced the end of the Hong Kong New Wave).

*Aces Go Places 3* (a.k.a. *Mad Mission 3*, 1984) was another installment in the successful *Aces Go Places* franchise from Cinema City (the earlier films were released in 1982 and 1983. The movies were the top films of each year (the first *Aces Go Places* grossed HK $26 million[23] when ticket prices were HK $15 (= U.S. $1.95).) It was produced and written by Raymond Wong Pak-min, and starred Sam Hui, Karl Maka and Sylvia Chang. According to Stephen Teo, 'Tsui's own dynamic style of filmmaking initiated a level of structural experimentation which was to be highly influential' (153).

The 'Cinema City style' emphasized comedy above all, stunts, visual effects, big budgets, and movies constructed by a creative team. For a period in the 1980s, Cinema City cornered the market for theatrical comedies. About 17% of films were comedies between 1985 and 1997 in Hong Kong.

---

23 There are typically 7.75 Hong Kong dollars to the U.S.A. dollar. (So when a movie makes HK $30 million in theatrical release in Hong Kong, that equals US $3.87 million).

In 1984 Tsui Hark founded Film Workshop with his wife, Nansun Shi Nan-sheng (he had decided to create a company during post-production of *Zu: Warriors From the Magic Mountain*; it was partly because Cinema City were only interested in making comedies). Film Workshop is based in Kowloon Bay.

Terence Chang[24] worked as general manager at Film Workshop in the 1980s (at Nansun Shi Nan-sheng's invitation). Following Tsui Hark's dispute with John Woo over *The Killer* and *A Better Tomorrow 3*,[25] Chang left with Woo. Chang described his time at Film Workshop thus:

> The first year was really exciting. The company was new, vibrant, and a lot of great films came from that time. Tsui Hark was very idealistic. He wanted to round up the best directors in Hong Kong and put them under one roof. He wanted to create an environment where all the directors, under his leadership, could be given the opportunity and nourishment to make artistic, yet commercial pictures.

The productions of Film Workshop include: *Shanghai Blues* (1984), *The Master* (1989), *King of Chess* (1992), *The Swordsman 2* (1992), *Wicked City* (1992), *New Dragon Gate Inn* (1992), *Once Upon a Time in China 2* (1992), *The East Is Red* (1993), *The Magic Crane* (1993), *Iron Monkey* (1993), *Once Upon a Time in China 3* (1993), *Once Upon a Time in China 4* (1993), *Green Snake* (1993), *A Chinese Ghost Story: The Tsui Hark Animation* (1997), *Knockoff* (1998), *Time and Tide* (2000), *The Era of Vampires* (2002), *Xanda* (2004), *Seven Swords* (2005), *Triangle* (2007), *All About Women* (2008) and the *Detective Dee* movies.

Tsui Hark has worked with Golden Harvest for much of his career; they have enjoyed many successes. However, they have also fallen out – over the release of *Zu: Warriors From the Magic Mountain*, for instance. And in the late 1990s, Golden Harvest sued Tsui for over-runs on 8 films (and Tsui's lawyers responded with a counter-suit for revenue from the *Once Upon a Time In China* pictures).

---

24 John Woo's regular producer, Terence Chang (b. 1949), had studied in New York and Oregon before working at Golden Harvest and in TV before joining Film Workshop. Chang also worked at D. & B.
25 He rushed his own sequel to *A Better Tomorrow* into theatres, for instance (which he had co-produced), to beat John Woo's sequel (altho' Woo doesn't like doing sequels).

## SOME GREAT MOMENTS IN TSUI HARK'S WORK

- Avoiding the cannibals in *We're Going To Eat You*
- The finale of *Zu*
- Meeting under the bridge in *Shanghai Blues*
- Backstage in *Peking Opera Blues*
- Chow Yun-fat versus the tank in *A Better Tomorrow 3*
- Maggie Cheung in *New Dragon Gate Inn*
- The first act of *Once Upon a Time In China*
- The ladders duel in *Once Upon a Time In China*
- Leslie Cheung in the haunted inn in *A Chinese Ghost Story*
- Wu Ma's Taoist dance in *A Chinese Ghost Story*
- Jet Li versus Donnie Yen in *Once Upon a Time In China 2*
- The Lion Dance competition in *Once Upon a Time In China 3*
- Jet Li in a clinch with Brigitte Lin in *The Swordsman 2*
- The watery finale of *Green Snake*
- The musical/ romantic montage in *The Lovers*
- The final duel in *The Blade*
- The motorcycle chase in *Black Mask*
- The market chase in *Knock-Off*
- The apartment fire-fight in *Time and Tide*
- The arrival of the warriors in *Seven Swords*
- Jet Li vs. Gordon Liu in *Flying Swords of Dragon Gate*
- Andy Lau and Jinger in *Detective Dee*
- The sea monster in *Young Detective Dee*
- The snow tiger scene in *The Taking of Tiger Mountain*
- The Battle of the Buddhas in *Journey To the West*
- The monster battle in *Detective Dee 3*

Tsui Hark on the sets of the Detective Dee films.

# 2

# TSUI HARK:
# ASPECTS OF HIS CINEMA

FAST FILMS.

This man is *fast*!

Not only does Tsui Hark produce and direct more movies than five filmmakers put together, his movies zip along at a cracking pace. 'Tsui's films move with such breakneck speed that one is hard put to find a Western equivalent,' noted Stephen Teo (153). He can't slow down.[1]

Tsui Hark should offer a competition to movie fans: a $10,000 prize to anyone who can come up with a camera angle [2] he hasn't used in a movie.

One of the great pleasures of Tsui Hark's cinema is the length of his movies. So many filmmakers are tempted into out-staying their welcome, into lingering over scenes, often because they actually don't have much of a story to tell, or their stories simply aren't that compelling in the end.

The typical Tsui Hark movie comes in at 80-90 minutes, a perfect and satisfying length for a picture (filmmakers such as Jean-Luc Godard, Woody Allen and Ingmar Bergman also thankfully keep to that sort of running time). Why carry on into 110, 120 or 140 minutes, when you've said everything you wanna say, done everything you wanna do, and told the story you wanna tell?

❃

A master showman, the two most entertaining segments of a Tsui Hark movie tend to be the opening act and the final act.[3] The first acts tend to be incredibly busy, as the filmmakers cram in everything they can think of – not only to set-up the rest of the movie, but to evoke a huge world (and to dare the audience to be bored). The first acts seem to acknowledge that the audience, if it's watching this movie in a theatre, has just walked in off the streets of Hong Kong which, as we know, can be crazy, busy and loud.

And the final acts are among the greatest finales in movies of recent

1 Grady Hendrix noted in 2013: 'All of his collaborators over the years feel that his movies would be better if he focused on fully expressing one idea rather than several, but Tsui doesn't have the time. He's saving China from extinction and if he has a thousand ideas in the three months when he's making a movie, then that movie will contain a thousand ideas.'
2 Tho' Tsui Hark is fond of high angle shots, but he doesn't film them himself – he has a fear of heights.
3 George Lucas often spoke of the importance of a good beginning and ending.

times. Make the opening and the ending special, they say, and the cinema of Tsui Hark certainly does that. At least half of the final act is filled with action, usually comprising several action sequences which run together. And Tsui Hark's movies also know that their audiences are busy people, and they haven't got time to hang about after the plots have been resolved. Thus, the *dénouements* are mercilessly (and quite correctly) short.

SCRIPTS AND ACTS.

As to the issue of who originates the idea for the movies he produces and directs, Tsui Hark is a little ambiguous: he says that most of the ideas come from him first, then he starts to gather the people together to produce the movie (which is what a film producer does). But just who writes the script, and who is originating most of the ideas is a bit vague (LM, 27). However, rewriting scripts is pretty much mandatory: you 'rewrite it and rewrite it and rewrite it' (ibid.). Finding a script that's ready to shoot without requiring rewriting hasn't happened yet for Tsui.4 Of his relationship with writers, Tsui remarked: 'My common experience is to fight with [writers] all the time. As a result some people think I'm very demanding'.

In 2011, Tsui Hark said (in *Twitch*):

The best thing actually to do is write according to what you feel. If you feel your heart would take you to the point where you would want to express something to do with the story or the film. Sometimes it's not the story; sometimes it's the way you tell the story. Sometimes it's the attitude you have with the story. The attitude is something you build and you accumulate for a long time for no reason and no logic, it's there. When you write that way, you might want to make it that way.

For Jean-Luc Godard, having a good script and a good subject were not the same thing. Having a *subject*, 'a meaning, a belief in something' was more important than having a good script or story. 'A pretty woman is not a subject', Godard asserted (1998, 177). North American cinema tended to have 'no subject, only a story'. For Godard, it's a 'good script when you know the subject and try to [explore] it' (ibid.). And a beginning, middle and an end, as Godard famously observed once (to Claude Lelouch in 1965), 'but not necessarily in that order'.

In her excellent study of Tsui Hark's cinema, Lisa Morton asserts that Tsui doesn't use conventional structures (of acts, or three-act models) for his movies. Actually, yes, he does. Right down the line. In fact, not only Tsui's movies, but almost all Hong Kong movies employ conventional narrative structures. (However, the way that Tsui tells stories is quirky, and it's that which makes his pictures look as if they avoid narrative conventions).

Instead of the three-act model, a better way of thinking of acts in film scripts, however, is to see them as 25-30 minutes narrative units

4 As to storyboarding, Tsui Hark said that he uses animatics now, and used to storyboard a lot for a while, until it became restricting.

(following Kristin Thompson in *Storytelling In the New Hollywood*). Thus, a two-hour movie will have *four*, not *three* acts. However, in Hong Kong, the industry usually releases films of 85-90 minutes, so that, yes, they are three-act movies. (And thus, for the action movies of Hong Kong, the *second act* is the big challenge – because any decent action movie can deliver a couple of great action scenes in the first act, and a Big Finale for the third act. But coming up with something in the middle which keeps the movie (and the audience) afloat is trickier).

For Tsui Hark, it's not necessarily the era or other elements that attracts him to a project, it's the characters (LM, 24). This is certainly true of movies such as the *Swordsman* series, the *Detective Dee* films, and of course the *Wong Fei-hung* series.

Grady Hendrix noted in 2013:

> Tsui's characters are neither here nor there, subject to sudden, traumatic changes in status and identity. Demons become human, men become women, swordsmen become monks, criminals become heroes, and heroes become villains. Shape-shifting aliens become bangable pinball machines, robots turn into sexy sirens, human bodies are pulled apart, hung from hooks, deflated, de-faced, skinned alive, castrated, amputated, and exploded. Twins and endlessly replicating time travelers proliferate exponentially.

Tsui Hark has taken up Chinese folktales and fables and classic stories many times as sources for his films, with movies such as *Zu: Warriors From the Magic Mountain*, *Seven Swords*, *Green Snake*, *A Chinese Ghost Story*, *The Swordsman*, *Detective Dee* and the *Once Upon a Time In China* series. In fact, Tsui is extremely fond of exploiting ancient and mediæval fables and tales (and not simply, as with the Walt Disney corporation, because they are well out of copyright!). The ancient and Middle Ages tales offer Tsui a framework that are well-known and familiar to audiences, which're also loose enough for him to do whatever he likes with them.

These folk, mythic and historical stories don't only appear in Tsui Hark's movies – they are the subject of many versions, and every famous Chinese tale will have not one but several television series produced from it. For example, the butterfly lovers theme has been remade many times, including on TV; the *Detective Dee* movies are not Tsui's invention – there are C.C.T.V. series (in the early 2000s), and many writers (such as Robert Van Gulik) have explored Judge Dee as a character; the mythic martial arts movies of Tsui's like *Zu* and *Green Snake* are regular topics on Chinese TV; and of course Wong Fei-hung is a central figure in literally 100s of movies and TV shows.

TSUI HARK THE MEDDLER.

Tsui Hark has been known to muscle in other film directors' projects (which seems to be more common in Hong Kong cinema than in the West).[5] Tsui admits that when he produces movies, 'I get too involved in the project, and there is not enough room for some directors to breathe'.

David Chung claimed that Tsui Hark 'took things over completely' during *I Love Maria* (a.k.a. *Roboforce*, 1988), which Tsui was producing and Chung was directing; Peter Wang complained that Tsui 'interferred' with his movie *The Laser Man* (1986); John Woo maintained that Tsui 'wrested away control of the sequel to my greatest masterpiece [*A Better Tomorrow*], and when I left to make the movie I wanted to make, rushed his version out just to make sure that it was a flop'. Rumours of Tsui's influence have also been suggested for *A Chinese Ghost Story* and *The Swordsman*.

However, there are a number of assumptions about this tendency of Tsui Hark's to hijack movies that he wasn't directing and their directors. One is that Tsui has the time to do that. Another is that he even *wants* to. Another crucial point is the assumption that the film directors that Tsui co-opts are weedy people with no defences. Many film directors are actually tough cookies who're over-seeing a large group of creative people. (Another factor is that the roles of director, producer and manager can be more vaguely demarcated than in the Western film industry, which's thoroughly unionized).

But there's no doubt that Tsui Hark is a force of nature, an immensely talented, ambitious and driven personality with seemingly boundless energy who's dedicated a substantial part of his life to movies and television. And apart from directors such as Wong Jing, few talents in Hong Kong cinema or Chinese cinema have been so productive. (Also, the accusations that Tsui has stepped into a director's territory have occurred too many times for there not to be some truth in it).

TSUI HARK THE ACTOR.

As an actor, Tsui Hark has done brief cameos, longer cameos, and full roles. As well as cameos in his own movies, Tsui has worked for other directors (such as *Yes, Madam!*, Corey Yuen Kwai, 1985, and *Final Victory*, Patrick Tam, 1987). His finest turn was as 'Big Bo' in *Final Victory*, according to Stephen Teo (1997, 157).

Tsui Hark also appears in *It Takes Two* (1982), *The Winter of 1905* (1982), *Twinkle Twinkle Little Star* (1983), *All the Wrong Spies* (1983), *Run, Tiger, Run* (1985), *Kung Hei Fat Choy* (1985), *Happy Ghost 3* (1986), *I Love Maria* (1988), and *The Big Heat* (1988).

Here's a fuller list: Tsui Hark has appeared in the following movies:

• *It Takes Two* (Karl Maka, 1982), with Tsui as a priest who poses as a gangster.

• The first two *Aces Go Places* movies: *Aces Go Places* (Eric Tsang, 1982), as a ballet stage manager, and *Aces Go Places 2* (Eric Tsang,

---

5 This has also occurred with Jackie Chan – during *Crime Story*, for instance, where Chan apparently took over from Kirk Wong.

1983), with Tsui as a madman.

• *All the Wrong Spies* (Teddy Robin Kwan, 1983), a spy spoof sequel to *All the Wrong Clues* (which Tsui helmed), with Tsui as 'Hiroshima Tora'.

• *Run, Tiger, Run* (John Woo, 1985), a reworking of *The Prince and the Pauper*, which was made in Taiwan and had Tsui as a grandfather figure.

• *Yes, Madam* (Corey Yuen Kwai, 1985), known as the break-out movie for Michelle Yeoh, featured Tsui as one of three con men (John Sham and Mang Hoi were the others);

• *Happy Ghost 3* (1986) was part of Cinema City's comedy franchise; Tsui was the 'Godfather' who matches up spirits with their homes.

• *Final Victory* (Patrick Tam, 1987), playing a nasty gangster ('Big Bo') in a white suit.

## TSUI HARK AND CHINA.

Tsui Hark is heavily invested in the theme of nationality, and China, and Chinese nationality, and Chinese identity, and Chinese history. It is a central theme in his cinema. Even in the fantasy martial arts movies, issues such as Chinese history are also being explored. It's not only the *Once Upon a Time In China* series that tackles the question of China's relationship with the rest of the world. Some of Tsui's movies are *very* Chinese, and *very* dense with Chinese tradition – so that Western audiences confess to confusion. 'Tsui has always been the most tradition-ally Chinese of Hong Kong directors' (Lisa Morton, 98).

In fact, one aspect of Tsui Hark's cinema, both as producer and director, is that it is entirely grounded in Chinese characters, Chinese stories, and Chinese issues. Nearly all of Tsui's films feature Chinese characters as the main characters, for instance. Thus, it might not be a coincidence that the two movies regarded as disappointments, the two 'American' films, *Knockoff* and *Double Team*, had a white European as the main protagonist.

Tsui Hark has tended to focus on making films in China – in Hong Kong and the New Territories, mainly, but also in Mainland China and Taiwan (his first movie, *The Butterfly Murders*, was filmed in Taiwan, and he was filming on the Mainland from early in his career). Why? Because Tsui is concerned with Chinese history and culture: most of his films feature Chinese characters in the main roles, for instance. Not Americans in China, not Europeans in China, but Chinese in China (or Chinese abroad).

Of course, an international filmmaker such as Tsui Hark has also filmed in locations such as South France, Italy, Paris and Los Angeles. And for film festivals and awards and the career that goes with being a film director, Tsui is everywhere.

Tsui Hark has raided Ancient Chinese legends several times – *The Four Great Tales of China*, for instance, are *The Tale of the White Snake* (used in *Green Snake*), *The Story of a Tragic Love* (adapted in *The Lovers*), *The Cowherd and the Weaving Maid* and *Seeking Her Husband At the Great Wall*. Tsui remarked he wanted to make movies with Hollywood's production values but with a Chinese sensibility.

Tsui Hark said he has always wanted to make a movie featuring the Monkey King,[6] a famous mythological figure in Chinese culture. In the end, it was Jet Li who appeared as the Monkey King instead, in *Forbidden Kingdom* (2008). But there have been many appearances of the Monkey King in recent movies and television shows – the *Journey To the West* story has been told many times in the Chinese media. Indeed, one of Tsui's biggest hits economically as a director was the *Journey To the West* sequel of 2017, which finally featured the Monkey King.

Altho' we think of Tsui Hark as a supremely Chinese filmmaker, he was in fact born in Saigon in Vietnam, and only moved to Hong Kong when he was thirteen or fourteen (so he is really a Vietnamese/ Chinese filmmaker). Tsui has become devoted to notions of Chineseness and the history of China in his cinema. Stephen Teo relates Tsui's deep fascination with Chinese history and culture to his background as a Vietnamese/ Chinese citizen, to being an overseas Chinese, not born on the Mainland or in Hong Kong.

Tsui Hark has been criticized for his nationalistic politics, and the denunciations of foreign cultures in his movies. But you can probably find issues of nationalism in most major film directors, and certainly most film cultures around the world use nationalism of some kind in most of their movies. In the West, we almost can't see it, because it's everywhere. But if you watch a lot of Asian movies then come back to a North American movie, it's striking just how strong the nationalism is. (However, some nations neighbouring China have an ambiguous attitude towards the country, and they certainly don't admire it as passionately as Tsui does).

And after a while, you get sick to hell of watching North American movies which crow about the U.S.A.'s dumb family values, its vacuous but all-pervasive capitalism, and, most disturbing of all, North America's war-mongering, its insistence on maintaining, at colossal expense ($798 billion a year in 2021), the military-industrial machine, its pro-military politics, and its insistence on the right to bear weapons: this is what I call 'Amerika Über Alles'.

That Tsui Hark is keenly interested in Chinese history and modern politics is easy to spot: it forms the background of some of his most celebrated works, from *Once Upon a Time In China* to *Seven Swords*. But Tsui doesn't employ historical events to stage spectacle cinema (in the manner of David Lean or Steven Spielberg); there is more to it than that (not least is Tsui's unabashed nationalism, his devotion to the idea of China). Tsui says: 'China has such deep cultural resources – it's just that we haven't utilised them yet'.

Stephen Teo, one of the better critics on Chinese cinema, pointed out that Tsui Hark's movies employ some of the icons and clichés of Chinese culture (such as acupuncture, martial arts, Peking Opera) in order to help make the movies appealing to outsiders. Yes – but as Tsui himself has noted, in the New Wave of Hong Kong cinema, the filmmakers were producing movies for the *local market*, *not* for the global market (that came

---

6 And a monkey-man does appear in *Iron Monkey*.

later). But there's no doubt that Tsui in the movies he directs likes to evoke traditional, Chinese culture and practices – but you could see that as a way of presenting the clichés and icons back to the home audience (just as every American Western flick contains numerous iconic elements which sell the cowboy and frontier lifestyle back to the American audience).

Stephen Teo also talks of 'cultural nationalism', more an emotional desire among Chinese people living abroad for Chinese culture. Chinese nationalism, Teo asserts, is found everywhere in Chinese cinema, from *kung fu* flicks to New Wave films, from Mandarin historical epics to Cantonese melodramas (1997, 110-1). In the *kung fu* movies of the 1970s, Teo identified an abstract nationalism in which *kung fu* heroes were using traditions (often from Shaolin) to fight foreign Manchus to restore the Chinese race (1997, 113).

As more of the Hong Kong film industry angled its products at Mainland China, Tsui Hark was conscious of the limitations that it put upon filmmakers: 'In the last 10 years Hong Kong movies have been gradually moving to the market in China', Tsui said in *Hyphen* magazine in 2011. 'And in that market, there is some degree of restriction on the subjects of the films we can make. We are very much constrained by the kind of rules and taboos of the censorship bureau'.

IDENTITY.

French philosopher Julia Kristeva (b. 1941) has developed a fascinating conception notion of the 'outsider'. Being exiled from Bulgaria helped Kristeva see both her own country and her adopted country (France) more clearly. Her experience of displacement was an ingredient in her idea of the 'cosmopolitan' individual, the 'intellectual dissident'. As Kristeva knows, strangeness or otherness (being a foreigner) is fundamental to being human: as Kristeva put it, *étrangers à nous-mêmes* (we are strangers to ourselves). In *Strangers To Ourselves* Kristeva describes the foreigner as the 'cold orphan', motherless, a 'devotee of solitude', a 'fanatic of absence', alone even in a crowd, arrogant, rejected, yet oddly happy (1991, 4-5). The stranger is always in motion, doesn't belong anywhere, to 'any time, any love' (ib., 7).

Julia Kristeva's notion of strangeness or otherness relates directly to the poet Arthur Rimbaud's 'Je est un autre ('I is an other')', Rimbaud's sense of exile and otherness. Living with a foreigner, then, in Kristeva's view, means not just accepting them but being them:

Rimbaud's *Je est un autre* was not only the acknowledgement of the psychotic ghost that haunts poetry. The word foreshadowed the exile, the possibility or necessity to be foreign and to live in a foreign country, thus heralding the art of living of a modern era, the cosmopolitanism of those who have been flayed. (1991, 13)

This throws light on Tsui Hark's cultural identity as an overseas

Chinese man, always dreaming of China, the homeland.

TSUI HARK'S COLLABORATORS.

Tsui Hark has worked with pretty much everybody in the Hong Kong film industry (and more recently on the Mainland). This is a partial list: the following actors have been important in the development of Tsui Hark's career:[7] Sylvia Chang, Brigitte Lin, Jet Li, Eric Tsang,[8] Leslie Cheung, Karl Maka, Chow Yun-fat, Jacky Cheung, Maggie Cheung, Waise Lee, Lau Shun, Sammo Hung Kam-bo, Rosamund Kwan, Anita Mui, Tony Leung Ka-fai, Joey Wang, Teddy Robin,[9] John Sham, Sally Yeh, Raymond Wong Pak-min, and Vincent Zhao.

Other regular actors in Tsui Hark's cinema include: Kenny Bee, Yuen Biao, Cheriie Cheung, David Chiang, Paul Chun, Paul Chu, Norman Chu, Kent Cheng, Adam Cheng, Andy Lau, Lau Ching-wan, Lau Siu-ming, Carman Lee, Loletta Lee, Leon Lai, Sam Hui, Dean Shek, George Lam, Michelle Reiss, Max (Benny) Mok, Carrie Ng, Tony Leung Chiu-wai, Wu Ma, Anthony Wong, Kenneth Tsang, Elvis Tsui, Donnie Yen, Ti Lung, Fennie Yuen, Charlie Yeung, Yan Yee-kwan, Nicky Wu, Jean Wong, Yu Rong-guang, Anita Yuen, Kenny Lin, Zhou Xun, Stephen Chow and Yuen Wah.

Producers Raymond Chow, Nansun Shi Nan-sheng, Leonard Ho, Terence Chang, Karl Maka, Chen Kuo-fu, Huang Jianxin and Ng See-yuen. (Tsui clearly learned plenty from producers such as Chow and Ho, and rapidly became a major player himself – founding Film Workshop five years or so after directing his first feature film). Writers such as Roy Szeto Chak-hon, Charcoal Cheung Tan, Ng Man-fai, Koan Hui, and Sharon Hui Sa-long.

An important collaborator with Tsui Hark was writer Sze-To Cheuk-Hon (a.k.a. Roy Szeto or Szeto Chak-Hon, b. 1954), the author of *All the Wrong Clues, Dangerous Encounter, Zu: Warriors From the Magic Mountain, Shanghai Blues* and *Once Upon a Time In China and America*. Szeto also wrote the *Lucky Stars* movies, the *Mr Vampire* movies, *The Emperor and the White Snake,* and Jackie Chan movies such as *Armor of God* and *Dragons Forever.*

Composers James Wong Jim, Joseph Koo, Lowell Lo, Mark Lui Chang-dak, David Wu, Romeo Diaz, William Hu, Teddy Robin Kwan, Kenji Kawai, and Woo Wai-laap. (This stable of composers is not to be under-estimated: music is a very big deal in Tsui's cinema).

Composer James Wong Jim has delivered more pieces of music (and songs) for Tsui Hark than anyone else; the incredible Wong, one of those composers who can turn his hand to anything (*very* useful to have on any production), has also appeared as an actor many times. Joseph Koo is another oft-used composer (beginning with *The Butterfly Murders* and the *Better Tomorrow* films).

7 The same actors crop up in movies of the 1980s and 1990s which Tsui Hark either directed, produced, co-wrote or acted in: Sally Yeh, Sylvia Chang, John Sham, Joey Wong, Eric Tsang, Teddy Robin, Karl Maka, Chow Yun-fat, Tony Leung, Leslie Cheung, Kenny Bee, Jet Li, Carrie Ng, Waise Lee, Brigitte Lin, Sammo Hung, etc.
8 Eric Tsang is another Tsui collaborator – a Cinema City honcho, a director/ writer/ producer with numerous credits, he has worked many times with Tsui.
9 Teddy Robin Kwan is one of the key figures in Hong Kong cinema of this period – he provided the score for *Black Mask*, directed the *All the Wrong Clues* sequel, and acted in *Working Class, All the Wrong Clues, Twin Dragons* and *It Takes Two.*

For some of the foreign prints of the movies of Tsui Hark (and John Woo), Western rock music was added – Peter Gabriel, the Alan Parsons Project, Jeff Beck, etc (presumably by distributors or companies or producers who thought that rock/ pop music would appeal to Western audiences). But it isn't a good fit – either cinematically or culturally. Altho' we can enjoy the pop music on its own, the original scores would be much preferred, for numerous reasons.

Editors Marco Mak Chi-sin, Gam Ma, Angie Lam On-yee, Poon Hung, Peter Cheung and David Wu Tai-wai (also composer). The significance of editors hardly needs to be mentioned in connection with the films directed, produced and written by Tsui.

DPs such as Arthur Wong (who's probably worked with Tsui Hark more than any DP), David Chung, Peter Pau (*Crouching Tiger, Hidden Dragon*), Lau Moon-tong (Tom Lau), [10] Hermann Yau Lai-to, Andrew Lau Wai-keung (not the singer/ actor – later a director of very Tsui-ian movies like *The Stormriders*), Poon Hang-sang, and Wong Wing-hang. Johnny Choi Sung-fai became Tsui's regular DP from *Seven Swords* onwards.

For such a visually sophisticated and inventive director as Tsui Hark, the on-set relationship with the cinematographer is absolutely vital.

Sometimes five or more DPs are credited on some productions. Why? Because Tsui Hark goes thru DPs like no one else – some only last a day before they're fired. Keeping up with Tsui is very challenging. As Arthur Wong explained:

> Tsui is very creative, but he changes his mind every minute. So sometimes, even though you've done a lot and a lot of preparation, suddenly he comes up with an idea and changes everything! And, he won't even give you enough time! That's the problem! He keeps pushing you, pushing you, pushing, squeezing you, and hurrying you. (D. Vivier)

Production designers William Cheung, [11] Bill Lui and Ma Poon-chiu. (Tsui has done production design himself, as has his ex-wife, Nansun Shi Nan-sheng).

And action directors Tony Ching Siu-tung, Yuen Woo-ping, Yuen Bun, Xiong Xin-xin, Cheung Yiu-sing, Wong Shu Tong, Ma Yuk-shing, Stephen Tung and Corey Yuen Kwai.

Action directors such as Yuen Bun, Yuen Woo-ping, Tony Ching Siu-tung and Xiong Xin-xin are vital in the cinema of Tsui Hark: they are the people, with their tough, hard-working stunt teams, who co-ordinate the action sequences (often appearing in them, too, as actors). Bun, for instance, has credits on a large number of Tsui movies.

MORE ON TSUI HARK'S COLLABORATORS.
NG SEE-YUEN.

A key influence on Tsui Hark's career, and in the *Once Upon a Time In*

10 DP for *The Magic Crane, Once Upon a Time In China 5, The Swordsman 2* and *3, A Chinese Ghost Story 1* and *3*, etc.
11 Cheung has credits on many of Tsui Hark's movies, and most of Wong Kar-wai's films.

*China* movies, was the producer, Ng See-yuen (known as 'N.G.'), who had backed Tsui Hark's first movie, *The Butterfly Murders* (Ng also co-produced *New Dragon Gate Inn* with Tsui, plus *We're Going To Eat You, Twin Dragons* and others). Ng (b. 1944, Shanghai) was a major force in Cantonese cinema, starting out (like so many others) at Shaw Brothers (in 1967), and forming his own production company, Seasonal Films, in 1975 (some say 1973). N.G. was one of the first to recognize the importance of Bruce Lee, and tried to convince Run Run Shaw to sign Lee to Shaws.

N.G. has directing credits, writing credits, acting credits and producer credits. He is an industry advisor on many boards and festivals. N.G. is also the founder of Ultimate Movie Experience International Cineplex, a chain of cinemas in China (including an IMAX theatre in Beijing).

Ng See-yuen's movies included the *Secret Rituals* films, *Anti-Corruption* (1975), *Bruce Lee: The Man, the Myth, The Invincible Armour* (1977), *Dance of the Drunk Mantis* and *Drunken Master 2*. N.G. saw the potential of Jackie Chan, and put him in the two important early Chan movies *Snake In Eagle's Shadow* and *Drunken Master* (both 1978, and both directed by Yuen Woo-ping), which made Chan a superstar. ('It was a partnership that was as good as any I've had in my life', Chan said: 'in every way that mattered, this was the first *real* Jackie Chan picture').

Ng See-yuen also introduced Jean-Claude van Damme to the world (in *No Retreat, No Surrender*) – van Damme would later star in two of Tsui Hark's movies, *Knockoff* and *Double Team*. Other credits of N.G.'s include: *Game of Death II, Ninja in the Dragon's Den, The Unwritten Law, The King of the Kickboxers, Superfights, The Soong Sisters, Legendary Assassin, Bloodmoon, Evening of Roses, Kung Fu Wing Chun,* and *The Grandmaster.*

MARCO MAK CHI-SIN.

Marco Mak Chi-sin (b. Nov 6, 1951) is Tsui Hark's regular editor (along with David Wu Tai-wai and Angie Lam On-yee). He has edited not only a high proportion of Tsui's movies as director but also Tsui's producer movies (such as the *Swordsman* and *Chinese Ghost Story* series, plus *The Magic Crane, The Era of Vampires* and *Iron Monkey*). Other credits include *The Stormriders,* the *Conmen* films, and *The Duel* (and several for Wong Jing). Mak is thus a vital collaborator in the world of Tsui's cinema, which puts such a high premium on editing. (Mak has been editing since 1977, and has also directed fifteen movies, including *Xanda, Dancing Lion, Set To Kill, The Wall* and *Haunted Office*).

David Wu Tai-wai (b. 1952) is another of many unsung contributors to the Tsui Hark empire – a regular editor and composer, Wu has directed as well as appeared in Tsui's movies. Wu also edited most of the celebrated John Woo movies. As Bey Logan pointed out, Wu is a key influence on the editing of action cinema, not only in Hong Kong (purely for his work with Woo – add Tsui and Ronny Yu, and you have a very formidable editor of action movies). Wu said he didn't have to talk with Tsui or Woo – they were in sync, and knew what they were doing.

Angie Lam On-yee (b. 1965) is another superstar cutter in Hong Kong. She is particularly brilliant with cutting action sequences. Her C.V. includes *Hero, House of Flying Daggers, Tai-Chi Master, Fong Sai-yuk 2, The Bodyguard From Beijing, C.J. 7, Kung Fu Hustle, The Warlords,* and numerous movies for Tony Ching, John Woo and Tsui Hark (beginning with *Once Upon a Time In China 2* in 1992).

What must it be like being Tsui Hark's editor?! Does the director visit the editing suite and ask of Angie Lam, Marco Mak or David Wu, 'can we make it go even faster?'!

Sometimes it seems as if editors Mak, Lam and Wu are like the crazy cannibals in *We're Going To Eat You*: when Mak, Lam and Wu get going on the celluloid pouring through the cutting rooms each and every day during production, they are chop-chop-chopping like mad axemen who haven't been fed for days. *Slash!* – there goes a gag they liked for about the first 22 times they saw it; *chop!* – there goes a bit where Jet Li turns to grin at Rosamund Kwan (we don't need that, it's covered elsewhere); and *whee!* – there goes an entire action sequence which took the stunt team weeks to film. Why was it cut out?

*Because it's not fast enough!*


JET LI.

Jet Li was born on April 26, 1963 in Hebel, China. (In Cantonese, Li's name is Lei Lin Git; in Mandarin, it's Li Lanjie). Li is short (5' 6"), but can take on anyone in movies. Li won the first national *wushu* competition in China since the Cultural Revolution (aged 9); he was the Chinese Men's All-round National Wushu Champion at the age of twelve. (*Wushu* is a form of martial arts as performance, combining Peking Opera, gymnastics, and colourful costumes, developed during the Cultural Revolution). Li moved to San Francisco with a Chinese actress (Huang Qiuyan) in 1988; they married (1987-90) and had two daughters. In the U.S.A., Li received his Green Card. Li later married actress Nina Li Chi (they have two daughters).

Jet Li appeared in several martial arts movies[12] right after the first *Once Upon a Time In China* film, including *Tai Chi Master, New Legend of Shaolin* (about Hung Gar), the *Fong Say-yuk* films, *Last Hero In China,* and *Kung Fu Cult Master* (a.k.a. *Evil Cult*).

Tsui Hark didn't want Jet Li to play villains, and always cast him as the hero. Tsui wasn't convinced by Hollywood's use of Li as a villain (in movies such as *Lethal Weapon 4*); it didn't work, and Li didn't look right, Tsui said. Tsui wanted Li to play the hero, the character who tries to do the right thing. 'When he stars in my movies, he must be a heroic figure'.

One should also note here Tsui Hark's genius with casting. Rarely commented upon by critics (tho' discussed endlessly by fans), casting is enormously important in a movie. And it's not an easy job. Tsui certainly has a knack for finding new talent, for getting the right people for the roles (he has also created roles specially for certain actors), and also for filling in the secondary roles and the character roles with suitable people.

---

12 Jet Li didn't make much money from his Shaolin pictures (he was paid a State subsidy).

BRIGITTE LIN.

Brigitte Lin is… Brigitte Lin. Lin was born in Sanchong, Taiwan on Nov 3, 1954.[13] (she is Lam Ching Hsia in Cantonese, and Lin Qinhxia in Mandarin; she is also known as Venus Lin). Lin was in many Taiwanese films (beginning in 1973) before appearing in Hong Kong films such as *Zu, All the Wrong Spies, Police Story, Peking Opera Blues*, the *Bride With White Hair* films, the *Royal Tramp* films, *New Dragon Gate Inn,* Wong Kar-wai movies such as *Chungking Express* and *Ashes of Time,* and the *Swordsman* series.

Brigitte Lin is one of the most remarkable of all recent Asian stars. She 'must certainly be one of the most fearless performers in the world' (Lisa Morton, 101). Lin, tho' straight, is known for playing lesbian and crossdressing women in films such as *All the Wrong Spies* (a lesbian disguising herself as a guy), *Fantasy Mission Force* (she shoots the clothes off a tied-up woman), *The Swordsman 3* (she's a lesbian transsexual superhero), *New Dragon Gate Inn* (steals another woman's clothes for herself), *Peking Opera Blues* (she wears men's military uniforms), *Boys Are Easy* (she's a lesbian cop), *Ashes of Time* (she plays both a brother and a sister), *Eagle Shooting Heroes* (she's a butch princess), and *Fire Dragon* (she's a masked male warrior).

Brigitte Lin's crossdressing or transgender character in the *Swordsman* movies (as Dongfang Bubai = Asia the Invincible) draws on the Peking Opera tradition (where actors can be both warriors and princesses. Indeed, the Tsui Hark movie *Peking Opera Blues* explores issues of gender[14] at length).

Brigitte Lin, according to Bey Logan, was one of the few bankable female stars in Asia: 'basically, all the ageless Ms Lin has to do is wave her arms and smile enigmatically and local audiences will pay to watch' (166).

Tsui Hark has tried to entice Brigitte Lin back to acting – for the remake of *Zu: Warriors From the Magic Mountain* in 2001, for instance, and to play the Empress Wu in *Detective Dee and the Mystery of the Phantom Flame*. Lin retired from acting in 1994, when she married businessman Michael Ying and had children.

❀

OTHER ACTORS.

Lau Shun is one of Tsui Hark's favourite character actors, and he's appeared in probably more Tsui movies than anyone else. Lau can do anything – from bumbling, comical servants to imperious government officials to insane sorcerers and deities. (Tsui had originally brought Lau in to advise on Peking Opera culture in *Peking Opera Blues*).

Charlie Yeung Choi-nei (b. 1974) is one of Tsui Hark's favourite actresses: following her winning turn in *The Lovers*, she appeared in *Love In the Time of Twilight*, *Catching Monkey 3-D* and was the lead in *Seven Swords* (among others, such as *Ashes of Time, Fallen Angels* and *Dr Wai*).

---

13 Some sources say 1957.
14 Peking Opera had a huge impact on the young Tsui Hark – including the play with gender.

Yeung is the classic Tsui Hark Girl – small and slightly-built, tomboyish yet feminine, soft but also tough, and with classical, Chinese features. Yeung retired in 1997, at the height of her fame, but returned to movies in 2004 (with *New Police Story*, and she appeared in *Seven Swords* in 2005).

Xiong Xin-xin (b. 1965), has numerous credits as a stunt co-ordinator and actor. He's one of those faces that you see in many Chinese movies of the 1990s and 2000s, including many of Tsui Hark's films. Xiong has been Jet Li's stunt double since 1986 (on *Shaolin Temple 3*).

✿

One should note again that actors – and crew too – are attracted to great filmmakers like Tsui Hark (or Ken Russell or Orson Welles or Akira Kurosawa) because they get to do things that few others ask them to do. The canvas, the world, the stories that the great film directors move in are huge.

Jean-Luc Godard said that it was natural for him to say to his actors and crew: 'give me more. Let's do what has not been done'.[15] One gets the impression that it's the same with Tsui Hark.

Altho' Tsui Hark has a reputation of being a little demanding on set at times, I would imagine that many actors and crew are happy to work with him. For the simple reason that they know that their work will be seen by millions of people. Which's what it's all about. They also know that Tsui is one of the great, celebrated talents in Asian cinema, and that working on a Tsui movie raises their own profile considerably.

Another reason that actors and crew want to work with Tsui Hark is that he is a powerful presence in the Chinese film business – his movies will get released, a lot of people will see them, they won't be re-cut by studios or backers (or censored – usually), the marketing and promotion will be good, they will be reviewed, and they will have an after-life on TV, cable, DVD, etc.[16]

CASTING POP STARS.

In casting many performers from the world of pop music, Tsui Hark said he and his production teams did that partly because they were seeking acting styles that were different from the stylizations of the old Shaw Brothers movies (which they grew up on), and different from the stylizations of television acting. And, besides, it didn't hurt that pop icons already had a built-in audience and fan base (include teens). Also, pop stars were used to performing and expressing themselves: as Tsui explained:

I like to use singers in my films because they are already experienced in communicating their feelings to an audience.[17]

Cantopop stars include Alan Tam, Andy Lau, Karen Mok, Aaron Kwok,

15 Quoted in A. Sarris, 1968.
16 All actors, East or West, have been in or know about projects that were sat on for years, or never got released, or were distributed poorly, or were hacked about by distributors or studios.
17 Quoted in B. Logan, 181.

Jacky Cheung, Leslie Cheung, Anita Mui, Ekin Cheng and Leon Lai (most of whom have appeared in Tsui Hark's movies).

The 'Four Golden Kings' – singers Leslie Cheung, Andy Lau, Jackie Cheung and Leon Lai – were hugely popular in the 1980s and 1990s. And, as Bey Logan noted, and as we know well, the 'Four Golden Kings' have appeared in numerous Hong Kong movies. In the West, Logan reckoned that it would be like the Osmonds and the Jackson Five uniting for a remake of *The Wild Bunch* (179).

In Asian cinema, casting pop stars has worked so many times. There isn't the stigma attached to using pop musicians as there is in the West (even so, Western cinema has cast from the world of pop and rock numerous times, with some incredible results: Prince in *Purple Rain,* Mick Jagger in *Performance*, Kris Kristofferson in *Pat Garrett and Billy the Kid* and *Heaven's Gate,* and David Bowie in *The Man Who Fell To Earth* ).

COMICS.

Tsui Hark is a big fan of Japanese *manga* and *animé*[18] (who isn't?!), and also Asian types of comicbooks, such as *manhwa* (Korean *manga*), and *manwua* (Chinese *manga*).[19] As his wife Nansun Shi puts it, comics are 'Tsui's one big vice' (LM, 224). 'I wanted to be a comic artist', Tsui remembered of his youth (LM, 19).[20] He reads lots of *manga* and other comics: 'because those things are very interesting to me' (ibid.). Tsui draws a lot, including when he's shooting, and he also paints. For Tsui, drawing is a great way of expressing visual ideas.

*Manga* have moved into many Asian territories, such as Taiwan, Hong Kong, Thailand and South Korea (Thailand is a major market for Japanese *manga*, and all of the main Japanese boys' and some girls' magazines are published there). And Korea has developed an animation industry increasingly in the past few decades (so it's now the third largest producer of animation after Japan and the U.S.A.).

Conversely, one of the biggest markets for Chinese action movies, and Hong Kong action cinema in particular, is Japan. You only have to look at any *manga* or *animé* to see the influence of Chinese action movies (and in particular anything starring Jackie Chan).

And the influence of comicbook style and visuals on the cinema of Tsui Hark is obvious everywhere. Tsui has deployed the comics approach many, many times – even the epic sweep of the history of China evoked in the *Once Upon a Time In China* series is cartoony. And comics pacing and storytelling – which, in Japanese *manga*, is *incredibly* fast, and yet has time for 'pillow moments' and interludes, for character-based scenes (the real impact of Japanese *manga* is in the areas of characters and storytelling). By contrast, Tsui finds N. American comics over-rich (their colours) and too slow (LM, 19).

And Tsui Hark has had a go at making artwork for comics – such as

18 'I like Miyazaki a lot' (LM, 31).
19 One reason that *manga* proved popular in Korea, Taiwan and Hong Kong was because the reading system was the same: from right-to-left and from top to bottom. Which meant that publishers didn't need to flip and re-format the pages.
20 He drew a lot as a kid partly because he was inspired by animated films (LM, 31).

Ma Wing-shong's *Red Snow* (1999). Using Photoshop software, Tsui has created images for comicbooks (he says it takes 4 hours to produce an image). Tsui appreciates how cheap drawing is for trying out ideas:

> with drawing you can just start over and do it again. You put it down and look at it and you see the right reaction without really costing a lot of money or causing a lot of commotion because of something going wrong. (LM, 19)

There are numerous *manga* that one could cite in connection with Tsui Hark's cinema: samurai epics are obvious choices (*Lone Wolf and Cub, Vagabond, Yongbi, Lady Snowblood, Blade of the Immortal*), historical stories (*Buddha, Hero Tales),* fantasy and horror comics (*Akira, Ogre Slayer, Urotsukidoji, Hellsing, Mushishi*), alien babes and goofy guys and harem stories (*Urusei Yatsura, Love Hina, Oh! My Goddess*), gangster/ thriller adventures (*Lupin III, Gunsmith Cats*), hi-tech cyber yarns (*Ghost In the Shell, Appleseed*), and of course the giant franchises of *manga* like *One Piece, Bleach* and *Naruto*.

Indeed, some *manga* come across as Tsui Hark movies: deadly female assassins in *Lady Snowblood* and *Ghost In the Shell*; wispy, wistful other-worldly women and goddesses in *Oh! My Goddess*; epic re-interpretations of ancient history in Osamu Tezuka's incredible *Buddha;* action-adventure in *Lupin III*; and ninja hurtling thru the treetops in *Basilisk* and *Naruto*.

The first animated movie that Tsui Hark saw was *Bambi* (1942) – and it's the same for many filmmakers: many saw a Disney movie as their first movie of any kind (Steven Spielberg, Woody Allen, Hayao Miyazaki, etc). Tsui recalled that his mom wouldn't let him see *Snow White and the Seven Dwarfs* (1937) because there was kissing (!), and because the heroine wore a low-cut dress. But *Bambi* – all animals – was OK. When Tsui later saw *Snow White*, he called it 'my most favorite movie', with a level of artistry and intricacy that's almost impossible to reproduce today.

VISUAL EFFECTS AND TECHNIQUE.
Tsui Hark is a filmmaker who foregrounds the tricks and visual effects of cinema, often in a self-conscious, stagey manner. Western filmmakers who also take this approach include: Orson Welles, Jean Cocteau, Walerian Borowczyk, Sergei Paradjanov, Tim Burton, Vincente Minnelli, Terry Gilliam, Powell & Pressburger, Ken Russell, and Francis Coppola.

Visual effects are one of Tsui Hark's chief concerns in cinema: from *Zu: Warriors From the Magic Mountain* onwards,[21] Tsui has attempted to develop a sophisticated and technically accomplished visual effects resource in China. This has involved nurturing visual effects teams and technical back-up and the infra-structure to make it all possible from scratch. Critics find this aspect of Tsui's cinema very difficult to analyze.

It's the same with crucial elements such as editing and cinemato-

---

21 As well as the optical and comping visual effects, there is animation, stopmotion, miniatures, and special make-up.

graphy. Critics have no idea how movies are edited, and how vital the process is. Film critics will mention that Tsui Hark's movies are ✂✂✂ rapidly, but that's as far as they go. They have little knowledge of the editorial process.

Tsui Hark says that special effects are there to help the story – but they're not the *raison d'être* of the film, nor the reason why the film is good or bad.

WOMEN AND FEMINISM.

Unlike many of his contemporaries, the films directed/ produced/ written by Tsui Hark offer many great roles for women. Not only are there juicy dramatic roles, but plenty of comical ones, too. Tsui's movies celebrate *active* women, proactive women, busy women, women who drive the plot with their desires, their hopes and dreams.22 While ancient, mediæval and modern Chinese society might be patriarchal through and through, Tsui fills his films with strong and resourceful women, who are three-dimensional characters. Tsui remarked:

> I think I'm trying to do something where the women are less predict-
> able and a stronger character.

The turning-point for Tsui Hark in terms of the roles of women in his cinema was 1984:

> So, I think 1984 was a very critical moment when I decided to write
> about women and simply ignore the men's characters for one project
> that was called *Shanghai Blues*. I know so many friends that were
> actresses like Brigitte Lin and they felt very frustrated for having no
> scripts written about women. That's why after all these experiences
> with these people; I decided to start making movies with these people
> being the priority character of the story.

The crossdressing and gender-bending in Tsui Hark's cinema focusses on women – women dressing up as men. No one can fail to notice that the women tend to be tomboyish (the Tsui Hark Girl is short, slim and a tomboy), hinting at the homoeroticism of the romances with men, as well as father complex women (in common with most women in adventure and fantasy fiction). Another recurring motif is a gorgeous woman who turns out to be either an ugly woman underneath, or a guy.23

In the historical pictures, the Tsui Hark Girl is typically a proud warrior, a tomboy great at fighting assailants (and with a few moves of her own). She's stubborn, even difficult, but has a soft, feminine side underneath (which she only reveals reluctantly, and only to the hero). Sometimes the Tsui Hark Girl is a punky, aggressive personality, with suitable accessories like tattoos and jewellery. Another Tsui-ian female type is the Kook. She's batty, scatter-brained, clumsy and adorable. She dresses

22 A woman who defies tradition is 'something that's very dramatic' for Tsui Hark (LM, 21).
23 Maybe Tsui had a terrible experience with a woman who was actually a man or trans-
vestite, because this scenario pops up so many times in his cinema!

funny, and wears big, Eighties glasses (i.e., she's a female version of Tsui himself).

Far fewer critics tackle the issues of feminism and the role of women in Tsui Hark's cinema.[24] It's not one of Tsui's primary themes, for sure (altho' some critics claim it is),[25] but in the subplots of his pictures (and not only in the romantic subplots), issues revolving around women are explored. 'Tsui Hark's women triumph by remaining or becoming feminine', reckoned Lisa Morton (LM, 13). On the one hand, there is certainly a proto-feminism at work in Tsui's cinema, tho' I'm sure many feminists could find plenty of material to back up their argument that women are portrayed in negative, demeaning and exploitative lights in Tsui's movies (the lesbian lovers in *Time and Tide,* for instance).

The cinema of Tsui Hark features strong, independent women, yes, but some Hong Kong movies have gone further in depicting wild women who can wield guns and kick ass – the *Naked Killer* movies, for instance, or the films of Wong Jing.

SEQUELS AND FRANCHISES.

Many of Tsui Hark's movies as producer and director have been remakes and sequels. But Tsui does something very different with the existing material every time: there is never a feeling that Tsui is rehashing a story, or warming up a corpse. (Compared to Western sequels and remakes, those of Tsui are in a wholly different realm). Tsui has even remade earlier movies he's directed (*Zu: Warriors From the Magic Mountain* and *Flying Swords of Dragon Gate*), as have filmmakers like Alfred Hitchcock and Tim Burton.

Among the franchises and series that Tsui Hark has contributed to as producer and director are: *Black Mask, Once Upon a Time In China, The Swordsman, Detective Dee, Aces Go Places, All the Wrong Clues, A Better Tomorrow* and *A Chinese Ghost Story.* Very significantly, Tsui has been the originator of many of those movie franchises and series, including *Once Upon a Time In China, The Swordsman, Detective Dee* and *A Chinese Ghost Story.*

As with most filmmakers, the majority of the movies directed/ produced by Tsui Hark are adaptations of existing material. Among the movies and stories that Tsui has originated himself are *The Master, Detective Dee, Shanghai Blues, Peking Opera Blues* and *Dangerous Encounters of the First Kind.* (Tsui is not a filmmaker who works predominantly from scripts which are completely original ideas, like Ingmar Bergman and Woody Allen).

REMAKES AND UPDATES.

A very important element of Tsui Hark's cinema is updating and remaking previous movies. Tsui is clearly enamoured of cinema from previous generations, and intent on updating it for a contemporary

24 'He may also be the world's greatest feminist director', reckoned Lisa Morton (6).
25 For Lisa Morton, 'the single most defining theme in the œuvre of Tsui Hark, beginning with his very first film', is the deconstruction of male and female roles (LM, 68).

audience. Even though Tsui has occasionally insisted that he is not remaking old movies, because it's disrespectful (*pace Flying Swords* of 2011), some of his most well-known and celebrate movies are remakes and updates: *The Blade* reworks *The One-Armed Swordsman,* the *Once Upon a Time In China* series delivers the familiar *Wong Fei-hung* legend to new audiences*, A Better Tomorrow* is a remake of *True Colors of a Hero, The Taking of Tiger Mountain* is a remake of the famous 1970 production, and *Flying Swords of Dragon Gate* updates both the King Hu-helmed movie of 1967 and Tsui's own *New Dragon Gate Inn* of 1992.

Maggie Lee Man-yuk calls Tsui Hark 'the king of remakes, or, rather, reinvention, drawing on diverse sources and blending genres, tones, and technique with the most imaginative abandon' (2021).

'Not only has he produced or directed films in nearly every conceivable category, he's consistently recreated, resurrected and revitalized dying or stagnant genres', noted Lisa Morton (10). In discussing why he keeps reviving old genres and movies, Tsui Hark said:

> I feel that much of it has to do with my childhood memories, my childhood impressions and my childhood preferences. When I look back at those movies, because of their dated approaches... it's impossible to share these special feelings with the audience today. That's why we're shooting those [old] stories with a contemporary approach.

The adherence to previous genres, forms and movies in Tsui Hark's cinema isn't mere recycling or mindless exploitation (tho' it is that, too). There is more to it than that. At one level, yes, business-wise, it makes sense for all the obvious reasons to update stories and movies that're familiar to audiences (which Hong Kong cinema has always done). But Tsui is doing much more than that. I think he is a true visionary filmmaker, going beyond what many forms of commercial cinema do.

In thriving film cultures, like France, Japan, Korea or the U.S.A., it is completely expected and normal to remake movies and stories all the time. *New actors in old stories* is one of the definitions of the Hollywood movie machine in the glory days of the 1930s thru 1960s, but the phrase still sums up a large proportion of the output of any flourishing filmmaking centre. Often, the remakes and updates are simply old stories dressed up in new clothes, with some new gimmicks to help sell them (such as 3-D,[26] or visual effects, or a postmodern spin on an old chestnut).

But the remakes and updates of Tsui Hark are in a different class, coming from a different place, and operating in a different arena. While Tsui clearly has an *incredibly* keen eye for commercialism and showmanship (you could hire Tsui to over-see any of the big spectacles in the modern era like the Oscars, the Golden Globes, or the opening of the

[26] Tsui Hark was interested in 3-D filmmaking immediately it became a possibility again in the 2000s. It would help cinema to compete with TV, the internet and all the other forms of entertainment that audiences could enjoy: 'I think also because movies are sharing audiences' time with TV and the Internet, even with a bigger screen, movies still have to be different from other mediums. Thus when the possibility for 3D came up, it was right away an attraction to me as a filmmaker'.

Olympic Games, whatever, and you'd be guaranteed a real treat), he is also doing much more as a filmmaker.

Hong Kong audiences are used to movies from Canton being different. They know, said Tsui Hark, that a Hong Kong movie won't be normal, will experiment, might not even be understandable or easy, but it will be different (LM, 28).

TSUI HARK'S FLOPS.

Among the movies of Tsui Hark regularly derided by fans and critics are: *The Magic Crane, Twin Dragons, The Master,* both *Black Masks,* with *Double Team* receiving the fiercest venom. *Green Snake* and *Knockoff* divide admirers. (Some also add *Once Upon a Time in China 4* ).

I don't agree: *all* of the above movies have their enjoyable aspects, and even *The Master* and *Double Team* aren't as woeful as fans and critics make out. But I care little for *Triangle, Missing* and *All About Women* (movies of 2007 and 2008). And, you'd have to admit, that some of Tsui's choices in the latter part of his career have been a little wayward: *Black Mask 2, Double Team, Triangle, All About Women, Missing* and maybe even *The Legend of Zu* (and yet *Black Mask 2, Double Team* and *The Legend of Zu* contain plenty of entertaining sequences, and some outstanding ones). Of all his attempts at remakes and updates, *The Legend of Zu* was probably a mis-use of his energy and resources. But Tsui roared back to masterpiece form with *Seven Swords,* with the *Detective Dee* movies, and with *Flying Swords of Dragon Gate.*

EDITING.

Tsui Hark's cinema seems to come from someone who never sleeps, who is never bored, who finds every aspect of living in the contemporary world fascinating, and who can operate at a higher level of energy and fever than the rest of us. Lazy, work-shy, boring and restrained are not characteristics you can hurl at Tsui! His stamina and energy are legendary.

Tsui Hark's movies are being edited as he shoots: Tsui likes to see what he's got as he films it. With digital editing workflows, Tsui and his editors can put together scenes quickly (using temporary visual effects, timing and colour grading). Versions of the film, before it's complete, can be sent to producers, distributors, visual effects houses, etc.

Baiyang Yu, Tsui Hark's editorial consultant, commented:

We had a very good workflow going for several pictures using Final Cut Pro 7. Tsui likes to see things assembled while we shoot, and typically that involves a lot of temporary visual effects compositing, color grading, and retiming. But that meant a lot of time waiting for things to render, and Tsui doesn't like to wait.

And like many filmmakers (such as Stanley Kubrick, George Lucas and Francis Coppola), Tsui Hark likes to work on his productions right up to the very last moment. As Tsui's editor Baiyang Yu noted:

> On *Flying Swords of Dragon Gate* we went through 15 versions and ultimately had to stop when the distributor reminded us the film was about to be released. It's going to be the same for the [*Detective Dee*] prequel. Our editing will not be complete until the last possible moment. We're changing everything all the time.

Like many Chinese action movies, the movies directed and produced by Tsui Hark often employ slow motion, and also step-motion. Indeed, step-motion (a.k.a. step-printed film) occurs just as much as slow motion. True slow motion is of course filmed on the set, with the camera running at higher speeds (48 frames per second or 96 f.p.s. being typical speeds). But step-motion is created after the fact, in the editing room and by optically treating the celluloid in the processing lab (where you can also select different kinds of step-motion). Sometimes Chinese action movies play whole beats of an action scene in step-motion, but with heightened sound effects (and usually a big music cue).

POST-PRODUCTION.

As noted above, the editor of *Flying Swords of Dragon Gate*, Baiyang Yu, said that the movie went thru fifteen different versions in the editing room before they decided on the final cut. Tsui Hark is a film director who, like many filmmakers, works right up to the premiere or general release date, fine-tuning, altering, cutting, re-cutting, rewriting and re-dubbing the movie.[27] So, well, yes, a Tsui Hark movie isn't really 'finished' – rather, the movie is released in the state it reached before the final, absolutely final, definitely-this-time-is-the-real-true-final date.

If they had their way, filmmakers would probably keep tinkering with their movie for days and weeks, which would drag on to months and then years. Orson Welles, Martin Scorsese, Michael Cimino and Francis Coppola, among numerous other filmmakers, liked to spend a *long* time in post-production. The trouble with that is, backers, financers, producers and film studios start crowing for the movie that *they*, *not* the filmmakers, paid for. Yes: commercial filmmakers *don't* pay for the movies they direct and produce and write! It's the financiers, the investors, and the film studios that actually fork out the dough. Consequently, they want a return for their investment, which can only occur when the darn movie is released!

Furthermore, post-production isn't cheap! If it's just Orson Welles and an editorial assistant and one of the Movieolas that Welles carted around Europe, fine, yes, that's not too expensive. And by that time (1950s thru 1970s), Welles was operating outside of the film studio system, and working on very low budget productions.

But in the commercial film business, post-production can be costly, and can involve quite a few people (if it's a visual effects blockbuster show

---

27 Tsui Hark described post-production as a 'very sensitive, emotional stage', when you are polishing and shaping, and you are very emotionally attached to the movie (LM, 30).

in the West, we're talking sometimes hundreds of people). For a filmmaker with an established reputation and proven track record, like Tsui Hark, it's much easier to exert the power to exploit resources and man-power on a production.

A minor but significant factor in the post-production of movies from the 1990s to today is digital technology: movies are now often cut using Avid or similar systems (Tsui has employed Final Cut Pro, Apple's editing software). For a director like Tsui, this means that multiple versions of scenes and sequences can be created and organized: Tsui is the kind of director who likes to edit scenes and whole movies in a number of ways. You could still do that with celluloid and Movieolas, of course (filmmakers such as Jean-Luc Godard and Steven Spielberg like to edit using real celluloid), but digital editing systems allow for multiple versions to be saved and viewed and compared very quickly. Also, optical effects can be applied instantly, such as fades, wipes, dissolves, slow motion, speed ramping, etc (in the celluloid days, optical effects had to be sent to the film labs, so you had to wait to see them).

CHANG CHEH AND KING HU.

Two Chinese film directors loom large over Tsui Hark's output: Chang Cheh (Zhang Zhe) and King Hu, the directors who pioneered *wuxia* films. They both hailed from Northern China, spoke Mandarin, and employed the Northern styles of the Peking Opera.

Tsui Hark has re-made movies by both directors (as well as working with King Hu on *The Swordsman*), and has clearly been heavily influenced by them. But then, it's impossible for a Chinese filmmaker working in action cinema *not* to be influenced by Chang Che and King Hu – between they directed many of the classics of *kung fu* and martial arts cinema. (Also, many of the performers and crew in Tsui's movies will have worked with both directors).

King Hu (1931-1997), born in Beijing, was the director of classics such as his 'Inn Trilogy' – *Come Drink With Me* (1965), *Dragon Gate Inn* (1967) and *The Fate of Lee Khan* (1973) – and his 'Buddhist Trilogy': the epic (and, for a martial arts movie, very long) *A Touch of Zen* (1970), *Raining In the Mountain* (1979) and *Legend of the Mountain* (1979). Hu worked at Shaw Brothers.

*A Touch of Zen* is the movie which's King Hu's crowning achievement for many, and which was a big hit at Cannes. *A Touch of Zen* was based on the same material used for the *Chinese Ghost Story* movies: *Liaozhai Zhiyi* by Pu Songling.

For King Hu, *kung fu* was choreographed like dance: 'I've always taken the action part of my films as dancing rather than fighting', Hu said (many others, including Jackie Chan, have thought the same). For him, the tradition of the Peking Opera was crucial in developing a way of staging action in cinema. For critics, the choreography in Hu's films was movement for movement's sake, rather than exploring themes or ideas or stories: altho' Hu's movies touched on Zen Buddhism, Confucianism, chivalry, history, nationalism and the supernatural, Sek Kei remarked, they were really interested in 'a free and unfettered state'.[28]

As well as influencing how martial arts was depicted in Hong Kong cinema, Hu also emphasized roles for women in his movies (which further endears him to Tsui Hark).

Chang Cheh (b.1923, Zhejiang Province, d. 2002) developed a team of collaborators which included Lau Kar-Leung as action director (along with Tang Jia), Bao Xueii, Wu Ma and John Woo. Chang wrote many of his own scripts (often with Ni Kuang). Chang's directing career was based around *wuxia* movies, and then the *kung fu* genre (they were produced at Shaw Brothers).[29] Chang's famous works include *The One-Armed Swordsman* (1967, updated in 1970), *The Golden Swallow, The Chinese Boxer, The Water Margin, Man of Iron, The Brave Archer* and *The Assassin*. (At one time, Chang produced 70 movies in 5 years at Shaws).

*The Blade* is a swordplay action movie, a re-make of *The One-Armed Swordsman* (*Dubi Dao,* Chang Cheh, 1967). The Shaw Brothers' *The One-Armed Swordsman* was the first Hong Kong movie to gross U.S. $1 million in Hong Kong. *The One-Armed Swordsman* starred Jimmy Wang Yu in 'a muscular, angst-ridden epic of blood-thirsty masculinity that ushered in an entirely new sensibility for martial arts cinema', according to Jeff Yang (50).

TSUI HARK AND JOHN WOO.

One would've expected Tsui Hark to have been the filmmaker who made it biggest in North America[30] (he 'out-Spielbergs Spielberg', quipped Roy Hoban in the *Village Voice*), but John Woo seems to have made the move into the North American film industry more successfully than Tsui. Both are Chinese filmmakers with a keen sense of what works commercially, both possess a strong style, both like making genre pictures (and remaking old movies), and both deliver movies to the key market of young males. (Timing has played a part, as has the kind of movies that Woo creates – blood and guts amongst guys and cool gangsters in thriller formats, the sort of films which critics exalt, and which are perhaps easier to sell to audiences than some of Tsui's movies). As to Tsui's influence on Woo, critics such as Tony Williams have noted that Woo's films prior to *A Better Tomorrow* are undistinguished (2002, 153).

Critics trot out plenty of guff about the theme of male friendship or brotherhood in the movies directed by John Woo, but there's just as much in the cinema of Tsui Hark. Really? Sure – to cite some titles: *Lake Changjin, Knockoff, Double Team, Time and Tide, Once Upon a Time In China, Blade, Aces Go Places, Seven Swords, The Master, The Flying Swords of Dragon Gate,* and *Black Mask*. Men fighting alongside each other, men looking after each other, men competing with each other – Tsui's cinema is full of those themes (as well as the proto-feminism).

28 S. Kei: "Xingzhe de Guiji", *Film Biweekly*, 13, 1979.
29 They ranged from 'cookie-cutter dreck to creatively innovative masterpieces', as Rovin and Tracy put it (245).
30 Deals such as a co-production with Francis Coppola came to nothing.

Altho' John Woo's form of slow motion, balletic action is utterly compelling, it is *waaay* too slow for Tsui Hark! Tsui's metabolism in cinema runs very, very hot! While Tsui is all for stretching out big dramatic or action-fuelled moments (and much longer than in Western movies), he would never go as far as Woo and editor David Wu Tai-wai in using multiple film speeds to create lengthy, post-Eisensteinian montages of fluttering doves, spattering blood and guttering guns.

TSUI HARK AND AKIRA KUROSAWA.

That Tsui Hark is a huge admirer of the cinema of Akira Kurosawa is obvious (but who isn't?!): the whole look of Tsui's *jiangzhu* and historical pictures derives from Kurosawa's movies (from the meticulously researched costumes and props, to the use of real locations and three-dimensional sets, to the enormous emphasis on environmental elements such as wind, rain, fire and snow). Ever since he saw *Yojimbo* (1961) as a teenager, Kurosawa has been a favourite for Tsui.

For Tsui Hark, Akira Kurosawa managed to produce movies that transcended their cultural origins in Japan. Kurosawa's films are universal, Tsui said, going way beyond the limitations of language and culture (yet you can also argue that Kurosawa's movies remained *very* Japanese).

Tsui Hark has produced his own version of *The Seven Samurai* in *Seven Swords,* and of samurai classics such as *Yojimbo* and *Sanjuro* in *The Blade* and *New Dragon Gate Inn.* The way that Akira Kurosawa filmed royalty, pageants and palaces, the way that he included a huge panorama of human life, from peasants up to kings, the way that he never loses sight of the individual in the epic stories, all have been absorbed by Tsui.

Akira Kurosawa's was a grand cinema that magically crossed international borders, to become one of the great bodies of work in the second half of the 20th century. Kurosawa's cinema is also very big on action, which of course has impressed so many filmmakers as well as Tsui Hark.

Akira Kurosawa's influence has been immense on world cinema. Paul Verhoeven said he put on *Rashomon* or *The Seven Samurai* from time to time to remind himself that films could be art. Terry Gilliam spoke highly of *Rashomon.* Bernardo Bertolucci said Kurosawa (with Federico Fellini) was one of the reasons he wanted to become a film director. And John Woo said he watched the last reel of *The Seven Samurai* before making his films, for inspiration on action. The influence of Kurosawa on Woo is clear to see (a movie such as *Bullet In the Head* is distinctly Kurosawan).

There are Akira Kurosawa moments in Paul Verhoeven (the battles with bugs in *Starship Troopers*); Francis Coppola (the extravagant machine gun death of Sonny Corleone in *The Godfather* recalls Macbeth's demise by arrows in *The Throne of Blood,* or the mythical soldiers in *Apocalypse Now*); George Lucas raided Kurosawa's mediæval *samurai* for the Jedi knights in his *Star Wars* saga; the *samurai* warriors also popped up in *Brazil* (Terry Gilliam); the elaborate gun battles in John Woo's Hong Kong action cinema, and the warrior ethic also appears in John Milius's films; and Bernardo Bertolucci made his own version of a Kurosawa epic in *The Last Emperor*. Other filmmakers who've cited Kurosawa as a key influence include Hayao Miyazaki, Wes Craven and Katsuhiro Otomo.

Akira Kurosawa was one of Ingmar Bergman's favourites. Bergman said he had studied *Rashomon* dozens of times (one can detect the influence of Kurosawa on films helmed by the Swedish genius such as *The Virgin Spring* and *The Seventh Seal*). Bergman said he regretted being so heavily influenced by Kurosawa. 'I want to say now that *The Virgin Spring* was a misadventure, a wretched imitation of Kurosawa. It was a period in which I surrendered so completely to the Japanese film that I almost became a bit of a samurai myself' (*Bergman On Bergman*, 120). That seems unnecessarily harsh.

GENRES.

A large proportion of Tsui Hark's movies are action movies. Comedy is key ingredient, as is violence, along with themes such as China, Chinese culture, nationalism, women, feminism, and food.[31] Doing the right thing and how to live in the world, are key moral concerns.

A huge proportion of the movies directed and produced by Tsui Hark have been historical movies: *Detective Dee and the Mystery of the Phantom Flame, The Blade, Green Snake, The Lovers, Peking Opera Blues, Shanghai Blues, New Dragon Gate Inn, Flying Swords of Dragon Gate, The Swordsman, Zu: Warriors of the Magic Mountain, Seven Swords* and the *Once Upon a Time In China* series. (The movies set in the present day tend to be thrillers and action movies). So Tsui and his film teams have spent years and years exploring the past, from the latter part of the 19th century (in the *Wong Fei-hung* series), to the mediæval period of *The Lovers,* and the ancient world of the *Detective Dee* series.

The *jiangzhu*[32] (= martial arts world) and the *wulin* (= martial forest) is where Tsui Hark gravitates towards in history – the wandering world of a China that never really existed (depicted in *The Blade, New Dragon Gate Inn, Flying Swords of Dragon Gate, The Swordsman, Zu: Warriors of the Magic Mountain, Seven Swords, The Butterfly Murders, A Chinese Ghost Story* and *The Lovers*). Indeed, among filmmakers of his generation, no one else has spent so much time imaginatively in the *jiangzhu* as Tsui.

Tsui Hark said he's had a special affinity with *wuxia pian* since childhood: around a quarter of his output as director is martial arts/ *wuxia pian*, and many more as producer.

*Wuxia* means swordsman/ martial fighter/ knight-errant (*wu* = military or armed; *xia* = hero, chivalrous. Known as *Mo hap* in Cantonese). Thus, *wuxia* movies were swordplay pictures, and they tended to be filmed in Mandarin. *Kung fu*, meaning fist fighting, and were usually made in Cantonese (with the *Wong Fei-hung* movies as the typical product).

31 Food? Oh yes – it's a motif in movies such as *We're Going To Eat You, Once Upon a Time In China* (eating Western food), *New Dragon Gate Inn, Iron Monkey* and *The Chinese Feast.*
32 'In *The Blade*, the *jiangzhu* exists in various manifestations that are no longer so abstract. It is country, community, locality; it is the person's character; it is the hero who knows how to develop his talent and achieve victory through the human dimension of speed rather than the superhuman one of flight', commented Stephen Teo (1998, 156).

*Wuxia* movies were regarded as more historical and 'authentic' than *kung fu* movies; their trademarks included fantasy, the supernatural, performers flying, and visual effects. *Kung fu* movies (from Canton) tended to be more 'realistic', emphasizing training and the body.

A significant proportion of Tsui Hark's movies are not only action movies, they are martial arts movies: *The Blade*, the *Detective Dee* series, *Green Snake, Flying Swords of Dragon Gate, The Butterfly Murders, Zu, Seven Swords* and the *Once Upon a Time In China* series. Most of the martial arts movies directed and produced by Tsui are set in the past.

Stephen Teo:

Tsui Hark's world is inclusive, blending the outrageous with the normal, the paranormal (as in his horror films) with the natural world (as in *The Blade*, with its contortions of mud, sand, and wind), and the supernatural (the notion of flight), with the mundane (the notion of speed). (1998, 154)

ROMANCE.
Love. Hearts and flowers. Romance...
Altho' it's the action movies, the historical movies, the thrillers, and the visual effects extravaganzas that Tsui Hark is usually known for (all masculine genres), and celebrated by film critics (most of whom are men), his cinema is filled with love and romance. Jean-Luc Godard wondered if love between a man and a woman was actually *the* chief subject of cinema; it's true of Godard's cinema, certainly (where romantic and erotic relationships are everywhere), and also true of Tsui's cinema. (Tsui comes from a very large family, which probably influenced the depiction of families in his cinema).

There is just as much romance, love and emotion in Tsui Hark's cinema as action, spectacle, history and visual effects. Some of Tsui's finest achievements have revolved around relationships and families: *Shanghai Blues, The Lovers, Green Snake, A Chinese Ghost Story*, etc. The fantasy and adventure movies, for instance, like *Green Snake* and *A Chinese Ghost Story*, are primarily love stories, and it's the love between a man and a woman that is at the core of the stories (and is what powers the stories along). 'I think we filmmakers often find ourselves trying to fill up the missing something of the audience's emotions and psychological needs', Tsui said.

Love crops up even in the titles of Tsui Hark's movies – *Love In the Time of Twilight, The Lovers, Love and Death In Saigon*, etc. Is Tsui, for all his pioneering achievements, his technical brilliance and action-heavy filmmaking, really a softie? Yes. Even in the harsh world of the *jiangzhu* of *Seven Swords* or *New Dragon Gate Inn*, love and romance are absolutely central (*romantic* is a key term in Tsui Land. Tsui thinks that 'women are more romantic than men'; 'romantic is the most key word in everything' [LM, 22]). Is he romantic? Tsui replied that you'd have to ask his wife.

'Romantic' – the word is uppermost in Tsui Hark's conception of cinema and entertainment – alongside 'emotion'. Cinema, Tsui asserts, must be emotional, there must be an emotional investment from the audience:

> I am looking for ways to make my audience feel. If your audience
> doesn't have a strong feeling from your story, you fail as a storyteller.

COMEDY.

Too few critical appraisals of the cinema of Tsui Hark emphasize the importance of *comedy* his work. But comedy is everywhere in Tsui's movies: *Peking Opera Blues* is a backstage comedy, as is *Shanghai Blues*; *Aces Go Places* and *All the Wrong Clues* are Cinema City comedies; black comedy is integral to *We're Going To Eat You* and *The Butterfly Murders*; horror comedy appears in the *Chinese Ghost Story* and *Swordsman* movies; the romances contain humour (*The Lovers*, *Green Snake*, *Love In the Time of Twilight*); and comedy is found throughout the *Once Upon a Time In China* series. And Tsui Hark added humour to films he produced, such as *A Better Tomorrow* and *Iron Monkey*.

Tsui Hark is particularly fond of gags using crowds – where mobs act as one. Like the crowd gathered outside the nightclub in *Shanghai Blues* which tilts its head to follow the moving sign of a fan covering the breasts on a billboard of a showgirl; like the villagers who cower in fear behind Leslie Cheung in *A Chinese Ghost Story*; like the guys who hide behind each other when the Chief is ranting in *We're Going To Eat You.*

AVAILABILITY

A *major* problem with approaching the cinema of Tsui Hark (and all Chinese cinema) is availability. You will smack up against the issue of availability as soon as you try to see anything other than the movies released in the Western world. Most of Tsui's films (and TV work) was produced for a Chinese market: the markets of Hong Kong and Mainland China are absolutely crucial. (Hence, Tsui's films are usually released with a Cantonese and a Mandarin soundtrack, which's the norm in Chinese cinema). This doesn't mean, tho', that the movies travel outside of China, either in their original form or in dubbed versions.

The language issue – Cantonese, Mandarin, English, whatever – is a minor one compared to general availability (subtitling is yet another issue). It's true that some of the key works directed and produced by Tsui Hark are easy to obtain in the West – the *Once Upon a Time In China* series, for instance, *Zu: Warriors From the Magic Mountain, Detective Dee and the Mystery of the Phantom Flame,* and of course those produced by or in conjunction with North American distributors (such as Columbia/ TriStar/

Sony), like *Double Team* and *Knock Off*. But many important movies are not easily available in the West: *The Butterfly Murders, Peking Opera Blues, Shanghai Blues* and *Dangerous Encounters of the First Kind* (gems of China cinema like *Peking Opera Blues* should be available in supermarket racks like Disney cartoons). It doesn't get better with more recent works, either: *All About Women, In the Blue, The Warrior, Young Detective Dee: Rise of the Sea Dragon* and others of the 2000s and 2010s are hard to source in the West.

Consequently, the following movies, directed by Tsui Hark, have not been explored fully in this study: *Search For the Gods* (1983), *Working Class* (1985), *Spirit Chaser Aisha* (1986), *The Banquet* (1991), *The Chinese Feast* (1995), *Tristar* (1996), *In The Blue* (2005), and *Catching Monkey 3-D* (2013).

The issue of availability affects many celebrated filmmakers – you simply can't find many of their key works. The issue of quality is another consideration: many movies are only available in substandard prints, with bad soundtracks, or in butchered versions (some Hong Kong movies look like they were copied from beat-up release prints that have been kicking around Central for years, then re-copied onto video and back again). Despite new distribution systems like the internet, or streaming, or DVD and Bluray (or older ones like video, or broadcasting on television), it's amazing how many jewels of cinematic art remain in limbo, or are lost, or can only be bought in scrappy versions from dodgy, one-eyed Buddhist monks in the scuzzy end of town for extortionate prices.

Another issue is that the international and Western versions of Hong Kong and Chinese movies sometimes change the following: the music; the dialogue; the scripts (scripts are rewritten during dubbing); add new sound mixes; and whole scenes are dropped.

Thus often the Western/ international cuts of Asian movies are *not* in the form the filmmakers preferred. Tsui Hark has complained many times that distributors have altered his movies for releases overseas.

The practice of dubbing the sound on afterwards in Chinese movies also extends to the stars: it was many years before Chinese movie audiences heard the real voices of Jackie Chan and Jet Li, for instance. Another consequence of dubbing is that the same group of actors tend to be heard in every movie.

For research online, the Hong Kong Movie Database and Hong Kong Cinemagic are excellent (they have photos of the cast and crew, for instance – very helpful when Chinese movies are filled with unusual names (and many alternative names and spellings) in both Mandarin and Cantonese). Love Hong Kong Film has useful reviews.

The critical reception/ interpretations of Tsui Hark's movies tend to use some of the following approaches:

NATIONALISM AND IDENTITY.
Chinese identity and nationalism – the 'Chineseness' in Tsui Hark's cinema.
What it means to be Chinese, what Chinese history and society is, how Chinese culture relates to the rest of the world – these're some of Tsui Hark's primary concerns, at the thematic level. Chinese identity is a theme that crops up many times in Tsui's movies – in particular how contemporary Chinese identity relates to recent Chinese history.

POLITICAL ALLEGORY.
Politics – ideology – movies as political allegories/ statements.
There are many articles discussing Tsui Hark's cinema as political allegories which explore (1) China's place in the new world order, (2) Hong Kong's political situation *vis-à-vis* Mainland China, (3) Hong Kong as a colony, and, inevitably, (4) Hong Kong during the 1997 hand-over.
Critics often draw attention to the allegorical/ analogical/ metaphorical aspects of Tsui Hark's cinema, how he includes political commentary or side-swipes at authorities, then they castigate the films for not doing more. They forget that movies are *primarily* commercial entertainment – if you want allegory/ metaphor/ political diatribes, look elsewhere. Or, if you've got the guts, make your *own* movie which features hyper-intelligent political satire, pro-socialist/ left-wing propaganda, philosophical essays and metaphysical arguments, while still being highly entertaining, state of the art technically, and cheap to produce.
'Tsui Hark is skillful in channelling the general anxiety of the people in Hong Kong into his films and in manipulating the audiences' responses', noted Leung Ping-kwan (in "Urban Cinema and the Cultural Identity of Hong Kong").[33]
Tsui Hark has not shied away from tackling ideological and political issues head-on: his series about Wong Fei-hung, for instance, *Once Upon a Time In China*, is explicitly political. And the series that sort of follows up *Once Upon a Time In China*, the *Detective Dee* films, also deliver political messages.
For Leung Ping-kwan, Tsui Hark's cinema is explicitly political:

Among Hong Kong directors, Tsui Hark is the one most obsessed with and skilful in making films into political allegories. In films he produced or directed, in his retelling of old tales as well as in his play with mixed genres, he always weaves in indirect political commentaries as well as references to contemporary issues. (In P. Fu, 242)

A good deal of the political and ideological content of the *Once Upon a*

---
[33] In P. Fu, 242-3.

*Time In China* movies boils down to simple dramatic oppositions:

West = guns (bad) ••• East = martial arts (good)
West = technology (bad) ••• East = tradition (good)
West = modern medicine (bad) ••• East = Chinese medicine (good)
West = exploitation (bad) ••• East = mercantile capitalism (good)
West = individualism (bad) ••• East = communities (good)
(And you'll find these oppositions throughout Hong Kong cinema).

The *Once Upon a Time In China* series pits the Chinese values of the family, neighbours, communities, tradition and righteousness against Western egotism, selfishness, cynicism, money, science, and negative imperialism.

ACTION, IMAGES, SPECTACLE.

'The imagery is one of the aspects I like about movies. It's like creating a virtual world with a lot of imagery, creating an illusion as well as the storytelling.'

That Tsui Hark's cinema is obsessed with creating spectacular and vivid movies everybody agrees. That Tsui is an image-obsessed filmmaker, a guy who can create extraordinary visuals with apparent ease, is central to his cinema (he has one of the most remarkable eyes for an image in film history). But this is an element of his cinema that critics find challenging to discuss, apart from making obvious statements about the beauty and power of Tsui's imagery.

As to action and choreography, Western critics are hopeless. They don't have the background knowledge of how movies are made. Many of them have probably never been on a soundstage.

And yet altho' issues like political allegory and Chinese identity are important in Tsui Hark's cinema, they are *not* the whole story! In the *Once Upon a Time In China* movies, for example, two minutes might be spent in a scene discussing China's role in the modern era (between Wong Fei-hung and a visiting dignitary, for instance), but seven minutes will be spent on a giant fight scene! And that fight scene will consume *far* more attention from the filmmakers than a little bit of dialogue about China and 20th century politics! (three days to shoot the fight scene, and half-an-hour to shoot the political discussion. Or as Jackie Chan put it, half a day for the talky bit, and four months for the action scene!).

But what will film critics talk about? – the two minutes of blether about Chinese politics! And what do audiences love? – the seven minute action sequence, where Jet Li rolls down the back of Iron Robe, or spins round a pillar twelve feet in the air, or whups the bad guys with an umbrella or a rolled-up shirt!

MORE ON ACTION.

Is Tsui Hark the finest director of action in recent cinema? Anywhere in the world? Even despite fierce competition? You could make a case that, *yes*, he is – even amongst the heavyweights of North America movies like Steven Spielberg, James Cameron, Michael Bay, Gore

Verbinski, Stephen Sommers, Michael Mann and Oliver Stone, or the token Brits (Ridley Scott), or one or two Europeans (Wolfgang Petersen, Renny Harlin, Roland Emmerich, Luc Besson, etc). Plus the stalwarts of the Hong Kong/ Chinese industry, such as John Woo, Tony Ching Siu-tung, Yuen Woo-ping, Johnny To Kei-fung, Ringo Lam Ling-tung and Jackie Chan.

You could cut together two or three full-length documentaries about martial arts and action cinema from Tsui Hark's movies alone. Or just one movie: *Knockoff* or *Time and Tide,* among the more recent contemporary thrillers, or the *Once Upon a Time In China* series, naturally.

And of course, Tsui Hark has worked with some of the great action stars – Sammo Hung Kam-bo, Jackie Chan, Jet Li, Yuen Biao, Michelle Yeoh, Jean-Claude van Damme – and some of the great action choreographers: Yuen Woo-ping, Tony Ching Siu-tung, Jackie Chan, Sammo Hung, Yuen Bun, Yuen Wah and Xiong Xin-xin.

> Action is not just by itself; action always comes with a story, it also comes with a style, it comes with extra information about what the director wants to show to the audience. These sorts of things are always with me. (2011)

MORE ON STYLE.

Tsui Hark is very much of the Akira Kurosawa School of Filmmaking – that is, plenty of natural, elemental material on screen – rain, fire, smoke,[34] wind, torchlight, candlelight, and more fire and more rain.[35] It means filming outdoors in sometimes tough conditions. It means leading the production team up mountains and across rivers. And for the actors it means quite a bit of hardship.

To achieve those Kurosawan effects requires stamina, determination, and, perhaps above all, patience (plus the resources of a fully-equipped studio with its technical staff. You can't stage this kind of production on a shoestring budget). This is perfectionist filmmaking, getting every detail right, composing scenes and frames teeming with incident and gesture.

Tsui Hark has a suitcase full of motifs and symbols which he uses – including tigers, butterflies, rain, water, the sea, funfairs, mothers and babies, goldfish and fish in tanks.

(So many of the motifs of the later historical films directed by Zhang Yimou – *Hero, House of Flying Daggers*, etc – can be found in classics of the Hong Kong New Wave cinema such as *The Terracotta Warrior*, the *Swordsman* series, the *Once Upon a Time In China* series, etc. The floating leaves, the dripping water, the rainfall, the billowing hangings of white and red cloth, the slow motion, etc.)

---

34 Smoke in Hong Kong cinema is not a pretty effect that drifts in the background of a scene to enhance the lighting – it is used as a setting in itself, a real, physical presence in the scenes. Sometimes smoke provides the whole environment of a scene (and, yes, sometimes that billowing smoke is used to hide things).
35 On a Hong Kong film set, electric fans are always near the camera – clothes must flap and billow.

## STORYTELLING – STORIES AND CHARACTERS.

And yet, amazing as it may seem, one of the chief motivations for many filmmakers is simply storytelling. *Movies are stories*. That's all. Just stories. And *filmmakers are storytellers*. So all of the above elements and issues – the political rants, the anxiety over identity in a global marketplace, the critiques of capitalism and Communism, the exploration of women's issues or visual effects, etcetera – are all *secondary* to the *primary* concern. Which is: to *tell a story*.

Yes: that's what filmmakers do.

They tell stories.

Stories which involve characters and things happening and drama and conflicts and battles and goals and motivations and all the rest. That's one of the things that audiences crave: stories • characters • things happening.

This is the level in Tsui Hark's cinema (or any cinema) that's easiest to discuss, and doesn't require too much expertise. Everybody knows what stories they enjoy (even – *gulp!* – film critics!).

But when I say a movie is 'just a story', that doesn't under-value stories! Or filmmakers as storytellers! We love these stories, we want to hear and see these stories, we construct whole cultures and identities around these stories. (However, too many books about Hong Kong cinema focus solely on the stories and the characters, forgetting everything else. And Hong Kong movies are *supremely* and properly, fully *cinematic*. Ignoring the filmic aspects of the movies misses too much).


## FURTHER THEORETICAL APPROACHES.

For those readers/ students who appreciate suggestions for theoretical approaches to subjects, here are some more:

• The relation of identity to art, to being an artist/ filmmaker.

• Approaching the issue of cultural and national identity using postmodern theory is an obvious angle for looking at Tsui Hark's cinema, and Hong Kong cinema.

• Forms of identity: psychological, social, cultural, national, historical, ethnic: for example, one could explore the relation of the Asian/ Chinese cultural identity of Tsui Hark's cinema to the issue of working as a filmmaker.

On the set of Flying Swords of Dragon Gate (above).

# 26

# *THE LEGEND OF ZU*

# *Sook San Jing Huen*

THE PRODUCTION.

Tsui Hark's dissatisfaction with how his 1983 fantasy epic movie *Zu: Warriors From the Magic Mountain* turned out is well-known (and has been voiced often over the years). Many aspects of the movie irked Tsui (not least the visual effects).[1] No doubt fans have enthused about *Zu: Warriors From the Magic Mountain* to Tsui (it has many admirers), and even critics enjoyed it (yes, even *critics!*), calling it a pioneering masterpiece (with breakthrough technical effects for a Hong Kong production). But the warm response to *Zu: Warriors From the Magic Mountain* didn't change Tsui's disappointment. So Tsui, in common with filmmakers such as Alfred Hitchcock and Tim Burton, went back and re-made one of his own movies, resulting in the version of *Zu* for the 21st century, entitled *The Legend of Zu* (*Zu Warriors* in the U.S.A.).

The budget of *The Legend of Zu* (*Shu Shan Zhuàn* in Mandarin, a.k.a. *Zu Mountain Official Legend*), was about U.S. $35 million (one of the highest in Tsui Hark's career), produced by Film Workshop and One Hundred Years of Film Company, and distributed by China Star. Released Aug 9, 2001. 104 minutes.

The 2001 movie was not released theatrically in the U.S.A.;[2] the North American home release cut the movie down from 104 to 80 minutes (which inevitably left out important elements – as usual, the international cut kept the action and spectacle, but missed out some of the character-based

---

1 One aspect of visual effects that probably doesn't sit so well in the Hong Kong film industry is the high cost of them during post-production. In the race to get movies in theatres, studios and distributors in Hong Kong tend to prefer as short a time in post-production as possible. But in the 1983 movie of *Zu: Warriors From the Magic Mountain*, post-production visual effects (such as optical effects and matte paintings) aren't cheap. And when you get to digital and computer-aided material, which has become the norm for many high budget productions in Hollywood and the West, you are talking *lots* of $$$$$, and *lots* of time to produce those effects. All of that drives up the budget hugely, and also pushes back release dates. So that high budget Hollywood productions can take literally months and months to finish in post-production (and that's far too long for the Hong Kong film industry!).
2 The Weinsteins were involved in the movie as producers.

aspects which make the story work).

That *The Legend of Zu* is a Tsui Hark production, no one is in doubt! Tsui has not only director and producer credits (exhausting enough!),[3] but also a co-writer credit (the other writer was Lee Man-choi). Brian Cox and Anant Singh were the co-producers with Tsui. Yuen Woo-ping was the action director (along with Yuen Shun-yee and Ku Huen-chiu); Eddy Wong Wang-hin and Joe Bauer supervised the visual effects; Ricky Ho composed the music; the DPs were Herman Yau Lai-to, William Yim Wai-lun, Li Bao-quan and Poon Hang-sang; Marco Mak Chi-sin edited; sound design was by Martin Chappell; sound sups. were Koan Hui-on and Les McKenzie; and costumes were by William Fung Kwun-man, Mabel Kwan Mei-bo, Lee Pik-kwan, Huang Baorong and Thomas Chong Chi-leung (many in the team were Tsui regulars).

The cast of *The Legend of Zu* included Ekin Cheng,[4] Cecilia Cheung, Louis Coo, Wu Jing, Kelly Lin, Patrick Lam, Ng Kong, Lau Shun, Sammo Hung and Zhang Ziyi.[5] Many were part of the Tsui Hark Repertory Company. The three main characters are King Sky (Ekin Cheng), Enigma/Dawn (Cecilia Cheung), and Red (Louis Coo). Whitebrows (Smamo Hung) is the grandmaster who presides over a battalion of warriors in Omei. The villain is Insomnia (who resides in a flying skull composed from human skulls). Amnesia (Kelly Lin) plays a nasty fairy. Patrick Lam is Thunder, one of Whitebrows' acolytes. Ng Kong is Hollow, the wielder of the Thunder sword; this character is reborn as Ying, played by Wu Jing. Lau Shun, a veteran of many Hong Kong pictures (including the *Once Upon a Time In China* series), plays the Buddhist monk Master Transcendental.

(Altho' the *wuxia* genre is very masculinist, Tsui Hark was keen once again to promote female characters, and to include women in warrior roles. So Zhang Ziyi's role as the newbie fighter Joy (and general's daughter) was one that in another production would've been played by a man).

Sammo Hung is masterly as the aged patriarch Whitebrows from the 1983 *Zu* movie – playing the same role (tho' with even longer white eyebrows): now Whitebrows has the ability (like everyone else in the 2001 movie) to zoom into the skies like Superman.

If you gave a high budget to a bunch of Hong Kong filmmakers along with access to a batch of computers and work stations and asked them to come up with a wild ride of a movie based on ancient, Chinese mythology, it might be something like *The Legend of Zu*. It's mad, it's skittering all over the place, it's edited at the rate of a human heart about to explode. *The Legend of Zu* injects even Tsui Hark's hyper-kinetic movie-making with a dose of near-fatal adrenalin (once again, Tsui's regular editor, Marco Mak Chi-sin, was the cutter).

The form of *The Legend of Zu* updates the 1983 *Zu: Warriors From the Magic Mountain* with a glittering barrage of visual effects and high fantasy

3 Because also in 2001, Tsui Hark also found time to direct *Old Master Q*. Meanwhile, he had helmed *Time and Tide* in 2000, and *Black Mask 2* in 2002, and produced *Vampire Hunters* in 2002.
4 Ekin Cheng was already well-known for many TV and movie appearances by the time of *Zu* – his role as Wind in *The Stormriders* (Andrew Lau, 1999) was an obvious forerunner of King Sky in *Zu*.
5 Zhang Ziyi was riding high then on the success of *Crouching Tiger, Hidden Dragon*.

costumes – it's *The Wizard of Oz* meets *Star Wars* meets the Shaw Brothers, but, this being a Chinese action picture, there's a feeling of freedom and openness that you won't find in any similar Western action-adventure or fantasy movie. (It operates within rules, though, it's not totally 'free' – but the 'rules' are different for this movie, compared to the Hollywood/ Western equivalent).

Set in a mythological China, where the *jiangzhu* is exaggerated and stylized to a super-heightened degree, *The Legend of Zu* is a world of mountains, colossal palaces, ancient, Buddhist temples, waterfalls, lush, green valleys, and floating islands of rock (prefiguring *Avatar* (2009), but clearly drawing on *Laputa: Castle In the Sky* (1986).) This time, the location scouts consciously avoided the usual and very familiar sites of Hong Kong cinema (so, no 19th century village sets, no stony scrubland, no bamboo forests, and no hillside roads). Instead, *The Legend of Zu* exhibits a much more rarefied and mythological look, in keeping with its subject matter of god-like characters and the magical realm of Zu.

The key relationships in *The Legend of Zu* are not of lovers, friends, families or parents and children, but teachers and pupils (and with colleagues within a team). You hear the word *sifu* (teacher) a lot: you have pupils (Ying, Joy) begging to be taught, pupils (King Sky) haunted by their teachers, with Whitebrows as the Ultimate *Sifu*, etc (and Sammo Hung certainly convinces as a *sifu* – Hung has done *everything* in movies, and then some!).

*The Legend of Zu* is also a movie of silly hairstyles (poor Cecilia Cheung!), mad, pointy, gold headdresses (for Louis Koo), characters delivering near-meaningless dialogue wearing their best 'grim' expression (Ekin Cheng stays grim throughout), and continuously billowing cloaks and costumes (every shot has a wind machine placed two inches from the actors' noses, plus smoke, and clouds, and filters).

THE STORY.

The plot is simple in *The Legend of Zu*, tho' its delivery is not: it's heroes vs. villains. The villain is Insomnia, a shape-changing and very magical critter who aims to become ruler of the Zu mountains (and the *jiangzhu*). So Whitebrows and his acolytes, plus King Sky and Red (and other heroes gathered along the way, such as Enigma), assemble to combat Insomnia.

You will notice right away that one character is notably missing in the 2001 *Zu* update/ remake/ sequel: Yuen Biao's Dik Ming-kei. Yes, gone is our audience identification figure (thankfully, there's no dumb modern-day wrap-around story, though). Along with Biao, much of the humorous approach of the 1983 *Zu: Warriors From the Magic Mountain* is ditched too, which contributed considerably to the success of the movie. The 2001 *Zu* is an altogether more sombre affair. (For instance, the teaming up of King Sky and Red is played pretty straight, without the bickering and humour that characterized Ding Yan with Dik, or Dik with Yat Jan, in the 1983 version of *Zu*. Gone is Dik's goofing around. And there's nothing like the erotic/ flirtatious scene between the women in the palace and the monks).

Hang on, there *is* a character in the manner of Dik Ming-kei in *The Legend of Zu*, and, in typical Tsui Hark style, it's a young woman not a young man: Joy (Zhang Ziyi) takes on the role of the neophyte warrior. Unfortunately, Joy's contribution to the story of *Zu* is rather marginal (and doesn't exploit Ziyi's talents fully, either).6 Joy is not really the audience's identification or observer figure.

▶

So, to kick off the 2001 movie, Whitebrows announces the theme of the piece in the first minute: he tells his disciples gathered in the temple at Omei that they must guard against greed and jealousy. And that's what the whole movie is about.

The prologue of *The Legend of Zu* occurs in the Kunlun mountains, serving to introduce Dawn and her protegé, King Sky (and two of the main stars). It's filmed in mysterious greens in craggy, windswept heights and giant, Buddhist statuary (Zu exists between Heaven and Earth). The hint of a romance between Dawn and King Sky is evoked (partly thru the casting of Ekin Cheng and Cecilia Cheung), tho' romance is a very minor element in *The Legend of Zu* (indeed, Dawn sends King Sky away partly because of the emotions complicating their teacher-student relationship).

Insomnia attacks here, and re-appears when we shift to 200 years later. Among the assaults on our heroes that Insomnia tries are sending *doppelgängers* to duel King Sky and Red, attacking the general and his troops, and firing bolts of energy at Whitebrows in Omei. Whitebrows responds with his Sky Reflector weapon. Act one of *The Legend of Zu* closes (around the 30-minute mark, as usual), with a stalemate, as Insomnia retreats into the Blood Cave, and Whitebrows issues orders to the main characters.

The weaponry was conceived as energy rather than physical objects (tho' there are plenty of those, too). King Sky has a moon orb and a sun orb (gifted to him by Dawn, in the prologue); Red has an amazing set of steel angel's wings; and the magical swords (mandatory in a *wuxia* picture) are yards or even miles long (and are called Heaven and Thunder). This is magic of an elemental kind, of the forces of skies, suns and storms.

The second act of *The Legend of Zu* includes scenes where Whitebrows discusses the challenge of facing Insomnia with Master Transcendental, the Buddhist monk; Whitebrows disappears to find a suitable weapon (leaving the arena open for the younger heroes), after instructing them what to do (and leaving King Sky in charge); Hollow and Enigma training with the Heaven and Thunder swords; Enigma being healed by King Sky, and later vice versa.

The scene between the fairy Amnesia (Kelly Lin) and Red (who's guarding the Blood Cave) is a curious allusion to *Peter Pan*. As the scene unfolds, with the customary cuteness in depicting Amnesia the pixie, you

6 One character seems a little ill-served by the 1,000 miles-an-hour pace of *The Legend of Zu* and that's Joy: played with gusto by the lovely Zhang Ziyi as a tomboy in tanned make-up, more could've been made of Joy's psychological journey from general's daughter to magical warrior apprentice (to Thunder, played by Patrick Tam).

wonder where this is going. Until the Blood Cave gets restless (by growing enormous horns!), and poor Red becomes infected by the fairy (a re-jig of the scene in the 1983 *Zu*, where Ding Yan was poisoned by the Evil Sect).

The third act of four acts of *The Legend of Zu* (using a four-act model) features a rescue mission in the Blood Cave, led by King Sky (he's now self-revived, using one of the three skills outlined earlier by Whitebrows – the power of regeneration). Confronting his shadow, Red, still possessed by Amnesia the fairy, King Sky undertakes an epic battle, while Ying is sent to rescue the captured Enigma.

One of numerous intriguing gimmicks here has spirits being split from bodies – thus, Ying rescues Enigma's body, while King Sky magically yanks Enigma's spirit out of Red's skull. Very abstract/ metaphysical stuff, visualized with much use of ghostly vfx (and of course the obligatory magical zooming about).

The fourth, final act of *The Legend of Zu* brings the struggles between the heroes and the villains to a highpoint: now the Heaven and Thunder swords, wielded by Enigma and Ying (the swords are *yin* and *yang*, male and female), have successfully fused (exactly what that means, and how it works, is left too vague by the film). Now the villain, Insomnia, is covering the land of Zu in a Blood Cloud, and it takes all of the ingenuity of the heroes to best him. Characters are zipping across blood-red skies, firing bolts of energy, and wielding mile-long, green swords. The Buddhist monks jiggle their beads and chant as they (and Master Transcendental) try to counter the onset of the Blood Cloud. (One niggle: it's a pity that Sammo Hung doesn't appear in person to deliver a piece of Hungian action. Instead, Whitebrows materializes as superimpositions, and a flashback to his wise words. Was Hung busy elsewhere at this time? Whitebrows is also conspicuously absent from the *dénouement* and the 'didn't we do well?' scenes. After appearing so prominently in act one, it's a big omission having Whitebrows bow out of the ending).

The finale of *The Legend of Zu* plays out as expected: the villain is trounced, and the heroes are victorious. Red has sacrificed himself to the cause (begging King Sky to kill him because of his infection by Amnesia/ Insomnia), King Sky vows to rebuild his clan, and order is re-established (and with a final flurry of his cloak, he vanishes into a blood-red sunset).

VISUAL EFFECTS.

The technical qualities of the filmmaking in *The Legend of Zu* are superb – particularly the integration of visual effects achieved on the set and the vfx added in post-production. By this time, the filmmakers at Cinefex and Menfond Electronic Arts had developed very sophisticated techniques to blend a variety of effects together.

The visual effects and the action in *The Legend of Zu* don't 'over-whelm' the story, they *are* the story. While Western critics complained about *The Legend of Zu* that was the story was confusing, and that the characters were thinly-drawn, the movie *is* telling a story all of the time, even when it's assaulting the audience with an extraordinary collection of effects and tricks. It's true, tho', that the characters are definitely sketchily presented, so that their feelings, their desires, their goals and their motives are only pencilled in at best. The trouble with that superficial approach to characterization is that it can weaken the story and the action (and charas become interchangeable – thus, the characters of King Sky and Thunder are very similar).

The combination of digital and post-production visual effects with the earthy, in-front-of-the-camera form of filmmaking in *The Legend of Zu* is dazzling. Virtually every shot in *The Legend of Zu* has had visual effects of one sort of another added to it, as Tsui Hark and the team aim to have a higher vfx shot count than comparable Western movies of the period such as *Star Wars: The Phantom Menace* (1999), *X-Men* (2000) or *The Matrix* (1999).

On seeing *Star Wars: The Phantom Menace* for the first time, Tsui Hark said he wasn't keen on the animation:

> When everything you see is created by animators, it starts to feel hollow. No weight. You want some weight. After a while you feel kind of left out. (LM, 24)

*The Legend of Zu* was advertized as having more visual effects (or visual effects shots) than *Star Wars: The Phantom Menace*. Almost impossible to say (and meaningless, anyway), because *The Phantom Menace* is wall-to-wall visual effects, like *Zu*. But not a minute of *The Legend of Zu* goes by without some action or other, and almost every shot seems to include visual effects. *The Legend of Zu* could be seen as Tsui's answer to *The Phantom Menace* (yet detractors could point out that the visual effects in *Zu* are just as floaty and uninvolving as in the *Star Wars* prequel movie. In *Zu*, tho', the charas are *literally* floating all the time. Few characters keep their feet on the ground for long).

*The Legend of Zu* also seems like Tsui Hark's reply to the *Stormriders* franchise, which covers very similar territory, and *The Stormriders* (Andrew Lau, 1998) was very clearly a movie made in the shadow of Tsui. It even used personnel from the Tsui Hark Circus, including his editor, and many actors. Did Tsui look at *The Stormriders* and say, 'that's *my* movie!' Because it is. (However, *The Stormriders* is a superior movie to *The Legend of Zu*).

Chinese filmmakers take a completely different approach to visual effects movie-making from their Western/ Hollywood counterparts: In the West, filmmakers are still tied to notions of 'realism' or 'naturalism', to delivering visual effects which simulate 'reality', and have some aspect of being 'believable'. Chinese filmmakers couldn't care less about that! The visual effects filmmaking in *The Legend of Zu* is so wild it approaches abstraction quite often, so that the swirling clouds, the zipping trails of flying martial artists, and the seemingly continuous storms and churning, volcanic interiors come across like the experimental *avant garde* work of a cutting edge, postmodern video and computer artist who's exploring the outer reaches of the cyber realm.

The colours of *The Legend of Zu* are marvellous – by the end of the movie, the filmmakers must've delivered every hue (and type) of sky possible (visual effects houses around the world must have huge databanks of skies – and *The Legend of Zu* is a strong contender for the Most Skies In A Movie award); they are not afraid of being extremely abstract at times (so that, when the human figures exit the frame, those images of nothing but scarlet light and orange clouds resemble a Mark Rothko canvas).

The flying skull-shape vessel in which the villain Insomnia resides is a superb piece of conception and digital execution – the skulls flow thru the sky, as streams of skulls that thunder by, reforming the dragonish skull in the air (the approach was reprised in *Journey To the West*).

In a way, the traditional and very old-fashioned fables and folktales of Ye Olde China are the perfect vehicle for the outrageous visual effects movie-making to be found in *The Legend of Zu* . Because there's no need to think about the story much at all – it's a simple structure comprising: the good guys versus the bad guys, with the heroes caught in the middle (i.e., the standard narrative structure for most Hong Kong action movies, and for many Tsui Hark movies, and for most action movies everywhere).

The archaic story elements in *The Legend of Zu* also mean that Tsui Hark and the vast team of filmmakers don't need to bother themselves with complex storytelling – however, they *are* telling the simple story using *very* complex means. Every shot in *The Legend of Zu* looks as if the filmmakers were challenging themselves to come up with something that hadn't been seen before. So they add new colours, new movements, new colourful skies, new morphing or digital elements, until the *Zu* remake is very far from the regular photography of regular filmmaking.

The *Star Wars* prequel movies (1999, 20002 & 2005) are virtually animated movies with the live-action footage of actors pasted into the scenes (a trend taken up by other action-adventure flicks in the West – but only those with the enormous budgets to accomplish this kind of post-production filmmaking). *The Legend of Zu* is in the same vein, so that it's more accurate to consider it as an animated movie with live-action additions[7] (the newer, postmodern conception of filmmaking), rather than a live-action movie enhanced with some visual effects (the older model).

*The Legend of Zu* is thus Tsui Hark's whole-hearted entry into digital filmmaking, into post-production filmmaking, the sort of movie which doesn't come together until the post-production period. (And yet, of course there are numerous practical effects, employed on set – smoke, fire, water, fog, interactive lighting, and lots of pyrotechnics).

Pyrotechnics? What Hong Kong action movie *doesn't* have petroleum in barrels exploding at some point?! Yes, part of the tiny budget of every Hong Kong actioner is set aside for the pyrotechnician to set alight parts

---

7 The actors are often reacting to nothing on the set, just staring and reacting where the assistant director or the director tells them to look. In the case of Tsui Hark, however, actors have been doing that for decades, because Tsui has been a pioneer in vfx filmmaking in Asia.

of the set or blow up a car. And fire and explosions are a part of *every* Tsui Hark action movie. So in *The Legend of Zu*, the characters duel by firing at each other – bolts of energy which leave smoke trails, and impact with a big explosion. It's the skills of the Taoist priest in the *Chinese Ghost Story* movies (punching with the palms outwards) taken to a wilder level.

THE SCORE.

Ironically, altho' the visuals are insane in *The Legend of Zu*, the movie is let down at times by its soundtrack: there is a way too busy sound design (by Martin Chappell), adding multiple channels of whooshes, zings, rumbles, grumbles, creaks and yet more whooshes to every movement (how many sounds can you concoct to accompany a martial arts character zooming up into the sky?! – they are all here!). So the soundtrack of *The Legend of Zu* is very different from the Hong Kong action pictures of the 1950s thru 1990s: it assumes the multi-layered approach of Hollywood action cinema, which uses 70 channels of sound effects where three would do perfectly fine. In the regular Hong Kong action picture, sound effects are loud and punchy, but they are few (and atmos is seldom included). They don't confuse, they add clarity and exaggeration to the scenes. But in *The Legend of Zu*, sound designer Chappell and the large sound team have gone nuts with weeks and weeks of sound effects editing and mixing. The result is at times a mishmash that confuses the movie, and overwhelms the audience. (However some of the sounds are marvellous: the grating, distorted scraps and grinds for the appearance of the skull of skulls, for instance).

Similarly with the score for *The Legend of Zu*, composed by Ricky Ho. Oh dear, what a pity! *The Legend of Zu* has opted for one of those *continuous* musical scores, so that the music is burbling along in pretty much *every* scene. Which means there is no let-up, no interludes, no pauses. And no build-up of tension and release, few changes of mood or tone, all of which are music's most fundamental elements.

As with the 70 channels of sound effects, the music is just *too much* in *The Legend of Zu*.[8] Stuffing a movie with too much music swamps the picture (the *Lord of the Rings* series, any superhero movie, and anything directed by Steven Spielberg are recent examples). So there's no escape from the constant, puttering music in *The Legend of Zu*. (I would love to see *The Legend of Zu without* the music – and *without* the too-busy sound effects in the action scenes).

Also, Ricky Ho and co. have opted for a Western, orchestral sound, where traditional, Chinese music, folk music, and percussive drumming might've been more suitable.

THE ACTION SCENES.

*The Legend of Zu* seems to be a case of a bunch of filmmakers challenging themselves to come up with a script that would contain more

8 It doesn't help, either, that the home entertainment releases of *The Legend of Zu* (on DVD) mix the music far quieter than the sound effects (this occurs a lot in home enter-tainment releases).

action scenes than any comparable movie (after all, by this time, Tsui Hark, Yuen Woo-ping and co. had certainly done it all before – many times!). In the second half of *The Legend of Zu* – no, throughout *The Legend of Zu* ! – nary a minute goes by with some action flaring up. This is a movie that is bored rigid if more than a minute unfolds without some action erupting. The speed of the storytelling is beyond neurotic, beyond anxious, beyond cocaine-hyped.

The pace of *The Legend of Zu* is so frenetic that it might've benefited from inserting some more 'air' into the scenes, or allowing for the audience to breathe a little![9] But this is not a movie that breathes normal air – it is hyper-ventilating on some magical ingredient from China's ancient herbal past which gives the user the dynamic energy of someone who can't rest, doesn't know when to sleep, and can't keep their mind on anything longer than 10 seconds. But, as *The Legend of Zu* is pretty much a constant battle, there is no let-up, and no rest until the end credits run.

Meanwhile, the narrative of *The Legend of Zu* is taking fabulously mad twists and turns (don't try to keep up, just enjoy the craziness of it all): there are characters flying all over the place (it's difficult to think of a similar movie of recent times in live-action with so many flying scenes – this is like all of Kung Hu's movies crammed into one film), often flying using swords (including the colossal, magical Thunder Sword, an outrageously phallic totem that's near-impossible to control); Enigma's spirit is trapped inside Red (and is extracted magically); battles rage in weightlessness inside the Blood Cave; Ying and Enigma fuse their spirits (or something) in order to have the power to defeat Blood Cloud, and so on.

When the villain Insomnia emerges from the Blood Cave in the form of a Blood Cloud to wreak havoc in the land of the immortals, in the 2001 movie's final act, the narrative boils down to one battle after another. The repetition of the story ideas (which might be wearying in another movie) is forgotten by the audience in the rapid assault of colourful imagery and sounds – Blood Cloud covering the sky with a gloopy, shiny, red mass (that clearly recalls the climax of *Princess Mononoke*, 1997);[10] the giant demon head that lurches out of the crimson blob, a stunning piece of animation; Amnesia the fairy who possesses Red using phantom troopers to attack the heroes in their compound, Trojan-horse style (this comprises one of the fastest-moving battles in a Tsui Hark movie – and his action scenes're already faster than everyone else's!),[11] and so on.

COMPARING THE TWO *ZU*s.

Inevitably, some critics compared the *Zu* of 2001 with the *Zu* of 1983, which was a much-liked movie, as well as being regarded as a classic by critics, and a pioneering outing for its use of visual effects. And you could argue that the '83 *Zu* has a more appealing cast (and a stronger centre to it, in the figure of Yuen Biao).

9 There *are* breather moments, but too few. About three, in all!
10 And also another 2001 movie, *Evolution* (Columbia/ DreamWorks).
11 The scene looks as if the filmmakers challenged themselves to come up with a speedier fight scene than ever before – it's a triumph for Yuen Woo-ping and the stunt team.

The 2001 *Zu* is *not* the 1983 *Zu* updated, reworked or rewritten: no, the 2001 version is a new take on the material. Many elements are carried over from the 1983 *Zu* (the super-villain, Whitebrows, the mythical *jiangzhu* setting, etc), but many elements disappear: the Ice Queen, the Ice Palace, Dik Ming-kei, the Evil Sect, Yat Jan and the Buddhist monks, the healing-of-the-monks middle act, and the frame story.

The middle acts of *The Legend of Zu* have versions of the healing episodes in the 1983 *Zu*. For example, Hollow (Ng Kong) is killed in a training session, when he and Enigma try to merge their Thunder and Heaven swords. Enigma falls to Earth – head-first, in a blaze of fire. Handily, King Sky is on hand to rescue her (from a waterfall's pool out of a travel brochure), and to use the moon orb as a healing aid (later, the situation is reversed, with Enigma tending to King Sky, who's been burnt to a crisp). At this point, King Sky has been told (by Whitebrows) that Enigma is really Dawn, his *sifu* from 200 years ago. Hollow, however, is re-made by Whitebrows, no less: but he's a different person, now called Ying (and played by charming innocence and high, athletic energy by actor Jacky Wu Jing – later the hero of the two *Lake Changjin* movies), who's lost his memory. Enigma sort of updates the character of Yat Jan in the 1983 *Zu*.

THE OUTCOME.

Sadly, *The Legend of Zu* turned out to be something of a disappointment for the filmmakers, and for Tsui Hark, just as the 1983 *Zu: Warriors From the Magic Mountain* had been. All of that money (U.S. $35 million – which's *a lot* in the Hong Kong film industry! – most of the classic movies we know and love from Hong Kong cost U.S. $0.5-4 million), and all of that immense effort didn't quite deliver the movie that Tsui hoped for (and the 2001 update was partly conceived to specifically crack the issues with the first movie). And *The Legend of Zu* certainly wasn't as well-received as the original *Zu: Warriors From the Magic Mountain*.

The casting, I think, could have been more star-oriented. Accomplished as the three lead actors (Cecilia Cheung, Ekin Cheng and Louis Coo) are, *The Legend of Zu* really does need actors of the marquee value of Andy Lau, Leslie Cheung, Chow Yun-fat, Maggie Cheung or Tony Leung.

Part of the problem with *The Legend of Zu* as storytelling is that altho' the over-arching plot is simple – a villain with godly powers is disrupting the world and needs to be stopped (i.e., it's the standard plot of all action-adventure stories) – the way that the plot is related is a little indistinct and over-complicated. For instance, how the heroes are working to combat the super-villain Insomnia contains several abstract elements. Whitebrows, for ex, talks in metaphysical and theological terms (of regeneration, for instance). But how those philosophical and metaphysical concepts can be turned into action and drama that'll work in a movie is something else. And you have to admit that the filmic solutions that *The Legend of Zu* conjures up are not wholly satisfactory, or dramatically compelling.

Take the villain, Insomnia: after zooming around the clouds as a skull made from human skulls, he or it retreats to the Blood Cave. And despite it/ he being visualized as an ugly demon-like figure for a short time (courtesy of intricate special make-up), the villain sort of disappears for too long. (The cuts back to the Blood Cave and red goopiness oozing about don't function convincingly as a movie villain who's Up To No Good. Again, it's too vague, abstract, and dramatically static, no matter how many channels of grating, screeching sound effects are added).

Much more successful is a movie baddie like the Tree Demon in the *Chinese Ghost Story* flicks: a monster with a killer tongue and tendrils. However, Tsui Hark and the team have Been There, Done That with those sorts of villains and that sort of cinematic approach (with practical effects, puppeteering, animatronics, special make-up, and men in monster suits).

▶

But if you come to *The Legend of Zu* as a style piece, a visual effects piece, an action piece and a spectacle piece, you won't be disappointed (the phantom troopers action sequence is worth the price of admission alone). Not every movie has to be 'serious' and sober like *War Horse* or *Medea*. *The Legend of Zu* is designed from the outset as a crazeee romp, and *The Legend of Zu* trumps most of its contemporaries for the sheer daring of its visual effects. (Once again, you are reminded that Tsui Hark and his production teams are fearless – they really are not afraid of trying *anything* to see if it works).

And if you put the story aside, and forget what characters are supposed to be doing what and why, and consider *The Legend of Zu* as a visual extravaganza, it is very impressive. *The Legend of Zu* features not just one or two spectacular shots, but many; many images are beautiful, with a dreamy, floaty quality amidst clouds and smoke (verily the 'floating world' of Japanese art); the landscapes are cleverly integrated with the visual effects and background art to create a suitably magnificent mythological realm; the imagery of the characters flying in every direction is amazing; the shots of the warriors of Omei soaring thru the sky *en masse*, like a phalanx of archangels out of a Gustave Doré engraving, are genuinely incredible.

One wonders if *The Legend of Zu* might've been more satisfying conceived wholly as animation (the influence of Japanese *animé* is particularly strong here, down to details like the giant, golden sunsets). Tsui Hark had already attempted a full-length animated movie with *A Chinese Ghost Story* not long before *The Legend of Zu* (tho' that production also had its problems). But in animation, the storytelling in *The Legend of Zu* wouldn't have been hampered by the restrictions of live-action. (However, limitations have never bothered Tsui – indeed, he recognizes that all movies are produced with limitations).

Tsui Hark called *The Legend of Zu* 'a disaster'. Well, we know that Tsui is not fond of his own films, seeing only the flaws (and he regards every work as 'unfinished'). But *The Legend of Zu* is by no means a 'disaster': not like the following movies which are duds: *The Lion, the Witch and The Wardrobe* (cost: $180m), *Prince Caspian* (cost: $200m), *Voyage of the Dawn Treader* (cost: $140-155m), *Spider-man 3* (cost: $300 million),

*The Brothers Grimm, Tin-tin, Home On the Range* (cost $110 million), *Snow White and the Huntsman* (cost: $170 million), the *Bourne* series, *Quantum of Solace, Casino Royale, The Hunger Games, Hannibal, Kingdom of Heaven, G.I. Jane, Batman Begins, The Beach, 8MM, Alien vs. Predator, Chocolat, Vanilla Sky, Amélie, About a Boy, Billy Elliot, Punch-Drunk Love, 8 1/2 Women, The Hulk, Oceans 11,* the *Charlie's Angels* movies, *Unbreakable, Jungle Book 2, Lemony Snicket, Sin City, Lara Croft, King Arthur, The Village, X-Men Origins: Wolverine,* the *Bridget Jones* films and *Where the Wild Things Are.*

Altho' *The Legend of Zu* wasn't well-received by Western critics (and it didn't even get a theatrical release), it is certainly superior to all of the above duds and flops (there are 100s more I could cite). Some of the above movies are not only abysmal, they are offensive ideologically and politically.

But a movie with Tsui Hark at the helm and with Yuen Woo-ping orchestrating the action, and featuring Chinese, mythological characters, is probably going to have something worthwhile in it. And *The Legend of Zu* does.

# 27

# *BLACK MASK 2: CITY OF MASKS*

## *Hak Hap 2*

*Black Mask 2: City of Masks* (*Hak Hap 2,* 2002) would probably rate as the most demented of Tsui Hark's recent movies as director – an insane superhero movie edited at 1,000 miles per hour, with action orchestrated by geniuses Yuen Woo-ping and Yuen Bun and, included in the price of admission: ex-porn star Traci Lords as a super-bitch superhero.

*Black Mask 2: City of Masks* was produced and directed by Tsui Hark, made by Film Workshop and One Hundred Years of Film, distributed by China Star in Hong Kong, and starred newcomer Andy On as Kan Fung/ Black Mask (in the Jet Li role in the 1996 *Black Mask* movie; On was voiced by Andy Lau in the Cantonese dub (also the narrator); this dub also includes familiar Hong Kong names like Raymond Wong, Patrick Lam, Cecilia Cheung, and Cherie Ying). Also in the cast of *Black Mask 2: City of Masks* were Tobin Bell, Scott Adkins, Jon Polito, Tyler Mane, Rob Van Dam, Terence Yin, Ko Shou Liang, Sean Maquette, and former-porn-star-turned-actress Traci Lords.

*Black Mask 2* was filmed mainly in English, with a partly Western cast. Yuen Woo-ping and Yuen Bun were back as the action choreographers.[12] Music by J.M. Logan. Bill Lui was art director. The DPs were Horace Wong Wing-Hang and William Yim Wai-Lun. Marco Mak Chi-sin and Angie Lam On-yee were the editors. Make-up by Poon Man-wa and Yip Lin-lui. Fx by Cinefex and Koan Hui-on. William Fung Kwun-Man was costume designer.

*Black Mask 2* was scripted by Charles Cain and Jeff Black, from a story by Tsui Hark, Julien Carbon and Laurent Courtiaud. It was produced by Tsui, Charles Heung and Tiffany Chen. *Black Mask 2* was released in the West (like many of Tsui's later works, by Columbia TriStar) on Dec 24, 2002 (Jan 9, 2003 in Hong Kong). 97 minutes. (102m in the Cantonese cut).

*Black Mask 2* is Tsui Hark's answer to the continuing stream of

---

12 Aided by Ku Huen Chiu.

superhero and comicbook movies pouring out of the Hollywood Film Factory (coupled with input from the video game industry, and also drawing on Japanese *animé*). Preposterous, ultra-violent, over-blown, over-cooked and over-the-top, Tsui and his team concocted a suitably ridiculously over-done visual style drawing heavily on the North American superhero movie model (with the *Batman* movies[13] as an obvious reference point, along with *The Green Hornet*). Saturated oranges, pale blues, multi-coloured shadows, tilted camera, and *very* rapid tracking shots, *Black Mask 2* was filmed like a comic, where every camera move is like a punch to the face in a panel in a comic, or like a speed line in Japanese *manga* emphasizing an action (the source of the *Black Mask* franchise is a Chinese comic, a *manhua*).

*Black Mask 2* also comes across as the work of a filmmaker trying to invent fresh ways of covering static dialogue scenes: *Black Mask 2* is not a movie comprising predictable shots like a close-up shot followed by an over-the-shoulder shot! Instead, the camera is roving across faces and spaces with the kinetic energy of an adrenalin freak, or a jittery video gamer who's been playing a computer game for 72 hours without sleep.

*Black Mask 2* is another movie where Tsui Hark throws down the gauntlet to those filmmakers (and critics) who demand that movies be constructed from perpetually moving cameras and editing which never holds on a shot longer than 2.0 seconds. 'You want fast?' *Black Mask 2* asks, and goes on to deliver the speed that few other filmmakers can achieve (let alone sustain). It's not the *speed* of the editing (i.e., cutting shots shorter than average), and it's not the rapidity of the mobile camera (i.e., moving the camera faster than average for mobile shots), it's the *storytelling*, and the construction of the beats within the storytelling.

In a Tsui Hark movie, you don't breathe, you don't pause, you don't wait, you use every moment of your 97 minutes (and yet there *are* pauses, and breathers). Instead, you hurtle on ahead. (However, Tsui remarked of the first *Black Mask* movie that he fancied doing *Black Mask* in a documentary style. But when *he* came to direct the *Black Mask* sequel, the documentary approach went out the window! – because the seduction of romance and mythology, of exaggerated, comic visuals, of going over-the-top is too much for Tsui to resist!).

*Black Mask 2* was also a densely worked-over visual effects movie (it opens in true Tsui Hark-style with an elaborate visual effects shot of a storm-tossed ocean (Cinefex and Koan Hui-on did the effects). That sets the tone: lashing rain, flashing lightning, nighttime, a tilted, restless camera, a raging sea, and all achieved using digital technology). In *Black Mask 2*, lightning is flashing even when there isn't a storm, and lamps are flickering for no apparent reason, other than it looks cool.

By this time (2001-2002), Tsui Hark and his teams were heavily into post-production visual effects, where computers and digital jiggery-pokery were deployed not only to enhance existing shots, but to tell the story with entirely digital shots. There are zooms into eyes, interior microscopic

13 Composer J.M. Logan spoofs bombastic superhero movies, including the parping brass stings by Danny Elfman in the *Batman* movies.

views of bodies (and machines), dives into suitcases, digital make-up on faces, full-body digital doubles, digital rain, animated cityscapes, and plenty more vfx.[14] Hong Kong film production had certainly come a long way in the 20 years between *Zu: Warriors From the Magic Mountain* in 1983 and *Black Mask 2* in 2002!

Setting aside the insane story and characters of *Black Mask 2*, you can appreciate how a filmmaker such Tsui Hark is the perfect artist to explore the amazing possibilities of digital imagery. There is no timidity in Tsui's form of filmmaking, no feeling of settling back into safe naturalism or ordinary, domestic melodrama. No! Tsui is a genuinely adventurous filmmaker, and when he and his teams are given the budget to deliver digital effects and special make-up[15] and the like on a big scale, they relish the opportunity. (And, coming from a different, Asian mind-set, they are not locked into the photorealism of North American visual effects, with their tiresome and deadening emphasis on 'realism').

Altho' Tsui Hark is the biggest name associated with *Black Mask 2* creatively, and altho' in a book about Tsui Hark, it's easy to say, 'Tsui did that', and 'Tsui did that', we should remember that he didn't write the script – Charles Cain and Jeff Black did. Tsui has a 'story by' credit, but that is shared, too – with Julien Carbon and Laurent Courtiaud. Thus, five people contributed to the script (not to mention the producers and others).

In the first ten minutes, *Black Mask 2* had staged plenty of action, including fire-fights, and a remarkable action sequence showing Black Mask doing his thing: battling a horde of bad guys in cars (at night, of course), using several martial arts forms plus some *James Bond*-style stunts (Black Mask is flying under, over and beside the cars).

The concrete, steel and glass *mise-en-scène* of *Black Mask 2* derives partly from filming in Thailand (it recalls the look of *Total Recall* (1990), which was staged in Mexico City). Tsui had already filmed in Thailand for *A Better Tomorrow 3*. Certainly, *Black Mask 2* is very gritty and flashy, and even ugly in parts (in, for instance, the portrayal of the wrestlers as long-haired, greasy louts).

▶

As to the story and the characters, *Black Mask 2* followed the North American superhero model closely, while also departing from it to pursue its own eccentric agenda. For instance, yes, there's the romantic subplot[16] involving Dr Marco[17] Leung (Teresa Maria Herrera) as a brilliant scientist (shades of *The Hulk*), reprising the role of ditzy librarian Tracy (Karen Mok) in the 1996 *Black Mask*. But she can't stand to be touched by a man! At all! And when she does, she jumps a mile, or she freezes into a hysterical catatonia, so she becomes rigid like a corpse! (A delightfully insane take on the Tsui Hark female empowerment theme).

14 The monsters and hybrids are marvellously portrayed, with the leaping praying mantis (Rob Van Dam) as a particularly formidable foe.
15 There is special make-up all over *Black Mask 2*.
16 The work colleague hoping for a dinner date with Leung, and Kan's romantic rival, is dispatched in the hospital with a claw thru the chest, leaving the way clear for Kan.
17 Is the name Marco a reference to Tsui Hark's regular editor, Marco Mak Chi-sin? Probably, as the first *Black Mask* also used names from Tsui's buddies – Shek, Szeto, etc, and called its hero Tsui.

It has to be said, tho', that the klutzy comedy performed by actress Teresa Maria Herrera expressing the kooky, jumpy, irritated aspects of the character of Dr Marco isn't wholly successful (and gets a little tiresome at times). Freezing limbs from the mere touch of a man is used one too many times, and gags like the doctor being stripped[18] down to a bra and panties in the back of a speeding car by accident don't quite work.[19] (Hong Kong cinema is fond of portraying the female romantic leads as nervy, goofy (but attractive) personalities, like Karen Mok in the first *Black Mask* movie. And Tsui Hark is fond of casting impish, svelte, eccentric women in his movies).

It's thus a pity that there isn't any chemistry between Teresa Herrera and Andy On (but emotional heat isn't necessary – or even desired – in this movie). They are teaming up, after all, to battle the DNA programme of the villains. But it certainly enhanced the first *Black Mask* that the chemistry between Jet Li and Francoise Yip was plain to see.[20]

Craziest of all in *Black Mask 2* (in a *very* crazy mix of kitsch pop Americana, Chinese martial arts, hi-tech futurism and comics culture), was the group of misfit wrestlers (so that *Black Mask 2* is another movie which explores the crossover between professional wrestling as glossy entertainment and movies. Performers such as the Rock (Dwayne Johnson), Dave Bautista and John Cena also took up acting in movies).

The wrestlers, Black Mask's adversaries, are a motley rabble who look (and act) like a moronic rock band (aside from the slinky shape of Chameleon, the only woman among them). Grizzled, long-haired, ugly, crude, and with only one brain cell to fight over among them, the wrestlers are a bizarre parody of the crass and tasteless values of Middle America (note that the wrestlers are cast from North American actors, so they become yet more representations of *gweilo*, foreign white devils in Chinese culture). And they're an easy target for the satire of Oriental veteran filmmakers like Tsui Hark! (When Tsui takes up North American pop culture, he can't help sending it up).

❱

Meanwhile, the other main female character, Chameleon, is played by (former) porn star Traci Lords[21] as a sleek super-bitch avenging her lover's death (Chameleon is a reprise of the Yuek-lan character in *Black Mask*, played by Francoise Yip). Costume designer William Fung Kwun-Man puts Lords in red-orange hair, green eye-shadow, and an L.A. punk rock groupie costume of black leather jacket, black tights, and cutaway top (perfect for a night out cruising the clubs on Sunset Boulevard). *Black Mask 2* teases with portraying Lords nude[22] by having her play scenes invisible or semi-transparent (and with a digitally-created body in many scenes). Because she's called Chameleon, right? In a mid-film fight,

18 The heroine is portrayed semi-clad several times.
19 She's trying to escape from Black Mask – by hurling herself out of a car doing 80 m.p.h.!
20 Or in *Dr Dee*, between Andy Lau and Lin Bingbing.
21 Traci Lords has had an extraordinary life and career by any standards, creating shock-waves thru the adult video industry when she was found out to have been under-age in pornographic movies.
22 Several movies have similarly titillated audiences by referencing Lords' earlier career in porn – which she would prefer to forget.

Chameleon chases Black Mask sliding down an enormous banner (advertizing Black Mask on TV) on the side of a building, and then duels with him underneath the fallen banner, in between cars). So you've got a famous American porno star, who's naked, but (almost) invisible, battling humans mutated into monsters in outrageously OTT martial arts duels! It's pretty wild. (Lords performs some of her stunts, tho' elsewhere in the movie; here it's mainly stunt doubles and digital animation).

Andy On is a handsome young chap who can move well. But he's not Jet Li – On might be a car valet guy at your hotel in B City. Good-looking, certainly, but no superstar.

Added to the mix in *Black Mask 2* is the MacGuffin of transmuting humans using DNA and chemical treatment (so the wrestlers become semi-human monsters... So welcome, ladies and gentlemen: Iguana Man! And Snake Man! And Wolf Man! And Claw Man!). Very silly, and sort of fun, in a bone-headed, dumb-and-dumber sort of way. (The filmmakers have a lot of fun with the different attributes of each human-monster hybrid, introduced in the first act). Thus, Doctor Marco is vital to the plot, because she can limit the effects of the drugs that Moloch and co. are developing.

There is also an epic scale to the opening teaser of *Black Mask 2* involving a super-computer-brain called Zeus who lives in a colossal hi-tech facility on an island like something out of the *Ghost In the Shell* manga or the updated *animé* version of *Metropolis* (2001). Here god-like Zeus turns out to be the orchestrater of the powers that have mutated Black Mask and his chief adversary in this movie, Dr Laing (Scott Adkins). Zeus plays the scary crime boss in a thriller, ordering the deaths of a bunch of scientists worldwide that Black Mask will try to visit. Zeus is the super-capitalist, too, who invents super-human bodyguards to sell to giant corporations, a riff on hi-tech Pacific Rim companies. (This leads on to the opening action scene of *Black Mask 2* where Laing and co. are after the Japanese scientist that Kan Fung has just reached. All of which inaugurates the man-on-the-run plot, as Kan flees Zeus's mob, and battles Moloch's crew, while also trying to secure healing, taking scientist Dr Leung, also a target of Zeus's, in tow).

So the first act of *Black Mask 2* introduces us to the hero, the villains, the gang of wrestler-mutants, their boss, King (Jon Polito), and another Mr Big, Moloch (Tobin Bell). Among the many action beats in act one are Black Mask and Dr Laing duking it out (a teasing glimpse of their later smackdowns, of course); Black Mask taking on Laing's henchmen in cars; Iguana (Andrew Bryniarski) beating up (and apparently killing) several bystanders; and the set-piece duel between Black Mask and Iguana.

The big action sequence in the first act of *Black Mask 2* is a monster-on-the-loose scenario, as Iguana completely transforms into a mini-Godzilla. From the stadium (where Iguana creates merry hell in the bleachers), the action moves up to a tall building and a radio mast. Exactly why isn't made clear (Iguana has Hellraiser's kid as a hostage, but why he becomes King Kong and climbs up the building carrying the boy doesn't make sense) – except that it's a suitably impressive setting for the crazy duel btn Black Mask and Iguana (while the crowds below react with hysteria, matched by the frenzy of the press). The location also provides the spectacular setting for the inevitable literal cliffhanger, plus Iguana's high fall (onto, of course, a car). Everything is played in *Black Mask 2* at a high pitch, as if only out-size acting is acceptable in the over-blown leviathan of a superhero movie.

The fury of Chameleon at her lover's death (when Iguana falls to his doom – this is a form of suicide), is something to see: Chameleon sets upon Boss King with a vengeance. That it's an American actress not known for body-slamming action and stunts playing Chameleon makes the scene even juicier. But when the sinister Moloch enters the scene, and the offer of a million bucks seems to placate the wrestling team (but not Chameleon, of course!), we reach the end of the first act.

❱

Because *Black Mask 2* follows the North American movie model for superhero stories, the story is sort of automatically ridiculous and barely worth exploring at any length. Ditto with the characters, who're drawn in the usual simplistic, one-dimensional manner of the superhero format (so you don't empathize with these characters on any level – they have as much dramatic substance as pixels in an arcade game).

Tho' the narrative model of *Black Mask 2* might draw on North American superhero movies and comics, there's no doubting that the style and approach of *Black Mask 2* is completely Hong Kongian. Nobody produces movies quite like Hong Kong filmmakers, and this version of superhero yarn set in a futuristic steel and glass city (dubbed 'B City')23 is self-consciously and gloriously Asian.

❱

Take your brain out and sit back and enjoy the terrifically insane action sequences which Yuen Woo-ping, Yuen Bun and their teams have cooked up! In the big mid-film bust-up (staged in – where else in a Hong Kong action movie? – another harbour and warehouse!) – you can see the filmmakers kicking ideas around at a production meeting and arguing, *darn, what can we do that we haven't seen before?* And what did they come up with? Only an action scene filled with stampeding elephants!24 Only the hero pursuing the bad guys on top of a galloping elephant! And a martial arts duel right on top of, in and around of the beasts!

Meanwhile, the stunt and action teams have a go at turning a man (Robert Allen Mukes) into a snake: arms by the side, legs locked together, and wearing a huge snake mask, this is a fun, try-anything character (which is one of the appealing features of Hong Kong cinema – they will try anything for a laugh, or to see if it can be done).

Black Mask vs. Praying Mantis (Claw) and Snake is yet another superb action sequence. Once again, it's staged partly on the side of a

---

23 B City is perhaps a reference to Bangkok, as the movie was filmed in Thailand.
24 A logistic nightmare, this sequence betrays a lack of spending in the budget, with ship containers being used as a set yet again in a Hong Kong action movie (and the street that the beasts march along is obviously not a real street).

building. For no particular reason, opponents are always dragging or chasing Black Mask up buildings (one suspects that the real reason is simply that Hong Kong action teams like to use multiple levels, and are especially fond of staging action in vertical spaces). The scene is also a reprise/ re-hash of the tower scene in the first *Black Mask*, when there were characters hanging off buildings, and fights on scaffolding.

The outrageous herd of elephants sequence is just one of many action beats in the middle act of *Black Mask 2*, which also includes: a fierce fight in a hospital (a favourite locale for Hong Kong action movies); Black Mask and Dr Leung fleeing the bad guys in a car; Black Mask punishing King in his office; Black Mask versus Chameleon; the wrestlers assaulting a compound to get some iridium, etc.

Much of this material is narratively simple, as each side struggles to gain control of the genetic technology, and one group battles against another (i.e., it's standard narrative development for the second act of an action movie). But writers Charles Cain and Jeff Black also include a classic scripter's device: a countdown (here, it's the revelation, discovered by Chameleon, that the genetically-modified wrestlers have a very limited life-span, and will be terminated within a matter of hours).

❯

In the third act of *Black Mask 2,* the concept of a 'DNA bomb' is introduced, to up the stakes and involve the whole of the futuristic city in the villains' plans. Now Dr Laing, on the orders of Zeus, includes the bad guy Moloch in the nefarious scheme to infect everybody in the city with mutant DNA, to turn them all into monsters (tho' Moloch ends up as a head being kept alive in a machine, an ancient science fiction trope).

Black Mask (who's also been infected) teams up with Dr Marco and Iguana's son Raymond (as a sidekick) to defeat the villains. This involves a series of duels in a stadium which consume most of the finale of *Black Mask 2* (echoing the finale of *Double Team*). The two Yuens (Woo-ping and Bun) and their stunt teams utilize every area of the concrete maze, including, as usual in a Hong Kong action picture, the upper levels. So characters're forever leaping onto concrete pillars or struts and back down again. There are so many duels, with Black Mask at the centre of them, the 2002 movie becomes One Giant Fight, using buses, motorbikes, guns, pipes, chains, statues, and anything else the filmmakers can get ahold of.

The finale of *Black Mask 2* plays out as expected, and, this being a Chinese action movie, extends the dramatic conflicts into very lengthy brawls. The only thing that spoils the finale is that it really should take place at night, in a smoke-filled, intricately-lit environment, or outside under lightning flashes, to do justice to the hi-tech *milieu* of this thriller. The concrete *mise-en-scène* of the sports arena looks like the car lot of any shopping mall. And you have to admit that we have seen much of this material before, and done better by both Yuens (Bun and Woo-ping) and by director Tsui Hark and his crew. (For instance, the big duel between Dr Laing and Black Mask, the set-piece of the finale, a-punchin' and a-kickin' on top of the statues outside the stadium, while impressive, lacks some of the zing and invention of other duels from the incredible cinematic resumés of the Yuens and Tsui. However, it's cute that Dr Marco and Raymond get to have their moment to shine, trouncing a henchman with a pile of enormous pipes – in the mandatory factory setting).

Minor charas Chameleon and Claw are finished off in a perfunctory manner – a sort of dual suicide, as they fall to the concrete in the midst of the chaos. (Well, it's Chameleon who decides fall to her doom, now she's found out about her limited life-span. She asserts, in a line that seems written especially for Traci Lords: 'I'm not gonna disappear!' Sadly, because Chameleon's left the team, she doesn't know about the antidote that Dr Laing waves in the face of the other wrestlers to get them to co-operate. With Black Mask defeating Laing within a few minutes outside the stadium, Chameleon could've been saved).

❱

*Black Mask 2* is hampered by a lack of money in some areas, and a ropey sound mix (for the English language release). The movie doesn't quite flow in some sections. Items such as the 'DNA bomb' don't come across strongly enough, but are played out chiefly in dialogue. The casting isn't spot-on. Some of the characters are under-written (and lack the calibre of actors to flesh them out, as good actors can do with a flimsy script). The Zeus giant brain scenes are amazing – the movie could've done with more scenes on this scale. Many of these flaws are flashed up if one views *Black Mask 2: City of Masks* as an American-Chinese hybrid, and references the American superhero models that *Black Mask 2* draws upon. Seen as an insane, Hong Kongian action movie stuffed with visual effects, and as a send-up of mind-numbingly dumb, Hollywood actioners, it's much more successful.

It goes without saying that *Black Mask 2* is the sort of movie that film critics loathe – because it reminds them that movies are entertainment, and 99.99% of them are crude, crass and idiotic (and thus movie reviewing is a stoopid exercise, because it applies solemn critical approaches to trash). Critics hate this kind of movie, too, because (1) it doesn't make any difference what they say about them, and (2) the target audience couldn't care less what critics say.

❱

But *Black Mask 2* is also a movie which is below Tsui Hark's talents. Not that it's easy (or enjoyable) producing a movie as enormous, complicated and intricate as *Black Mask 2* (it isn't; it must've been hell to film in parts, not least because of all the night shoots). It's that, well, somehow this superhero material is just too throwaway and superficial and inconsequential to merit the amount of attention and time and energy it's been given by Tsui and the production team.

Whichever way you slice it, *Black Mask 2* is founded on baloney, and Tsui Hark is worth more than building mountains out of junk. Maybe if *Black Mask 2* was funnier, or even stoopider… (certainly it couldn't be camper!).

We should also note that Tsui Hark was still moving at 1,000 miles-an-hour around 2002, directing and producing movies with astonishing rapidity: at the time of *Black Mask 2*, these included: *Time and Tide* in 2000, *The Legend of Zu* and *Old Master Q* in 2001, and *The Era of Vampires* and *Black Mask 2* in 2002.

You can argue, though, that the trashy, Neanderthal qualities of *Black Mask 2* are precisely what make it appealing. To take a bunch of hairy wrestlers and turn them into mutant-beast superheroes is wonderfully dim-witted. So you can place *Black Mask 2* alongside other send-ups of superhero movies, such as *Superhero Movie* (2008) and *Mystery Men* (1999) (and, in Hong Kong cinema, films like *City Hunter*, or Wong Jing's comedies, or the Tsui Hark-produced *Wicked City*). Of course, many superhero flicks are already so OTT they're beyond parody (or, like the *Batman* movies of 1989-1997, they wisely parody themselves before anybody else can).

And if you ask, what is Tsui Hark doing making a movie so retarded?, the answer is: having a blast!

# 28

# *SEVEN SWORDS*

# *Cat Gim*

*Seven Swords* (2005, *Qi Jian* in Mandarin) sees Tsui Hark white-hot, operating at full power. *Seven Swords* is a contender for the greatest swordplay movie ever – it's got everything, and then some.

It is ecstatic cinema.

PRODUCTION.

*Seven Swords* was written by Tsui Hark, Chi-Sing Cheung and Chun Tin-nam. It was exec. prod. by Bong-Chui Hong, Raymond Wong Bak-Ming, Yong Zhang and Nansun Shi, and prod. by Tsui, Lee Joo-Ick, Zhong-Jun Ma, and Zhizhong Pan. Angie Lam On-yee edited. The DPs were Johnny Choi Sung-fai and Venus Keung Kwok-man. Kenji Kawai was composer. Zhanjia Yang was prod. des. Art. dir. by Eddy Wong. Costumes by Shang Li-Ya. Yun-Ling Man was key make-up artist.25 Steve Burgess was supervising sound editor. Sound by Chung Wai Leung and Chung-Hau Leung. Chia-Liang Liu was action director (along with ten action choreographers such as Lau Kar-leung, Xiong Xin-xin and Stephen Tung-wei).

In the vast cast were Donnie Yen,26 Charlie Yeung Choi-nei, Lau Kar-leung (also one of the action directors), Leon Lai-ming, Duncan Chow, Lu Yi, Tai Li-wu, Sun Hong-lei, Kim So-yeon and Zhang Jing-chu. Released July 25, 2005. 153 mins.

The budget was rumoured at eighteen million U.S. dollars – in the West, a movie of this scale would be 150-200 million. (Also, movies such as *Knock-off* ($30 million) and *Double Team* ($35 million) cost far more!).

*Seven Swords* is based on the historical novels by Liang Yusheng – *Saiwai Qixia Zhuan* and *Qijian Xia Tianshan* (= *Seven Swords Descend*

25 The make-up in *Seven Swords* goes for a 'no make-up' look (Yun-Ling Man was key make-up artist) – a sort of 'realistic' look which, ironically, is achieved with plenty of make-up. However, while the villagers are deglamourized, the villains take up the painted faces approach, with scary body paint (not quite Peking Opera, but getting there).
26 Yen was a replacement for the Korean actor Song Seung-heon, who left before filming began.

*From Mount Heaven*). They were first published in 1956-57, in serialized form in the *Ta Kung Pao* newspaper.

The novels of Liang Yusheng had been filmed in 1959, as *Swordsmen Leave Tianshan*, by the Emei Film Co. in Hong Kong. *Seven Swords* was conceived on a grand scale as part of a multi-media franchise (and a six-part series of films) – which included a TV series (*Seven Swordsmen* internet and cel phone games, comics, and even clothes. The follow-up, *Seven Swords 2*, was rumoured over the years since 2005. The TV series, *Seven Swordsmen* (a.k.a. *Seven Swords of Mount Heaven*), appeared in 2006.

The score for *Seven Swords* was by the Japanese composer Kenji Kawai (b. 1957, Tokyo), one of the great composers of film and TV music of recent times. Kawai provides thrilling action cues with jagged strings and percussion (drums are one of Kawai's specialities), and sweeping, plangent cues for the slower scenes (some of which are very beautiful). Kawai played in rock bands (such as Muse) b4 moving into film soundtracks (a path many others have taken, such as Danny Elfman, Rick Wakeman, Thomas Dolby, and Vangelis). Kawai has scored *Devilman, Vampire Princess Miyu, Blue Seed, Sorcerer Hunters, Deep Fear, Hyper Princess, The Samurai, Kibakichi, Death Note, Eden of the East, Gantz, Sleeping Bride, Princess Minerva, Mikadroid, Mermaid Forest, Ip Man, Ghost In the Shell, Ranma 1/2, Maison Ikkoku, Gantz, Moribito, Ring, Ring 2, Chaos, Dark Water* and *Kaidan*.

The filmmaking of *Seven Swords* is on an epic scale, with enormous outdoor sets, location shooting in remote parts of China (including Xinjiang and the Tien Shan), as well as studios in Beijing, lavish costumes, intricate props (such as weaponry), 100s of extras, grandiose fight choreography, and luxurious production values everywhere.

The production of *Seven Swords* was based in Beijing (which was increasingly in the 1990s a second production base for Tsui Hark). Here, before principal photography, the main actors took part in horse-riding lessons, and martial arts classes run by Lau Kar-leung and the other action directors (once again, many in the cast hadn't done any martial arts or action). From Beijing, the production spent months filming in the remote region of Xinjiang.

Everybody who worked on *Seven Swords* attests to the challenges of filming in the wilder regions of China, and up in the mountains (the extreme cold, for a start, plus the high altitudes – the dizzy reactions to the altitude were included in the movie). This was a movie production which was an adventure in itself. But the tough schedule paid off, because the vistas that appear on screen are just amazing.

CASTING AND WOMEN.

*Seven Swords* is a kind of summary of Tsui Hark's cinema – or the historical/ fantasy/ martial arts aspects of it. All of Tsui's previous historical movies are referenced in *Seven Swords* – some in a joky manner. Like the umbrella that one of the heavies wields, a riff on the icon of Wong Fei-hung (but now it decapitates victims when it closes). The narrow corridor duel at the end comes from *Once Upon a Time In China 2.* Charlie Yeung Choi-nei, meanwhile, is introduced in a pastoral manner, riding a donkey and playing a flute, a reference to her break-out role in *The Lovers* (the flute is also linked to the magical sword that Wu is given, with holes to cover to control it and *New Dragon Gate Inn*).

Talking about Charlie Yeung Choi-nei – you can't miss the fact that *Seven Swords* makes Yeung's Wu Yuanying one of the chief protagonists. In the first act, we are seeing events thru her eyes often, and we follow her (and Han Zhibang) up into the heavenly mountains, to call for help from the magical swordsmen (she insists that they go). And Yeung also seems to have top billing – alongside Leon Lai and Donnie Yen (Yeung had recently returned to acting).

Charlie Yeung might be another of Tsui Hark's transformations from male to female in terms of characterization. In the archaic sexual politics of the era, it's only Yeung among the women) who becomes a member of the Seven Swordsmen (and only by dressing as a man). And altho' Yeung is one of Tsui's favourite actresses, he is certainly tough on her, too: right after she's been introduced riding the donkey, she's attacked by one of Fire-wind's heavies, punched repeatedly and dunked in a pool several times so she loses consciousness! (Oh yes, Chinese cinema is certainly harsh in its treatment of female charas at times!).

*Seven Swords* continues Tsui Hark's insistence on promoting roles for women. While some women are concubines and traded and treated as such (this is set in the *jiangzhu* after all), such as General Fire-wind's mistress Green Pearl (So-yeon Kim), there are several strong female roles, including two among the heroes (Charlie Yeung, playing the main protagonist, Wu Yuanying, and Jingchu Zhang as the young teacher Liu Yufang, a.k.a. Fang), and, to even things up, one amongst the villains (Jiajia Chen, playing one of the Twelve Guardians, Kualo).[27] There is a kind of love triangle evoked in *Seven Swords* – Wu and Han were once an item. But Han decides later he prefers Fang.

No one can miss the fact that the film producers have cast small and *very* skinny women in the three lead roles (and one amongst the villains) – Charlie Yeung, Kim So-yeon, Zhang Jingchu and Jiajia Chen. This is a female type seen in plenty of Tsui Hark movies, of course – and, let's not forget, across so much of contemporary, Chinese cinema.

According to Zhang Jingchu, she requested a meeting with Tsui Hark and the writers because her role didn't have enough (or any) action in it (Zhang is a young teacher and mother figure to the village children). Possibly the scene where Zhang's Fang picks up a blade and dispatches the traitor Dongluo was the result of that meeting.

Appearing as an actor (and action director) in *Seven Swords* is Lau Kar-leung, a true legend in Hong Kong cinema: born in 1934, he was taught

---

27 The lovely Chen as Kualo was given a striking punky look with white make-up and piercings, and sadomasochistic behaviour and lesbian longings. Kualo licks her blade, drawing blood on her tongue, and lusts after Green Pearl.

*kung fu* by his father Lau Charn who in turn was taught by Lau Sai-wing, the most famous follower of the real Wong Fei-hung. He appeared in the *Wong fei-hung* film series, worked at Shaws, action choreographed movies for Chang Cheh, and directed classics of action cinema such as *The Executioners From Shaolin, 36th Chamber of Shaolin, Legendary Weapons of Kung Fu, The Spiritual Boxer, Scorpion King, Martial Club* and *Drunken Masters 2* and *3*.

Lau Kar-leung plays the ageing martial artist (and former executioner) Fu Qingzhu (a.k.a. Unlearned Sword), who brings together the denizens of Martial Village ((Wu Village) and the mythical heroes (it's also Fu Qingzhu was starts up the narrative of *Seven Swords*, as a survivor of the invasion by Fire-wind's crew in the opening reel). As the plot unfolds, Unlearned Sword is often the go-to character for explanations, and he also advises and leads the band of heroes (as befitting an actor and director like Lau, who is one of the patriarchs and wizards of Hong Kong action cinema).

ROMANCE.

There's a teensy bit of romantic subplot between Wu Yuanying and Transience, as well as the romantic triangle between Han, Wu and Fang; if Han moves towards Fang romantically, there needs to be someone for Wu (who was originally linked to Han) – you can't have the top-billed female star, Charlie Yeung, being boyfriend-less; hence Transience steps up (and he's played by one of the top three billed stars, Leon Lai, one of the 'Four Heavenly Kings' of Cantonese pop music, who's often cast in romantic roles). Thus, it's Transience who teaches Wu how to use the Heaven's Fall sword, for instance, in a training scene which possesses a romantic subtext (and a clearly sexual undercurrent, too – they've both got their hands on a phallic sword, and you have to put your fingers over the holes in the sword's hilt to make it work).

There is also a teensy subplot where Liu Wufang looks up to Dragon/ Chu Zhaonan (where Fang and Han are about to make love, and Fang declines, saying she can't love two men). There is more of this subplot in the deleted scenes (it doesn't really exist in the movie as is, tho' it is evoked in the dualogue between Fang and Green Pearl by the stream).

The second love triangle among the minor subplots in *Seven Swords* features Green Pearl, General Fire-wind's concubine, who's taken away by Chu Zhaonan (much to Fire-wind's irritation). The relationship that develops over the course of the movie between Green Pearl and Chu is touching – they are both Korean (sharing the same language is the first step in the development of their relationship).[28] Both Chu and Green Pearl are portrayed as troubled souls, and presumably their displacement from their country of origin is part of their woes (the scene where Dragon takes Green Pearl to a hill and shows where her homeland lies is very moving – aided by an exquisite strings cue from Kenji Kawai. The concept of 'home' has become increasingly significant in Tsui Hark's cinema. This is also where he casts her ashes at the end).

---

28 This reflects Tsui Hark as growing up in Vietnam, not Mainland China.

Green Pearl, meanwhile, is an enigma, viewed with suspicion by the villagers (as an outsider and potential threat), befriended by Liu Wufang, and kept under the protection of Chu Zhaonan. The performance of Green Pearl by So-yeon Kim emphasizes her nervous, fearful demeanour, with much breathy, gaspy acting. (Kim is very beautiful, and has been given a pale make-up (by Yun-Ling Man and the team) and is usually lit by DP Johnny Choi with a strong top-light which brings out her amazing features).

The image-making capability of Tsui Hark is in full effect in *Seven Swords*. Some of the most memorable images in *Seven Swords* are of the greatest visual effect in history – the human face. There's an astonishing close-up of Charlie Yeung, for example, as she turns away from the re-united couple of Han and Fang, with Yeung's face three inches from the camera lens. (And the camera holds and holds on the faces of many of the cast – Yen, Kim, Zhang, Leon, etc).

EDITING.

The truly awesome Angie Lam On-yee was editor of *Seven Swords*, and her contribution is absolutely fundamental to the impact of the movie. Yes, this brutal, macho martial arts epic was cut by a woman! If you are a fan of brilliant editing, *Seven Swords* is a sublime example (maybe only a few viewers would watch a movie just to consider the editing, but in a movie such as *Seven Swords*, you can't help but be aware of it).

*Seven Swords*, in its later acts, finds a clever means of including many more scenes, and squeezing in more material into its already long running time: it uses flashbacks and montages (two final versions were prepared – 120 and 150 minutes. And no doubt the movie went thru numerous variations, as usual with a Tsui Hark movie, and particularly movies cut using digital tools).29 Thus, instead of laying out scenes which require more gradual lead-ins and dramatic set-up, the movie can cut into the meat of the scene directly, because the framing of the flashback (and some narration occasionally), does the narrative work. Similarly with the montage form of editing, where longer scenes can be compressed.

When the Seven Swordsmen give up their weapons in General Fire-wind's compound, for ex, each of them receives an emotional flashback about the sword (which also reminds us just how much we've seen in this fantastic film – all the way back to the heavenly mountains).

Also, the flashbacks and montages make the finale a more complex sequence narratively: instead of parallel action happening at the same time, the movie zigzags across time. So now the Big Action Finale is intercut with scenes of Fang and the children fleeing the murderous traitor Dongluo, and with the later scenes of the Chu Zhaonan and Green Pearl story (when General Fire-wind's captured them).

The time shifting is pretty complicated, but it does the job of separating the multiple plots in the finale of *Seven Swords*. This sort of storytelling demands a good deal from an editor, and Angie Lam On-yee rises to the challenge: after all, this is a Tsui Hark movie, where time and

---

29 In typical Tusi-ian style, the opening shot of *Seven Swords* is a goat!

rhythm and pace don't flow as they do in any other movie (and certainly not in other action-adventure and *wuxia* movies).

The rough cut of *Seven Swords* came in at four hours – understandable for a film of this scale. Distributors of course wanted a film two hours or under; the 150-minute cut was selected because it was a more satisfying version – the 120-minute cut left out too much.

*Seven Swords* is structured in five acts, following the model of Kristin Thompson (where each act is 25-30 mins). Tsui Hark described the plot of *Seven Swords* as a kind of origins story for the Seven Swordsmen, relating how they came down from Mount Heaven.

Some Western viewers, not familiar with the source material by Liang Yusheng, found the plot of *Seven Swords* confusing. Part of the problem perhaps is that *Seven Swords* is an ensemble piece – it's a group of heroes tackling a bunch of oppressors (it's *The Seven Samurai*). The hero is split into three – Han, Yang Yuncong and Wu Yuanying, and they're aided by a bunch of swordsmen, plus assorted villagers, including teacher Liu Yufang and her father Chief Liu Jingyi. (Names likely continue to confuse Western audiences – but the novels by Liang Yusheng feature a vast assembly of characters. More appear in the *Seven Swordsmen* TV series).

BACK IN THE *JIANGZHU*.

*Seven Swords* can be seen as one of the big, prestigious Chinese action movies that's part of the cycle that began with *Crouching Tiger, Hidden Dragon* and continued with *Hero, House of Flying Daggers* and *The Curse of the Golden Flower* (and continued with *The Warlords, The Banquet, Red Cliff, An Empress and the Warriors*, etc). Like some of those movies, *Seven Swords* was filmed partly in Mainland China (and in Mandarin). It's another movie aimed at the Mainland Chinese market (as well as an international audience).

The *milieu* is the *jianzghu* once again, the mythical realm of the martial arts where Tsui Hark has spent years, cinematically. But it's not the whimsical, fantastical *jiangzhu* of *Zu: Warriors From the Magic Mountain*, but the earthy, tough, desperate martial arts world of *New Dragon Gate Inn* and *The Blade*. Just surviving takes all your energy (that's what Fire-wind says – survival is all).

*Seven Swords* features a large cast: the seven swordsmen of myth, three young characters, the villagers (including the Chief), plus the bad guys (General Fire-wind, plus Twelve Guardians, plus minor charas). The 2005 movie is one part of a much larger story, which might easily be a long-running TV series, or a series of movies. (Indeed, it was the forerunner of a 2006 TV series, *Seven Swordsmen* – see below).

General Fire-wind has a band of captains called the Twelve Guardians: they are each given an elaborate look (tattoos, piercings, jewellery, wonderful black-and-white face make-up, and decorated armour), and a unique weapon (such as shields with blades, a net of knives, scythes, a deadly umbrella, etc). The Twelve Guardians have names like Bald Lion, Hair Wolf, Dagger Peak and Stone Beast.

Everything is fake in a movie, but in a Chinese action picture and costume picture, you get a strong feeling that the actors really *are* in those places, you can feel the bright sunlight, the chilling cold,[30] the textures of the clothes, and so on. Oh, it doesn't make the slightest bit of difference whether a movie's made in studio or on location or in a cardboard box outside Burger King. Who cares? The audiences doesn't – they just want a good couple of hours entertainment.

Are *The Wizard of Oz, Sunrise* or *The Red Shoes* lesser movies because they were filmed entirely in a studio or backlot? No! But there's no denying the real, physical pleasure of the real, physical landscapes that a movie like *Seven Swords* employed. The films directed by Tsui Hark have an *acute* sensuality. You can find this full-on sensuality in the cinema of Andrei Tarkovsky, Pier Paolo Pasolini and the king of this kind of grand cinema, Akira Kurosawa.

But with the films of Tsui Hark, following on very much from Akira Kurosawa and epics like *The Seven Samurai, The Hidden Fortress* and *Yojimbo*, the sensuality is combined with astonishing action choreography, mobile, totally confident staging and blocking of actors, and piercingly exquisite cinematography (the photography by Johnny Choi Sung-fai and Venus Keung Kwok-man is truly exceptional in *Seven Swords*).

This is masterclass filming, in short, breathtaking in its ambition and scope. It is, I would venture, as genuinely 'epic' and 'visionary' as the films of David Lean or Akira Kurosawa or Cecil B. DeMille or D.W. Griffith (the usual film directors cited numerous times as filmmaking aiming for something Epic and Grand).

In *Seven Swords*, the seven swords of the title are: Transience, which Yang Yuncong wields, Star Chaser (Xin Liongzi), Celestial Beam (Mulang), the Deity (Han Zibang),[31] the Dragon (Chu Zhaonan), Heaven's Fall (Wu Yuanying), and the Unlearned (Fu Qinzhu).

▶

Tsui Hark remarked that the theme of *Seven Swords* is very simple: righteousness. That is, how to live in a society properly (this is also the theme of the *Once Upon a Time In China* series). But for each character, how to attain that is different and challenging. (In the aftermath of the attack of the Fire-wind mob on Martial Village there is a brief introduction of the pedagogic theme of being and acting righteous, when Leon Lai (Transience) talks to a child).

The script for *Seven Swords* (by Tsui Hark, Chi-Sing Cheung and Chun Tin-nam) is complex, orchestrating a large ensemble cast, and giving the main characters goals, motives and challenges. In the editing (often regarded as another rewriting process), the script becomes even more multifold – with the addition of flashbacks.

---

30 You can see the actors' breath in many scenes.
31 Han Zhibang, played by Lu Yi, is a reprise of the Daki (ethnic minority) character from *New Dragon Gate Inn* (he even looks like Xiong Xin-xin, who was Ngai) – he performs the Peking Opera tumbles that Tsui Hark absolutely loves. Don't bother *walking* across a space when you can flip and somersault across it.

Structurally, *Seven Swords* is telling several plots simultaneously, but the over-arching narrative scheme is boldly clear: an Imperial (Manchu) edict has been issued banning martial arts, and some enforcers are taking that literally, by wading into communities and slaughtering all of the martial artists. So, yes, it's the common people versus the Imperial court again, it's the peasants against the Manchu, it's the underdogs versus the oppressors, the staple of literally 100s of *wuxia pian* (and plenty of Tsui's earlier pictures).

The narrative background of *Seven Swords* is set out clearly and violently in the opening scenes, in a rural community, where the officers of General Fire-wind (the Twelve Guardians) arrive to create chaos. As in thousands of Chinese movies, the Imperial forces are portrayed as vicious bastards who smile gloatingly as they slice and dice their victims. (Their reign of terror is enhanced by digital grading, which picks out red, one of the symbolic colours of China, in the banners, sashes and of course the blood).

The first act of *Seven Swords* sets up the heroes, from Martial Village (300 miles away from the first village), and the antagonists, General Fire-wind's crew, and the quest for the superheroes from Mount Heaven who're going to Save The World. The set-up is basically *The Seven Samurai*, with a team of warriors defending a village (a narrative scenario that's been used many times since the original, tho' the 1957 Japanese movie remains the supreme rendering of the theme in cinema).

Notice how the movie cuts into the middle of scenes sometimes – par for the course in a Tsui Hark movie, which speeds along at 1,000 m.p.h. It suggests that plenty was cut out (and it was – the home releases contain some of the deleted scenes, and there's a longer version). For ex, the key scene in act one, when General Fire-wind's mob start their killing spree in a village, we cut right into the midst of a heated argument between the villagers and the assassins – there's no build up of the heavies on horseback entering the village, for instance (but, for a Chinese audience, there doesn't need to be: all we need to know is that the heavies this time are brutish Manchu threatening the peasant class).

Act one of *Seven Swords* culminates with Han, Wu and Fu reaching the heavenly mountains and successfully summoning the magical swordsmen. We are now in a wholly fantastical realm – mediæval China as it appears in myth and fairy tale. The photography, up in the snowbound mountains of Xinjiang, is staggeringly beautiful, and does as much as anything else in conveying mythical power. (Incidentally, Johnny Choi Sung-fai joined the Tsui Hark Circus on this movie, and became Tsui's regular cameraman).

‣

Act two of *Seven Swords* comprises two enormous action sequences at the start and the end of the act. It's the customary back-and-forth struggle of heroes and villains of action-adventure stories, as each side in the rival communities tries to gain the upper hand, of the peasant-class underdogs versus the Imperial predators. The action scenes are now coming thick and fast, culminating in a truly sensational sequence where General Fire-wind's crew makes a night-time assault on Martial Village (right in the middle of a scene where Fang was about to be hung as a scapegoat for the apparent betrayal by Unlearned Sword).[32] Fang is a teacher, protecting the children of the village – a reprise of very similar scenes in the *Once Upon a Time In China* series (played by Rosamund Kwan).

Everyone has their moment to shine in the night raid episode – this is the first time we see the Seven Swordsmen going into battle, and they don't disappoint. The action choreographers fully exploit the possibilities of the unique weaponry of the Twelve Guardians. (Notice how the heroes wield the sacred weapon of all Asia, the sword, while the Twelve Guardians have invented a bizarre array of crude tools. In Asia, you never ignore the sword – at your peril!).

Once again, the beauty, the speed, the athleticism, the dexterity, the skill and the intensity of the choreography in a Chinese movie achieves levels of transcendence, of poetry.

If ecstatic cinema ever existed, it's right here.

The heroes fight back with the action climax to act two, the mirror of the two halves of act two of *Seven Swords*, with a raid on General Fire-wind's compound. Again, everything is working at full power, with numerous stand-out beats, including a rapidfire duel between Kualo and Chu Zhaonan (Donnie Yen). The furious clash takes place on and under horses, in the inner sanctum of Fire-wind's digs. (Tsui Hark can't resist sneaking in lesbian subtext in a movie – so Kualo launches herself on top of Green Pearl, right in the middle of a life-and-death action sequence. It's highly improbable, but typical of Tsui's eccentric vision).

▶

Act three of *Seven Swords* is primarily a chase, tho' it involves the entire village: Martial Village has upped sticks and left, with General Fire-wind not far behind. There are many scenes where the villagers have halted on their journey, and the pell-mell pace of the movie is set aside. Editor Angie Lam On-yee has included breather moments, such as the intriguing two-hander between Fang and the Korean courtesan Green Pearl.

The breather scenes thicken the characterizations (important when there are so many charas), as well as allow the audience to get its breath back. Many Tsui Hark movies include scenes like this, despite his reputation as a 1,000 miles-an-hour filmmaker. However, a movie running to 80 or 90 minutes can't include so many of them. The 153-minute cut of *Seven Swords* features more than the 120-minute version did (because scenes like this are often the first to go).

Movies with so many characters need scenes like this for everything else to possess some dramatic substance.

▶

General Fire-wind is humanized a tad in his romantic longings for

32 Some of the Martial Village scenes are played at a hysterical level, whipping up the fervour of the underdogs fighting for survival against the Imperial hunters.

Green Pearl (which aren't reciprocated). But he is also given eccentric habits (laughing like a cartoon dog), and kinks (biting Green Pearl's bare back as she stuffs herself with food, in an unusual twist on a domination and rape scene). Sun Hong-lei[33] plays General Fire-wind with relish (how often do you get to play a cruel baddie on a cinematic canvas this large?): and despite the humanization of the super-villain, he is still the ruthless super-villain. For ex, his view of life is nihilistic: for him, humans might start out as fun-loving, innocent children, but they grow up to becoming man-eating beasts. It's the very bleak view of earlier Tsui Hark films like *The Blade* and *Dangerous Encounters – 1st Kind*. (Actor Sun said that Fire-wind had been killing for so long it didn't have any impact on him anymore, he just killed people as part of his job. Actually, this is how prehistoric people were millions of years ago. Did they fret and angst and feel guilty in the liberal manner about having to kill animals or aggressors who moved in on their territory? I doubt it).

One of the subplots of *Seven Swords* is a subject very close to Tsui Hark's heart: *home*, the idea of home, and being displaced from your homeland. The whole of Martial Village is disrupted, and becomes a caravan on the move, for instance. The notion coalesces around the concubine Green Pearl, and also Chu Zhaonan: both are Korean, both are far from home. In a poignant scene, Dragon takes Green Pearl to a spot in the mountains and shows her where her homeland is, far to the East. Dragon's command to Green Pearl is central to Tsui's life-philosophy: never forget your name, and never forget your home, where you came from.

THE FINALE.

The finale of *Seven Swords* follows the recipe for action-adventure and *wuxia* pictures – it comprises a giant action sequence in the Big, Villain's Lair set. Here the Seven Swordsmen have run to the rescue of one of their member, Chu Zhaonan, who's been captured by General Fire-wind and his crew (and is introduced chained to several horses, about to be pulled apart). The action is broken up into sections, with the Seven Swordsmen rescuing Dragon, battling the remaining Twelve Guards of Fire-wind, and many other beats, climaxing with the expected duel between the heroes and General Fire-wind. It's the two top-billed male stars of *Seven Swords* – Leon Lai and Donnie Yen – who get to face off against the super-villain, Fire-wind. Not only do they share the limelight, they also share a sword (Trans-ience),which they throw to each other.

The action is *stupendous*. It's filmed at night for added atmosphere (and no doubt meant weeks and weeks of gruelling night shoots for the cast and crew – but it was so worth it), and features a multitude of practical fire effects, creating a constantly flickering light. Everybody gets their moment to shine in a series of simply incredible duels.

And Charlie Yeung's Wu masters her tricksy sliding sword and dispatches a tough opponent in a very intense grappling fight. Also, it's

---

33 Sun Hong-lei wasn't a martial arts movie fan, and was sceptical, until he met the director and found out how the character could be played.

Wu who ultimately kicks off the hostilities in the climax: everybody else has given up their sword, but Wu won't: at that point, all hell breaks loose. (A superb gag has the lackey who's been gathering up the magical swords being lifted in the air, so the warriors of Mount Heaven can grab their weapons).

Transience (Leon Lai) takes up the first half of the furious smackdown with General Fire-wind, which occurs around the throne at the top of a flight of steps (the inclusion of flames and sparks adds even more thrills to the duel). The duel then shifts into several zones – a maze of columns behind the throne, to a narrow corridor, and finally an armoury.[34] (A memorable addition to the duels is the energy that the unfinished sword Transience exudes, shaking the banners and flames in the vicinity.)

Donnie Yen is a ball of energy: he escapes from the horses, but is still tied up with chains, which he employs as a weapon against Fire-wind. How the chains are eventually cut is another inventive beat in an action sequence stuffed with them.

Once again, Chinese action directors demonstrate that nobody else anywhere can stage action and sword fights like they can: the duel in the tall corridor (itself a call-back to the climax of *Once Upon a Time In China 2*) is fiendishly ingenious and almost impossible to carry off (let alone to stage and film).

Things get extremely brutal in the Fang-and-cave part of the plot of *Seven Swords*: Dongluo (Kuan-Chun Chi) is the spy inserted in the Martial Village group by General Fire-wind, feeding them with information. Fang watches in despair when Dongluo goes on the warpath – killing her father Liu Jingyi, the village Chief, and many others, including the unforgivable crime of slaughtering children. Just how the tiny, slight and terrified Fang dealt with this opponent is delayed until the *dénouement* scenes (she manages to slay Dongluo).

DELETED SCENES.

The deleted scenes, included in the home entertainment releases of *Seven Swords,* contain the usual scenes which were presumably cut for length (such as Transience meeting up with the Seven Swords at Tien Shan). With so many characters and the potential for numerous subplots, it's no wonder the rough cut came in at over four hours.

Some of the deleted scenes from *Seven Swords* thicken the romantic subplots (such as the love triangle between Wu, Han and Fang). Another scene depicts the additional romantic subplot which has Fang falling for Dragon (Chu). In true over-melodramatic style, Fang chooses to tell Han just as he's on top of her about to make love. (Of course, it's Wu Yuanying who accidentally spots the lovers wrestling in the hay).

An action scene was dropped: in the cave, Transience finds one of Dongluo's men going thru his gear. This would've played further into the subplot of Dongluo being the traitor.

Other scenes include a horse-lovers' sequence: Han has to say

34 Where the piles of gunpowder and cannon balls will provide the expected explosions. But for once, they don't (tho' Fire-wind does try, and Transience manages to prevent him).

goodbye to the horses of the village, including his beloved mount Joy Luck. If you like to watch horses galloping in spectacular settings (and who doesn't?), this is a fine scene.

One scene shows General Fire-wind and Green Pearl where the concubine refuses to play and sing for him. Another intercuts Fire-wind and an underling with the children playing in the cave. Another has the Chief and villagers worrying where the Seven Swordsmen are.

*SEVEN SWORDSMEN*

The TV series adaptation of the 1956-57 novels by Liang Yusheng appeared in 2005-2006: *Seven Swordsmen*, also known as *Seven Swords of Mount Heaven* and *Seven Swords of Mount Tian*. This was the television companion to the *Seven Swords* movie. Like the *Once Upon a Time In China* TV series, *Seven Swordsmen* was a big, prestigious production comprising 39 hour-long episodes (actually 46 minutes each). It was produced by Ciwen Pictures and Film Workshop for C.C.T.V., and filmed on video.

The *Seven Swords of Mount Heaven* series was produced by Tsui Hark, Cheung Sim-yam, and Wang Yong, and written by Tsui Hark, Cheung Chi-sing, Chun Tin-nam, Wu Jiu-xi, Liu Yu-zhu, and Li Chang-fu. The directors included Tsui, Jacob Cheung Chi-lung, Clarence Ford, Marco Mak Chi-sin, Gary Sing, and Lam Kin-lung.

In the enormous cast of the TV series were Vincent Zhao,[35] Yu Cheng-hui, Ji Chun-hua, Ada Choi Siu-fan, Sang Wei-lin, Gallen Law Ka-leung, Ray Lui Leung-wai, Liu Yue, Leung Kar-yan, Ai Dai, Kiu Chen-yu, Patrick Tam Yiu-man and Wong Hok-ping.

❀

The background story of *Seven Swordsmen* is the familiar one of Imperial (Manchurian) oppressors versus martial artists and political rebels. It's the 17th century in China and once again, the forces ruling the land are stamping out martial arts and its practitioners. Their target in the first episodes is the Martial Village, which houses the Red Spears Society, a secret, anti-Manchu organization of martial artists (the Manchurians have defeated the Ming Dynasty and established the Qing Dynasty.

Episode one of *Seven Swordsmen* introduces the background plot, some of the main characters, stages some swordplay action, and kicks off the story. Popping out immediately is the impressive photography and the glorious settings high up in Alpine mountains, which was also the environment of Mount Heaven in the *Seven Swords* movie.

Struggling through real snow (and fake snow) on Mount Heaven, three swordsmen from Wu Village (led by Fu Qingzhu – Yu Chenghui) hope to

---

[35] Vincent Zhao was Wong Fei-hung in the later films, and in the TV series, and also in *The Blade*.

obtain the aid of Master Shadow Glow, the aged swordsmith. The Master's charges, the four swordsmen of Mount Heaven (Chu Zhaonan, Yang Yuncong, Xin Longzi and Mu Lang), are first introduced training with wooden swords in among caves and glaciers, flying all over the place as they chase a white, floating flower.

The Imperial, Manchurian bullies are first depicted acting brutally and without remorse – they issue orders and castigate anybody who defies them. There's an attempt on General Nalan Xiuji's (Er Yang) life by a lone assassin which's swiftly rebutted (with death). During this scene, a Peking Opera performance plays out on a stage, a very Tsui-ian notion (the performers have to continue with blood spattered on their face make-up).

A more recent take on the *Seven Swords* material appeared in 2019 from Tencent Penguin Pictures/ Yinbo International Film (plus sequels), helmed by Francis Yam.

The Legend of Zu (2001).

Black Mask 2
(2002).

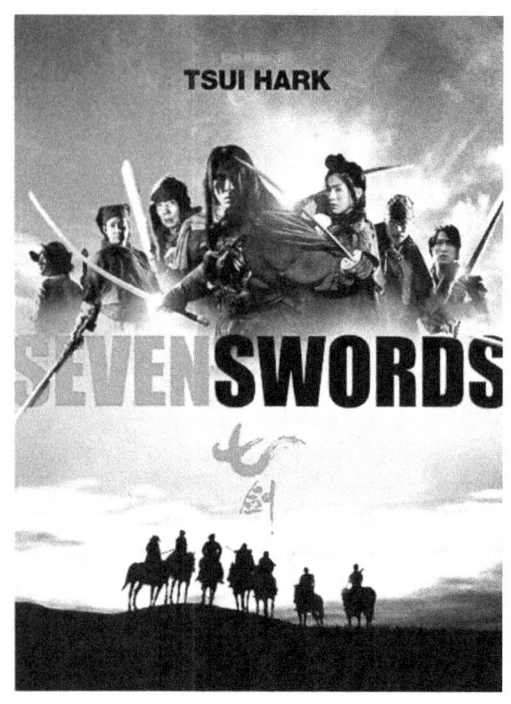

Seven Swords (2005). This page and over.

# 29

# *TRIANGLE*

## *Tie San Jiao*

*Triangle* (*Tie San Jiao,* 2007, a.k.a. *The Iron Triangle* a.k.a. *Jigsaw*) was a three-segment movie directed by Tsui Hark, Ringo Lam Ling-tung and Johnny To Kei-fung. It was written by Half Leisure, Kenny Kan, Sharon Chung, Yau Nai-Hoi, Au Kin-Yee and Yip Tin-Shing, produced by Tsui, To and Lam for Milkyway Image/ Film Workshop/ Polybona Films/ China Film Co-production Corp./ Media Asia Group (the latter seem to be the distributors of many recent Asian movies in the West). Cheng Siu-Keung was DP; music by Dave Klotz and Guy Zerafa; edited by David M. Richardson; and action dirs. were Chin Kar-lok, Yuen Bun and Bruce Maang Lung. The cast included Simon Yam, Louis Koo, Sun Honglei, Lam Ka-Tung, Kelly Lin, You Yong, and Lam Suet. Released: Nov 1, 2007. 92/ 100 mins.

Ringo Lam Ling-tung (1955-2018, Hong Kong) is best-known for the *On Fire* series, *Burning Paradise* and *Full Contact.* He had worked with Tsui Hark on *Twin Dragons.* Johnny To Kei-fung (b. 1955, Hong Kong) helmed *The Heroic Trio* and *The Eighth Happiness.*

Unlike most multi-director, anthology movies, *Triangle* isn't conceived in episodes (or episodes with a common theme or motif), but has a single story and a single set of characters (Tsui Hark initiated the concept, which revolves around three themes: temptation, jealousy and destiny).

Set in and filmed in Hong Kong, *Triangle* is a Cantonese thriller/ drama based around three middle-aged, Chinese losers (Fei, Sam and Mok) who get involved in crime (in this case, the heist of long-lost treasure). Inevitably, things go wrong, and keep going wrong for the three hapless and rather useless, wannabe criminals.

Yes, it's tough to survive in the heartless, big, bad old city — everybody needs money, everyone feels 'hard-pressed' (as the subtitles put it), as the pressure of survival in the contemporary world becomes difficult to sustain. Guns... knives... endless cel phone calls (cel phones are everywhere in Tsui Hark's later work), cars (*duh*, of course!), car lots, busy, city streets, television, a subway train, heavies in suits, dingy bars and fast food restaurants – *Triangle* has all of the usual ingredients of a contemporary thriller (whether it's made in Hollywood, Bollywood, London, Sydney or Hong Kong). Yes, let's face it – Cantonese cinema has churned out *thousands* of these movies.

So that's the A-plot of *Triangle:* the B-plot is – hey! guess what?! – a romantic story of sexual betrayal, as Sam's wife Ling fools around with cop Wen (Sam is one of those weak-willed, nervous husbands, the worst sort of person to put in charge of a gun or a car or a heist). Ling, meanwhile, begins the 2007 movie as the adulterous, long-suffering wife who wants to be rid of her useless spouse (she thinks he's going murder her, like his first wife, tho' she seems to have died in a car crash); but halfway thru Ling becomes Lady Macbeth, screaming and attacking her cop lover Wen (actually, the continuity of the characters and the stories is all over the place in *Triangle*, as if each successive director promptly ignored much of what the previous director had done! Which sort of defeats the aim of the piece!).

So we have seen this movie many times before. Well, sure, you can say that about pretty every movie in the arena of commercial cinema (and underground, *avant garde* and experimental cinema is also stuffed with repetitions and copies). But in *Triangle,* the feeling is instant and long-lasting. In book publishing, thrillers account for a quarter of all new fiction published. It's the same in cinema: thrillers make up a huge proportion of all movies released. So we've all seen 100s perhaps 1,000s of thrillers and crime and drama movies.

Thus, not a single element of *Triangle* is 'original' or 'new'; also, the approach taken with the material offers nothing we haven't seen a zillion times before. In which case, why even watch *Triangle* at all? Well, sometimes movies are able to persuade us to hear and watch the same old stories by the flair of their filmmaking, or the extravagance of their action and set-pieces, or their music, or the charisma and vitality of their stars, or the compelling nature of the old chestnuts they're telling.

*Triangle* has none of that: the actors, the performances, the technical aspects, the music, the set-pieces, the action, the costumes, the settings, the themes, the motifs, the politics – not a single element compels the audience. There's no Jackie Chan, no Jet Li, no Michelle Yeoh, and no Maggie Cheung to hypnotize us. The music (by David Klotz and Guy Zerafa) is mediocre (tho' moody and interesting at times). The cinematography (by Cheng Siu-Keung) is run-of-the-mill thriller stuff (more backlight! more smoke!). The action and fights are aiming for 'realism', but that's a meaningless concept in Hong Kong cinema! (and perhaps in all cinema).

*Triangle* is scuppered too by a total lack of identification with the characters and their situations: we just don't give a hoot about any of these dumb, vain, narcissistic, selfish, crude and unappetizing people...

we don't care what predicaments they get into (which become increasingly silly as the narrative unfolds)... and we don't care what happens to them in the end.

So a lot of energy and time (and Hong Kong dollars!) is expended on *Triangle,* and three veterans are at the helm: Ringo Lam Ling-tung, Johnny To and our own Tsui Hark. Add up all of the movies those guys have directed (and produced), and you have an incredible slice of Chinese cinema. But here, saddled with such unappealing, and unchallenging material and themes and characters, they skid into a wall like a car in a car chase (BAAAM!), and burst into flames.

There's just nothing especially gripping here in *Triangle.* Even the scenes which're supposed to deliver some wacky humour don't work (like the scene where the gang, fleeing a bungled post-heist confrontation, have their tyres punctured by a garage mechanic on the make who offers to fix them all for $HK 2,000. It's a sort of Jean-Luc Godard piece of black comedy (out of *Weekend* perhaps), or like something out of a North American road movie of the 1970s, when Warren Oates and Gene Hackman might've encountered some wild hill-billies off the beaten track).

Meanwhile, even the customary Tsui Harkisms, which form such a large part of his appeal as an outstanding filmmaker, are thin on the ground in *Triangle.* Why oh why can't Tsui come up with material befitting of his colossal talents? Why does he direct 10,000 miles below his potential? This is a guy who can direct *anything*, who can deliver incendiary movies like *Zu: Warriors From the Magic Mountain, Once Upon a Time In China, The Blade* and *Seven Swords,* but he comes up with yet another Hong Kong, action thriller drama that isn't dramatic, isn't thrilling, and contains little action.

❖

Let's approach *Triangle* from a different angle: forget the Tsui Hark angle (difficult!), and that Ringo Lam and Johnny To were co-directors, and look at *Triangle* on its own merits, as a movie that we watch and listen to.

It's not very good, is it?

Because it doesn't compel our attention, it doesn't excite us, or move us, or do any of the emotional-psychological-spiritual-visceral-physical-sensual things that we want (or hope) movies to do! It isn't interesting either on an intellectual level, or a political or ideological level. And not on a technical level.

By comparison with, say, *Knockoff* and *Time and Tide* (among Tsui Hark's later work), which were also contemporary thrillers, with a strong crime-in-Hong-Kong element, and which were thoroughly clichéd and predictable at the story and character level, *Triangle* is really poor. Because *Knockoff* and *Time and Tide* had many other ingredients that made them compelling, entertaining and enchanting.

By contrast, *Triangle* is one of those movies that you have to ask yourself: *why am I watching this?* Life is short, and there are thousands of other movies to see, so why this one, why this one now? Because it's a Tsui Hark movie? For me, that's a big part of it. Well, nearly all of it. Without

Tsui (or Lam or To), I wouldn't bother watching *Triangle.* Who would?

Sometimes it is interesting and insightful to see a great film director taking on a routine or clichéd story or genre. In the case of *Triangle,* however, no it isn't. Similarly, the experiment of having three directors and their writers tackle the same set of characters and develop an initial dramatic set-up is potentially interesting, but doesn't bear fruit (*Triangle* delivers shrivelled figs instead of juicy melons!).

By the third act of *Triangle* (directed by Johnnie To), the audience doesn't care a jot about that stupid, ancient jacket with gold buttons, or the money, or the endless gun battle in the long grass and bushes on a scrap of land next to the water in some out of the way section of the New Territories.

So a cop shows up. *So what?* So an alligator swims through the water. *So what?* So the darn lights keep going out in the riverside restaurant, and everybody stands there, waiting for someone to do something in the darkness. *So what?*

The third act of *Triangle* is like a bunch of actors waiting around for someone to write a fucking script so they can deliver their fucking lines and fucking go home. It's five a.m. again already! We've been shooting all night! For terrible money! So the night shoots go on and on as the filmmakers try to decide who's going to fire at whom, who's going to get away scot free, and who's ordered the chow mein and who's got the noodles.

Or something like that. Because *no one cares.*

Death by a thousand cuts. Or in this case, death by boredom... and the cicadas go *krrk-krrk* in an empty theatre in Kowloon. How many in the audience made it to the end of this 90-minute thriller?

Well, shoot, it *can* be interesting to consider a great filmmaker's failures – like Orson Welles and *Mr Arkadin* (1955), or Alfred Hitchcock and *Family Plot* (1976). But sometimes, as with Jean-Luc Godard and *King Lear* (1987) or Steven Spielberg and the depressingly bad *Tin-Tin* (2011), *Triangle* doesn't justify the amount of investment an audience might put into it.

# 30

# *MISSING*

# *Sam Hoi Tsam Yan*

So we are back in Tsui Hark Land with *Missing* (= *Sam Hoi Tsam Yan*, 2008), a horror thriller set in the world of scuba diving and clinical psychiatry. Zhang Zhao, Zhao Haicheng, Jiang Tao, Chi-wai Yan, Wu Chi-ming, Peter Ho Sun-chan, Eric Huen, Hiu-ping Lee, Kim-wah Lou, and Tsui produced for China Film Co-Production Corporation/ China Film Group Corporation/ Beijing Enlight Pictures/ Film Workshop/ Mandarin Films/ Dong Tian Motion Picture Investment/ Applause Pictures; the presenters were Raymond Wong Pak-ming, Nansun Shi Nan-sheng, Sanping Han and Changtian Wang (10 producers and 4 presenters!); script by Tsui from a story by Lau Ho-leung (other sources credit Tsui and Ho with the script and Tsui and Kwak Jae-yong with the story); music by Ricky Ho Kwok-kit; Sakamoto Yoshinao was DP; costumes by Silver Cheung Sai-wang; editing by Yau Chi-wai; and art. dir by Kenneth Mak Kwok-keung. In the cast were Angelica Lee Sin-je, Isabella Leung Lok-sze, Chang Chen, Guo Xiaodong, Tony Leung Ka-fai and Chang Chen-yue. Poon Cheuk-ming, Pang Mei-seung and Lau Ho-ngai also appeared. Released: June 9, 2008. 118 mins.

There are five main characters in *Missing* : the heroine, Dr Gao Jing (Angelica Lee Sin-je), her boyfriend Dave Chen Guo Dong (Guo Xiaodong), his sister, Xiao Kai Chen (Isabella Leung Lok-si), a psychic, Simon (Chang Chen) and a fellow psychiatrist, Dr Edward Tong (Tony Leung Ka-fai).

For Angelica Lee Sin-je, it's a major role, requiring the actress to perform in most every scene, plus diving scenes, action scenes, and several high emotion scenes (yet Lee was encouraged to tone down her performance many times, perhaps with a view to 'keeping it real', as they say, or to ground the ghost story in a more conventional form of acting, rather than the usual exaggerations and eccentricities of the Chinese horror genre. So no eye-rolling and hysterical outbursts *à la* Jacky Cheung or Anthony Wong here).

❀

*Missing* was filled with Tsui Harkisms, from the elaborate opening credit sequence (an aerial shot of the shoreline with the credits superimposed over the sea and the rocks, filmed by a flying swordsman), to the numerous Tsui-ian motifs (fish, water, unusual camera angles, disorientating subjective views, etc).

Once again, Tsui Hark opted for a female lead (Dr Gao), aided by another woman (her boyfriend's sister, Xiao-kai Chen), in this story of mysteries and threats buried beneath the ocean, and hauntings by ghosts.

*Missing* is familiar horror movie fare: subjective camera, shadowy interiors (even when folk are at home, they opt to turn off the lights to encourage ominous shadows), and, most obvious of all, horror film music. In a horror movie, as we all know, the *music* is cueing the viewer throughout. Thus, composer Ricky Ho Kwok-kit might be regarded as a co-creator of *Missing*, as he's doing so much of the dramatic work to make the movie fly. In the first act alone, the music is covering all sorts of possibilities, including the mandatory whooshes and rumbles of the horror film genre. The score is largely orchestral (rather than the usual electronica and synths of Hong Kong horror movies), which is a result of a bigger budget.

Some of the music in *Missing* is shamelessly, cheesily romantic – in the scenes where Dr Gao encounters her dead boyfriend at her apartment. For the love scene across the divide between life and death, Ricky Ho delivers indulgent orchestral sounds, with strings prominent. Less appealing are the many plinky piano cues – a form of movie music which I think should be outlawed (on pain of death – by drowning). Folks, we have heard enough teardrop piano music to last several lifetimes! There *are* other forms of music you can put underneath lovey-dovey-kissy scenes! It doesn't *have* to be bloody piano played in pseudo-Chopin tinkles!

In addition, the sound design in *Missing* – overseen by Tommy Ho Chi-tong – is going all-out to create suspense and mystery from what are visually often rather pedestrian scenes (say, a woman in an apartment looking at a glass of water, a woman walking thru a dimly-lit apartment, a woman entering an elevator).

painting*Missing* rightly won the award for Best Sound Effects at the 45th Golden Horse Awards in 2008 – it is stuffed with everything the sound team can think of, plus some kitchen sinks. Sound-wise, this is more over-stuffed than the acting, the camerawork, the editing, or other technical aspects. *Missing* has had a lot more time and effort spent on it than the usual Hong Kong horror movie (where one or two sound effects at most were all that many scenes required). Instead, *Missing* is layered with sounds (and the soundtrack has been built from the ground-up, as usual in Chinese cinema, including the dialogue, which's mostly added later).

The editing pace is slower than the usual Tsui Hark picture, and the storytelling, too. The cinematic approach is more like television, a TV movie, in its pacing. Scenes run on longer than usual in a Tsui movie, and there is much more setting up of scenes, and more building of suspense.

*Missing* is a much smaller scale production than the ones that Tsui Hark was taking on before it (*Seven Swords*) and after it (*Flying Swords of Dragon Gate*). Instead, the approach is similar to *Triangle* (2007) and *All About Women* (2008). And maybe the effort of producing *Seven Swords* was exhausting (it certainly looks like an exhausting production), because something happened with Tsui's mid-2000s movies: *Missing*, *All About Women* and *Triangle*. These movies are simply below par for Tsui, lacking the overall cohesion and suitably compelling concepts at their foundation. While there are flashes of brilliance in them (as in all of Tsui's work), they don't appeal like the crowd-pleasers such as *Seven Swords* or the first *Detective Dee* movie, made just before and afterwards. (It's worth noting, too, that these three films, *Missing*, *Triangle* and *All About Women*, are set in the contemporary era (and in China, as usual), while most of Tsui's films in the 2000s and 2010s were historical pictures).

❁

A four-act movie in this genre might be expected to feature some themes or subtexts – but it's not clear what the themes are in a movie such as *Missing*. Tsui Hark and the team don't seem to have much they want to say using this story and movie. The themes in a movie such as *Once Upon a Time In China* or *Detective Dee* are loud and clear, but *Missing*, beyond its romantic subplot, seems vague, insubstantial, unsure.

*Missing* is a genre outing, which requires adhering to forms, structures and – God forbid – rules. Even a satirical, parodic horror movie usually follows some of the basic principles in terms of characters and narrative structure. *Missing* is no different.

Thus, Angelica Lee Sin-je is required to spend most of the 2008 film in a state of anxiety, jumping at noises in the night, fearful of shadows in the corner of the room (the mechanics of a chiller require that someone in the cast is needed to act/ react scared, and it's often a young woman in horror cinema – and not in just recent movies). Nothing is what is seems at first, and once one mystery is solved, another one materializes out of the mist behind it.

*Missing* is Tsui Hark's *Jaws* (1975), an undersea adventure/ mystery/ horror flick – or maybe more akin to the cash-ins and rip-offs of *Jaws*, such as *The Deep* and *Piranha*.[1] And *Missing* is Tsui's *Poltergeist* or *The Exorcist* – it's another Chinese ghost story, with spectres popping up in act two, when the story shifts to Dr Gao at home and at work. *Ghost* (1990) is in there, too, as Dr Gao yearns for her dead lover and encounters him as a spectre.

---

[1] The amazing success of *Jaws* led to cash-ins, among them: *Grizzly* (William Girdler, 1976), about a giant grizzly bear, *Orca... Killer Whale* (Michael Anderson, 1977), with Richard Harris in the Quint role, *The Deep* (Peter Yates, 1977), from another Peter Benchley novel, starring Robert Shaw, Jacqueline Bisset and Nick Nolte, *Cujo* (Lewis Teague, 1983), a Stephen King story about a rabid St Bernard dog, *Tentacles* (1977), *Day of the Animals* (William Girdler, 1976), *Squirm* (Jeff Lieberman, 1976), about sandworms, *Alligator* (Lewis Teague, 1980), *The Jaws of Death* (a.k.a. *Mako: The Jaws of Death*, William Grefe, 1976), another shark flick, *Jaws of Satan* (Bob Claver, 1981), about a snake, *Great White*, *Eaten Alive* (a.k.a. *Death Trap*, Tobe Hooper, 1976), about a psycho with a crocodile, *Tentacles* (Oliver Hellman, 1976), about a giant octopus, and *Piranha* (Joe Dante, 1978). A-list movies such as *Alien* could also be seen as highly influenced by *Jaws* (it was dubbed '*Jaws* in space').

Yet *Missing* also feels way below Tsui Hark's talents as a filmmaker. It's the kind of movie that might've been better served ifTsui had produced it but handed over the direction to someone else. Instead,Tsui receives the triple-threat film credits: produced by, written by and directed by (though the story was by Lau Ho-leung).

❥

Halfway through act one of *Missing* the narrative takes a sudden turn – Dr Gao's boyfriend Dave Chen dies. But the movie doesn't show that: instead, it moves forward two weeks (with a caption) and we cut to the funeral, where the boyfriend's body lies in state – but headless.

So, corpses without heads – swiftly followed by more ghosties and mysterioso occurrences.2 The boyfriend's demise is thus the inciting incident, the mystery that needs to be solved by her heroine, Dr Gao. Meanwhile, out in the ocean somewhere between Japan and Taiwan3 (note the political aspects of the watery interzone), there's an underwater city (Yonagunni) which divers explore and then they disappear.

In act two, the psychic Simon (an over-the-top performance by Chang Chen) is introduced: he's Dr Gao's unstable, unpredictable accomplice in the exploration of the supernatural (Dr Gao also has a spiritual adviser in the form of her fellow psychiatrist Dr Tong (played by Tony Leung).) Dr Gao has been undergoing hypnotism from Dr Tong, and treating Simon for mental illness.

The background setting for *Missing* is thus psychiatry and the mental health industry – automatically conjuring up the familiar oppositions of science vs. religion, matter vs. spirit, the known vs. the unknown. But *Missing* isn't the most compelling nor the most sophisticated investigation of the paranormal, of the boundaries between the living and the dead, between this life and the after-life.

Some of the shocks and scares in *Missing* are deftly handled, as one would expect from a film director who has been dabbling in horror movie material since his first feature film, *The Butterfly Murders,* in 1979 (and following that up with a cannibal outing in *We're Going To Eat You* in 1980). Tsui has always enjoyed the mechanics of horror cinema, and how it takes him back to the first influential movies he saw as a child, where it's OK to evoke primitive emotions in a childish manner.

Sometimes it seems as if Tsui Hark also has his eye on recent Asian chillers of the late 1990s/ early 2000s such as *The Ring, The Grudge, Dark Water* and *The Eye* – the latter starred, by the way, Angelica Lee Sin-je. Tsui's cinema is at its weakest and least appealing when it too obviously follows trends rather than setting them. Tsui is at his best when he is a trail-blazer – like when he re-invented the grand, historical, action-adventure genre (and the sub-genre of Wong Fei-hung pictures) with the *Once Upon a Time In China* series, or when he re-invented the fantasy adventure swordplay epic for a modern audience with *Zu: Warriors From*

2 *Missing* features ghosts a-plenty – in the credits they are described as Noodle Ghost, Old Lady Ghost, Bald Ghost, Thin Ghost, Police Ghost, etc. Many of the ghosts feature the expected special make-up jobs.
3 The Ryukyu Islands.

*the Magic Mountain*, or when he showed everybody what a faster-than-light historical romp could be in the *Detective Dee* series.

When you put a film like *Missing* into the Tsui Hark *œuvre,* it can only be regarded as a minor work at best. And it's not as compelling as other second tier work from Tsui such as *The Raid* or *Double Team*.

‣

Towards the end of the third act (around the 1h 20m point), *Missing* shifts into a re-set and re-cap section: voices of authority (or at least alternative viewpoints) now suggest that the heroine, Dr Gao, has lost it completely. She undergoes some treatment which erases many of her memories (don't ask the obvious questions: how? What treatment is this?).

Anyway, the emphasis on Dr Gao as the proactive heroine is reversed: now she's the victim who has to be looked after by charas such as Xiao Kai Chen and Tang. This comes after a lengthy section of hauntings, encounters with her ghost boyfriend, and attempts by Dr Gao to evade the murderous manœuvres of a white-haired ghost (Su Zhenjing, a girl who drowned a year before in the same undersea ruins).

Improbably, video footage is part of the re-setting section of *Missing* – a video camera just happened to be filming the events underwater when Dr Gao was suffering from too much nitrogen and her boyfriend Cheh expired. (Photographs are also used for explanations in *Missing*).

In a four-act narrative structure act three can be a danger time, as Tsui Hark knows well: dangerous because the audience has already seen pretty much everything the film can offer (unless it is saving some stupendous material for the finale. But, as highly experienced movie-goers like us know, the finale will likely be a bigger and louder version of material we have already seen, such as the climax to act one). Anyway, Tsui knows that if the movie is going to run to nearly two hours and have a four-act structure, the third act needs pepping up. Hence the long sequence of re-setting the plot, plus the dramatic reversal of Dr Gao's predicament, so that now she's a victim.

Dr Gao wants her man – even if he's definitely dead, definitely not of this world anymore, and is clad in a bizarre deep sea fisherman's outfit of damp black (with his face lost in shadow beneath the hood – he lost his head, remember?[4]). And when they embrace they are engulfed in flames (a clear sign that embracing is not possible, unless you don't mind being burnt). *Don't touch!* – Chen warns Gao away, but she can't resist touching.

So by the time of act four, the 2008 movie seems to say, To Hell With It! – let's go all the way into wispy, romantic lyricism. The movie employs one of Chinese cinema's favourite devices, which you see towards the end of so many Chinese flicks: the musical montage. It's always a ballad, it's always about love and loss and death, and it always features a montage style of filmmaking, with dialogue jettisoned in favour of the cinema of images.

So *Missing* enters Chinese M.T.V. territory with Dr Gao following her

---

4 Don't ask how he can communicate with Dr Gao while being headless.

dreams and yearning to join once again with her beloved Dave Chen. She's forgotten so much, but somehow (with the aid of some medication), she's able to track down the beachside shack that her boyfriend used for a photographic studio. Then she lights a lantern and sits on the beach staring out to sea, lost in a lovey-dovey stupor (we've all done it). It's cute – and the music is doing all it can to make us buy it. But it doesn't quite gel with the rest of the movie.

Anyway, while Xiao Kai Chen is desperately seeking Dr Gao, the lady has disappeared. The editing flits back and forth in time and depicts what happened: Dr Gao followed her heart all the way into the ocean. The camera holds on a close-up of Angelica Lee Sin-je and pans with her as she walks into the surf. It's a suicide trope, but it's not suicide by this time in this movie (even though mental health has been one of the dramatic backgrounds). It's not suicide because it's about eternal love, and living beyond death, and being re-united with your beloved in the after-life.

It's mythology. It's a fairy tale. And it's Tsui Hark delivering some wish-fulfilling magic. Tsui is actually much more of a romantic softie than his media image as an all-round showman would suggest. Sure, he delivers slambang action with flying swordsmen and incredible adventures of Chinese folk heroes like Wong Fei-hung and Detective Dee. But he's also hopelessly in love with love – with love, that is, as it's depicted in movies (when it's been cinematized, when it's been transformed through video cameras and computer editing). This is the man, after all, who produced a film called The Lovers, and immediately followed it up with More Of The Same (Love In the Time of Twilight ).

Yes, Tsui Hark loves love. But it's the mythical, fairy tale sort of love of the movies. It's Disney love, in effect: and what does Missing end with but an evocation of the folk tale of the Little Mermaid! Yes, folks, Dr Gao wades out into the briny and sinks into it, to be transformed into a mermaid, re-uniting with her boyfriend Dave Chen (and he's a mer-man!).5

---

5 There's even a shiny ring as part of the ultra-romantic shenanigans at the end of Missing (discovered by Dr Gao on the beach).

# 31

# *ALL ABOUT WOMEN*

# *Nurén Bú Huài*

*All About Women* (*Nurén Bú Huài = Not All Women Are Bad,* 2008) was directed/ produced/ co-written/ and co-edited by – guess who?! – Tsui Hark. It was produced by Dong Yang Huan Yu Media/ Polybona Films/ Beijing Enlight Pictures. It was produced by Tsui, his wife Nansun Shi Nansheng, Huang Jianxin and Elvis Lee; Tsui co-wrote the script with Kwak Jae-yong;[6] the score was by Paul Lee and Lee Shih-Shiong; Johnny Choi Sung-Fai was DP; and it was edited by Tsui, Hideyuki Mako and Chan Ki-Hop. It starred Zhou Xun, Kitty Zhang, Kwei Lun-mei, Alex Fong, Geoffrey Gao, Eddie Peng, Stephen Fung and Shen Chang. Released on December 11, 2008.

Filmed in Beijing[7] (in Mandarin), *All About Women* was partly conceived as a remake of *Peking Opera Blues* (continuing Tsui Hark's penchant for remaking his earlier movies), and as a companion to the previous two movies centred on women: *Shanghai Blues* and *Peking Opera Blues. All About Women* focussed on three young women (like *Peking Opera Blues*), but was a very different movie from the 1986 hit (and not in the same class at all).

Zhou Xun (b. 1974) is one of the 'Four Dan Actresses' of China (the others are Zhang Ziyi, Zhao Wei and Jinglei Xu). Zhou's roles include *Suzhou River, Balzac and the Little Chinese Seamstress, Painted Skin, The Emperor and the Assassin, The Banquet, Confucius, Meet Miss Anxiety* and *The Yinyang Master.* Tsui later cast her in *Flying Swords of Dragon Gate.* For *The Equation of Love and Death* (2008), Zhou won best actress awards at the Shanghai Film Critics, Golden Rooster Film, Chinese Film Media and Asian Film Awards.

▶

*All About Women* is a good example of all of the things that people

---

6 Kwak Jae-yong is a Koren filmmaker who was already working on a similar sort of script; Tsui Hark ditched his script, and worked with Kwak to produce a story together (which Kwak wrote in Korean; it was translated into Chinese for Tsui to rewrite (then back again).)
7 Btn Jan and Apl, 2008.

*don't* like about the cinema of Tsui Hark – it's too busy, too gimmicky, jammed with too many ideas, too many scenes, and too many bits of business. It lacks focus, cohesion. *All About Women* is maddening – it's too impatient and too anxious to be bothered tell a story in a routine manner, so it's jumping about like a young monkey (or a hyper-active child), dipping into this, fiddling with that.

The editing style of *All About Women* (courtesy of editors Tsui Hark, Hideyuki Mako and Chan Ki-Hop) is nervy, impatient, and even cranky. Looking at just two minutes, one can imagine that the movie went thru numerous versions (like so many of Tsui's later movies). The editing slows somewhat for the middle acts of *All About Women* – partly because the movie's script and propulsion starts to waver.

*All About Women* is in a screwball comedy form – where dialogue is delivered rapidly, and much of the humour is found in the dialogue. *All About Women* features the usual clutch bag of Tsui Hark motifs – tigers,[8] fish in tanks, clocks, etc.

Self-consciously 'feminist', yes – *All About Women* not only foregrounds women in the lead roles, it happily (and aggressively) jams the portrayal of male characters into pigeon holes, as men do to women. So men are turned into babes and models, sexually objectified by women (in a proto-feminist reversal). They are secretaries and assistants. They trail along in the wake of women, trying to keep up with them. Mo Qiyan is enamoured of Tie Ling, and follows her about; for his stalker-like behaviour, she smashes him on the head with a brick.

*All About Women* is what critics continue to insist on calling 'stylish'. Well, shoot, *everything* has a style! *Everything* is 'stylish'! (What they mean by 'stylish', of course, is a slick, glossy and usually urban/ thriller/ gangster/ contemporary sort of movie where charas sport fashionable clothing and accessories.) Anyhoo, *All About Women* is rather too concerned with a gimmicky visual style which tends to overwhelm the rest of the picture. It's one of those visual approaches which's full of show-off trickery like multiple screens, speed ramping, captions, lots of visual effects and post-production gimmicks, and a battery of trendy music. In many another movie, this kind of filmmaking becomes wearying after a while – and too self-satisfied, too contrived, too self-conscious. (Indeed, some viewers found *All About Women* bewildering, and tiring. It does seem as if this movie is aiming to please just person – Tsui Hark – and that the director is doing just what the hell he likes).

The desperate-to-be-cool tendency mars some of Tsui Hark's other later works (particularly the contemporary-set thrillers like *Time and Tide* and *Knock-off*). But, you have to admit, this is part of the point of *All About Women* – it really is putting design/ fashion/ style at the forefront (William Cheng's costume design is one of the stars of this 2008 movie, but then, costume is foregrounded throughout Tsui Hark's cinema). Another flaw with *All About Women* is the too-talky script – like some other later films helmed by Tsui, there are scenes where actors rattle off *way* too much

8 When her boyfriend persuades her (aggressively) to try a cigarette, Fanfan imagines the smoke in the form of a tiger snarling at her.

dialogue, as if everyone's speeding on cocaine (and as if everything needs explaining, and all the time. It's too much – hell, there's too much of everything in *All About Women*! ).

When you put aside the upper levels of froth and wow-look-at-me camerawork, the desperate-to-be-trendy hip-hop/ dance music, and the almost obsessive emphasis on fashion and design in *All About Women*, you find an entertaining portrait of three young women living in what for Tsui Hark is by far the greatest nation on earth – China. At its heart, underneath the over-abundance of quirky style and cinematic excess and too-nervous editing, *All About Women* is a character study. The foregrounding of young women is as if Tsui is attempting his version of the movies directed by Pedro Almodovar or Rainer Werner Fassbinder about women (the title, *All About Women*, is very Ingmar Bergmanesque). So, altho' there *is* a story in *All About Women*, that isn't what this 2008 movie is about – no, it's about women (as the title states. The 21st century *Charlie's Angels* movies might also be a point of reference here – slick, hip, postmodern (and rather empty and pointless) portrayals of young women in the contemporary world. This is life as a pop promo, as a TV commercial, as an I-Phone screen, where information is delivered in snippets, as in women's magazines).

▶

So there's Ou Fanfan (Zhou Xun), the kooky, clumsy, awkward nurse/ doctor/ scientist, and a daydreamer. The giant glasses giving her an owl-like appearance are part of Fanfan's eccentric accessories;[9] yes, once again there's a short, skinny, neurotic woman with short, bobbed hair and huge glasses, a recurring type in Tsui Hark's cinema. Fanfan's boyfriend is musician Sima Xiaogang (Stephen Fung).

Fanfan enjoys a huge number of costume changes.[10] *All About Women* interweaves multiple levels of reality – so we have fantasies and dreams playing in amongst the 'real'/ everyday scenes, rather like the colourful fish in the fishtanks that Tsui Hark likes to place in the foreground of his shots. (An early scene in *All About Women*, for instance, has Fanfan fantasizing about her dance instructor, and tango-ing with him. He twirls her around like she's a mannequin (in classy, black clothes), until, at the end, he unceremoniously drops her on the floor).

Fanfan also freezes at the mere touch of the opposite sex – this is a reprise of a gag over-used in *Black Mask 2*, where Dr Marco Leung (Teresa Maria Herrera) froze when touched by men. In a later scene, Fanfan is immobilized when she's in bed with rock star X (Godfrey Gao). (Fanfan is the same character as in *Black Mask 2* – she's even a doctor in a prim, white coat in a hi-tech facility). Does Tsui Hark have experience of this? one wonders.

So there's Tang Lu (Kitty Zhang), a high-powered businesswoman who can melt the heart of every man within a five-mile radius (the scene where she enters a fancy city office, and all of the guys blush scarlet[11] and

9 Tsui Hark used to wear big glasses like this – very Eighties!
10 Including a variety of wigs (one, for some reason, has a crooked fringe).
11 *À la* Japanese animation.

fumble and gawk and fall over, is wonderful). Mo Qiyan (Eddie Peng) is her long-suffering secretary, trailing along after her (who fancies Tie Lung).

So there's Tie Ling (Kwei Lun-mei), a punky, goofy (and kooky) girl of 19 years-old. Another dreamer, another artist (she's a novelist and rock singer), and also – *very* improbably – a boxer[12] (!), Tie is given a visual look that is instantly recognizable as Tsui Harkian (the hat is the giveaway – like Pier Paolo Pasolini, Tsui is *very* fond of hats!). Tie has a imaginary boyfriend, X (Godfrey Gao) (don't we all?!). Unfortunately, you soon tire of Tie when she becomes a spoilt brat in too many scenes (in contrast to the way that Kwei Lun-mei is usually cast), including at a concert (this scene goes on and on, as Tie tries to keep a show together that's descending into chaos very ineptly). Much more convincing for Kwei was her role in *Flying Swords of Dragon Gate* as the fierce Tartar warrior, Bu Ludu).

▶

It's a romantic comedy, but *All About Women* is not particularly romantic, and only occasionally comedic. Actress Zhou Xun, playing Ou Fanfan, carries the funniest moments – like the scene where, blind as a bat, she tries to put in contact lenses (reminiscent of a young Woody Allen, in the clumsy physical schtick he did in *Sleeper, Bananas, Play It Again, Sam*, etc).[13] And the pheromone patch plot provides some laughs in *All About Women* – when single women're surrounded by hordes of male admirers, for instance, when the patches go flying when Fanfan uses her handbag[14] to (unsuccessfully) whack Tie Ling. (*All About Women* closes with a series of romantic scenes which tie up the plots, including a wedding, and Fanfan fantasizing about being in a bridal gown).

▶

*All About Women* resembles a magazine article in one of those trendy lifestyle magazines – women's magazines like *Cosmopolitan*, *Vogue*, *Marie Claire*, etc, are full of this sort of combination of lifestyle/ character portrait/ fashion/ design/ urban setting. *All About Women* even looks like a lifestyle magazine (or the splash page of a website), with its mix of slick photography, upmarket settings (plush offices of metal and glass, a fashion photography shoot), sports cars, designer clothing, cel phones, laptop computers, multiple screens and superimposed captions and ideograms.

At times, *All About Women* comes across as so sleek and slick and glossy, it seems to be a commercial funded by the People's Republic of China's PR department to promote contemporary China as a hi-tech, super-chic country with all modern amenities, a solid and efficient infrastructure, and a host of pretty people to keep you company when you invest your billions of petro-dollars in this renewed super-state (*Come To Beijing! Learn Mandarin! Make mMoney In a Reborn City!*). The steel and glass offices with their postmodern curves, the minimal apartments, the white, spotless medical facilities, the clean subway trains and stations,

---

12 This teeny girl is flattened with a single punch – is that a Tsui-ian joke about *Xanda*, which he produced for his editor Marco Mak in 2004?
13 Allen admitted that he stole his moves from Bob Hope and the Marx Brothers.
14 Handbags are prominent in *All About Women*.

the fancy restaurants, even the punky lair of quirky Tie Ling is chic (like the fashionable trash in *Blade Runner*) – this is a far cry from the usual portrayal of modern China in movies (even more incredible, it's not a thriller/ triad/ gangster/ *yakuza* movie, it's a romantic comedy!).

If Tsui Hark wanted a job as a poster boy/ PR chief for the Chinese government, he's got it. No need to audition – just walk in and spend those Chinese Yuan on advertizing to attract foreign investment and overseas tourism. *We love China!* this movie seems to be crowing – irrespective of the ditzy, romantic plotlines and the proto-feminism (yes, even modern China is trying to overcome its image as an all-patriarchal nation riven by superstition and poverty!).

But then, hell, this *is* one of Tsui Hark's aims in his movies – to explore contemporary China in all its forms. Which includes how twentysomething women're living these days. Who cares if the depiction of the lifestyle is rather superficial and trite (this *is* a romantic comedy, after all! – a chick-friendly genre in which some leeway with credibility is accepted/ expected!).

The beauty of *All About Women* is... the movie itself, as a hi-tech, postmodern, hyper-fashionable object in itself. *All About Women* is at times simply a *thing*, an artefact, a series of images and sounds, it's something that passes thru your eyes and ears, it's pop culture in a cheerful, slick form, as easy to digest, in its way, as the trashiest Hong Kong, low-brow thriller or comedy.

Sports cars... posh restaurants... shiny elevators... freeways that glitter at night... glass skyscrapers that sparkle in the sun... and of course a colossal wardrobe of designer clothing... *All About Women* is Tsui Hark's entry in the Cool, Minimal, Postmodern Movie Genre. This is a vision of Beijing after the Olympics as a flashy, postmodern realm. That *All About Women isn't* a thriller/ gangster flick, and that it *doesn't* star a bunch of handsome guys in sunglasses (wannabe Chow Yun-fats), that *All About Women* is a romantic comedy, whose chief topic is L♥O♥V♥E, and which stars three young(ish) actresses – is remarkable. (It is, tho', a little smug – like many romantic comedies, a little too proud of its coolness, its flashy visuals, its high fashion *milieu*. Again, that self-satisfied haughtiness is a hallmark of the world of fashion and style).

❧

At two hours, *All About Women* is too long – it's too much time to spend on such a nervy, jittery cinematic form. This is one instance where the movie would benefit from being prised out of Tsui Hark's mitts (not easy!), and placed in the hands of a film producer and an editor who could lop out half-an-hour, bringing it down to the usual 80-90 mins for a Hong Kong movie.

An example of the over-long sequencing of scenes occurs in the charity auction. Gags (like Fanfan accidentally bidding during the auction while she pops in her contact lenses), are extended too long. OK, we get the joke – now move on! It's certainly curious that a movie that's moving at the speed of postmodern hyper-activity should allow such *longueurs*.

Retrogressive and non-feminist is the ending of *All About Women*: it's a church wedding. But the expected unions are subverted, and two of the three women remain single (Tang Lu walks away from her boyfriend, and Tie Ling cracks assistant Mo Qiyan on the face in the boxing ring and sends him flying). Only Fanfan seems to enjoy a clinch, with her on-off boyfriend, musician Sima Xiaogang.

As a comedy, *All About Women* seems to be attempting anything and everything that might raise a laugh, and hoping that one of the routines or bits of shtick will stick. It's a scattershot ploy that Hong Kong comedies have undertaken regularly, but it doesn't quite suit the material, or the characterizations.

And the directorial style is so over-bearing, it swamps the movie. There are several well-known stars in *All About Women*, but the real star is the dizzy, hyped-up form of the movie itself (and its originator, Mr Tsui).

Triangle (2007), above. All About Women (2008), below.

Missing (2008).

# THE *DETECTIVE DEE* MOVIES

## 32

## *DETECTIVE DEE AND THE MYSTERY OF THE PHANTOM FLAME*

## *Di Ren Jie Zhi Tong Tian Di Guo*

INTRO.

*Detective Dee and the Mystery of the Phantom Flame (Di Ren Jie Zhi Tong Tian Di Guo,* 2010) was an action-adventure movie directed and produced by Tsui Hark, starring Andy Lau Tak-wah and action directed by Sammo Hung Kam-bo. Those three names alone constitute an entire history of recent Chinese cinema: Tsui, Lau and Hung! So you know you're in safe hands.

*Detective Dee* is an outstanding movie on every level, with Tsui Hark directing at full throttle, employing his boundless energy and extra-ordinary vision to the maximum. Tsui when he's on fire is an unstoppable railroad train, he's a force of nature, he's a dragon master of world cinema.

Tsui Hark, born in 1950 and thus 60 when he directed *Detective Dee and the Mystery of the Phantom Flame,* shows no sign of slowing down. *Detective Dee and the Mystery of the Phantom Flame* is staged with the verve and passion of an idealistic, athletic youth in his 20s with infinite stamina, eager to please a global audience with absolutely sensational visuals and action. You can see, looking at any two-minute segment of *Detective Dee and the Mystery of the Phantom Flame,* that it was exhausting to create. Of course, Tsui was aided by a vast team of professional filmmakers – but this is clearly a Tsui Hark movie (as much as a giant production like this can be attached to a single person. It can't, really – it takes a huge organization to mount a movie this big).

Peggy Lee, Nansun Shi Nan-sheng, Chen Kuo-fu,[1] Zhang Dajuin, and Tsui Hark executive produced for Huayi Brothers/ Taihe Film Investment Co./ China Film Co-Production Corporation/ Film Workshop; Wang Zhonglei and Wang Zhongjuin produced; Chen Kuo-fu and Zhang Jialu wrote the script (it was based on *Detective Dee and the Mystery of the Phantom* by Lin Qianyu, about Di Renjie); music by Peter Kam; Parkie Chan and Chan Chi-ying were DPs; editor: Yau Chi-wai; costumes: Bruce Yu Ka-on and Choo Sung-bong; prod. des. by James Chiu; sound by Wang Danrong and Ziao Ying; sup. sound ed.: Nan Zhao; vfx supervisors: Phil Jones, Lee Yong-gi and Nam Sang-woo. Sammo Hung Kam-bo headed up by the action choreography team (which, on big shows like this, was considerable – the other action dirs. were Yuen Bun (Tsui's regular action dir.), Chi Kit Lee (assistant) and Alan Lam). Released: Sept 29, 2010. 122 minutes.

In the cast were Andy Lau (Lau Tak-wah), Carina Lau, Li Bingbing, Deng Chao, Yao Lu, Richard Ng, Teddy Robin, Liu Jin-shan, and Tony Leung Ka-fai.

The movie was filmed in Mainland China (based in the Hengdian World Studios in Zhejiang), from May, 2009 onwards, using Red One digital cameras.[2] The budget was U.S. $20 million. The film did well at the Hong Kong Film Awards.

The *Detective Dee* productions were filmed at 'Chinawood', the Hengdian World Studios in Zhejiang, China – you will recognize many of the buildings and sets from movies such as *Hero, The Warlords* and *The Forbidden Kingdom*. It's true that there is an element of the settings having a 'theme park' feel (the Hengdian World Studios are also a theme park). But that suits movies about Chinese history – altho' postmodern critics deride Western movies which turn history into a theme park, Disneyfying history, in out-and-out fantasy stories such as *Young Detective Dee,* where there are sea dragons and flying warriors, it fits.

One of the most remarkable aspects of *Detective Dee and the Mystery of the Phantom Flame* is the budget: according to Wikipedia, it was U.S. $20 million. You have *got* to be kidding! It must be *impossible* to make a $200-250 million movie like *Detective Dee and the Mystery of the Phantom Flame* on a budget of $20 million! There are many factors involved, of course – principal among them must be that labour and resources in China are, compared to the West, much cheaper. How can China flood the world with low-priced goods? Partly because the people producing them are paid much less than their counterparts in the Occident.

*Detective Dee and the Mystery of the Phantom Flame* was another of the high profile Chinese productions which benefitted from co-production with companies in the People's Republic of China (as well as government incentives.) *Detective Dee and the Mystery of the Phantom Flame* was filmed in Mandarin, in keeping with its Mainland China setting, and like many movies which employed Mainland Chinese companies. Access to

---

1 Producer Chen Kuo-fu (b. 1958) became a regular collaborator with Tsui Hark around this time. Chen produced the *Tai Chi Zero* series.
2 This was a challenge to the crew, who were used to shooting on celluloid.

the increased resources meant that it had to play to a Mainland Chinese audience. (But it is also a bigger budget version of the sort of movies that Hong Kong cinema has been producing for decades).

≈

THE CAST.

Andy Lau Tak-wah[3] plays Detective Dee who's been hired to uncover the mystery of an assassination plot. The setting is Imperial China in 689 A.D., in the lead-up to the coronation of Empress Wu Zetian, the first woman emperor of Ancient China. Dutch author Robert Van Gulik, among others (such as Frédéric Lenormand, Zhu Xiao-di, Sven Roussel and Eleanor Cooney and Daniel Alteri), has written novels about Judge Dee (such as *The Canton Murders* and *The Red Pavilion*, a TV series from C.C.T.V.)[4] featuring Judge Dee had appeared prior to these movies, in the early 2000s (and another TV series in 2017, no doubt influenced by the financial success of the movies. *Detective Dee*, a.k.a. *Legendary Di Renjie*, a.k.a. *Tong Tian Di Ren Jie*, starred Ren Jia-lun as Dee, and Jiao Jun-yan as the Empress and was scripted by Chan Sap-sam).

Detective Dee (a.k.a. Di Ren-jie a.k.a. Judge Dee/ Di) lived in the Tang Dynasty from about 630 to 700 A.D. He was a magistrate and judge. Wu Zeitan (*c*. 625-705) was a concubine of Taizong; she became Empress in 655; her accession was in 690 (the period of the movie), and she declared herself 'Holy and Divine Emperor'. Wu Zeitan's husband was Gaozong; her father was Wu Shihou, and her mother was Lady Yang. In *Chronicle of the Chinese Emperors*, Ann Paludan describes Wu Zeitan as 'an extraordinary woman, attractive, exceptionally gifted, politically astute and an excellent judge of men'. Wu ruthlessly suppressed any opposition to her regime; a purge of 697 resulted in high families and scholars being exiled, disgraced or killed. Wu also appropriated religion, assuming titles such as 'Sage Mother' (from Taoism) and 'Maitreya the Peerless' (from Buddhism).

The court and palace context of *Detective Dee and the Mystery of the Phantom Flame* will be very well-known to anybody who's seen a few Chinese, historical movies or TV shows. It's the familiar world of palaces, luxury, a strict hierarchy, ritual, deference, numerous ministers, lackeys, armed guards and ladies-in-waiting. Paranoia rules supreme, nobody's to be trusted, food is tasted, everyone is hiding their real motives, and operating in disguise.

One of the amazing things about *Detective Dee and the Mystery of the Phantom Flame* is that it energetically revived so many clichés and staples of Chinese cinema. Watch a few Chinese movies, and you will have seen everything here before; and for Chinese audiences, they will have seen this stuff *thousands* of times before. Yet, thru imagination, will power – and sheer balls – the producers somehow manage to encourage an audience to buy into this hackneyed material *yet again* (I do think that Tsui Hark is a really ballsy, gutsy filmmaker – his bravery is colossal; he will dive in, he will do things that many other filmmakers would back off

---

3 Tsui had considered Tony Leung Ka-fai, Tony Leung Chiu-Wai, and Jet Li for Rie. All would've been great.
4 Early TV series included 1969 and 1974.

from).

The equivalent in Western cinema would be the *Indiana Jones* movies (a clear forerunner of aspects of *Detective Dee and the Mystery of the Phantom Flame*), and also the cycle of superhero movies of the 2000s and 2010s (*Spider-man, X-Men, Transformers, Avengers* etc), which trotted out the same rubbish using new actors and some new visual effects ('old stories, new actors' is one of the watchwords of Hollywood cinema. But that was a mantra way back in the 1920s).

The casting of the principals in *Detective Dee and the Mystery of the Phantom Flame* is spot-on: around Andy Lau Tak-wah's Detective Dee an appealing group is assembled, comprising Shangguan Jinger (Li Bingbing), assigned by the future Empress to watch over Dee; Minister Pei Donglai (Deng Chao), a fearsome albino swordsman; and Donkey Wang (Richard Ng/ Teddy Robin), a crusty, old helper figure. Tony Leung Ka-fai plays Dee's former buddy Shatuo Zhong who turns out to be the fiendish super-villain behind everything (one clue is that he's introduced in the opening scenes), and Carina Lau makes a tough, wily future leader of Imperial China, Empress Wu Zeitan. Lau, who appeared in several Tsui films prior to this, is married to Tony Leung, and is a big celebrity in China. (Actually, the casting is great across the whole movie. And, as we know very, very well, if the concept is strong and the script is tight, and the cast is solid, you are most of the way there).

And Andy Lau is Andy Lau – how can Andy Lau Tak-wah look exactly the same as he did 25 years earlier?! Lau is one of the marvels of recent Chinese cinema, an actor who can really act, who looks beautiful, who can submerge himself in a character (so you're not aware it's Lau), and who can also move well and perform many of the stunts (including swimming with real, live killer whales![5]).

The chemistry between Andy Lau Tak-wah and Li Bingbing, who have the most scenes together in *Detective Dee and the Mystery of the Phantom Flame,* is a delight to see – mostly astonishingly expressed in the love scene at the start of act two, which combines sex and nudity with incredibly rapid and imaginative martial arts. The love scene beautifully plays out the familiar sparks and antagonisms between rivals who're attracted to each other (you put your two stars together in a room at night), but in a manner unique to Chinese action cinema. It's remarkable that these filmmakers can turn a cliché upside-down, and re-present love and sex between two people as something new. (Shangguan Jinger is another of the strong, independent women in Tsui Hark's cinema, someone who can handle herself fantastically well in any situation. Her speciality – a whip – is marvellously integrated into the action).

This is not only Andy Lau Tak-wah's show, altho' he's the top-billed actor – in fact, all three of the principals – Li Bingbing, Deng Chao and Lau – are contributing a good deal. Both Chao and Bingbing are wonderful in the action scenes.

*Detective Dee and the Mystery of the Phantom Flame* is a Chinese

---

5 In *Moon Warriors* (1992).

action movie with Sammo Hung Kam-bo as the chief action director. That alone makes it worth watching! With a budget this big (for a *Chinese* movie), and a giant canvas upon which to work, Hung – who has, like Tsui Hark, done everything in cinema *and then some* – manages to out-do himself. And Yuen Bun is Hung's equal. *Detective Dee and the Mystery of the Phantom Flame* is absolutely stuffed with spectacular action scenes, from one-on-one sword fights (and sword-and-whip fights, and sword-and-axe fights), to mass battles with one swordsman (often it's Detective Dee) versus an army of soldiers.

There are assassination scenes involving ninjas[6] racing across rooftops and letting loose hundreds of darts... there are fights on top of galloping horses... there are duels with shape-changing assailants, with the hero hallucinating from sleeping powder...

In *Detective Dee and the Mystery of the Phantom Flame*, assassins pop up everywhere, as several groups vie for power. There's always a danger of being overheard. You can't trust anybody – the atmosphere of political paranoia is strongly evoked.

There's lots of Chinese magic in *Detective Dee and the Mystery of the Phantom Flame* – not only the poisons, potions, medicines and acupuncture, but also talking stags,[7] villains who can split apart, and robotic, metal assassins.

Disguises and masks are employed throughout *Detective Dee and the Mystery of the Phantom Flame* – everyone is hiding something. In a novel but thoroughly Chinese twist, acupuncture changes people's faces – so that Shangguan Jinger appears as the Imperial Chaplain, and Donkey Wang[8] (Wang Lu) is played by both Richard Ng and Teddy Robin Kwan (veterans who've been part of Tsui Hark's output, and Cinema City, for decades).[9]

The characterization of Dee Renjie is another of Tsui Hark's righteous men – someone trying To Do The Right Thing. He's Wong Fei-hung in Ancient Chinese history, acting as the intermediary between the rival factions in Tang Dynasty China. Tsui and co. aged Dee down, so he's not the slower, middle-aged character who has sidekicks who're *kung fu* experts. Instead, he can fight himself. He's someone who can be in jail one minute and chatting with the future Empress in the next. He's the character who has the larger view, the liberal who uncovers corruption everywhere. (The critique of the government of the People's Republic of China is implied yet obvious. Anyway, in most of Tsui's films, the authorities ruling China have always had elements of corruption. And it's also a staple ingredient of historical, Chinese movies that the Imperial authorities or someone linked to them will be corrupt or at least downright weird).

The mystery of the title – *Detective Dee and the Mystery of the*

6 Some of the action scenes featuring the Chinese ninjas look like the work of Yuen Bun.
7 Early on, the Empress consults the Imperial Chaplain – who's in the very unexpected form of a talking deer. (However, in Asia, deer are seen as messengers of the gods).
8 When Donkey Wang is revealed as the court physician, the exposition takes place in a Christian church (anachronistic, to be sure).
9 According to Bey Logan, Tsui couldn't decide actor to use, so, thanks to the acupuncture gag, both were cast.

*Phantom Flame* – is a plot to overthrow the government and Empress Wu Zeitan (and the idea of a female leader – a true rarity in Chinese history. Many aren't happy that a woman is going to be crowned Emperor).

When we first meet Dee Renjie, he's in a *Count of Monte Cristo* scenario, in prison, aided by a blind, old man.[10] The fierce action scene which follows includes two rival groups,[11] with assassins on the rooftops attacking the government officials going about their business (the scenario is reprised several times).

It's tough being Dee Renjie – as the initial scenes show. He's in jail, then he's attacked, and then he's set upon again after being given his official task. (Yes, there's not even time to shave off that over-done beard, so we can see the famous Andy Lau cheekbones, before the room's filled with barbed darts).

The plot of *Detective Dee and the Mystery of the Phantom Flame* is set in motion by the conventional motif in a mystery story – a death/murder (followed by another one; Jia (Yan Qin), overseeing the building of the Buddha statue, is the first). Here the phantom flame ingredient – burning people from inside – is given a gruesome and spectacular representation. It occurs during another convention of epic movies – the guided tour of some of the Big Sets (for an Italian visitor):[12] there are production value views of the colossal interior of the statue of Buddha, all flaming torches, wooden walkways, smithies with molten metal and construction workers. And the head of the Buddha statue set allows for some impressive views over the Ancient Chinese capital.

ও

The *delight* in filmmaking, the sheer *joy* of putting action on screen, bounces off the screen in *Detective Dee and the Mystery of the Phantom Flame*. The stunt teams are working at full stretch (as so they usually do in most Chinese action movies), so that you really can feel the effort being expended on the screen, you really can feel the hits and the pain. When a stunt guy lands on the ground on his back in slow motion in a Chinese action movie, it really does hurt (try it without breaking your back!). In a Chinese action movie, the *physicality* of combat is portrayed more viscerally and imaginatively than in any other form of cinema. And the sensuality (and beauty) of it, the speed and tempo of it, the inter-connectedness of it, and the consequences of it.

Technically, *Detective Dee and the Mystery of the Phantom Flame* is a masterpiece: James Chiu oversaw the set design which includes the colossal interior of a statue of the Buddha (both the base and the head), the gorgeously over-the-top Gothica of the Phantom Bazaar, many temples and monasteries, and many impossibly lavish palace interiors (where the amazing vistas of the Hengdian Studios are exploited to the full. There are also scenes filmed in Beijing featuring a semi-circular archway that we've seen in many Chinese movies). As a series of spaces,

10 And sporting a giant fright wig. Many actors, including well-known ones, enjoy using very different looks.
11 The setting – the raised platform and the fire at night is reminiscent of a similar scene in *The Era of Vampires*.
12 General Asper, played by Jean-Michel Casanova.

*Detective Dee and the Mystery of the Phantom Flame* is a triumph of fantastical concoction, as rich as the paintings of Gustave Moreau.

Tsui Hark's regular costume designer, Bruce Yu Ka-on (aided by Choo Sung-bong), creates a wonderful vision of Ye Olde China – because when you have Imperial splendour as your fundamental look, you can really go to town (as Chinese cinéastes always have done – for opulence, no other cinema can touch them). And Yu and Choo do: red and gold is everywhere; Shangguan Jinger is clad in white; Dee in dark tones. Meanwhile, the albino official pei Donglai was given a complicated white make-up.

*Detective Dee and the Mystery of the Phantom Flame* wasn't the first production about Judge Dee – there were several earlier scripts for this film, including one written for Jet Li. Also, the character had appeared in several TV series in Hong Kong and China such C.C.T.V.'s *Detective Di Renjie* series, 2004-2012), as well as movies (Kent Cheng and Liang Guanhua appeared as Dee, for example). And Empress Wu Zeitan was also the subject of TV series and films.

One of the changes that Tsui Hark made to the script by Cheng Kuo-fu and Zhang Jialu was to turn the character Shangguan Jinger into a woman (a typical Tsui-ian move). Shanggan was a real person, a politician and poet in the Tang Dynasty; Tsui felt it would give him more leeway if he created a new character. It was typical that Jinger is not only a sort of reluctant sidekick to the hero, Detective Dee, but also has a romantic liaison (of a kind) with him. It's also typical of Tsui that Shangguan Jinger should be cast with another small, slender, tomboyish woman.

The slickness of the filmmaking in 2010, compared to the Hong Kong New Wave of the late 1980s and early 1990s, is readily apparent in *Detective Dee and the Mystery of the Phantom Flame* in the arena of sound, for instance. *Detective Dee and the Mystery of the Phantom Flame* is technically much improved from the movies of 20 years earlier, aurally. Much of the dialogue is looped, as usual in Hong Kong cinema, but the dubbing is so much smoother, neater and cleaner. Meanwhile, the sound design and the sound effects are as multi-layered as a high-price Hollywood movie.

ACTION.

For action fans, *Detective Dee and the Mystery of the Phantom Flame* is a cauldron of delights: one of the stand-out sequences is the journey to the Phantom Bazaar,[13] with its submerged caves and corridors, its chasm forms, its flickering light, its candles and torches, its lost souls, its boatman out of Greek mythology, its piles of broken planks and disused mine workings, and the feeling of a threat from every corner. (Narratively, it's a visit to a haunted house or castle to get some intel from an aged weirdo – a great turn from Hong Kong regular Richard Ng[14] as the comically named Donkey Wang). Once a sequence like this gets going (with a giant

---

13 This climaxes act two.
14 Casting Richard Ng gives the audience a shorthand characterization for Donkey Wang – in the West, it'd be like casting a well-known comic actor like Will Ferrell.

bell crashing through the roof as an assassination attempt), you forget every other action scene you've enjoyed, because the filmmakers command your attention with total authority and imagination.

*Imagination*! Yes! These filmmakers *really* know how to let fly with one gag, one inventive move, one trick upon another. When the Imperial Chaplain (or what appears to be the Imperial Chaplain) materializes in a scarlet cloak, with the ability to split apart and re-assemble, *Detective Dee and the Mystery of the Phantom Flame* is elevated into the realm of action *plus* magic, which is one of Chinese cinema's specialities (especially when directed by Tsui Hark). It takes all three of our heroes (Dee, Jinger and Pei) to tackle the witchy Imperial Chaplain, and even then they don't nail him for a long time. In *Detective Dee*, Tsui Hark wanted 'to do something like he'd never done before, which is so difficult. Something he's never done before means we have to find a new ground for understanding.' (2011)

The swords, the axes, the whip, the kicks – one of the reasons that you hire an action director like Sammo Hung Kam-bo and his Hung Bar team, and a genius like Yuen Bun, is because not only have they done everything before (so they are true veterans), they are also interested in doing something new.

Everything in the Phantom Bazaar sequence has been seen/ done before, but somehow *Detective Dee and the Mystery of the Phantom Flame* makes us feel as if it's truly new – or it persuades us to pretend that it's new. It's certainly exciting. (Deng Chao is terrific in this scene, where we get to see what Minister Donglai can really do).

Filming in the cave was tough – a water set which also included plenty of fire effects. Sammo Hung Kam-bo said the set was too big to make the stunts look good.[15] It's water plus fire plus martial arts plus flying gags plus puppeteering flying logs and boats and other parts of the set. Very tough to pull off, but so worth it.

Another of the many, many incendiary action scenes in *Detective Dee and the Mystery of the Phantom Flame* has Detective Dee visiting the Infinite Monastery to confront the shape-changing Shangguan Jinger, who turns out to also be the Imperial Chaplain (the device of acupuncture is employed again – the Chaplain, who appears as a handsome youth, is revealed as Jinger when the acupuncture needles're removed). Their duel is remarkable, particularly how the filmmakers blend subjective point-of-view images with objective ones, how they combine visual effects with on-set action, how they employ the stone statuary, and even include something you've never seen before: charging stags who hurl themselves at the hero (deer! yes – and it works!).

Add to that the hero hallucinating from sleeping powder – so it's a kind of drunken *kung fu* scene combined with multiple visual effects which evoke wobbly sets, bubbling floors, wavy pillars and flames, plus Jinger/ Chaplain zooming about the area in scarlet robes. At times the screen moves into near-abstraction, as the robes flying thru the air (a favourite

---

15 Hence, some scenes used smaller side alleys, or tunnels.

motif in historical, Chinese pictures) smear into billows of scarlet. (And the sequence ends with something unexpected – the hero Dee skewered and possibly dead).

And for fans of weaponry, *Detective Dee and the Mystery of the Phantom Flame* is heavily fetishized, and includes the full complement of Chinese action movie staples, including magical swords,[16] axes, whips, throwing stars, bows and arrows and spears (Sammo Hung Kam-bo is without superiors in the use of weapons in martial arts cinema). Known for his grounded action style, Hung is happy in *Detective Dee and the Mystery of the Phantom Flame* to stage many action scenes up in the air, with many actors attached to wires (actually, Hung had done many films using wire-work, such as *Eagle Shooting Heroes*). Combining the aerial action with stellar sets, intricate lighting, delightful costumes, and attractive stars, and you have an entertainment as thoroughly enjoyable as anything in the whole history of cinema.

And then there's visual effects. The mandate that Tsui Hark gave the filmmaking team seems to have been: *go nuts*. Or: *go even more nuts than usual! Detective Dee and the Mystery of the Phantom Flame* is crammed, jammed and *rammed* with visual effects, ranging from extensive miniatures and computer animated creatures (like rampaging deer!), to a Tsui Hark favourite device: helicopter shots floating over historical cities (with harbours and boats prominent).

Here is a vision of Ancient China that really captures its scope and grandeur (that previously might've been achieved with matte paintings and models). The result is sort of an animated matte painting, but now the camera is floating around the environments in 3-D (even so, *Detective Dee and the Mystery of the Phantom Flame* is also filled with traditional visual effects, in-camera effects, practical effects, and of course miniatures).

It is a *vision,* tho' – it's not 'real', not 'historical', even tho' there is historical research a-plenty on display. The vistas of Ye Olde China are of the order of historical paintings of the 19th century and 20th century which recreated ancient eras in super-detailed panoramas (John Martin, Thomas Cole, Lord Leighton *et al* in the West).

Tsui Hark is a filmmaker who has always revelled in the mechanics of cinema, and often how cinema achieves impossible images, like the vistas of Ancient Imperial China. In this respect, *Detective Dee and the Mystery of the Phantom Flame* is a very traditional movie, with its roots in the silent cinema of D.W. Griffith, Cecil B. DeMille and Géorges Méliès. If Griffith, DeMille and Méliès were making movies in 2010, this is what they might be doing (actually, they *already* did all of this in the 1910s and 1920s. If you go back and look at silent movies, you'll see, very rapidly, that pretty everything we see today had already been done 100 years ago).

Tsui Hark is a filmmaker who has the uncanny ability to celebrate the true magic of cinema. There's a child-like wonder of what visual effects can do, and what cinema can do, in Tsui's work. Tsui's movies really are

16 Dee wields a magical sword with a spinning element that breaks other swords.

genuinely amazed at the possibilities of cinema, taking a deep delight in the trickery that cinema is.

While the story of *Detective Dee and the Mystery of the Phantom Flame* is predictable in parts, and the overall concept and scenario of assassination plots on an Emperor in Imperial China has been worked over millions of times, the storytelling is actually intricate. For example, there is a clever and economical use of flashbacks (like how Detective Dee thinks back to the love scene with Shangguan Jinger, and how, when they were on the floor during the ninja attack, she didn't want him to touch one of her acupressure points, or how Dee received the special sword from the late Emperor, which links Dee with the former regime).[17]

And the storytelling in *Detective Dee and the Mystery of the Phantom Flame* takes many a twist and turn, as disguises are lifted, as motives are revealed, and as people's true natures are uncovered. So altho' *Detective Dee and the Mystery of the Phantom Flame* may be predictable in some of its broad strokes, it is also elaborately plotted (the central spine of the movie sticks to the mystery/ detective narrative form, with the enigma of the assassinations being examined step-by-step. *Detective Dee and the Mystery of the Phantom Flame* is a movie where a detective really does some detecting– in many 'tec outings, the footwork often amounts to talking to a few witnesses).

≥≈

*Detective Dee and the Mystery of the Phantom Flame* is a big, broad and furiously paced action-adventure yarn, but it does also contain subplots, including the romantic subplot between Detective Dee and Shangguan Jinger. It's the familiar romantic scenario of rivals/ opposites who become attracted to each other. Different goals, different motives, which are laid aside at times (tho' the antagonism between Dee and Jinger is revived a number of times: these are lovers who'll be deadly enemies fighting crazily one moment, then recovering in each other's arms the next).

Similarly, Pei Donglai begins the film as a government heavy, who's also ideologically opposed to Judge Dee (as are many of the characters – they all prefer to keep their heads down and avoid ruffling any feathers – especially those of the Imperial rulers). The affinities with today's People's Republic of China are obvious.

But both Shangguan Jinger and Minister Donglai come round to Judge Dee's point-of-view as the narrative progresses, when the twisted, sinister ways of the villains, who include the Empress, are exposed.

*Detective Dee and the Mystery of the Phantom Flame* is also another of Tsui Hark's explorations of China – its mythologies, its politics, its social structure, and its place in the contemporary world.

Chinese superstitions (of which Tsui Hark is very fond) are peppered throughout *Detective Dee and the Mystery of the Phantom Flame*, from the opening scenes, where the workers fear reprisals because some special amulets were removed, to evocations of Chinese medicine, acupuncture,

---

17 The film begins with the Emperor dead, and the build-up to the coronation of the Empress Dowager. The next *Detective Dee* films are prequels, with the Emperor still alive.

poisons, Buddhism, and of course numerous images of classical, Chinese art (*Detective Dee and the Mystery of the Phantom Flame* is another red-and-gold movie).

The bustling market scene comes quite late in *Detective Dee and the Mystery of the Phantom Flame* – it's an essential scene in any historical epic, of course, but it's usually delivered in act one (as a production value scene, and a watering hole scene, where the hero meets new allies). In *Detective Dee and the Mystery of the Phantom Flame,* this is where Dee encounters Prince Ling (Wang De-shun), who gives Dee the special sword.

᠉

Pacing is on the nail in *Detective Dee and the Mystery of the Phantom Flame,* too: though it's a storming action movie with few equals in contemporary cinema, *Detective Dee and the Mystery of the Phantom Flame* also knows when to slow down, when to focus on two characters on their own, by filming two actors in simple, over-the-shoulder close-ups. And *Detective Dee and the Mystery of the Phantom Flame* makes those quieter, intimate scenes *work*, gives them value and weight: these are not mere 'interludes' between the action set-pieces, they are not talky scenes which're necessary for us to plod thru in order to reach the next whammo. You can certainly feel the level of *engagement* between the filmmakers and their material, which transmits to the audience. There's no doubting that these filmmakers are really attuned to the material, and they are enjoying exploring it (again, this's down a good deal to the writers, Cheng Kuo-fu and Zhang Jialu).

So altho' there is a throwaway, fast and furious aspect to *Detective Dee and the Mystery of the Phantom Flame,* as well as a celebration of cinema as a spectacle of grandiose visions, it is also emotonally moving in parts, and does examine some of serious issues. Such as a perennial Tsui Hark favourite: what is worth fighting for? Is a political goal worth dying for? And: what is the cost of 'doing the right thing'?

Because the goals in *Detective Dee and the Mystery of the Phantom Flame* are explicitly political and social: they come to a head in the crucial scene between Detective Dee and dowager Wu Zetian, after the colossal statue her regime has built to itself has collapsed and crushed the palace. Dee reprimands Wu for aiming to succeed and become top dog at any cost, and seeing people as expendable. Wu accepts the critique (rather than chopping off his head). Dee also says, more unexpectedly, that while Wu might be punished in better times, her succession to the Imperial throne is probably best for the nation, despite her nefarious deeds. (A similar grudging recognition of the Emperor's significance occurs in 2002's *Hero*).

᠉

When the two old friends meet (in the statue of Buddha), Shatuo Zhong must realize that the authorities're closing in on him: now that Judge Dee has been brought out of prison, Shatuo knows that things are getting more serious. Dee, meanwhile, must also suspect Shatuo. Indeed, Pei Donglai's instincts are correct: he orders his guards to seize Shatuo and subject him to extreme torture. Dee over-rules that, perhaps because he wants Shatuo to remain at large a little while longer, to see what he's up to, and if anything else will come to light.

The finale features the expected smackdown between the hero and the super-villain – former old friend, Shatuo Zhong (tho' you could also argue that the Empress is partly villainous – as Dee tells her at the end).

The battle between Judge Dee and Shatuo Zhong is a full-on action-adventure tussle, exploiting every part of the Buddha statue to the max: first, they meet in the head, where we have the mandatory exposition scenes (this is a mystery, after all, which requires some explanations). Then the fights begin – and, in typically eccentric style, the opening hostilities occur halfway down the Buddha statue, in the elevator.

Cliffhangers, fire beetles, Shatuo Zhong's accomplices, sunlight (which ignites the beetles' poison) – the obstacles are piled on one after another. And once the Big Set has been used up, the action moves outside, onto galloping horses.

It's played out as broad, swooping action, quite wonderful to see. Sure, the outcome is as certain as anything is in cinema (this is Chinese Movie Hokum *par excellence*), but it's pulled off with a terrific energy and imagination.

The ending is all suggested in the opening scenes: we see images of molten metal being poured, and of the furnaces; the elevator (a big part of the finale); the walkways and chains; and of course Shatuo Zhong in the middle of it all. That takes place in the guided tour for a visiting European dignitary.

So the ending of *Detective Dee and the Mystery of the Phantom Flame* features not only the face-off between the hero and the villain, but also the big pay-off and the villain's crazy scheme – of toppling the statue[18] onto the Forbidden City and the Empress who wronged him years ago (and took his hand).

TSUI HARKISMS.

And *Detective Dee and the Mystery of the Phantom Flame* doesn't disappoint as a barrage of visuals – Tsui Hark's eye for image-making is unique in world cinema. While many images can be found everywhere in contemporary cinema – the slowly drifting tracking shots, for instance – Tsui can also stamp his vision all over a movie. The high angle crane shots,[19] for example, as if Tsui is channelling the spirit of Orson Welles, and Tsui's highly idiosyncratic feeling for close-ups (look at the variety of ways in which Tsui and his cameramen Parkie Chan and Chan Chi-ying film a face, for example). There are also two-shots out of *Persona,* the Ingmar Bergman movie of 1966 (with one actor in the foreground out of focus, in

18 And in *Knock-off*, the Buddha statue in Hong Kong exploded.
19 One notes the increase in overhead shots in cinema in the age of cameras on remotely-controlled booms, cranes, etc (along with the slowly-drifting camera move, another electronically-controlled movement). Tsui Hark certainly favours unusual camera angles, and there are numerous scenes which're covered in high angle shots which in the past would be dolly shots or tripod shots. (There are probably too many, though, in *Detective Dee and the Mystery of the Phantom Flame* – watching people converse from thirty feet above just isn't particularly interesting after a short time).

profile), sudden, very rapid handheld shots, and shots where the camera seems to wrap around the martial arts moves in an intricate dance. (The way that the camera dances in amongst the actors and stuntmen in Chinese action cinema is surely one of the reasons for its high impact).[20]

*Detective Dee and the Mystery of the Phantom Flame* is full of Tsui-isms: the visual ones include Andy Lau Tak-wah taking off white pieces from his eyes, when he pretends to be blind; looks into camera; shape-shifting in comical close-up; overhead angles; and a tiger in a cage.

And numerous Tsui Harkisms of staging and themes: the crossdressing; Gothic horror; haunted areas; the love tussle between Lau and Li; a talking stag; Chinese medicine; Chinese customs and superstitions; and Buddhism.

There are obvious allusions to the *Swordsman* films, to the *Chinese Ghost Story* series, to King Hu's cinema, etc. (The scenes with the Imperial Chaplain in the Infinite Monastery recall the formidable Invincible Asia in *The Swordsman 2*).

20 The camera operator was Marc Ehrenbold.

# 33

# *YOUNG DETECTIVE DEE: RISE OF THE SEA DRAGON*

## *Di Ren Jie Qian Zhuan Zhi Dou Long Wang*

*Young Detective Dee: Rise of the Sea Dragon* (2013) revealed Tsui Hark and a vast team of filmmakers in full effect with a take-no-prisoners, Chinese fantasy adventure extravaganza. A remarkable movie in every respect, *Young Detective Dee* embodied the terms 'epic' and 'spectacular'. It's a masterpiece.

Wild, beautiful, silly, outrageous – *Young Detective Dee: Rise of the Sea Dragon* has the force of nature that is Tsui Hark looking like he's having a whale of a time (a sea dragon of a time), concocting yet another slice of Ancient Chinese Hokum.

If anyone's going to tackle Chinese history and fantasy and do it properly, it's got to be Tsui Hark! Who, among contemporary filmmakers, is so passionate and knowledgable about Chinese art, culture, society, politics and history?[21] No one. Who can package all of that research and wisdom into thrilling, breathtaking cinema? No one.

Tsui Hark co-produced, co-wrote and directed *Young Detective Dee: Rise of the Sea Dragon*. It was produced by Chen Kuo-fu, Addi Ng, Helen Li, Bernard Yang, James Tsim, Zhang Dajuin, and Tsui's ex-wife Nansun Shi Nan-sheng for Film Workshop/ Taihe Film Investment Co., Ltd/ Huayi Brothers. The story was by Tsui and Chen Kuo-fu, with a script by Tsui and Zhang Jialu. The action was directed by Yuen Bun (Tsui's regular action choreographer) and Lin Feng. DP: Johnny Choi Sung-fai. Editor: Boyang Yu. Music: Kenji Kawai. Casting: Mo Lan. Prod. des. and art dir.: Kenneth Mak Chung-man. Costumes: Pik Kwan Lee and Bruce Yu Ka-on. Make-up: Sau-Han Chan. Hair: Lin Tai Lee. Released: Sept 28, 2013. 133 mins.

*Young Detective Dee: Rise of the Sea Dragon*  starred Mark Chao

---

21 'It involves historical figures, but we're not basing our story on historical facts,' Tsui explained.

You-ting, William Feng Shao-feng,Kenny Lin Geng-xin, Ian Kim (Bum Kim), Angelababy, Dong Hu, Chen Kun, Shan Zhang, Guoyi Chen, Nan Tie, Jie Yan and Carina Lau Ka-ling. (Feng Shao-feng is an appealing actor who might well have played Detective Dee himself. Action-wise, Feng steals the show with some very flamboyant action sequences.)

*Young Detective Dee: Rise of the Sea Dragon* was filmed with 3-D cameras (5K 3D using RED EPIC cameras (and was converted to 1080p ProRes), and edited with Final Cut Pro X (Tsui Hark was able to edit on set,[22] using Final Cut Pro on a MacBook Pro with Retina display).)[23]

One of the highlights of *Young Detective Dee: Rise of the Sea Dragon* is the score – by Japanese superstar Kenji Kawai, who worked with Tsui Hark on *Seven Swords* (the only gripe is that the music is mixed way too low on the DVD home release, as often occurs. Oh, if only the sound team for the home entertainment releases of movies ditched the dialogue and the sound effects, and let the music from geniuses like Kawai let rip!).

৯৮

*Young Detective Dee: Rise of the Sea Dragon* was a prequel to *Detective Dee and the Mystery of the Phantom Flame*, with Mark Chao You-ting in the title role of the young Sherlock Holmes in the Imperial Police, the Da Lisi (played by Andy Lau Tak-wah in the first *Detective Dee* movie). As Tsui explained:

> When we read stories about Di Renjie, we realized he wasn't an
> amazing detective, but a judge. While making the first Di Renjie film,
> we talked a lot about how Di Renjie would have developed as a judge
> when he arrived in Luoyang. That's how the story for the new film took
> shape.

It's unusual, perhaps, to go for a prequel movie in only the second outing in a series, but not unusual in the world of Tsui Hark. Also, in commercial, blockbuster cinema, prequels and reboots have become the thing to do in the 2000s-2010s.

It's a prequel, but it's also a sequel – that is, *Young Detective Dee: Rise of the Sea Dragon* features most of the same elements as the first movie of 2010, and most of the same sort of characters (tho' switched around). Constants such as Empress Wu Zeitan and Dee Renjie and palace ministers, guards and lackeys appear in each movie.

Dramatically, the *Detective Dee* movies are essentially stories about a cop/ detective who's protecting the State from nefarious forces within and without. The historical context turns this familiar narrative form into a Sherlock Holmes or Agatha Christie tale, to use Western equivalents. But in a contemporary setting, the *Detective Dee* movies are no different from 100s of cop shows and detective shows on television.

The political background of *Young Detective Dee: Rise of the Sea*

---

22 Cutting the film digitally, the filmmakers were able to send versions of the movie before it was completed to different VFX vendors, the music composer, the sound editor, the marketing team, and the distributors.
23 'In addition to consulting with the editor, director assistant, and producer, I sent different versions of the film to many people to get their feedback. Although I know the film I shot very well, the feedback from other people is a good reference for me.'

*Dragon* concerns rival states/ communities within Ancient China (it's set in 665 A.D., 24 years before the 1st film): the Tang Dynasty rules the Mainland, but other nations/ territories resent their domination. Among these are the Dondo people,[24] with their leader, Huo Yi (Dong Hu), as one of the chief villains/ opponents in *Young Detective Dee.* Huo Yi seeks revenge for the diminishing of Dondo, and hopes to rule an empire of his own.

The background story of *Young Detective Dee: Rise of the Sea Dragon* is thus huge: it concerns the whole of China, no less – China as a state, as a political system, as a group of communities/ territories/ nations, as a mix of ethnicities, as multiple cultures and traditions, and also China as ideas, as mythologies, as philosophies. These are issues that've deeply concerned Tsui Hark for many years (they run throughout the *Once Upon a Time In China* series, of course, where the issues are foregrounded).

In this respect, Dee Renjie is another of Tsui Hark's noble, righteous characters – like Wong Fei-hung. And, like Wong, Dee is almost too good to be true,[25] too brilliant at everything and, darn it, he is *always right!* But that is what a hero is, in Tsui's conception: someone who fights for right, who knows what is right (and, more incredibly, someone who can work out what to do to solve a problem and, even more astonishingly, is capable of carrying out that solution!). Dee boldly states the theme in the *dénouement*: someone has to stand up for what is right, and to attack privilege.

Of course, Dee Renjie, like Wong Fei-hung, isn't a 'real person' but a set of ideas, a feeling, or a dramatic mouthpiece – to express the filmmakers' thoughts on issues like contemporary China.

The 2013 movie is an action-adventure-fantasy with few peers in the contemporary era, but it is also freighted with some political messages. One is that in-fighting and internal conflicts weaken Tsui Hark's beloved China. The *Detective Dee* movies are critical of the too-dictatorial policies of Empress Wu Zeitan (Dee tells off Wu at the end of the first *Detective Dee* picture), and the second movie is also suspicious of the ruling powers.

But just as detrimental to the future of the nation is the squabbling amongst institutions and communities – which was one of the key themes of the *Once Upon a Time In China* series. Dee Renjie is a counterpart, of course, to Wong Fei-hung, as Tsui Hark's vision of a righteous person who tries to fight against the world's ills (or, more correctly, the corruption within China).

In the politics of Tsui Hark, the world needs people like Wong Fei-hung and Dee Renjie – and if you can't create them, you can tell stories about them, and make movies about them.

ɞ

Visual effects are not only employed in the action sequences in

24 The Dondo heavies, who act like secretive ninjas, sport a silly mask and fright wig combo which makes them stand out a mile.
25 And Mark Chao does play Dee Renjie a little smug and smirky at times.

*Young Detective Dee: Rise of the Sea Dragon* – this is a movie that's been heavily worked-over in post-production, with visual layers and flourishes added to existing scenes. In talky exposition scenes, for instance, the talks're livened up with superimpositions (from foreground to background, so we see a head in the foreground narrating events show in the background). To depict Dee Renjie's photographic memory and invest-igative powers, the camera crash-zooms into an object (like a name tag), or the object's flying out towards the viewer. In one highly self-conscious sequence, Dee's memory for maps is illustrated with video game-style imagery, where the camera arches up over a hanging map, turns it into three dimensions, then races thru the city streets on the map which morph into the real streets. True, it's over-kill (i.e., way beyond the dramatic requirements of the script), and it looks a little plasticky, computery and gimmicky, but it's also fun. The gimmicks are typical of 3-D movies. (This sequel has many more editorial gimmicks than the first *Detective Dee* movie, as if the producers are continually aware of having to re-invent the historical fantasy movie, and to make it appealing to a new (and young) audience. Movies of this sort will try anything to liven up a scene; movies have to attract new punters all the time.)

Introducing the world of the story was Dee Renjie in voiceover: very quickly the audience was immersed in Ancient China *circa* 665 A.D. Customary shots of lavish royal processions, the Emperor and the Empress in a carriage, the Imperial buildings, thousands of extras, exotic costumes, and a production design (by Ken Mak Chung-man) that was simply astounding. *Young Detective Dee* had the filmmakers going all-out to evoke the grandest of Chinas, a fantastical China that never existed, that can only exist in art, in cinema, in literature, etc – and in the imaginations of filmmakers insane enough to try to put it on screen.

The complex etiquette and strict hierarchy of the Imperial palace and its numerous levels of interaction and its myriad rules were carefully evoked in *Young Detective Dee* – it's one of those worlds where everybody knows their place, and deference is everywhere (bowing, scraping, kneeling, etc. When in doubt, get on your knees and grovel). Every scene features a hierarchical social structure, even when there's only two people in a room (this is where a Chinese audience is way ahead of overseas audiences, who don't always understand the intricacies of the social world. Especially in a Tsui Hark movie, where the pace is so rapid, and shorthand is used to depict social relationships).

And yet, for all its huge scale and its 100s in the film crew, *Young Detective Dee* is actually not much different in aim or feel from Tsui Hark's 1983 movie *Zu: Warriors From the Magic Mountain* (or even his first film, *The Butterfly Murders*). There is the same irrepressible urge to entertain, to thrill and to dazzle the audience. You simply can't help but be won over by the energy of this kind of movie-making from a master showman.

Even the sea god battles, tho', are something that Tsui Hark had done before – remember the outrageous duels between the snakes and the Buddhist monk in *Green Snake*? And Pirate-Time in the *Once Upon a Time*

*In China* movies? The sequences in *Young Detective Dee: Rise of the Sea Dragon* are of a similar order (tho' with more sophisticated visual effects).

*Godzilla, Beauty and the Beast, Snow White, The Butterfly Lovers, Pirates of the Caribbean, The Creature From the Black Lagoon*, Ray Harryhausen flicks – these and many more crop up in *Young Detective Dee: Rise of the Sea Dragon*.

'Big, big, big' seems to have been the *mantra* of Tsui Hark and the team here: one can imagine the conversations during preproduction, between the storyboard artists and visual artists at the drawing board and the production designer: how about this shot? No, no: *bigger!* *Bigger!*

Thus, the opening establishing shot of the Imperial city of China in *Young Detective Dee* was another of the enormous, aerial, harbour images that Tsui Hark loves to put in his historical films (again emphasizing borders, edges, travel, immigration, transience – as if Tsui has never forgotten getting off the boat from Vietnam to Hong Kong in the 1960s, or visiting New York City for the first time in the 1970s).

By 2013, the filmmakers in Hong Kong and Beijing have become so adept at depicting a fantastical Ancient China that the audience takes it for granted. Oh yes, there's another amazing Chinese building (a temple, say), which looks simply exquisite... Oh yes, and here's another grandiose Imperial interior art-directed by Ken Mak Chung-man (look at the use of red and gold in this film, and how Johnny Choi Sung-fai's cinematography captures it).

Production designer and art director Kenneth Mak Chung-man and the enormous art department are one of the stars of this production – it boasts a design and a look that is stupendous – it's so good, you wonder why everybody else in the film industry doesn't give up and go home. For imagination and beauty, this production design can't be beat. This is a work of genius for Ken Mak.

*Young Detective Dee: Rise of the Sea Dragon* presents an impressive series of social spaces at a bewildering pace: one minute we're in a teahouse (Tranquillity Teahouse), then a doctor's clinic, then an Imperial reception hall, then a back street, then a brothel, a jetty, a tower, the Da Lisi police HQ, a lively market, and on and on. It seems as if every square inch of the Hengdian World Studios was employed in *Young Detective Dee: Rise of the Sea Dragon* (and they are vast).

Red and green are the signature hues of *Young Detective Dee: Rise of the Sea Dragon* – red is everywhere in the Imperial settings – anything that can be painted red is painted red. (The art dept. nought all of the supplies of red paint in China). Meanwhile, for night scenes, instead of the customary blue, green is deployed (which picks up with the green theme in the sea monsters, the greenery in the gardens, and the sea itself).

Once again, a Chinese, historical movie has drawn heavily on historical research and in particular Chinese art: many scenes are designed and filmed like Chinese landscape paintings or court paintings. Watching *Young Detective Dee: Rise of the Sea Dragon* is like seeing an ancient scroll unfurl. Long lenses flatten out three-dimensional scenes into flat images (despite the use of 3-D camera technology).

The art direction and compositions are exquisite – if the narrative wasn't hurtling along like an express train, *Young Detective Dee: Rise of the Sea Dragon* might be a moody, poignant drama about separated lovers (which, in act two, it is). The flattened space, the heightened and stylized colours of red and green, the flickering lamps and candles, the constantly billowing,[26] layered clothing – it all evokes another tale of lovers existing in the too-short time in between desire and death, like butterflies.

*Young Detective Dee: Rise of the Sea Dragon* opened with a colossal action sequence that probably cost more'n twenty or thirty average-budgeted Hong Kong movies. It delivered an attack on the fleet of the Imperial Navy at sea at night using the whole arsenal of visual effects available to filmmakers in the contemporary period[27] (water is of course very challenging to pull off in visual effects – and the sea dragon sequence had water in pretty much every shot, swiftly followed by fire effects, also difficult to achieve in vfx). Models, computer-assisted animation, full-size sets, green screens, and pretty much every computer-assisted effect available (and all of the usual practical effects) were included in the sequence, along with a suitably high volume sound mix, with crashing waves and splintering wood as each vessel was ripped apart by the sea dragon passing beneath. The sea dragon attack sequence provided a suitably gigantic opening to the 2013 Chinese movie – with devastation on a vast scale.

*Young Detective Dee: Rise of the Sea Dragon* has elements of a buddy movie, when Dee Renjie teams up with prison doctor Shatuo Zhong[28] (an appealing comic turn by Kenny Lin Geng-xin). Why a doctor, of all people? Because slices of the plot of *Young Detective Dee* revolve around poisons and antidotes; thus, handily, Shatuo is able to identify the parasites which're being hidden in tea (as well as poisonous plants), and can help with Dee's wounds, and Yuchi's bee-stings. (Meanwhile, there's a quack doctor, Wang Pu, and the Imperial Doctor – doctors are key figures in tales of Ancient China, where health is all-important). That the special Bird's Tongue tea is only drunk by the aristocracy is more satire in *Young Detective Dee,* which digs at the ruling classes repeatedly (the villains' plan is to wipe out the Imperial Tang dynasty using poisoned tea, because they all drink tea). Dee uncovers their nefarious scheme.

*Young Detective Dee: Rise of the Sea Dragon* is an action-adventure movie, tho', not a historical documentary. Thus, the second action sequence follows on swiftly from the Imperial Navy attack sequence: the precious beauty at the heart of *Young Detective Dee* is the young courtesan Yin Ruiji, who simply by existing causes mayhem amongst the men all around her (the movie underlines Yin's uncanny effect on guys – this's more than simply erotic desire or sexual magnetism. And yet she

26 *Young Detective Dee: Rise of the Sea Dragon* is another movie where it looks as if electric fans were employed in every single scene.
27 Ray Harryhausen and *Godzilla* and other Japanese monster movies were among the references.
28 A reworked version of the character played by Tony Leung in the first film.

hasn't done the deed with any of them).

A kidnapping attempt on Yin Ruiji by a group of underwater, ninja-like warriors turns into a storming sequence of rapidfire martial arts (with exotic weaponry a favourite);[29] in fact, there are multiple groups trying to snatch Yin (making this part of *Young Detective Dee: Rise of the Sea Dragon* – the second act – a kind of treasure hunt narrative, with living treasure). The spinning, flowing choreography has all the hallmarks of Yuen Bun's style (as well as Tony Ching Siu-tung's). It is quite, quite beautiful – the imagery of spinning bodies in the air is like a gymnastics event at a fairy tale level, like the Olympic Games if it was orchestrated by real gods, not mere humans. The speed of the movements seems even faster than before (is that possible in Hong Kong-style action? Which's already lightning fast!). The filmmakers have stuffed the *kung fu* action with visual effects, too – speed ramping, slow motion, weapon-point-of-view shots, and lots of blink-and-you-miss-them effects (many are computer-aided).

Now, in the midst of fights, the camera zooms into an arm, to reveal the effects of Dee Renjie's bruising punch on a victim, or switches from regular motion to slow motion, or uses computer-assisted animation to portray deadly weaponry scything thru the air into the viewer's face (a standard 3-D cinema tactic).

Each fighter is given their own fighting style – by far the most flamboyant is that of the Da Lisi Minister Yuchi Zhenjin. An acrobatic, whirlwind *kung fu* style, where flying and spinning at high speed is the norm. When Yuchi is in a hurry, he simply zooms upwards from his throne on a dais and crashes thru the roof! Forget about doors and windows! (And Yuchi handily carries all manner of weaponry with which to punch, knock over and halt victims in their tracks).

The action sequences continue, one after another, each one given its own choreography, style and look: a truly remarkable smackdown between arch villain Huo Yi and Yuchi (and assorted henchmen), in Wang Pu's clinic (another set art-directed by geniuses) • Yuchi battling the Dondo warriors • our heroes trying to control Yuan Zhen • the Dondoers summoning (and feeding) the sea monster • Dee, Yuchi *et al* encountering the sea monster (they fall into the water).

The action sequence featuring Minister Yuchi facing off against the Dondo warriors in the canals surrounding Swallow House seems almost impossible, combining underwater tussles with Yuchi zooming out the water while sword fighting. The intricacy, the timing, the flair and the beauty of the conflict is hypnotic. Nowhere else on the planet can you find such athletic, graceful scenes of mayhem.

✳

With the introduction of the water beast Yuan Zhen (at the start of the 2nd act),[30] *Young Detective Dee: Rise of the Sea Dragon* moves into *Beauty and the Beast* and *The Little Mermaid* territory (his appearance

---

29 Weapons fetishists will love this movie – the art and props department has really gone to town in concocting unusual (and highly detailed) weapons.
30 His design, as a green sea monster, references the famous monster in *Creature From the Black Lagoon* (Jack Arnold, 1954), a much-copied movie.

complicates the narrative significantly). Yuan Zhen in his poisoned state is a one-man army who requires many opponents to bring him down. As the plot unravels, it turns out that Yuan Zhen was actually Yin Ruiji's lover – and a poet, no less! Yes! This is a fantasy action-adventure movie which has time to stop the wild action for scenes where characters write poetry, recite poetry, and quote poetry. Wow! Only in a Chinese action movie!

So, yes, there is a love story in *Young Detective Dee: Rise of the Sea Dragon* (playing a distinctly secondary role, however). Yin Ruiji is such a magnetic courtesan, she has the élite of the capital paying *hommage* and hoping to be her first client (Yin possesses a sexual heat comparable with Cleopatra – which no actress, of course, can quite embody, tho', among Cleopatras on screen, Liz Taylor probably got closest. Angelbaby, the latest in a long line of pale, skinny, beautiful young actresses in Chinese cinema, doesn't quite fit the bill).

The romance of Yuan Zhen and Yin Ruiji is told in flashback in a very heightened, fairy tale manner (it's back to movies such as Tsui Hark's *The Lovers*). For the scene where they make love, they are depicted nude, floating in an abstract space of coloured banners. Again, the movie is very old school – the love token, for instance, is a jade hairpiece, a cliché of Chinese stories (there are movies from the 1930s called *The Jade Hairpiece*).

In *Young Detective Dee: Rise of the Sea Dragon*, there are only two really significant female characters: Empress Wu Zetian and Yin Ruiji. As played so impressively by veteran Carina Lau Ka-ling, the Empress is a wily operator, cool-to-chilly, sly, cunning, and a formidable presence (you do not want Empress Wu as your enemy!). The Empress is also the effective ruler of the Tang Dynasty, while the Emperor is ailing. A *female* ruler of China? Believe it! (And with Lau performing the Empress, you can believe that she *could* rule China).

Yin Ruiji, meanwhile, is essentially a Fairy Tale Princess; she's at the centre of several plot strands (she becomes a target when she's chosen as the human sacrifice for the sea god). There is an element of the *Snow White* fairy tale here, with sexual jealousy bubbling underneath Empress Wu Zeitan's relationship with Yin, evoking the Queen in *Snow White* and the heroine. Empress Wu enjoys being top dog, and so is happy that a mere courtesan, whose fame outweighs her beauty, should be banished.[31]

＊

Tsui Hark is fond of Chinese superstitions and customs as well as Chinese history and mythology. *Young Detective Dee: Rise of the Sea Dragon* contains many examples – like the perennial issue of immortality. Like poisons. Like tea drinking. Like calligraphy. Like medicine. Like food.

Lion Dances appear in *Young Detective Dee: Rise of the Sea Dragon*, along with several festive scenes and processions: the procession of the Imperial court thru the streets, for example, along with the dancing sacrifice, Yin Ruiji; at the end, an enormous ceremony to honour the defeat of the sea dragon, and the success of the parasite case.

31 From her first big scene, the Empress expresses her scorn that so much trouble is being caused by a mere courtesan.

Indeed, *Young Detective Dee: Rise of the Sea Dragon* is another opportunity for the filmmakers to incorporate a host of Chinese customs, issues and artforms. They are everywhere, in every single shot. The undercurrent of proud nationalism is strong in *Young Detective Dee: Rise of the Sea Dragon* – Tsui Hark's cinema has never been timid when it comes to celebrating all things Chinese. *Young Detective Dee: Rise of the Sea Dragon* is another manifestation of the simple fact that China is a global power of awesome potential.

Poisons, a speciality of many Chinese tales (and of courtly intrigue yarns set in the ancient world everywhere), are a theme in *Young Detective Dee: Rise of the Sea Dragon* – the Dondoers are using parasites to ravage and weaken the Imperial court. A visit to cackling quack Wang Pu (Zhong Shatuo's *sifu*) reveals a wacky cure: eunuch's piss! So *Young Detective Dee* contains scenes of whole legions of folk in the palace swallowing bowls of golden soup. Yummy! And very gross! (But note that Empress Wu Zeitan is not shown drinking it, and neither is the Emperor – instead, there's a very long shot of the royal chamber and voices are heard). As if the rulers of China can't be included in gross-out scenes.

So it was parasites that turned poor Yuan Zhen into a rapacious sea monster (the Dondoers have used humans to breed the parasites, in another gross-out horror moment, late in the piece). Writers Tsui Hark, Chen Kuo-fu and Zhang Jialu exploit those nasty parasites to the max – they use them to place the hero in the ultimate jeopardy of an instant public execution. Courtesy of Shatuo Zhong and the Imperial Doctor Wang Pu (Chen Kun), Dee and Yuchi present the eunuch urine cure to Empress Wu Zeitan. If it doesn't work within two hours, off with their heads.

Thus, in true cliffhanger style, our heroes're pushed to the limit by the filmmakers – kneeling on the block, ready to take the executioner's blade. It's pure adventure serial hokum (and shamelessly contrived), but it works: the Hong Kong film industry has exploited this kind of cliffhanger a zillion times, just like any other film industry. The price, as Alfred Hitchcock noted, is never paid. No one dies. The heroine (Yin Ruiji) and the sidekick (Shatuo) rush in to the nighttime execution to beg for a little more time. No dice: continue with the execution, orders bitch-goddess Empress Wu Zeitan. Only when an aged test patient staggers in yelling of the cure's efficacy, is the execution stopped. (Empress Wu, like the Queen in *Alice's Adventures In Wonderland*, seems disappointed. She's a monarch who can order up an execution at night within moments, and she doesn't like her plans going awry).

Everyone is in on the pretence – the audience, the filmmakers, the actors, the producers – to be a member of a movie audience, you have to go along with the game. There's no point resisting – you are wasting your time. Go and do something else if you don't like cliffhangers and clichés like this!

Nobody believes that the hero will be decapitated. In which case, the enjoyment comes from the tease, and from the filmmakers playing with the audience's expectations (as the audience tries to work out how our heroes will get out of this one).

So why include such a sequence? Well, for one thing, it really does shore up the third act (in a four-act model) of *Young Detective Dee*. It's an artificial construction, of course, with its narrative countdowns (clocks) and its cliffhangers, but drama as a form is pretty darn artificial already. (Also, it shows our hero literally putting his neck on the line. And the outcome is that he's promoted, over Minister Yuchi's head, to lead the investigation of the sea monster. Empress Wu Zeitan recognizes a useful lackey when she sees one. And Yuchi has not come up with results so far).

૨

The finale of the second *Detective Dee* movie includes three sections: (1) an enormous battle in amongst poisonous plants on Bat Island at night, (2) an incredible duel between our heroes and Huo Yi on a vast cliff face, and (3) a sea battle with the sea dragon.

In the second action sequence, Huo Yi is now clad in special armour enabling him to cling to the rocks, and clamber up them (as well as to slash the ropes of the heroes). You can see that the cliff scene was tough to shoot, with actors and doubles and stunt guys hanging on wires for hours and hours – yet, somehow, the action choreographers Yuen Bun and Lin Feng and the stunt teams have discovered ways of coming up with new methods of delivering action, new moves, and new camera angles.

Once again, each of the three main heroes is given something significant to do (primarily, saving each other from falling to their doom). The scene is a variation on the Hong Kong staple of depicting a finale using verticality as a key ingredient: typically, it's a tower, a platform, a warehouse, the roof of a building, or the upper reaches of an inn (all of which Tsui Hark has employed several times).

The sea god,[32] of course, surges in for the spectacular finale of *Young Detective Dee: Rise of the Sea Dragon* – with a gloriously old-fashioned piece of storytelling (old school drama, but told with state-of-the-art technology). *Jaws, King Kong, Godzilla,* and *Pirates of the Caribbean 2*[33] are in there – and of course, the King of Visual Effects, Ray Harryhausen. There isn't the slightest whiff of jeopardy – no way will this kind of movie sacrifice any major character at this late stage. But we go along for the ride – come on, it's a sea monster attacking warriors and ships! What's not to like? (Hell, there's even a wonder horse that can swim underwater – here the filmmakers chuck away any semblance to 'reality', so they can include outrageous images like Minister Yuchi rescuing the drowning Dee on the horse, and the hero riding the horse across the remains of battered, wooden ships, while the sea monster looms behind him).

The underwater wonder horse is a classic piece of Tsuist hokum,[34] as is the sea god (a marvellous creation – resembling a manta ray, with squid-like tentacles, and the mandatory giant maw). The filmmakers add their

32 You can't introduce a giant monster like that and not pay it off with a big action scene.
33 The monster clearly draws on the Kraken attacking ships in the second *Pirates of the Caribbean* movie.
34 A horse in a beat appeared in *Pirates of the Caribbean.*

own twist to the sea monster motif by having the beast able to leap out of the water hundreds of feet, with the camera in a top shot next to the creature (a hero shot has the beast leaping over Dee Renjie in the foreground). The scene contains thousands of stunts, tumbling actors, tons of water, splintering wood and masts, and impressive computer-aided animation.

How is the beast defeated? Only by poisonous fish! (reprising the poison theme). Well, something that large and ferocious dying from poison isn't quite as amazing as having the thing blow up or duel another leviathan. So the filmmakers include a countdown motif – the soldiers with the crossbows and nets of poisoned fish are going to fire on the signal of flags[35] from another ship. Of course, it all goes wrong, the signaller is tossed into the sea, and it's up to our heroes to save the day.

Like many a finale of an action movie, the storytelling is unnecessarily complicated, but the visuals and the filmmaking are simply wonderful. This is Tsui Hark at his crowd-pleasing best, and working at maximum stretch, reminiscent of the endings of *Green Snake* and *Zu: Warriors From the Magic Mountain*.

The end of this very traditional piece of storytelling is a classic *dénouenent* scene (actually, there are several *dénouements* and plot tie-ups). Presided over by the Empress and the Emperor (now restored to health), Dee Renjie is honoured with a special sword (the meteorite mace he uses in film one). The reverse angle reveals the customary vista of the Imperial palace swarming with thousands of extras. Other short scenes resolve other subplots – such as the romance of Yin Ruiji and Yuan Zhen (they're depicted together, with Yuan now restored nearly to his former self – *aah*, how sweet! And off they trot, into the wilderness, with money donated by Dee). A too-smug scene btn the three heroes when the monster's defeated. And Dee Renjie ruminating on the story (in voiceover).

---

35 The flags are red, of course.

# 34

# *DETECTIVE DEE AND THE FOUR HEAVENLY KINGS*

## *Di Renjie zhi Sidatianwang*

Astounding!

A genuine roller-coaster of a movie, a true thrill-ride of a movie.

The pace of it, the energy of it, the imagination and invention of it – this is incredible filmmaking.

Co-written, produced and directed by Tsui Hark – who else could it be? There's probably only one person on the whole planet who could've made this film (though not on his own! The cast and crew involved thousands of people).

*Detective Dee and the Four Heavenly Kings* (*Di Renjie zhi Sidatianwang*, 2018) was co-written with playwright Chang Chia-lu (from a story by Tsui Hark and producer Chen Kuo-fu), and produced by Huayi Brothers Pictures/ Huayi Brothers Pictures International/ C.F.K. Pictures/ Youku Pictures/ Shanghai Tao Piao Piao Movie & TV Culture/ Wanda Film and Television Media/ Film Workshop. The producers included Nansun Shi Nan-sheng, Tsui Hark, Zhang Da-jun, Chang Chai-lu, James Tsim Tak-faat, Jerry Yu-ning, Chen Kuo-fu, and Bernard Yang Ting-kai. The presenters (producers) were: Dennis Wang Zhong-jun, Tao Kun, Wang Zhong-lei, Yang Wei-dong, John Zeng Mao-jun and Jerry Li-jie

DP: Johnny Choi Sung-fai, editors: Tsui Hark and Li Lin; prod. des.: Akatsuka Yoshihito; art dir.: Raymond Lee King-man; costumes: Lee Pik-Kwan; image supervisor Bruce Yu Ka-on; make-up: Maggie Choy Yin-ching; hair: Lee Lin-tai; score: Kenji Kawai; visual fx sup.: Chuck Chae; and sound des.: Steve Burgess, Jay Yin and James Ashton. The action directors were Lin Feng, Li Kai, Chen Hao-jie and Li Ming-liang (plus an enormous stunt team). And an immense number of vfx crew, working for effects houses such as Cubic Pictures, Cutting Edge, Mofac, Digital Frontier, Oscar F.X., V.F.X. Studio Ubuntu, W.2 Studios, I.O.F.X., Macrograph, Yannix, Anima, Nippon Effect Center, L.I.N.D.A., etc.

Released July 27, 2018 (China), Sept 13, 2018 (Hong Kong). Category II B. 131 mins.

Many in the crew had worked with Tsui Hark for a long time – Nansun Shi and Bruce Yu, for instance, going back thirty years and more.

In the cast were Mark Chao You-ting, William Feng Shao-feng, Kenny Lin Geng-xin, Ethan Juan Ching-tien, Sandra Ma Si-chun, Carina Lau Ka-ling, Sheng Chien, Yang Yi-wei, Bao Ri-fu, Zhang Ao-yue, Sun Jiao-long, Wang Xi-chao, Shi Sheng-gang, Li Bing-lei and Xu Ming-hu. And a vast army of minor roles and extras and stunt people.

ª

*Detective Dee and the Four Heavenly Kings* followed on narratively from the first sequel, *Young Detective Dee* (so it was still a prequel to the 2010 film, *Detective Dee and the Mystery of the Phantom Flame.* Indeed, the *Young Detective Dee* is referenced to remind us of it – in the important scene where Dee and Minister Yuchi talk). Several in the cast returned from the *Young Detective Dee* film (including Chao, Feng, and Lau). The script, as usual with Tsui Hark, went thru many iterations (and no doubt the editing did, too).

Once again, *Detective Dee and the Four Heavenly Kings* depicts the mythical China that didn't exist but *should* have existed. Or, if Tsui Hark and the team were allowed to rewrite history, this is what it would be like. Tsui seems passionately in love with recreating Ancient China on a vast scale: it's not just big, big, big, it's enormous.

And, once again, the *joy* of filmmaking comes across in *Detective Dee and the Four Heavenly Kings* – the movie revels in staging outrageous entertainment. This is one of the very appealing aspects of the cinema of Tsui Hark – he looks like he's having a great time. Maybe nobody else on the set is (this is exhausting filmmaking), but the director is! And that pleasure in making cinema really comes across.

ª

As to the background context of *Detective Dee and the Four Heavenly Kings,* in the first act, the adversaries are the Mystic Clan (= Fuyin Clan), a group of Taoist warriors from the *jiangzhu* hired by the Empress. Tsui Hark is very fond of fanciful and eccentric characterizations and designs (and unusual weaponry): here we have Huan Tian (the leader), Spectral Blades, Smoke Volant, Water Moon and Night Ghost (they demonstrate their peculiar abilities to the Empress Wu Zeitan in an early scene, while MinisterYuchi looks on scowling and fighting them off when they get carried away).

The 2018 movie opens out, however, to include deeper and older opponents and threats to the moral order: the Wind Warriors, a mysterious and dangerous band of rebels who use an Indian magic of illusion to scare the bejesus[36] out of their victims (they are led by the masked man called Faceless Monster – Jia Wei). The portrayal of the Wind Warriors directly evokes the White Lotus Clan in the second *Once Upon a Time In China* movie. The Wind Warriors seethe with anger from being nearly wiped out by

36 Or should that be the be-Ganesh?

the previous Emperor, even though they aided the establishment of his regime (*Detective Dee and the Four Heavenly Kings* is about several forms of civil war within China, and within the Imperial Palace, as different institutions are set against each other, each vying for the upper hand).

Altho' *Detective Dee and the Four Heavenly Kings* used state-of-the-art visual effects and technology, it is actually an old-fashioned piece of storytelling, in terms of its characters, its plot, and its themes. But few movies can deliver this kind of old-fashioned hokum at such a rapid pace, with so much energy, and with such imaginative skill.

The casting is perfect in *Detective Dee and the Four Heavenly Kings* – the lead actors are particularly fine, with some humorous interplay between Detective Dee and his sidekick Shatuo Zhong; the flirtation between Shatuo Zhong and new character Water Moon; and the more sober, brotherly relationship between former rivals Dee and Yuchi Zhenjin.

Although this is a *Detective Dee* movie, the story in fact presents two heroes in the forefront: Detective Dee (Mark Chao You-ting) and Yuchi Zhenjin (William Feng Shao-feng). They were adversaries in the *Young Detective Dee*, but now they're working together. The decision to bump up the role of Yuchi (so it's a kind of buddy movie) means that there is less for Dee to do in some sections of *Detective Dee and the Four Heavenly Kings,* because Yuchi takes up his function (however, in the fourth act, Yuchi disappears for some time, when he's been arrested and imprisoned after the Wind Warriors impersonate him, and the film shifts the focus to Dee). However, it's William Feng who steals this movie.

A key scene expresses the political philosophy behind the 2018 film: Dee Renjie gives Yuchi Zhenjin a painting that was commissioned to memorialize the events in the previous *Detective Dee* film. In the corner of it, Dee has added some words about protecting China from forces that threaten to consume it from inside. It's a touching scene between Dee and Yuchi in which the agreement to Do The Right Thing is asserted, captured chiefly in the way that actors Chao and Feng play off each other).

Kenny Lin Geng-xin as Shatuo Zhong (Dee Renjie's disciple in healing and herblore) nabs the best bits of the humour in *Detective Dee and the Four Heavenly Kings* – such as when Water Moon slaps him in the face; or when he tries to fly like Detective Dee, kicking off a wall, while Dee soars away and he lands back on the ground. Kenny Lin is a favoured kind of actor for Tsui Hark – he can play comedy (as in the Monkey King in *Journey To the West*), and he can play drama (as in *The Taking of Tiger Mountain*), and he comes across as a regular guy. Tsui has cast Lin in many roles in his recent cinema.

*Detective Dee and the Four Heavenly Kings* is a thoroughly masculine outing: there are only two female characters of note: the Empress Wu Zeitan and the assassin Water Moon.

Water Moon is first introduced in the scene featuring the Mystic Clan demonstrating their powers to the Empress: she is a black-clad, Japanese ninja. Later, however, that disguise is dropped, and she is often put in regular clothes (and spies from above but in regular form).

Sandra Ma Si-chun (b. 1988) is an appealing addition to the cast of the Tsui Hark Circus; playing Water Moon much younger, Ma is a classic Tsui-ian tomboy woman (small, pale, skinny), the sister of Charlie Cheung in *The Lovers*, for example, or the girls in *Peking Opera Blues*.

&

Much of *Detective Dee and the Four Heavenly Kings* is set in and around the Da Li Si, the Bureau of Investigations, and the Imperial Palace, plus two memorable visits to a rural Buddhist temple (and a rural dungeon).

The MacGuffin of *Detective Dee and the Four Heavenly Kings* is the Imperial Mace (the Dragon Taming Mace), a version of a magical sword seen in the 2013 prequel (there is much scurrying to and fro as rival groups try to wrest it free of Detective Dee, after Emperor Gaozong gives it to him. The Empress is furious that her husband and the Top Man In the Realm has presented it to Dee – she expresses her fury by hurling everything off several tables right after the outdoor presentation ceremony. She tells the Emperor that Dee might use the magical sword against them, though her real motives are hidden. This is the inciting incident in act one, setting off the train of events of the movie).

But, actually, the real MacGuffin of *Detective Dee and the Four Heavenly Kings* is the Indian magic of illusion which was created, it seems, to allow the filmmakers (and Tsui Hark in particular) to indulge in fantastical flights of fancy. These include a giant, white ape, a golden, Chinese dragon, flying lizards, colossal demons, enormous fish, tentacled thingies, and more (often, these immense creatures are Tsui's *hommages* to the monster movies he enjoyed as youth – in *animé*, in Japanese monster flicks, in *King Kong,* and in Ray Harryhausen's adventures).

Talking about monsters – the influence of Japanese animation can be discerned in many places in *Detective Dee and the Four Heavenly Kings*. Not only does *Detective Dee and the Four Heavenly Kings* boast a magnificent score from a genius composer of numerous animated classics from Japan, Kenji Kawai, it employs many motifs from *animé* (just as *animé* has influenced Hollywood production for decades now).

The device of mass hallucination handily allows the filmmakers to have it both ways, as they always prefer: to stage scenes with fantasy creatures as if they are really there, and simultaneously to play the same scenes without them. The illusion motif is another form of Tsui Hark's fascination with the mechanics of cinema. (Other forms of altered worlds in cinema include dreams, drugs, virtual reality, storytelling, etc).

&

*Detective Dee and the Four Heavenly Kings* is a whole wagonload of Tsui Harkisms: traditional, Chinese culture (acupuncture,[37] healing, poison, calligraphy, mythology); Peking Opera; the theme of righteous-ness versus hatred; wise, Confucian sayings; romantic flirtations; swordplay to the max; Buddhist religion; a visit to a temple; visual effects everywhere (in almost every other shot); a tiny, skinny, punky girl (Water Moon); animals (horses, fish, monkeys, and mythical beasts like dragons,

37 Acupuncture is referenced throughout the movie, with both Dee and Zhong using it on themselves or others (Dee is poisoned in several scenes, and uses acupuncture to help).

demons and apes); Japanese *animé*; and goofy comedy. And it is of course a Chinese story filmed in China with a Chinese crew and Chinese actors.

As for action, *Detective Dee and the Four Heavenly Kings* contains every type of action that Tsui Hark has included in his cinema, right back to *The Butterfly Murders*: every variant of swordplay; monster duels; and chases across rooftops, thru stables, on horseback, thru courtyards, atop statues, etc. Tsui seemed to be challenging himself and his action co-ordinators to come up with something he hadn't used before. That is an almost impossible task for possibly the greatest action director in film history.

Certainly, solely in terms of action choreography, *Detective Dee and the Four Heavenly Kings* is absolutely thrilling. The production employed more visual effects in some action sequences, as they tried to show audiences something they hadn't seen before (the weapons, for example, flying all over the place). But there is the same emphasis on rapid motion, acrobatic stunts, fluidity and beauty. (Some of the action scenes are explored further below).

Although Tony Ching Siu-tung wasn't involved with *Detective Dee and the Four Heavenly Kings,* there are numerous Chingian motifs in it – the flowing swordplay, with costumes billowing in the breeze; the chases across the rooftopos; the Wind Warriors flying through the air dressed in black like Japanese ninjas, and so on.

The score for *Detective Dee and the Four Heavenly Kings* is an outstanding assembly of Oriental styles from superstar Japanese composer Kenji Kawai (he provided the score for the first sequel, and for *Seven Swords*). If you hire Kawai to compose your soundtrack, you are in safe hands. You can leave everything to him and he and his team will deliver – big time. Kawai draws on all sorts of musical styles, as he often does for his scores. There are sweeping strings, as expected, and pounding percussion cues (one of Kawai's trademarks), and some really ballsy choral cues.

The costumes, hair and make-up are gloriously eccentric for the villains and the rivals, while Carina Lau Ka-ling looks as dangerously imperious (and ageless) as ever. Lee Pik-Kwan and Bruce Yu Ka-on oversaw the wardrobe, while Maggie Choy Yin-ching and Lee Lin-tai did the hair.

The sets (by Akatsuka Yoshihito and Raymond Lee King-man) are very self-indulgent, with over-the-top renditions of Imperial grandeur (the throne room in particular is a remarkable and vast wedding cake of Imperial, dynastic red and gold decoration). The photography is, as always in even the weakest films by Tsui Hark, stunning (Johnny Choi Sung-fai was DP, with Edward Chan Yiu-leung and Pan Zhen as cinematographers, and lighting by Lee Chi-wai).

Design-wise, there's no holding back in *Detective Dee and the Four Heavenly Kings*. As they say, if you are going to step up to ring the bell, then you'd better *really* ring it. Or as David O. Selznick put if, if you are going to do something like an epic movie, then you'd better *really* do it.

&

The first act of *Detective Dee and the Four Heavenly Kings* rapidly introduces the three main characters: the Empress, Dee Renjie and Yuchi Zhenjin. Dee is first seen training, on his own in a courtyard – but using a switch instead of a sword (to slice up falling ginko leaves). This scene is used as foreshadowing, when he uses the technique to immobilize one of the villains. Yuchi Zhenjin accompanies Empress Wu Zeitan to audition the assassins she's hired to steal the Dragon Taming Mace from Dee Renjie. The Mystic Clan – Huan Tian, Spectral Blades, Smoke Volant, Water Moon and Night Ghost – demonstrate their special skills (ninja Water Moon materializes out of the Empress's shadow, for example, while Spectral Blades hurls huge, curved spinning weapons). Yuchi protects the Empress when the projectiles get a little too close.

Much of the rest of act one of *Detective Dee and the Four Heavenly Kings* comprises a continuous action sequence, with the Mystic Clan attempting to steal the magical sword from Judge Dee's offices at night, while Dee and his men take on some of the villains. The action is exquisitely staged and completely thrilling. This is action filmmaking at the very height of flamboyant expression – the characters are racing along the rooftops, diving around pillars, evading plumes of acid, and melting into smoke. While all of this has been seen before in Hong Kong and Chinese cinema, here it's achieved with such flair it's breathtaking.

The Empress Wu Zeitan visits an old minister (Faceless Lord) being kept in a dank, water-logged dungeon in a subsequent scene (Tsui Hark has included a bit of *The Count of Monte Cristo* in several films), which thickens the plot (and reminds us that the Empress is the real superpower in the *Detective Dee* series). In the second visit, it's revealed that Faceless Lord died two years ago, and the Empress is also under the spell from the Wind Warriors, because she imagines that the old man leaps out of the dungeon to attack her.

And there's another training sequence, overseen by Yuchi Zhenjin, and of course it's another action scene (though more light-hearted – it features jokes about Yuchi always wearing his full battle armour, and Shatuo Zhong being unable to fly like Dee or Yuchi). When *Detective Dee and the Four Heavenly Kings* shifts into act two, Dee visits his mentors, the Buddhist monks Master Yuan Ce and Master Sanzang.[38]

&

The customary market scene[39] in a costume drama occurs at the start of act two (instead of its usual place, early in act one). It's Peking Opera Time, with acrobats tumbling thru the shots, magicians conjuring tricks, and there's a general festive atmosphere.

This is where Shatuo Zhong gets his own subplot in *Detective Dee and the Four Heavenly Kings*, which develops throughout the film (and includes his flirtatious relationship with Water Moon). So Zhong is our observer figure for the introduction of the mysterious and sinister Indian clan of the

38 The name of the monk in *Journey To the West*.
39 Favourite Tsui-ian motifs such as fish are prominent.

Wind Warriors (a little later, the exposition about the secret clan is delivered by Dee Renjie to Zhong).

Water Moon and Shatuo Zhong are the main charas in this section of *Detective Dee and the Four Heavenly Kings*. Even here, the staging is dynamic and full of movement. When Water Moon spies on the market and on Zhong, she is high up, and moves from position to position with graceful, flying leaps. Isn't this one of the joys of Chinese martial arts movies, this freedom of gesture? That people don't just walk up stairs, but jump from the ground to a pillar to a balcony? It's the same exhilaration as seeing Jackie Chan get over a locked gate by pushing off from one pillar, kicking off another, and using a palm on the top of the gate to twist over it.

The beautiful, flowing movements (culled of course from the Peking Opera tradition, which we know Tsui Hark is absolutely crazy for) enhance the scene with flow, colour and muscular staging. In the Shatuo Zhong subplot a romantic flirtation develops between the herbalist and the cool assassin, Water Moon (they share the same homeland, Tiele).

Taking its cue perhaps from *A Chinese Ghost Story*, which comically switched the traditional gender roles, this time it's the man who's spied on while bathing instead of the woman. So Kenny Lin Geng-xin is cast in the Leslie Cheung role as a guy washing himself while a young woman spies on him, then taunts him up close.

Back to the action: act two of *Detective Dee* features two stunning sequences. In the first, Yuchi Zhenjin performs the Sherlock Holmes routine, and discovers where Dee Renjie has hidden the magical sword: in a Buddhist temple presided over by huge statues of the four Heavenly Kings of the film's title.

But the heavies are on Yuchi Zhenjin's tail: Spectral Blades bursts into the scene by blasting through the gates and hurling himself at Yuchi (who's standing on one of the statues). A frenetic duel ensues, pitting swords against flying, spinning, curved blades, until Yuchi uses the Imperial Mace to take care of Spectral Blades (giving him some of his own medicine – the Mace fractures one of the blades so that shards split off and whizz right through Spectral Blades' body). The duel is superbly inventive in other ways – it exploits every part of the small, temple courtyard, including the upper levels.

Act two climaxes with a grandiose set (the impossibly luxurious throne room) and a grandiose set-piece (the appearance of a fearsome dragon): the conjuring tricks of the Mystic Clan which're swiftly overtaken by the hallucinations of the Wind Warrior Clan. Once again it's Yuchi Zhenjin who's our audience idenification figure in this scene, rather than Dee Renjie (who has gone into hiding as he tries to uncover who is really behind the plot to steal the Dragon Taming Mace. He suspects that it's Empress Wu Zeitan, but he doesn't want to believe it, or to pursue where that line of thinking will lead).

It took a while for the Asian film industry to match the level of quality of Western/ American visual effects, but it was worth the wait for scenes such as the golden dragon going wild in the throne room in *Detective Dee* and the Four Heavenly Kings. It's a crowd-pleasing scene in the manner of Ray Harryhausen's stopmotion animated adventure flicks, a scene which revels in the magic trickery of cinema.

෴

Act three of Detective Dee and the Four Heavenly Kings begins in fine style with Sandra Ma Si-chun's big action scene in the movie: it's a chase on horseback and across the rooftops outside the Imperial Palace, pursued by three agents from the Wind Warriors Clan (this section of Detective Dee and the Four Heavenly Kings opens with Dee Renjie attempting to confuse the enemy by sending several agents in different directions from the Bureau on horses (and Shatuo Zhong is given his own task – to visit the Buddhist monks upcountry).

Water Moon is eventually overcome by the Wind Warriors – they are able to fly (in their black cloaks, they resemble the ninjas that Tony Ching is fond of putting in his films. Indeed, this section of Detective Dee and the Four Heavenly Kings is very Chingian in its action). A great touch has the three henchmen combining into one human creature with long, insect-like arms and claws (and with the face of the Empress).

Before Water Moon's defeat, however, there is some marvellous stuntwork with horses (if Tsui Hark directed a cowboy flick, this is what it would look like), and furious flights across the neighbourhood's roofs. Both sides land blows, but the Wind Warriors also use poison, and Water Moon, severely wounded, scurries into some stables to hide. This is where Shatuo Zhong, changing horses on his important mission for the Bureau, finds Water Moon, in agony on the ground.

So there are two flirtation scenes in Detective Dee and the Four Heavenly Kings – one is the very common scene of a patient being nursed back to health, with erotic interplay emerging from the close proximity – between Water Moon and Shatuo Zhong. When Water Moon realizes that Zhong has undressed her and tended to her wounds, she slaps him (when the film cuts to Zhong on his horse, with his face puffed up, the gag is right out of Japanese animé).

The filmmaking employs several time-shifts here, cutting back from Shatuo Zhong on his journey thinking about the conversation with Water Moon about Tiele, their homeland (the film cuts to an image of the home country as a paradisal place of flowers and mountains). Water Moon plays the familiar stubborn (i.e., proud), angry patient who refuses any help, while Zhong has even taken some of the poison into his body when he sucked out the wound.

The second flirtation scene in Detective Dee and the Four Heavenly Kings is more dangerous, when the Empress Wu Zeitan visits Detective Dee's chambers at night, dressed to kill. Before the Empress is revealed to be Smoke Volant in disguise, the scene allows Carina Lau and Mark Chao to play a sexy seduction scenario. (It's a replay of the love scene between Andy Lau and Li Bingbing in the first Detective Dee movie. Again, this is a common Tsui Hark approach – to portray a love or sex scene that has a hidden agenda, or isn't really a love scene, or one of the participants is in disguise, or begins as a love scene but then becomes something else).

⋙

A trip to a remote Buddhist temple where Master Yuan Ce resides is a scene that might've come from any Tsui Hark picture from the past 40 years. It's the young monk Yuan Ce (Ethan Juan) who helps out the heroes in the end, rather than the usual wise, old sage. When Yuan Ce gallops into the finale riding the enormous, white ape, it's certainly a memorable entrance.

The temple, meanwhile, is designed like the settings in the New Territories of Hong Kong, where so many of the films of the Hong Kong New Wave were made. There's an ancient tree, signs, and an amusing riff on stone cairns. Maybe it's the influence of British artist Andy Goldsworthy, but you find towers built from pebbles everywhere these days.

The monk is so close to nature he's become part of it: Yuan Ce is sitting in the lotus position and meditating but he's being absorbed into the tree. Shatuo Zhong can't get through to him (he's forbidden to talk, though he tries to mug and grunt), until Yuan's spirit familiar, a giant, white ape thunders into the scene. The plot can't be explained by a roaring gorilla, however – that comes from another familiar, a floating fish (the creature summarizes the Plot So Far, in the usual place, before the climax).

⋙

The finale of *Detective Dee and the Four Heavenly Kings* is furiously paced and fiendishly complicated cinematically (and technically), even though it plays out in an old-fashioned manner. That is, the movie follows the *Action-Adventure Movie Handbook*, chapters 15 thru 18: *The Action Finale*, and includes the usual cliffhangers, snakepit scenarios and last-minute rescues. Everybody gets to do their bit, and the two main heroes – Dee and Yuchi – step aside for a moment to allow the Buddhist monk Yuan Ce to take on the arch villain, Faceless Monster (they observe Yuan battling Faceless Monster together on a watchtower).

Shatuo Zhong sadly informs Dee Renjie that Yuan Ce won't come to help them, but we know he will, because Water Moon has been dispatched to the Buddhist temple. (The preceding scene is given a big build-up – not only Yuchi but Dee and all of the Bureau of Investigations officers visit Water Moon to plead with her to help them).

The finale of *Detective Dee and the Four Heavenly Kings* begins with the preparations for the attack by the Wind Warrior Clan on the Bureau of Investigations. Yuan Ce has given our heroes some Buddhist sutras to chant which will combat the hallucinations of the enemy (the Dragon Taming Mace helps, too). Waves of attackers come at them, including an enormous demon with eyes all over its skin (this is a very Ray Harryhausenian scene, as the filmmakers pay a tribute to the God of Visual Effects, and *hommage* movies such as *The Seventh Voyage of Sinbad* and *Jason and the Argonauts*. There's another movie *hommage* – to *King Kong*, when the white ape battles the flying lizards).

The assaults by the Wind Warriors is a *tour-de-force* of action cinema (they vault over the very high walls of the Bureau using poles). The gags come thick and fast, involving shields, swords, spears, horses and ropes, on every level of the compound. There's a blissful intensity to the action, which passes by the viewer in the blink of an eye, but which took weeks to achieve (and many takes).

The motif of mass hallucination allows *Detective Dee and the Four Heavenly Kings* to stage all sorts of supernatural shenanigans, including a second giant demon and a barrage of writhing, red tentacles. And the Wind Warriors transform into huge flying reptiles with long tails which set about the guards of the Bureau.

Among the many other beats in the finale of *Detective Dee and the Four Heavenly Kings* are Yuchi Zhenjin taking on the Mystic Clan's Smoke Volant – trapping him in an underground chamber (where the enemy thinks the Emperor and the Empress are hiding). After that, Yuchi, who has been out of the picture for a while, is part of the finale in the Bureau of Investigations. He has his own duel with one of the flying reptiles/ Wind Warriors, and eventually teams up with Detective Dee (a great touch has Yuchi cutting down the ropes which have pinned Dee down then raised him into the air. So Yuchi gets to save Dee).

With our heroes close to being overwhelmed, a *deus ex machina* rescue is required. It arrives in the form of a real god – Monk Yuan Ce riding atop his spirit familiar, the albino ape.

Another moment of rescue sees Water Moon arriving just in time to protect Shatuo Zhong from the Wind Warriors who're clambering all over him. This is the final scene of their appealing, semi-romantic subplot.

Faceless Lord is finally unmasked, as he confronts the superhero Buddhist monk, Yuan Ce. The message of the 2018 movie is once again stated (letting go hatred and the urge to kill, transcending the past, and protecting what is precious). Mr Faceless can't let go, of course, and repeatedly attacks the monk. The outcome of the film, however, was never in any doubt.

The finale of *Detective Dee and the Four Heavenly Kings* is beautifully worked out, with a series of escalating threats and last-minute rescues. You can see that Tsui Hark absolutely relishes staging this kind of colossal action (if Tsui had his way, a movie would be entirely an act three climax, with one snakepit or cliffhanger scenario after another).

The *dénouement* scenes of *Detective Dee and the Four Heavenly Kings* are short (rightly), such as the Emperor thanking the Bureau guards. Some *dénouements* occur within the end credits. In one, we see the Empress Wu Zeitan humbled and praying (though we can guess that this new pious demeanour won't last long). In another, we see a continuation of the scene where Water Moon visited the Buddhist temple.

&

Critics found *Detective Dee and the Four Heavenly Kings* impressively visually and technically, though for some there was too much computer-assisted wizardry and superfluous eye candy. Some critics disliked the move from mystery and investigation *à la* Sherlock Holmes towards monsters and action.

Andrew Skeates in Far East Films reckoned that Tsui Hark 'delivers a wickedly fun fantasy romp full of wondrous fight actions and flights of fancy', while Edmund Lee in the *South China Morning Post* said:

> the director's supernatural whodunit is diverting at times but ultimately proves a disappointing third instalment in the series; pointless C.G.I. mayhem replaces its seventh-century mystery origins.

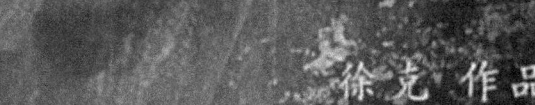

徐克 作品

狄仁杰之通天帝国

Detective and the Mystery of the Phantom Flame (2010).

DETECTIVE DEE
AND THE MYSTERY OF THE PHANTOM FLAME

王朝の陰謀
判事ディーと人体発火怪奇事件

DVD
VIDEO

Young Detective Dee (2013), this page and over.

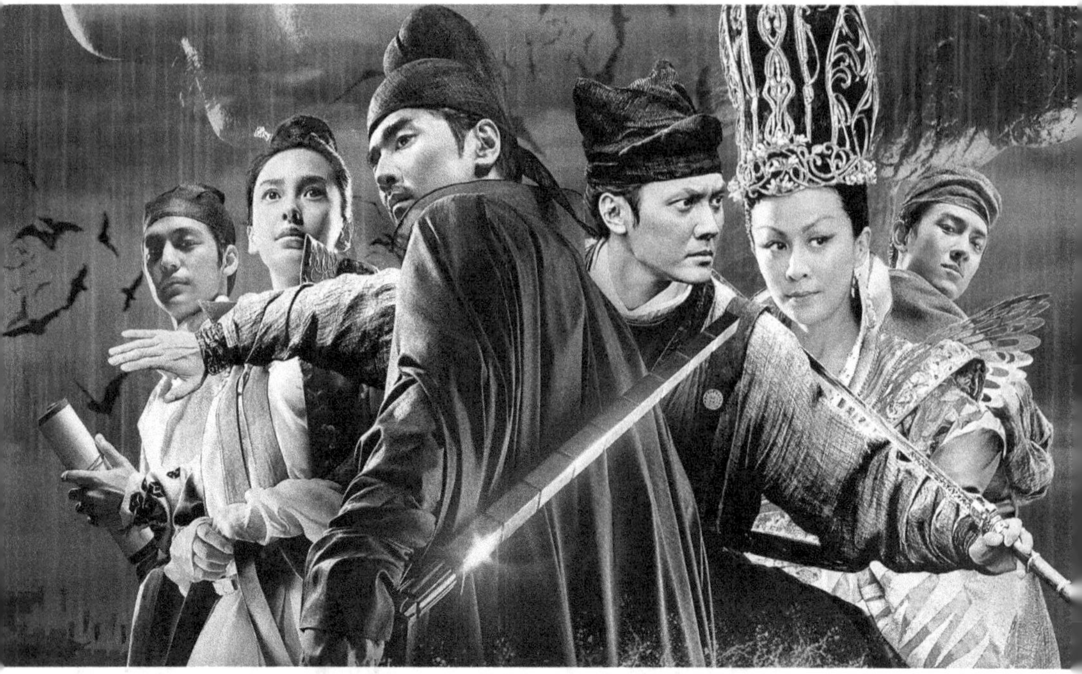

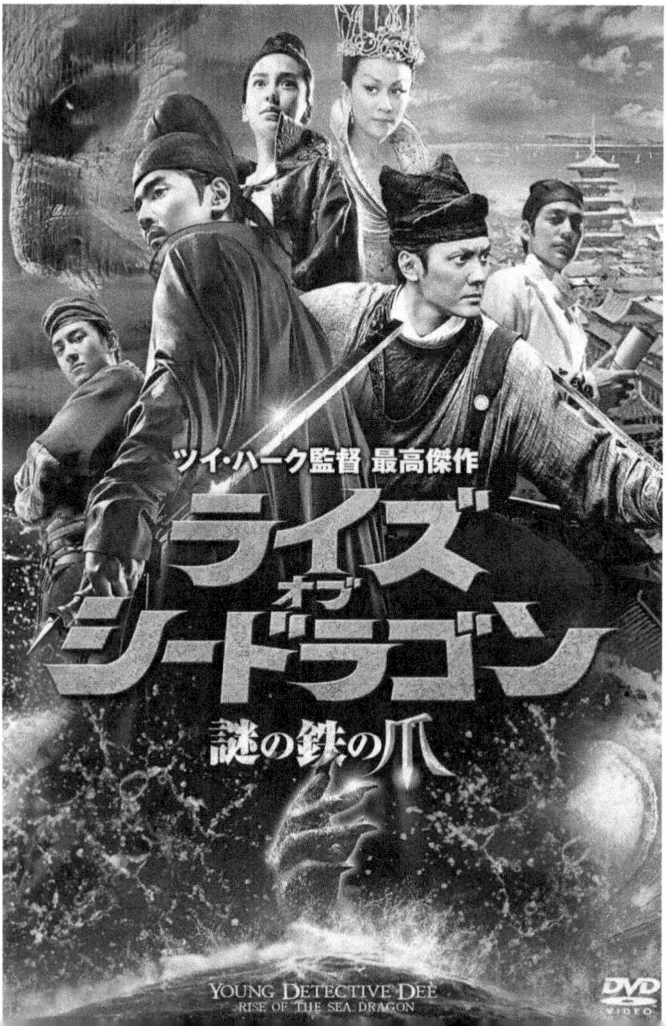
ツイ・ハーク監督 最高傑作
ライズ
オブ
シードラゴン
謎の鉄の爪
YOUNG DETECTIVE DEE
RISE OF THE SEA DRAGON
DVD
VIDEO

Detective Dee and the Four Heavenly Kings (2018).

# 35

# *FLYING SWORDS OF DRAGON GATE*

# *Long Men Fei Jia*

In 1992 Tsui Hark produced and co-wrote *New Dragon Gate Inn*, when he was riding high on the Hong Kong New Wave (following the smash hit of *Once Upon a Time In China* the year before). *New Dragon Gate Inn* was a remake of the 1967 classic helmed by King Hu, one of the influences on Tsui (as well as the co-director of *The Swordsman,* along with Raymond Lee, who directed the 1992 *New Dragon Gate Inn*). In 2011 Tsui produced, co-wrote and this time directed a remake (or continuation) of *New Dragon Gate Inn*, entitled *Flying Swords of Dragon Gate.* Tsui Hark commented:

> The new movie is not a re-make, but rather a continuation of the same story from the first *Dragon Inn.* I'm not a fan of re-makes because I always have strong impressions for the original, especially if they are good movies. So why re-make a classic? It's not the right manner or show of respect toward the original and the filmmakers who produced it.

(We'll come back to the remake/ sequel/ continuation issue.)

*Flying Swords of Dragon Gate* (*Long Men Fei Jia*, 2011) was prod. by Shanghai Media Group/ Film Workshop/ Polybona Films/ Bona International Film Group/ Liangzi Group/ Shinshow Co./ China Film Group Corporation; the producers were Nansun Shi Nan-sheng, Wenhong Yang, Dong-ming Shi, Xiaoli Han, and Tsui Hark; exec. prods. were Dong Yu, Rui Gang Li, Jeffrey Chan, and Sanping Han; Tsui has script credit; the action dirs. were Yuen Bun, Allen Lan Hai Han and Sun Jian Jui; music by Xin Gu, Han Chiang Li and Wai Lap Wu; DPs: Johnny Choi Sung Fai; editing by Chi Wai Yau; prod des. by Kenneth Yee Chung-man; art dir. by Ben Lau; costumes by Hsuan-wu Lai and Kenneth Yee Chung-man; and sound design by Suk-won Kim. Released: Dec 15, 2011. 125 mins.

In the cast were: Jet Li, Kwai Lun-mei, Chen Kun, Zhou Xun, Li Yu-chun, Mavis Fan Hiu-huen, Fan Siu-wong, Du Yiheng, Sun Jian-kui and Viann Zhang Xin-yu. The main characters were: Swordsman Zhao Huai'an, fellow warrior Ling Yanqiu, the chief villain Yu Huatian (also: Pu Cangzhou / Blade in the Wind), Lun-Mei Kwei as the Tartar chief, Gu Shaotang as a warrior, and Su Huirong (the escaped courtesan). Gordon Liu makes an entertaining cameo as a villainous eunuch in the opening duel.

It was a big budget, Chinese movie (rumoured at $35 million). It was touted in the P.R. as the re-uniting of Tsui with Jet Li, after their 'fall-out' over the *Once Upon a Time In China* movies (however, that disagreement was about money and the Golden Harvest studio (some said it was to do with immigration issues).[1] And, besides, Tsui and Li *did* work together after *Once Upon a Time In China*, such as on 1996's *Black Mask* and 1997's *Once Upon a Time In China 6*).

Jet Li steps into the role that seemed made for him in the 1992 version, which was played then by Tony Leung Ka-fai.[2] (Li was rumoured to have received $12 million in U.S. dollars for the role – a massive sum for a Chinese star in a Chinese picture, and a huge chunk of the budget).

2011 was a busy year for Jet Li in fantasy *wuxia pian* – he also starred in *The Emperor and the White Snake*, directed by Tony Ching Siu-tung, with whom Li has worked many times. (This was a partial remake of *Green Snake*, directed by Tsui Hark in 1993).

Chinese superstar Zhou Xun (b. 1974) appears in the role that Brigitte Lin played in *New Dragon Gate Inn*: if you had to pick a Chinese actress beloved enough in Asia to step into Lin's shoes, it might be Zhou. If she doesn't have quite the aloof mystery of Lin (who does?), Zhou has the star power to inhabit the role.

᠃

*Flying Swords of Dragon Gate* starred Jet Li in a truly fantastic, immensely enjoyable romp. The production was deliberately traditional and conventional, in terms of characters and storylines and themes, but it employed state of the art visual effects, including a huge amount of computer-aided work (*Flying Swords of Dragon Gate* announces its eye-popping vfx work in the opening shot, a very long, very complicated (and no doubt very expensive) computer-aided animated helicopter shot in a harbour, flying in between the masts of ships). This is a nod too to the opening image of *Wong Fei-hung* in 1991, which was a miniature shot, and it's the sort of shot that Tsui Hark would've included years ago if the technology had been available.

Tsui Hark is without doubt one of the great film directors of visual effects, the equal of any of the celebrated filmmakers of vfx, whether it's Géorges Méliès at the birth of cinema (and the father of all visual effects work), or masters in the West such as Ray Harryhausen and Steven Spielberg. Tsui simply *adores* visual effects, and stuffs his movies with

1 Also around this time, Jet Li's manager Jim Choi was shot dead as he stepped out of an elevator.
2 Apparently, Donnie Yen was approached by the producers, but he turned the role down, preferring not to repeat himself.

them. If there's a trick shot that Tsui and his team haven't tried, they'll have a go at it (but by 2011, and his fortieth feature as director, Tsui had already delivered every visual effect in the history of cinema). Tsui's movies *foreground* visual effects,[3] and make everybody aware that these are tricks and gimmicks and sleights of hand. Tsui doesn't want to *hide* the visual effects, to pretend they don't exist, but to *celebrate* them, just as the martial arts choreography in the movie celebrates the human body and incredible action. (Thus, *Flying Swords of Dragon Gate* opens with that extremely elaborate vfx shot, which's so obviously a vfx shot – it includes camera moves impossible even for remote devices, like zooming thru tiny openings. It's thus the point-of-view of a flying sword).

At a technical level, *Flying Swords of Dragon Gate* is outstanding – the team that Tsui Hark, Nansun Shi Nan-sheng and the producers have assembled are veterans. These guys are totally natural filmmakers. The design, the costumes, the make-up, the hair, the lighting, the props, the art direction, the sets, the cinematography, the sound design, the stunts, and the music – everything is top-notch.

And of course, with a cast headed up by Jet Li and this being a full-on martial arts epic, the action is simply stupendous. I mean, wow!, if you haven't seen a Chinese action movie for a while and then you happen upon something like *Flying Swords of Dragon Gate*, you have your neon-green socks knocked off! The action in *Flying Swords of Dragon Gate* rocks, big time.

*Flying Swords of Dragon Gate* features Tsui Hark working at full stretch, at the height of his powers. The movie, being a *wuxia pian* set in the very familiar *jiangzhu,* is a collection of Tsui's Greatest Hits, and is stuffed with Tsui-isms. So we have a big battle on a boat (from *Once Upon a Time in China 4*), Lun-mei Kwei is the loud, punky, dangerous woman, Chang Xiaowen (from *Seven Swords*), crossdressing Zhou Xun, and so on. The new take on Ye Olde Chinese tales included the feminist characters (from any Tsui), the computer-aided elements, and of course filming in 3-D. (Thus, *Flying Swords of Dragon Gate* was another technical challenge for Tsui and the team; Tsui likes to shake things up technically, after making so many movies).

Act one includes three action set-pieces set or near water: the harbour-side opening scene, a face-off beside a river (in a steep valley location used in other Chinese films), and aboard a State ship.

We also visit the courtesan's palace in act one of *Flying Swords of Dragon Gate*, where the background political plot of the movie is concocted: Yu Huatian is manipulating the strings as the grand puppeteer. Thus, the last of the courtesans, Su Huirong, is used as bait for the heroes, luring them to the river valley in the wilds. (As if he realizes that this is a trap, the real Zhao Huatian hides and watches, while the double Zhao is the one who saves the woman).

That Su Huirong is pregnant adds a layer of hopeful symbolism to the proceedings (though this film, despite its prominent female characters, is

3 There is plenty of green screen work (matching close-ups on a sound stage with location shooting, for example).

set within an oppressive patriarchal society, the usual totally masculinist world of Chinese historical pictures. For example, a woman is punched on the boat by the authorities, and Su is threatened with a blade pointed at her stomach).

*Flying Swords of Dragon Gate* is Tsui Hark working on a giant canvas – the first act sets out the huge scale of the movie, shifting from the harbour to the courtesan Wan's palace, to a remote, Buddhist temple, to a sandstone river gorge, to a ship at sea, and to the desert of the Dragon Inn itself. (Some of the locations are familiar to viewers of recent Chinese, historical movies – the river setting surrounded by cliffs, for example, and the same Imperial sets in Beijing).

In *Flying Swords of Dragon Gate* the production team get to play with all of the new toys available to filmmakers, including giant remote cranes, which can achieve those now-familiar, very high angle shots. But this also means that some scenes in *Flying Swords of Dragon Gate* were filmed with a gently drifting crane, in wide shot: pretty to look at, but a little flabby cinematically compared to having the camera right in amongst the actors, and tracking or moving around them. The big (and very expensive) remotely-controlled cranes create wonderful (and very steady) shots, but sometimes they lack the dynamism of putting the camera in with the actors (and compared to having camera operators atop a crane).

Part of the reason for this is that *Flying Swords of Dragon Gate* was filmed for 3-D presentation, which requires a slightly slower, more considered form of filmmaking, which needs to give shots time for the audience to see what's going on, for the three-dimensional effect to occur.

Jet Li said the technical challenges was so great for 3-D that they were only filming six shots a day at first. Well, that's not fast enough for any movie – and definitely not a Tsui Hark movie! But this was how *Flying Swords of Dragon Gate* was marketed – as China's first martial arts movie in 3-D.

Since *The Legend of Zu*, Tsui Hark and his vfx crews had been combining computer-assisted animation with live-action for human figures – by the time of *Flying Swords of Dragon Gate*, the mixes seem much more accomplished, as the movie switches from a computer-aided double of a character to an actor (sometimes in the same shot, and in daylight).

Computer-aided animation is integrated into the action seamlessly – now the filmmakers can stage flailing ropes attacking Jet Li (on the ship), as Yu Huatian unleashes his magical martial arts (and revealing again the influence of Japanese *animé*). Many Hong Kong movies look like Japanese animation, and Tsui Hark's films consciously draw on it; now, by mixing live-action footage with animated footage, Tsui's works can become even more like cartoons).

*Flying Swords of Dragon Gate* combines traditional, Hong Kong action filmmaking with computer-assisted animation at a ferocious rate. Still, many of the old school techniques were employed – like breakaway props, and like the wooden tower inside which the final duels take place. And wires are everywhere in *Flying Swords of Dragon Gate* – like the golden thread booby traps in the maze.

*Flying Swords of Dragon Gate* is another of the big budget, luxurious Chinese, historical movies of recent times, where production design, art direction, props, hair, make-up and costumes are intricate and extravagant. As with all of Tsui Hark's movies, there is no holding back in the realm of costume design: Hsuan-wu Lai and Kenneth Yee Chung-man deliver elegant, colourful wealth in the wardrobe for the West Bureau and the East Bureau. (The extravagance in the costume department is announced in the opening scene, where Gordon Liu as Wan Yulou wears over-the-top golden robes).

In some action scenes, it seems almost impossible for the actors and stunt crew to move in those elaborate, multi-layered costumes which include heavy robes and headgear. It's difficult enough to walk in clothing that goes right down to the ankles, let alone perform spins and kicks. (However, elaborate costumes have been a part of entertainment in China for centuries – the Peking Opera style, for example, always has fancy clothing, hair and make-up).

The score for *Flying Swords of Dragon Gate* (by Xin Gu, Han Chiang Li and Wai Lap Wu) is outstanding, a joyously old-fashioned Chinese soundtrack which includes pounding, hammering drums and percussion. (The movie announces its old-fashioned aims from the outset, with a clanging, jangling cue over the opening credits which might be the prologue of a Peking Opera performance or an old Shaw Brothers movie.[4] The Peking Opera cues continue in the 2011 movie, a nod to the original *Dragon Gate* movie of 1967. One imagines that Tsui Hark likes to think of his martial arts movies as exactly that – like sitting down to enjoy a Peking Opera show). However, there are also Western-style cues with a full orchestra.

*Flying Swords of Dragon Gate* was looped, as usual in Chinese and Hong Kong cinema. You can see one reason why in the behind the scenes material on the home releases: almost every shot had noisy wind machines blasting through them, making recording clean dialogue tracks impossible. Chinese filmmakers love texture and movement, and fans are everywhere blowing clothing, hair, leaves, petals, flames, you name it. (You can also see, in the documentary footage, why making a full-on action-adventure movie in the Asian film industry is absolutely exhausting, as actors and stunt people perform take after take of difficult shots featuring multiple beats and moves. And you can also see that large chunks of *Flying Swords of Dragon Gate* were made by the action directors and second unit teams).

❧

*Flying Swords of Dragon Gate* was deemed a continuation or sequel to *New Dragon Gate Inn* by the filmmakers, but it is also very much a remake and an update, just as the 1992 version was a remake/ update of the 1967 movie. There are variations, of course, and many new elements, but as the opening narration sets out the political background, it's the same setting:

4 That's part of Tsui Hark's aim to recreate the excitement of being a kid and going to the cinema.

the Imperial villains from the East Bureau and the West Bureau, pursuing rebels and dissidents and the good guys who oppose them. The central sequence is the same as the 1992 movie: everybody convenes on the Dragon Gate Inn as a huge storm rolls in (if it was a true sequel or continuation, there'd likely be new settings and adventures).

*Flying Swords of Dragon Gate* is not a step backwards for Tsui Hark, but it is certainly a movie he has made before, and pretty much all of the ingredients have appeared in previous Tsui movies. Well, come on, *Flying Swords of Dragon Gate* was Tsui's fortieth feature as director (depending how you count Tsui's movies as director).

But no director in China or anywhere else on Planet Earth can cook up a historical action fantasy movie quite like Tsui Hark. And in a global media teeming with products, Tsui puts his stamp on his movies.

Story-wise, *Flying Swords of Dragon Gate* is an old, wooden chest (found in a cave, of course) filled with very familiar martial arts motifs, including brutal officials, spies, disguises, betrayals, double-crossing, plus the usual settings – palaces, boats, inns, secret chambers, deserts and temples. (The bigger budget means that the sets're more plentiful, and larger. The 1992 *New Dragon Gate Inn*, for example, didn't have as many sets, or so many very large sets).

Indeed, altho' there are updates and new ingredients in *Flying Swords of Dragon Gate*, it is also very old-fashioned storytelling. The finale, for example, hits all of the dramatic beats one would expect – this is a *wuxia pian* which plays out just like all of Tsui Hark's other swordplay pictures.

You will notice a glaring omission from the 2011 update of *New Dragon Gate Inn*: the incredible character of Jade, played with genius by Maggie Cheung (the character is noted in the dialogue several times, having departed three years ago. However, being referenced in speech isn't quite the same as having Maggie Cheung right there in the flesh!). Instead, the character of the Tartar brigand, Chang Xiaowen/ Bu Ludu, sort of corresponds to the character of Jade from *Dragon Gate Inn*. (But Chang Xiaowen is not Jade Mark II; for instance, she speaks in Tartar, with her dialogue translated by her hulking lieutenant, so there isn't the entertaining bawdy banter that Cheung delivered in the 1992 movie).

As soon as the Tartar boss Chang Xiaowen is introduced, at the Dragon Gate Inn, there's a fight – because that's how things are done in action-adventure movies in China. It's a woman versus a man and employs a favourite device with action choreographer Yuen Woo-ping – a wooden table (it was used memorably with Michelle Yeoh in *Wing Chun*). As Tsui Hark recalled, some of the gags with the table were not planned, but they developed what happened on set.

*Flying Swords of Dragon Gate* is far less humorous than *New Dragon Gate Inn*, which delivered a brand of broad, black comedy. The cannibalism of *New Dragon Gate Inn*, for example, is included, but it's only a minor beat (well, by the time of 2011, Tsui Hark had cooked up several cannibalistic yarns). Maybe the movie decided to portray a more sober version of the 1992 film, which included comical antics from Maggie

Cheung, Tony Leung and Xiong Xin-xin. We don't have the comic-erotic interplay between Cheung and Brigitte Lin, either – such as in the famous scene where a striptease is combined with a duel.

ᵡ

The 2011 movie is totally in love with the body in motion, with bodies flying thru space, with the grace of bodies interacting. It's truly beautiful! It's magical! It's poetic! And it doesn't hurt that the movie is full of attractive stars, including Zhao Wei, Lun-Mei Kwei and of course Jet Li.

In *Flying Swords of Dragon Gate*, the art of cinema is glorified for all to see: it's one of the aspects of Chinese, action cinema that I *really* admire and enjoy. These movies *want* you to gasp in joy at the magic of cinema, they *hope* you are going to love the way the actors fly thru the air or end up balancing on top of a teetering pile of wood in another graceful fighting pose.

It all works, it all rocks, it all sings. *Flying Swords of Dragon Gate* is another reason why Tsui Hark is one of the giants of world cinema – towering way above many film directors who're regularly touted as being masters.

As an action movie, *Flying Swords of Dragon Gate* is jammed with fights in inns, fights on boats, in mazes, on collapsing wooden platforms, and the two-part duel that climaxes the movie, in the midst of the dragon-sized maelstrom, as Zhao Huai'anand the chief villain, Yu Huatian, duel with flying swords while chained together and hurtling thru the sky (this is a wild visual effects sequence, in the manner of *The Legend of Zu*, where the sandstorm and tornadoes are used as a justification for keeping the characters airborne for a lengthy period). There is an astonishing use of the steel darts of Chinese and Japanese martial arts (including how they attach themselves to others embedded in wood on hooks),[5] swords that fly, swords that break apart and whizz towards victims, chains, and, in the maze at the end, deadly golden thread. (The swords are individualized, as in *Seven Swords:*Tsui Hark admits that he adores swords, and he calls them the king of weapons. In *Flying Swords of Dragon Gate*, as in *Seven Swords,* every possible use of a sword is included in the action scenes. Now, however, swords are continually shattering into dangerous shards that hurtle at the victim, via computer-aided animation – Yu uses the shattering sword device to take down opponents).

Like many of the big martial arts movies coming out of China recently (from *Hero* and *Crouching Tiger* onwards), *Flying Swords of Dragon Gate* is a compendium of every type of fighting style, every stunt and gag imaginable, every trick shot and visual effect.

One of the highlights of *Flying Swords of Dragon Gate* pits two veterans of the *wuxia pian* genre against each other: Jet Li and Gordon Liu: they duel in a ferocious battle all over the sets, including amongst the confined space of under-floor red pillars and wooden supports. They had duelled erlier, in *Last Hero In China* (1993). (Liu, the star of classics such as *The 36th Chamber of Shaolin*, is given a wizened, aged make-up as the

---

5 As if the movie is trying to best *The House of Flying Daggers*.

eunuch commander of the East Bureau, Wan Yulou. It's ironic, because the amazing Lui seems ageless, and without make-up looks as young as he did back in the 1978 movie).

Jet Li is given an impressive introduction – zooming down from the sky towards Gordon Liu, while hurling a whole tree trunk at him. This is certainly a crowd-pleasing entrance for Li – introduced in the midst of a furious action sequence.

The duel also includes the ideological stance of Jet Li's swordsman, Zhao Huai'an: he's on the side of good and right, and he and his comrades are battling State oppression. The same sort of confrontation is reprised in the riverside action sequence (but with the double of Zhao doing the fighting), and again in the climax of act one, on the ship at sea (hundreds of Hong Kong action movies follow this same formula, where the climax of act one is simply a bigger version of the opening action scene).

❧

Zhao Huai'an is another of the Robin Hood/ Wong Fei Hung figures that Jet Li has played many times, the usual hero battling the forces of (State) oppression. The only criticism here might be in terms of Li's character is that we don't see him so much in the second act.[6] But when he's on screen, Li never disappoints: he is such a sensational, charismatic star (even when he *appears* to be doing nothing much at all. As with Marlon Brando or Marilyn Monroe – or Jackie Chan – you just can't take your eyes off Li).

One of the additions to the plot is the lure of treasure (yes, *that* old chestnut! It's worked for 115,294 action-adventure movies, why not this one?). Exposition is deliversed about the treasure, which adds a complication to the already-tangled knot of people and relationships in *Flying Swords of Dragon Gate* (and pushes the movie into a fourth act).

The middle section of *Flying Swords of Dragon Gate* slows down a tad for quite a few talky scenes (for a long time, we are stuck underneath the inn in giant, rocky sets, recalling sections of early Tsui Hark pictures such as *The Butterfly Murders* and *Zu: Warriors From the Magic Mountain*. Some of the group discussions are rather long for an action-adventure movie, and the clarification of allegiances and motivations are somewhat over-written. If these were trimmed, *Flying Swords of Dragon Gate* would be a three-act movie structure, losing 15-20 minutes). But that's partly because the first act of *Flying Swords of Dragon Gate* was rammed with action scenes, leaving far less time for exposition and talk (if you open a movie with plenty of action, that means it's got to slow down later). The complexity of some of the social relationships in the second and third acts of *Flying Swords of Dragon Gate*, with those fierce loyalties, government officials and arcane references, might confuse some audiences: there are many groups of people converging on the fabled Dragon Gate Inn, each with their own motives and goals (buried treasure is a major motivation). Untangling all of that is something I would imagine leaves some audience members behind.

6 That's partly because when Jet Li's playing a superhero like this, it's challenging finding significant things for him to do.

But it doesn't matter! You don't watch a Chinese martial arts movie wholly for the story and the characters! Besides, the visual storytelling is so elegant, the use of physical acting is so strong (actors never just stand and there and spout dialogue in a Chinese action flick), you can enjoy everything (and without subtitles, too).

The body!

Wow – Chinese action movies contain without question the most agile, athletic and awe-inspiring bodies in all cinema (including, yes, even porn! If Chinese action movie-makers produced porn like they deliver action, it would be unbelievable!).

The flow of movement, the speed of it, the elegance of it, the self-assurance of it, the timing of it, the shapes of it. These bodies are so alive, so full of energy. The actors communicate everything with their poses, with movement from one state to another state (and, yes, their facial expressions). It is acting with the *whole body*. Oh yes, sure, there are Western traditions of performance that emphasize the body, but too few movies offer actors the chance to explore those acting styles (you are more likely to see them in theatre, and very occasionally on TV).

This kind of cinema is so lively – when you compare it with live-action in the West, how *static*, how fixed in space like mannequins Western actors are! (Or how producers and directors (or audiences) like them to be). What's so wonderful about Chinese action movies is that movement can take place *anywhere* across the screen, not only in the centre. There's an *openness*, a *freedom*, to the movement and the performances in Chinese action cinema.[7]

Some critics have criticized Tsui Hark for remaining too much of a 'movie brat', and making genre pictures too often. Who cares?! Who cares about that when Tsui (and a vast team) is delivering movies of such high quality? I for one *don't* want Tsui to become all po-faced and gloomy like a 'serious' European art film director. I'm totally happy for Tsui to direct *Flying Swords of Dragon Gate* or *The Blade* or *Once Upon a Time In China*!

❧

Another striking aspect of *Flying Swords of Dragon Gate* is the prominence of female stars: the movies of Tsui Hark have always had a penchant for strong women (who also happen to be eye candy), and *Flying Swords of Dragon Gate* is filled with them. (Yes, from a second wave feminist perspective, Tsui's cinema is rather macho and chauvinist, tho' it has always been generous in terms of the front rank roles it gives to women). Both Zhao Huai'an's beloved, Ling Yanqiu, and the courtesan who's run away from the palace, Su Huirong, are travelling as guys; meanwhile, there's Blade of the Wind, and the marvellous character of Chang Xiaowen, the punky Tartar with a henna-ed face and a wicked, laughing, rebellious attitude (who is also Bu Ludu). *Flying Swords of Dragon Gate* is not afraid, either, of having women battling other women, which was part of the 1992 movie (tho' there is also some violence against

<hr>

7 I keep returning to David Bordwell's wonderful account of Hong Kong action cinema, which says it all.

women, which occurs in other Tsui-produced movies, which's off-putting).[8]

*Flying Swords of Dragon Gate* thus continues the crossdressing of *New Dragon Gate Inn* (and the *Swordsman* series). And the super-villain, Yu Huatian, is also travelling in disguise (Wind Blade impersonates Yu, and Yu lets his hair down in the finale and is feminized). Doubles and disguises provide, as in *New Dragon Gate Inn*, many of the twists in the plotting of *Flying Swords of Dragon Gate.* (It's another movie where no one is quite what they seem, and some of the reveals occur quite late in the narrative).

Actor Chen Kun gets to play both super-villain Yu Huatian and his double, the goofy Wind Blade. For this role, Kun resembles a young Jacky Cheung (in precisely the sort of role that Cheung did play in films such as *A Chinese Ghost Story 3*). Pu/ Wind Blade carries most of the humour in the second half of *Flying Swords of Dragon Gate*, along with the flustered innkeeper.

Another doubling effect occurs between Zhao Huai'an and Ling Yanqui, with Ling posing as Zhao (when she rescues the courtesan Su Huirong on the riverboat). Tsui Hark is fond of this motif (a good proportion of *The Swordsman 3* features imposters of Asia the Invincible).

Tsui Hark knows that if you put a spear into a woman's hands and corner her in a dangerous situation, it's so much more compelling than a guy in the same context. We expect the guy to fight his way out, to know the moves, but with a woman, it's a different effect. *Flying Swords of Dragon Gate* evens up the main characters by including as many women as men (and in the finale, the women out-number the men).

Notice that in the finale, the remaining characters (those that haven't been killed off), feature three guys but four women. It's typical of Tsui Hark's cinema that he should reverse the gender of the characters: Ling Yanqiu we know is a woman travelling as a swordsman (in the Brigitte Lin role); Ling would be sufficient in a conventional movie, but *Flying Swords of Dragon Gate* adds the courtesan Su Huirong, now revealed as a secret agent; and finally Gu Shaotang, another female warrior.

&

The finale of *Flying Swords of Dragon Gate* is actually two main sections of the movie: (1) the giant battle outside the Dragon Gate Inn, with the super-storm, the sand, the arrows, the flashing swords, the tumbling horses, and the first of the hero vs. villain duels. This climaxes act three. (2) We go into act four with the introduction of the buried city of gold (the intricate visual effects shot that reveals the city echoes the helicopter shot at the beginning, this time flying back and back to uncover more'n more of the palaces and temples of the hidden realm).

It's artificial, and we know it: in the middle of their ferocious duel, Zhao Huai'an announces to Yu Huatian, jump on a horse if you dare to fight me in the eye of a dragon storm. This is a feeble motivation for the change of setting of the duel from the sand to the sky, and the set-piece of the sword duel in the middle of a hurricane. Another contrived piece of screenwriting

---

8 Men are selfish, one of the women complains.

has the climactic duel in the sandstorm ending unresolved – now it's continued in the buried kingdom.

The double finales in *Flying Swords of Dragon Gate* have the bloated feel of over-cooked movies such as the *Pirates of the Caribbean* franchise, the *Avengers* series, or many recent superhero movies. We have one gigantic action sequence, and then the film works up to another one (there are two sandstorms, for example – one isn't enough!).

The Big Battle in act 3 of *Flying Swords of Dragon Gate* involves every gag and stunt imaginable – there's no point holding back now. With the sandstorm, the looming clouds overhead, the high wind, and the desert setting, *Flying Swords of Dragon Gate* resembles the celebrated finale of *The Blade* (which for some Tsui Hark has never bettered). Fights're exploding all over the place, and each of the main charas is given their moment to shine (like Chang soaring on a shield to attack the enemy, and Gu Shaotang duelling with deadly double swords, with Zhao Huai'an coming to her aid).

A piece of *The Wizard of Oz* flies into the movie here, when a chunk of the now-demolished Dragon Gate Inn is caught up in the twister (both Yu Huatian and Zhao Huai'an are flung into it). Cleverly, the out-house lands atop the sunken kingdom, and is used by the heroes as a makeshift escape route for the others still trapped in the grand hall below.

Before that, the style of filmmaking of 2001's *The Legend of Zu* is reprised for the swordplay in the midst of a hurricane, as Zhao Huai'an and Yu Huatian fly around each other, attached by chains. It's gloriously silly, a crowd-pleasing piece of hokum (and even the chain itself is used as a weapon by each of the duellers).

ఊ

In Round Two of the climax of *Flying Swords of Dragon Gate*, we are in the Big Finale Set (a lavish temple with out-size statuary, enormous walls, golden treasure and a maze of deadly booby traps of golden threads), several duels are staged, including the second (no, third) bout of the hero vs. villain duel.

The finale of *Flying Swords of Dragon Gate* also contains some of Tsui Hark's customary moralizing – Tsui can't resist inserting some philosophical/ ethical messages in his movies. Here, the issues of politics, conflict, life and death are evoked. You might haul out the gold from the buried palace, but to what end? You will die eventually.

Some of the dialogue is pure Hong Kong corn – about the value of money (a topic endlessly debated in Hong Kong cinema). And it's also dialogue that's found in many treasure hunt narratives: a bunch of characters converge on the treasure and decide how to split up and carry it out of the palace (here the second sandstorm provides a countdown which means everything has to be speeded up).

By 2011, Tsui Hark had been producing versions of the action-adventure movies he loved as a child for decades and decades. Tsui is a veteran of this kind of storytelling, where obstacle upon obstacle is piled on for the heroes. These include a second storm approaching, a maze, booby traps covering the way out, and the reveal of one of their number being an agent.

Thus, at the end of *Flying Swords of Dragon Gate*, the maid Su Huirong turns out to be an Imperial lackey, working for the arch villain, Yu Huatian. The reveal comes with a classic piece of Peking Opera-style boo-hiss melodramatics: Su takes the dagger that Ling Yanqiu gave her for protection, and stabs Ling from behind (repeatedly). Thus, Su transforms from helpless, pregnant courtesan who needs to be protected to venal villainness (and brilliant martial artist). The odds are evened up a little: instead of Gu, Chang, Zhao, Ling and co. versus Yu, Su fights alongside Yu.

Remember the smashed piece of the Dragon Gate Inn? Which Yu Huatian and Zhao Huai'an landed in? Here it provides one of the staples of Hong Kong action cinema set in the *jiangzhu*: the duel on (and inside) a wooden tower (seen in films such as *Fong Sai-yuk, Tai Chi Master* and of course *Once Upon a Time In China*). So we're not out of the Hall of Treasure yet – the heroes have to clamber out, while battling the villains with swords, throwing daggers, timber and pieces of razor wire.

And with a simple fade to black, it's all over.

And we're into the *dénouement* scenes of *Flying Swords of Dragon Gate* which are very traditional: they are no different, really, from films made 20, 30, 40, 50, 60, 70 or more years ago. They take place on the sanddunes in the desert, with the survivors convening before separating on horseback. This is one of Tsui Hark's favourite ways of ending an action-adventure yarn. (A coda's added – set in the temple weeks or months later, with Wind Blade and Chang colluding in the poisoning of the courtesan Wan).

# 36

# *THE TAKING OF TIGER MOUNTAIN*

## *Lin Hai Xue Yuan*

*The Taking of Tiger Mountain* (*Lin Hai Xue Yuan,* 2014, a.k.a. *Tracks In the Snowy Forest*) was directed by Tsui Hark, produced by Huang Jianxin and Don Yu Dong, and written by Tsui, Huang Jianxin, Wu Bing, Dong Zhe, Lin Chi-an and Li Yang, from Qu Bo's novel, *Tracks In the Snowy Forest.* It was backed by a large number of companies: Bona Film Group/ Huaxia Film Dis./ August First Film Studio/ Wanda Media/ China Movie Channel/ Youku Tudou Film/ Shanghai Real Thing Media/ Dream Sky Film/ Bona Entertainment.[9] The executive producers were: Yin Cao, Jeffrey Chan, Ruoqing Fu, Victor Koo, Rui Gang Li, Huijun Wu and Jerry Ye (14 other producers – administrative producers, associate producers, etc – are credited, including Nansun Shi Nan-sheng, Don Yu Dong and Huang Jianxin). Casting: Laicheng Zhu. Costumes: Yoo-jin Kwon, Zhuozhuo Lo, and Hua Wang. Art dir.: Zhenzhou Yi. Sound designer: Kinson Tsang. Sound: Wu Jing-Jing. Visual effects supervisors: Sameet Gupte and Wook Kim. Special fx: Wook Kim. Action directors: Yuen Bun and Liu Guo-Qing. Music: Wu Wai-lap. DPs: Johnny Choi Sung-fai and Gao Hu. Editor: Yu Baiyang.

In the enormous cast of *The Taking of Tiger Mountain* were: Zhang Hanyu as Yang Zirong, Tony Leung Ka-fai as Lord Hawk,[10] and Kenny Lin Gengxin as Shao Jianbo (a.k.a. Captain 203). These three were the main characters. Also in the cast were: Yu Nan as Ma Qinglian, Tong Liya as Little Dove, Han Geng as Jimmy, and Chen Xiao as Gao Bu. The secondary characters complement the lead characters with a huge ensemble of People's Liberton Army soldiers, villagers, and Hawk's bandits. *The Taking of Tiger Mountain* was filmed in Mandarin, and in 3-D (the flavour of the month in the 2000s and 2010s). Released Dec 23, 2014.

---

9 The film begins with at least eight film company logos.
10 In the opera, he's Vulture.

141 mins.[11]

*Tracks In the Snowy Forest* performed very well in Mainland China, with a gross of U.S. $150 million. Easy to see why – it's a thrilling action-adventure movie, brilliantly directed by Tsui Hark working at full power. It's a potboiler, in part a men-on-a-mission tale from World War Two, but delivered with breathtaking panache. And its subject matter is aimed at Chinese audiences (it's another Chinese story about Chinese people filmed in China by a Chinese cast and crew).

*The Taking of Tiger Mountain* was a remake – the story had filmed in 1970 as *The Taking of Tiger Mountain By Strategy*, produced by Beijing Film Studio, directed by Xie Tieli, and starring Shen Jinbo and Tong Jiling. *The Taking of Tiger Mountain By Strategy* was a popular film of the era (it was seen by 7.3 billion Chinese by 1974, according to the Chinese government, partly because this was during the Cultural Revolution, when seeing the film was expected. So it's a remake of a film seen by millions).

*The Taking of Tiger Mountain* was based on a Peking opera, drawn in turn on the same novel, *Tracks In the Snowy Forest* by Qu Bo. The opera of *The Taking of Tiger Mountain By Strategy* has ten scenes, which include: (1) advancing in victory – Winter, 1946, (2) Chiapi Valley pillaged – dusk (6) into the bandits' lair and (9) off to the attack – morning.

*The Taking of Tiger Mountain* is yet again about a Chinese subject, for a Tsui Hark movie, and it's another slice of Chinese history. With it's World War Two setting (it's based in 1946), *The Taking of Tiger Mountain* could be considered Tsui's first WWII movie as a combat picture (earlier films, such as *Shanghai Blues*, had used WWII, but they weren't really about the war. *The Raid* (co-directed with Tony Ching), is a forerunner of *The Taking of Tiger Mountain*). Tsui would follow this up with not one but two movies set in the Korean War in 1950, the two *Battle of Lake Changjin* films. *The Taking of Tiger Mountain* developed the cinematic form which the two *Lake Changlin* movies used.

Yet *The Taking of Tiger Mountain* is also about mythical China, the China that Tsui Hark sees as possessing an unrivalled treasure trove of stories and myths. Thus, altho' *The Taking of Tiger Mountain* is set just after World War Two, within a precise historical period in Chinese history, it also features elements that been around for millennia: survival, the cold, Winter, hunger, food, community, and wild nature.

*The Taking of Tiger Mountain* is linked to the foundation of modern China, of course (in 1949), and can be placed beside several other movies of this era which have tackled the same topic (such as the all-star *The Founding of the Republic*, 2009). Tsui Hark had of course explored these issues in the *Once Upon a Time In China* series (featuring the historical figure of Sun Yat-sen, for instance, who founded the Republic of China in 1912).

In some respects, *The Taking of Tiger Mountain* recalls action-adventure movies of the 1960s and 1970s of the West set in WW2, men-

---

11 One of Tsui Hark's longest films. And it's a movie, unlike 1,000s of Hollywood movies which run to the same length, which fully justifies running to two hours twenty mins.

on-a-mission movies such as *Where Eagles Dare* or *The Guns of Navarone* or *The Dirty Dozen*. And *James Bond*, which Tsui has mined several times already, is another jump-off point for *The Taking of Tiger Mountain* (the super-villain Hawk is very Bondian, and he even has gadgets like guns that rise out of the floor). It is also self-consciously old-fashioned in its approach to the material, as if it is remaking the *Tiger Mountain* film of 1970 but using the technology of the 2010s (indeed, many movies, Tsui Hark's included, employ the cinematic techniques of recent times (such as digital animation) to remake old movies).

ﹶ

Our heroes are the People's Liberation Army of China, and our villains (or rivals, at least), are the Tiger Mountain bandits (led by Lord Hawk) who're exploiting the vacuum in political influence following the defeat of Japan (and their surrender), during the Chinese Civil War. Caught in the middle are the inhabitants of Leather Creek village (which the brigands have been raiding, and where our heroes base themselves as they plan their attack on Tiger Mountain).

Even tho' the narrative context of *The Taking of Tiger Mountain* is highly political, the production team have consciously depoliticized the movie, focussing instead on delivering a rousing adventure tale. However, there's no mistaking the fact that the good guys are in the People's Liberation Army and the bad guys are bandits (pursuing the wrong kind of nationalism and capitalism, from the point-of-view of the Chinese Communist Party immediately after WWII).

Yang Zirong and Shao Jianbo (Captain 203) head up the large group of People's Liberation Army characters, and Lord Hawk is the top dog among the bandits. Yang Zirong goes undercover to infiltrate the bandits.

As Lord Hawk, the chief rival/ villain, chief of the bandits, Tony Leung Ka-fai's identity is teased for a long time – seen from behind, or in shadow, until some 50 minutes into the 2014 movie. He's given an elaborate make-up and hair job, and has a vulture as a pet. With his over-large, decorated fur coats[12] and bald pate, he might've stepped out of the *Road Warrior* movies (sometimes he looks like a hunting bird himself, his bald head in amongst frothy furs and feathers). It's a slice of ye olde movie hokedom, a character that's stepped out of old action-adventure serials. (Leung plays Lord Hawk with a jaded, tired manner – he's heard it all before, and he's bored by running an empire in the mountains of the North-East of China. He delivers his lines in a quiet, croaky voice, his head tilted down, which makes him all the more threatening. Everybody fears for their lives around him).

There are two heroes at the heart of *The Taking of Tiger Mountain*, true (and one out-size villain, Lord Hawk), but this movie is another of Tsui Hark's many ensemble pieces, with an enormous cast. Again, generous amounts of precious screen time are given to lots of secondary characters, who always, in Tsui's cinema, contribute to the piece. In films like his, it takes many people to make up the whole.

12 The enormous coats lend Tony Leung a bigger-than-life silhouette, which fits the superhero genre presentation of his character.

Bai Ru (Liya Tong), a.k.a. 'Little Dove', is a kindly combat medic who joins the People's Liberation Army along with Yang Zirong. Of course she's fond of Captain 203, in the usual unrequited, love-from-afar manner of traditional, Chinese movies.

The feral boy Knotti is a minor character who links together the People's Liberation Army with Lord Hawk at Tiger Mountain (unfortunately he's given a fright wig).[13]

The MacGuffin of *The Taking of Tiger Mountain* is a map outlining where the troops are situated following the surrender of the Japanese after WWII (actually, there are three maps). The maps are fully exploited as tokens of exchange and thus potentially betrayal, too (Yang, for instance, plants a map on Brother 2 (Shi Yanneng), who is searched and discovered with it).

There're healthy portions of Tsui Hark's *The Blade* in here, and *Seven Swords*, and going back to *We're Going To Eat You*, which depicted bandits and outlaws as very aggressive but very stupid men. Indeed, you could intercut parts of *We're Going To Eat You* from 1980 with *The Taking of Tiger Mountain* from 34 years later happily. Tsui must've chuckled to himself that a movie like *The Taking of Tiger Mountain* could be so successful at the Chinese box office, when *We're Going To Eat You* had covered much of the same macho, blustery territory, but nobody came to see the film, back when he was starting out in directing features, and he could only dream of having a movie take $150 million in Mainland China).

*The Taking of Tiger Mountain* is played straight throughout – it might not have as much humour or lighter moments of other films in the Tsui Hark œuvre, but it is conscious of its over-the-top social context. And it's a very boysy movie, with female characters this time relegated to minor roles (there are only two women of any significance).

*The Taking of Tiger Mountain* orchestrates familiar Tsui Harkian issues, too – such as the old and the new; the old China (of the bandits), and the new China (of the People's Liberation Army of China); such as: survival (manifested in simple, universal items such as food, and hunger, and cold).

*The Taking of Tiger Mountain* is the fourth gigantic movie directed by Tsui Hark in the five years between 2010 and 2014 (the other three were the two *Detective Dee* movies and the *Dragon Gate Inn* remake). Does Tsui ever sleep? Does he ever sit still for more'n five minutes? Does he have reserves of energy which other mere mortals can only dream about?

To make movies this big in that amount of time requires considerable amounts of stamina and determination, not to mention imagination and skill. *The Taking of Tiger Mountain* is once again a mammoth production, and much of it was filmed in real, snowbound locations. Certainly *The Taking of Tiger Mountain* benefits immensely from the rich texture of filming out of doors in real snow. No need for the actors to pretend being cold! You can see they're freezing! (If you are a fan of snow movies, as I am, you will enjoy *The Taking of Tiger Mountain*. Some of the snow is fake,

---

13 Which is later trimmed.

of course, but plenty of it is real).

৯৯

Style-wise, *The Taking of Tiger Mountain* contains the full arsenal of Tsui Hark's cinema. As in Tsui's movies from 2010 onwards, the crane was much in evidence, with numerous scenes covered in drifting, formal high angle shots. (*The Taking of Tiger Mountain* is another 3-D movie, with the filmmakers conscious of capturing scenes for that medium).

*The Taking of Tiger Mountain* contains images you've never seen before – such as a grenade exploding in reverse. *The Taking of Tiger Mountain* is full of Tsui-isms and tricks, yes, but it also contains simple and clear filmmaking where necessary: many scenes are covered in medium close-ups in shot-reverse-shot patterns. Many scenes are filmed with precise, slowly-moving shots. And, once again, everything is in service of the story and the movie.

The pace is frantic, as usual in Tsui Hark's cinema, but it does slow down in several places, such as a beat where Knotti hands Captain 203 some soup (at Bai Ru's behest).

As *The Taking of Tiger Mountain* unfolds, it seems more and more like an Akira Kurosawa epic movie. It has many affinities with the masterpiece that Kurosawa filmed in 1975 in the snowy regions of the Soviet Union, *Dersu Uzala* (which also includes a battle with a tiger, military figures carrying rifles, uneasy relations between Russians and Chinese, hunger and deep snow). Survival is a big theme in both *Dersu Uzala* and *The Taking of Tiger Mountain* (which are also, it has to be acknowledged, very manly, with women relegated to the sidelines – only one woman – the hero's wife – appears in *Dersu Uzala*, and only two in *Tiger Mountain*).

Technically, *The Taking of Tiger Mountain* is masterful on every level. The costumes (by Zhuozhuo Lo, Hua Wang and Yoo-jin Kwon) are perfect, from Lord Hawk's voluminous furs and luxury to the uniforms of the People's Liberation Army (Kwon, Wang and Lo have fun coming up with all sorts of fur-lined hats for the numerous secondary charas, and creating a variety of funky, eccentric outfits for the bandits. The make-up artists were Zhuozhuo Lo and Hua Wang). The sets, the look, the cinematography, the lighting, the sound design, the props – every element is outstanding.

*The Taking of Tiger Mountain* is another colossal visual effects movie (the effects were by Dexter Studios and Prime Focus). The post-production effects are seamlessly blended with the on-set plates. And by now in the Chinese industry, they have surpassed Western vfx houses. This time, tho', in a more 'realistic' movie, the post-production (digital) vfx are used in the conventional manner of the West – to extend sets, to replace backgrounds and skies, etc (rather than the very heightened, clearly abstract and spiritual effects deployed in movies like *Black Mask 2* and *The Legend of Zu*). And in front of the camera, this being a Chinese, action movie, there are thousands of practical effects and special effects. The cameras don't roll on a Tsui Hark production, it seems, unless there are wind machines, smoke and fog machines, flames and fires, and rain machines a-blowing and a-humming.

The fortress, where Master Hawk and his bandits hole up, is a very movie-ish construction: a spectacular location high up in the mountains, permanently snowbound, with a tall cliff/ outcrop of rock above it, and a crevasse surrounding part of it (acting as a natural moat). Although *The Taking of Tiger Mountain* is set in a real historical period (1946), it is also happily presents a mythical, fantastical China.

Inside, there's the Big Set, the villain's dwelling place which of course is destroyed during the finale. There's a raised dais and a throne (because Master Hawk is essentially a warlord from any time in the past four thousand years in China),[14] and multiple levels, with girders and pillars (because Chinese filmmakers like to have plenty of spaces to stage action).

೩

The framing story in *The Taking of Tiger Mountain* is curiously delivered – *The Taking of Tiger Mountain* opens with aerial shots of New York City (in the present day of 2014), moving down to the character of Jimmy (Han Geng). But then it shifts rapidly into the 1946 narrative. At the end, Jimmy calls on his grandmother (Lv Zhong) at New Year's, for a family get-together. The People's Liberation Army of China turns up, from the past, in a theatrical moment, to gather around the tables and the food. The scene acts as a curtain call for this epic movie, and the large cast (where it's smiles all round). In a classic Tsui Hark beat, an old, Chinese movie is playing on TV, which the characters watch (it's the Peking Opera version of the story seen in the prologue).

In the first part of the framing story, Jimmy is in Gotham at Christmastime (the film was released at Christmas) – so the movie opens with Disneyesque evocations of the holiday season.[15] Is this going to be a romantic comedy, with Jimmy meeting a cute Asian girl who's grandmother was Ma Qinglian? No, it's a piece of narrative wrongfooting.

In a karaoke bar (where everybody seems to be Chinese), Jimmy hooks up with his chums, and becomes fascinated by a movie playing on a TV. It's the original version of *The Taking of Tiger Mountain*. The Peking Opera fits to evoke the homeland (and we know how fond Tsui Hark is of it).

The framing story of *The Taking of Tiger Mountain* acts in the usual manner, connecting the present with the past, linking what the People's Liberation Army did for China in the past (and their sacrifices), to today (actually, it's not wholly 'today' as in 2014, when *The Taking of Tiger Mountain* was released – there is a cheating with the timeline. Knotti was Jimmy's grandfather).

Tsui Hark has used framing stories before – famously in *Dr Wai* (1996). That particular frame justified itself partly by having the past and the present interact directly, as Jet Li's character (Chow Si-Kit) comes up with stories (which his assistants rewrite). In *The Taking of Tiger Mountain*, the frame is not necessary, and reflects an uncertainty from the

14 Altho' it's not furnished with marble and granite, but wood and iron girders.
15 David Wu advised on the opening sequence.

production team. As several critics noted, it's not needed.

ঽৣ

*The Taking of Tiger Mountain* opens, in true Hong Kong, action movie style, with a giant fire-fight (following the brief exposition in voiceover), as we see the Chinese People's Liberation Army assaulting a bandit hide-out in a railroad yard in deep snow. The many visual effects shots and trick shots which draw on video game technology take the 2014 film far away from historical reality, or your average combat movie (there are bullet-view shots, freeze frames, speed ramping, and of course plenty of slow motion. What Hong Kong action movie from the 1980s-to-now plays without at least a little slo-mo?). Freezing the participants while the camera careens around them to take the reverse angle comes from computer games, where different viewpoints can be selected of some action. It's a little fussy and over-elaborate, but it's part of Tsui Hark's attempts to keep his movies up-to-date.

The fire-fight is a big production number which also introduces us to several of the main and minor characters, to the camaraderie of the People's Liberation Army of China (and their genius with military strategy), and to the *mise-en-scène* of the story, with its forest and mountain settings, its cold and snow, and one of Tsui Hark's key themes: survival (the issue of food is key, and the motif of food is rapidly delineated).

Combat is one thing, but just living presents plenty of problems. Like food = none. Like resources: poor. Like cold = very. As with Chinese cinema in general, Tsui Hark's work is very accomplished at selling realities such as cold. No need to add cold breath with computer animation here.

After the fire-fight, and the rapid introduction of the main characters in the People's Liberation Army, *The Taking of Tiger Mountain* gets into some of the goals of the heroes. A second action sequence erupts halfway thru act one involving Lord Hawk's spy Luan Ping (Du Yi-heng) and his gnarly chums, who capture the boy Knotti and his minder Jimmy, who rushes in to rescue him. The torture scene that follows is ugly – Chinese/ Hong Kong cinema doesn't hold back when it comes to portraying how nasty humans can be to each other.

*The Taking of Tiger Mountain* is certainly gory and over-the-top in its depiction of violence. The opening fire-fight sequence announces that this movie will show bodies being torn apart by gunfire and explosions. And the action will be in the heightened form that Hong Kong action cinema has made its own – so the boy Knotti, hung upside-down and being pushed around by thugs on either side, manages to grab a pistol and shoot it at Luan Ping (the gunshot alerts the People's Liberation Army nearby, and they rescue Knotti and Jimmy... So Lord Hawk whips his lady Ma Qinglian savagely when she fools around with Yang ZIrong (even tho' he ordered her to do it)...

Structurally, *The Taking of Tiger Mountain* follows the action-adventure template of Western cinema and Hong Kong action cinema: for example, the fire-fight in the opening scene (which sums up the film in a nutshell) is replayed at the end of act one, and of the finale (and several other times in the movie).

Lord Hawk and the Tiger Mountain stronghold is introduced with some elaborate visual effects shots – the kind of formal crane shots and chopper shots that Tsui Hark is fond of. The main set of the villains is a hokey, shadowy, torch-lit reception hall straight out of the *Action-Adventure Movie Handbook* (Chinese Edition, 1932). Tsui had been here many times before (three years previously, in *Flying Swords of Dragon Gate*, for instance, or back to *Zu: Warriors of the Magic Mountain* in 1983).

In the throne room, the compositions emphasize symmetry, with Lord Hawk the misshapen spider at the centre of this web of banditry and coercion. One of his first acts types his character as a venal villain – again, right out of the *Action-Adventure Movie Handbook*: the two underlings who managed to flee from the People's Liberation Army assault on the rail yard in the opening scene are bound to pillars and tortured – Lord Hawk's pet vulture attacks their faces.

*The Taking of Tiger Mountain* features a breathtaking and absolutely thrilling encounter between Yang Zirong (one of the two heroes) and an enormous tiger in a forest (Yang's on his way to infiltrate Tiger Mountain). Yang is alone on horseback in the snowbound woodland, where the horse is the first to apprehend the approach of the tiger. In a way, the fight is the film in a nutshell: it's survival, it's humanity struggling to thrive (or just stay alive) in an inhospitable environment, where the natural world is scarily, implacably and untameably *wild*.

The tiger scene is a technical marvel, exploiting digital and practical effects, wire work, stunts, sound effects, etc, to the full, and it takes place, in typical, Chinese action movie style, up a tree (with the clever creature climbing a nearby tree, to leap at the hero. Wow!).

*The Taking of Tiger Mountain*'s second act begins with several very talky scenes – the narrative slows down considerably, and the film is full of exposition. With the action sequence involving Yang Zirong versus the tiger, *The Taking of Tiger Mountain* shifts into very high gear, and continues like that as Yang is brought into Hawk's compound (which is designed very much like a mediaeval castle, with Hawk as the Emperor in expensive furs). This is another exciting sequence, with Hawk and his crew acting so suspiciously of Yang they have him perpetually at gunpoint. Following that nail-biting section, *The Taking of Tiger Mountain* moves into a series of trials for Yang, as the bandits test him.

One of the tests involves Lord Hawk's new wife, Ma Qinglian (Yu Nan), who's sent in by Hawk to seduce Yang Zirong (who of course circumvents that challenge). In the process, Yang alerts Qinglian to the survival of her son Knotti (who's back at the People's Liberation Army's camp in Leather Creek village). The scene is played close to a fever pitch, with Qinglian sobbing in relief, but, after all, this *is* a big, Chinese picture, when high emotions aren't only expected, they are mandatory!

One of the subplots in *The Taking of Tiger Mountain* is pure cheese – or corn – or popcorn: the mother Ma Qinglian who's desperate (hysterically desperate) to be re-united with her son Knotti. No way is that child going to be sacrificed, and not the mother neither: yes, they rush towards each other in the *dénouement* sequence. Hugs!

That it was a mother and child as the emotional subplot of *The Taking of Tiger Mountain* and not a romance (often the more usual subplot in action movies), tells you more about the sort of movie the filmmakers were aiming for. (However, there are romantic yearnings from afar – the Glasses Man Gao Bu for the nurse Bai Ru, and said nurse for Captain 203).

Yang Zirong comes up with novel ways of communicating with Shao Jianbo – such as hiding letters in tree bark; the most inventive method is to place a *communiqué* in the clothes of a guy who's executed and pushed off a cliff (which Jianbo picks up below). And when Yang arrives at the pre-arranged drop-off point, he pretends stomach ache and while he fakes relieving himself, stuffs a message in a pile of snow, marking it with a piece of tree bark (Tsui Hark's cinema has always enjoyed details like that).

Another scene of betrayal and accusations occurs in front of Lord Hawk, with Yang Zirong and Brother 2 being accused, while Ma Qinglian looks on (and suffers from Hawk's ire once again). Scenes such as this, and the later battle of wills between Yang and the spy Luan Ping, liven up *The Taking of Tiger Mountain* in between the big, action set-pieces. It evokes a community where everybody is on edge, ready to pull out a gun and shoot someone who accuses them.

The third act of *The Taking of Tiger Mountain* is largely taken up with one of the finest action sequences in recent cinema – it's a set-piece which can persuade you that Tsui Hark may be the finest director of action in movies. The third act depicts an assault on the Leather Creek village, where the Chinese People's Liberation Army are based, by the bandits – on horseback, on foot and – a new addition to the Tsui Hark Circus – on skis. (The skis were set up in a scene just before, when the People's Liberation Army recce the spot and how to reach Tiger Mountain via Eagle's Peak).

Everything that the freezing, hungry army can get hold of is used in the fight – machine guns, shotguns, pistols, knives, grenades, and improvized weaponry (such as oil drums turned into makeshift cannons. They are successful in persuading Lord Hawk's bandits that the People's Liberation Army has a whole regiment there, not just 30 men).

The fighting is desperate and ugly – but it's one of those action scenes where the brilliance of the filmmaking delivers an exhilarating experience for the viewer. At first, the People's Liberation Army of China seem to have the upper hand, rigging their digs with a series of boobytraps (such as a deep pit, a camouflaged cart, horse traps, etc), until the bandits gather themselves and fight back.

The Leather Creek village sequence involves 100s of gags, some of them flamboyant – soldiers ski-ing over the roofs of houses, massive explosions (such as the watch-tower), soldiers fighting while ski-ing, and more.

The raid exploits the dramatic possibilities of the characters, too – it puts a young woman and a boy in amongst the battle. And, in true Tsui Hark style, the woman – the nurse Bai Ru – receives her own story within the sequence (chasing down villains with a pistol, while also trying to keep the boy Knotti under control. Knotti has his own adventure, delivering some ammunition in a box to Tank). In the chaos, the spy Luan Ping escapes, and hurries back to Tiger Mountain. But his troubles are not over – he encounters a formidable opponent, Yang Zirong).

After the village battle seems to be done, and the participants are mourning their dead, the narrative structure shifts, going back in time to depict how the medic Bai Ru pursued the killer of Glasses Man Gao Bu.

Following the giant village battle sequence, there's a very loud, yelling scene when the spy (Luan) captured by the People's Liberation Army escapes back to Lord Hawk and his bandits, and faces off against Yang Zirong (it's played as a battle of wills between two men for Hawk's trust; Yang wins). The movie revels in the sight of grisly, middle-aged actors shouting at each other (the grungey costumes and make-up jobs are picked out with harsh lighting from above which creates unflattering shadows on the scowling faces).

This is more like a cowboy movie from the 1960s where nobody trusts anybody else and is perpetually drawing their weapons and waving them at angrily at each other. The slightest remark is seized upon as potential betrayal, and the trigger-happy bandits would be right at home in the *Fistful of Dollars* movies.

Lord Hawk is weary of it all, and pulls his pistol to shoot Luan (partly perhaps to shut him up). But he's a terrible shot, so it's down to Yang Zirong to do the deed.

The finale of *The Taking of Tiger Mountain* is everything you'd expect from the action sequences announced in the opening act. It revolves around the People's Liberation Army of China staging a raid on the bandits' fortress – on skis! This is the mirror of the bandit attack on the Army compound in act three. Here, it is played at night, during the Lunar New Year celebrations at the fortress (the '100 chicken feast' in the opera).

How do the People's Liberation Army of China reach Hawk's HQ, which's guarded by a deep chasm? Only by leaping across the gulf using ropes and skis! Who cares if 'reality' is left far behind in the finale of *The Taking of Tiger Mountain*, when the action is this sublime?

The climax of *The Taking of Tiger Mountain* contains everything you'd expect, but with numerous twists and new takes on old chestnuts, including: the heroes and the villains coming face-to-face, the heroine being put in jeopardy (several times), the storming of the fortress, several duels between the heroes and the right-hand men, the super-villain fleeing, and the final duel with the super-villain.

The set-pieces feature masterful choreography by Yuen Bun,Liu Guo-qing and their team. The sequence demonstrates many reasons why Chinese filmmakers are the greatest in the history of cinema at portraying action on screen. One reason is shot size, lenses, camera angles and camera movement: every gag and every stunt and every bit of business is given a shot which will show it off to the best, which will make it clear and readable to the audience, and which will intercut with other shots. No 'impressionistic' camerawork here (shots using long lenses which depict vague action), no pointless shaking of the camera, no waving the camera about in a desperate attempt to create excitement – instead, powerful, crisp, precise shots.

ﾆ﮲

Once again, Tsui Hark and co. wheel in a tank to deliver out-size gags – like firing upon the cliff that towers above Lord Hawk's stronghold, which brings down meteorite-sized rocks to topple down. (In the *Lake Changjin* movies, tanks are very prominent).

Amusingly, *The Taking of Tiger Mountain* features two endings: in the first, as Yang Zirong pursues Lord Hawk for the inevitable smackdown between the hero and the villain, he manages to nobble Hawk by sliding over the floor, underneath the gunfire. (This is set in the cavernous, storage halls deep below Tiger Mountain).

Not big enough for you? During the framing story in New York, a new ending is portrayed (it is motivated by Jimmy musing on whether Lord Hawk had an airstrip at Tiger Mountain): this one is the expected gigantic battle between the hero and the baddie: a colossal chase and duel and fight along a tunnel and then in a crevasse as the production unleashes 100s of visual effects shots, numerous gags, and many over-cooked, blockbuster-movie-sized action beats. The sequence with the runaway aeroplane is very *James Bond*, very *Indiana Jones* and – most of all – very much a Hong Kong cinema episode (tho' not every Hong Kong picture can afford to spend quite *this* much on the action!). It's also a variation on the climactic sequence in *Dr Wai* featuring a plane.

This is Tsui Hark having it both ways (or all ways): and he's done it before. The ending of *A Chinese Ghost Story*, for example, wasn't deemed big enough when the filmmakers looked at the rough cut. So a second ending was filmed.

ﾆ﮲

Western critics pointed out that *The Taking of Tiger Mountain* was another tale of a heroic, modern China, and that it wasn't critical of the ruling powers. But few movies of this scope are – truly revolutionary films tend to be much smaller (and they don't receive the backing of big studios or governments). And in the People's Republic of China, few or no movies of this scale are allowed to be critical of the Powers That Be.

For some viewers, *The Taking of Tiger Mountain* was too one-sided: the heroes were good all-round (and in the right), and the villains were ugly and cruel (and in the wrong). Certainly, *The Taking of Tiger Mountain* has the feel, like the original 1970 film and the opera, of a righteous, government-sponsored piece of propaganda. (The same criticisms would be levelled at the *Battle of Lake Changjin* films, this time from Western critics).

Flying Swords of Dragon Gate (2011).

Making Flying Swords of Dragon Gate.

The Taking of
Tiger Mountain
(2014).

# 37

# *JOURNEY TO THE WEST: THE DEMONS STRIKE BACK*

## *Xi You Fu Yao Pian*

*Journey To the West: The Demons Strike Back* (a.k.a. *The Demon Chapter*, 2017), known in Mandarin as *Xi You Fu Yao Pian* and in Cantonese as *Sai Jau Feok Jiu Pin*, was the sequel to 2013's *Journey To the West: Conquering the Demons*. A huge number of companies (and their producers) contributed to this, in Asian terms, mega-production (the budget was in the region of U.S. $64 million). The film was a monster hit (with a global gross of $329m, and 1.65593 billion Yuan in China), the biggest for Tsui Hark as a director thus far.

Tsui Hark directed, was co-producer and co-writer, and one of the editors. Yet this is not 'A Tsui Hark Film', despite that credit appearing in the main titles. No. This is a sequel and, like all sequels, it's also a remake (just as the first film was a remake of earlier versions of *Journey To the West*). *Journey To the West 2* sticks closely to the template set out in the first film of 2013. And the *Journey To the West* material has been adapted many times).

The backers of *Journey To the West 2* included these companies: Star Overseas Ltd/ Tianjin Maoyan Pictures/ Guanzhou Jinyi Media Corp./ Premium Data Associates Ltd/ Xiang Shan Zeyue Culture Media Co./ Huayi Brothers Pictures/ Shanghai Tao Piao Piao Movie & TV Culture Co./ Lian Ray Pictures/ Zhejiang Hengdian Film Co./ Dadi Century Company Ltd/ Dadi Century Company Ltd/ Hehe Pictures Corporation Ltd/ Maxtimes Culture Films Company Ltd/ China Film Co., Ltd/ and Wanda Film and Television Media Co.

Inevitably, many firms backing the movie means lots of producers: James Tsim Tak-fast, Tsui Hark, Stephen Chow Sing-chi, Hay Wei, Yang Wei, Chow Man-ki, Jerry Lu, John Zeng, Liu Rong, Chen Lizhi, Wang Zhongjuin, Cai Yuan, Xu Tianfu, Li Xioadong, Zheng Zhihao, Lian Jie, and Tsui's ex-wife, Nansun Shi Nan-sheng.

Tsui Hark co-wrote the script with Stephen Chow Sing-chi, Jia-jia Wei and Kelvin Lee Si-zhen. DP: Johnny Choi Sung-fai. Costumes: Lee Pik-kwan. Art dirs.: Liao Hui-li and Guo Zhong-shan. Image supervisor: Bruce Yu Ka-on. Prod. des.: Akatsuka Yoshihito. Make-up: Maggie Choy Yin-ching. Hair: Lee Lin-tai. Action dirs.: Yeun Bun and Yuen Tak. Editors: Tsui, Li Lin and Jason Zeng Wu-sen. Sound: Yang Yu-hui. Sound design: Kinson Tsang King-cheung and Yiu Chun-hin. Music: Raymond Wong Ying-wah. Visual effects dirs.: Park Young-soo and Wook Kim. Released Jan 28, 2017. 108 mins.

In the cast were Kris Wu Yi-fan (as Tang Sanzang), Kenny Lin Geng-xin (as the Monkey King), Yao Chen (as the Minister), Jelly Lin-yin (as Felicity), Mengke Bateer (as Sandy), Wang Li-kun (as Spider), Yang Yi-wei (as Pigsy), Tony Wang-duo (as the young Pigsy), Bao Bei-er (as the Emperor), and Cheng Si-han (as Tang's *sifu*, Master Nameless). Shu Qi appears in flashbacks as Duan (and in some present-day scenes), and the director and Stephen Chow have cameos in the theatre sequence. Principal photography began on August 6, 2015.

The cast in the 2017 sequel is changed around from the 2013 *Journey To the West*: it's a shame that Huang Bo wasn't back as the Monkey King (instead, one of Tsui Hark's favourite actors of the 2010s, Kenny Lin Gengxin, took up the golden fright wig (and the black fright wig) as everyone's favourite psycho ape, Sun Wukong). And Wen Zhang was similarly impressive as the main character, the bald, Buddhist monk Tang Sanzang, the part that Stephen Chow would've played in younger years (but he was replaced by Kris Wu Yi-fan – just as appealing, though not as deft with comedy. And Wu plays the movie bald, while Zhang had that ridiculous wig). Among the central four characters, Yang Yiwei and Mengke Bateer replaced the actors in the 2013 movie (it's a pity that some of the principal actors couldn't be in the sequel only four years later).

Many in the crew had worked with Tsui Hark many times before – such as composer Raymond Wong Ying-wah, DP Johnny Choi Sung-fai, designer Bruce Yu Ka-on, and action choreographers Yuen Bun and Yuen Tak.

*Journey To the West: The Demons Strike Back* is also very much like other big budget movies of the 2000s-2020s made in Mainland China by Hong Kong crews: it's a more expensive version of the movies they were turning out in Hong Kong in the 1970s thru 1990s. Sections of *Journey To the West* films are essentially pricier, splashier versions of scenes that Tsui Hark and his contemporaries had already delivered in the *Chinese Ghost Story* films and the *Swordsman* films. I'm thinking of the spider-women set-piece which climaxes act one of *Journey To the West: The Demons Strike Back* (that comes from the 16th century novel). The narrative structure of it, for example, such as the build-up, the erotic flirtation, the comical interplay of demons and heroes, the revelation of the monsters, and finally the shift into full-scale action.

Since his first big visual effects outing – *Zu: Warriors From the Magic Mountain* in 1983 – where he got to play in the sandbox of cinema on a big scale – Tsui Hark has been absolutely fascinated by cinematic trickery. He just loves very intricate effects (and also simple, physical effects), and he is happy to make them completely obvious to all. In fact, he *wants* the viewer to notice them (at least in a movie like *Journey To the West 2*, where notions of 'realism' or 'naturalism' are far, far away).

In *Journey To the West 2*, the visual effects were provided by, among others, Terminal FX, Dexter Studios, Intelligent Creatures, Yannix Thailand Co., Mofac & Alfred and Monk Studios. Park Young-soo and Wook Kim were the visual effects supervisors.

*Journey To the West: The Demons Strike Back* is another movie directed by Tsui Hark where visual effects threaten to overwhelm everything else (and not only in the finale, but throughout the whole picture. There are visual effects in pretty much every single scene. This is also a studio-bound production, and even locations are tricked out with digital additions and digital mattes. Nothing in *Journey To the West: The Demons Strike Back* is presented as is, everything has been transmuted using visual effects, including digital grading).

Viewers might discuss *Journey To the West: The Demons Strike Back* as a visual effects extravaganza, but it is also a feast for costumes, hair and make-up. Everything is stylized and heightened in the hair (Lee Lin-tai), make-up (Maggie Choy Yin-ching) and costume (Bruce Yu Ka-on and Lee Pik-kwan) departments – but even more so than a conventional, Chinese historical picture, because this is a candy-coated, Peking Opera version of a Chinese legend. Nobody turns up in jeans and a Tee shirt and walks on set. Oh no, everybody in this movie – including all of the extras – has been made up and dressed. It's no surprise that the film won the award for Bruce Yu and Lee Pik-kwan for costumes at the Hong Kong Film Awards. (There are 25 assistant make-up artists credited, 16 assistant hair stylists, 3 special make-up artists and 8 assistant special make-up artists).

The score for *Journey To the West: The Demons Strike Back* (by Raymond Wong Ying-wah) is the expected boisterous, action-adventure music (thankfully, no raindrop piano here – slow strings are employed for the emotional scenes instead). As it's a comedy movie, there are several quotes from famous pieces of music, such as traditional, Chinese movie music, and from Richard Strauss's *Also Sprach Zarathustra*.

٠

The 16th century novel by Wu Chen'en is one of the most well-known works of literature in Asia. In it, Tang Sanzang (a.k.a. Tripitaka) travels to the West (to India and Central Asia) in search of Buddhist scriptures (the *sutras*), aided by three accomplices: Sun Wukong (the Monkey King), Zhu Bajie (a.k.a. Zhu Wuyeng, or Pig or Pigsy), Sha Wujing (a.k.a. Sandy), a monster, and Sha Wujing, a white horse (Tang's steed). Along the way the travellers have all sorts of adventures. The themes of *Journey To the West* include seeking enlightenment, in the Buddhist manner, redemption and forgiveness (for former sins).

*Journey To the West 2* is not a Tsui Hark movie as a personal project, or one that he had been burning to make for decades, but it is full of familiar Tsui-isms. One is portraying large crowds as aggressive idiots – and in *Journey To the West: The Demons Strike Back*, they are particularly belligerent, demanding double their money back from the clumsy performance of the heroes in an early scene. Surely this isn't how the filmmakers see their audience, is it?[1]

This is Tsui Hark as the circus showman, the master of ceremonies of an Oriental pantomime. And it's movie-making as a circus (the film opens in a circus, and includes another set-piece at a festival),[2] and as a magic show (the Biqiu city is very fond of magic tricks, even the Minister herself performs them). And it's a brash, over-done comedy movie released at New Year (like the first film).

So it's Fairy Tale Time in Movieland once again – this is an unapologetically silly film, stuffed with bright colours, monsters, out-size performances and plenty of Peking Opera flourishes. *Journey To the West* is Tsui Hark's *Wizard of Oz* and *The Arabian Nights*, like *Shanghai Blues* was his *An American In Paris* or *Singin' In the Rain*. It's candy thru and thru, self-consciously light-hearted and lightweight.

And yet *Journey To the West* is also a true Tsui Hark film in being made in China, all about China, starring a Chinese cast, filmed with a Chinese crew, and based on a famous Chinese legend.

*Journey To the West 2* seems as if Tsui Hark is making a movie for his 12 year-old self (or for the son or grandchild he never had). It's for twelve year-olds kids everywhere, with its set of misfit (but powerful) superheroes, its silly comedy, its over-bright colours and *animé*-style action.

It's interesting to compare the two directing styles of Tsui Hark and Stephen Chow Sing-chi in the first film and the sequel: Chow is a master of comedy and comic timing, and wonderful at bringing out the pathos or surreality of people interacting. But Tsui's vision is truly colossal and dazzling; he loves to fling everything into the pot (the more colours, the more action, the more chaos, the more sounds, the better). *Journey To the West 2* is an absolutely massive movie; and Tsui's directing style is incredibly bold and muscular.

᠄

The world of *Journey To the West: The Demons Strike Back* is thoroughly patriarchal – as Ancient China always is in art and cinema, and always was in reality and history. But the 2017 movie manages to squeeze in some prime roles for beautiful women by simply turning them into demons so that the four male heroes have to vanquish them (but not before they've first been introduced as young women). Thus, the giant spiders that lure the heroes into their lair in act one are first depicted as gorgeous girls. Similarly with Felicity, the White Bone Spirit. And in a typical Tsui-ism, the Minister who works for the Emperor is a woman, a role

---

1 The movie dares the viewer to ask for double his money back!
2 *Journey To the West: The Demons Strike Back* has fun with presenting the circus folk as cynical entertainers, led by their boss, who is of course a small person (called Midget – Shuang Li).

usually played by an old character actor[3] (it looks as if the production team considered the script and the casting and simply changed the gender of the Minister. That occurs quite often in Tsui's cinema).

And no one can miss the depiction in several places in *Journey To the West: The Demons Strike Back* of ugly women and fat women and snarling, nasty women (the king's harem in act three, for instance, or the boisterous crowd at the circus in act one).

The first movie made the temptation of romantic love and women one of the key subplots: it's a staple of Chinese comedy movies to portray Buddhist monks struggling to resist the advances of the most incandescent starlets that the Hong Kong and Chinese industry can conjure up.

*Journey To the West 2* continues that moral dilemma subplot, throwing Monk Tang Sanzang into close proximity with a number of women (usually played for comedy. This element of *Journey To the West: The Demons Strike Back* reprises the humorous seduction scenes in *Green Snake*). And it also presents Monk Tang as haunted by the figure of Duan, the dead beloved torn to pieces by the Monkey King in the climax of the previous movie of 2013 (when Monk Tang watches Felicity dance for the Emperor, for example, he sees Duan doing her moonlit dance. This is a scene, by the way, when the movie stops for a dance number – and forms a reprise of the song and dance performed in the first *Journey To the West* film to lure the giant boar).

Jelly Lin-yin is impressive as Felicity the White Bone Spirit – flirtatious, sexy, and enigmatic, but also a vulnerable country girl who was the victim of bandits.

Some of the appearances by Duan (Shu Qi) are in the form of flashbacks as well as dreams, using footage from the first film. But Duan also appears in the flesh – she returns in the *dénouement*, for example (where the love between Tang and Duan is re-affirmed, and there's a humorous confusion between Duan and the Monkey King as they walk beside Tang in the desert).

In taking a Buddhist monk as the hero, you could regard *Journey To the West: The Demons Strike Back* as another version of Tsui Hark's many cinematic explorations of righteous figures like Wong Fei-hung. How to do the right thing in a chaotic, cynical, exploitative and repressive society is something that Tsui's heroes wrestles with.

However, that theme seems buried in *Journey To the West: The Demons Strike Back* in the flood of silly, superficial but amusing antics, action set-pieces, music cues and visual effects. There isn't a big or important theme in *Journey To the West: The Demons Strike Back*, let's face it, as there was in, say, the *Once Upon a Time In China* series. The figure of Tang Sanzang does carry issues as a character such as righteousness and integrity (and holiness), but they are integrated into the picture more as mere functions of plot to make the movie work. The 2017 movie isn't *really* interested in how you can act in a noble or

3 Often it was Lau Shun in Tsui's movies of the 1990s.

compassionate manner, as if it's encouraging the audience to read and follow the Buddhist religious *sutras* right after they leave the theatre (even tho', yes, you could argue that *Journey To the West: The Demons Strike Back* actually does present Buddhist precepts, and that Tang is another of Tsui's figures, like Wong Fei-hung or Detective Dee, who is wrestling with the issue of How To Do The Right Thing. The big argument scene, for example, in act three, is played straight, and brings out those issues).

There are some obvious parallels with Tsui Hark's earlier works: how Monk Tang is struggling to keep his band of demon hunters in order (and the Monkey King in particular), and to keep them on the right path, which evokes Wong Fei-hung and his workers at the Po Chi Lam Clinic. Notice that Tang's master, Master Nameless, is largely absent from the sequel – because Tang himself is now the teacher and the leader.

The film doesn't allow Monk Tang and the Monkey King to absorb all of the limelight: it gives scenes to Pigsy the pervy porker who drools at the sight of anything female (or food), and the giant, melancholy fish Sandy.

*Journey To the West: The Demons Strike Back* is built around set-pieces, in the usual manner of Chinese action-adventure movies (or action-adventures movies from anywhere): an action set-piece to open the movie, an action set-piece to climax act one (plus a smaller one in the middle of act one). Act two introduces back-story, subplots and exposition, plus of course a big set-piece for its finale. Act three (*Journey To the West: The Demons Strike Back* has a three-act structure) builds into a final act action sequence and stays there for the duration, until the end.

Structurally, *Journey To the West: The Demons Strike Back* is a road movie format. It features a band of heroes on their travels, having adventures along the way. Some are hunting demons in the action set-pieces (the spiders, the fake Emperor), but some are comical scenes where they meet a new group of characters.

*Journey To the West: The Demons Strike Back* isn't entirely episodic, however: there are one or two subplots which recur throughout the picture. One concerns Tang Sanzang's desire to become an enlightened monk, a Buddha-in-the-making, so to speak (and to be acknowledged by his master). This goal is outlined in the dream sequence that opens the movie (dreams in movies often illustrate what a character is hoping for, or desires – or fears).

The constant bickering between the two main characters is another subplot (which fuses with the main plot of the adventures of the heroes). *Journey To the West: The Demons Strike Back* is in part a buddy movie between magical beings. Cleverly, the subplot about Tang trying to keep the Monkey King in check is tied to the romantic subplot (it's often the Monkey King who questions Monk Tang about his quasi-romantic relationship with Duan, and then again with Felicity).

Another subplot in *Journey To the West: The Demons Strike Back* is the romantic longing that Tang experiences – these coalesce around the figure of the dead Duan. This is also raised in a dream – again, in a comical manner, when Tang is dreaming of Duan with the Monkey King right next to him, and clutching him. (Meanwhile, Pigsy, being the horndog in the band of brothers, also raises the issue of Duan and their leader's relationship with her).

No doubt some of the set-pieces in the 2017 sequel were elements that the 2013 *Journey* film hadn't included, as is common with sequels. The two *Journey To the West* films are episodic in narrative structure, with set-pieces that can be taken out or swapped with others.

So *Journey To the West: The Demons Strike Back* opens with the *Gulliver's Travels* dream, rapidly segues into circus performance scenes, which soon introduce the characters (though with humorous reversals – instead of superheroes, they're an odd bunch of misfits). The mid-act one set-piece sees the mayhem created by the Monkey King and his pals escalating (while Monk Tang tries to keep them under control). In the second half of the first act, the film slows down for some important exposition, the introduction of the Duan romantic subplot (again, in a humorous fashion), and the continuing bickering between the Monkey King and Monk Tang (which forms the real foundation of *Journey To the West: The Demons Strike Back* – brothers who put up with each other, or the significance of friendship).

A nest of spiders provides the amazing climax of act one, as the band of sort of brothers stumbles upon a palace of beautiful women who turn out to be monsters (led by Wang Likun as the chief spider-woman). Following that, *Journey To the West: The Demons Strike Back* moves into slower scenes before entering the spectacular city of Biqiu. The scenes build up to the introduction of the fake Emperor, climaxing with the Monkey King taking on the Emperor in a series of colossal action gags.

ॐ

The *Gulliver's Travels* skit in the prologue sets the tone for the rest of the 2017 movie: Tang Sanzang is dreaming of being the giant amongst Liliputians, who want to worship him. His *sifu,* Master Nameless (Si-Han Cheng), appears to bestow him a halo (which he happily wears, sitting in the lotus position as Buddha). The *Gulliver's Travels* sketch introduces how this movie will approach the *Journey To the West* material, with its over-the-top design, its rainbow colours, its pantomime characters, and its blend of live-action with cartoons.

The spider-women set-piece that rounds off act one of *Journey To the West: The Demons Strike Back* is Tsui Hark as the master showman, staging chaotic monster action within an elaborate setting (the first of the big sets), which evokes a palace and the ubiquitous tea-house of 1,000s of Hong Kong historical romps).

The build-up to the action set-piece that climaxes act two of *Journey To the West: The Demons Strike Back* is long and detailed: there's a lengthy procession thru the streets (one of Tsui Hark's favourite forms of including big production value scenes along with traditional, Chinese culture). The Minister (Yao Chen) is the key new character in Biqui City, interacting with Monk Tang in many scenes (the comical bits of business, like the magical tricks that don't quite work or seem fake, baffle Tang). The Minister voices a Tsui-ism: it doesn't matter if the tricks are real or fake.

*Journey To the West: The Demons Strike Back* arrives at the big set at Hengdian World Studios – the same stage was used for the Imperial reception room in *Detective Dee: The Four Heavenly Kings* the following year. Production designer Akatsuka Yoshihito (along with art directors Liao Hui-li and Guo Zhjong-shan) has gone all-out to present a fantasy of Ye Olde China: nothing is too lavish, too over-the-top (or too stupid).

Simpering underlings, a harem of ugly, over-weight women, a spoilt brat of an Emperor and grovelling subservience are among the ingredients in the confrontation, which is cleverly reflected by a falling-out between the two main characters, the Monkey King and Monk Tang.

There's no need for Tsui Hark to make another cartoon using Japanese *animé* talent in Tokyo (as he did with the animated adaptation of *A Chinese Ghost Story*), because *Journey To the West: The Demons Strike Back* is just that. And especially here, when the foolish Emperor reveals himself to be a mechanical toy (a sort of Chinese-Indian robot – Astro Boy if he grew up in Delhi), taking on the Monkey King in a storming sequence of ridiculous, superhero shenanigans (the Emperor summons a sphere of flames inside which armed cavalry ride).

The early stages of act three feature some intriguing notions: Monk Tang negotiates with the Emperor for the possession of Felicity, the new concubine. Tang suspects that she is a demon, who needs to be dealt with; but Tang is torn because he sees in her the spirit of his beloved Duan (when Tang thinks back Felicity's erotic dance, it is intercut with Duan dancing, using the same gestures). Tang's judgement is not quite clear, then, as he confuses Felicity with Duan, tempered by his repressed desire for Duan.

ꝗ

The preamble to the action set-piece of the finale, *Journey To the West: The Demons Strike Back* presents a fascinating scene where the two main characters argue with each other. This looks like a scene scripted by one of the other writers – Chow, Wei and Lee, rather than Tsui Hark (judging from the tone, and the rhythm of the dialogue). The Monkey King has insisted all along that Felicity is a demon (and she is), but Tang refuses to believes it. The Monkey King sets about the people of Felicity's homeland, while Tang tries to stop him, and to protect Felicity.

Only later is all of this revealed as a clever ruse by the heroes to trick the powers behind the demons, the Emperor and the Minister. But the argument between Tang and the Monkey King is striking for its length and ferocity (in what is essential a comedy adventure flick). However, it does illustrate what is at stake in this movie – the friendship among the heroes.

When, at the end of the argument, the Monkey King balloons up to his King Kong-size (memorably visualized as a cluster of grey rocks with red lava underneath), it announces the beginning of the climax.

The finale of the *Journey To the West: The Demons Strike Back* sequel is the expected out-size showdown between the heroes and the demons (big? No, *bigger*! No, no, sweetie, even *bigger*! Thus, even the real Lord Buddha makes an appearance, intoning solemnly from somewhere in the star-spangled cosmos. Indeed, the finale of *Journey* is a Battle of the Buddhas – the villains summon three golden Buddhas to duel with Tang and the Monkey King, but the heroes have got the *real* Buddha on their side! And against *that* Buddha, no one stands a chance!).

It's striking just how much the climax draws on the example of *Green Snake*,[4] a movie released in 1993 (which Tsui Hark is fond of). *Journey To the West: The Demons Strike Back* employs some of the same ingredients, such as the elements of water (enormous floods), fire (walls of fire and the Monkey King and the Buddha burning with fire), and earth (huge rocks are hurled about).

The Minister and the Emperor begin the attacks, which the Monkey King repels (for part of the finale, Monk Tang is hiding in the Monkey King's ear or on his back). The Monkey King deploys his magical staff. In one of the numerous vivid scenes, our heroes are plunged into an ocean.

In the midst of the maelstrom the human figures are tiny, dwarfed by the battle raging between the King Kong-sized[5] Monkey King – Tang, Felicity, Sandy, Pigsy, and the two demon villains, the Minister and the Emperor (Pig and Sandy do their bit, but the finale is mostly about the Monkey King and Tang taking on the Minister and the Emperor. Felicity cowers behind some rocks).

The setting is a mountainous region of Asia – the misty ranges of the *jiangzhu*, where each of the figures can be placed atop a peak, on a small plateau, hurling insults at each other from 100 of yards away (it's similar to the environment of *The Legend of Zu*).

Indeed, most of the finale of *Journey To the West: The Demons Strike Back* is a giant cartoon with live-action elements such as the actors composited into the image. For a long time Tsui Hark has been an animation director in large part – numerous action set-pieces in *Journey To the West: The Demons Strike Back* are actually animation (like so many big budget Hollywood movies these days).

This section of *Journey To the West: The Demons Strike Back* is also very much like Japanese *animé*, and many a Saturday morning cartoon: superheroes are zooming about the sky, hurling rocks, fire, water and bolts of energy at each other. This duel is simply a flashier, pricier version of the finales of 1,000s of cartoons aimed at kids.

Anyway, the visual effects teams deliver entertaining, flashy animation involving towering waves, golden statues of the Buddha, and rocks being slammed here and there. Actors yell, percussion thuds on the soundtrack,[6] and lightning flashes.

For the finale, the writers opted to bring back the Minister and the Emperor; now, apparently, they have used Felicity to sow the seeds of

4 *Journey To the West: The Demons Strike Back* is in part a remake of the *Chinese Ghost Story* movies and *Green Snake*.
5 Remember how Tsui Hark disliked being called King Kong when he was studying in the U.S.A., and that partly encouraged him to change his name to Tsui.
6 Percussion because it has to be something loud to cut through the chaos.

discord between Tang and the Monkey King (with the minor theme of sexual jealousy). Meanwhile, the Minister reveals herself to a demon, too (the multi-headed, Immortal Golden Vulture), while the Emperor is a manic metal toy with six arms.

Although the enemy summons three Buddhas, who dispense tidal waves and fire, Monk Tang has his golden, Buddha palm – and this time, it's the real Buddha who appears (he admonishes the Minister for her behaviour and mistaken beliefs).

Felicity (the White Bone Demon) receives a moving death scene in the Japanese *animé* manner (her body dematerializes into white-purple tendrils of light and disappear into the sky, heading for the full moon). Poor Felicity was the victim of a gang rape, no less, and left to die. Her bitter resentment has kept her in a demonic state: the death scene is partly played as a love scene, with Monk Tang holding Felicity in his arms as she confesses her love for him (even while knowing that there is no space for her in his heart because Duan is still there).

This is Tsui Hark the romantic softie, including a poignant love-and-death scene as the emotional-spiritual catharsis at the end of the climax. With Felicity's soul spiralling to the heavens, the story is over, and we are into the *dénouement* scenes.

The chief *dénouement* is a Tsui Hark staple – the heroes are on their way once again (this time in a desert). Tsui ended films such as the *Swordsman* series, *The Magic Crane* and *New Dragon Gate Inn* like this – usually, it's on horseback, with the heroes riding off into the sunset. So the bickering resumes between Tang Sanzang and the Sun Wukong; the Tang-and-Duan romantic subplot is evoked humorously (and Duan appears walked beside Tang, joking with him); Sandy and Pigsy shrug and follow their master and the credits roll.

The credits of *Journey To the West: The Demons Strike Back* are endless, naming the thousands of the crew who made this mega-movie possible. The director and the co-writer (Tsui and Chow) themselves appear in a humorous skit which sends up the notion of a post-credits scene. As they clean up a movie theatre in China with black bin bags, they tell the audience that no, this isn't a blockbuster, and it doesn't have an after-credits scene.

It's easy to see why *Journey To the West: Conquering the Demons* (*Chu Mo Chuan Qi Sam Zang Fu/ New Chinese Odyssey*, 2013) was a mega-hit in the People's Republic of China: it's a very enjoyable romp of an action comedy. It's got spectacle, action, drama, romance and comedy, and the spirit with which it delivers it all is appealing. The film earned most of its colossal $215 million global box office gross in P.R.C., which for a Chinese production is a *lot* of dollars.

*Journey To the West: Conquering the Demons* is usually considered another Stephen Chow Show, but in fact he co-wrote it with seven other writers, no less (Derek Kwok, Xin Huo, Yun Wang, Fung Chi-chiang, Lu Zheng Yu, Lee Sheng-shing and Iy Kong), co-directed it with Derek Kwok, and was one of no less than 9 producers (the other 8 were: Zhonglei Wang, Ping Dong, Ellen Eliasoph, Samping Han, Ivy Kong, William Kong, Dajun Zhang, and Zhongun Wang). Chinavision Media Group/ E.D.K.O Films/ Huayi Brothers/ China Film Group/ Village Roadshow Picture/ Bingo Movie produced. Released Feb 7, 2013. 110 mins.

In the cast were Shu Qi, Wen Zhang, Huang Bo, Chen Bing-qiang, Lee Sheung-ching, Show Lo, Cheng Sihan, Xing Yu, Chiu Chi-ling, Chrissie Chau and Yang Di.

It's a terrific cast, but it's Huang Bo who steals the movie as the Monkey King (a.k.a. Sun Wukong). He's first introduced as an ashen grey, aged hermit in an underground cave (he's been imprisoned by Buddha for 500 years). He pounces on Monk Tang as a whispering weirdo.

Wen Zhang, in the role that Stephen Chow would've played had he been younger, was superb – as the Buddhist monk and demon hunter Tang Sanzang (and Zhang also performs the part something like Chow would do). Both Huang Bo and Wen Zhang were replaced in the 2017 sequel (as were Chen Bing-qiang and Lee Sheung-ching).

Perhaps the biggest surprise with *Journey To the West* was the casting of Shu Qi as a kick-ass action heroine, the demon hunter Duan. It's not the sort of role that you associate with Qi[7] (a former Category III star later known for romantic roles – she was the girlfriend of Jackie Chan in *Gorgeous*, 1999); but it works. Qi (b. 1976, Xindian, Taiwan) is a quirky presence on screen, a striking departure form the usual, Chinese starlet or serious actress (she has worked in Korea and Taiwan as well as Hong Kong). Qi is an eye-opener as a tough, apparently veteran demon hunter who scorns Monk Tang's approach of singing love songs to demons (at first).

Unusually, *Journey To the West: Conquering the Demons* presents a woman chasing a man, as Shu Qi's Duan pursues Wen Zhang's Monk Tang, convinced that he is the man for her – despite many signals that he is not, and that he rejects her many times. He's a Buddhist monk, too, of course, which is used for comedy in Chinese cinema.

This wasn't the first time that Stephen Chow had taken on the famous

---

[7] Actually, Qi has played some action roles (such as in 2015's *The Assassin*).

*Journey To the West* legends – he had starred in a version in the 1990s entitled *Chinese Odyssey* in the West (so *Journey To the West* is in part a remake for Chow). The mythology of *Journey To the West* has been a staple in Chinese television and movies for a long time.

ॐ

There's a charming sense of play in *Journey To the West: Conquering the Demons* – in the silly costumes, the fright wigs,[8] and the mix of contemporary comedy with ancient mythology.

*Journey To the West* is mounted very much in the contemporary Hollywood manner of franchises such as *Pirates of the Caribbean* and *Indiana Jones*, though the humour is much *much* quirkier and sillier. Like many Hong Kong comedies, *Journey To the West* shifts from seemingly straight drama into goofy comedy very rapidly. *Journey To the West* features jokes that wouldn't appear in similar Hollywood fare.

*Journey To the West: Conquering the Demons* is funny, though the sense of humour is mighty strange at times (there's nonsensical humour and black humour). But the movie is well-meaning, and returns to the moral middle ground, despite its many diversions.

Some of the humour in *Journey To the West: Conquering the Demons* derives from playing with stereotypes and expectations, turning around what audiences might expect from a scene or a character. After all, there's little interest in simply trotting another straight adaptation of the *Journey To the West* legends. So the 2013 movie puts its own spin on well-worn scenarios and characterizations.

Tsui Hark didn't direct this 2013 movie (he directed the sequel in 2017), but there is some very Tsui Harkian humour in *Journey To the West: Conquering the Demons* – such as the grizzled villagers on the river and their Neanderthal reactions *en masse* to the demon hunters.

Transformations are everywhere in *Journey To the West: Conquering the Demons*: most characters are introduced as one thing but become another (and then another).

The stops-all-out finale of *Journey To the West: Conquering the Demons* features several Tsui Harkian ingredients – such as the giant, golden Buddha who hovers above the Earth and squashes the Monkey King under its enormous palm (this is reminiscent of the ending of *Green Snake* and *A Chinese Ghost Story 2*. Tsui's sequel also drew on the finale of *Green Snake*).

---

8 Wen Zhang sports a send-up of the sort of wigs that Stephen Chow used to wear – it's bushier and wider.

# 38

# THE BATTLE AT LAKE CHANGJIN

## Changjin Hu

*The Battle At Lake Changjin* (*Chángjin Hú,* 2021) was a super-production from companies including Bona Film Group/ August First Film/ Beijing Dengfeng International Culture Communciations/ Alibaba Pictures/ China Film Group/ Huaxia Film Distribution/ Shanghai Film Group. The producers included Chen Hong, Nansun Shi Nan-sheng, Candy Leung, Jian Defu, Don Yu-dong, Huang Jianxin, Quji Xiao-jiang and Yu Shu-qin (plus the 3 directors). Huang Jianxin and Lan Xiaolong scripted. Tsui Hark co-helmed with two other directors: Chen Kaige (*Farewell My Concubine, The Emperor and the Assassin*), and Dante Lam Chiu-yin (*Operation Red Sea, That Demon Within, Guarding Our City*). And three co-directors: Huang Jianxin, Haiqiang Ning and Ju-chun Park. Music by Wang Zhi-yi, Li Ye and Elliot Leung;9 editing by Marco Mak Chi-sin, Tsui, Li Danshi and He Yong-yi; art dirs.: Le Wei, Lam Wai-kin and Ho Chi-hang; and 6 DPs: Peter Pau, Ding Yu, Choi Man-lung, Gao Hu, Luo Pan and Horace Wong. Released: Sept 30, 2021. 178 mins.

In the (almost all-male) cast were Jacky Wu Jing, Jackson Yee, Duan Yihong, Zhang Hanyu, Jerry Li Chen, Hu Jun, Elvis Han Dong-jun, Oho Ou-hao, Shi Pengyuan, Tang Guo-qiang, Liu Sha, Liu Jin, Wang Wu-fu, Wang Jian, and Zhu Ya-wen.

*The Battle At Lake Changjin* was a mammoth production with a huge budget (some U.S. $200 million), making it one of the most expensive pictures produced in China by Chinese companies (and the biggest picture that Tsui Hark had been involved with – although several of his recent movies were also big budget productions). Around 70,000 soldiers from the People's Liberation Army were used as extras (*The Battle At Lake Changjin* is no different from many large-scale war movies in enlisting real soldiers to act as extras. One reason is that they are disciplined, and respond to being organized in groups). The visual effects budget was substantial.

9 The score was of course the expected Big, Heroic Music (recorded in Vienna).

*The Battle At Lake Changjin* was a mega-hit in China, taking in over 5.77573 billion Yuan (U.S. $900 million). The success of *The Battle At Lake Changjin* inevitably led to the release of a sequel. (The sequel – *The Battle At Lake Changjin 2: Water Gate Bridge* (*Changjin Hu Zhi Shuimen Qiao*) – appeared a year later, with much of the same cast and crew).

The two productions were filmed back-to-back (thru 10 months): the sequel, entitled *The Battle At Lake Changin: 2 Water Gate Bridge*, was released a year later (on Feb 1, 2022). Filming during the C.O.V.I.D. incident, plus the weather, added to the difficulties of the production.

*The Battle At Lake Changjin* was an epic war movie (nearly three hours long) set in China, about China, with Chinese characters and themes (which is in tune with Tsui Hark's cinema, most of which has been about China). The subject was an incident during the Korean War in 1950 – the Battle of the Chosin Reservoir (a.k.a. Lake Changjin); the second film focussed on the struggle over the Sumun Bridge, to stop the enemy's retreat.

*The Battle At Lake Changjin* is another of the recent, Chinese movies which ape Western historical epics, though the emphasis is entirely on the People's Republic of China. The overall issue of *The Battle At Lake Changjin* is defending China from invaders – this time, it's the forces of the United States of North America (and the United Nations). So it's China versus the world, and in particular China versus the West, those clever, white, Imperialist *gwailo*.

The message is loud and clear:
• China is wonderful!
• China can overcome any obstacles and win any war!
• The Chinese people are the finest on Earth!
• COME AND LIVE IN CHINA!

The two *Battle At Lake Changjin* movies evoke the troubled political relations between the People's Republic of China and the U.S.A. Everything has changed since the Korean War. Or has it? Who spends the most on the military today? Yes – it's the United States of America, which spent $778 billion in 2021. And who spends the most after the U.S.A.? Yes – it's China, which spent $252 billion. (Both the U.S.A. and China are way ahead of other nations, such as: 3. India: $73 billion. 4. Russia: $62 billion. 5. Britain: $59 billion and 6. Saudi Arabia: $57 billion).

❧

Some Western critics saw *The Battle At Lake Changjin* as government-sponsored propaganda, but the same can be said of many North American war movies, or Russian war movies, or French war movies, etc. It would be foolish to expect a movie of this size and with this subject matter to be anything but a film celebrating Chinese politics and Chinese culture. (Plus, it was commissioned by the propaganda department of the Chinese Communist Party, to celebrate their 100th anniversary). Some territories in the region of the world regard China with suspicion).

Part of the unease with a Chinese epic movie like *The Battle At Lake Changjin* for Western film critics is that it's the *Americans* who are now the invaders, the enemy, the ones who have to be killed in order to stop them going any further. The Yanks are, in the dumb jargon of U.S. movies, the 'bad guys', and the duty of the Chinese heroes is to expel them from their beloved Motherland at all costs.

In Western war/ action/ adventure/ fantasy movies, it's reversed, so that it's *normal* and *expected* that it's Asians who're going to be blown to bits, that it's Asian villages that will be over-run, that it's Asians who pay the price. If you have seen a lot of American or European or British or Western war movies[10] (and action movies), you will have seen all sorts of groups of people being decimated. In a way, it's refreshing to see the moral-political balance being shifted in favour of the people usually portrayed as the enemy.

Many American/ Western action/ war/ fantasy movies are 'America Über Alles' ideologically, which promote the American way of life, and the American military machine; in short, American political domination. Sometimes it's good to have a change, and move away from having the U.S.A. smother all with its ideology.

*The Battle At Lake Changjin* doesn't demonize the enemy, however, but grants many scenes to the American commanders and the soldiers in several HQs and encampments (altho' for some Western critics, yes, *The Battle At Lake Changjin did* portray the Yanks in a negative light – as war-mongers, with MacArthur angling for using atomic weaponry). But the Americans are definitely the enemy here, and some observers regarded *The Battle At Lake Changjin* as reflecting the uneasy political relationship between China and the U.S.A. of the period when the film was produced (it has been an uneasy relation for decades).

ᶓ

Tsui Hark's impact on *The Battle At Lake Changjin* can be discerned in the many visual effects sequences, including the many aerial scenes (Tsui loves any chance to put cameras in the sky); in the rapid cutting style (a staple of all of Tsui's cinema); in the grand, mobile crane shots (seen throughout Tsui's later work); and of course in the subject matter – a Chinese story about Chinese people defending China and set in China.

Although Tsui Hark shares the directing credits with two other directors (Chen Kaige and Dante Lam) and three co-directors (Huang Jianxin, Haiqiang Ning and Ju-chun Park)), there are indications that Tsui had substantial input in the production of *The Battle At Lake Changjin*. For example, the presence of many of Tsui's former collaborators (some going back to the 1980s in Hong Kong – such as stunt overlords Bruce Law Lai-yun and Stephen Tung-wai), plus his ex-wife Nanshun Shi as producer, and his regular editor, Marco Mak Chi-sin, and that he shares a producer credit and an editing credit (along with two other editors, Le Danshi and He Yong-yi, plus editing supervisor, Marco Mak).

However, *The Battle At Lake Changjin* is clearly, like any big movie production, a massive team effort. It's not an *auteur* work at all. Most of the time was spent on organization, as is obvious from any of the big

10 And not only Vietnam War movies.

scenes, which required months of planning by large groups of people, and weeks to set up at the location (all of the important work for *The Battle At Lake Changjin* would've been accomplished during pre-production. Or as Jean-Luc Godard put it, everything is already done before the cameras roll).

&

Visual effects are everywhere in this very expensive Chinese movie: among the vendors supplying the many vfx shots were: D.N.E.G., Double Negative, Scanline V.F.X., Tau Films, Terminal F.X. and Asymmetric V.F.X. Dennis Leung was the vfx supervisor. Many of the locations were enhanced with vfx additions, much of the aerial photography used visual effects, and many of the stunts were altered in post-production.

Sometimes the visual effects became a little fussy and self-conscious: in the amazing dry river bed sequence, for instance, where the Chinese troops are pinned down by a couple of U.S. fighter planes, the camera is skittering about in an attempt to generate even more excitement (it's an effort to capture everything in a single long take. It was a 4,000 frame shot that stitched together 15 different plates). It's over-done, a mite clumsy, and actually dramatically unnecessary (but then, *The Battle At Lake Changjin* is not a movie that holds back!). There are also some video game-style sequences which seem out of place in a movie which's very traditional in its storytelling, despite the fancy technology used in the production (such as when an officer is killed in the finale, and the camera floats around him suspended in mid-air, *Matrix*-style, or when exposition is parcelled out over frozen, computer game-ish imagery).

&

*The Battle At Lake Changjin* is staged in the gritty, gory manner of war films of recent times, where *Saving Private Ryan* (1998) is the template. The wastage of wartime is emphasized throughout the piece, and is always countered by the assertion that the Chinese military must defend themselves from their enemies. No matter what it costs in terms of lives, the People's Republic of China must not allow the foreign devils into their much-loved country.

If you are feeling a little vulnerable or queasy, don't watch the two *Battle At Lake Changjin* pictures. You might be thrilled by the action, and your spirits might soar at the scenes of brave, hearty Asians uniting in the common cause of fighting off the invading demons, but it's also a film littered with corpses, with gruesome gore, and with blood a-plenty. (So it's one of those war movies that's ambiguous – it wants to glorify the Chinese nation but does so by emphasizing chaos and brutality).

In fact, parts of the two *Lake Changjin* movies are disgusting in how they emphasize the gore and suffering when they portray what humans do to each other in wartime. But then, Asian cinema has often exaggerated gore and horror to an alarming degree.

Don't bother looking for feminist or feminine material in *The Battle At Lake Changjin,* either. Like most war movies of this type, it's extremely manly, malesy, masculinist. *The Battle At Lake Changjin* presents China in

1950 as a thoroughly patriarchal society. Women are only glimpsed on the sidelines – like the pretty girl at the railroad station seen by Wu junior as the train leaves when the soldiers move out, or a soldier's wife in a brief flashback in the finale of the second film).

*The Battle At Lake Changjin* is a war movie as an action-adventure movie, and it's filled with incredible scenes of mayhem: the Yanks attacking Chinese ports and ships at sea; a bombing raid on a train; fighters strafing soldiers on the ground; an astonishing battle in a village; and the extensive, stops-all-out finale.

Thus, the two Wu brothers embody two familiar oppositions of combat movie themes: Wu junior imagines wartime as pure adventure and opportunity. He is innocence, youth, gullibility. Wu senior has already been in the conflict, and sees it as necessary but horrific. He would rather be doing anything but this. But by the end of the 2nd installment, Wu junior has seen all he could ever want of war and catastrophe.

There isn't any subtext in *The Battle At Lake Changjin* – it's all in the top two layers of the movie: the first is the fight against the foreign devils to protect the sacred soil of 'Our Land', the People's Republic of China. The second is family – which is an extension of the patriotism of 'Our Land'.

Comedy is inserted in *The Battle At Lake Changjin* from time to time to lighten the gloom, gore and chaos. Much of it revolves around the character of the very young Wu Wanli, played by Jackson Lee. He is the butt of joshing in Seventh Company, the naïve and vulnerable rookie who is teased. But that relationship also provides exposition, as the older soldiers explain to Wu junior (once the joking has finished) about parts of the plot and the political background.

꙳

*The Battle At Lake Changjin* rapidly introduces the historical context following a prologue depicting a familiar motif: the Return of the Soldier (where Wu Qianli (Jacky Wu Jing) goes back home, meets his family, and delivers the ashes of his brother, Wu Baili. The scenes are echoed at the end of the 2nd movie, when Wu Wanli brings home his brother Qianli in an urn).

The home-coming scenes establish the all-important issues of family and home-life – i.e., this is what is at stake in *The Battle At Lake Changjin,* and what the Chinese forces in the People's Volunteer Army are fighting to protect. A later scene, on a railroad train carrying the soldiers to the front-lines, offers another angle on the issue of What Are We Fighting For? – in the middle of an argument, the soldiers stop suddenly when they see a beautiful vista of the Great Wall of China at sunset. It's an image of China the Great, China the Mythical Land of Ours.

Tsui Hark makes his style of epic filmmaking known following the prologue with a colossal, million-dollar visual effects shot: it's pure Tsui Hark, a sweeping, continuous shot which takes in fighter planes, destroyers, bombing raids, missile launches, and several kitchen sinks. Everything and then some is loaded into the shot. It puts the money upfront, and announces to the audience that this movie is going to be Big – Very, *Very* Big! And like so many of Tsui's establishing shots, it occurs over water with a simulated, helicopter-style aerial view.

The exposition in *The Battle At Lake Changjin* occurs with a series of high-level political meetings halfway thru act one, with Chairman Mao Zedong prominent. Played by Tang Guoqiang, Mao is portrayed as a cool, shrewd operator, keen to advance China's place in the world, but careful to carry his team along with him. (*The Battle At Lake Changjin* cuts back to Mao in Peking once or twice later on, to remind us of the wider issues at stake). We also meet the 9th Company officers who gather at Chengfang-dong to orchestrate the operations (we return here many times).

*The Battle At Lake Changjin* thus portrays the conflict between China and the U.S.A. on several levels, as is customary in the war genre. One of the models structurally is of course *War and Peace*. So the character of Wu Qianli is a guy in the thick of things, commanding a unit of young soldiers, the 7th Company (including his kid brother Wu Wanli (Jackson Lee), who tagged along without him knowing). Wu is our audience identification figure, an everyman from a humble background. When the 2021 movie resets itself, or moves into an aftermath sequence, we always return to Wu, along with his brother Wanli (so *The Battle At Lake Changjin* is also yet another brotherhood format in narrative terms).

Jacky Wu Jing is an officer, so he has some impact on the story, but he's really there in many scenes to provide a focus (notice how the movie includes Wu's point-of-view throughout, so we are always witnessing events through his eyes (just like Pierre Bezukhov in *War and Peace*). Sometimes the camera moves in close to Wu, and circles around him, to look over his shoulder, as if we are right next to him, seeing events from his perspective).

ઢ.

Some of the action set-pieces in *The Battle At Lake Changjin* are as accomplished as any movie about war. The prolonged skirmish in the rural village in the mountains, in act three of *Lake Changjin,* is a masterpiece of really intense armed combat, with everything thrown into the mix – tanks, jeeps, grenades, rifles, machine guns, pistols, knives, snipers, fire (and full-body burns), and plenty of explosions. The use of point-of-view shots is remarkable, placing the audience right into the thick of things. Every technique of cinema is deployed to generate a visceral sense of chaotic combat.

The thrilling tank vs. tank battles, the sniper vs. sniper duels, and the images of soldiers running amok are surpassed by the highly over-cooked ruckus in a building between a few Chinese soldiers and a few American soldiers. It's one of those close combat sequences which Chinese cinema is more skilled at delivering than any other cinema. The physicality of bodies entangled in a bitter fight to the death is brilliantly achieved in Chinese films. The scene is played at maximum hysteria, as Wu Qianli yells at his brother Wanli to stab the Yank behind him who's got his arms pinned. Little Wanli eventually does kill a guy – his first – in this horrific baptism by fire and blood.

The village *melée* closes with a tank duel, as the Chinese troops (led by the hero Wu Qianli, of course) take on an enemy tank. The scene where both tanks careen down a hill, unable to brake, while piling thru (and smashing up) houses recalls the famous sequence in the classic Jackie Chan movie *Police Story* (1985).

※

The 2021 movie depicts the difference in technological resources: the Chinese troops have no air support whatsoever,[11] while the Yanks have many forms of aircraft, including early helicopters (this would be replayed in the Vietnam War, and movies about the Vietnam conflict sometimes drew attention to the difference in technology between the two sides). So the Chinese hope to win by swamping the enemy with much greater numbers.

The finale of *The Battle At Lake Changjin* is going to be even bigger than everything we've already seen, as usual in the action-adventure genre. It starts not in act 6 (the movie is 6 acts long), but in act 5. (i.e., the action finale takes up most of acts 5 and 6). To set out the terrain of Lake Changjin (a.k.a. Chosin Reservoir), there are many shots flying over the mountains and the (frozen) lake (these are combinations of live-action plates and visual effects).

The build-up to the finale of *The Battle At Lake Changjin* contrasts the North American forces eating a hearty Thanksgiving dinner with all the trimmings and the Chinese soldiers holed up in the mountains, shivering with the minus 40° C cold, with only tiny potatoes frozen solid to eat. *The Battle At Lake Changjin* certainly sells the feeling of being very, very cold (even tho' many scenes were filmed amid fake snow in the suburbs, and in the studio, and on the backlot at Hengdian World Studios). And how the Chinese troops have to wait for hours in the mountains, in full battle gear, until they receive the 'Go' signal from the command centre at Chengfang-dong.

Much of the finale of *The Battle At Lake Changjin* comprises a gigantic assault on an American command outpost at Chosin Reservoir. The Chinese overwhelm the Yanks by sheer numbers. The action gags are astounding, combining trucks, jeeps, tanks, rocket launchers, mortars, machine guns, rifles, pistols, flares, explosives, oil drums, and anything else the filmmakers can get hold of. (The movie restrains itself from including some dragons, some flying swordsmen and of course a golden Buddha).

So *The Battle At Lake Changjin* closes with the Chinese troops forcing the Yankie *gweilos* to retreat and go home – the 2021 movie ends with a preposterous scene of thousands of Chinese soldiers charging down to the beaches carrying red flags and cheering at the departing ships of the Americans as they head back to the New World. (This was used as the ending to the second movie).

*The Battle At Lake Changjin* is too long. Several scenes are

11 In a scene, the soldiers hope one day they'll have similar technology.

redundant, repeating material seen elsewhere. There are unnecessary returns to the American command centre, for example, and there are too many scenes of the Chinese troops regrouping. An aerial bombardment of a forward command post of the Chinese Army is not needed.

Technically brilliant and very moving in parts, the two *Battle At Lake Changjin* movies are vivid reminders that the human species is completely insane and very dangerous. So the movies are pretty depressing.[12]

12 The body count in the two *Battle At Lake Changjin* movies is enormous.

# 39

# *THE BATTLE AT LAKE CHANGJIN 2: WATER GATE BRIDGE*

## *Changjin Hu Zhi Shuimen Qiao*

The sequel to *The Battle At Lake Changjin* was entitled *The Battle At Lake Changjin 2: Water Gate Bridge* (= *Changjin Hu Zhi Shuimen Qiao*, 2022). It appeared a year later, with much of the same cast and crew. Huang Jianxin and Lan Xiaolong scripted again. Released: Feb 1, 2022. 149 mins.

Running to two-and-a-half hours, *The Battle At Lake Changjin 2: Water Gate Bridge* was shorter (though still a prestige movie length). And it was another mega-hit at the box office in the People's Republic of China, taking a gross of 4.07007 billion Yuan. (Altho' it's the opposite of the usual comedy fare of a New Year's release).

*The Battle At Lake Changjin 2: Water Gate Bridge* continues the nationalistic celebration of all things Chinese (dubbed propaganda in the West). In a scene halfway thru the movie, as the troops prepare their assault on the Sumun Bridge, which's heavily defend by the Yanks, they stand in a group looking at their Motherland in the distance. A rising sun shines brightly behind snow-capped mountains and they all salute and chant:

Long live the People's Republic of China!

The film holds back from super-imposing an image of Lord Buddha smiling down on them from the heavens (it has the sun instead – just as good. No, better. If ever there was a godly, divine, mystical entity, it's our nearest star).

ﻌ

*Water Gate Bridge* doesn't hang about: following the numerous film company logos, and a brief summary of the Story So Far (as depicted in the first *Lake Changjin* movie), and the introduction of a new character

(Commander Yang – Geng Le), we are straight into another series of massive battles. So the Chinese and the Yanks are butting heads (and machine guns, and tanks, and grenades, and bazookas, and planes) immediately. It's as if there wasn't a year's break between the release of the two films. Or it's as if the fight has been continuing in the interim – while we've been snacking on pizza or checking our e-mails, Wu Qianli, his kid brother Wanli and his chums in the 7th Company of the People's Volunteer Army have been fighting the North Americans in the snowy wastes of mountainous Korea.

Thus, the two movies tell a continuous story, without a time shift between film one and film two. Typically, film sequels move on some time (such as the *Star Wars* series), or they tell a different story but in a similar time frame (such as the *James Bond* series). Instead, *The Battle At Lake Changjin 2: Water Gate Bridge* carries on directly from the end of *The Battle At Lake Changjin,* with our Chinese heroes nearly on top of the American air-base at Hagaru-ri (where the 1st Marine Division are based).

First, there's another bombing raid by the North Americans from on high (by U.S. Navy Corsairs), demolishing and scattering the troops of the 7th Company and their comrades in the People's Volunteer Army (who're trudging thru deep snow on their way towards the American airfield at Hagaru-ri. They are looking battered and exhausted, but their fighting spirit seems undaunted).

Following this scene, a run of enormous action sequences front-loads *The Battle At Lake Changjin 2: Water Gate Bridge*. This time, it's an assault on the airfield we saw at the end of the first *Lake Changjin* picture. Once again, the Chinese troops overwhelm the defending Americans with sheer numbers and their determination to never give up. They are not going to rest until the demon invaders have been expelled from the Fatherland of China.

Regrouping and aftermath scenes follow, with the discussions on how to take the Sumun Bridge from the enemy. Both sides hunker down over maps – the Chinese are holed up in a freezing cave, huddled over a scrap of paper with a pencil drawing on it. By contrast, the American HQ at the Bridge features a flashy model of the area, hot coffee and even a Christmas tree. There is a touching memorial to a fallen officer. The Wu brothers converse and share a moment (the score is of course teardrop piano).

The deadly cat-and-mouse games begin with skirmishes around the perimeter of the Sumun Bridge (at night, with searchlights hunting down Chinese soldiers). This is stirring, *Boy's Own* stuff, with both sides trying to out-manœuvre the other (the Yanks have laid a trap for the Chinese, for example, hiding away and waiting for them to get closer).

The filmmaking employs many big, high, sweeping camera moves, to explain the geography of the scene to the audience: the camera zooms up from the Sumun Bridge then back down again to show how far Wu Qianli and the 7th Company lads are from the pipes (in the crags above the Bridge), or swooping around the American gun emplacements on tall, wooden towers and down to another squad of Chinese soldiers waiting for the signal to attack.

When the Chinese sappers blow a hole in one of the pipes, they're able to infiltrate the enemy stronghold rapidly, running inside the pipe to the pump room. The action is filled with intricate bits of business involving grenades, machine guns, bazookas, sniper rifles and revolvers. Wu Qianli gets his own action sequence – throwing himself down the mountain (leaping from place to place), and taking the enemy's headquarters single-handed.

Sections of *The Battle At Lake Changjin 2: Water Gate Bridge* are unnecessarily gory to tell the story or to show that war is an ugly, dehumanizing experience – guys dying underneath tanks, for example, or bodies being blown to bits, or engulfed in flames. It's part of the 'war is hell' kind of war movie, of course, but it's over-done. Maybe it's unsettling because the two movies are so long – and it takes *two movies* to tell this story (which would usually be covered in a single installment).

The soldiers we've spent a little time with are expiring all over the place in *The Battle At Lake Changjin 2: Water Gate Bridge*, so there are fewer and fewer recognizable faces in the cast who survive.

In fact, after the final assault on the Sumun Bridge by the Chinese troops, everybody is killed, even Wu Qianli, with only his brother Wu Wanli somehow surviving, against all the odds (Wu junior *has* to survive – the demise of both brothers would be too much, and this sort of patriotic war film won't go there). So the form of *The Battle At Lake Changjin 2* is also the familiar, Chinese tragedy, very popular in China, when everybody expires at the end.

Desperation is the order of the day now: the remnants of 7th Company of the People's Volunteer Army have precious few resources or ammo (they count out their remaining ammunition in the snow), and no reinforcements. Meanwhile, the Yanks have been fully re-supplied (though their spirits are low. Nobody, it seems, wants to be fighting this war).

Thus, the ending of *The Battle At Lake Changjin 2: Water Gate Bridge* depicts the familiar scenario in the war movie genre of the few against the many, the tiny army facing overwhelming odds. The survivors in 7th Company launch themselves against the Americans on the Bridge (and when they've run out of bullets, they still attack, and are mown down).

Wu Qianli makes a final assault on the Sumun Bridge, armed with only his trusty revolver and a tank shell snaffled from the enemy. It becomes a heroic sacrifice, and Wu is killed (while also managing to blow up the shell). He dies in his brother's arms, a poignant and moving death, as the brothers look at each other (dialogue is left aside, making the moment even more bittersweet).

The *dénouement* scenes of *The Battle At Lake Changjin 2: Water Gate Bridge* are lengthy and milked for every ounce of emotion (for example, there are several montages of flashbacks thru the film and from the first film. Wu Qianli's death also inaugurates another series of touching flashbacks). The 2022 film visits many of the key personnel among the secondary characters (such as General Douglas MacArthur, President Truman in the White House, the U.S. officers in Korea, and the Chinese generals who oversaw the operation). There are scenes at graveyards where officers pay their respects to the fallen, when half of China seems turned into a burial ground.

But the emphasis at the end of *The Battle At Lake Changjin 2: Water Gate Bridge* is on Wu Wanli taking his brother's ashes back home. His brother Qianli materializes for a final bow, to say farewell to his younger brother – and to the audience; after all, Jacky Wu Jing has been the star of this show (even tho' it's very much an ensemble piece). The end credits feature another montage of memorable moments from the movie (while a ballad  plays). And altho' the *Lake Changjin* films don't include images of Lord Buddha, they do feature a suitable stand-in in several scenes: a golden sunset.

&

西遊記2
妖怪の逆襲

Journey To the West 2 (2017).

西遊2
大年初一

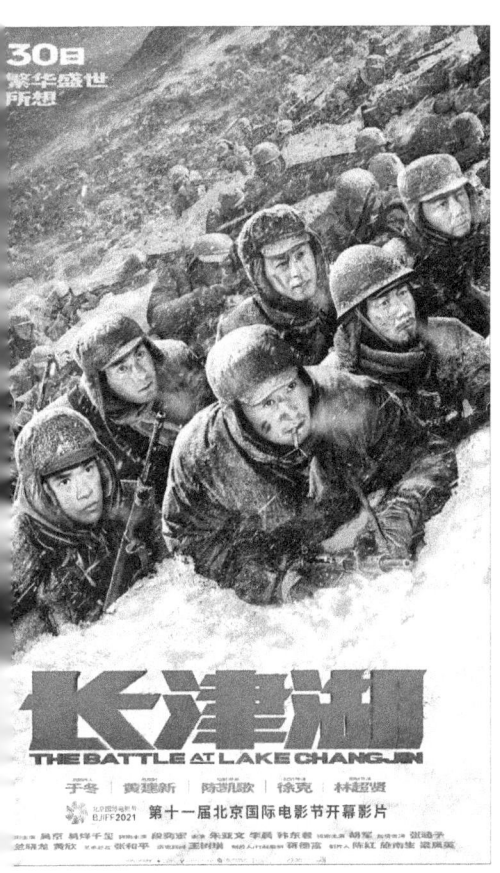

The Battle At Lake Changjin (2021), left and above.

The sequel (2022), below.

# 40

# OTHER MOVIES DIRECTED BY TSUI HARK

*WORKING CLASS*

*Working Class* (1985) was about three guys in a noodle factory (played by Sammo Hung, Teddy Robin Kwan and Sam Hui) who clash with the management. Also appearing were Joey Wong Cho-Yin, Anglie Leung Wan-Yui, Kwan Hoi-San, and Nam Hung. Cham Gan-Kuen wrote the script, Yiu Yau-Hung was art dir., David Wu Tai-wai was editor, Joe Chan Jun-Git was DP, Mau Sau-Nung was costume des., and Teddy Robin Kwan composed the score. Released Aug 10, 1985. 94 mins.

*THE BANQUET*

*The Banquet* (*Hao Men Ye Yan*, 1991) is one of several benefit movies that Tsui Hark has been involved with – this one was made to help the victims of flooding in Mainland China in 1991. Tsui is one of several directors in *The Banquet*. Ng See-yuen and John Sham produced. Written by Choi Ting-ting.

The cast included pretty much everybody in Hong Kong movies, such as Eric Tsang, Maggie Cheung, Jacky Cheung, Anita Mui, Gong Li, Michael Hui, Andy Lau, Sammo Hung, Aaron Kwok, Leon Lai, Leslie Cheung, etc. Released Nov 30, 1991. 95 mins.

*THE CHINESE FEAST*

*The Chinese Feast* (*Gam Yuk Moon Tong*, 1995) was a foodie comedy produced by Tsui Hark, Raymond Wong Bak-ming and Li Ning, written by Tsui and Philip Cheng, and starring Leslie Cheung, Anita Yuen, Kenny Bee, Law Kar-ying, Vincent Zhao, Xiong Xin-xin and Lau Shun (all Tsui Hark regulars). Jan 28, 1995. 106 mins.

Cooking, restaurants, competitions, rival chefs and mobsters, with the Qing Han Feast (of 108 dishes) as the focal point, *The Chinese Feast* is another Tsuian pæan to traditional Chinese culture (it's set in Beijing). As Tsui recalled, 'it's fun making a movie about food. We had four or five different chefs on the set cooking all the time' (LM, 121).

A big hit for Tsui Hark, *The Chinese Feast* was a script that had been on the shelf for several years (back from the days of *Once Upon a Time In China*) – it was written by Ng Man-fai, Che Chung-taai and Tsui. In fact, according to Tsui, Yuen Biao had stolen the idea after Tsui had told Biao the story (Biao & co. made *Shogun and Little Kitchen*). So Tsui halted production on *The Chinese Feast*; but when Tsui heard that *Eat, Drink, Man, Woman* was being produced, he put the film aside again.

*TRISTAR*

*Tristar* (1996, *Daai Saam Yuen* in Cantonese = *Big Three Round*) was produced by Mandarin Films, Cinema City and Film Workshop, co-written by Tsui Hark, Che Chung-taai and Tiu Wan, produced by Tsui and Raymond Wong, with art direction by Bill Liu, photography by Arthur Wong and Chris Doyle, editing by David Wu Tai-wai, Tony Chow and Chan Kei-hop, action direction by Xiong Xin-xin, music by Lowell Lo, and starred Anita Yuen, Leslie Cheung, Lau Ching-wan, Moses Chan, Sunny Chan, Elvina Kong, Raymond Wong, and Xiong Xin-xin. Released: Feb 15, 1996. 107 mins.

*TriStar* is a sort of follow-up to *The Chinese Feast*. In this comedy, Leslie Cheung plays a Catholic priest, Father Zhong, with Anita Yuen as a hooker, Baiban.

Altho' *TriStar* was a hit in Hong Kong (HK $25m gross), Tsui Hark commented that *TriStar* 'didn't come out as what I wanted', and that he hadn't handled the material or the characters right (LM, 208). But he had always wanted to tackle religion as a topic.

## CATCHING MONKEY 3-D

*Catching Monkey 3-D* (*Zhua Hou,* 2013) was prod. by Bona Film Group, pod. by Nansun Shi Nan-sheng, wr. and dir. by Tsui Hark.

In the cast were: Charlie Yeung Choi-nei, Yu Nan, Li Guang-jie, Liang Jing, Wen Zhang, Daniel Chan Hiu-tung, Li Guang Jie and Liang Jing


## THE LEGEND OF THE CONDOR HEROES: THE GREAT HERO

Tsui Hark's next movie as director after the enormous *Battle of Lake Changjin* pictures was *The Legend of the Condor Heroes: The Great Hero* (*She diao ying xiong zhuan: Xia zhi da zhe,* 2025), produced by H.G. Entertainment/ Union Pictures/ Film Workshop/ Lian Ray Pictures/ China Filim Co., produced by Fu Ruoging, starring Zhan Xiao,[1] Dafei Zhuang, Tony Ka-fai Leung, Wenxin Zhang and Ada Choi, and released at Chinese New Year in 2025. The production was based at Xanadu Studios in Inner Mongolia. Tsui scripted the movie from the fiction of Louis Cha (Jin Yong), which has been adapted often in Chinese TV and movies (and Tsui has taken on Cha's novels several times – such as *The Swordsman 2*).

---

[1] The role of Yang Guo has been played in previous adaptations by Andy Lau, Louis Koo, Richie Ren, Chen Xiao, Huang Xiaoming and Christopher Lee.

The Banquet (1991).
The Chinese Feast (1995).
Tristar (1996).

PART THREE

TSUI HARK

MOVIES AS PRODUCER

# THE *BETTER TOMORROW* MOVIES

# 1

# *A BETTER TOMORROW*

## *Jing Hung Bun Sik*

There are three official *Better Tomorrow* movies:

*A Better Tomorrow* (1986)
*A Better Tomorrow* (1987)
*A Better Tomorrow: Love and Death In Saigon* (1989)

The third *Better Tomorrow* picture is discussed in the chapter on Tsui Hark's movies as director (there are 'official' and 'unofficial' remakes, too – see below). Let's look at the *A Better Tomorrow* movie first:

*A Better Tomorrow* (1986) was directed by John Woo, co-produced by Tsui Hark, and starred Chow Yun-fat, Ti Lung and Leslie Cheung. Need we say more?! What a combination! Woo + Tsui + Chow + Cheung + Lung! Can't lose, can it? It doesn't!

*A Better Tomorrow* (*Jing Hung Bun Sik* in Cantonese, *Ying Xiong Ben Se* in Mandarin = *Heroic Character*, a.k.a. *The Color of a Hero, Gangland Boss* and *True Colors of a Hero*), was produced by Tsui Hark and Wan Ka Man for Cinema City and Film Workshop; written by Chan Hing-ka, Chan Shuk-dut, Leung Suk-wah and John Woo; Wong Wing-hang was DP; Lui Chi-leung was prod. des.; Bennie Lui was art director; Gam-Jan Yeung was costume des.; Blacky Ko and Stephen Tung were action directors; Joseph Koo composed the music; and Ma Gam and David Wu Tai-wai were editors. It was a big hit for all involved – the number one movie of 1986, with a gross in Canton of HK $34.6 million (so a sequel was inevitable).[1] Released: Aug 2, 1986. 95 mins.

[1] The *Better Tomorrow* movies inevitably inspired cash-ins – such as *Return To Better Tomorrow* (Wong Jing, 1994), *Hero of Tomorrow* (1988) and *City War* (1989).

Tsui Hark had invited John Woo to Hong Kong in 1985, to make *A Better Tomorrow* (he had been appearing in *Run Tiger Run*, helmed by Woo, in Taiwan; at the same time, Tsui was preparing *A Chinese Ghost Story*). According to Tsui's wife Nansun Shi Nan-sheng, Tsui and Woo 'would go drinking, and tell stories, and pour their hearts out'. Woo said of *A Better Tomorrow* that 'a lot of the emotion behind the film reflects my friendship with Hark'.[2]

John Woo said he was feeling down because he was making comedies and he wanted to make character-driven dramas. Tsui Hark, Woo said, encouraged him to return from Taiwan to Hong Kong to direct *A Better Tomorrow*: 'he produced and helped me to write it'.

Karl Maka recalled meeting John Woo and Tsui Hark to discuss *A Better Tomorrow* at Cinema City – they told him the story: 'I never want to hear the story!' Instead, Maka asked who was in it, then how long it would be, then how much it would cost. When they told him, he said OK.

This is the movie that really launched the mature John Woo gunplay style, where guns[3] replace swords in stories of male brotherhoods, gangsters, frantic (yet balletic) action scenes, a contemporary Hong Kong setting, and of course all couched within the thriller and crime genre. Brotherhood or the 'essence of honour' is called *yi* in Chinese – a system of honour, justice and fraternity. *Yiqi* is a system of personal loyalty. *A Better Tomorrow* launched a new cycle of 'hero' or *yi* films. (Critics who drool over Woo's filmic gunplay typically discuss this movie and the others up to *Bullet In the Head* – the Woo Golden Age thus runs from 1986 to 1992, and comprises the two *Better Tomorrow* flicks, *The Killer, Hard-Boiled Egg* and *Bullet In the Shed* – *Just Heroes* (1989) and *Once a Thief* (1991) aren't usually included).

*A Better Tomorrow* has pretty much every element we've come to expect (and enjoy) from a John Woo-directed movie: men being men (*real men*, men who are brave and noble, but with soft hearts), and all of the aspects of brotherhood, male bonding, and patriarchal power: loyalty, determination, bravery, integrity and of course generous doses of vanity and self-absorption (narcissism being a key element in the gangster genre), and the undercurrent of homosocialiity (and maybe homoeroticism, denied by Woo, but quite definitely part of the mix). The movie revived the career of Ti Lung, and made stars out of Leslie Cheung and Chow Yun-fat.

Stefan Hammond and Mike Wilkins described a John Woo picture as

packed full of rapid mood swings. Good-natured horseplay gives way to brooding nostalgia, followed by tear-drenched melodrama – and then a big fight scene. (38)

The story comes from *True Colors of a Hero* (a.k.a. *Story of a Discharged Prisoner*), a movie of 1967 directed by Lung Kong. So *A Better Tomorrow* is a remake (which follows *Story of a Discharged Prisoner*

---

2 Woo has remarked that he drew on his friendship with Tsui Hark in the development of the relationships in *A Better Tomorrow*.
3 Woo maintains that he's not a violent individual, and isn't a gun nut.

closely). *The Brothers* (1979) was also an inspiration, and *The Brothers* was in turn a remake of *Deewaar*, a 1975 Bollywood film. John Woo recalled that he had wanted to make a male version of *True Colors of a Hero* (no surprise there!), and Tsui Hark wanted to do a female version of it (again, no surprises!).

> I remember clearly wanting Michelle Yeoh playing the Chow Yun-fat
> role [recalled Tsui Hark]. Rather than examine the relationship
> between a group of men, I wanted the relationship to be between
> women. From very early on, I wanted to do movies without any guys.

And Tsui did just that with *Peking Opera Blues,* and in *his* version of *A Better Tomorrow*, the second sequel, *A Better Tomorrow 3: Love and Death In Saigon.*

The story of *A Better Tomorrow* is cretinously dumb – and the filmmakers know it! Hell, this is a Hong Kong action movie, after all! You've got gangsters who produce fake money,[4] and sell it. You've got a duo of gangsters (Mark Gor[5] and Ho Sung) – who're already veterans of the crime game – who operate with the self-satisfied cool of hardened samurai. You've got the kid brother (Kit) who's training to be a police inspector, who doesn't know about his brother Ho's nefarious deeds (both Kit and Jackie are the most 'ordinary' or 'regular' types among the characters).

The remakes of *A Better Tomorrow* included:

• *Diamond Kingdom* (1988), which drew heavily on *A Better Tomorrow.*

• *Aatish: Feel the Fire* (Sanjay Gupta, 1994) was an unofficial remake.

• *A Better Tomorrow* (Song Hae-sung, 2010) was an official remake, with John Woo acting as executive producer. It was produced by C.J. Entertainment/ Formula Comics Entertainment/ Fingerpint Pictures/ Michigan Venture Capital/ Lion Rock Prods./ C.J. E. & M. Film Financing/ Fortune Star Media/ Frontier Works Comic/ Zuzac. Released: Sept 16, 2010.

• *A Better Tomorrow 2018* (Ding Sheng, 2018) was produced by Film Workshop/ Beijing Jingxi Culture & Tourism/ CoolBoy Culture Communication/ United Entertainment/ Beijing Skywheel Entertainment/ Beijing Sparkle Roll Corporation/ Chongqing Shuimu Chengde Capital. Released: Jan 18, 2018.

In *A Better Tomorrow*, the 28 year-old Chow Yun-fat [6] (b. May 18, 1955, Hong Kong) cuts one of the coolest of super-cool gangsters in contemporary cinema. You haven't seen *anyone* look cooler than Chow. He really is a gorgeous-to-look-at creature in *A Better Tomorrow*: tall, handsome, clad neatly in suits, with a long, black coat,[7] always lighting a cigarette (*always* with the cigarettes! – and with a matchstick in his mouth). Chow has 'superstar' written all over him, and it's no wonder that

---

4 Counterfeiting is the criminal background of the sequel, too.
5 Mark Gor means 'Brother Mark'.
6 Chow Yun-fat in Cantonese is Jau Yun-faat and Zhou Runfa in Mandarin.
7 Which became fashionable – the 'Mark Coat'. Costume designer Gam-Jan Yeung should be credited, too.

he has been one of the biggest stars in Asia for decades, and why Chinese audiences just *adore* him! (Ironically, the powerful Hong Kong film distributors weren't sure about the casting of Chow – according to Tsui Hark, 'everyone was against it. *Everybody* was against it' (LM, 64); but after Chow became a celebrity, not long after *A Better Tomorrow,* they would beg to have him star in a movie).

Forget the North American equivalents – Robert de Niro, Al Pacino, Mickey Rourke, Jason Stratham, etc. Are you nuts?! Chow Yun-fat effortlessly out-cools them all! The influences, according to John Woo, include Alain Delon in *Le Samouraï* (a movie and a character that's influenced quite a few filmmakers – Delon should really charge royalties!), and Ken Takakura in his many Japanese thrillers. (*The Yakuza* (Sydney Pollack, 1975) might be another inspiration).

The narcissism of gangsters in cinema has often been remarked upon, and it has always been a part of the gangster movie. Gangsters have always been well-dressed, and have often admired themselves in mirrors. Chas in *Performance* (Donald Cammell and Nic Roeg, 1970) is supremely narcissistic, and confronts himself in mirrors more than most movie characters. Masculine narcissism was a fetishized spectacle in 1995's *Casino*, most obviously in Robert de Niro's character, who had 52 costume changes. Part of director Martin Scorsese's ritual each morning was choosing the suit, shirt, tie and jewellery with the costume designers (Rita Ryack and John Dunn) for each day's shoot.[8]

Chow Yun-fat's turn as Mark 'is so deeply impassioned that actors as dependable as Ti Lung and Leslie Cheung nearly cease to exist in scenes with him', noted Lisa Morton (61).

Chow Yun-fat's mobster Mark Gor is aided by a young Leslie Cheung (playing Tse-Ho Sung's kid brother Kit), Ti Lung (as Tse-Ho, Mark's accomplice), Tien Feng plays the father, Sung, Waise Lee is the rival boss, Shing, and Emily Chu is the romantic interest, Jackie.

Chow Yun-fat is an impossible-to-compete-with force in *A Better Tomorrow*, but after the first act, he does disappears for long stretches, so we're spending time with either Ti Lung or Leslie Cheung. Thirty years-old at the time (but looking much younger, though – ironically, Cheung is older than Chow Yun-fat!), Cheung is sensational as the desperately ambitious Kit, a guy who simply hasn't got quite what it takes to be the super-cop he so wants to be. So it's ambition plus self-doubt, honour and justice conflicting with family and personal issues.

Ti Lung, meanwhile, was a Shaw Brothers veteran, having appeared in numerous Shaws productions, often paired with David Chiang, and often directed by Chang Cheh (Zhang Zhe), including playing the lead role in many *kung fu,* swordplay and action movies (such *Shaolin Temple* and *Duel of Fists*, both helmed by Chang Cheh, John Woo's mentor. Woo dedicated *Just Heroes* (1989) to Chang). Lung in *A Better Tomorrow* thus needs no introduction for a Hong Kong audience – they've already seen him in, well, everything. Lung's role as the elder brother who's trying to go

---

8 "Interview", *Sight & Sound,* 6, 1, Jan, 1996, 10.

straight chimes with Lung's acting career (he became an alcoholic, and retired from acting in 1994, after appearing in *Drunken Master 2*).

The central psychological and emotional tension in *A Better Tomorrow* is not between the hero and villain, or the hero and his girl, or the hero and his boss (tho' there are elements of that), but between Kit and his brother Ho. In the latter part of the second act of *A Better Tomorrow* (which meanders somewhat, and comes over as awkward soap opera), Kit is stressing mightily over his brother Ho. What do you do when your brother is a criminal? Or when he's a criminal trying to go straight?

Folks, we've been here many times before! *A Better Tomorrow* sort of gets away with these old *policier* genre chestnuts largely thru the force of Leslie Cheung's and Ti Ling's performances. This is the heart of *A Better Tomorrow* – literally – these scenes between Kit and Ho, between Ho Sung and Mark, and then between all three of them in the final shoot-out.

It's always struck me as odd that when a former criminal hopes to go straight, the mob won't let him! And they expend a lot of time and effort in persuading or coercing or beating up the guy to make him stay or re-join their syndicate! Days and weeks (and numerous henchmen) are wasted in trying to force the ex-con to come back to the fold. It's bizarre: wouldn't that time and effort be better spent running the business? Like, *err*, making money? Or, if you *really* need a new employee for the mob, train up some guys to take the ex-con's place!

Meanwhile, Waise Lee plays Shing, the gangster on the make: he's the ambitious Prince out of Greek tragedy who'll murder his boss to remove any obstacles in his path. At the beginning of *A Better Tomorrow*, Shing's over-shadowed by Mark Gor and Ho Sung; after the botched job and the assassination in the restaurant, Shing moves into the ascendant. Yet altho' he seems to be a character who's looking towards the future, eliminating people blocking his way to the top, he is also mired in the past, spending too much time and effort in trying to persuade Ho to return to the organization. (Shing is thus the villain in *A Better Tomorrow*, not the two criminals, Mark and Ho, altho' they are on the wrong side of the law. In the Woo-ian code of honour, it doesn't matter so much which side of the law you operate in, it's about how honourable, loyal and chivalrous you are). *A Better Tomorrow* was not a gangster movie, Woo insisted: 'it's a film about chivalry, about honour, but set in the modern world'. *Last Hurrah For Chivalry* was a sort of dry run (or a prequel) for *A Better Tomorrow*, Woo said.

Produced by Cinema City[9] and Tsui Hark's Film Workshop, *A Better Tomorrow* was executive produced by Wan Ka Man. So what's Tsui's input in *A Better Tomorrow*? Altho' the story does seem to be John Woo-ish through and through (altho' let's remember, it was a remake of *True Colors of a Hero* – it was *not* written solely by Woo, but with three other writers), you can spot all sorts of Tsui Harkisms: the knockabout comedy of Jackie with her cello case, for instance (which smashes into everything, including

9 Cinema City was reluctant to get involved with serious dramas.

the window of a car driven by Tsui!). The sweetness of Jackie, too, and her relationship with Kit, seems particularly Tsui-ian. To the point where the Jackie-and-Kit scenes don't really fit in with the rest of the 1986 picture. (Meanwhile, Tsui has a cameo as one of the music examiners listening to Jackie give an audition in a theatre, which goes horribly wrong. Tsui adds his customary silent comedy touches. One hopes this is not an indication of how Tsui behaves during auditions, as fidgety and bored!).

Jackie is another of the girl-next-door types which Chinese action cinema likes to place next to the hero/es. That is, a kind, sweet, pretty, young woman who presents no (sexual) threat, but can be put in jeopardy sometimes (as the Princess Who Needs To Be Rescued). Jackie thus carries both the (slight) romantic subplot, and most of the comedy in *A Better Tomorrow* (unfortunately, the comedy virtually disappears after the first act. And the tenderness that Jackie tries to evoke in Kit only lasts for a while, because he's so obsessed with the police case). Jackie, in short, is sidelined, and the movie isn't interested in her (and the scenes involving Jackie are indifferently directed).

▼

*A Better Tomorrow* has a charm and even naïveté which's actually adolescent. This 1986 movie has a mental age of about 14. It's what a 14 year-old kid might think a gangster's life is like. Ho's father Sung tells him to get out of the game while he can (where have we heard that before?!). He also remarks that what Ho is doing is 'cops and robbers'.

Well, pretty much most gangster movies are nothing more sophisticated, psychologically and dramatically *and* ideologically, than 'cops and robbers'. That's all they are: you've got the guys on this side shootin' guns, and the guys on the other side shootin' guns. Civilization as capitalism performed by children dressed up as gangsters.

But that's part of the charm, I think: that, altho' the big cityscapes seem 'contemporary' and flashy, altho' the look of the gangsters, with their sharp suits, cigarettes and slick haircuts, seem super-cool, altho' the attitudes and the behaviour seem 'adult' or 'grown-up, and altho' the guns seem real and the costs of the lifestyle're severe (life or death), what these movies actually boil down to is men behaving like kids.

*A Better Tomorrow* really is, like most gangster pictures, a grown-up or adult version of a children's game. Don't let the suitcases full of money, the flashy cars, the Big City setting, the cigarettes, the guns and the fire-fights fool you. This is really a cartoon of 'cops and robbers', a comicbook version of gangsterism (the shoot-outs, choreographed and filmed so brilliantly, are pure comicbook stuff. Black Ko Shou-liang and Stephen Tung Wai were the action choreographers for *A Better Tomorrow*).

Ditto with the grand themes that run underneath John Woo's movies – brotherhood, loyalty, justice, chivalry. They *seem* to be dramatic themes given the high culture treatment, as if Woo, Tsui Hark & co. were really making *Macbeth* or *Othello* in contemporary Hong Kong instead of a schlocky crime story. No: this element too of Woo's cinema has been over-praised by film critics (meanwhile, the phrase 'heroic bloodshed', coined by Rick Baker, is only part of the mix: single words like 'brotherhood' or 'loyalty' or 'chivalry' are more accurate descriptions of the Woo-ian world. The blood and guns isn't that important in the end – that's simply the trimmings, the visuals, the gimmick, and the manifestation visually of what the films're really about – tho' of course it's what everybody (film censors included!) see when they first set eyes on it).

Altho' critics go on (and on) about the theme of brotherhood/ friendship in the cinema of John Woo, in fact it's a common theme in Hong Kong action cinema (and Chinese cinema in general). And it's all over North American cinema, of course.

The lighting and camerawork in *A Better Tomorrow* isn't the finest in John Woo's cinema (the DP was Wong Wing-hung). For example, the lighting is too much like regular television, where sets're lit too brightly (because video technology requires plenty of light, they say. And because broadcasters reckon that audiences like to see everything). Technically, *A Better Tomorrow* has the somewhat slapdash quality of many Hong Kong movies (which were produced, let's not forget, to play to the local market in the local theatres: *A Better Tomorrow* is not meant to be 'art' or prestige cinema. It's a schlocky, exploitation kind of picture).[10]

Musically, *A Better Tomorrow* sports a synth-heavy soundtrack typical of the mid-Eighties (but there's also a cut from one of Peter Gabriel's albums, featuring the familiar, slow, Fairlight synthesizer drones which Gabriel & co. employed *ad infinitum* – you can hear them in the score for *The Last Temptation of Christ*. The Western music might have been added for overseas versions – it occurs in other Cinema City/ Film Workshop movies of this period). At times the music comes across as a low-rent version of Ennio Morricone. Other times, it's as hokey and schmaltzy as a TV soap opera on its *n*-th re-run, even tho' it was composed by the veteran Joseph Koo. (*A Better Tomorrow* is, like most Hong Kong movies of the era, looped throughout. And the sound mix is patchy in parts. With many scenes played at a hysterical pitch in the latter part of the 1986 flick, it's such a pity that the looping isn't wonderful: this sort of drama really demands the audience gets the full force of the actors' performances. And that means live sound!).

▼

*A Better Tomorrow* takes a while to get going in its first act. There are the major characters to be introduced, of course (partly so that their subsequent deaths have more resonance when they occur). It's like a video game or a game of bowling: you set up the pins only so you can knock them down.

The atmosphere of smugness and vanity is important (particularly between the two gangsters, Mark Gor and Ho Sung) in the first act,[11] so that when the job in Taiwan goes crashes and burns, the consequences

10 Lisa Morton remarked that *A Better Tomorrow* looks like the work of a 1970s 'chopsocky' movie director, with the fight in the apartment like a parody of a 1970s slasher film, forced humour (the cello scene), and over-used zooms (LM, 61).
11 Chow Yun-fat plays his role with an easy-going grin, for instance. Life is good for him – until it goes very wrong (in the assassination scene, where his legs're shot).

have more impact.

There's a rather silly scene at the beginning of the second act of *A Better Tomorrow*, where three people, no less (including a police officer), are unable to deal with a lone assassin (when the heavy enters the apartment where the brothers' pa Sung is convalescing). It doesn't convince (and thus weakens the movie), and it's an example of an action scene in a Chinese action movie running on too long (some comedy would lighten the load here – but taking itself so seriously is one of the failings of John Woo's cinema). Also in this scene, poor Jackie is smashed across the face twice by the goon – it's really nasty stuff.

With the music swelling into strings, and the giant close-ups lingering over teary-eyed, staring faces, and the evocations of suppressed emotions, you might think, switching channels on TV and finding *A Better Tomorrow* playing halfway through, that you're watching a bad daytime, television soap opera. Parts of *A Better Tomorrow* play as cheesily and hokily as one of those awful Ozzie soaps.

Also, some of John Woo's cops and robbers pictures come across as some of the most homoerotic outings in recent cinema. Woo and his team bring the stirrings of homosexual desire to the surface, so that the screen is fairly teeming with repressed emotions between men. One man looks at another, in close-up, his hands on the other's shoulders.

Whew! It's hot stuff! And instead of sex we have extended action scenes (choreographed like musicals, about the gayest of cinema genres), and instead of erections we have guns (which you point at the victim, and have to re-load!), and instead of ejaculations there are exploding squibs spurting blood!

The cinema of John Woo is a veritable feast of Freudian symbolism, and barely concealed phallic desire. How big is your gun?! How many times can you shoot before you have to recharge your ammo?! Who can be stuffed with the most bullets and still survive?!

John Woo has denied repeatedly that any homoeroticism was intended in his movies.[12] It's homosociality, not homoeroticism. But the scenes of men in pain, of men suffering, and of soap operatics and mock-opera hysteria (in genre terms associated with women's movies), say otherwise. The irony is that these 'men's men' can also be seen as a bunch of screaming queens.

On one level the John Woo Action Scene is filmmaking brilliance; on another level, it's revoltingly violent; on another level, it's pathetically childish, surreal and unbelievable; on another level, it's phallic and Freudian; on yet another level, it's really creepy and disturbing.

One could also argue that the John Woo Action Sequence negatively aligns homosociality with violence (you see this also throughout North American action cinema) – that male bonding and the concepts of brotherhood and chivalry should always have an aggressive or deathly

---

12 Critics see what they want to see, Woo said. In the world of Woo's cinema, 'man is man, woman is woman, friendship is what it seems', as Bernice Reynaud put it, and there is no ambiguity, no homoeroticism.

component (or even just a colossal dose of suffering). *Oooh baby*, it *hurts* to be a man! And it hurts even more to be 'man's man'!

The participants shoot each other with phallic substitutes until they're spattered with bodily fluids, leaking away until they die – it's an exciting orgy of blood and movement and bang-bang sound, yes, but it's also negatively linking homosociality to death and destruction (self-loathing being one of the most disturbing aspects of recent cinema – and it's all over Asian cinema).

The final act of a John Woo-directed actioner has the heroes and the anti-heroes dissolving into a bloodbath which simultaneously glorifies them and condemns them. They die heroically but also unintentionally pathetically. The deaths're meant to lend an air of tragedy and pathos to the proceedings (this's what the movies want the audience to respond to), but the characters and their deaths are also self-destructive to an alarming degree (and they injure those around them), self-absorbed, narcissistic, and misguided. The stories and the characters and the filmmakers aim for tragedy and catharsis and grandeur, but they also unwittingly attract derision and disgust. The movies and the filmmakers want to have it both ways (as they always do!): they want to resolve their stories with ultra-violent (and preposterous) action, yet also reach for grandiosity and tragedy.

There is an affinity between the brotherhood movies of John Woo and gay *manga* aimed at women in Japan. Women enjoy *yaoi, shonen ai, June*[13] and gay *manga* which depict boys in love, beautiful young men (*bishonen*) in pain. *Yaoi* comes from the *yama-nashi, ochi-nashi, imi-nashi*, which means 'no climax, no punchline, no meaning'. It typically involves pretty boys (*bishonen*). The boys and young men are figures who combine elements of both sexes: they are sensitive, feminized men, but also tough, masculinized women. Female readers enjoy the portrayals of friendship between men, and their bravery (especially in extreme situations such as war). Tho' the characters in *yaoi manga* are gay men, Fred Schodt points out, 'they are a manifestation of females, they're like young women wearing cartoon-character costumes' (2002, 122-3).

In his study of Hong Kong cinema, Stephen Teo calls *A Better Tomorrow* as 'the single most representative, most classically perfect Woo picture' (1997, 176). Thomas Weisser enthused about the *Better Tomorrow* flicks in *Asian Cult Cinema*:

> These movies are anthems to heroic bloodshed. They contain the most over-the-top, bullet-splitting, machine gun-cracking, blood-splattering scenes of all time. In any movie. From any country. Ever. (23)

Chow Yun-fat maintained that he didn't think that *A Better Tomorrow* would be a major success: nobody was optimistic about its prospects

---

13 The term *June (ju-ne mono)* comes from the magazine.

(including the boss of Golden Princess,[14] Lawrence Louey):

> But then, going to see the première, you can feel the atmosphere in the cinema. The audience is very excited, shouting, clapping hands. This never happen in a Hong Kong movie. I love it. (F. Dannen, 80)

[14] Golden Princess was a film production company, active in the 1980s up to the mid-1990s. It invested in Cinema City and backed movies such as *I Love Maria, The Killer, Bullet In the Head, Hard Boiled, Wicked City, The Swordsman, The Swordsman 3, A Chinese Ghost Story 3, Peking Opera Blues, Wild Search, King of Chess, Shaolin Warrior, The Royal Scoundrel,* and *Blue Lightning.*

# 2

# *A BETTER TOMORROW 2*

## *Ying Hung Bun Sik II*

*A Better Tomorrow 2* (1987, *Jing Hung Bun Sik II* in Cantonese, *Ying Xiong Ben Se II* in Mandarin = *Heroic Character II*) was produced and co-written by Tsui Hark for Cinema City (Tsui has 'story by' credit), directed and co-written by John Woo (Ng Yu-sam), exec. prod. by Tony Chow Kwok-Chung, edited by David Wu Tai-wai, music by Joseph Koo,15 Lowell Lo and David Wu (also music editor), action choreography by Tony Ching Siu-tung, art dir./ prod. des. by Andy Lee Yiu-Gwong, Chi Fung Lok and William Yam Wai-Leung, photography by Horace Wong Wing-hang and Bob Thompson, costumes by Pauline Lau Bo-Lam, Nancy Tong and Liu Mei-Chow, and starred Chow Yun-fat, Leslie Cheung, Ti Lung, Dean Shek, and Emily Chu. It was released on Dec 17, 1987. 104 mins.

Well, with those credits, *A Better Tomorrow 2* is going to be worth watching even if it stinks! Three major directors (Woo, Tsui and Ching), plus three great stars (Chow, Cheung and Lung)!

The sequel seemed inevitable – because the first *Better Tomorrow* (1986) had been a big hit for all involved – the number one movie of 1986, with a gross in Canton of HK $34.6 million (the *Better Tomorrow* movies inspired cash-ins – such as *Hero of Tomorrow* (1988), *City War* (1989) and *Return To A Better Tomorrow* (Wong Jing, 1994)). The Hong Kong industry had been churning out gangster movies before *A Better Tomorrow*, of course, but when one comes along that proves a big hit with local audiences, and seems to develop a new cinematic style (and a hot star in Chow Yun-fat), inevitably the rip-off movies pile in.

There are four great performances in *A Better Tomorrow 2* – Leslie Cheung, Dean Shek, Ti Lung and Chow Yun-fat.16 A movie can't go wrong with a cast like that – add to that action sequences choreographed by

15 Koo and James Wong Jim composed the theme song, performed by Leslie Cheung.
16 Chow is sensational in this movie.

Tony Ching Siu-tung, and even if *A Better Tomorrow 2* reeked, it would have something worth watching. There is also a wonderful supporting cast, featuring many regulars in the Hong Kong movie business – Kenneth Tsang-kong and Shing Fui-on, for example, also pop up in the next film that John Woo directed, *The Killer*.

Among the many Woo-ian elements in *A Better Tomorrow 2*, apart from the mandatory ingredients of gun-play, brotherhood and old-fashioned chivalry, are a church (of course!), a hospital, a young girl who gets injured in a fire-fight, tearful reunions and sorrowful farewells.

Tsui Hark's input can be discerned in *A Better Tomorrow 2* in the introduction of not one significant female character, but two; in the romantic relationship surrounding Cantonese heartthrob Leslie Cheung; Kwok-wing and in details such as the artist's studio featuring images of Chow Yun-Fat in his break-out role in the first *Better Tomorrow* movie (it's as if the audience is clamouring for Chow in the first act, so we visit an artist who has produced numerous images of Chow's Mark in the Pop Art style, as if the movie is already selling its merchandize in the first act). In the third act, Ken Lee appears in the studio, and dresses in Mark's gear: instead of being creepy and disturbing, it's played as a movie-movie moment (Ken poses beside an image of Mark in the same outfit. Hell, Ken even has a match in his *bouche* like Mark did).

There were disagreements over *A Better Tomorrow 2*: John Woo said that he delivered a cut that ran to 2h 40m, which had to be reduced to two hours, within a week. So Tsui Hark also cut the movie[17] – he 'took half and I took half and we cut our parts separately. I didn't get to see the whole picture until its opening night. Naturally, the result was uneven and unsatisfying'. Woo complained that the two halves did not match up. Consequently, *A Better Tomorrow 2* is not one of Woo's favourites among his own movies.

Most of the first act of *A Better Tomorrow 2* looks like it could've been directed by anybody, aside from only one or two Woo-ian flourishes (such as the over-done orchestral music, more suited to a day-time soap opera, and the long, lingering looks the men give each other. There are a few Woo-ian quirks in the editing, however, such as some freeze frames). Much of the first act of *A Better Tomorrow 2* is talky and low power, dramatically (the scenes are also lit flatly, without any texture or imagination). If John Woo's heart wasn't in doing this sequel, it certainly shows in act one. Dean Shek's Uncle Sei Lung is the focus, a man who's betrayed by his bosses (Shek is terrific in the scenes following his betrayal). And Leslie Cheung Kwok-wing (as Kit/ Billie) is effortlessly wonderful, as always (was there ever a more luminous star in recent, Chinese cinema?). The focus in act one is also on Ti Lung in prison: the scenes deliver exposition and characterization.

Apart from a brief montage (which forms the nightmare of Sung-chi Ho (who's in jail), we don't see Chow Yun-fat until the start of act two of *A*

---

17 Seven editors are credited.

*Better Tomorrow 2* (at around 26m). Here the action switches to Gotham,[18] where Chow is running a Chinese restaurant in Chinatown (Chow is basically the same character as Mark from *A Better Tomorrow*, tho' now he's Ken Lee, Mark's brother.[19] Ken is portrayed as the leader of a bunch of Chinese/ Chinese-Americans in New York City; they defer to him, and are distressed when he opts to return to China with Uncle Lung).

The face-off between Ken Lee and the Chinese restaurant employees and the North American heavies who come demanding protection money re-plays familiar Asian vs. American conflicts (which Tsui Hark depicted in *Zu: Warriors From the Magic Mountain* and *The Master*): the *gweilos* ('white devils') are portrayed as crude, rude, and insanely aggressive, and the Chinese guys are polite and placatory (at first, at least, until they're pushed). Chow Yun-fat delivers a marvellous performance here, a lengthy monologue which uses rice/ food as a pretext for a riff on current issues (the movie lingers over a medium close-up of Ken, without bothering to include reverse angles of the guy listening).

Following the customary action that climaxes act one (every Hong Kong action movie has a Big Scene to close the first act), *A Better Tomorrow 2* moves into some unusual territory, in particular the troubled relationship between Ken Lee and Uncle Sei Lung. *A Better Tomorrow 2* is more extreme than your usual crime/ gangster flick in not only having Lung undergo exile and suffering, he is also put into a strait jacket and installed in a hospital. Thus, for much of act two, Lung is played by Dean Shek as insane (and, this being directed by John Woo, it's a hysterical portrayal of madness – he has hospital orderlies forcing food down him while he writhes on a bed).

In the second act, *A Better Tomorrow 2* cuts between the Hong Kong scenes, involving mob boss Ko and the gangsters, and Sung-chi Ho and Kit, and the Ken Lee and Lung Sei scenes in Gotham. There are many opportunities for action scenes – Boss Ko and co. want to get rid of Lung, for instance, and send several teams of gunmen to the U.S.A. after him – but Lung has Ken as his heroic bodyguard (so no matter how many armed guys in suits lurk in corridors or stairways, Ken manages to trounce them all). It's typical of the over-egged narrative style of Hong Kong action cinema that Uncle Lung should regain his senses smack in the middle of an action scene (and to help Ken, too, who's fallen to the ground as the heavies approach in a car).

There are bombs, too, which go off in the restaurant (when Ken Lee is looking after Uncle Lung). It's witnessing a girl being injured during one of the Triad attacks on the restaurant that sends Lung over-the-edge into madness.

And there are action scenes back in China, too – in one, Kit manages to take advantage of a gangsters' hand-over, impressing mobster Ko's men. This is Leslie Cheung as James Bond, taking on hordes of armed henchmen when the hand-over of counterfeit money at night by the sea

18 Aside from the second unit images of New York City (which might belong to any movie), the interior scenes look like we're back in Hong Kong.
19 Some accounts have Ken as Mark's cousin.

ends in yet another shoot-out. Cheung's Kit is leaping about, and diving onto a power boat (boats and harbourside fire-fights occur in the next film in the John Woo canon, *The Killer*).

In the second nighttime, action scene, Sung-chi Ho is coerced to shoot Kit at close range (so that Boss Ko will trust him). It's certainly a very distressing scene – within the story of the movie, but also in seeing such a beloved actor as Leslie Cheung being shot twice. That is simply something you *don't* want to see. (And Ti Lung plays his remorse vividly, returning to the scene to hurry Kit to hospital. It's heavily ironic that Boss Ko uses shooting Kit as an initiation test for Ho, after Ho comes to him looking for work. The scene is replayed in the finale, when Ken Lee brings Kit to the hospital, and is met by Ho outside).

❀

Inevitably, *A Better Tomorrow 2* moves back to Hong Kong for the resolution of the plot (and of course the blam-blam[20] shoot-out which you know is a dead certainty in a Woo-and-Tsui action movie): Uncle Lung and Ken muse on the concept of 'home' (a very poignant theme in both Woo's and Tsui's cinema), which has multiple resonances (of the 1997 Handover, of the Chinese abroad, of exiles, etc).

Wait – is that *Mark*? No, it's *Ken*. Both Kit and Sung-chi Ho are taken aback for a moment. Chow Yun-fat loudly, jokily insists that he's 'Ken, Ken', not Mark. Before the giant shoot-out, there's a charming scene set in a cemetery in sunlight: regardless of what the text or the subtext is saying in this scene, what impresses is observing these four great actors together within the same scene. For once they're not running around firing weapons while riddled with bullets, or crumpling to the floor in hysterical insanity, they're just talking. Scenes like this are as valuable as the action set-pieces. The scenes where Chow Yun-fat plays opposite Leslie Cheung are delightful, and to be treasured.

❀

So *A Better Tomorrow 2* moves towards its shoot-out climax, in a plush manse up in the hills outside Hong Kong, where Boss Ko and his mob are celebrating the success of their money counterfeiting operation (out comes the Peter Gabriel music – for at least the third time). Ken Lee suits up in Mark's old (bullet-ridden) duster coat and shades (hanging grenades inside it like he's a travelling salesman. Chow Yun-fat adds little bits of comical business here).

The finale of *A Better Tomorrow 2* is thus another stops-all-out, guns-'n'-grenades sequence, a men-with-guns smackdown, with one stunt after another – an explosion in slo-mo, a twisting dive, a two-pistol blammy moment, blood smeared on white walls, squibs bursting inside actor's shirts, while the sound of gunfire is mixed high.

But the finale of *A Better Tomorrow 2* features so many henchmen, all of whom are absolutely useless in a fight, and so many gags and stunts, it's more like a parody (both Tony Ching Siu-tung and Tsui Hark are big on comedy, but John Woo isn't known for inserting much humour into his

20 The silent, cool assassin wearing shades uses a silencer – oh no, not on a John Woo movie, where every gun is fitted with a 'loudener'!

dramatic finales, even tho' he's directed comedies). For ex, the gunmen are endless, tumbling out of doors into corridors, in groups, so they're not human any more but objects to be shot by the heroes.[21] For ex, Sung-chi Ho snatches up a samurai sword, so we have some swordplay action for a few action beats (I bet that was Tony Ching's idea. Ti Lung, of course, had appeared in many swordplay pics). Ho uses the sword to dispatch Shing Fui-on (who's armed with an axe), then sets about some more heavies.

Three of the heroes survive (Lung, Ho and Ken) in *A Better Tomorrow 2*, but poor Kit bites the dust (halfway thru act three, prior to the mansion bust-up). In a moving scene (played for Maximum Tear Effect by Chow Yun-fat and Leslie Cheung), Kit speaks to his wife Jackie who's just given birth (while Ken Lee stands beside him in a call-box. Kit can barely string two words together, but he does name the child just before he expires.

A woman giving birth is 100% of the time a wholly artificial dramatic-narrative device in movies of this kind (and 99.99% of the time in all other movies – consider how editor David Wu Tai-wai is cutting together the hospital, the mansion, Leslie Cheung and co.). Death and birth, the end and the beginning, loss and hope, the present and the future – there's no point complaining now, halfway through the final act of a movie! Especially about a film with such over-cooked melodrama! (and it's no use pointing out that stopping for a phone call instead of carrying straight on to the hospital is nuts. Kit is seriously injured, and they pause for a chat!). So Kit dies – he's given a moving and protracted death scene, slipping to the ground as the camera moves backwards while Leslie Cheung sings on the soundtrack. (I can't be the only viewer who finds scenes where Leslie Cheung dies unsettling. I'm willing the movie – don't kill Cheung! He's too special).

If you take *A Better Tomorrow 2* straight, it's very impressive; if you step back a little, it's ridiculous, comical and over-the-top; from the perspective of conservative politics, it's offensively violent, shamelessly crude and irritatingly stupid; from a feminist viewpoint, it's prehistoric and chauvinist; from a social realist standpoint, it has no relation to the real world whatsoever and has little of value to say about contemporary society; from a liberal political view, *A Better Tomorrow 2* is ideologically backward, employing over-done histrionics and mindless mayhem to convey garbled nonsense; but if you're a fan of action cinema, it's one of the great movies.

Sometimes contemplating a movie like the two *Better Tomorrows* and *The Killer* (which are not so much a trilogy as basically the same movie), I wonder if I'm watching: –

• A commercial *for guns* or a plea to *ban guns*?;

• Is it pro or anti violence?;

• Is it more than a morally murky cartoon about men running around buildings going *blam-blam, you're dead!* – just like kids in the playground?

• Is it a treatise on just how moronic humans really are, and the only

<hr>

21 A critic compared them to clowns in a circus.

hope for civilization is a bunch of righteous (self-righteous) crooks?

• Is it a movie about the corruption of the human soul via the technology of warfare?

• Are the heroes (actually, they're anti-heroes) different from their rivals (Boss Ko and his mob) just because they talk about being righteous?[22]

• Is it a modern version of an Ancient Greek tragic play – Sophocles with guns instead of swords? (– wait, there *is* a sword!).

• Is it a commercial for the return of fascism or for the Chinese Communist Party? (The MacGuffin is counterfeit money, after all; both fascists and Communists enshrine money, though for different reasons).

I guess I have to admit that part of me is thrilled by the brilliance of the filmmaking, entertained by actors as electric as Chow, Cheung, Shek and Lung, while another part of me is thinking, *this is garbage*. Ideologically, it's junk, and it's politically offensive. So it's classy trash, a corny cartoon (as hokey as the shooting star that Leslie Cheung reckons is an ill omen).

---

22 It's the joke in *Jane Austen's Mafia* (1998): in *The Godfather*, Don Corleone famously drew the line at narcotics: thieving, racketeering, prostitution and other crimes were OK for da Corleone family bizniz, but not drugs. The way that distinction was made in *The Godfather* seemed so serious, coming from Marlon Brando (despite the hypocrisy of it). In *Jane Austen's Mafia!*, the Don laments the old days: 'we steal things, we kill and dismember people. Now it's all drugs. Where's the honour?'

# THE *CHINESE GHOST STORY* MOVIES

# 3

# *A CHINESE GHOST STORY*

## *Sin Nui Yau Wan*

INTRO TO *A CHINESE GHOST STORY*.
The *Chinese Ghost Story* movies are:

*A Chinese Ghost Story* (1987)
*A Chinese Ghost Story  2* (1990)
*A Chinese Ghost Story  3* (1991)
*A Chinese Ghost Story: The Tsui Hark Animation* (1997)

*A Chinese Ghost Story* was remade in 2011 (and dedicated to Leslie Cheung).

*A Chinese Ghost Story* (1987, Mandarin: *Qiannu Youhun = Sien: Female Ghost*, a.k.a. *Fair Maiden, Tender Spirit*), was one of those movies where everything works, and the mix of elements is just gorgeous. This is a golden, 100% killer of a movie.[23]

*A Chinese Ghost Story* has everything going for it: it is among the finest fantasy and action movies ever; it boasts a finale as grand as any in cinema; it tackles the most profound themes; it possesses a perfectly achieved tone and attitude; it features two incandescent stars; it is helmed by two of the greatest action directors in history; and it is brilliant filmmaking.

*A Chinese Ghost Story* was produced by Film Workshop/ Cinema City written by Yuen Kai-Chi, produced by Tsui Hark, Claudie Chung Jan and Qianqing Liu, exec. prod. by Zhong Zheng, and directed by Tony Ching

23 For more on the *Chinese Ghost Story* films, see my companion book.

Siu-tung. Music was by the great James Wong Jim,[24] Romeo Diaz, David Wu and Dai Lemin, editing by David Wu Tai-wai, production design by Hai Chung-Man, art dir. by Kenneth Yee Chung-man, costumes by Shirley Chan and Kitty Ho Wai-Ying, hair by Peng Yen-Lien, make-up by Renming Wen and Man Yun-Ling, visual fx by Ma Xian Liang, sound by Xiaolong Cheng, David Wu and Qun Xue, with photography by Poon Hang-Sang, Sander Lee, Tom Lau Moon-tong, Wong Wing-Hang, Yongheng Huang, Jiaogao Li and Putang Liu. Action directors[25] were Tony Ching Siu-tung, Philip Kwok Chung-fung, Lau Chi-ho, Alan Tsui Chung-sun and Bobby Woo Chi-lung. Released: July 18, 1987.

In the cast were Leslie Cheung Kwok-wing, Joey Wong Jo-yin, Wu Ma, Lau Siu-ming, Lam Wai, Xue Zhilun, Wong Jing, Huang Ha, Yeung Yau-cheung, Shut Mei-yee, Elvis Tsui and David Wu Tai-wai. The budget was HK $5.6 million (= US $650,000). It was showered with awards (including Fantafestival Rome, Fantasporto Porto Film Festival, and Avoriaz Fantastic Film Festival, and Hong Kong Film Awards for best score, best song and best art dir.), took HK $18.8m gross, and it ran for a blissful 98 minutes.

*A Chinese Ghost Story* is very much in the same mold as *The Bride With the White Hair* and similar Hong Kong films. It's a romantic tale couched in horror/ fairy tale/ fantasy movie packaging, an impossible romance between a human man and a supernatural woman.

Tsui Hark produced *A Chinese Ghost Story*, and his stamp is all over it: he was involved in developing the project, in creating the script, in the casting, in the visual effects, etc (as Tsui remembered: 'actually, I was thinking of [directing] all of them!'). It was produced by his Film Workshop company (with Cinema City), and his Cinefex Company created the visual effects. The frenetic pace is clearly something close to Tsui's filmic sensibility. It's safe to say that *A Chinese Ghost Story* is very much a Tsui Hark concept (and production). However, he says that it was Tony Ching Siu-tung who directed it, and that he helped out, and directed some parts. As well as Ching's contribution as director, it's also worth noting that the screenplay credit goes to Yuen Kai-Chi: one of the reasons that this movie is so good is because of the brilliant script.

*A Chinese Ghost Story* marks the first of the really great Tsui Hark and Tony Ching Siu-tung movies: no doubt about it, the two trilogies – the *Chinese Ghost Story* and the *Swordsman* films – are among the finest in fantasy and action cinema, and one of the greatest collaborations in the history of cinema between a film director and a film producer (see my book on Tony Ching).

It's not bad going, either, for Tony Ching to have a masterpiece as his third film as director – and a much-loved film, too (altho' some critics, including me, would count *Duel To the Death* as a masterpiece, too). Thus, Ching is the man behind not one but two greatly admired and enjoyed

---

24 This was the first James Wong Jim contribution to Tsui's movies (along with *Shanghai Blues*).
25 Jin Guo, Zhilong Hu, Zhihao Liu and Zhongxin Xu are also credited as martial arts directors.

series of films – *A Chinese Ghost Story* and *The Swordsman*.

Tsui Hark said that Ching Siu-tung had been reluctant to accept the directing assignment, partly because his previous movie, *The Witch From Nepal*, which also had supernatural and fantasy elements, hadn't done well at the box office. Ching wasn't feeling great about helming another movie, including one which was a romantic story. As they continued to talk, Tsui said, Ching eventually agreed to do it.

*A Chinese Ghost Story* was important in Tony Ching's career because it was a hit – his pet project, *Duel To the Death*, hadn't set the box office aflame, and *The Witch From Nepal* had fared poorly, too. But *A Chinese Ghost Story* did great business.

According to Tsui Hark, *A Chinese Ghost Story* went through some reworking: after the film had shot for some 30 days, and had been cut together, they looked at it and decided that it needed more elements in certain areas. The ending, for instance, was revamped: Tsui, with his producer's hat on, decided that the movie required something bigger. (And yet the giant battle between the Tree Demon and our heroes would be plenty for many movies. *A Chinese Ghost Story*, however, is definitely Something More).

THE PRODUCTION.

*A Chinese Ghost Story* was based on the 17th century (Ming Dynasty) stories (found in *Strange Stories From a Chinese Studio*)[26] by Pu Songling (Pu-Sing Ling, 1640-1715), known as 'Master Liaozhai', tho' much altered (Liaozhai lies behind the Chinese horror tradition).[27] Songling's stories are all about the human body (which makes them perfect for Chinese action movies, which foreground the body constantly), about keeping the body intact (for reincarnation), and about ghosts/ spirits seeking bodies for reincarnation. (Tsui Hark had considered a movie based on Pu Songling's works since 1978; he had pitched it to T.V.B.). The movie changed Pu Songling's stories – to the point where it didn't look much like the original, Tsui commented (LM, 75).

The 1987 movie also references ghost stories from Japan (such as *Ugetsu Monogatari* (1953), and is a remake of *The Enchanting Shadow* (Li Hanxiang, 1960), which gave *A Chinese Ghost Story* its title). *Dragon Gate Inn* (1967) and *Legend of the Mountain* (1979) might also be influences (certainly when Tsui Hark came to direct movies such as the *Once Upon a Time In China* series and *The Blade*, the nighttime scenes especially have a *Chinese Ghost Story* feel).[28] Forerunners such as the wonderful Sammo Hung comedy horror flick *Spooky Encounters* (1980) are also in the mix.

Chinese ghost stories pivot around the theme of reincarnation, and Hong Kong horror movies are defined by ghost stories. It's the *whole body*

26 The stories have also been published as: *Strange Tales From Liaozhai, Strange Tales From the Liaozhai Studio, Strange Tales From Make-do Studio* and *Strange Stories from the Lodge of Leisure*.
27 For Chinese audiences, the beliefs and superstitions presented in horror movies aren't fake: 'Hong Kong horror films reflect the genuine beliefs and fears of a superstitious people', pointed out Bey Logan (101). They were also the basis for *A Touch of Zen* (1971).
28 Hong Kong critics said that *A Chinese Ghost Story* looked like a TV commercial; quite a few movies of the 1980s drew on this look (as well as pop promos and MTV).

that's important in the Chinese philosophy of reincarnation (as in Ancient Egyptian religion). Thus, shape-changing or missing limbs is not good, and the body must remain intact (so that decapitation is a major setback, because it means no reincarnation).

The female ghost is one of the principal characters of the Chinese ghost story: typically, the woman is young and unmarried (so that she has no son or husband to burn incense and give offerings so she can find a decent spot in the after-life). The female spirits search for the romance among the living that they didn't experience when they were alive. So that Chinese ghost stories tend to be romances, between human men and ghostly women. Two figures usually crop up as well: the Taoist monk, who tries to protect the man from the ghost (and from his own earthly desires), and a demon or monster, who wants the ghost for itself.[29]

The female ghost or spirit is a *juli*, a seductress, and sometimes a *xian*, a fairy (she is usually beautiful, proving the necessary eye candy, and also suggesting 'she was a victim of a love that went wrong').[30] The man tends to be an effete, harmless, goofy guy.

There were two sequels to *A Chinese Ghost Story*, as well as the inevitable quick cash-ins from rival Hong Kong film teams. In *Portrait of a Nymph* (a.k.a. *Picture of a Nymph*), for instance, released the following year (1988), some of the same cast (including Joey Wong and Wu Ma), run thru exactly the same story (some folk prefer it to *A Chinese Ghost Story*). As a partial tribute to Leslie Cheung Kwok-wing, *A Chinese Ghost Story* was re-released in a restored version in 2011 (and there was a special screening, which cast and crew attended).

The *Chinese Ghost Story* sequels added cast members such as Jacky Cheung (another pop music icon in China). Cheung, one of the four Canto-pop stars (and dubbed 'the King of Canto-pop'), is wonderful in *A Chinese Ghost Story 2*, and also appeared in many other movies in this period, including action thrillers (such as *Bullet In the Head*), and Tsui Hark's films, such as *Wicked City*. Meanwhile, Tony Leung Chi-wai took over Leslie Cheung's role for the second *Chinese Ghost Story* sequel of 1991. A remake of *A Chinese Ghost Story* (a.k.a. *A Chinese Fairy Tale*), was produced in 2011 by Golden Sun Films.

In 1987, when the top-grossing movies around the world were *Fatal Attraction*, *Beverly Hills Cop 2* and *The Living Daylights*, *A Chinese Ghost Story* is a hugely enjoyable flick which can compete favourably with anything released that year (or any year). For example, the movies in the horror and fantasy genre in the U.S.A. of 1987 included *Predator*, *RoboCop*, *The Witches of Eastwick*, *Nightmare On Elm Street 3*, *Batteries Not Included*, *The Lost Boys*, *Innerspace* and *The Running Man*. Sure, we've all seen all those movies (and enjoyed them!), but *A Chinese Ghost Story* trounces them for imagination, style, wit and action (and beauty – what actors in those North American flicks can compete with Joey Wong

29 J. Yang, 2003, 76, 77.
30 S. Teo, 1997, 222.

and Leslie Cheung?!).[31]

By comparison with North American ghost romance pictures of the same period, such as *Ghost* (1990) and *Always* (1989), *A Chinese Ghost Story* is marvellous. It doesn't have time for anything approaching 'realism' or everyday reality (why bother? you're surrounded with it!). *A Chinese Ghost Story* is a movie-movie that celebrates its movieness with every shot. In *A Chinese Ghost Story*, 'the story of undying love and Good vs. Evil is told in the style of an American horror film on speed', as Lisa Morton put it (LM, 72).

*A Chinese Ghost Story* is a feast of a movie, deliberately corny, popcorny, cheesy, silly, over-the-top, and it doesn't take itself seriously for a second. It's glorious fun, the movie equivalent of a pantomime, or a fancy dress party. The pacing and editing is spot-on: just enough is spent on establishing the hero Ning[32] Choi-san's character, for instance, but not too much; the action scenes are stuffed with beats and gags, but the action is pinned to the central conflicts of each scene, and never allowed to run on simply for the sake of more action, and the 1987 movie has plenty of time to explore the intimate, romantic moments between Ning Choi-san and Nip Siu-shin.

If you rush the slower scenes in your haste to get to more action or more horror, the audience hasn't spent enough time with the characters, or their relationships, or the situations. It is, after all, the *characters* and their *relationships* and the *story* which really make a comedy work. Great comedy comes out of the drama and the characters and the situations (as all of the major comedy filmmakers assert); *A Chinese Ghost Story* follows this all-important tenet (which Tsui Hark wholly understands). But that also applies to great horror movies or great action movies or great romantic movies.

Or put it like this: *A Chinese Ghost Story* has a terrific, cleverly written script that hits all of the right notes at the right time. Oh, it's not *The Cherry Orchard* or *Twelfth Night*. But it's not meant to be! It's a piece of candy, but brilliantly executed.

The script of *A Chinese Ghost Story* is once again constructed along classical lines: act one, for instance, climaxes with the Swordsman Yin versus ghost battle; act two has a similar but bigger conflict between Yin and the monsters, but closes instead with the comical courtroom scene (and Ning Choi-san and Yin agreeing to join forces). The court scene (where Ning reports a murder) lightens the proceedings, providing a farcical breather before the two finales in act three. The court scene is important, too: after it, the relationship of Ning and Yin is cemented: now they are resolved to combat the ghosts and monsters.

As Thomas Weisser put it:

this is a brilliantly conceived fantasy featuring two very likable Asian performers, Leslie Cheung and Joey Wong. But the real star is Ching

---

31 'Where *A Chinese Ghost Story* is way ahead of its American counterparts is in its use of romance and sensuality', noted Lisa Morton (LM, 72).
32 Some translations used the name Ling.

Siu Tung and his extraordinary camerawork. (40)

Ric Meyers summed up *A Chinese Ghost Story* thus:

Ching Siu-tung's splendid fantasy of a thousand-year-old unisex tree demon with a mile-long tongue, pimping a beautiful spirit for 'the big evil'. Sit back – you literally haven't seen anything like this before.[33]

Kozo in Love HK Film reckons that

the most compelling thing about *A Chinese Ghost Story* is probably its sheer cinematic energy. People fly, jump, and engage in situation comedy with little pause for breath… *A Chinese Ghost Story* is primo eighties Hong Kong Cinema, which means a complete disregard for any attempt at realism. Everything here is so hyperrealistic and over-the-top it makes Hollywood musicals look like the very model of restraint.

THE CAST.
There are three main characters in *A Chinese Ghost Story*:
• Ning Choi-san, the hapless scholar and debt collector
• Nip Siu-shin, the beautiful ghost (*kuei*) of the story
• Yin Chik-ha, the Taoist demon hunter[34]
The cast of *A Chinese Ghost Story* is terrific, headed up two of the most beautiful people in Chinese cinema of recent times: Leslie Cheung Kwok-wing and Joey Wong Jo-yin. You can look at these two lovely actors all day. They are simply sensational. Cheung is especially fine with the comedy in *A Chinese Ghost Story* (always an attribute that's under-valued by film critics), but he's also prime leading man material: Cheung is *hot!*

LESLIE CHEUNG.
Leslie Cheung Kwok-wing[35] was a much-revered star in both the pop music and film worlds. In Asia, pop stars regularly move into movies and television (just as they do in the West). Somehow, the stigma of a rubbish pop idol trying to achieve plaudits in cinema isn't attached to Asian stars – many of the most memorable turns in recent Asian cinema are from pop stars.
Leslie Cheung Kwok-wing was born on Sept 12, 1956 in Hong Kong (his father was a tailor). Sadly, he committed suicide in 2003 by jumping from a 24 storey Hong Kong hotel. He suffered from depression. His suicide note said he'd had enough (altho' he had been seeing doctors). Cheung starred in many movies, some of them first-rate, including *Ashes of Time, A Better Tomorrow 1 & 2* and *Happy Together*. At the time of *A Chinese Ghost Story*, Cheung also appeared in the critically acclaimed *Rouge*, as well as *A Better Tomorrow*. Cheung was often paired with fellow

---

33 Quoted in F. Dannen, 373.
34 The *fat-si* is a Taoist priest or shaman who has spells and magic to deal with ghosts and spirits. The *fat-si* takes on physical and scientific as well as religious tasks.
35 Leslie Cheung's name in Cantonese is Jeung Gwok-wink and Zhang Guorong in Mandarin. He is sometimes billed as Leslie Cheung Kwok-wing.

pop star and actress Anita Mui. Cheung's sexual identity was a focus of attention; he dated both men and women, and said it was best to describe him as bisexual (some of his film roles explored his queer media image, such as *Farewell My Concubine* and his films with director Wong Kar-wai).

Educated in England (like many Hong Kong actors), in Norwich and Leeds, Leslie Cheung began his pop singing career in 1977. He worked for the R.T.V. network in Canton (many future stars of Hong Kong cinema started out in television). Cheung gave up singing in 1989[36] to concentrate on acting ('as an actor, you can go much further – travelling back and forth in time, playing different characters. It's like having more lives during your lifetime', he explained).[37] Cheung later returned to live performance, embarking on several successful tours.

*A Chinese Ghost Story* is one of Leslie Cheung's most enjoyable performances (he was really hitting his stride at this time – he also delivered a scorching performance in *A Better Tomorrow,* the year before *A Chinese Ghost Story*). Cheung's Ning Choi-san is well-meaning but cowardly, naïve (even simple) and unremarkable. He's the everyday guy hero, the ordinary guy who finds himself in extraordinary circumstances.[38] He doesn't want to be where he is, and he wants to stay out of trouble. He's poor, and doesn't like his job, but does it anyway (all attributes that everybody can identify with! Ning is a very Tsui Harkian characterization).

Leslie Cheung is carrying *A Chinese Ghost Story* for long stretches – where he's the only character on screen (for instance, in the earlier scenes which are essentially a guy in a haunted house scenario. And just one guy, not a couple or a group). This is a *tour-de-force* comedy turn: one of the reasons that the *Chinese Ghost Story* films are so effective and so entertaining is down to Cheung's performance.

The 1987 movie also gleefully delivers gender reversals, too – by having Ning Choi-san play a feminized role (to the point where, in the 1990 sequel, he's taking a bath when the monster appears, a cliché of the horror genre, where it's usually an opportunity to see a starlet unclad).

Amazingly, Leslie Cheung looks about 18, altho' he was 30[39] at the time of the first *Ghost* movie (Cheung also plays Ning Choi-san much younger than his real age, 20 instead of 30, but he carries it off). Like Maggie Cheung, Brigitte Lin and Chow Yun-Fat, Cheung is an ageless actor.

JOEY WONG.

Meanwhile, Joey Wong is… Joey Wong! A face that can melt the lens, the 20 year-old Wong Jo-yin (b. Jan 31, 1967, Taipei, Taiwan) needs to do nothing except just stand there to be incredible (tho' she does plenty more'n that in *A Chinese Ghost Story*! Critics unfairly carped that thankfully all Wong has to do is show up; but no, she is acting her socks

36 After giving sell-out concerts on 33 consecutive nights at the Hong Kong Coliseum.
37 However, Tsui Hark said that Cheung had been reluctant to take on the role, because he'd had bad experiences in playing in period roles (in TV).
38 Lisa Morton describes Leslie Cheung's Ning Choi-san as 'idealistic without being naïve, clumsy without being foolish, romantic without being maudlin, and frightened without being weak' (LM, 73)
39 He's 11 years older than Joey Wong.

off too. And she is terrific in other Tsui Hark-related movies, such as *Green Snake* and *The Swordsman 3*).

Joey Wong Jo-yin would later appear as one of the snake-women in *Green Snake* (1993), a movie which's essentially the same plot as *A Chinese Ghost Story*.[40] (Casting the female ghost was probably the toughest casting job in *A Chinese Ghost Story* – finding character actors to play mad, Taoist monks or scary Tree Demons isn't so difficult! But the actress selected to play Nip Siu-shin had to be other-worldly and convince as a ghost, but also be attractive, and a good actor. Sounds easy to find? Trust me, having done casting myself, it's not that easy! What you find with casting is that if you have five boxes to tick, many actors you see will cover three or four of the requirements, but not all five).

Incidentally, Joey Wong was not Tsui Hark's first choice for the ghost in *A Chinese Ghost Story* – he thought she looked too contemporary and too tall – she's 5' 8" (his choices included Japanese singer Akina Nakamori and May Lo). But when Tsui and the team saw Wong in the costume, it was obvious she was perfect.

Ching Siu-tung wanted Joey Wong and Leslie Cheung for *A Chinese Ghost Story* precisely because they were very contemporary actors: they would revive the genre with new blood. (Ching took the same approach by casting singer and TV actress Kelly Chen in *An Empress and the Warriors*, another of his big, romantic movies).

The actors in *A Chinese Ghost Story* throw themselves into the roles – it's very physical stuff. Apart from the action scenes, the actors're drenched with rain, wading waist-deep in water, close to fire, or falling into the sea (Leslie Cheung gamely does this a number of times – not counting the takes we don't see!). A Chinese action movie is no easy ride for the cast, as many visiting Western performers have found out.

THE SECONDARY CHARACTERS.

And – this is also perfect casting – Wu Ma plays the Taoist monk hunting down the spirits. Wu Ma (1942, Tianjin – 2014), sometimes known as Feng Wuma, is a veteran of literally hundreds of movie appearances (around 250), as well as a prominent film director (he was A.D. to Chang Cheh, and directing from 1970 onwards).[41]

Wu Ma steals every scene he's in. His introduction, for instance, is genius: instead of having Ning Choi-san encounter Yin Chik-ha creeping around the temple at night, or stumbling upon him in the village by day, Ning Choi-san runs into Swordsman Yin in the midst of an epic sword duel with an arch rival, Hah Hau (played by Lam Wai). So, cleverly, the screenwriter (Yuen Kai-Chi) weaves in exposition about the temple and the spirits in the middle of a juicy slice of furious swordplay and wire-work. And we see Yin in his element, at work, *showing* us what he does (instead of him *telling* us about it).

---

40 Joey Wong became a favourite for Tsui – perfectly cast in *The Swordsman 3* and *Green Snake* as doomed, tragic heroines.
41 Wu Ma has directed movies with similar man-and-ghost romances to *A Chinese Ghost Story*, including *Portrait of a Nymph* and *Burning Sensation*.

On this same crazy night, the rival swordsman Hah Hau encounters Ning Choi-san in the wilds, in the midst of another swordplay scene; later, the rival swordsman becomes one of the ghost's sorry victims (as he nurses his wounds beside a campfire; Nip Siu-shin materializes as a seductive water nymph, and Hah Hau is soon engulfed in a monstrous tongue and sucked dry).

A Chinese Ghost Story is happy, too, to portray a powerful and predatory woman. Nip Siu-shin is depicted seducing and tupping two victims before she meets scholar Ning Choi-san. However, the movie lets the beautiful ghost stay this side of murder, when the lovemaking scenes cut to a point-of-view, Steadicam shot (the classic, subjective monster shot of 1980s horror cinema) of the thing or monster approaching rapidly. While Siu-shin looks on, it's the monster that does the actual killing (it's not revealed in full until later).

CASTING.

One should also note here Tsui Hark's genius with casting. Rarely commented upon by critics (tho' discussed endlessly by fans), casting is enormously important in a movie. And it's not an easy job. Tsui certainly has a knack for finding new talent, for getting the right people for the roles (he has also created roles specially for certain actors), and also for filling in the secondary roles and the character roles with suitable people. In A Chinese Ghost Story, everyone can agree that Leslie Cheung was the perfect choice.

Tony Ching has used many pop stars in his films as film director – the ones produced by Tsui Hark, obviously, but also his more recent works, such as Kelly Chen appearing in An Empress and the Warriors, and Xiao Zhan in Jade Dynasty (both Chen and Zhan are wonderful, and, being the main characters, they have to be).

ROMANCE AND HORROR.

Nip Siu-shin is enslaved to the Tree Demon, a.k.a. Old Dame (Lao-lao): she is forced to procure men for the Tree Demon by having sex with them: the Tree Demon then rushes in to suck out their energy – with a giant tongue! (presumably their chi is high during lovemaking). It's a grotesque version of a sadomasochistic, master-and-slave, pimp-and-prostitute arrangement.

The horror genre aspects are the packaging in A Chinese Ghost Story, as Tsui Hark explained, that covers what is really a romance story. Horror and romance would be plenty, but, this being Cantonese cinema at its finest, two other elements're added: action and comedy. Getting the mix right is so important, and A Chinese Ghost Story is perfectly pitched in terms of tone and attitude as well as its balance between action + comedy + romance + horror.

And notice how each element complements the other: there are genuinely creepy moments in A Chinese Ghost Story (it is a perfect Hallowe'en movie), but they are always balanced by comedy before and after. The romance, meanwhile, is genuine (there is definitely a chemistry between Leslie Cheung and Joey Wong), but again the humour lightens it (and inevitably interrupts it). Meanwhile, the action, as one might expect, is truly extraordinary – in live-action, Chinese filmmakers have *no competition* from any filmmakers anywhere on Earth.

*A Chinese Ghost Story* is also the first grand expression of the importance of romance and romantic desire in the cinema of Tony Ching Siu-tung (it was a subplot in his previous two movies as director, *Duel To the Death* and *The Witch From Nepal*). It's surprising just how much romance is a key ingredient in Ching's films, even tho' he's known as one of the premier action directors on the planet. One of the memorable aspects of *A Chinese Ghost Story* is the lovers crying 'Ning Choi-san!' or 'Siu-shiiiin!' to each other.

The romantic plot in *A Chinese Ghost Story* reaches a heightened point in the finale, when the lovers share a final moment together, and then Nip Siu-shin is gone. Forever.

When a movie gets the *balance* between horror and comedy right,[42] it's very satisfying. In *A Chinese Ghost Story*, the filmmakers might have had recent (pre-1987) outings in the U.S.A. such as *Ghostbusters* or *E.T.* or *The Evil Dead* in mind. More recently, the humour in the *Pirates of the Caribbean* series hits a very similar tone (lavish vistas, great visual effects, and spooky moments, but not too gory or nasty – and, at the heart of it, a well-meaning but klutzy guy. In fact, Johnny Depp has affinities with Leslie Cheung, in the way that Depp played Captain Jack Sparrow in *Pirates*. And in the *Chinese Ghost Story* sequel of 1990, when Cheung has his beard and moustache, he's even more Depp-ish).

COMEDY.

*A Chinese Ghost Story* is very funny. In the bustling village scene (mandatory in any historical movie, East or West, always in the first act), everybody regards Ning Choi-san as a doofus. When he asks about the temple where he wants to spend the night because he's broke, everyone mutters behind his back that he's a dead man, very much in the Mel Brooks mold when someone mentions Dracula's Castle (and Tsui Hark is very fond of such comical crowd scenes). There's some inventive comedy using rain and water: the debt collector's account book is a soggy mess of smeared black ink, and Ning Choi-san has charms against spirits imprinted on his back when he's pushed against a store display (again, it's likely that Tsui Hark was behind these gags).

As so often in Chinese, fantasy movies, there's some pantomime-style crossdressing in *A Chinese Ghost Story*: the Tree Demon, Old Dame, is played by Lau Siu Ming, a veteran of numerous *kung fu* movies (and like many supernatural foes, s/he has an imperious, echoey voice).

And, just as in a pantomime, there is a lengthy comical sequence where the Mother-In-Law From Hell comes to visit: the Tree Demoness pays a visit to Nip Siu-shin's chamber, announcing that she's got to marry

42 The humour in *A Chinese Ghost Story* is perfectly pitched – it's very funny, but it doesn't detract from or stop the story, and it doesn't lessen the atmosphere of dread.

the Lord of the Black Mountain in three days. Siu-shin, meanwhile, hides Ning Choi-san in a wooden bathtub (so that the Old Dame can't smell him – this's also why Siu-shin meets her lover out on the water, in the pavillion). Comedy, farce, hiding lovers from stern, parental figures – it's all delightfully silly (Ning catches glimpses of Siu-shin half-dressed... her sister Siu Ching, is on her case... and the Old Dame catches the scent of the human Ning several times). And it's sexy – the moment when the topless Siu-shin leans down into the water to kiss Ning underwater is iconic.[43] And *A Chinese Ghost Story* is absolutely jammed with memorable images like that.

TECHNICAL ASPECTS.

Technically, *A Chinese Ghost Story* is a marvel. The production design, the costumes, the hair, the make-up, the editing, the cinematography, the sound design – all departments are working at their optimum. There is a wonderful use of props, for instance: Swordsman Yin has his anti-demon charms and a magical sword, and much is made of the painting of Nip Siu-shin which Ning Choi-san spots in the village market (that prop does a *huge* amount of narrative work in the first two *A Chinese Ghost Story* movies).[44] Meanwhile, texts and words are everywhere – from the cemetery stones and the wayside markers, to the paper charms deployed by the Taoist monk and Ning's soaked tax account book. There's even time for the lovers to indulge in some Chinese calligraphy during one of their (all too brief) sojourns together.

All of the *Chinese Ghost Story* films, like many historical movies, are costume movies: *A Chinese Ghost Story* is filled with flapping, floating and very long pieces of material (Shirley Chan and Kitty Ho Wai-Ying were the costume designers). Joey Wong Jo-yin, as the chief female star of the movie, receives the most lavish treatment from the hair, make-up and costume departments: Wong's Nip Siu-shin is more a bundle of white or red cloth fluttering in the wind than a former human being now ghost.[45] The movement of the clothes, one of the hallmarks of Chinese, historical movies, perfectly embodies her in-between status, in a limbo between life and death. (In Chinese costume dramas, clothes don't hang statically on the body, they are photographed in motion, which enhances their beauty).

The acting style and the staging in *A Chinese Ghost Story* is inventive and, by Western standards, unorthodox. For example, characters standing and spouting dialogue, the default performance style in Western TV and film, is only part of the mix in *A Chinese Ghost Story*. Just as common are scenes where a character leaps up into a tree, or performs a weepy, emotional scene lying on the floor. The Peking Opera style of performance, beloved of Tsui Hark, is displayed throughout *A Chinese Ghost Story*, and not only in characters such as the Tree Demon and Nip

43 'One of the loveliest kisses in all of modern cinema' (Lisa Morton 73).
44 When Nip Siu-shin's not on screen, it's a reminder of her; Ning sees the picture before he meets Nip; Ning goes back to buy it; it's handed back to Ning by Nip; the art dealer tells Ning Choi-san that the model has been dead a year; it reminds Ning of Nip at the end of act two; Siu-shin tells Ning to keep ahold of it, and it's the only memento of her he'll have; and, yes, he's clutching it in the final scene.
45 The filmmakers use several techniques to give Siu-shin a gliding, floaty motion.

Siu-shin.

Seven cinematographers worked on *A Chinese Ghost Story* (probably more if you count second unit and visual effects teams – and some celebrated names, such as Tom Lau Moon tong, Poon Hang-sang, etc), but the result is completely unified[46] – and absolutely gorgeous. This 1987 movie is a photographic feast, and it's got the lot, technically: lamplight, candlelight, firelight, sunset, dawn, night (many ways of lighting a night scene), lightning, explosions, and visual effects.

The sound editing, mixing and dubbing (by Xiaolong Cheng, David Wu Tai-wai and Qun Xue) on *A Chinese Ghost Story* has had a little more time and energy spent on it than your average Hong Kong movie (in any genre). There are some wild sounds in *A Chinese Ghost Story*: tapping, bubbling sounds for the creatures in the temple; loud, echoing voices for the demons; every variation on whooshes for the swordplay and ærial flights; comical, spooky noises when Nip Siu-shin uses her ghostly magic; and extraordinary screams in the underworld sequence.

The score – by James Wong Jim, Romeo Diaz, David Wu Tai-wai and Dai Lemin – includes the expected traditional, Chinese music, and electronica and breathy synthesizer effects for the supernatural scenes.

Editing orchestrates the boundaries between life and death in *A Chinese Ghost Story*: several times, it's simply a single cut, and not a grand visual effect accompanied by 50 channels of noisy sound effects, that takes someone away (to death) or brings them back (to life). For instance, our heroes pick up a bunch of funeral urns, each containing a ghost. Swordsman Yin asks the ghosts to take their urn and leave – they do, and in a cut to the reverse angle, they have already gone. Similarly, when Nip Siu-shin appears to Ning Choi-san in the inn, there's a cut to the reverse angle and Siu-shin is already there, standing behind the scholar. Finally, in the deeply moving climax of the movie, Nip Siu-shin disappears in between the shots, as the camera stays on Ning and we hear Yin's voice off-screen: 'she's already gone'.

Forget wild (and expensive) visual effects, whooshing sound effects, wreathes of smoke and flashing lights, the most formidable effect in cinema, as all good filmmakers know, is the simple cut. With just one cut, you can create – or destroy – anything.

VISUAL EFFECTS.

*A Chinese Ghost Story* is another of Tsui Hark's visual effects feasts. The visual effects were delivered by his company, Cinefex Workshop, and overseen by Ma Xian Liang. Altho' the visual effects budget was in the region of $160,000 (!), they are marvellous, because of the way that they are integrated into the storytelling. That is, the $160,000 spent on the visual effects in *A Chinese Ghost Story* was more successful by far than the million$ spent solely on effects in Hollywood blockbusters such as

---

46 No matter how many photographers shoot a Hong Kong movie, the results always seem to be in sync.

*Snow White and the Huntsman*[47] or *Where the Wild Things Are*. Because those movies reek! And *A Chinese Ghost Story* simply *sings*.

Among the notable visual effects in *A Chinese Ghost Story* are the stopmotion animated creatures, very much in the Ray Harryhausen mold (and marvellously integrated with the live-action). There are also matte shots, miniatures, animation, and optical printing (the movies of Tsui Hark are especially fond of integrating matte paintings with live action, to create those impossible, vast vistas vital to much of fantasy cinema). And, with all those inanimate objects to animate, like giant tongues or swords or tree roots or tentacles, there is a lot of on-set puppeteering in *A Chinese Ghost Story,* plus some animatronics, and special make-up.

Many of the effects were of course created on the set, in front of the camera. *A Chinese Ghost Story* is, like *The Blade* or *The Bride With White Hair*, a fantastically sexy movie in its evocation of *texture* and *atmosphere*. Rain effects, fire effects, smoke effects, lightning effects, wind effects and wire effects – *A Chinese Ghost Story* has got the lot. Every shot has smoke billowing through it (and leaves), wind machines blowing clothing, and, for the lighting, deep blues for the nighttime scenes and reds and orange for the fires and the lamps and the candles.

ACT ONE.

Let's have a look at some of the scenes: –

*A Chinese Ghost Story* opens with a pre-credits teaser featuring the Chinese ghost of the title, in the form of Joey Wang, preying upon a hapless scholar working at his books late at night (one of those places where the windows are always open, where drapres're always fluttering, where the art direction and lighting are exquisite). The spectre appears outside the room, then moves inside to seduce the scholar. The dreamy atmosphere is enhanced by the flapping, white drapes, and the female voice singing.

Ning Choi-san is introduced travelling on his own through the countryside on his way to collect taxes (a thankless job). The rigours of travel (and Ning's characterization) are evoked with some basic realities of life – food (inedible) • and theft (unavoidable) • and death (instant) • and terrible weather (cold and wet).

Sheltering from a rainstorm, Ning Choi-san finds himself witnessing a savage and bloody running battle, with a swordsman pursing and nobbling several thieves (this is a kind of send-up of Akira Kurosawa's cinema – rain, countryside, swords, sudden violence, etc).[48] The scene evokes the proximity of comedy and violence, which's a recurring feature of the *Chinese Ghost Story* movies.

After delineating Ning Choi-san's characterization and predicament (as a lowly but diligent tax collector), *A Chinese Ghost Story* continues with the marvellous bustling village sequence. It's packed with incidents –

---

47 *Snow White and the Huntsman* cost an astonishing $170 million! What a shocking waste of money! Just think what the Chinese film industry could do with $170 million – in 1987 – or now!

48 Ning might be starving, but after the swordsman's left, he immediately throws the gift of some bread away.

selling paper charms,[49] an art dealer,[50] a street brawl, looking for somewhere to stay, finding something to eat, tax collecting, the search for wanted men,[51] the superstitious crowd, and the painting of the ghost.

The rapid shift from day to night[52] takes us into horror movie territory, with Ning Choi-san heading for the Hotel From Hell, the Lan Yeuk Temple, through a forest of wolves. All of the clichés of the horror genre are included with such charm and ingenuity, no one minds if we've seen this hokum 1,000s times before.

The Lan Yeuk Temple is the setting for the introduction of the third major character in *A Chinese Ghost Story*, the Taoist sword master, Swordsman Yin. Once again, Ning Choi-san has the habit of stumbling into trouble; wherever he is, things go wrong. The staging of the scene is masterful, with Ning caught in the frenetic battle between two ancient, fierce rivals, Yin and Hah Hau – he's trapped literally between the two of them, at sword-point. (Here, one of Ning's only weapons – talk – doesn't quite work, tho' Hah Hau storms off in the end).

We're still only part-way through act one of *A Chinese Ghost Story*, because we haven't even got to the nighttime romance yet, or the conflict between Swordsman Yin and the monsters. *A Chinese Ghost Story* doesn't feel rushed, yet it is also racing along at the frantic pace of the city of the Hong Kong itself.

For example, *A Chinese Ghost Story* has time to depict an exposition scene between Ning Choi-san and Swordsman Yin, a scene of Ning bedding down in the Temple, the awakening of the corpses in the attic above, the demise of Swordsman Hah Hau, and the beginning of the romance of Ning and Nip Siu-shin in the waterside pavillion.

A romance between a human man and a spirit woman is a sub-genre of Chinese romance tales (but it's also found in Western folklore and fairy tales – men and mermaids, for instance). In *A Chinese Ghost Story*, it's staged as a highly stylized scene out of a mediæval painting, unreal and dreamy (torches placed in the water as well as in the pavillion is a great touch, and Nip Siu-shin plays a *qin*), but also delightfully comical.

The climax of act one of *A Chinese Ghost Story* is also the finale of both act two and act three, as usual in many movies. That is, it's a conflict between Swordsman Yin and the monsters, with Ning Choi-san caught in the middle (at this point, Ning doesn't quite know who or what Nip Siu-shin is).

Swordsmen and ghosts leaping up trees (and down them, and through them, and around them, and between them), is a form of action that Ching Siu-tung has been delivering for decades. Ching is the King of Forest Fights, of wire-work amongst leaves and branches.

The finale of act one of *A Chinese Ghost Story* is fast and frantic, but

49 Folklore and superstition are evoked throughout *A Chinese Ghost Story*.
50 There's a great gag of the art seller turning all of his wares away from onlookers when he discovers that Ning is poor.
51 The belligerent and dim cops armed with swords looking for the criminals on the wanted posters are a classic running gag (very Tsui-ian). Later, a guy's dragged in who's the spitting image of Swordsman Yin. (Tsui used the gag later, with the impostors in *The Swordsman 3* and *Iron Monkey*).
52 Via some optical wipes.

also includes several romantic clinches (Ning Choi-san lands atop Nip Siu-shin with his hand on her breasts, a Japanese *animé* joke, for instance), and some crude comedy (Swordsman Yin urinates in the bushes where Ning is hiding).

ACT TWO.

Act two of *A Chinese Ghost Story* repeats many of the elements we've already seen in act one: more romantic scenes btn Ning Choi-san and Nip Siu-shin, more of Swordsman Yin (his comical song), more of Ning in the scary temple (and the undead), Ning in the woods again (now with three lanterns), Nip snaring another victim, etc.

But there are complications – the biggest is Ning Choi-san coming face to face (or to nose) with Old Dame, the Tree Demonness, and her entourage. If the Old Dame isn't enough as a potential problem to overcome, there's Nip Siu-shin's sister Siu Ching (Sit Chi-Lun), who suspects that Nip is hiding something (or someone).

This lengthy sequence, where Ning Choi-san is hidden by Nip Siu-shin in a bathtub, is played chiefly for laughs (there are many bits of actorly business, as Ning is nearly-but-not-quite-discovered, taking *A Chinese Ghost Story* into romantic farce or comedy of manners territory. Tsui Hark (likely the creator of this part of the film) had already delivered variations on this sort of scene in both *Shanghai Blues* and *Peking Opera Blues*).

But there's also barely suppressed aggression, too. For ex, Old Dame whipping[53] her daughter Nip Siu-shin (and it's not the first time that Nip has been punished). We also see the monsterish side of the Tree Demonness, with glimpses of the giant tongue (tho' the two aren't put together in a single shot yet).

Comedy, aggression – and romance (the first time that the lovers kiss is when Nip Siu-shin gives Ning Choi-san air under water in the tub (a bath scene in movies is also often an excuse to have the lead actress undressing, as here, and kissing under water to give someone air is a common motif. Tony Ching used it recently in *Jade Dynasty*, 2019).

In the resuming of the romantic scenes, Nip Siu-shin and Ning Choi-san consummate their love in the water pavillion, filmed, as always with the pavillion scenes, with drapes fluttering in front of the camera. There's a second song here (following Yin's Taoist song), which turns the love scene into a montage of the lovers' courtship (and a 'Story So Far' summary of the film).

This is a very common narrative device in Hong Kong movies, where an ecstatic moment is riven with evocations of nostalgia and sadness. The lovemaking in the present tense seems overwhelmed by memories, set to a melancholy tune ('Let the Dawn Never Come', sung by Sally Yeh). The song and the montage editing transforms the present moment into a sum of the past, turns lovemaking into memory, and reminds us that although this is sort of the happiest of times, it is also the saddest, because the lovers cannot stay together.

---

53 The whip neatly links to the giant tongue.

The romance in *A Chinese Ghost Story* has, after all, one of the biggest obstacles you can imagine between two lovers: one of them is dead. They're not from rival clans, not from different social classes, but separated by death.

Hence the bitter poignancy of the scene at the end of act two, when Ning Choi-san and Swordsman Yin visit the cemetery, and Ning confronts the cold, hard fact by the light of day: Nip Siu-shin's gravestone, with her name on it. These are tried and tested ingredients of folklore, bringing together love and death, and they always work.

ACT THREE.

*A Chinese Ghost Story* isn't content with one finale: it has two! And both *rock*, big-time. Indeed, *A Chinese Ghost Story* has a final act as stupendous as any other movie ever made. The ending of *A Chinese Ghost Story* is a *tour-de-force* of filmmaking; it features a barrage of practical effects and visual effects which overwhelm the audience with thrills and invention. As a series of gags and ideas, the final act of *A Chinese Ghost Story* is truly remarkable – but these are not just effects for the sake of effects, they are all tied to the storytelling. And yet, they are not the true ending and resolution of the whole movie: that occurs in the scene in the inn, over two or three close-ups of three people in a room.

The finales of *A Chinese Ghost Story* incorporate every trick and visual effect in film history – pixillation, puppeteering, optical printing, superimpositions, slow and speeded-up film, animation, animatronics, special make-up, and wire-work.

And let's not forget the editing (by David Wu Tai-wai), which cuts the ending within an inch of its life, yet gives everything its proper weight and place, and doesn't shred it with pointlessly rapid editing (as so many other movies do). The two finales of *A Chinese Ghost Story are* cut very fast (as usual in a Tony Ching and Tsui Hark movie), but the pace is in sync with the storytelling and the performances.

In the first half of the finale of *A Chinese Ghost Story*, the Taoist monk Yin Chik-ha and the hapless scholar Ning Choi-san go up against the dreaded Tree Demon, Old Dame. What are they fighting for? Why, the luscious Nip Siu-shin, of course! Only she just happens to be a ghost! (But by this time, Ning has promised Siu-shin that he'll make sure her spirit is laid to rest, which involves digging up her remains in a nearby grave. Swordsman Yin is resistant to the notion: ghosts and humans do not mix, he reckons. But Ning, realizing at last that Siu-shin is a supernatural creature (she acknowledges this to his face), and there's no hope they could be together for long, does the right thing, as a romantic die-hard).

A well-meaning but useless scholar, a crazy, old, Taoist monk, an outsize Tree Demon villain (who has the longest tongue[54] in history), and a beautiful princess who's dead – ahh, it can only be a Chinese, fantasy-action-comedy-horror-romance movie based on a 17th century tale and centuries of superstition and folklore.

---

54 That tongue is 'horror and high camp, kung fu and special-effects fantasy, it is hyperactive, pathological and multi-dimensional', noted Stephen Teo (1997, 228).

✦

The first finale of *A Chinese Ghost Story* would be enough to cap any movie (but the filmmakers, looking at what they'd shot later, opted to go back and add some more). It's centred around the Lan Yeuk Temple, but also takes in much to-ing and fro-ing to the water pavillion (where Ning Choi-san and Nip Siu-shin tryst), and running around the woodland, with occasional visits to an over-grown cemetery (all set at night, of course, with blue lighting, smoke, wind, and flickering flames). The action is spell-binding, with the visual effects, the stunts, the flashing swords, the explosions, and the wire-work coming thick and fast. It's fantastically furious fantasy filmmaking, one of those set-pieces where the movie-makers chuck in everything they can get hold of, not caring whether it looks 'real', whether it's 'believable', or whether it even makes sense! Who cares? It's simply sublime!

But, folks, this is not miraculously achieved action and visual effects for the sake of it – the filmmaking is always telling a story, is always dramatizing the struggles between the four protagonists: the young scholar Ning Choi-san who just wants to save Nip Siu-shin and be with her (and help her achieve a peaceful quieting of her restless spirit); the Taoist demon-buster Yin Chik-ha, who wants to vanquish the monsters for once and for all; Siu-shin who hopes that her soul can be laid to rest (and be free of enslavement to the Tree Demon), but also to be with her lover; and the fiendish monster Tree Demon, who wants to slaughter anyone who opposes it (and who won't let Siu-shin go without a fight!).

The scenes in *A Chinese Ghost Story* of the colossal tongue slithering around the temple so it envelops it are brilliant updates of schlocky, 1950s monster movies. There's a Wall of Tongue out there! ('Don't let it get in your mouth!' the heroes yell at each other. Damn right! No French kissing with that demon!).[55] Once the tongue's inside the building, the gags and stunts are amazing – amazingly *rapid*, too, and very funny (As director Ching Siu-tung explained, it took a *lot* of work to make that giant tongue look good. But it was worth it).

As a sequence of in-front-of-the-camera practical effects, this is one of the finest in all cinema, worthy of the maestros of German silent cinema like F.W. Murnau or Fritz Lang. There is the same energetic, try-anything spirit of 1920s German cinema, and the levels of imagination and skill on display are astounding.

Yes, when it comes to puppeteering an entire environment, with breakaway props, walls, floors, ceilings, rafters, tables, windows, balconies and pillars, Hong Kong cinema has no equal. It's as if Hong Kong action cinema is always part-animation, but these guys are animating real things, not drawings or pixels – *whole buildings* as well as people and props and monsters!

Anything can move in Hong Kong action cinema – and frequently does. You thought that chair was just going to sit there quietly throughout the scene? No, Jackie Chan is going to spin it, bounce it to and fro on a

55 We've already seen a ghostly point-of-view shot of the tongue entering a victim's body and sucking the life out of it.

victim's head, and then break it over him. You thought that at least the walls might survive intact – no, that giant tongue is smashing through them.

The filmmakers of *A Chinese Ghost Story* also deliver inventive variations on the monster that can transform – so they are throwing tentacles at the audience, then roots that wriggle along (and under) the ground, then branches that leap at the hero, then a giant beak, and even then the monster doesn't – won't, can't – die (another horror movie staple).

The creature is slithering into and out of a hole, sliding under the ground, grasping Yip Siu-shin, and Ning Choi-san, and the Swordsman (at different times), and performing impossible transformations. The filmmakers worked tirelessly to make a giant tongue appear as a fearsome opponent, and they succeeded. It's ridiculous – a giant tongue! Everyone knows that, but one of the tricks in making it work was to approach the whole thing with just the right tone and attitude (the *tone* of *A Chinese Ghost Story* I reckon is absolutely perfect). Thus, there are comical touches, but not too many (the threat is not deflated with laughter); the humour is delicately balanced with the thrills and suspense.

So Swordsman Yin is comically covered with goop but he could still die at any moment. So Ning Choi-san is desperately trying to avoid the tip of the tongue entering his mouth in a humorous manner, but it looks like he might lose.

✦

The second finale of *A Chinese Ghost Story* starts when the heroes visit a new locale, another inn. Here the lovers are re-united (following some business with the multiple funeral urns, which contain ghosts of young women, sort of Nip Siu-shin's sisters. This is played for both comedy and pathos). There are some sweet touches, too – such as Swordsman Yin's embarrassment when he sees the lovers together.

The second finale in *A Chinese Ghost Story,* producer Tsui Hark explained, came about when the filmmakers decided what they had initially scripted wasn't satisfying (the script went thru a number of variations). As they didn't have the $$$$$ for a Big Set (where most action movie finales take place – often it's the super-villain's lair, which is destroyed at the end), they decided they could put the climax in a spaceless space. That is, just a piece of ground (at night, of course), which, with the aid of *tons* of smoke and clever lighting (and slow motion, and a battery of visual effects), they could persuade the audience that it was the underworld (of course, audiences can be easily persuaded: if an actor tells them they're in the underworld, the audience believes it. There's no point *not* buying into it – especially this late in the movie. And, anyway, who knows what the underworld looks like?).

There are so many imaginative ideas erupting all over the place in the second finale of *A Chinese Ghost Story*, it's impossible to cite them all. Many of the images and beats are memorable: the running, galloping army that's transparent (carrying Nip Siu-shin in a palanquin[56] to her wedding)…

56 Tony Ching is very fond of galloping palanquin scenes – they appear in his first film, *Duel To the Death.*

Swordsman Yin kicking Ning Choi-san to soar over the army towards Siu-shin (a p.o.v. shot shows him flying over the army below)... the skull motif – the skulls in the inn, and the mountain of skulls that the Black Mountain Demon stands on... Siu-shin and Ning Choi-san flying through the air, as she rescues him yet again... Ning and Siu-shin crashing into a cliff and being engulfed by clutching arms... Yin taking on the whole army single-handed (and later with a sword crackling with energy)... Yin writing heaven and earth spells on his palm in blood and firing them at the enemy... the Black Mountain Demon's knight disappearing and re-appearing behind Swordsman Yin's back... the screaming heads that shoot out from under-neath the Black Mountain Demon's cloak, hurtling at Siu-shin and biting her...

The *confidence* of the filmmakers, their *invention* and *creativity*, and the *joy* they have in entertaining the audience, are very infectious in *A Chinese Ghost Story*. You can't help but be blown away by it, swept along by it, and energized by it. The *spirit* of this movie, its *tone* and *attitude*, are so appealing (sometimes you can't believe just how many marvellous scenes the film team have produced in *A Chinese Ghost Story* – but the montage of the movie's highlights that plays over the end credits reminds you, while Leslie Cheung sings the theme song).

And there is a *genuine* feeling of movie magic in *A Chinese Ghost Story* – of filmmakers who're delighting in the magical effects that cinema can create, just like Géorges Méliès was over-joyed like a child when he discovered what movies and cameras could do back in the early 1900s (Méliès would've utterly *adored A Chinese Ghost Story*! This is a Mélièsian movie if ever there was one!).

✦

Let's look at the climactic scene in the inn, when our heroes make it back from the underworld after the battle with the monsters and demons and army of the dead – how they crawl out of thin air into the shadowy interior of the temple just before sunrise (a special effect very reminiscent of *The Wizard of Oz*, *The Invisible Man* or *Stairway To Heaven*). Look at the staging of the scene – how the three actors are exhausted, on the floor,[57] until Ning Choi-san moves to the window, where the sun is streaming in (sunlight is fatal to Nip Siu-shin, like a vampire). Ning can't bear to turn to look at Siu-shin, because he knows he's got to say goodbye to her forever. He faces the window and the light, turned away, and tells her to return with her ashes. A final medium shot of Siu-shin lying on the floor... Then there's a brilliant use of off-screen dialogue, and a cut – when Yin Chik-ha says, 'she's already gone'. And in the blink of an edit made on 35mm celluloid, it's over, the romance is ended.[58]

This scene, not the giant battle in the underworld, resolves the primary plot of *A Chinese Ghost Story* – the love story. Notice how poignant it is, how effective, and how economical – it's played largely over

57 A previous conversation btn the lovers was also played on the floor – in the midst of the giant tongue attack.
58 The movie closes with our heroes galloping away under a rainbow (several Hong Kong action movies of this period close with the heroes on horseback, including *Peking Opera Blues*, *New Dragon Gate Inn* and the *Swordsman* movies).

close-ups of the principal actors. And notice too that it's very short, and all the more emotional for it. Many comparable movies, especially in the 21st century, would milk and milk that scene. I find the ending very moving – partly because we are mourning the loss of a much-loved star, Leslie Cheung.

Parts of the window's wooden blinds crumple, letting more light in – the human-and-ghost romance has ended (as it has to), but the light caught on film says otherwise: it is a rich, juicy, orange light, so vibrant you could bathe in it. It's the light of morning: there's no need to draw attention to the countless symbols that the light of sunrise embodies. And *A Chinese Ghost Story* as a whole doesn't really want or need spiritual or religious or metaphysical interpretations. But they are certainly there if you want to evoke them. (And yet there is something so luscious about the golden light flooding into the inn, and the way that it has been photographed, that's mysterious and sensual. Like many Chinese, fantasy movies, *A Chinese Ghost Story* is in love with light. It's a movie which uses light itself as a primary dramatic device, like films such as *Close Encounters of the Third Kind*[59] or *Princess Mononoke*).

WE ARE ALL GHOSTS.

There are many poignant moments in *A Chinese Ghost Story*: sure, it's a stops-all-out, fantasy rollercoaster ride, but it also exhibits an acute awareness of issues like time passing and death, like the fleetingness and impermanence of human existence, like the frailty of love and romance. There are scenes in *A Chinese Ghost Story* where the headlong rush of the narrative halts, for instance: such as when Taoist monk Yin Chik-ha has a crisis of conscience, and wonders what the hell he's doing (remarking that he's set himself outside of life, but he's not a ghost, either: he's lost somewhere in-between. To humans, he deliberately appeared as a ghost, but when he's among ghosts, he is the human who wants to vanquish them).[60]

And there's time for a jokey courtroom scene: Ning Choi-san is beaten on the floor while the judge and his assistant berate him (the assistant's played by one of the movie's composers and a major creative talent in Hong Kong cinema, David Wu Tai-wai, and the judge is Wong Jing, one of the moguls of Cantonese cinema).

*A Chinese Ghost Story* also has time in its jam-packed 98 minutes for some musical montages. There's a delightfully bonkers scene where Swordsman Yin delivers a musical rap about Taoism ('Dao, Dao, Dao, Dao!') as he performs a marvellous sword dance (a set-piece also in the 1960 film). As the lovers make love, we have the customary slow ballad ('Let the Dawn Never Come' by Sally Yeh) playing over close-ups of two

59 The deep orange of the sunlight recalls the ball of light on the other side of the door that the child Barry opens in *Close Encounters of the Third Kind* (1977). When he was asked to provide an example of a 'signature shot' or 'master image' in all of his films, Steven Spielberg chose the shot in *Close Encounters of the Third Kind* of the bright orange UFO light outside: 'that beautiful but awful light, just like fire coming through the doorway. And he's very small, and it's a very large door, and there's a lot of promise or danger outside that door'.
60 In *A Chinese Ghost Story*, one of the Taoist swordsman's tasks is to keep the world of ghosts, the *yin*, separate from the world of humans, the *yang*.

beautiful people, Leslie Cheung and Joey Wong. In many a movie, these MTV-a-like[61] montages of lovemaking and togetherness have no dramatic or emotional heat at all, but in *A Chinese Ghost Story* they are delicious.

Because we are all ghosts.

Because we are all here for a moment, then we're gone.

A great fantasy movie, like *A Chinese Ghost Story*, can evoke those spiritual issues so magically, exploring them, yet somehow also offering a kind of emotional/ religious catharsis.

This is great storytelling.

61 Ching Siu-tung said the design of *A Chinese Ghost Story* was 'like watching a Chinese MTV'.

A Better Tomorrow (1986).

A Better Tomorrow 2 (1987).

A Chinese Ghost Story (1987), this page and over.

# 4

# *A CHINESE GHOST STORY 2*

## *Sin Nui Yau Wan II – Yan Gaan Do*

Most of the principals of the first *A Chinese Ghost Story* movie returned for the first sequel, including the director, producer and stars. *A Chinese Ghost Story 2* (1990, *Qiannü Youhun Zhi Renjian Dao* in Mandarin = *Sien Female Ghost II: Human Realm Tao*) was written by Lau Tai-mok, Lam Kei-to and Leung Yiu-ming (with a story co-credit for Tsui Hark and Yuen Kai-Chi), with the same cast (Leslie Cheung Kwok-wing, Joey Wong Cho-yin, Wu Ma, and Lau Siu-ming), plus newbies Jacky Cheung (as Chi Chau/ Autumn), and Michelle Reiss (a.k.a. Li, as Yuet Chi/ Moon.) Also in the cast were: Ku Feng, Waise Lee Chi-hung, Lau Shun, Wong Fue-chun, Do Siuy-chin, Johnny Koo, Fei Sing, Wong Hung and Ng Kwok-kin. (Ching Siu-tung directed all three *Chinese Ghost Story* movies, and Tsui Hark was producer on all three). DP: Arthur Wong, editor: Marco Mak Chi-sin, art dirs.: William Chang Suk-Ping and Ho Kim-Sing, sound: Miu Gik Luk Yam Sat, Kwok Wing-Kei, Lam Wing-Cheung and Wong Choh-Keung, costumes: Kitty Ho Wai-Ying, hair: Chau Siu-Mui and Peng Yen-Lien, music: James Wong Jim, Romeo Diaz and Tang Siu-Lam, special fx by Nick Allder and David Watkins, make-up: Man Yun-Ling, and the action dirs. were Cheung Kan Chow, Ching Siu-tung, Bobby Woo Chi-lung, and Lau Chi-ho. Released in July 13, 1990. 98/ 104 minutes.

Produced for around HK $7 million (= US $1 million)[1] – an impossibly tiny budget! – *A Chinese Ghost Story 2* is a typical sequel: More Of The Same, tho' slightly different (however, it develops the Chinese ghost plot into the future, rather than, like many sequels, and most in Hong Kong cinema, re-hashing the same elements but with a new yarn). The first movie was a ghost story and romance; the second focusses on more human issues, or morals and ethics.[2] Altho' film critics made their usual

---

1 Bey Logan reckoned the budget was US $7 million, but that seems too high; it might stem from the confusion between Hong Kong and North American dollars. In fact, the first movie cost $650,000, so a step up to $1 million seems correct.
2 There were many meetings, Tony Ching recalled, as they decided what to do in the *Chinese Ghost Story* sequel.

complaints about *A Chinese Ghost Story 2* being less successful than the first movie, I'm sure it played well with viewers (I bet an audience in a multiplex theatre in Kowloon in 1990 enjoyed the scares, the jokes, the romance and the swordplay. It's a perfect Friday Night Movie). After all, you get more Leslie Cheung Kwok-wing (and that's enough for many fans!), and you also get more Joey Wong, and you get Jacky Cheung, and you get Wu Ma! What's not to like?!

Like many sequels, *A Chinese Ghost Story 2* not only draws on the first film in every way, it quotes directly from it, in the form of several montages. *A Chinese Ghost Story 2* opens, for instance, with a montage of images which summarize the story of the first outing. In the middle of act two, to evoke the tragic romance of Ning Choi-san and Nip Siu-shin, there's another montage, which includes the iconic scene of the underwater kiss. Joey Wong sings on the score, along with a female chorus.

Altho' Tsui Hark, among others, were part of the high-powered team of collaborators working on *A Chinese Ghost Story 2*, this is still a Tony Ching movie. And not only in the action scenes: many of the romantic scenes in *A Chinese Ghost Story 2* are far more indulgent, stylized and dreamy than those in the work of Tsui. *A Chinese Ghost Story 2* doesn't feature just one image of the lovers in a close embrace, but many. Often these're filmed in slow motion, with exaggerated lighting. Backlit, floating, the lovers drift across the set or have their faces pressed together on the ground. The camera lingers long over the incredible faces of Joey Wong and Leslie Cheung (and Michelle Reiss).

Ching Siu-tung's cinema pushes romantic motifs into extreme stylization, holding on slow motion images of the lovers far longer than similar movies. The *mise-en-scène* is intricately art-directed, carefully composed, meticulously costumed, with perfect make-up and exquisite lighting. These images have had a lot of time and energy expended in staging them.

Technically, *A Chinese Ghost Story 2* is absolutely amazing: with the legendary Arthur Wong heading up the photography department, this is one of the most ravishing looking of all Hong Kong movies. A huge proportion of the show occurs at night or dusk, requiring a massive amount of lighting equipment. And as it's a historical fantasy, there is plenty of opportunity for highly stylized lighting schemes.

It wasn't easy, though: Arthur Wong recalled an incident on this movie:

> I was hanging from a big crane set above a 100-feet deep cliff. I had to move away from the edge. But they wrongly calculated my weight and when I was in the harness, with the camera and the batteries, I was too heavy. When I just took off, I was upside-down, head down. Wow, it was very scary. And it was very hard to get me back once I was

upside-down. People had to come to the edge of the cliff and grab me. (D. Vivier)

All of the departments in charge of the visuals are stellar: costumes by Kitty Ho Wai-Ying, hair by Chau Siu-Mui and Peng Yen-Lien, make-up by Man Yun-Ling and art direction by William Chang Suk-Ping and Ho Kim-Sing (many of whom worked for Tony Ching and Tsui Hark on other productions).

The editing of A Chinese Ghost Story 2 keeps the movie in perpetual motion, yet with many opportunities for reflective interludes, and emotional montages. Tsui Hark's regular editor, Marco Mak Chi-sin, cut this film. One of the chief reasons that A Chinese Ghost Story 2 is so satisfying is because it is so well-edited.

Finally, the score, by James Wong Jim, Romeo Diaz and Tang Siu-Lam, should be cited as a key ingredient in the success of A Chinese Ghost Story 2: as with the Once Upon a Time In China films, A Chinese Ghost Story 2 employs a traditional, Chinese score in the main. As it's also a fantasy movie and a horror movie, however, it uses electronica for suspense. Also, there are several songs in A Chinese Ghost Story 2, sung by Leslie Cheung, Joey Wong and a chorus.

✦

One of the delights of a sequel is seeing how the filmmakers employ the elements of the previous movie/s. In A Chinese Ghost Story 2, these included finding inventive ways of bringing back props like the painting of Nip Siu-shin, or using the charms, or the demon fights, or the eye candy (male and female) and semi-nude bathing scenes.3 But a sequel doesn't usually change everything, if it's got sense (if you change too much, it's not a sequel, it's a different movie). The trick with a sequel of this kind of fluffy, commercial, popcorn cinema is to give the audience something that seems 'new' yet is also exactly the same (because that's also what the audience want).

It's a tricky balancing act that inevitably means that you keep many ingredients just the same. So in A Chinese Ghost Story 2 many of the elements are straight repetitions from the first movie: thus, Ning Choi-san is back as the hapless debt collector with his backpack, arriving in a town on his travels; there's a visit to a haunted house, a creepy night spent there during a storm (with a monster appearing), a rough restaurant, wanted men posters, the painting of Nip Siu-shin, another mad Taoist monk, a procession, an arranged marriage, comical bathing scenes, farcical/ partial nudity scenes, romantic kisses, more battles with monstrous foes, more swordplay, etc.

After all, the filmmakers involved in producing A Chinese Ghost Story 2 are Hong Kong veterans. They are out-and-out capitalists, experienced showmen who aim to make money from their movies. Yes – money! So A

3 The 1990 movie decided that fans would want to see Leslie Cheung taking a bath. So, in the Righteous Villa, Ning Choi-san pops into a wooden bath which's handily nearby. And that's when the monsters show up, just as in a horror movie when the heroine's taking a shower. It's here too where the rap version of Tao Te Ching is reprised from the first movie, with Ning singing it now as a protection against evil spirits.

*Chine$e Gho$t $tory 2* is a wholly commercial proposition. Yes, and once the end credits start to roll, the house lights are already up, and you're being hurried out of your seat to make way for the next showing (common practice in Hong Kong!).

✦

Among the most pressing challenges in *A Chinese Ghost Story 2* was what to do with Joey Wong's character, Nip Siu-shin, who eventually received the peace she desired (a proper death and burial for her soul) in the finale of the first movie. Instead of reviving the character (a cinch to do in a fantasy flick – especially one about life and death and ghosts!), which must've been tempting, the writers and producers opted to have Joey Wong appear as a new character, Windy (who's pretty much the same, of course, but not so wan and pale and ethereal – tho' just as beautiful).

Windy is part of a group that follows Elder Chu – so she is very human, very not-ghostly (but she does have a supernatural moment), and is introduced brandishing a sword which she holds up at Ning Choi-san (thus she is now one of the many female warriors in Hong Kong cinema). They meet following an extravagant nighttime fight scene outside the Righteous Villa, where the rebels dress up as ghosts in white and duel with Autumn (halfway thru act one). This fight scene contains stupendous images – like the would-be ghosts floating down behind Ning.[4] And when Ning catches a glimpse of Windy, he does a double-take, as do we – actors like Joey Wong are literally breathtaking.

*A Chinese Ghost Story 2* is a haunted house movie – we spend *a lot* of time in the shadowy Righteous Villa, and far less outdoors, as in the previous *A Chinese Ghost Story* outing. *A Chinese Ghost Story 2* is part comedy horror movie, part *wuxia*/ martial arts movie, part romantic drama, and part farce.

As Windy inevitably falls for Ning Choi-san (and who wouldn't when he's played by the divine Leslie Cheung?!), she agrees at times to pretend to be his lost love, Nip Siu-shin. Ning, meanwhile, spends part of *A Chinese Ghost Story 2* in exhausted or altered states, imagining that Windy is really Siu-shin.

And while Ning Choi-san pines for Nip Siu-shin (even when the wide-awake side of him knows that he'll never see her again – they said farewell forever at the end of the first flick), *A Chinese Ghost Story II* includes a few scenes where both Windy and Moon are looking at Ning lovingly, from afar. The scenes play into the celebrity status of Leslie Cheung, of course – he's the kind of super-babe actor that fans at film premieres scream over. In some scenes in *A Chinese Ghost Story 2*, there isn't even a reverse angle depicting what the women're looking at: instead the camera stays on Moon and Windy, bashing their heads together in their eagerness to try to get a better glimpse of Ning. (As the movie progresses, Moon seems to accept that Ning seems more interested in Windy than her. She

---

4 One of the many marvellous images in *A Chinese Ghost Story 2* features the introduction of the rebels: dressed as ghosts in white, in a forest night scene, they are lowered into the frame out of focus behind Leslie Cheung as if they're corpses hanging from ropes from trees. It's a genuinely creepy image, and the *Chinese Ghost Story* movies are full of such scenes.

sulks and pouts, but in the finale becomes more attached to the Taoist monk Autumn, even tho' this relationship is also doomed. Because when Autumn revives the couple by kissing *chi* back into them, he avoids Moon because she's a woman. A romance between a woman and a Taoist monk is never going to fly in a Chinese action movie! Even when that monk is played by the appealing pop star Jacky Cheung!).

And *A Chinese Ghost Story 2* is funny. Putting Ning Choi-san in prison with a wily, old coot played by Ku Feng (who's also near-crazy) was a fun skit on *The Count of Monte Cristo* (and the prison genre). Having Ning then being mistaken for Elder Chu, a highly-respected scholar and philosopher, was wonderful (Ning grows a beard in jail, as you do – he's in there for months – so he looks like the Elder. Later, he shaves it off to become the familiar Ning and Leslie Cheung without a beard). In an instant the beardy guise switches the hierarchy of the relationships around, and now Ning is elevated to the leader of the pack, instead of being the rather hopeless youth who's just trying to get along and stay out of trouble. The gag is extended to a scene where Ning shaves off his 'tache, only to find that the rebel group dismiss him as just anyone – without those whiskers, he's a nobody! (Director Ching Siu-tung remarked that he was thinking of Tiananmen Square and the suppression of political rebellion in the personality of Elder Chu, a writer who's imprisoned for apparently politically subversive works (which aren't at all).)

Certainly the political/ ideological opinions of the writers, and Tsui Hark, can be heard in the speech that the old man gives in the cell – he mentions that if he writes history, he's accused of criticizing the present, and if he writes fairy tales, he's charged with purveying superstition (i.e., whatever he does as an artist/ writer, the powers-that-be will find some fault with his work). The Communist ideology of Mainland China is critiqued here.

✦

One of the finest scenes in *A Chinese Ghost Story 2* had the group of rebels eavesdropping on Ning Choi-san and Windy talking following their amazing encounter in the forest. Here is the brilliant use of the painting prop – the calligraphy that Ning and Nip Siu-shin performed in the first *A Chinese Ghost Story* movie (and spoke in voiceover), drawn into the painting, is now switched about. Now the rebel group is thrilled to think that Ning is going to recite some amazing poetry, and they get to hear it. Which he does! And lo and behold, the poem contains clues which the rebels decipher as referring to their Master and the water pavilion (it must've taken some time for the screenwriters to work this out! The comedy, complete with group reaction shots, is very Tsui-ian, as is the mistaken identity gag).

Wu Ma only appears towards the end of *A Chinese Ghost Story 2*: instead, it's Jacky Cheung who takes up the role of the crazy, Taoist demon hunter and companion to Ning Choi-san in the adventure. One of the four pop singers known as the 'Four Golden Kings' (along with Leslie Cheung, Andy Lau and Leon Lai), Cheung is terrific in the comic/ action/

sidekick role of the priest Autumn (he has the same charms and protections against the demons, but he can also burrow under the ground at speed – one of the ninja techniques that Tony Ching is fond of). Cheung gets the tone of these movies spot-on, revelling in the OTT masquerade of it all (*A Chinese Ghost Story 2* is like a Chinese *Abott and Costello* picture – tho' certainly made with more visual panache!). A year later, Cheung was back in a comical role for Tsui Hark, as 'Buck Tooth' So in *Once Upon a Time In China,* and after that in *Wicked City.*

✦

The script of *A Chinese Ghost Story 2* is dense with subplots: the romance between Ning and Windy; the erotic triangle of Ning, Windy and Moon; the romantic rivalry between Windy and Moon; Moon's fondness for Autumn; the Imperial persecution of Windy's father, Lord Fu; the mistaken identity of Ning as Elder Chu; the conflict between the rebels and the government; Official Hu realizing the Imperial court is corrupt; the introduction of the High Priest and his lackeys, and so on.

Multiple identity is another theme in *A Chinese Ghost Story 2* – Ning Choi-san is mistaken for Elder Chu by the rebels (despite his protestations); Windy isn't Nip Shui-sin (but Ning wants her to be); and the High Priest turns out to be a demonic Buddha and then a mad monster.

The narrative in the second act of *A Chinese Ghost Story 2* replays many moments from the first *Ghost* picture (act two is the trickiest part of any commercial movie), but you barely notice it. The characters, motifs and scenarios are switched around, but played for similar sorts of comedy, farce, awkwardness, embarrassment, suspense, etc.

The filmmakers, for instance, milk every ounce of thrills and comedy from a bunch of youths trapped inside a haunted house (the Righteous Villa). They squeeze every cent out of the giant monster and its animatronic head (it spooks Ning Choi-san and Autumn, with a series of gags about the freezing palm charm; it startles Windy taking a bath; and it creeps up on Moon. The monster fights continue outside, with the Imperial official taking it on, as well as Autumn. In some scenes, there's a flying monster hand or just the torso attacking the rebel group).

The filmmakers take great delight in dumping a ton of nasty gunk on their beautiful leading lady, with Joey Wong's Windy turning into a demon for some fun visual effects battles reminiscent of *The Exorcist* (1973), until she's kissed back into reality by Ning Choi-san, as the lovers spin and spin in the air. This provides both a supernatural scene for Joey Wong, where she's ghost-like as in the first flick, but she's a nasty spectre who breathes out snakes, and our Movie Kiss between the two main stars, a reprise of the first film, as a series of cuts show Windy becoming more'n more human. At the end, the lovers drift gently to the floor and Ning seems blissed-out – only for Autumn to exchange his *chi* – it's OK for a Taoist priest to perform mouth-to-mouth on a guy, isn't it?

One bathing scene isn't enough. So the filmmakers have their other main star (Joey Wong) undressing and taking a bath (to wash off the goop the prop department have dumped on her). And of course the giant monster is still lurking around. And of course there's French sex farce comedy when Ning Choi-san tries to cover Windy's modesty from the rest of the rebel gang (this is a replay of the scene where the Old Dame appeared in Siu-shin's chambers in the first film). Ning goes to great lengths to preserve Windy's virtue. Woven into this is the romantic rivalry between Windy and Moon.

Another ingredient added to *A Chinese Ghost Story 2* were the cannibal outlaws: Ning Choi-san is hapless enough to stop over at their inn and restaurant not once but twice! Cue images of severed hands and toes mixed in the stew, and a dog with a hand in its maw. Yuk! (One can imagine that this part of the script came from Tsui Hark; he had made much of mad cannibals in *We're Going To Eat You* ).

Either you buy into the comedy or you don't – the sex comedy stuff, the French farce stuff, the cannibals stuff, the monster creeping around and nearly-but-not-quite grabbing the heroine stuff, and the women drooling over a man stuff. But you have to admire the light-hearted spirit in which this 1990 movie is delivered: this is a film that knows it's a pile of fluff, and revels in it. It's a Friday night, popcorn and candy and yelling at the screen sort of movie. It's the movie equivalent of a theme park ride, a haunted house ride at the fairground (plenty of Western movies are like this, and some, like *Pirates of the Caribbean* and *The Haunted Mansion*, are even based on theme park rides!).

✦

A new character, an Imperial official, Hu (played by veteran actor Waise Lee), thickens the plot of *A Chinese Ghost Story 2*, arriving at the end of act two – by first pursuing our heroes into the haunted Righteous Villa, then switching ideological sides when he sees how brave they are, and, when he encounters the super-villain High Priest, how corrupt the Imperial circle is. Hu is a thematic character, then – not essential to the central plot, but he exposes the corruption of the Imperial government. *A Chinese Ghost Story 2* was made not long after Tiananmen Square. (Hu is part of an Imperial guard escorting Windy's father, Lord Fu, to his execution; his scene is filmed, once again, at the stony cliffs and dirt track in the New Territories. The scene features Hu going up against the Taoist priest Autumn).

The sequence where Hu enters the High Priest's lair in *A Chinese Ghost Story 2* is genuinely imaginative and chilling: it's a palace arrayed like a court of law lit by flickering torches where Imperial ministers have been kidnapped and eviscerated, so that only hollow husks remain. It's a terrific satire on the 'hollow men' who rule the land – the literal emptiness and nothingness of civil servants and governments. They're not even corpses, they're just shells. (Meanwhile, out back, Hu stumbles into the charnel pits where bits of bodies are heaped, some still partially alive. And three of the heroes have been imprisoned inside red cocoons, presumably the first stage of evisceration. Hu sets them free, which leads to the finale).

✦

The finale of *A Chinese Ghost Story II* has to top the first movie of 1987, as sequels often try to do: it becomes a giant monster movie, when the new villain, the chief Buddhist monk and adviser to the Emperor, the High Priest, arrives in town. A formidable opponent, a self-righteous religious figure, who hides behind the paraphernalia of organized religion, the High Priest is played by Lau Shun (a Tsui Hark regular – he was Swordsman Zen in *The Swordsman 2,* the aged Asia in *The Swordsman 3,* Wong Fei-hung's father in *Once Upon a Time In China 3*, and appeared in numerous movies of this period). Crossdressing in villains in Chinese fantasy cinema is once again evoked, when the High Priest speaks in a high-pitched woman's voice. However, that's only part of it: the High Priest is also an adept at spell-casting, reciting enchantments in Sanskrit to over-power his rivals.

When the villain turns into a giant, golden statue of the Buddha,[5] you know you are wholly within Asian folktale territory – this sort of imagery, with talking statues of gods, simply doesn't appear anywhere in Western cinema. At the climax of a North American action or fantasy movie, no villain would be allowed to turn into Jesus!

In the finale of *A Chinese Ghost Story 2*, the heroes call on the aid of the crazy, old monk Yin Chik-ha from the first *Ghost* movie: Wu Ma makes a very welcome return as Swordsman Yin, from his bolthole in the Lan Teuk Temple from the first film.[6]

✦

The visuals in the finale of *A Chinese Ghost Story 2* are stupendous – out come the coloured lights, the glowing miniatures and matte paintings, the optically-printed bolts of magic, the smoke and fire practical effects, and actors and stuntmen are flying all over the screen. The camera is often at ground level, hurtling along. The visual effects are wild, with no holds barred: the earth is cracking open, a giant beastie emerges – a centipede![7] – and our heroes take refuge in a magic circle of flying, golden swords. Every possible visual effect and special effect and practical effect is employed, furnishing so many rapidfire gags. There is, as in the first *Ghost* movie, a joyous celebration of the trickery that cinema can conjure up.

For instance, there's a stunning battle against invisible assailants, as Hu the Imperial official duels with the High Priest's henchwomen, who hurtle at him using ninja-ish invisibility (Tony Ching had employed invisible warriors before – it's irresistible to a filmmaker who enjoys the trickery of cinema). The sword fight is a set-piece all of its own, with Hu playing part of it as a one-armed swordsman (a favourite staple of Chinese *wuxia* cinema), when his arm's cut off early on in the fight. There are incredible details in the scene – such as blood spattering out of invisible wounds onto the dirt (but when they're killed, the ninja lose their invisibility, then disappear).

---

5 The orange and gold lighting accentuates the symbolic colours of Buddhism.
6 This is one reason why Windy and Ning Choi-san get separated from the others. They're pursed by the wolves from the first film, where the mere mention of the dread name Lan Teuk Temple has the beasts fleeing.
7 Like something out of William Burroughs, a critic remarked.

In the same sort of rocky, threatening arena of stones and night that the first *A Chinese Ghost Story* movie used for its finale, *A Chinese Ghost Story 2* has our heroes battling a giant monster. All sorts of inventive beats and twists are concocted to surprise and delight the audience. In one memorable shot, as the monster appears, the ground erupts, forming a wall of broken stones behind our heroes (instead of the usual flames), who're running towards the camera. In another scene, the two Taoist monks, Yin Chik-ha and Autumn, are eaten by the monster (Yin dives in to save Autumn). Trapped in the yucky goop of the monster's belly, Yin reckons that they could separate their spirits from their bodies and flee. It's a suitably magical escape – a *deus ex machina* sort of escape, and a kind of cheat. But within the context of this high-powered, supernatural movie, where life and death are continually being fought over, the filmmakers get away with it. (However, poor Autumn isn't able to return to his body – there's a startling point-of-view shot, with the power and anxiety of a bad dream, when Autumn's semi-transparent spirit flies right over his body lying on the ground, and off into the black sky. Moon hurries after him, but she can't grasp his spirit).

✦

*A Chinese Ghost Story II* closes with an audience-pleasing happy ending (thus, because Windy isn't a ghost or dead, our couple can be legitimately together). First, there's another elaborate street procession,[8] echoing the one in the first *Ghost* movie, where Ning Choi-san spots Windy parading thru the village. Windy, sporting an elaborate headdress[9] in a covered palanquin,[10] is going (reluctantly) to her arranged marriage (an echo of the finale of the first *Ghost* flick, where Nip Siu-shin was due to wed the Lord of the Black Mountain). Ning, hurrying into the crowd, generously wishes her well (passing his blessing to her via Moon).

Ah, but we can't leave our hero like that, can we?, watching wistfully and mournfully as the heroine is carried away by fate to a marriage she doesn't want. So the filmmakers close the 1990 *A Chinese Ghost Story 2* with a big reunion scene, out on the hills, staged on horseback so they can have that cliché of all movie clichés: the heroes riding off into the sunset.[11]

Everything about this movie has been designed as a crowd-pleaser – the filmmakers want to entertain the audience more than anything. And they succeed! So *A Chinese Ghost Story 2* duly closes with the lovers re-united (and, please, geeks and crrritics, *don't* remind us that Windy isn't Ning Choi-san's true love, that his beloved is really Nip Siu-shin![12] We know that! And, anyhoo – he's going to be dating a flesh-and-blood woman – and she's played by Joey Wong!).

8 Filmed on the Shaws' backlot set.
9 Joey Wong in one of her finest incarnations. The image of Wong in the headdress was employed in the marketing of the movie.
10 No one uses palanquins more than Tony Ching in cinema. Maybe Ching simply enjoys the image of a palanquin (or maybe that's how he thinks the film director should be treated on set!).
11 This occurs in several Hong Kong movies of the period.
12 Or that there'll be repercussions from the arranged marriage.

# 5

# *A CHINESE GHOST STORY 3*

# *Sin Nui Yau Wan III: Do Do Do*

*A Chinese Ghost Story 3* (*Qiannü Youhun III Dao Dao Dao*, directed by Tony Ching Siu-tung, 1991) is a visual effects action comedy masterpiece. At a technical level, it is absolutely staggering. Like many Hong Kong movies (even the bad ones!), *A Chinese Ghost Story 3* is perfect fare for a rowdy, Friday night crowd in a cinema in teeming, neon-bright Hong Kong or Macau (its primary audience). *A Chinese Ghost Story 3* makes no pretence at being anything other than a straight-ahead slice of polished, incredibly sophisticated (yet grungey) entertainment. *A Chinese Ghost Story 3* is a winner in every area.

Many of the cast and crew of *A Chinese Ghost Story 3* had worked on the previous installments in the *Chinese Ghost Story* series (this one appeared a year after the second movie). Tony Ching Siu-tung was back directing (and he was one of the action directors, along with Ma Yuk-shing, Yuen Bun and Cheung Yiu-sing; Bruce Law handled the fire and burn stunts); Tsui Hark produced and co-wrote the script with regular collaborator Roy Szeto Cheuk-hon; Cho King-Man co-produced; exec. producers: Chui Bo-Chu and Roger Lee Yan-Lam; music by James Wong Jim, Chow Gam Wing and Romeo Diaz; edited by Marco Mak Chi-sin; art directed by James Leung; photographed by Tom Lau Moon-Tong; costumes by William Chang, Bruce Yu Ka-On, Bobo Ng Bo-Ling and Chan Bo-Guen; make-up by Chi-Yeung Chan; hair: Chau Siu-Mui and Lee Lin-Dai; and sound by Chow Gam-Wing. Released July 18, 1991. 99 mins.

Joey Wong Jo-yin and Jacky Cheung Hak-yow reprised their roles (Cheung's Swordsman Yin was altered – now he's not a Taoist Master, but a money-hungry treasure seeker, happy to slaughter anybody foolish enough to steal his *geld*); Lau Siu-Ming was the Tree Demon again; but Leslie Cheung bowed out, to be replaced by Tony Leung Chiu-wai (however, Cheung does appear in the opening prologue of *A Chinese Ghost Story 3*, which reworks the climax of the first movie, with its giant tongue – tongues play a key role in *A Chinese Ghost Story 3*). Also appearing were Nina Li-chi (as Butterfly), Tiffany Lau Yuk Ting (as Jade), Cheung Yiu Sing, Hoh Choi Chow, and Lau Shun (as Reverend Bai Yun, Fong's *sifu*).

*A Chinese Ghost Story 3* is a hugely enjoyable third entry in the *Chinese Ghost Story* series: it's pretty much a re-run of the story of the first movie of 1987, with two Buddhist monks taking shelter in a temple haunted by ghosts. So back come the four main characters: the hapless youth, Fong, the gorgeous ghost, Lotus, the crusty, old, Buddhist monk *sifu*, Master, and the chief villain, the Tree Demon, with Jacky Cheung playing Swordmaster Yin.13

The tone and attitude and atmosphere of *A Chinese Ghost Story 3* are absolutely spot-on. The cast hit exactly the right note of mock seriousness, playing the adventure straight, but leaving plenty of room for the goofy helplessness of Tony Leung's Fong, the jokey asides of Jacky Chueng's Swordsman Yin, the sweet, yearning melancholy of Joey Wong's Lotus, and some of the craziest, over-the-top performances in Hong Kong cinema – from Lau Siu-Ming as the Tree Demon and Lau Shun as the *sifu* Bai Yun.

Lau Siu-Ming's Tree Demon/ Priestess is a diva of gargantuan dimensions. By comparison with the most out-there performances of actors in the West as derranged bad guys in Western action flicks, Lau is completely excessive. Robert de Niro, Ian McKellen, Mickey Rourke, Joe Pesci, Ben Kingsley, Jeremy Irons *et al* – they are well-known for playing crazy antagonists in action cinema in the West. But, accomplished as they are, and fun to watch as they are, they are utterly eclipsed by the scorchingly high energy of Chinese performers, who start big then get bigger and bigger, where the Peking Opera traditions survive in actors who can turn their own faces into wild masks of horror, terror, ecstatic glee and truly creepy sadism.

And let's not forget Tony Leung Chiu-wai ('Little Tony Leung'), with his bald pate and wide, dark eyes: a remarkable actor (who can do anything), and one of the stalwarts of Hong Kong New Wave cinema, Leung does a fine job of stepping into Leslie Cheung's shoes (a tough act to follow – because Cheung, tho' he makes it look so easy, is a truly formidable talent). Tho' Leung doesn't quite have Cheung's incandescent star quality, Leung hits just the right note of earnestness, goofiness and cowardice; he is acting his socks off. It's a terrific comic performance which gets the balance spot-on between drama and humour (that is, for the comedy to work, *A Chinese Ghost Story 3* has to function first as a story and as a drama, and you have to buy into these characters and the situations). Known for serious roles like the gangster flicks directed by John Woo (*Bullet In the Head, Hard-Boiled*, etc), and later on for romantic roles (in the films of Wong Kar-wai and others), it's great to see Leung playing comedy (which he has done more than you'd think).

---

13 Yin makes a short speech about being trained by the older Taoist Master, to connect the two charas – altho', if this movie is meant to take place 100 years later, he would be too old (indeed, Yin says that the Master has died).

It's impossible not to enjoy *A Chinese Ghost Story 3* – you'd have to be a really miserable, really cranky and really stick-in-the-mud so-and-so not to like *A Chinese Ghost Story 3*. Seriously. Yes: this movie is going all-out to entertain *you*, the audience, and it succeeds magnificently.

The look of the 1991 *Ghost* movie is sensational, with DP Tom Lau Moon-Tong, production designer James Leung, costume designers Bruce Yu Ka-On, Bobo Ng Bo-Ling, William Chang, and Chan Bo-Guen and all the others (in make-up, practical effects, sound, editing, casting and so on) really coming up with the goods. James Wong Jim, Chow Gam Wing and Romeo Diaz compose a suitably mysterioso score for the ghostly sequences, and jaunty pop cues for the lighter scenes. (The score supports the action at every twist and turn, almost as if the musicians are playing the music live to the picture). The action choreography (by Tony Ching, Yuen Bun, Ma Yuk-shing, Cheung Yiu-sing *et al*) is of course absolutely outstanding (with cable-work creating truly awe-inspiring flying scenes, as fluid and imaginative as in any movie in film history).

Not content with staging a single performer flying on wires – across enormous distances – the stunt team hook up a host of performers on cables (and not only people, but also numerous props, including, in the finale, giant pillars of stone which erupt from the ground). And there's a new development for this film, actors are now flying in curves and circles. There is no wire-work in cinema anywhere that comes near this!

✦

*A Chinese Ghost Story 3* is another love story – between a weak, effeminate man and a ravishing female ghost (the staple format of Chinese ghost stories). Turning the two humans caught up in this tale into Buddhist monks accentuates the battle between the two realms of religion and magic on one side and evil and bad karma on the other. Fong and Lotus are thrown into the middle of the battle between Bai Yun and the Tree Demon, between Buddhism and corrupt magic, between doing the right thing and doing evil. (The duels between the monks and the ghosts in *A Chinese Ghost Story 3* allow the filmmakers to indulge in evoking numerous ancient beliefs, superstitions and practices of Chinese culture and Buddhist religion: promoting such folkloric material, even if it's in a completely hokey movie-movie manner, is one of Tsui Hark's passions).[14]

Act one of *A Chinese Ghost Story 3* includes a lesbian love scene – well, a scene that skirts very close to lesbian erotica without delving into Category III (porn) territory. In a scene that might've come out of *Green Snake,* Lotus and Butterfly are first introduced in *A Chinese Ghost Story 3* in a close embrace in their chambers (where all is pieces of floaty, coloured cloth), sharing what seems to be smoke from an opium pipe. It's girls together in a teasing, intimate set-up that's a recurring motif in Tsui Hark's cinema (drugs, beautiful girls, sex, and even tattoos are laid out in a voluptuous scene lit and photographed by DP Tom Lau Moon-tong like a

14 The talisman in the 1991 *Ghost* movie is a golden statue of the Buddha (which performs many duties, not least reminding Fong of his spiritual calling as a Buddhist monk). The monks are transporting the precious Buddha statue, and of course the hapless Fong loses it.

Chinese painting. As usual in a Tony Ching film, every single scene has wind machines billowing the hair and costumes).

The lesbian scene leads directly on to the let's-show-how-nasty-the-villains-are sequence, where the Tree Demon presides over a decadent court of ghosts who slay a band of ruffians. The centrepiece is, of all things, a pool (a more extravagant version of the wooden baths of the previous *Chinese Ghost Stories*). Lotus and Butterfly play the sirens that lure the men into their deadly domain, from which there is no escape. Out flicks the Tree Demon's tongue (in a remarkable monster p.o.v. shot, across the surface of the water), and into the gullet of its first victim. (And in a nifty piece of screenwriting, the brigands sneaked into this area in the first place because they caught a glimpse of the golden Buddha that the two monks were carrying in a restaurant; even cleverer, it's Swordsman Yin who accidentally slices open the cloth hiding the statue).

The lure of gold in *A Chinese Ghost Story 3* brings in once again the issue of money in a Hong Kong picture, that hyper-capitalist city of, as Chinese movies have it, gamblers, gangsters, hookers and hustlers (there are two treasure-seeking groups in *A Chinese Ghost Story 3*).

Yes – this's how Swordsman Yin is introduced in the first reel of *A Chinese Ghost Story 3* (in the opening sequence) – cutting up the thieves who've stolen his money: it's the replay of the sheltering-from-a-storm scene in the first *Ghost* film, where the hapless scholar found himself in the midst of a bitter feud. Comedy is uppermost, tho', as poor Fong has blood sprayed over him repeatedly and – in a classic, Tsui Harkian joke – body parts too (and afterwards, he's told to bury the corpses by his *sifu* who, in a great gag, just happens to have a little hoe in his robes!).

✦

Love – and sex... *A Chinese Ghost Story 3* squeezes an entire second act out of Joey Wong's spirit Lotus trying to seduce Tony Leung's monk Fong. That's all it is, for 20 or 30 minutes: a man, a woman... one wants it, one doesn't want it... the movie happily trots out the old narrative chestnuts of a beautiful, willing woman and an unwilling (but handsome) man (that it's two famous and attractive stars of the early Nineties period, Wong and Leung, enhances the sequence no end – Leung was something of a pin-up at the time, too).

And the first act of *Ghost 3* had already delivered that scenario between Lotus and Fong – intercut with scenes of Bai Yun trying to draw out the ghosts using his Buddhist magic (Bai Yun has to be taken away from the scene, so that Lotus can go to work on Fong). Lotus attempts many times to seduce Fong, resulting in all sorts of amazingly dynamic physical acting: this is the polar opposite of a romantic comedy where two people stand and spout clever-clever quips that a team of writers have spent months re-writing. Instead of Western cinema's continual and dogged insistence on dialogue-heavy romantic comedies, and the static blocking of two actors just standing there, the Chinese action approach, steeped in Peking Opera performance styles, is gloriously kinetic and inventive.

In their first encounter, Lotus flutters into the Orchid Temple when Fong foolishly opens the front door, and wafts about in distress, crying about ghosts like a scared child. Joey Wong captures the mock fear and sneaky seduction of Lotus as she dances around Fong, trips, falls, and pulls him on top of her (repeatedly). The Peking Opera approach puts bodies in continual motion, striking amazing poses – all across the floor, and other parts of the set.

This is the Hong Kong film equivalent of a seduction scene in a Hollywood musical – musical cinema (and musical theatre) is really the closest equivalent to something like this, where movement, rhythm, timing, music, lighting, costumes, and practical effects work together to form a dazzling combination that evokes romance, beauty, comedy, and danger.

This is mesmerizing cinema, where each shot is conceived as if starting from scratch, as if each shot stands alone, as if each shot could be The One, as if each shot has the potential to become the Greatest Shot Ever Filmed.

Indeed, this is how Hong Kong cinema films action: instead of filming all of the shots from one side (from one actor's point-of-view), then adjusting everything (lights included), to film from the other side, which is the Western/ Hollywood way, Hong Kong cinema films each shot and each piece of action individually.

But the shots *are* conceived as part of a sequence, with a flow, a rhythm, a timing. Hong Kong action cinema is more compelling than many other forms of action cinema perhaps because it constructs its action sequences in this manner. The camerawork and the editing follow the rhythm, tempo and the flow of the movement as it was filmed on the set, rather than a pre-conceived series of storyboards, for example, or sticking to a rigid shot-counter-shot pattern, or filming tons of footage and hoping it will will cut together.

So now in the second act of A *Chinese Ghost Story 3* the silly-but-fun device of the extra-long tongue that the villain deployed so memorably in the previous A *Chinese Ghost Story* movies (and seen in the prologue of this movie), becomes a motif in the seduction scene, as Lotus French kisses Fong. And French kisses him again (to get out some snake venom, she claims; snakes are everywhere in this movie. And there's the business of the lost Buddha statue (which is then found to be broken), which also adds to the comedy in act 2).

Really, all we we're watching is a couple of actors goofing around on a lavish temple set (with occasional appearances from a third actor, Lau Shun), but it's amusing, it's entertaining, it's fun. Sure, it's very conventional romance-plus-comedy, and this time not even a fervently radical film critic could link this humorous, romantic sequence to the 1997 Hand-over in Hong Kong! (Tho' that wouldn't stop them trying! There are some critics who see *every* movie made between 1982 and 1997 in Hong Kong as relating in some form or other to the 1997 Hand-over!).

But A *Chinese Ghost Story 3* is very clearly designed mainly as a piece of entertainment in which the local, Cantonese audience can *forget* about all of that, and simply watch a pantomime about ghosts and monks and demons (it's a high-class panto delivered by a team of *very* talented veterans).

A Chinese Ghost Story 3 has an impressive scope and size, with its village sets and hills, fields and forests, its temples and palaces, yet much of the film comprises only three actors: Tony Leung, Joey Wong and Lau Shun. But they are so good, you don't notice for a moment that whole scenes and then whole sections of the film slip by which feature only two actors on a single set (such as the Orchid Temple at night).

✦

Act two of *A Chinese Ghost Story 3* climaxes, as expected, with a Big Action Sequence: the re-appearance of the Tree Demon, and an absolutely remarkable magical duel between the Tree Demon and Master Bai Yun – the combination of practical effects and optical effects is as inventive as any in fantasy cinema. The imagery of the Buddhist *sifu* balancing on his staff and the Tree Demon conjuring a battery of elemental forces to kill him are incredible – water effects, fire, explosions, etc (the film uses one of Tony Ching's signature images – a wall of water exploding upwards behind a sorcerous figure, also seen in the *Swordsman* series). The feeling for texture and atmosphere is so acute, you can feel the elements of fire and water as they interact with the characters. (No need for movie enhancements like I.M.A.X., or 3-D, or flight simulator platforms, or smell-o-rama, when you've got movie-making this sensuous).

Meanwhile, the more comical and romantic aspects of the battles between humans and ghosts occur in the scenes between Fong and Lotus, as a counterpart of the epic Bai Yun versus Tree Demon scenes: here's Fong hurrying about, torn between helping his Master and feeling sorry for Lotus.

The magical staff (a *khakkhara*, also known as a Zen stick and pewter staff) that Bai Yun carries is exploited inventively here – the monk throws it at Lotus, pinning her painfully to the wall of the Orchid Temple. Bai Yun calls for help from Fong, and Fong, having freed Lotus from the staff, takes him the staff. The act two climax includes numerous bits of intricate, physical business that play out very rapidly. But all of the action – and the comedy – is still fixed firmly to the fundamental characterizations of the four principal players (the two monks and the two spirits).

As Tsui Hark has explained many times, action comes with a story, and a style, and a look – it's not merely action for action's sake. Thus, the wild and over-the-top action sequences in a movie such as *A Chinese Ghost Story 3* are always rooted in the narrative context, in the character-izations, in their relationships, their conflicts, their goals and their motivations.

✦

Many, many elements in *A Chinese Ghost Story 3* are pure Tsui Hark: the scene where money-grubbing Swordsman Yin finds his coins on the ground talking back to him and scooting into a nearby pool to disappear (as charmed by Bai Yun) is pure Tsui (and pure Walt Disney). Animated in stopmotion, the coins talk back to their owner (and they also bow to prove they belong to him). Money is such an important motif in Hong Kong cinema, it's no surprise that Tsui would eventually include animated, talking coins.

Another very Tsui Harkian sequence is the crowded village scene, where everybody it seems is a sword-maker or a sword-seller (including some swords with ridiculous designs, like a convention of fantasy cosplayers and their homemade weaponry). Tsui also loves scenes where whole crowds act as one, in a humorous fashion – doing a double take altogether, for instance.

The rivalry between the two female ghosts (Joey Wong's Lotus and Nina Li Chi's Butterfly) is another Tsui Harkian ingredient in *A Chinese Ghost Story 3*. The twitching of Bai Yun's over-large ears is another Tsui-ism[15] (later, they grow and cover his eyes, when the Tree Demon captures him).

The floppy ears bit of business occurs at the close of the act two finale – really, it's a rather artificial way of delaying the final smackdown between the heroes and the villains: Bai Yun tells his pupil to hurry into town to have the golden Buddha statue fixed (it's needed to defeat the Tree Demon).

✦

So the golden Buddha statue MacGuffin is still doing some narrative work in act three of *A Chinese Ghost Story 3* – Fong heads into town to get it repaired, only to have the blacksmiths and ruffians get the better of him (there was a hint of that when they spurned Bai Yun begging for food[16]). It's here that Fong bumps into Swordsman Yin, which re-introduces Yin into the proceedings, in time for the finale. (Yin saves Bai Yun from the thugs, but for a price. He constantly calculates his fee on his abacus, while knowing that Bai Yun is penniless like him. Yin agrees to help Bai Yun rescue his Master with the promise of remuneration).

In act three of the second *Chinese Ghost Story* sequel, the French romantic farce elements are re-introduced, involving Fong and Lotus with the added complications of greedy Swordsman Yin, and the catty, resentful sister of Lotus, Butterfly (this occurs just before the action section of the finale). The many jokes include the worldly Yin, who doesn't have a problem fooling around with women, having to watch the supposedly chaste monk Fong being kissed into submission by Lotus. It's just not fair! (The humour is enhanced by the casting of pop star Jacky Cheung as Yin – a singer who's used to the adulation of girls).

Two guys, and two girls: the sequence is played like French farce and screwball comedy: very fast, and very silly. Lotus hurls herself at Bai Yun, after Butterfly has also burst into the temple to do the same. Swordsman Yin watches in disbelief as not one but two beautiful women throw

15 'Tsui Hark's ability to make something incredible and outlandish out of ordinary facial features such as eyes, ears and tongue must mark him as a unique filmmaker', remarked Stephen Teo (1997, 229).
16 Food is another Tsui-ian motif in *A Chinese Ghost Story 3* – Fong is perpetually hungry. His Master talks about prayers and the spiritual life, but Fong can't exist on words alone.

themselves at Bai Yun's feet (in frustration, he performs a sword dance, this movie's version of the dance of the Taoist Master in the first film. Unusually, *A Chinese Ghost Story 3* doesn't have Jacky Cheung sing).

There's a raid on the Tree Demon's digs by Fong and Swordsman Yin, where they dash in and out rapidly, with the action as swift as a manic kids' cartoon (but with the rescue of Bai Yun put off for the finale). The stunt crew somehow depict *sifu* Bai Yun and Lotus zipping across the ground. Butterfly and Lotus are prominent here, and there's a third sister, Jade (Tiffany Lau Yuk Ting), who unfortunately gets in the way of the bitchy rivalry between Lotus and Butterfly. And the Tree Demon has his arm cut off (by Swordsman Yin) – but it grows back again.

✦

To climax the 1991 *Ghost* installment, and all three *Chinese Ghost Story* movies, Tony Ching Siu-tung, Tsui Hark and the team conjure up a truly remarkable barrage of action sequences which assault the audience like World War Three. As with the previous two *Chinese Ghost Story* flicks, the finale is an enormous battle between the good guys (the two monks and the Swordsman) and the villains (the Tree Demon, plus the Mountain Devil, Butterfly, and their henchmen) – with Lotus as the wild card caught in the middle of the crossfire.

The action sequences in the finale of *A Chinese Ghost Story 3* are simply insane,[17] with nothing in Western cinema coming anywhere near them. By the time of this third movie, the filmmaking team had achieved a sophistication of visual effects cinema which blows everyone else out of the water.

There's so much enjoy in the climax of *A Chinese Ghost Story 3* – how about, for starters, the scene where the heroes fly on a magic carpet (made from the *sifu*'s cloak) in between stone pillars smashing upwards thru the ground? How about the insanely hysterical performance by Lau Siu-Ming as the Tree Demon, battling the heroes while poor Fong is strung up in the air with red ropes?[18] How about the Tree Demon impersonating Lotus at the night festival (so you get two Joey Wongs running in slow motion)? How about the Tree Demon's demise in an extraordinary full-body burn scene? How about the conception of the Mountain Demon as a grimacing head of dirt and dust, and a walking temple with arms? How about Fong being turned by his *sifu* into a man-sized, golden Buddha and flying high above the clouds to greet the sunrise and reflect the spiritual light down into the underworld built by the Mountain Devil, to dissolve the monster in a series of incredible explosions? How about the beautiful, vibrant orange colours and shafts of light to depict the sun bursting into the netherworld?

Tsui Hark inserts his beloved Lion Dancing into *A Chinese Ghost Story 3*, as he did in every historical movie he produced in this period. In a scene of flaming torches and a boisterous crowd, Lion Dancers perform:

17 The finale of *A Chinese Ghost Story 3* employs every trick cinema has ever developed, and invents some of its own, too.
18 And Butterfly trying to seduce him – Fong is fated to have beautiful women throwing themselves at him in *A Chinese Ghost Story 3*.

only after the movie shifts back to the Orchid Temple at night is it revealed that our heroes have never escaped: they've been caught in an illusion of the Tree Demon.

The welter of visual effects stomp across the finale like the Imperial Army: as soon as the giant tongue of the Tree Demon has been attacked with flying swords and bombs by the heroes, and the Tree Demon burns to death, the second villain erupts from Hell: the Mountain Devil. The sequence is a variation on the finales of both of the previous *Chinese Ghost Story* pictures, this time with a temple coming to life to stalk the heroes, who're fleeing on a magic carpet.

It sounds amazing, and it is: the combination of models, puppet-eering, animatronics, and astonishing practical effects (pyrotechnics, smoke, dust, fire) is spellbinding. Whole segments of the sets are puppeteered using wires to create wild images of devastation, of crumbling stone pillars, of billowing dirt from explosions.

Even with the film sped up, the action directors (Ching, Ma, Yuen, and Cheung) conjure up remarkable stuntwork – performers are sent flying into every corner of the sets and the frame; actors slide across the ground at 50 m.p.h.; Lotus grabs Bai Yun and dives into the ground.

The pell-mell approach resembles a quickfire comedy with one gag hot on the heels of the one on the screen. This movie simply does not acknowledge that something *can't* be done, that conventional physics would not allow the human body to travel that fast, or to bend like that. No one says 'no' to Tony Ching!

Anything seems possible here, as cinema is re-invented in scenes of breathtaking imagination. Often it's the miracle of *editing* that is making it all work: Tony Ching, Tsui Hark and editor Marco Mak Chi-sin possess a feeling for how images cut together as skilful as anyone in the history of cinema or television.

# 6

# A CHINESE GHOST STORY: THE TSUI HARK ANIMATION

## Siu Sin

*A Chinese Ghost Story: The Tsui Hark Animation*[19] (1997, *Siu Sin* in Cantonese; *Xiaoqian* in Mandarin), was the first feature overseen by Tsui Hark in animation – a dream of his, probably, of many decades (ever since he started making movies in his early teens).

The voice cast of *A Chinese Ghost Story: The Tsui Hark Animation* is a bunch of Tsui Hark regulars: Nicky Wu, Charlie Yeung, Anita Yuen, Raymond Wong, Eric Kot, James Wong Jim, Sylvia Chang and Kelly Chen (all the usual suspects – 'my friends, performers and stars'), with Tsui voicing the dog, Solid Gold. Writer: Tsui Hark. Produced by Triangle Staff/ Film Workshop. Dis. by Golden Harvest. Directors: Andrew Chen Jun-man and Tetsuya Endo. Producers: Nansun Shi Nan-sheng, Tsuneo Leo-sato, Charles Heung and Meileen Choo. Music: Ricky Ho and James Wong Jim. Animation director: Tetsuya Endo. Character designers: Frankie Chung and Takashi Nakamura. Editor: Chi-sin Tsui Kak. The budget was U.S. $7 million. Released July 31, 1997. 84 mins.

If *A Chinese Ghost Story: The Tsui Hark Animation* looks like a Japanese *animé*, that's because it is: the animation was produced by Triangle Staff in Japan, an *animé* house whose credits include *Macross Plus, Serial Experiments Lain, Space Pirate Mito, Catnapped, Ultra Nyan* and *Hyper Doll*. One of the animation directors was the remarkable Takashi Nakamura (b. 1955, Yamanashi Prefecture), the chief animator on *Akira* (for many the greatest animation ever), with credits including: *Robot Carnival, Fantastic Children, Peter Pan, Nausicaä of the Valley of the Wind,* and he directed *Catnapped* and *Tree of Palme.*

Triangle Staff worked with Film Workshop to produce the movie, so *A Chinese Ghost Story: The Tsui Hark Animation* is a kind of Chinese-Japanese hybrid, tho' the style and the approach is very Japanese; while

19 The subtitle, 'The Tsui Hark Animation', has a mogul's air about it – as if Tsui was now of the stature of Alfred Hitchcock or Steven Spielberg (well, for some, he was – and he is).

the subject – Chinese supernatural tales, is distinctly Chinese.[20] But anyone who's seen any *anime* will know that Japanese cartoons are full of this kind of fantasy and adventure, and Chinese mythologies have popped up in Japanese animation many times.

Thus, the influence of Hayao Miyazaki is easy to spot. Walt Disney is in there, too, of course[21] (the first animation that Tsui Hark – and many of us – encountered was Disney), as well as more recent Western animations. The ghost town has distinctly Tim Burtonian influences (including *The Nightmare Before Christmas,* 1993).

Tsui Hark expressed disappointment with the animation in *A Chinese Ghost Story,* the use of 3-D,[22] the variations in the quality in the animation, and with the production set-up. Tsui discovered that animation requires a different kind of organization from live-action: it's a discipline that demands an enormous amount of work which has to be sustained over months and months (setting up an animation production team and pipeline from scratch for a feature film is a massive undertaking. The animation business, too, is *very* different from the live-action business). It appears that there were disagreements about the look and the approach of *A Chinese Ghost Story: The Tsui Hark Animation*; Tsui complained that the traditional animators in Japan didn't want to work with the Chinese designs (LM, 129).

However, there's no doubt that some of the production crew in Japan were veterans of animation, whereas Tsui Hark, despite his enormous experience in filmmaking (including animation added to live-action plates), probably had less experience of *anime*.

✦

*A Chinese Ghost Story: The Tsui Hark Animation* is a fun, fast-paced and colourful version of the Pu Songling stories and the three *Chinese Ghost Story* movies. There's plenty of action, plenty of goofy humour, some wistful romance, and of course spectacle. There are songs, too (mostly by James Wong Jim, who also plays Red Beard).

And there's no doubt that *A Chinese Ghost Story: The Tsui Hark Animation* is another of Tsui Hark's pæans to the riches of Chinese history and tradition.

It's got the superpower battles between Buddhist monks flying around the sky, it's got the hapless tax collector caught in the midst of this out-size, supernatural world (now aided by a classic dog sidekick), and a ghost town. The Reincarnation Train is a fun concept – a flying train that clearly draws on the famous Cat-bus[23] in *My Neighbor Totoro* (Hayao Miyazaki, 1988), though in the form of a Chinese dragon.

The ironic commentary in *A Chinese Ghost Story: The Tsui Hark*

20 The animated *Chinese Ghost Story* is 'as much a reworking of *Zu* as any of the *Chinese Ghost Story* films' (Lisa Morton, 127).
21 *A Chinese Ghost Story: The Tsui Hark Animation* was 'a deliberate attempt to make a cross between Japanese *anime* and American Disney', Tsui Hark said in 1998.
22 The 3-D technology was still in its infancy in 1997, and there were problems with it.
23 The Cat-bus – the *nekobasu* – is one of Hayao Miyazaki's original and most memorable creations, a giant, stripey ginger cat, with eyes as headlights, and mice eyes illuminating the front and rear. As a magical transport, the Cat-bus is a perfect creation: it looks like it has always existed, like the best artworks. There must have always been a Cat-bus, surely? The Knight-Bus in the *Harry Potter* books seems to have drawn on the Cat-bus.

*Animation* on Chinese myths and movies about Chinese myths is amusing – and of course, Tsui Hark was more responsible for the recent spate of Chinese fable/ fantasy movies than most individuals on the planet.

The characters were aged down – to early teens, to match the target audience, perhaps. Which inevitably scuppers the intensity and operatic tragedy of the romance of the 1987-1990-1991 *Chinese Ghost Story* movies (that was Tsui Hark's decision – to make it funnier, to have 'a totally cute version of the story' (LM, 130), to have early teens expressing emotions more suited to late teens). And at the end, an amusing sequence has all of the characters regressing to babyhood.

The 1997 cartoon, of course, lacks the two superpowers of the live-action movies – the actors Leslie Cheung Kwok-wing and Joey Wong Cho-yin. (The character animation of Ning Choi-san can't compete with an actor as incredible as Leslie Cheung. Indeed, most of the time in *A Chinese Ghost Story: The Tsui Hark Animation,* Ning is gawping in awe or fear, or he's yelling, 'Siu Shin!!').[24]

But *A Chinese Ghost Story: The Tsui Hark Animation* is very romantic, with romance as a key element: Ning Choi-san has been jilted by his girlfriend, Lan, and in the first act dreams of her, remembers her, and encounters another beauty, Shine (in a procession in the ghost town). So women as aloof, beautiful and frustratingly unattainable figures are one of the motifs of *A Chinese Ghost Story: The Tsui Hark Animation.* It all ends happily, of course – Ning is re-united with his beloved Shine, as humans, on Earth.

On the down side, *A Chinese Ghost Story: The Tsui Hark Animation* is marred with too many action scenes looking and sounding the same – this is an issue of tone and of the script, which Tsui Hark, as co-writer and co-producer, might've addressed.

The characters zooming thru the air recall *Zu: Warriors From the Magic Mountain* (the re-make of *Zu* would use digital animation to send its characters flying around the sky). Maybe it works for a ten year-old audience, but there's a lack of weight and substance to the animation and the action (precisely what Tsui Hark complained about in regard to *Star Wars: The Phantom Menace,* a couple of years later – and the 2001 *Legend of Zu* was Tsui's reply to *The Phantom Menace*).

---

24 To be fair, Leslie Cheung also spends quite a bit of time shouting, 'Siu-shin!!'

A Chinese Ghost Story 2 (1990),
this page and over.

倩女幽魂II

人間道

A CHINESE
GHOST STORY II

A CHINESE
GHOST
STORY 2

A Chinese Ghost Story 3 (1991),
this page and over.

A Chinese Ghost Story (1997).

# THE *SWORDSMAN* MOVIES

# 7

# *THE SWORDSMAN*

## *Siu Ngo Gong Woo*

The *Swordsman* movies[1] were adapted from *The Smiling, Proud Wanderer* by Jin Yong (Louis Cha, 1924-2018), which have been used for five or so TV series (and a Shaw Brothers movie of 1978). So the *Swordsman* films are by no means the only interpretations of the novels of Jin Yong, one of the best-known authors of *wuxia* stories. In fact, a TV series is a probably more fitting form for adaptation, because Jin Yong's stories contain a huge cast of characters and numerous events. Those depicted in the *Swordsman* movies are but one small segment (and a loose adaptation at that).

The film is usually credited to Raymond Lee (but in fact six directors are known to have worked on it, including the original director, King Hu, and Tsui Hark and Ann Hui).

*The Swordsman* (Cantonese = *Siu Ngo Gong Woo,* Mandarin = *Xiao Aoi Jianzhu* = *Laughing and Proud Warrior*), was produced by Tsui Hark, Tommy Law Wai-Tak and Chu Feng Kang for Film Workshop.[2] It was written by six people: Kwan Man-Leung, Daai Foo Ho, Huang Ying, Tai-Mok Lau, Yiu-ming Leung, and Jason Lam Kee To; costumes: Cheung Sai-Ying, Cheung Kam-Kam, Lui Siu-Hung, Shing Fuk-Ying, Edith Cheung Sai-Mei, and Bo-Ling Ng; hair by Sam Biu-Hoi and Lee Lin-Dai; A.D.: Kuo-Han Yuan (and 8 other A.D.s); music by Romeo Diaz and James Wong Jim; the DPs were Andy Lam, Lee Tak-Wai, Joe Chan Kwong-Hung, Horace Wong Wing-Hang and Peter Pau; art direction by Leung Wah-sang; make-up by Lau Gai-Sing, Poon Man-Wa and Cheung Bik-Yuk; editing by Marco Mak Chi-sin and David Wu Tai-wai; the action choreographers were: Tony Ching

1 For more information on the *Swordsman* movies, see my companion book.
2 According to Tsui Hark, the investor backing *The Swordsman* was not convinced about the movie, because it had been done before, and failed. Tsui insisted that he could make it work (LM, 24).

Siu-tung, Lau Chi Ho, Bruce Law, and Yuen Wah. It was released on Apl 5, 1990, and grossed about HK $16 million.[3] 115 mins.

The production apparently wound on for 2 years (LM, 172). It boasts 9 assistant directors, six costume designers, five DPs, etc – and six writers. At around 115 minutes, *The Swordsman* is significantly longer than many Hong Kong action pictures (which're usually 80-90 mins, tho' this length might be not sanctioned by the filmmakers).[4] It won Hong Kong Film Awards for Best Action and Best Song and the Golden Horse Award for Best Film and Best Supporting Actor (Jacky Cheung).

✦

*The Swordsman* was completed by Tsui Hark after King Hu walked out (after ten days of filming), and other directors (such as Ann Hui, Andrew Kam Yeung-Wa and Raymond Lee) were tried; Tsui co-directed the remainder of the movie with action director Tony Ching Siu-tung. (Nothing remains in the film of Hu's footage, according to Lisa Morton [LM, 172]). *The Swordsman* was credited as being co-directed by Tsui Hark, Raymond Lee, Tony Ching Siu-tung and the two directors who left: King Hu and Ann Hui (Andrew Kam also appears in some credits).

For filmmakers of the Hong Kong New Wave, King Hu was a key figure, a pioneer of the martial arts movie (and of making *wuxia pian* artistic and poetic as well as visceral and commercial). Hu's swordfighting films were typically set in the Ming Dynasty, 1368-1644 (like this one), featuring swordsmen (and women) and eunuch villains (emissaries of the oppressive Dongchang, the Imperial authorities). Hu was known for treating action as choreography as something lyrical and abstract, and stylized.

By inviting King Hu to work on *The Swordsman,* Tsui Hark and co. were expressing their appreciation for a veteran of the kind of cinema that they loved (and grew up with). However, Hu's health was failing, which didn't make the disagreements between him and the filmmakers easier (Hu died in 1997, aged 66).

✦

Sam Hui Koon-kit (who had worked with Tsui Hark in 1984's OTT *James Bond* spoof *Aces Go Places*, and in *Working Class* in 1985), plays the lead role in *The Swordsman*, Linghu Chong, the Hua Mountain student and swordsman.[5] Hui's Linghu is confident and calm, one of the most easy-going figures in movies of the *jiangzhu,* played with a light-hearted charm by Hui. (Jet Li continued with that light touch in the *Swordsman* sequel).

Among the supporting cast in *The Swordsman* were a bunch of Hong Kong regulars (this is a terrific cast), including: Cecilia Yip as Yue Lingshan (a.k.a. 'Skinny Boy'), Linghu Chong's sidekick (another of the many crossdressing charas in Hong Kong cinema, and another of Tsui Hark's cute tomboys); Yuen Wah plays one of his customary nasty

---

3 *The Swordsman* series was parodied in *Royal Tramp* (1992), directed by Wong Jing and Gordon Chan and starring Stephen Chow.
4 It's true that some of the scenes in act 3 of 4 do meander somewhat, with maybe a subplot too many.
5 It might've been tempting, tho', to play up to Hui's comical persona.

bruisers,[6] Zuo Lengshan, a practitioner of 'dark' martial arts (Wah was also one of the action directors); Jacky Cheung Hok-yau is Ouayang Quan, eunuch Gu Jinfu's ambitious, cunning henchman; Sharla Cheung is Ren Yingying, leader of the Sun Moon Sect; Fennie Yuen is Blue Phoenix a.k.a Lan Fenghuang (Ren Yingying's aide); Wu Ma is Liu Zhengfeng, one of the retiring Sun Moon warriors; and the ever-dependable Lau Shun is Gu Jinfu, the eunuch villain from the Eastern branch of the Imperial forces. (*The Swordsman* casts three beautiful actresses to counter-balance the masculinist bias of martial arts movies: Fennie Yuen, Cecilia Yip and Sharla Cheung. Placing two women as leaders of the Sun Moon Sect – Cheung and Yuen – is very much part of Tsui Hark's project of re-instating roles for women in movies. And it's typical of a Tsui-produced *jiangzhu* movie that the sidekick of the hero is a boy played by a girl).

The casting of *The Swordsman* is marvellous, and each of the principals embodies their characters as well as popping out of them – there is always a feeling in Chinese, historical action movies of this kind that it's all a pantomime, that it's pure entertainment, and should be taken as just that – a wild show. Actors aren't allowed to wink at the camera (rightly), but the movie does. The cast play it straight – but also with plenty of Peking Operatic over-acting. They don't need to nod at the audience, because the situations are so outlandish.

*The Swordsman* is a gorgeous *mix* of elements: comedy, romance, spectacle, music, characterization, history/ mythology, Chinese culture – and of course action and martial arts. *The Swordsman* is also a truly inspired vision of the *jiangzhu*, the martial arts world, which Tsui Hark explored many times (in fact, *The Swordsman* marks the first major entry in evoking the *jiangzhu* in the 1990s became home-from-home for Tsui and his contemporaries in Hong Kong); and, of course, Tsui had dived into the *jiangzhu* in his very first feature film as director, *The Butterfly Murders*, while Tony Ching had lived in the cinematic *jiangzhu* since the 1960s (working on his father's films at Shaws).

The editing of *The Swordsman* – by Marco Mak Chi-sin and David Wu Tai-wai (regulars in the Tsui Hark Cinematic Circus) – is fiendishly intricate. Tracking the ensemble cast and their subplots with sword-sharp precision, the cutting weaves a story stuffed with incidents and bits of business.

The theme song of *The Swordsman*, 'Chong Hoi Yat Sing Siu', was composed and written by James Wong Jim; Sam Hui performed it (several times – the film fully exploits Hui's pop star status). Like the theme music of *Once Upon a Time in China*, 'Chong Hoi Yat Sing Siu' has a sad, lyrical tone which enhances the atmosphere of nostalgia and history (and you'll be humming it immediately).

✦

*The Swordsman* helped to create many of the staple scenes of the 'New Wave' of historical action movies in Hong Kong – the *jiangzhu;* the

---

[6] Yuen Wah was an actor and martial artist, who doubled for Bruce Lee at Golden Harvest; he was one of the 'Seven ILttle Fortunes' from *sifu* Yu Jim Yuen's Peking Opera school. Yuen appeared countless times as heavies in Hong Kong movies (such as *Eastern Condors, Kid From Tibet, Dragons Forever* and *Iceman Cometh*).

nighttime attack on the inn or palace; the sword fight in the trees (again at night); *ronin* warriors; the gratuitous, nude bathing scene involving a beautiful woman (plus crossdressing comedy); a wild brawl on a boat; inter-clan rivalries; a musical interlude; rebellion against oppressive/corrupt regimes, etc.

The sequels to *The Swordsman* continued with most of the same elements and characters. Much of the cast was changed for the sequels, however, tho' returnees included Fennie Yuen as Blue Phoenix, and Lau Shun (it's not a Tsui Hark-produced movie unless Lau Shun is in it).

✦

*The Swordsman* teems with plots and counter-plots. Much juice is elicited, for instance, from disguises: so Ouyang Quan acts as Lin Pingzhi, Skinny Boy is a girl, an old man (Feng Qingyang – Han Ying-chieh) is really a master martial artist, and Gu Jinfu and the Imperial guards are forced to pretend to be Lam's bereaved family.

Clans and communities are a very prominent feature of *The Swordsman* (as in many Chinese, historical movies), and they're pitted against each other: the Mount Hua clan, the Sun Moon Sect, the emissaries of the Imperial Court, etc. Meanwhile, Linghu Chong and the *Sunflower Scroll* are at the centre of the tussles for power. Each group is vying for the upper-hand, imagining that the secret techniques of the *Sunflower Scroll* will give them the advantage. Within the strict hierarchy of each group (where the authority of the leaders or the *sifus* must never be questioned), there are traitors (such as Ouyang Quan). But Linghu Chong, being the hero, is of course good and straight and true (he embodies the element of righteousness that is a primary issue for Tsui Hark).

The MacGuffiin in *The Swordsman* is that old chestnut of Chinese *jiangzhu* stories, the sacred scroll (the *Sunflower Manual* contains martial arts secrets, including telekinesis and the ability to walk thru walls). In the opening scene, it is stolen from the Imperial Palace. The (nighttime, rooftop) theft kickstarts the narrative of *The Swordsman*, with the Imperial Court ordering the return of the scroll to the Imperial Library. (As is customary in Chinese, *wuxia* films, the Imperial Court scenes are placed upfront, to offer some spectacle, to orientate the movie in time and place (it's the Ming Dynasty), and to provide the impetus for part of the narrative – an Imperial order, a move against rebels, a kidnapping, or the theft of something important. But those Imperial Court scenes soon fulfil their dramatic function, and movies tend to shift rapidly to the *jiangzhu*, the martial arts world).

And the *Sunflower Scroll* is a martial arts manual which's confused in the finale for a music manuscript (a telling comment on what is important in life). The M.S. is a scroll called 'Xiao-ao Jianghu', the 'proud and laughing martial arts world' (which's the song that Liu Zhengfeng and Qu Yang sing on the boat).

The pursuit of the thieves thought to possess the *Sunflower Scroll* provides the first part of act one of *The Swordsman*, with Gu Jinfu leading the Eastern forces of the Chinese Empire. Exposition is woven into these scenes but, as the audience in this movie is chiefly a Chinese-speaking one, it contains far less exposition than movies aimed at an international market. We are thus introduced to the villains and the narrative engine that ignites the plot first, before moving on to the heroes.

We first meet the heroes Linghu Chong and Yue Lingshan (a.k.a. 'Skinny Boy') when they visit the den of Lin Zhennan, to deliver messages from the Mount Hua Sect (yes, once again a buddy duo is set up in a Tsui Hark movie, but with a lovely actress playing one of the guys). The tone of *The Swordsman* is set out here, deftly combining comedy and action, with Sam Hui's Linghu Chong played casually and humorously. For instance, to prove who he is, Linghu launches into an elaborate sword dance (the scene also demonstrates that he's an experienced swordsman).7 (The house is one of those traditional buildings seen in 100s of martial arts movies – a large interior of wood with upper balconies, perfect for staging action all over the place. It could be intercut with the buildings in the *Chinese Ghost Story* flicks or *Once Upon a Time In China,* or the inn in *Crouching Tiger, Hidden Dragon*). Gu Jinfu and his henchmen soon attack, providing one of the first action sequences in *The Swordsman* (the finale also takes place here).

Zuo Lengshan, acting for Gu Jinfu and co., is a malicious piece of work all-round: in a scene of extraordinary barbarity, his heavies torture Lin Zhennan's wife by tearing out her eyes, then her tongue (the gore, including a bloody eyeball, is typical of Hong Kong cinema, but also seems unnecessary and over-the-top). Lin is nearby, listening to Zuo's taunts, and unable to retaliate because he's injured.8 All of this takes place in long grass at night where no one can see what's going on. As if Gu Jinfu and his army aren't enough, Zuo and his thugs up the threat even more.

✦

One of the stand-out sequences in *The Swordsman* is a delightful musical interlude that occurs at the start of act two – 'Xiao-ao Jianghu' ('Hero of Heroes' or 'A Laugh At the World'), by James Wong Jim and Tai Lok-man, a song about the 'proud and laughing martial arts world' (the *jiangzhu*). Finding refuge on a boat, Linghu Chong and his sidekick Skinny Boy meet some fighters from the Sun Moon Sect, Liu Zhengfeng (Wu Ma) and Qu Yang (Lam Ching-ying), who are retiring. They sing and play the song 'Xiao-ao Jianghu', which acts as a pop promo within the movie (a not-uncommon practice in 1980s cinema, and songs and pop stars are common in Hong Kong movies). It's moving, too, that Liu and Qu are fatally wounded in the giant action scene that follows, and opt to go out in style: Liu dies, as they play the song of the *jiangzhu* one last time, then Qu sets fire to the boat, and they expire in flames on the sea. (*The Swordsman* is partly concerned with the passing of the *jiangzhu*, in common with many *wuxia pian* in this period – it's a gesture towards nostalgia, it's a swansong for the movies of a generation's youth, nostalgia for the movies that the

---

7 Using flames flicked from candles on the sword blade; the dance goes slightly wrong (Linghu Chong invents some of his own moves); later, there are huge explosions when gunpowder is accidentally set off.
8 By Linghu Chong and co. – as if Linghu unconsciously realizes that Lin Zhennan is not all he seems.

filmmakers grew up with, nostalgia for a vanished world (that never existed in the first place, but *should* have), it's a pæan to historical as well as mythical China, plus a commentary on the state of modern China. And it's also a passing of the torch from the older generation to the younger generation).

Indeed, music is one of the most direct methods for accessing those historical, mythical, romantic realms, as filmmakers know well (the *ronin* Feng Qingyang tells Linghu Chong that emotions are more powerful than martial arts). The composers of *The Swordsman* (Tsui Hark regulars Romeo Diaz, Tai Lok-man and James Wong Jim) employ many traditional musical forms; and there's a *qin* (stringed instrument) which Linghu carries (and plays). The 'proud and laughing martial arts' song is reprised several times (including in the midst of the action finale, when Linghu sings it again, and when he is recovering from being poisoned).

Linghu Chong encounters another older, wiser figure, in the guise of Feng Qingyang (mid-way thru the movie, in the second half of the second act): as the Imperial heavies close in, a fierce battle ensues (again staged at night). Feng turns out to be a master swordsman, despite his age (at first he seems to be a weak, old man who's only interested in cooking some food): this is one of the outstanding action scenes in *The Swordsman*, definitely directed by Tony Ching Siu-tung, with its miraculous feeling for wire-work and speed and practical effects. Feng defeats one of Gu Jinfu's most vicious henchmen and his crew, with some help from Linghu; the non-stop stunts include the lightning-fast passing of swords from hero to hero, Ching's penchant for airborne swordsmen slicing through dust, and Feng and Linghu working together, culminating in the extreme (and very Chingian) physical gag of a body in flight being sliced in half. (And the sequence offers another master-pupil relationship, with Feng showing Linghu the 'Nine Swords of Dugu'. Feng also tells Linghu that all is not well in the *jiangzhu*, and that Yue Buqun (Lau Siu-ming – the Tree Demon in *A Chinese Ghost Ghost Story*), the leader of the Mount Hua Sect, is also corrupt. In the final fight of *The Swordsman*, Linghu uses the 'Nine Solitary Swords' moves to defeat the crooked leader, Yue Buqun).

✦

In the third act (using a 4-act model), *The Swordsman* travels to the exotic realm of the Sun Moon Sect in Miao: their HQ is an inn[9] in a bamboo forest. This part of *The Swordsman* is very reminiscent of the central section of *New Dragon Gate Inn* (the latter film is almost a remake of *The Swordsman*) – you've got several groups travelling in disguise, numerous cat-and-mouse manœuvres (as each group tries to gain the upper hand), creeping about at night, evocations of erotic desire (including lesbianism), eating and carousing, a powerful female leader, etc.

Each of the *Swordsman* movies comes even more to life when it depicts the Sun Moon Sect – out come the scarlet[10] costumes and sets,

9 The bamboo inn is exploited to the max.
10 Red is the signature colour of this film.

the wonderful headdresses[11] (the costume design by Cheung Sai-Ying, Cheung Kam-Kam, Lui Siu-Hung, Shing Fuk-Ying, Edith Cheung Sai-Mei, and Bo-Ling Ng is outstanding), the use of wood and bamboo, the exaltation of superstition and ritual. One imagines that Tsui Hark and the teams could create whole movies around the Sun Moon Clan – a band of warriors led by a beautiful, young woman who oppose corrupt regimes seems to inspire them (Tsui is especially fond of evoking ancient traditions and beliefs). But, like many exotic and unusual communities, they have a greater impact when they're set against regular, everyday folk. (However, there aren't many communities that are 'normal' in the *Swordsman* movies!).

In the Sun Moon Sect sequence, suspicion and distrust play out in the primary plot, while the secondary plots include some romantic comedy; disguises/ crossdressing; and the poisoning of Linghu Chong. Our heroes arrive, but are treated suspiciously; Ouyang Quan appears in disguise as the dead Lin Pingzhi; and there are tussles for supremacy.

Altho' critics continually deride Hong Kong action movies for what they see as their poor scripts, the characters and their relationships are carefully worked out in *The Swordsman*: for ex, in the Sun Moon Sect section of *The Swordsman*, the antagonism between Ren Yingying and Blue Phoenix (over the leadership of the clan), between Linghu Chong and Yue Buqun (whom he now distrusts), over the secret messages from Lin Zhennan, between Linghu and Blue Phoenix, and many other charas are all evoked clearly.

Historical Chinese movies often squeeze a *lot* of dramatic mileage out of rivalries, loyalties, betrayals and disguises. The issue of loyalty and doing the right thing is vital. *Where* you put your loyalty is absolutely crucial here: are you for the Eastern branch of the Imperial Court or for the Sun Moon Sect? Or, like Ouyang Quan, are you out for yourself?

In the Sun Moon Sect part of *The Swordsman*, the struggle for the superior position politically is played out visually and dramatically in a marvellous series of kinetic scenes, with charas sneaking about, leaping thru open windows, hiding, spying, over-hearing, and occasionally fighting.

*The Swordsman* happily and nimbly switches genres and moods, moving from deadly serious statements about doing the right thing and opposing corrupt regimes to goofy comedy (Linghu Chong sits on Blue Phoenix when she's hiding and sings), romantic farce (Blue Phoenix seducing Skinny Boy), and mystical healing montages.

In the midst of it all, our hero, Linghu Chong, is poisoned (the filmmakers employ a lengthy three-shot, as poisoned cups of wine are passed back and forth in an elaborate, well-rehearsed dance). But this time, instead of the cup being knocked out of the hero's hand by accident, or something distracting the drinkers, Linghu is poisoned. Luckily, there are experts in Ancient Chinese medicine on hand (thus, Tsui Hark and the filmmakers shoehorn some more traditional, Chinese culture into a movie

11 The Miao (a.k.a. Hmong) are known for their elaborate embroideries (for wedding attire); and their jewellery – silverwork, coil necklaces, spiral earrings, and headdresses.

– altho' scenes of restoring the hero via magical and medical means are a standard trope in Chinese, historical movies).

In *The Swordsman*, Linghu Chong experiences a rough regime of healing via worms – yes, wriggly worms, administered thru pipes (by Blue Phoenix) into the nostril (ugh!). In his fever dream, Linghu thinks back to the Sun Moon Sect Elders he met, and here the footage of the song on the boat and the subsequent battle is recycled in a montage. But the recycling is not wholly shameless padding, because Linghu's visions seem to be apprehended by Ren Yingying, proving Linghu's trustworthiness (two beats before this, Ren was all for dispatching Linghu).

✦

Tsui Hark is fond of creating buddy duos, but subverting them by having the counterpart to the hero (or top-billed star) being played by an actress. The ruse works on several levels: the masculine relationship of the buddy set-up is maintained (they are 'men' in a man's world, or 'men' in public); being men, the characters can interact in the strictly patriarchal society of historical China; there's inevitable erotic attraction/ teasing between the two; and there's crossdressing and disguises (which're eventually uncovered); the crossdressing also provides opportunities for misunderstandings, embarrassments, and farce.

The quasi-lesbian scene in *The Swordsman* is pure Tsui Hark – it combines crossdressing with lesbianism. So, Blue Phoenix is given a lusty characterization (dropped from the later *Swordsman* films): she takes a shine to Yue Lingshan, Linghu Chong's companion (Skinny Boy), who travels as a man. Blue Phoenix flirts with Lingshan (who's drunk), then carries him/ her into a side room and is about to have her wicked way with her/ him, only to discover that she's a woman as she rips apart her clothes. It's not the first time (nor the last!) where Tsui teases audiences with some woman-on-woman action.[12]

Further romantic elements in *The Swordsman* include Yue Lingshan's unspoken affection for Linghu Chong (witness her dismay at being ordered to marry Lin Pingzhi), and the erotic, quasi-lesbian undercurrent in the antagonism between Ren Yingying and Blue Phoenix.

One of the issues tackled in *The Swordsman* is the Sins of the Fathers, and the troubled relationship between the older generation and the younger generation: this is a staple of martial arts movies, and is always featured in Tsui Hark's interpretation of the genre. Thus, both Gu Jinfu and Yue Buqun are corrupt patriarchs (and are duly punished in the finale). Meanwhile, a good and true patriarch, Liu Zhengfeng (Wu Ma), is killed by the Imperial bruisers. The lust for power is loudly scorned in *The Swordsman*, with the crooked Elders and Ouyang Quan hungering for the *Sunflower Scroll*.

✦

With some great directors of action involved (Lee, Hu, Tsui), plus Tony Ching Siu-tung, Lau Chi Ho and Yuen Wah as action choreographers, *The Swordsman* doesn't disappoint as an action movie. Among

12 The comic goofing around, when Linghu Chong sits on Blue Phoenix's head when she's sneaked into his room, is another example of Tsui Hark's brand of erotic but ditzy comedy.

the delights in *The Swordsman* are a fierce bust-up on a boat; several nighttime duels in smoky forests; an attack on a house; a brawl in an inn; and duels involving flying snakes and bees. The action is of the swordplay variety – fantastical and exaggerated, with much use of cables, rigs and flying, the manipulation of props, and intensely acrobatic movements out of Peking Opera. The *wuxia* genre is presented here via action which emphasizes energy and magic – there are numerous stunning evocations of high energy, and different forms of energy, in conflict with each other. (Several scenes are Chingian: the nighttime display of special swordsman-ship by the hermit Feng Qingyan; the battle on the boat; and the final duel between Linghu and his *sifu* Yue Buqun, which shows Linghu Chong using the sword forms on Yue).

In the boat sequence, most of the vessel is destroyed as our heroes beat off Yuen Wah's Zuo Lengshan and his henchmen. Linghu Chong and Skinny Boy are travelling by sea with the retiring Sun Moon Sect members. Following the lovely song scene, Zuo's boat rams the ship, and an all-out battle ensues. The boat offers plenty of opportunity for stuntmen to go crashing into sails, for masts to topple, and – a Chinese speciality – characters to fly up out of the water. This is a beautiful sequence of flowing movement and inventive stunts, with a poetic use of water and light.

Yuen Wah suffers a nasty (but well-earned) death: attacking the Mount Hua house, he is set upon by Ren Yingying's bees as well as Blue Phoenix's snakes. In a disgusting, nightmarish image,[13] Zuo Lengshan's face and shoulders are crawling with bees (a call-back to *The Butterfly Murders*, perhaps). This occurs after a wonderfully staged fight in amongst the long grass once again, where Blue Phoenix and Ren are pushed to the limit against Zuo (while carrying a comatose Linghu Chong, whom Ren is trying to resuscitate even as she flies thru air, fleeing from Zuo).

As all trails lead back to the Lam house, there's the delightful sight of the Imperial eunuch and his underlings having to don disguises, and pretend to be the grieving family of *sifu* Yue Buqun. The film exploits the reversal of political power as Gu Jinfu is forced to kowtow repeatedly. The tables are turned once more, before the finale, when Yue Buqun is brought to his knees and Gu Jinfu holds court again.

The action in the finale of *The Swordsman* is remarkable for its physical and technical complexity. In the small, enclosed space of the interior of the Lam household, with its upper balconies and pillars, the filmmakers stage a series of fierce battles. There's barely any room to swing a sword, let alone fly a stuntman thru the air in that building, but Tony Ching Siu-tung, Lau Chi Ho and Yuen Wah and the team deliver absolutely outstanding choreography.

Prior to the demise of the villains, the MacGuffin of the *Sunflower Manual* scroll is brought into play several times; it's repeatedly confused with the 'proud and laughing martial arts world' music scroll (and Linghu Chong gets to sing the catchy tune once more).

---

13 I've had nightmares like this with bees! I can't watch this scene again!

The Imperial eunuch, Gu Jinfu, is set upon by pistols and a rifle (brought by clever Blue Phoenix), plus swords (from Linghu Chong) and finally Ren Yingying adds the last touch, tearing the guy apart with her whip. And Linghu, in the closing duel, brings the over-bearing *sifu* Yue Buqun down a notch or two (including cutting his meridian points), using the 'Nine Swords of Dugu' forms he learnt from Feng Qingyan. Only the intervention of Skinny Boy stops the hero running her father thru with his sword.

The duel is a very Chingian swordplay scene – to portray the deadly *chi* emanating from *sifu* Yue Buqun, the environment is puppeteered – wooden fences split apart, for example, and the ground is sliced with energy lines. Tony Ching's penchant for very extravagant aerial spins and somersaults, complete with flapping clothing, is much in evidence. Ching would later make this kind of highly romantic action choreography famous in the West in the 2002 film *Hero*.

*The Swordsman* closes with what became one of Tsui Hark signature motifs (which he used many times): the heroes riding off into the sunset on horses under a big sky in the countryside (this time in slo-mo), as if the producers have decided to go for the most clichéd ending they can imagine. Thus ends one of the great Hong Kong action movies.

# 8

# *THE SWORDSMAN 2*

# *Siu Ngo Kong Woo II Dung Fong Bat Baai*

THE PRODUCTION.

Jet Li plus Brigitte Lin plus superstar action director Tony Ching Siu-tung with Tsui Hark as producer and an outrageously over-the-top story combine to produce one of the great fantasy swordplay movies of recent times. It starts at full speed and doesn't let up! The prologue alone contains a horse being sliced in half, flying horses and warriors, decapitation, a swordplay battle in an Imperial palace, and a god-like being in scarlet who declaims from the tops of trees.

*The Swordsman 2* is a work of genius. It's a masterpiece of pure popcorn movie fantasy, and can stand beside any of the great action movies in the history of cinema. 'Ecstatic cinema', 'giddily demented', 'eye-popping', and a 'gender-bending, gravity-defying, mystical-surreal fantasy beyond your wildest dreams' (F. Dannen, 339), are some of the critical assessments of *The Swordsman 2*.

*The Swordsman 2* (Cantonese: *Siu Ngo Kong Woo II Dong Fong Bat Baai;* Mandarin: *Xiao-ao Jianghu II Dongfang Bubai = Laughing and Proud Warrior: Invincible Asia,* 1992) was directed by Tony Ching Siu-tung, and starred Jet Li, Brigitte Lin, Rosamund Kwan, Michelle Reiss (Lee), Waise Lee, Lau Shun, Chin Kar Lok, Yen Shi Kwan, Candice Yu On-on, and Fennie Yuen (that's one of the best casts in a 1990s Chinese movie). *The Swordsman 2* was a re-thinking of the first *Swordsman* movie, with the major roles being re-cast. (Others in the ensemble included: Kwok Leung Cheung, Kwok-Ping Choi, Man-Kwong Fung, Choi-Chow Hoh, Kwok-Kit Lam, Yeung-Wah Kam and Chi Yeung Wong).

Tsui Hark was producer, Chi-Wai Cheung and Wai Sum Shia were assoc. producers, Hanson Chan, Elsa Tang Pik-yin and Tsui Hark wrote the script, Tom Lau Moon-tong was DP, Marco Mak Chi-sin was editor, music was by Richard Yuen, action directors were Tony Ching Siu-tung,

Yuen Bun, Ma Yukshing, Bruce Law and Cheung Yiu-sing (plus 6 assistants), costumes: Bruce Yu Ka-on, Kwok Mei-Ling, Shiu Ching-Yee, Chan Bo-Guen, Yeung Lin-Mui and William Chang, make-up by Man Yun-Ling and Lai Ka-Pik, hair by Chau Siu-Mui and Wan Yuk-Mui, prod. des.: Yee-Fung Chung and Wah-Sang Leung, sound rec. and ed.: Kam Wing Chow.

It was produced by Film Workshop/ Long Shong Pictures/ Golden Princess. It was a big hit in Canton, with a gross of HK $34,462 million (great business for any Hong Kong movie, and one of Jet Li's biggest hits in China). Category IIB. Released on June 26, 1992. 108 mins.

The Swordsman 2 has everything – all you could desire from characters, a story, action, visuals, music and film stars. And for film critics it delivers a strong political commentary, while cultural theorists can delight in the transgender play.

Jet Li (Li Lanjie) and Brigitte Lin (Lin Ching-hsia) head up the terrific cast of The Swordsman 2 : both have never been better, and both were at the peak of their powers. With Once Upon a Time In China and The Swordsman 2, Li established himself as a major force in Chinese cinema (The Swordsman 2 and Once Upon a Time In China 2, another masterpiece, were both released in 1992). Li is at his winsome, charming best[14] in The Swordsman 2 – yes, and he moves like a dream! He really is one of the most beautiful creatures ever put on film. (Western cinema has many male babes, pin-up stars, and great actors who're charismatic, talented and beautiful – but can they move like that?!).

JET LI.

Jet Li was born on April 26, 1963 in Beijing, China. (In Cantonese, Li's name is Lei Lin Git; in Mandarin, it's Li Lanjie). Li is short (5' 6"), but can take on anyone in movies. Li won the first national wushu competition in China since the Cultural Revolution (aged 9); he was the Chinese Men's All-round National Wushu Champion at the age of twelve. (Wushu is a form of martial arts as performance, combining Peking Opera, gymnastics, and colourful costumes, developed during the Cultural Revolution). Li moved to San Francisco with a Chinese actress (Huang Qiuyan) in 1988; they married (1987-90) and had two daughters. In the U.S.A., Li received his Green Card. Li later married actress Nina Li Chi (they have two daughters).

Jet Li first appeared in some movies about the Temple of Shaolin.[15] His break-out role was playing Wong Fei-hung in the Once Upon a Time In China series. Li appeared in several martial arts movies right after the first Once Upon a Time In China film, including Tai Chi Master, New Legend of Shaolin (about Hung Gar), the Fong Say-yuk films, Last Hero In China, and Kung Fu Cult Master (a.k.a. Evil Cult).

With Ching Siu-tung, Jet Li has appeared in the Swordsman films, Hero, The Warlords, The Terracotta Warrior, The Sorcerer and the White

---

14 Jet Li is not serious and dour in The Swordsman 2, as some critics complain – he plays a drunken warrior in an appealing manner (he's introduced riding on a horse, drinking). Indeed, Li follows how Sam Hui played the character in the first Swordsman film.
15 Li didn't make much money from his Shaolin pictures (he was paid a State subsidy).

*Snake,* and *Dr Wai.*

BRIGITTE LIN.

Brigitte Lin is... Brigitte Lin; Lin was born in Sanchong, Taiwan on Nov 3, 1954.[16] (She is Lam Ching Hsia in Cantonese and Lin Qinhxia in Mandarin; she is also known as Venus Lin). Lin was in many Taiwanese films (beginning in 1973) before appearing in Hong Kong films such as *Zu: Warriors From the Magic Mountain, All the Wrong Spies, Police Story, Peking Opera Blues,* the *Bride With White Hair* films, the *Royal Tramp* films, *New Dragon Gate Inn,* some Wong Kar-wai films such as *Chungking Express* and *Ashes of Time,* and the *Swordsman* cycle.

Brigitte Lin is one of the most remarkable of all recent Asian stars. She 'must certainly be one of the most fearless performers in the world' (Lisa Morton, 101). Lin, tho' straight, is known for playing lesbian and crossdressing women in pictures such as *All the Wrong Spies* (a lesbian disguising herself as a guy), *Fantasy Mission Force* (she shoots the clothes off a tied-up woman), *The Swordsman 2* and *3* (she's a lesbian, transsexual superhero), *New Dragon Gate Inn* (she steals another woman's clothes for herself), *Peking Opera Blues* (she wears men's military uniforms), *Boys Are Easy* (she's a lesbian cop), *Ashes of Time* (she plays both a brother and a sister), *Eagle Shooting Heroes* (she's a butch princess), and *Fire Dragon* (she's a masked male warrior).

Brigitte Lin's crossdressing or trans-gender character in the *Swordsman* movies (as Dongfang Bubai = Asia the Invincible) draws on the Peking Opera tradition (where actors can be both warriors and princesses. Indeed, the Tsui Hark movie *Peking Opera Blues* explores issues of gender[17] at length).

Brigitte Lin, according to Bey Logan, was one of the few bankable female stars in Asia: 'basically, all the ageless Ms Lin has to do is wave her arms and smile enigmatically and local audiences will pay to watch' (166).

Tsui Hark has tried to entice Brigitte Lin back to acting – for the remake of *Zu: Warriors From the Magic Mountain*, for instance, and to play the Empress Wu in *Detective Dee and the Mystery of the Phantom Flame*. Lin retired from acting in 1994, when she married businessman Michael Ying and had children.

Brigitte Lin delivers a career high with her powerful and unforgettable turn as a human-becoming-a-god in *The Swordsman 2*, Asia the Invincible. In a cinema jammed with truly insane villains/ monsters/ crime lords and all-round psychos, Lin manages to fashion a transgendered character all of her own in the world of Hong Kong movie-making. Of course, let's not forget that the role of Asia/ Dawn was actually created by the writers and the filmmakers (plus the costume designers, the hairdressers and the make-up artists. The film won the Hong Kong Film Award for Best Costumes and Make-up). But, as directors and producers and writers

---

16 Some sources say 1957.
17 Peking Opera had a huge impact on the young Tsui Hark – including the play with gender.

know all too well, they can only go *so far* in putting a character together: because, ultimately, an actor needs to embody that character on screen. And Lin achieves that magnificently.[18]

Tsui Hark said he had the idea for the character of Asia the Invincible when he was filming *Zu: Warriors From the Magic Mountain* – it was a chara tailor-made for his friend Brigitte Lin[19] (LM, 90). The character came out of Jin Yong's book, but was considerably expanded from the ten pages in the novel. Tsui told Lin not to read the book, but to read the script; he also wanted to dub her voice; Lin agreed. (However, as Tsui recalled, 'virtually everyone, including the author Jin Yong (Louis Cha) was vehemently against' casting Lin).

After *The Swordsman 2*, the character of Dongfong Bat Baai became a popular gag in movies – and the next *Swordsman* movie acknowledged the popularity of the character, by building the entire plot around him/ her.

It's a wonderful fantasy of Imperial, political oppression – and if you're going to be oppressed, at least Asia the Invincible is charismatic and beautiful (if also insane and brutal). Brigitte Lin's Asia makes a change, too, from the usual Imperial tyrants in Chinese, historical movies, who tend to be twisted, eunuchized sickos.

✦

*The Swordsman 2* also conjures kick-ass roles for the other women in the cast: the lovely Rosamund Kwan, as Ren Yingying, leader of the Miaos (taking over from Sharla Cheung in the first film), gets to wield whips and daggers with an impressive confidence (and she rips assailants to shreds, too!). Michelle Reiss/ Lee is cute, naïve, playful and charming as Yue Lingshan (Kiddo), the hero's sidekick (replacing Cecilia Yip). She's the familiar tomboy woman in Chinese cinema (and a recurring motif in Tsui Hark's films), dressing like a man, and joining the Wau Mountain Sect as one of the boys. The character of Blue Phoenix (Lan Fenghuang), played by Fennie Yuen again, is intriguing: another tomboy, who looks up to her chief, Ren Yingying (Kwan), with hints of distant, unrequited lesbian desire (tho' Blue Phoenix subsumes her emotions into the goals of her group, the Miaos).

The rest of the supporting cast of *The Swordsman 2* is very fine: Candice Yu On-on is suitably attractive and tender as Asia the Invincible's concubine Snow (a.k.a. Cici),[20] adding a running commentary on the transformation of Asia from male to female (and finding Asia becoming more diva-like and difficult as the magic of the sacred scroll takes hold). Among the guys, Lau Shun, one of the great character actors of this period of Chinese cinema (who seems to have appeared in everything, and was certainly a favourite of Tsui Hark's), is superb (as always) as Swordsman Xiang Wentian (a.k.a. Zen), part of the Sun Moon Sect. Yen Shi-kwan plays the imprisoned former chief of the Miaos, Ren Woxing (a.k.a. Master Wu), with a cackling intensity. Waise Lee, another actor

18 Tsui Hark said he didn't include Asia the Invincible in the first *Swordsman* movie, because her character would've upset the balance (LM, 90).
19 Brigitte Lin as Asia may not look masculine, but her presence, her attitude and the expression of her will persuade us to accept her as male.
20 The name of one of the only two Empresses of China.

who is everywhere in Chinese cinema, was impressive as the *ronin* leader Fubu Qianjun (a.k.a. Hattori), who aligns himself with Dongfang Bubai. Cheung Kwok-leung was Eunuch Hong (whose fate is to be another of Asia's victims – decapitated), and Chin Kar-lok was another mad cackler, as Yuanfei Riyue (a.k.a. Saru), Hattori's henchman.

THE CRITICS.

*The Swordsman 2* has everything going for it, *and then some*. The action is completely spell-binding, with the 39 year-old Tony Ching Siu-tung, the king of wire-work and flying actors and stunt people everywhere, at the top of his game.[21] Once again, one is struck by the feeling of total freedom that Ching's films as director or action choreographer possess. The sheer beauty and grace (and speed) of the movement thru the frame is gorgeous to contemplate. *The Swordsman 2* is one of Ching's finest outings – as the fantastical and exotic elements are allowed to run riot. Ching explained the approach:

We tried something new in every action scene, like Brigitte Lin's *zhang feng* [palm power]. In other films *zhang feng* causes only an explosion, but I tried disintegrating an entire person.

Barry Long on *The Swordsman 2* noted:

Bordering on expressionism, this contains all of the classic elements of a Tsui Hark Film Workshop production – crisp action choreo-graphy, an ensemble of A-list performers, a visual flair that is always eye-popping, and plenty of gender confusion.[22]

Lisa Morton adds:

one of the most giddily demented films ever made... This is gonzo filmmaking, with a complexity of vision and a surety of skill that are continually jaw-dropping. (LM, 87)

Stokes and Hoover describe *The Swordsman 2* thus:

Ching plays it over the top with Dionysian abandon, creating 'ecstatic cinema' captured by multiple cameras dramatically careening at all angles and sundry color schemes of permeating blues, reds, and browns. The wire stunts come fast and furious... (104)

THE SCRIPT.

Check out the script of *The Swordsman 2*. So often critics complain about the quality of the scripts in Hong Kong cinema, insisting that they are patchy, don't make sense, and are ignored in favour of action and spectacle. Sure, many times, yes (but you try writing scripts for five or more movies per year!).

21 'The physical effects are genuinely amazing', Lisa Morton said (LM, 88).
22 Quoted in F. Dannen, 36.

Actually, the screenplay for *The Swordsman 2* (by Hanson Chan, Tang Pik-yin and Tsui Hark) is as neatly worked-out as any good film script: the structure is rock-solid, heading from an initial crisis (Asia the Invincible taking over the Sun Moon Sect), through the reactions of the Mountain Wau Sect to the problem, up to the bloodshed and multiple deaths in the finale, as everybody converges on Asia in her/ his Imperial stronghold. Like a tragic play, the narrative in *The Swordsman 2* has an unstoppable inevitability about it – a continuous descent into turmoil, you might say. The writers make sure, for instance, that the opponents and obstacles are piled up high for our heroes: not only the Imperial court, and Asia the Invincible, and the Sun Moon Sect, and Japanese ninja/ *ronin,* but even one of their own – Master Wu, Ren Woxing (who, upon his release from prison, turns out to be something of a psychopath,[23] and once Asia is (apparently) vanquished, Wu embarks on a cruel programme of elimination).

Also, the script for *The Swordsman 2* is tightly-plotted and mixes up the tempo: it's not all slambang action; not only are there character-led scenes, there are musical and nostalgic interludes, humorous scenes, and a series of seduction/ flirtation scenes. There are moments, for example, when the characters stop and reflect on what it all means, and on the passing of time. (Tsui Hark said he put all of the characters onto a white board, to work out with the production team what to do with them [LM, 90]). 'What makes *Swordsman II* a great film (instead of merely an interesting curiosity) is that the emotions are as intense as the action (and the warped morality)', remarked Lisa Morton (LM, 89).

*The Swordsman 2,* set in 1572, continues to use the same narrative ingredients of the first *Swordsman* movie of 1990, but the new cast and the new approach makes it feel like a different story with different characters (there are rival clans, Imperial heavies, a magical scroll, a wandering warrior and his sidekick, etc). There's no doubt that Jet Li blossomed into a huge star at this time, filling the role of the drifting, drinking warrior with a wonderful, self-deprecating humour, as well as of course the agility and grace of a dancer. As Linghu Chong, Jet Li (taking over the role from Sam Hui in the first film) is a delight from his introduction onwards (swigging at a bottle on a horse, accompanied by his sidekick, Kiddo, played with sweet charm by Michelle Reiss/ Lee. So, yes, Li is evoking another version of the drunken swordsman, a staple of many a *kung fu* flick. And that wine flask crops up repeatedly – and is also part of the flirtation scene between Linghu and Asia the Invincible – staged, with typical eccentricity, with both characters waist-deep in the sea).

*The Swordsman 2* is also a companion to the first *Once Upon a Time In China* movie, released in 1991: there's a similar romance, for instance, between Jet Li and Rosamund Kwan (there's no doubting that, in this period, Li and Kwan made a gorgeous couple – and both exude a fresh-faced, rosy-cheeked innocence that only exists in movies. If people were

23 In the jail, Master Wu reveals his nasty side when he kills five guards – and Linghu Chong remarks that it's not necessary.

really like this, Earth would be Heaven!).[24]

The Swordsman 2 has time for character scenes, for love scenes, for humorous scenes, and for musical scenes: there are several musical montages: music is a key component in this 1992 movie (Linghu Chong plays a *qin*, to charm Kiddo),[25] the Wau Mountain Sect sing the 'Hero of Heroes' song repeatedly round the fire, and music provides the springboard for nostalgic and poetic interludes.[26] There's even a *Count of Monte Cristo* prison sequence, when Linghu's captured by Asia the Invincible's mob, and discovers that Master Wu is chained up in the cell opposite his (with an inventive use of rats to carry messages between the cells).

STYLE AND LOOK.

Technically, The Swordsman 2 boasts an all-round cinematic brilliance, some lavish and intricate costumes, a battery of visual and practical effects, and incredible cinematography. This is a very, very beautiful film. The lighting is truly magical, with firelight, flaming torches, moonlight, stormlight, smoke-filled nights,[27] candles and natural light deployed with absolute mastery and lyricism. The textures and atmospheres are beyond even the celebrated Hong Kong films. *The Swordsman 2* is I think one of the greatest movies to come out of Hong Kong, and certainly one of the finest movies anywhere for lighting and photography.

Look at the use of locations in the New Territories, for instance. Even tho' fans of Hong Kong cinema will have seen some of these locations before (many times, some of us! – that same beach, that same piece of cliff and rocks, that same forest, etc), DP Tom Lau Moon-tong lends them a delightfully heightened, lush look, as if China were being re-invented all over again. The ocean, forests, mountain roads, roadside inns, and Imperial palaces – *The Swordsman 2* creates a magical dream of a China that never existed (but *should* have existed!).

The extensive night shoots out-of-doors enhance the 1992 movie with atmospheric scenes lit by burning torches and campfires. You get the impression that if the electrical power was suddenly cut for the lighting rigs, the cinematographers and the sparks would find a way of lighting the entire movie using wood fires, candles and oil-fuelled torches.

*The Swordsman 2* is also a giant visual effects movie, in the Hong Kong New Wave tradition of never letting the limitations of the budget hold you back. Smoke billows thru every scene (indoor or outdoor), and the air is full of leaves, fire, kicked sand, flying snakes, branches, logs, and swords. Wind machines, rain machines, smoke machines, full-body burns, explosions, pyrotechnics, optical super-impositions, special make-up,

---

24 And yet Earth *is* Heaven — we just don't realize it.
25 He sings a James Wong Jim song, 'Jek Gei Gam Woo Siu'.
26 Linghu Chong, with his irrepressible charisma, leads the singing of the theme song ('Xiao Hongchen') of the movie in act one, at the Mountain Wau Sect's hide-out in an inn; *The Swordsman 2* seamlessly segues into the Sun Moon Sect also singing the song, as the musicians sway, while Ren waits for Linghu's return. That's clever screenwriting.
27 By this time, Hong Kong camera and lighting crews had enough lamps and electrical power to really make outdoor night scenes work.

models, animation, puppetry, and of course lots of wire-work – is there a visual effect that *The Swordsman 2 doesn't* use? Not really – and yet all of the effects are deployed in the service of the story and the characters. Or put it like this: *The Swordsman 2* is such a great visual effects movie because the script is solid. And most of the effects occur in front of the camera. (Again, altho' Tsui Hark is known as a master of visual effects, Tony Ching Siu-tung employs them just as brilliantly).

*The Swordsman 2* is edited by Tsui Hark's regular editor, Marco Mak Chi-sin, a genius editor if ever there was one: one of the chief reasons for this movie being a masterpiece is the brilliance of the editing (which's true of many classics). Contrasts are made by cutting on visual rhymes (from one set of characters sitting around a camp fire at night to another, for example, or by cutting from one group singing a song to another). Mak doesn't simply join one scene to another: he conjures up several incredible montages – and not only poetic montages over music, but also parallel action. The most melodramatic slice of action in parallel occurs when the hero Linghu Chong is making love with Snow (Candice Yu – thinking she's Asia the Invincible), while the *real* Asia is out and about wasting all of his cohorts! Wow!

How do you portray a god or demi-god on screen? The solution in *The Swordsman 2* is inventive, to say the least. Verticality and height is emphasized – Asia the Invincible stands on top of trees,28 or in their branches,29 as if s/he is nature itself. When s/he talks, her voice echoes around the landscape everywhere, as if the Earth is speaking.30 Characters are rushing upwards into the sky or the branches of a tree, or diving downwards following their swords onto an opponent, or leaping into the ground. And a vast battery of practical effects are deployed to dramatize the powers that the god-like Asia possesses.31

ASIA THE INVINCIBLE.

In *The Swordsman 2*, Dongfang Bubai, Asia the Invincible (sometimes called Dawn), is using the sacred scroll to achieve great power. The cost? His masculinity, his male identity – or, as Master Wu chortles, his penis – he has to castrate himself (when Wu reads the sacred scroll, he roars with laughter). There's more: the characterization of Asia the Invincible not only uses the cliché of eunuchs, he is transforming into a woman (the movie tracks the change bit by bit, so that, in the finale of *The Swordsman 2*, Asia is making himself/ herself up as a woman in front of a mirror, and his/ her voice changes (in most of the movie Asia seems to be dubbed by a male actor; halfway thru, his voice becomes hoarser, and when the change is nearly complete, it seems to be Brigitte Lin's voice). The 1992 film plays with how people perceive leaders and political power – Asia's followers notice that his/ her voice has altered, but they still follow the

28 Meanwhile, Ren Yingying and Master Wu also spend time on the roof of the inn.
29 In one amazing shot, Brigitte Lin stands in the branches of a huge tree, as Dawn converses with Master Wu in the distance.
30 But Asia doesn't move her mouth in her first encounter with Linghu.
31 Using wind machines, smoke machines, special make-up, puppetry, models, optical printing, and of course wires.

commands).

The Swordsman 2 is a movie where a flirting scene between the two main stars is played waist-deep in water off a sandy beach in the late afternoon. A mysterious scene, with the threat of antagonism (and violence) being put aside momentarily when Asia the Invincible finds him/ herself being instantly intrigued by this bold trespasser on his/ her realm. A scene where the anti-hero alters the weather and kills birds[32] out of the sky with his/ her new-found magical powers. A scene where the hero, in his drunken, youthful energy, spins in the air for sheer joy, flying out of the water.[33] Remarkable – it's like no other flirtation scene in cinema (especially when we know that Asia the Invincible is a demi-god, and is transforming from a man to a woman. In this scene, s/he seems to reveal herself/ himself as an attractive heterosexual prospect to Linghu Chong). And of course, the scene is performed by two of the loveliest stars in Hong Kong cinema, Brigitte Lin and Jet Li (both of whom have blurred the categories of gender, and have also played gender-bending roles). So that if the issue of homoeroticism is raised by the ruse of Asia the Invincible finding Linghu attractive, it is offset by having Asia played by a woman. So the film producers cover all bases (which they always prefer to do!).

Most of the love scenes btn Linghu Chong and Dawn the Invincible are played with Dawn staying mute, so his/ her voice doesn't give him/ herself away (it's a wry commentary on the relation between power and communication, on identity and expression, and also on gender roles – how Dawn acts the coquettish lover when s/he is still partly a man, how s/he laughs exaggeratedly, like Harpo Marx,[34] at Linghu's jokes). When Asia finally speaks to Linghu, in his/ her womanly guise, the first thing s/he says is Linghu's name.

The gender-bending in The Swordsman 2 (which continued in the sequel of 1993, of course), fascinated Western critics. Of The Swordsman 2, Raymond Murray commented in Images In the Dark: 'the film's ultimate plot twist involves Jet spending the night in Brigette's bed, before realizing it means he's had sex with a eunuchized man!' (373). And yet, of course, he doesn't – we see Linghu Chong in a clinch with Snow (a.k.a. Cici), Dawn's lover (tho' they haven't made love for 6 months, according to Snow – that is, when Asia was still a guy). Linghu Chong is not sure – he demands that Asia tell him the truth in the finale, but s/he remains, of course, a mystery.

Men meant to be men but played by women, and vice versa, and men pretending to be women, and vice versa, and the voices of men or women being dubbed by their opposite, are staples of Chinese cinema (also drawing on the theatrical tradition of all-male troupes), but seem to titillate Western film critics. Well, there is a tradition in the West of men playing women's roles, which Western critics keep forgetting (the history of theatre going back to Ancient Greece, for example, where everybody,

32 And notice how Linghu Chong and his Mountain Wau chums don't waste those dead birds! If they fell on many places around the world, they'd be cooked immediately! And the lads do just that.
33 The phallic aspects of Linghu's delight are obvious.
34 Brigitte Lin doing Harpo Marx?! Why not?!

male or female, on stage was played by a guy). But in North American and Western cinema, characters that're meant to be men are almost always played by men (and vice versa). However, in Chinese cinema (and Japanese cinema), having women play guys, but not in a disguise or as a gender switch, is a convention.

With the *Swordsmen* movies, the fact that Brigitte Lin was doing the gender-bending added immensely to the tease for Western film critics – because Lin is a fantastically attractive woman (and also already possesses a masculine/ tomboy appeal even before she steps into men's clothes). And, in portraying three other women in strong, kick-ass roles – Michelle Reiss/ Lee, Fennie Yuen and Rosamund Kwan – *The Swordsman 2* was adding to the gender reversals (a running gag, for instance, has the boys in the Mountain Wau Sect joking about Kiddo being a woman).

✦

In act two of *The Swordsman 2*, there are seduction scenes between the hero and the heroine who's still partly the anti-hero. Linghu Chong opts to investigate Asia the Invincible's quarters (along with Swordsman Zen). This is one of several mid-film action sequences: Linghu doesn't simply sneak into Asia's palace, or knock on the front door: this is a flamboyant section of *The Swordsman 2*, involving much flitting about at night on rooftops, hanging from rafters, battling guards who erupt from underneath the ground (a classic Chingian motif), and a complex duel between Linghu and Asia the Indivisible in his/ her chambers. The editing is as nimble and swift as one of Asia's flicked needles or pebbles, and the choreography is some of the finest in a Tony Ching Siu-tung movie (notice how both characters are moving very close to the floor, never more than waist high).

To illustrate just how venal Asia the Invincible could be, Chimp (Chin Ka-lok) had already been cornered and executed earlier: Asia controls his body with a well-aimed needle at a pressure point. In a grotesque moment (which also doesn't make sense), the shape of Chimp's body is imprinted on the wall of Asia's chambers in blood (and Chimp collapses on the ground soaked in blood and very dead).

Butterflies or moths fluttering inside a paper lamp (likely a Tsui Hark addition)[35] are one of myriad details in this sequence, and in the follow-up seduction (of course, the insect is nailed by a flying needle). Yes, those flying needles do a lot of work in *The Swordsman 2*. How wonderful is Chinese cinema in being able to turn something so domestic and 'feminine' (and *small*) – embroidery and needlepoint – into fearsome weaponry which can control the victim's pressure points. (The flying needles are reprised several times in *The Swordsman 2* – during the Linghu Chong and Asia the Insatiable seduction scenes, Linghu gets entangled in the threads,[36] a terrific *femme fatale*-as-spider motif; and in the finale, Master Wu is ensnared by a battery of needles which Asia unleashes in her/ his fury.)

And yet this elaborate scene, which displays the bodies of Brigitte Lin and Jet Li in an inventive, very graceful and tangled choreography, is only

35 A reference to his first film.
36 And there are playful jokes – like when Linghu tears the embroidery, so there are two dragons. (A reference to the movie *Twin Dragons*).

one of many packed into this part of *The Swordsman 2*, which also includes a scene of Swordsman Zen versus Hattori and his guards, Linghu Chong and his cohorts in disguise as gypsies, and Linghu carrying Asia the Invisible away from the palace, to drink with his buddies round a fire. And in this frenetically-paced movie, there is a moment where Linghu speaks longingly of a time outside of war and politics, a time when he can just drink (these anti-war, anti-oppression interludes are a recurring motif in Tsui Hark's cinema).

(This sequence also contains one of the signature romantic motifs in *wuxia* pictures of this era: the hero and the heroine flying side by side through the tops of trees, accompanied by a lush music cue – moments that become iconic, and are tailor-made for the trailers).

WOMEN IN ACTION.

*The Swordsman 2* is full of women, too: there are not one, not two, not three, but four prominent female roles in *The Swordsman 2* (plus Snow). The clever script gives them all things to do,[37] plus goals and motivations, and none of them are simply 'girlfriend of the hero', or 'stay at home mom', or 'girl next door'. *The Swordsman 2* is a movie which foregrounds women in action – as only Hong Kong action cinema can! Each actress has her own scene (actually several scenes) in which to shine: Rosamund Kwan[38] explodes flying warriors with her whip; Michelle Reiss takes on numerous swordsmen, spinning like a top; Fennie Yuen is an incredible snake-handler and martial artist;[39] and Brigitte Lin is, well, simply astounding as the demi-god Asia the Invincible.

Ah, how happy for Jet Li! – because each of the women in *The Swordsman 2* is in love or half in love with Linghu Chong. Thus, *The Swordsman 2* has not one romantic subplot, but several (Linghu has four admirers – a harem). And the 1992 film carefully tracks each of the women's feelings for Linghu – consider how the numerous looks and quips are integrated into the scenes (yet again negating the common view among critics that the scripts and dramas of Hong Kong movies are not carefully worked out). How, for ex, Kiddo looks at Linghu hugging Ren Yingying enviously, and how Blue Phoenix notices that (Fennie Yuen is great at sly smirks). The barely-suppressed jealousy is a delight to see in characters such as Ren (Kwan) and Kiddo (Reiss) as they squabble in the background over Linghu. (Kiddo, for instance, is keen to primp up herself to attract Linghu – the film includes humorous scenes where Kiddo's new hairstyle[40] causes surprise and pratfalls, and when her make-up is switched with ingredients for the soup. Kiddo's scene at the mirror depicts

37 Presumably Tsui Hark, as co-writer, had some say in bumping up the roles of the women in *The Swordsman 2*. Because it doesn't really need five women – it could get by, as many action movies do, with one or two.
38 It's great to see Rosamund Kwan's demure Aunt Yee from *Once Upon a Time In China* as an action heroine. And she's given a whip! In one scene, she's pulling along a swordsman with her whip snagged on his foot, while he holds himself up with his sword, which sparks as it's dragged thru the dirt.
39 'One of the most non-traditional martial arts films ever made', opined Lisa Morton (LM 87).
40 The buns on the side of the head are a classic, Chinese hair-do, but also might be a *Star Wars* joke.

another gender reversal: Kiddo has been dressed as a man, and here feminizes herself with the aid of make-up and a new hairstyle. The comedy thus plays into the central theme of gender confusion).

Indeed, the love/ romance elements are no mere subplot/s in *The Swordsman 2*, but bear upon the main plot of clan/ political rivalry many times. Dawn the Invincible's feelings for Linghu Chong, for instance, prevent her/ him from slaying Linghu's countrymen (well, for a moment, at least!).

Jet Li and his women! – because there's another woman for Li, when Asia the Invincible coerces her lover Snow to seduce Linghu Chong (thus neatly circumventing the notion of the (apparently) straight hero of an action movie having sex with a man who's castrated himself and is transforming via magic into a woman.[41] But when that 'man'/ 'woman' is played by the incandescent Brigitte Lin, what's the problem?!).

Even more remarkable, in a movie stuffed with remarkable sequences, while Linghu Chong is taking the lovely Snow at Asia the Invincible's place, his cohorts are embroiled in to-the-death battles with Asia and his/ her crew. Yes, the action hero is having sex while everyone is getting slaughtered left, right and centre! (Thus, when the lights go out in Asia's chambers, and the switch of Asia for Snow occurs, it's not played for farce. It's an erotic scene, but played straight, because editor Marco Mak intercuts it with Asia demolishing Linghu's colleagues. Another detail in this sequence has Asia sensing what Snow is feeling, and perhaps regretting it).

ACTION SCENES.

It's pure pleasure all the way in *The Swordsman 2*: among the many delights are the action scenes. First up, in the prologue, there's a sword battle and escape in an Imperial palace, and a battle between Linghu Chong and Kiddo on a mountain trail with Asia the Invincible. The Japanese ninja-style attack on the inn is the highlight of act one of *The Swordsman 2* – it boasts a sophistication and invention with wire-work and movement beyond even 99% of Hong Kong filmmakers. Scenes where the warriors spin flying blades and then hop on them to soar into the building are simply astonishing. (Nothing in Western cinema has ever come close – right up to today).

There are many points in this 1992 Hong Kong movie which seem miraculous – as if we are witnessing the Birth of Cinema all over again. To achieve that (or even attempt it) is absolutely amazing. And this occurs many times in Hong Kong cinema. (This is not a pompous or pretentious statement: it *feels* like this is the Birth of Film because the filmmakers take such delight in their work; they are artists in their child-like mode, where making art has a significant and very appealing sense of *play*).

But then our heroes fight back with – what? – *snakes*. And that means snakes, Chinese-style! Draped all over the actors, whizzed on wires, and sliced to pieces by flying swords (in a huge cascade of snakes, in slo-mo).

---

41 But why does castration equate with becoming a woman?!

Blue Phoenix shines in this part of *The Swordsman 2* (check out the *physical* acting here, the rapid changes of pose as Blue Phoenix trills on her high-pitched whistle to call up the serpents. Tony Ching has a brilliant feeling for bodies in movement, and how the camera can frame and follow that movement). The Japanese *shinobi* respond with scorpions – so it's scorpions vs. snakes. And Linghu Chong later takes up a scorpion and puts it in his flask of wine, to enhance the flavour – this is one of the numerous comical touches woven into the slambang action sequences in *The Swordsman 2*).

The exploitation of space in *The Swordsman 2* is also exceptional – the Chinese filmmakers use every inch of the inn, upper and lower levels, including having characters (like Kiddo) crash thru the floor, hurtle thru windows, fall from upper to lower levels, and fly up to the roof. [42] The attack on the inn continues into the forest outside, with Ren Yingying and Blue Phoenix duelling swordsmen using snakes, whips and flying swords (in *The Swordsman 2*, the participants announce their martial arts techniques before they use them, as often in swordplay films: 'Flying Sword!').

Oh, this is glorious cinema, so self-assured, so inventive – and so silly! As if being human is simply not enough for mere humans – they must be able to zoom up into the trees on cables, or disappear into holes in the ground, with their swords leaving an energy line of sparks.

The assault on Asia the Invincible's palace is another outstanding sequence: the traditional, Chinese rooms, with their veils and patterned screens, provide tight, enclosed spaces where the action choreography at times emulates lovemaking (after all, this is Linghu Chong entering Asia's chambers). The editing (by Marco Mak Chi-sin) is especially fine in this sequence, combining extreme close-ups of flying needles with shadowy rooms and partially-lit close-ups of stars Jet Li and Brigitte Lin.

The penis – the sword – the needle – the canon – so many phallic tropes; there's no need to tease out the sexual subtext in *The Swordsman 2*, because the movie deconstructs itself for your pleasure in front of your eyes. Yes, this is a movie stuffed with Freudian, castration imagery, too – guys have their heads torn off, Dawn castrates himself, and both Swordsman Zen and Hattori cut off their own arms!

In a movie which reinvents fantasy swordplay yet again, as if from scratch, and also pushes what has already been achieved in *wuxia* movies even further, the Swordsman Zen versus the Mountain Wau warriors sequence is remarkable. Zen is the lone swordsman, mysterious and super-powerful (later, he's revealed to be a member of the Highlanders who's disfigured himself to elude capture. He's played by the ever-dependable, awesomely versatile Lau Shun).

So it's one man against seven or so, including Linghu Chong, and *everyone* is flying on cables (set in, of course, a smoke-filled forest at night). This is a ballet of ferocious energy and high speed. The photography and framing is another object lesson in filmmaking, the

42 Several characters spend time on the roof – Wu, Ren and Blue Phoenix. Indeed, roofs are a major location in many Chinese action movies – filmmakers can't resist taking the action upwards.

editing and rhythms have a mesmeric flow, and it's quite, quite beautiful (and details like the spinning swords, the swords rotating around the wrists, in and out of the grasp, has the vertiginous ecstasy of Japanese animation. Yes – in Chinese action cinema, it's as if all inanimate objects become alive, and the environment too is a force that can't be ignored).

In the climactic love scene in *The Swordsman 2*, where Linghu Chong arrives at Asia the Invincible's quarters and discovers that s/he has flattened many of her/ his underlings, the filmmakers orchestrate space and light with a deft, skilful ease. How, for instance, Asia rapidly douses the lamps so that s/he can slip away and have Snow stand in for her/ him in the love scene. How Linghu stands some way off, so he doesn't see Snow (she's behind the door).

Martial arts that can reverse the flow of blood, or momentarily paralyze the victim, is a recurring motif in the *Swordsman* series, and in many Hong Kong action pictures (in *The Swordsman 3: The East Is Red*, Koo has his blood flow reversed by Asia the Intractable, and in *The Swordsman 2*, Blue Phoenix immobilizes Kiddo during the massacre, so she can take on Asia alone[43]).

Not simply killed – victims are torn to pieces in *The Swordsman 2* in grotesquely over-the-top ways. In the massacre by Asia the Invincible in the outdoor, nighttime battles at the start of act three, the demi-god uses his/ her magic to shatter the survivors of the Wau Mountain Sect into pieces. Like a tragic play (and like many a Chinese action movie), the finale becomes wholesale slaughter – most of the Wau Mountain Sect are killed, Hattori is decimated by Master Wu, and Snow poisons herself (staying alive long enough to gloat at Asia when s/he returns).

*The Swordsman 2* is stuffed with gross-out moments, too – not action, but pure horror: Master Wu's 'essence-absorbing' stance provides a few. Like, in his duel with Hattori, Wu withers Hattori's arm, and then shrinks his head to rubbery goo (while Hattori's headless corpse staggers about). To rejuvenate himself, in the impressive prison sequence, Master Wu sucks the life out of the guards, compressing the hapless victims down to football-size bundles of clothes. At the end of the movie, Swordsman Zen cuts off his own arm (in order to save face and not return to Master Wu empty-handed, so to speak, when he's sent to accost Linghu Chong and his chums, as they leave on a ship).

Asia the Invincible on her/ his nighttime rampage is the first part of the finale of *The Swordsman 2*, and at times bests the action sequence in the Imperial palace. It contains some thrilling duels – such as (1) Master Wu against Hattori (ending in Hattori's head being shrivelled then simply yanked off Hattori's body); (2) Blue Phoenix against the Japanese ninjas; (3) Kiddo taking on the ninjas single-handed; (4) Kiddo and Ren Yingying battling more *shinobi*; (5) Asia the Invincible as a one-woman-man army, slaughtering the Mountain Wau brothers; and (6) Blue Phoenix taking on Asia using snakes and poison.

The sequence, one of Tony Ching Siu-tung's finest as a director, is

---

43 Eventually, it wears off, and Kiddo returns to the fray.

freighted with many memorable images, such as Asia the Incredible against a burning building... the Japanese ninjas riding on spinning throwing stars pursing Blue Phoenix crawling on the ground... and the Mountain Wau lads being literally ripped to shreds by Asia's magic...

The strength of the imagery here is far more than making pretty pictures: every single camera angle and camera set-up is designed not only to express exciting action, and to tell the story (tho' that's enough), but to create mysterious, magical events.

The sequence has a powerful dramatic countdown added to it, too – Blue Phoenix has been attacked with one of Asia the Invincible's needles, and is ailing fast (despite managing to halt the damage temporarily using pressure points). So there's a girl to save on top of everything else. (This is a reprise of the scene where Linghu Chong was poisoned in the first film.) Incredibly, Blue Phoenix has enough strength to attack Asia the Inflexible with a flying snake; when that doesn't work, she simply eats a snake and spits the poison back at Asia.

Yet *The Swordsman 2* is *not* wall-to-wall action in the finale (tho' it feels like that). In fact, there is a touching scene where Linghu Chong and his pals bury their Mountain Wau colleagues in graves (in pouring rain, of course). Linghu scratches their names on the wooden posts. Kiddo hurries back to the grave of her horse, where she left her sword, now determined to have her revenge on Asia the Invincible.

Most action-adventure movies don't have time for lengthy burial scenes – often it's just three shots lasting four seconds each for maybe two of the main characters, and then we're back to the rushing around, the yelling, the motorcycles and the explosions.

*The Swordsman 2* also has time in the final act for a key scene, also between Master Wu and Linghu Chong: beside a bonfire at night they discuss the sacred scroll. Linghu is stunned to discover that to master the magic you have to lose your penis; Wu, of course, continues to laugh and laugh. (Linghu is also confused now about just who – or what – he had sex with at Asia's digs[44]).

The second half of the finale of *The Swordsman 2* is set back in the Imperial palace at Black Cliffs, with Asia the Invincible single-handedly taking on the heroes. Among the many, many fantastic gags in this sequence is one where, having launched a spinning, flaming cauldron at the heroes, Asia simply turns back to work on his/ her embroidery! It's very seldom you see the master villain in any action movie doing some needlework[45] right in the middle of a giant action scene! S/he sits there and ruminates pensively in voiceover, as if it's a sleepy afternoon of falling cherry blossom, while our heroes battle balls of fire in the air (once again, Linghu Chong rushes to Kiddo's aid).

The finale of *The Swordsman 2* features a vast battery of props that're spinning, flying and exploding across the screen – cauldrons,

44 If this was a Wong Jing or Stephen Chow movie, that part of the plot would be much cruder!
45 One of her needles wraps around Linghu's sword and pierces it.

hooks, needles, wooden pergolas, even whole buildings. Linghu Chong of course attacks first (Jet Li is the star, after all), and manages to wound Asia the Invincible; s/he responds with multiple flying needles, as each of the heroes launches themselves at her/ him. Master Wu's life essence absorbing skill is used on Asia the Invincible repeatedly, until blood gushes out from the sword wound made by Linghu (as weapons, in an inventive touch, he brings along the metal hooks that Asia used to string him up in prison. But Asia is able to stop them with her/ his flying needles).

The battle includes almost every gag and stunt you can think of, yet the psychodrama isn't forgotten (as when Asia the Invincible foxily lets slip that s/he and Linghu Chong have had sex – much to the distress and outrage of both Ren Yingying and Kiddo fighting alongside Linghu. They make catty remarks about it during the tussle). The action continues up onto a building at the end of the court, which crumbles and crashes down a cliff, topped by several more flying gags, where Linghu can't help saving Asia, even though s/he's killed his comrades (he also rescues Kiddo and Ren).

✦

Serious points are made in *The Swordsman 2*, even tho' this is very much a popcorn movie. For instance, at the end, Master Wu becomes the guy sitting on the throne in the Black Cliffs Imperial palace,[46] replacing Asia the Invincible. And what does he do? Only order the ruthless annihilation of anyone who opposes him.[47] And he cackles like a madman while heads are rolling and blood's splashing up the palace walls. So, yes, you replace one brutal head of government (Dawn the Invincible) with another (Master Wu) and, for the populace, and the law, and the nation, what's the difference? (That *The Swordsman 2* is making political comments about modern China seems obvious – but they are there if you want to take them up. After all, the background context of *The Swordsman 2* is the struggle for power in a nation riven by conflicts between warring groups. The vaguely historical context includes references to the Maindlanders, the Highlanders, and the Japanese ninjas brought in to help the Sun Moon Sect. References to the brutality of the Chinese government resonate throughout 1990s Hong Kong cinema, and to events such as Tiananmen Square).

The pursuit of Master Wu's new regime continues to a harbour, where Linghu Chong and Kiddo are preparing to leave (Ren Yingying suggests they find sanctuary for a while in Japan; she remains in China, opting to stay loyal to her father, even tho' he's turned out to be a psychotic tyrant). Zen the Swordsman is sent to bring back Linghu, giving us an unexpected final swordfight on the boat and the dockside. It's here that Zen slices off his arm, so he can return to Master Wu severely injured (and this's after he's already disfigured his face!).[48]

All of which ties up the plots so that the heroes can sail off into the

---

46 Seen in a low angle shot which tracks into an ugly close-up.
47 Most of the victims (who appear on a list, including Linghu's name), are youngish types – which we can take to refer to students and radicals in modern China.
48 But, as he puts it, he can't fight, can he, with his sword arm amputated?

sunset on a ship amidst drifting smoke and the final reprise of the heroic song, 'Hero of Heroes' (Ren Yingying watches from the harbour then a beach; the 1992 film cuts back repeatedly between her and Kiddo and Linghu Chong on the boat, underlining the poignant motif of departure and change, a recurring theme in Chinese cinema).

*The Swordsman 2* also performs the familiar work of re-setting the characters back to their default positions: now it's Linghu Chong and his companion Kiddo on their travels again, which's how they were introduced 105 minutes ago. So they're ready for a new set of adventures in the next movie (except *The Swordsman 3* decided to take a different approach, and dispensed with Linghu Chong and Kiddo altogether).

# 9

## THE SWORDSMAN 3: THE EAST IS RED

## Dung Fong Bat Baai 2 – Fung Wan Joi Hei

Move over Supergirl. Your days are numbered Wonder Woman. Asia the Invincible, the first transsexual lesbian superhero is now the reigning queen! This spectacular *kung fu* fantasy is 95 minutes of non-stop action featuring awesome special effects and enough flailing bodies and exhilarating fight sequences to keep any fan of the genre enthralled.

Raymond Murray, *Images In the Dark* (373)

*The Swordsman 3: The East Is Red*[49] (1993, *Dongfang Bùbài – Fengyún Zàiqi* in Mandarin = *Invisible Asia 3: Turbulence Again Rises*), was directed by Tony Ching Siu-tung and Raymond Lee Wai-man, co-written by Tsui Hark, Charcoal Tan and Roy Szeto Chak-Hon, produced by Tsui and Lau Jou for Film Workshop/ Long Shong Pictures/ Golden Princess, and crewed by many of the same people who made *The Swordsman 2* or who were regulars in Tsui's movies of the era, including: music: William Hu and Woo Wai Laap, DP: Tom Lau Moon-tong, editing: Chun Yu and Keung Chuen-tak, set dec.: Chung-Sum Lam, art dir.: Eddie Ma Poon-Chiu, costumes:[50] Kwok-Sun Chiu, William Chang Suk-Ping, Chan Sau-Ming and Pat Tang Yu-Hiu, make-up: Hon-Wan Tung and Chan Kok-Hong, hair: Jane Kwan Yuk-Chan (and 4 others), sound mixers: Wai-Luen Cheng and Kam Wing Chow, and action directors Ma Yuk-shing, Tony Ching and Dion Lam

[49] Fans and critics often refer to *The Swordsman 3* as *The East Is Red*. The title comes from an opera written during the Cultural Revolution. And *The East Is Red* is the title of a 1965 movie (directed by Wang Ping).
[50] The costumes in *The Swordsman 3* are outstanding: Kwok-Sun Chiu, William Chang Suk-Ping, Chan Sau-Ming and Pat Tang Yu-Hiu designed the wardrobe. With several Hong Kong stars to dress up, the costume dept go to town with colour and shape (plenty of loose robes for the stars, so they can float in Tony Ching's customary slow motion, aerial scenes).

Dik-On. Category II. Released on Jan 21, 1993 (a Chinese New Year release).[51] 93 minutes.

*Swordsman 3* fared less well at the Canton box office (with HK $11.248 million) than *The Swordsman 2* (and it is, in the end, a lesser movie than *The Swordsman 2*, and, in a way, it's a side-story, focussing mainly on Asia the Invincible).[52]

The production of *The Swordsman 3* was 'chaos', Tsui Hark recalled, 'because we ran out of people, we ran out of actors'. Everybody seemed to be working on at least one other movie simultaneously (Tony Ching was working on two other flicks, and Brigitte Lin was shooting another film). Consequently, the picture writes and shoots around actors such as Lin who weren't always available (as well as using doubles, etc). Thus, by now in the *Swordsman* franchise Asia the Invincible has a feared reputation, so s/he can be referred to in dialogue but not seen, because the audience knows that character. And instead of the 'original' Asia, we now have impostors.

As Tsui Hark recalled, it was the backers who asked for a third helping of the *Swordsman* (because, yes, sequels and franchises are originated and orchestrated by studios and financers, not writers and directors, in the East as in the West. Sequels are usually produced in order to make money). Tsui thought he was done already with the *Swordsman* world, and with the character of Asia the Invincible (and s/he seemed to have died. However, a high fall doesn't always mean instant death in Movieland – there's no shot of Asia dead on the ground (or in pieces) in the second *Swordsman* film).

So coming up with a story for a third *Swordsman* flick required some finagling with the mechanics of the narrative: Tsui Hark and his co-writers Charcoal Tan and Roy Szeto Chak-Hon opted for a 'Death of the Costumed Swordplay Movie' concept, in which everybody is trying to cash in on the mythical status of Asia, copying her/ him (a sly dig at the rip-off ethic of the film industry in Canton, and actors playing the same role in multiple movies. The *Swordsman* movies had their own cash-in films, of course, as any box office hit does – in the West as in the East).

*The Swordsman 3* is built around the usual three-act model of most Hong Kong movies (which fits an 80-to-90-minute picture). However, the problems in making the film are obvious: it really only has enough decent material for two acts (also, the film recycles both previous *Swordsman* movies in order to bump up its running time). It might've been more honest to deliver a 60-minute movie, but for a theatrical release in Canton and East Asia, that wouldn't satisfy the audience. Several of the great Walt Disney movies are a shade over 60 or 70 minutes. But audiences expect more from a live-action feature.

*The Swordsman 3* is a kind of cruder, exploitative version of the previous *Swordsman* movies and of the swordplay genre: it's got sleazy scenes with hookers, gory violence, and gratuitous lesbian scenes.

51 To make that release date, *The Swordsman 3* would have been filming not long after the release of the second *Swordsman* movie, in June, 1992.
52 The name Dongfong Bat Baai is on everybody's lips – they repeat it all the time.

*The Swordsman 3* lacks a strong story to tell: there isn't an over-arching plot which compels the viewer – or compels the characters. For example, what is at stake isn't clearly defined: in *The Swordsman 2*, Asia the Incredible is a major threat because he/ she's destabilizing part of China, breaking up the clans, and ruling with a iron fist.[53] In the first *Swordsman* film, we had the brutal Eastern branch of the Imperial forces, among other villains, intent on demolishing the Sun Moon Sect.

In *The Swordsman 3*, Asia the Inconsolable seems more interested in pretending to be one of the girls in a brothel, or lording it over former lovers (like Snow), or pursuing her/ his impostors (like a multi-national corporation hunting down copyright theft and licensing pirates).

✦

Brigitte Lin Ching-hsia was back as the great, wild, unpredictable and very dangerous Dongfong Bat Baai (who else could it be?!); Joey Wong Cho-yin played Xue Qianxun (Snow), Asia's former lover (the Cici role in the 2nd film, played by Candice Yu On-on), and now an Invincible Asia impostor (and leader of the Sun Moon Sect; however, Snow poisoned herself in *The Swordsman II*); Yu Rongguang was Gu Changfeng (General Koo), the government official tasked with discovering what really happened with Asia the Nasty years ago (he's not a replacement for Linghu Chong, tho' Koo is the main male role in *The Swordsman 3*). The rest of the cast included Lau Shun (playing Asia the Crossdresser in her/ his aged guise, whom we meet first),[54] Eddy Ko (the Chief from *We're Going To Eat You*, and one of the leads in Tony Ching's first directorial effort, *Duel To the Death*), Jean Wang, Lee Ka-ting, Dion Lam Dik-On, Lau Chi-Ming and Kingdom Yuen.

Yu Rongguang (b. 1958), a Peking Opera performer and former martial arts boxer, is I reckon a very fine actor, looks great, moves well, and is often overlooked in accounts of this period of Chinese cinema (where he's overshadowed by stars such as Jet Li, both Tony Leungs, Sammo Hung, Sam Hui, Andy Lau, Chow Yun-fat and Jackie Chan). But in movies such as *Iron Monkey, The Terracotta Warrior, Supercop 2, Rock 'n' Roll Cop* and *My Father Is a Hero,* Yu is a strong leading man, as well as a suitably cruel villain (however, in *The Swordsman 3*, Yu has the tough job of following Jet Li – as with Vincent Zhao in the later *Once Upon a Time In China* movies, that proves a challenge).

Yu Rongguang trained in Peking Opera performance (in Beijing – he is a Mandarin speaker). He had already appeared in movies and TV before starring in Tsui Hark productions; he was the lead in *The Terracotta Warrior*, directed by Tony Ching. Later, he moved into producing and directing.

✦

The principal charas in *The Swordsman 3: The East Is Red* are General Koo and Asia the Incontrovertible, Snow (Asia's lover), and Dai (Snow's lover) – with Koo hoping to humanize Asia (good luck with that!), trying to tame him/ her (or at least to stop her/ him childishly, selfishly, and

53 A fist clutching needles and colourful threads, though.
54 In the credits, Shun is known as 'Warden of the Holy Altar'.

rather pointlessly wasting anyone who gets in her/ his way). Yet the 1993 movie wrongfoots the audience with regard to Koo – introducing him as the hero (as he leads the band of Spaniards to Asia's resting place in act one), where the real emphasis is on Asia, Snow and Dai.

*The Swordsman 3: The East Is Red* is a reworking of the *Swordsman's* themes and elements: this time General Koo takes up the role of the Swordsman Linghu Chong, tho' his government official is a departure from the conception of the character in the previous movies (and in Jin Yong's stories). Koo doesn't joke around, or drink, like Linghu, for instance, and he's not a heroic swordsman, he's a government employee. Gone too is some of the rivalry between the clans and groups (tho' the Sun Moon Sect is back – and up to their usual decadent antics, with a harsh leader – Snow). And most of the characters from *The Swordsman 2* have been ditched, too, with the focus now on Asia the Insatiable and her/ his clones.

*The Swordsman 3: The East Is Red* politicizes the myths and legends of the *jiangzhu* by including Spanish conquistadors in the mix, as well as the Japanese military (in the form of samurai and ninja), and referencing attacks from the Dutch Navy (a caption says the film is set in 1595). Thus, once again it seems as if the adventures of swordsmen and beautiful but deadly semi-demons are being presented within a quasi-historical context which refers to the formation of early, modern China in amongst international forces (Japan and Russia on one side, and Europe on the other).

The foreigners are sent up, as usual in a Hong Kong movie (and especially in a Tsui Hark's production): the Japanese are portrayed as humourless – they go to sea dressed in full samurai armour, clad all in black. Their fiendishly clever inventions (flying ninja, a submarine) are no match for Ancient Chinese magic. And their samurai leader is a midget. The Spaniards are fools who don't understand the language, trailing along their witch doctor, the Catholic priest to cleanse the land.

The prologue recycles the climactic ending of *The Swordsman 2* for three or so minutes (helping to bump up the running time of this troubled second sequel): from *The Swordsman 2,* we see Asia the Invincible battling our heroes at the Black Cliffs palace, and Asia falling to her/ his doom. Notice a glaring omission from the recycled footage: no close-ups of Jet Li whatsoever (even tho' he was the most prominent chara in the finale of film two); it would mislead the audience. Sorry, there's no Jet Li in this movie, folks! (This film was released in Jan, '93, seven months after *The Swordsman 2* ).

General Koo and his Chinese buddies Ling and Hon Chin (Eddy Ko), for instance, arrive with the Spanish contingent on their ship (and we know that the Spaniards are after something different from the Chinese). The opening sequence takes us 23 years[55] after the end of *The Swordsman 2* ), with our heroes landing at the mysterious, foreboding Black Cliffs (where, the last time we saw Asia the Inalienable, s/he was leaping to her/ his ruin). The Spaniards have brought along a Christian priest in order to exorcise

---

55 Or is it 100 years? Or is it 4 months?

the evil land of China – but of course European Catholicism is no match for Oriental magic! So Asia the Unwastable is soon breaking loose from her/ his grave (appearing first as a wizened, slightly sinister woman with wild, white hair, played by the ever-amazing Lau Shun – Lau went from playing the evil, Imperial eunuch in film one to the disfigured warrior Zen in film two to the aged Asia in film three!), before the reveal of Brigitte Lin Ching-hsia in all her glory, as a rubber mask is tossed away – another bit of Chinese Opera business. Asia also dispenses with his/ her silly white fright wig).

Thus, as Asia the Invincible is now one of the two main protagonists, she/ he is given goals to achieve and things to do: when General Koo informs her/ him that there are folk going about impersonating her/ him and debasing her/ him image, s/he flies into a rage, and vows to wipe them out (Koo's sensible pleas of 'no more killing' we know are not going to last long!). Wow! – Asia is a true diva, flying off the handle at the slightest slight (in this pumped-up sort of movie, everything is played at a hysterical level, from the performances of the actors to the visual effects, the costumes and the action). 'One of the most outrageous examinations of feminine power ever committed to film' (Lisa Morton, 99-100).

The introduction of the existence of the fake Asia the Invincibles is a clever gimmick to exploit the now-popular character with multiple versions (as well as playing to Asia's vanity, her/ his hunger for power, and ensuring that Asia's journey back from the wilderness to the centre of the story has some dramatic weight behind it. And it also solves the scheduling issues – if Brigitte Lin isn't always available, other actors can play one of the impostors).

It's a narrative hook that works well enough as a means of stirring up some conflict between the groups – the Chinese, the Spaniards, the Japanese, and the rivals (the Spanish declare that they too are seeking the sacred scroll).

The first Asia-as-impostor sequence features Snow and her Sun Moon Sect cohorts on a ship at sea being attacked by Thunder and his Japanese crew: the scenes of two ships shelling each other, one of the staples of the pirate genre are, in the hands of this group of filmmakers, merely one element in a panoply of visual effects, tricks, stunts and gags – including Japanese ninjas on flying kites, multiple sword fights, the Nipponese vessel turning into a submarine, and Joey Wong going into battle as Snow at her huffiest and fiercest.

Another Asia-impostor sequence (we're still in act one!) has Asia the Indescribable and General Koo weightlessly travelling to a forest where a more primitive, tribal form of ritual and worship is taking place (wild dancing, a roaring fire, ethnic masks, a mad mob, and sacrifical victims who are happy to be burnt as offerings to the deity Asia). Poor Koo isn't able to stand in the way of the real Asia's rage at these heathens (how *dare* they worship a fake Asia?!) – which extends to blasting out the hearts of the soldiers ranged against him/ her (one of numerous *ugghh* moments in the *Swordsman* series – including the willing sacrifical victim having *her* heart yanked out by the head priest). This ridiculous scene, which tops act one of *The Swordsman 3*, is a return of the horror genre for Tony Ching and Tsui Hark, but played for gruesome fun, like the haunted house in the funfair.56

✦

So much for the background story of *The Swordsman 3: The East Is Red* – this is 'ecstatic cinema', remember, and traditional/ conventional elements such as 'character' and 'story' and 'theme' are only part of the mix! Yes – because this is an action-adventure movie directed by Tony Ching Siu-tung and Raymond Lee, and it's produced by Tsui Hark, and it's stuffed with action.

Among the numerous ecstasies in *The Swordsman 3: The East Is Red* are the many scenes filmed at sea. This is a maritime version of a *wuxia pian* (it's really a pirate movie in many respects), with ships blasting away at each other, fights in the rigging, stunt people flying about on ropes, masts toppling, and many other of the expected gags in a pirate or sea-based adventure movie (much of the *Once Upon a Time In China* series occurs at harbours – border zones between China and the rest of the world, and also stages fights on ships). But, this being Hong Kong cinema, there are all sorts of eccentric elements added to the mix, like: flying needles; like: Japanese ninja flying from ship to ship on flags like kites; like: fighters holding up cannons in one arm and firing them; like: Asia the Invincible riding a swordfish57 (!); like: Asia the Inviolable collecting all of the bullets fired by the Spaniards in the air, and flicking them back, to kill them (another version of Chinese using traditional means (i.e., magic), to trump the *gweilo* invaders with their guns and bullets); like: ships running aground and also flying; like: a ship turning into a wooden submarine (yes, of course it's the fiendishly tech-minded Japanese who pull off this trick! This outrageous gag is likely a Tsui Hark idea).

For this version of swordplay-meets-pirates-meets-*kung-fu*-meets-fantasy, the filmmakers have procured some full-size boats (as well as the usual models and scaled-down sets).58 Filming models on water is a giveaway of scale, of course, so inter-cutting with full-size sets helps a lot. 59

The sequence where Asia the Invincible in her/ his furious god-like persona attacks Snow and her ship is simply extraordinary – the filmmakers create enormous explosions of water,60 and place Asia rising up out of the sea on a swordfish, unleashing waves of energy (with the screen filled with sparkling, back-lit waterdrops). And all of this is filmed at night. 61

It's like seeing a Las Vegas show combined with a Disney theme park

---

56 Or the second *Indiana Jones* movie.
57 Almost certainly Tsui Hark's idea – like a stag, of all things, popping as the wise oracle in *Detective Dee*.
58 The filmmakers happily have some grips manhandling a scale model ship in front of cliffs or against the sky, to stand in for the full-scale vessels they haven't got. Orson Welles did that in *Othello* (1952).
59 The budget is still stretched, here, though it thankfully doesn't resort to the Hollywood approach of filming boat scenes in the studio, against either panoramas or green screens.
60 First seen in *The Swordsman*, but here taken to extravagant heights. In one extraordinary shot, water explodes around the whole perimeter of the ship.
61 This would've be a tough series of nights for everyone involved. Logistically, these scenes are very challenging.

show combined with a Japanese *manga* brought to life. Again and again, Hong Kong cinema reminds us that *anything is possible*.[62] Well, at least in movies it is!

*The Swordsman 3* contains action which 'makes John Woo's *The Killer* seem like a Bergman opus', according to Raymond Murray (*Images In the Dark*, 373). 'One of the most audacious works of genius in the history of the fantasy film' (Lisa Morton, 98). '*Swordsman* is a mad, muddled and marvellous 90s update of *wuxia* films', said Stephen Teo (199).

And seeing Brigitte Lin Ching-hsia let rip as a one-womany army is worth the price of admission alone: despite the 1993 movie not fitting together narratively, or thematically, or dramatically, it features some wonderful scenes. Like Joey Wong, Lin's screen persona in many movies is of a gentle, intelligent and somewhat enigmatic actress. But Lin convinces as an arrogant, ultra-violent tyrant (partly because, as with Wong, the contrast is so extreme, and what Lin gets to do is so over-the-top. Similarly, the pert, winsome, rosy-cheeked Rosamund Kwan is dressed in dominatrix black in the *Swordsman* movies and wields a whip).

The mad laugh, the scornful looks, the sudden switches in emotion – Brigitte Lin Ching-hsia has movie villain-dom down pat. And when s/he's standing proudly on the arm of the mast, sweeping her/ his robes to one side, looking down on everyone, Lin's Asia the Infrangible is a memorable image, an Errol Flynn or Burt Lancaster pirate gone very, very bad. Even the *Pirates of the Caribbean* films, much as we love them, with their state-of-the-art visual effects and colossal, 200 million dollar budgets (probably 100 times what *The Swordsman 3* cost), couldn't match this.

✦

For beauty, *The Swordsman 3: The East Is Red* boasts two of the great faces of recent Chinese cinema: Brigitte Lin Ching-hsia and Joey Wong Cho-yin. The filmmakers shamelessly exploit the sexual heat that their starlets generate, too, by putting them together physically as lovers. Both are women impersonating men (Wong's Snow, now pretending to be Asia), or sort-of-women that were once men (Lin's Asia). That Snow is pretending to be Asia the Invincible complicates the erotic subterfuge (and her lover Dai turns out to be a guy) – this is the kind of thing that makes postmodern critics go ga-ga. Gender-bending, transgender and lesbianism – all in one scene! *Sooo* postmodern! *Sooo* radical! Oooh, *sooo* transgressive!

It's staged as a flashback for Snow (a.k.a. Xue Qianxun), who has never stopped loving Asia the Invincible (Snow reprises the role of Cici in the 2nd *Swordsman* picture), when Asia was Dongfong Bat Baai, it seems (i.e., a man). It's intercut with Snow and *her* lover, Dai, in another lesbian, opium-sweet clinch. But on screen we see Joey Wong and Brigitte Lin (and Jean Wang) kissing, sharing opium on their tongues, and pouring wine into each other's mouths (in one of those luxurious boudoir settings, complete with painted screens and candles, exquisitely lit by DP Tom Lau Moon-tong – not forgetting the make-up by Hon-Wan Tung and Chan Kok-Hong,

---

[62] Lisa Morton speaks, *pace The Swordsman II*, of 'the dizzying idea that human beings are capable of anything, whether it's flying or changing sex at will' (LM, 88).

the costumes by William Chang Suk-Ping and others, and the hair by Jane Kwan Yuk-Chan and others. The colours in the boudoir setting are of course red and gold). The camera lingers over the faces of Lin and Wong, and Wong and Wang, in giant, glowing, back-lit close-ups... by Ganesh, these are fantastically beautiful people!

The romantic subplot of *The Swordsman 3* pays off in several ways. For a start, it is one of the few things that can humanize or redeem Asia the Inestimable (tho' not in the end!), it reminds the characters that there are other things at work and worth fighting for/ living for than taking over China as a demi-god, and of course it provides the eye candy of Joey Wong and Brigitte Lin in a Lesbian Kiss Scene, and Joey Wong and Jean Wang in *another* Lesbian Kiss Scene.

Having Joey Wong Cho-yin playing a jilted lover, a spurned and hurt lover, works perfectly (tho' Asia the Inexpiable isn't going to be sucked into a guilt trip! If anyone's going to be ladling out guilt, it's Asia). It plays to Wong's strengths, too, as an actress (Wong can evoke the pain of love perfectly – she can sulk and huff and pout at an Olympic Games level. Wong is terrific in *The Swordsman 3* – her screen persona is so æthereal and gentle, it makes a striking and appealing contrast when she lets fly as a tyrant). And it works well too because this side of Snow's personality is introduced *after* she was depicted as the brutal leader of the Sun Moon Sect (where her followers see her as a man. Once again, there's an important political point being made when Snow is revealed to be a woman, and the soldiers realize they've been ruled by an impostor. Yes, your leaders are never quite what you thought!).

But for an impostor of Asia the Indivisible, Snow is doing pretty well. She has many aspects of Asia down pat: the needles-as-weapons *kung fu*, the imperious, impatient, declaiming tones, the kingly demeanour, and even a devoted concubine. (Unfortunately, Dai the concubine turns out to be a Japanese ninja in disguise – his/ her face's ripped off as a mask, revealing an ugly, middle-aged guy who's near-naked in a loincloth. Snow is, naturally, *very* enraged, and their duel, filmed amid the upper levels of the Sun Moon Sect vessel at night, and then out onto the ocean, is one of the highlights of *The Swordsman 3: The East Is Red*. It includes remarkable images such as Snow flying in slo-mo against a giant, full moon, while slicing the air with her/ his sword, and conjuring explosions out of the ocean. Like the real Asia, when Snow is crossed in love, she is *very* disgruntled!).

Two women, one man – *The Swordsman 3* again turns the tables, gender-wise, and also adds a hysterical, sadomasochistic vibe, so that Snow offers her life to Asia the Indefectible when Asia's fury is unleashed when s/he finds out that Snow has been posing as her/ him, and Koo, who seems to be the hero (and casting Yu Rongguang suggests that), becomes dangerously obsessive.

In keeping with Tsui Hark's ambition to make a 'Last Of' movie (the Last Swordplay Film, the Last Costume Epic, etc), there's a raw, apocalyptic atmosphere to *The Swordsman 3*, which's expressed in the high energy, the multiple deaths, the insanity. (Tsui would take this martial-arts-movie-as-apocalypse even further two years later with *The Blade*).

✦

In its third and final act, *The Swordsman 3: The East Is Red* loses its way somewhat, narratively. There are several sequences which don't do justice to the premise and the themes (or the characterizations), or the goodwill that the *Swordsman* series has generated thus far (for the audience) – so that, when the final smackdown occurs (as we all know it will!), it lacks the full dramatic resonance (altho' it *is* extremely spectacular).

For instance, following the superb dust-up between Asia the Indivisible and Snow (where Snow comes off worst, as expected), the filmmakers spend maybe too much time with scenes that meander a little – like General Koo and his cohorts in a mutinous face-off with the Sun Moon Sect crew on the ship, or arguing amongst themselves, or taking care of an ailing Snow and escaping on the ship's sail like a kite, and later a wooden raft. (Some of these scenes are simply not very gripping: like, the Spanish ships approach the Sun Moon Sect's vessel, but after shelling them, they sort of vanish. Like, the scene where Koo and Snow bond on the makeshift raft runs on too long, and doesn't contain enough dramatic juice).

However, what happens is truly unexpected: the 1993 movie lurches drunkenly into a side alley marked 'Crazy-Weird' (which in Hong Kong cinema is not a tiny alley, of course, but a very wide boulevard lined with neon-drenched skyscrapers and monsters). We follow Asia the Indefinable into, of all places, a harem of prostitutes who serve a military encampment:[63] this is Asia wondering what it's like to be ordinary and human. He/ she impersonates a mysterious woman who joins the camp – the narrative of *The Swordsman 3* is undergoing lots of sudden narrative jumps which don't quite make sense.[64] How, for example, Asia wants to be regarded as just one of the girls, only to immediately subvert that by being antsy and sly and ruthless (s/he just can't help him/ herself taking command of any situation. No one is going to boss Asia around, and Asia simply has to control everything).

So there are scenes where Asia the Inequable challenges the Japanese visitors (including the midget samurai leader, Thunder) to a deadly dice game (where the stake is losing your legs! – very Tsui Hark), and also allowing her/ himself to be captured and imprisoned (and in jail, apparently, Asia realizes that to be an ordinary human sucks just as much as being a demi-god. Anyway, we don't *want* to see Asia as an 'ordinary' person!).[65]

On the plus side, this part of *The Swordsman 3: The East Is Red*

---

63 The setting of the military encampment at night is skilfully portrayed – it's striking how much time we viewers spend out of doors, at night, where it's always breezy, and a half or full moon shines, amongst campfires, and drinking, carousing soldiers.
64 The flow of scenes judders a little, suggesting that scenes were curtailed or left out.
65 But has Asia forgotten what it felt like to be human? Well, it has been a long time since s/he was human!

allows Brigitte Lin Ching-hsia to go all-out with the characterization of Invincible Dawn. And Lin rises to the challenge, turning Asia the Incalculable into an unpredictable force of nature – you don't know what he/ she is going to do next. For instance, nobody would guess that Asia would turn all homey and cosy and folky, when s/he picks up a *pipa* (lute) and sits by the campfire to sing a song (and the movie turns into an MTV pop promo for a minute or two, lit by flickering light, as the whores gather round to wonder who this amazing new recruit could be. It's nothing out of the ordinary, tho', for a Hong Kong movie to include several musical montages).

As wayward as the brothel sequence is, though, Brigitte Lin Ching-hsia looks as if she is enjoying herself here – this is Lin at her most arrogant, cunning, catty and teasing. The scenes where Lin pretends to laugh along with the hookers, or to be best friends and all girls together, are funny but also scary – we've already seen Asia the Intolerable literally tearing people apart in the Highlanders ritual scene. (The brothel madam (Kingdom Yuen) is rightly suspicious of Asia, but when she sees the newbie getting the better of the rough, demanding men, she warms to her/ him).

♦

Meanwhile, the writers – Tan, Szeto and Tsui – struggle to find new obstacles/ complications to the *Swordsman* plot and themes: anyone can spot what *The Swordsman 3* desperately lacks: a strong central plot which'll tie all of the characters together. Or to put it in simpler terms: the screenwriters didn't have a satisfying ending.

So the authors return to the concept of multiple impostor Asia the Invincibles. Thus, now the commander of the encampment, General Tin Kai-wan (an overblown performance by Lee Ka-ting), is also having delusions of grandeur, imagining himself to be another Asia the Invincible (and having his concubines dressed up as a bunch of little Asias in red – this's where *The Swordsman 3: The East Is Red* derails itself in digressions that don't really go anywhere, and also repeat what we've already seen. Yes, it's a *second* encampment of hookers! With a similar atmosphere of drunk, out-of-control guys lurching about, ogling the prostitutes dressed as their arch enemy).

This part of *The Swordsman 3: The East Is Red* becomes Chaos Night, Topsy-Turvy Time, when things go just a little crazeee – so that even General Koo is taken over the mood of power-madness. Generals Tin and Koo are soon coming to blows as they fight over the beautiful Snow. Yes, Koo has brought Snow along with him (and his faithful aide Chin). Just by lying there looking coy and superior, and by being luscious, Snow seems to cause trouble – Tin is besotted.

The duels between Koo and Tin are deftly portrayed – using one of the staples of historical, Hong Kong movies, a tall, wooden tower, just the thing for aerial combat. So once again it's night, it's smoke, it's fire, it's weightless action on wires and flailing swords.

And the action keeps coming: in the military camp scenes Snow has her moment of glory when she teases and bests the Japanese commander, Thunder, who's revealed to be a tiny imp.

The military camp sequence is a kind of free-for-all, narratively, so that anyone who has an idea for something that Snow, or Tin, or Koo could do gets their idea put in the film. Like, one of the make-up girls suggests: what if Snow arrogantly teases General Tin, like she did with Shogun Thunder? Or, one of the sparks comes up with this nugget: how about General Koo waking from delirium to discover General Tin banging a gong (!) up on the look-out tower, while Snow lolls about on his lap?

The introduction of so many narrative sidetrackings and artificial conflicts weakens *The Swordsman 3: The East Is Red* considerably in its last half-hour. Whereas *The Swordsman 2* had a tightly-controlled narrative that managed to keep the primary plot in focus as well as giving the large ensemble cast interesting (and spectacular) things to do – all the way to the Grand Finish – *The Swordsman 3* stumbles and staggers. It veers off into swordplay btn Generals Koo and Tin, into Snow horsing around with Tin (just to spite Koo, perhaps – but also because Snow remains the masochistic devotee of Asia the Unobtainable to the very end. Indeed, the filmmakers have retained Snow as a character to embody what Asia has lost – love, humanity, etc. Snow becomes the precious beauty in life which Asia has cast aside in his/ her bid for power. But they also don't quite know what to do with Snow, apart from having Joey Wong lie there and look beautiful. Which of course Wong can accomplish with ease. Thus, in the Big Battle at the end of the third *Swordsman* flick, Snow has little to do except to look pained that Asia seems to be ignoring her (and she's injured, too). Snow's strategy seems to be to sulk and pout her way back into Asia's heart).

Anyway, after emphasizing too many minor and strange elements, *The Swordsman 3: The East Is Red* hurtles around the corner of the Hong Kong Movie Race Circuit, heading for the Final Stretch – with the Finish Line in sight (10 minutes away). And just what is a Hong Kong swordplay/ fantasy/ action flick going to do? Only have scenes of Big, Wild Action! For the finale, everybody else seems to have gone home (including all of the extras), and only three charas remain: Asia the Insane, Snow the Wistful Masochist, and General Koo the Paranoid Intermediary (who just wants everybody *to stop fighting, already! And to just get along!*).

No. No – because Asia the Unpleasable is a divinity as a spoilt child who, if it/ he/ she can't get what it/ he/ she wants, is going to *destroy* it! Yes – the signs were displayed in the scene in act one of this third *Swordsman* celluloid outing where Asia attacked Snow viciously. For being an impostor, yes, but also perhaps for simply being someone who really got to him/ her, who got under her/ his skin, and whom s/he really loved. Asia is the supreme egotist (vain but vicious), who demands total servitude from his/ her lovers. *Love me or die!* might be his/ her mantra. So Snow must die – and it can only be Asia who kills her.

The moral teaching in the finale of *The Swordsman 3* is: recognize and love what you have, not what you desire. Very Taoist/ Buddhist: be *here* (not *there*). Or as North American schmaltz like *The Wizard of Oz* or a Disney cartoon might put it, *there's no place like home*. Ain't that right, Toto? Oh yes, ma'am, it is – especially when 'home' is a colossal nation like the People's Republic of China! (Which has a head-start on North America of several thousand years for weaving myths and legends about heroes and gods).

For the finale of *The Swordperson 3*, the filmmakers have brought back the national navies – so the smackdown takes place on wooden ships at sea. Unfortunately, we have already seen this in the incredible nighttime sequence where Asia the Naughty laid siege to Snow and the Sun Moon Sect's vessel (the finale, filmed in full daylight, simply doesn't have the same impact and atmosphere).[66] But Ancient, Chinese magic does allow for scenes not often used in the Western pirate/ maritime movie – flying ships! (Asia's magic raises ships out of the water: as well as flying boats, we have boats landing on top of each other, boats running aground, and of course, boats exploding). And other non-Western scenes occur – the heroes soaring on sails ripped from ships thru the sky, pounding each other with bolts of energy shot from the palms.

The finale of *The Swordsman 3* is filled with endless bits of business in the cat-and-mouse tussle between General Koo and Asia the Inflammable – such as Koo wielding a cannon to fire at Asia, Asia responding by using her/ his flying needles to pin Koo to the cannon, and then Koo to the bulwark. One moment we're up in the air on the masts, the next we're in the hold. A memorable beat has Asia and Koo using sails (still attached to the square yard-arms) as weapons, striking each other with them, while hurtling thru the air.

The 'anything goes' approach to filmmaking is one of the appeals of Hong Kong action (and comedy) cinema – here it includes Asia the Indomitable's military costume, as if he or she's the commander of an empire of one soul, her/ himself.

But this final segment of the climax of *The Swordsman/woman 3* lacks many dramatic and cinematic elements to make it convince. The staging doesn't make sense at times, as if much of the footage was achieved with stand-ins, and there wasn't enough coverage to smooth over the cracks (which happens occasionally with Hong Kong movies). A giveaway is the decision to have Asia the Intractable and General Koo placed always far apart – so in the reverse angles (and in the wide shots, of course), Koo or Asia can be a double.[67] But if the production team were also making one or more films at the same time, all of this is understandable.

Yes, like many Hong Kong pictures, the ending of *The Swordsman 3: The East Is Red* has everything falling apart, emotions running wild and unchecked, and a high body count. General Koo, for ex, seems to expire in a boiling mass of fire as a ship explodes, and Asia the Inexplicable spirits the dead Snow away on a flying sail into the sunset (there's a

---

66 The flat, cloudy skies don't help.
67 That diminishes Asia, though: such as how s/he demands that Koo hand over Snow, from a distance, when s/he is clearly much more powerful than Koo, and can stride in and take Snow at any time.

lovely, weepy close-up of the two stars, Joey Wong and Brigitte Lin). Asia the Unstoppable, we note, survives.

It's not always a convincing dramatic/ aesthetic solution, it's not always a satisfying ending in terms of narrative or thematic structure, but the Chaos plus Death[68] plus Shouting plus Explosions ending of many a Hong Kong movie is certainly crowd-pleasing (in the noise and mad visuals, the filmmakers hope the audience will forget about the flaws in the script). So, yes, lots of stuff blows up, fires rage, and characters die… Roll the credits!

---

68 'It could be argued that *everything* in *The East Is Read* leads to death, for it may be the bloodiest film with the highest death count in Tsui Hark's filmography' (Lisa Morton, 100).

The Swordsman (1990),
this page and over.

Classic Tony
ing imagery –
g swordsmen.

The Swordsman 2 (1992).

The Swordsman 3 (1993), this page and over.

# 10

# *THE BIG HEAT*

# *Sing Si Dak Ging*

*The Big Heat₁* (*Sing Si Dak Ging* in Cantonese, dirs. Johnny To and Andrew Kam, 1988) was written by Gordon Chan and produced by our man (some sources have Tsui Hark as an uncredited director). Music: David Wu Tai-wai and Lo Tayu. Editor: David Wu Tai-wai. DP: Horace Wong. Art dirs.: Raymond Chan Kam-Ho and Benny Lui Chi-Leung. Costumes: Bruce Yu Ka-On. Produced by Film Workshop and Cinema City. Released: Sept 22, 1988. 98 mins.

Waise Lee Chi-lung headed up the cast as the cop John Wong; also appearing were Philip Kwok, Paul Chu-kong, Stuart Ong Sai Kit, Matthew Wong Hin-Mung, Lionel Lo King-Wah, Betty Mak Chui-Han, Peter Lai Bei-Dak, Michael Chow Man Kin, Ken Boyle and Joey Wong (many in the cast were Tsui Hark regulars, many have been in, well, *everything*, and actors like Philip Kwok (he's one of Waise Lee's team, Kam), are also directors, producers and writers; and Kwok was one of the action adirectors. Tsui has a cameo as Inspector Yiuming Butt).

*The Big Heat* was a difficult production, apparently, with directors dropping out,₂ and a script that, according to Gordon Chan, went thru fifteen drafts (and was no doubt changed again on set and then in post-production). It took nearly 2 years to complete.

Directors are always cited by critics, but this is a producer's movie (or even a distributor's movie: *get me this star, and that actress, and you've got a deal*). You could intercut *The Big Heat* with movies of the period directed by John Woo, or Tsui Hark, or Ringo Lam, or Jackie Chan, and not know the difference (for ex, *The Big Heat* has the slo-mo, gangster cameraderie and big explosions of Woo, the nimble editing, girl power and quirky bits of Tsui, the slamming stuntwork of Chan, and the gritty, grimy, bloody *milieu* of Lam).

*The Big Heat* is a fairly typical Hong Kong actioner narratively and

---

1 The Western title is of course from the celebrated *film noir* of 1953, helmed by Fritz Lang.
2 Jimmy Leung Chi-Ming and Tony Ching Siu-tung were also part of the production.

conceptually: a police story focussing on Waise Lee's cop John Wong, but with a higher quality of mayhem than the average Cantonese cop flick. Critics drew attention to the gory, brutal scenes (fingers blown away, full body burns, decapitations, dissections, etc). Rookie cops throwing up is a recurring gag (tho' *The Big Heat* is a much more serious outing altogether than some Tsui Hark-produced films, and the occasional bits of humour don't shift this picture out of its fundamentally sombre tone).

John Wong is the familiar troubled policeman of Hong Kong thrillers – his problem this time? A paralyzed right hand – the one that cops shoot with! (guns are a *very* big deal in *The Big Heat* – by the time act one is through, we have already seen *numerous* moments where pistols're being brandished, fired and loaded left, right and centre. It's in the mold of the *Dirty Harry* films).

As this is an action thriller about cops and robbers, the female roles are few, and under-written. Joey Wong plays Ada, a nurse, and Betty Mak Chui-Han is John Wong's girlfriend Maggie (who helps out with the case by analyzing the container for the drugs). Maggie is killed for her involvement, and Ada is knocked about (tho' she survives; her boyfriend Kam doesn't).

Parts of *The Big Heat* are filmed in a routine, television style[3] (principally, the talky scenes, in the police station),[4] but when the film moves out onto the streets of Hong Kong (where passers-by are gawking at the actors all the time), it possesses an energetic, frantic quality. For the rest of the time, outside of the action scenes, *The Big Heat* is a movie of guys in suits (always blue suits with blue ties and white shirts)… of men riding around in cars… of men in shades wielding guns… of men joshing with each other… It's the cops on one side (John Wong plus his three colleagues), and the gangsters on the other (but the gangsters look like legitimate businessmen). As in 1,000s of other *policiers*, the mobs have nicer clothes, swankier cars, plusher offices, and better houses; and the cops seems to be in perpetual struggle – against their bosses, the authorities, the government, the city, their environment, their lovers – and each other.

In *The Big Heat,* the MacGuffin is drugs, once again. Drugs and money in super-capitalist Hong Kong. That's the outer story, the thriller element: what's really at stake is the Tsui Harkian theme of 'doing the right thing', or stemming the tide of corruption (of drugs entering Canton).

The action in *The Big Heat*, as one has come to expect from Hong Kong action movies, is very impressive – this is a movie where the first Big Action Scene includes a guy being set on fire then shoved by a Jaguar car into a pile of gasoline barrels which – *of course!* – explode. And soon we're treated to car chases, foot chases, fire fights, etc, as another Hong Kong movie goes through its paces and delivers what audience clamour for.[5] It's a movie where Kirk Wong plays a character called in the credits: Gangster Who Gets Hand Blown Off.

3 David Wu Tai-wai and Lo Tayu's mainly electronic music has some fine moments,
4 You can sense the impatience of the filmmakers: do we have to be in this office yet again doing another scene which sets up the next bit of action? Can't we go play outside and blow cars up?!
5 Bruce Law and his team were probably responsible for the car and fire stunts.

Act two of *The Big Heat* features an extraordinary fire-fight in the corridors of a hospital (a favourite setting in Hong Kong actioners), followed by a cat-and-mouse chase in the elevator shafts. The sequence fully exploits the fear of heights, of enclosed spaces, and of falling – and you can guess how the henchman ends up (snared in cables and falling elevators).

It's a given that the finale of *The Big Heat* is going to feature the following items: (1) gunplay, (2) chases, (3) explosions, (4) blood, (5) outrageous stunts, (6) loud music, (7) slo-mo, (8) rapid editing,[6] and (9) a spectacular demise of the villain/s (among many other elements).

*The Big Heat* delivers all of that – this is hard-hitting, powerful action, tho' the costs are high: John Wong's lady Maggie is killed (and receives a moving funeral scene), as does Kam, the boyfriend of Ada (Joey Wong); the other charas are severely wounded (tho' of course Wong survives to the end, having dispatched the drug-dealing bad guys). There is also a cemetery scene, where the survivors visit the new resting place of the rookie. (Tsui Hark takes his cameo in the *dénouement*, tho' his long-haired weirdo doesn't really lighten the proceedings of this grim movie).

The finale has numerous flamboyant touches – such as the street lit in red one way and in deep blue the other way.[7] Joey Wong isn't merely the princess who must be protected (tho' she is that, too). She gets to whack a henchman around the head with a plank, and helps her lover drive the truck which pummels the villain's auto until it's smashed up inside a building (one of many suitably out-size car stunts in *The Big Heat*).

6 It's the distinctive editing style of David Wu.
7 It takes a *lot* of lights to punch through coloured filters.

# 11

# *KING OF CHESS*

# *Kei Wong*

*King of Chess* (*Kei Wong*, 1988/ 1992) was the subject of a dispute[8] with director Yim Ho: he walked off the picture due to disagreements with Tsui Hark, who was producing it.[9] It was made in 1988, 'and was shelved before it was given the Tsui Hark 'treatment' and finally released in 1992', according to Stephen Teo (1997, 155). Tsui wanted a unified, comedic tone throughout the film. As L. Stokes and M. Hoover remarked, *King of Chess*

> has a curious double nature: two directors, time frames, places, tones, chess kings, chess sets, and identities. Mainland scenes are dramatic, Tapei scenes more comic. (157)

Released on Sept 25, 1992, *King of Chess* was written by Yim Ho, Zhong Acheng and Tony Leung from two novels by Chang Shi-kui and Zhong Acheng, and starred Yim Ho, Tony Leung, John Sham, Chin Shih Chieh, Jue Waai Fei, Wong Sing Fong, Yang Lin, Danny Deng An Ning and Chu Feng Kang. *King of Chess* is set in two periods – during the Cultural Revolution, and in the present day, and in Tapei and Hong Kong. It's filmed in two different styles (Yim Ho said he was responsible for directing the scenes in which he appeared).

John Sham is the link between the two eras of *King of Chess*, as he remembers his time as a child during the Cultural Revolution.[10] In the present day scenes, Ching encounters another young chess prodigy (Wong Sing Fong). In the hyper-capitalism of the late 1980s (seemingly a world away from the Communist Cultural Revolution of the late 1960s), Ching and his cohorts use the kid to help them wheel and deal.

Chess as a motif for exploring political differences is not a new idea,

8 Yim Ho said he met Tsui Hark years later at a disco, but all Tsui said was that he had been young.
9 According to Terence Chang, working at Film Workshop, Tsui had asked him to fire Yim.
10 When it goes into the past, a kid with frizzy hair and glasses appears as the young John Sham.

of course. Several films and shows in the West have done it, with Russian chess masters and Western ones (such as in the musical show *Chess*, 1984).

One of the striking aspects of *King of Chess* is the newsreel footage of the Cultural Revolution, edited into a montage that opens the movie. The prologue is fascinating: it's longer than it needs to be, the footage is cut to music by Lo Ta-yu and David Wu Tai-wai, and the montage focusses on young people caught up in the fervour of the Cultural Revolution. The imagery of crowds waving the *Red Book*, and of Chairman Mao doing the rounds as a high ranking politico, assume an enhanced significance in the light of the run-up to the 1997 Handover, and in the wake of Tiananmen Square. (The newsreel is included later, too. It also adds, as usual with newsreel, a lot of production value to the film – it includes scenes involving 1,000s of people which would be costly to recreate).

The finale of *King of Chess* is, of course, a chess match (on television, of course): the child prodigy plays against John Chan, typed as the chief rival. Here, Ching's memories of the past pile upon each other, with the movie cutting back and forth repeatedly. The child is injured (in some rather artificial action), but all turns out well.

In the *dénouement*, the charas from the 1960s are brought into the present day, and there are some final montages pitting the Cultural Revolution against present-day Hong Kong.

Tsui Hark's influence can seen throughout *King of Chess* – the emphasis on comedy, the setting of the TV station (which echoes where Tsui first started out, at T.V.B.), the focus on a female character (Jade – Yang Lin – she's the first character to be introduced), a woman in a largely male-dominated world of work, and motifs such as food,[11] two time zones, and survival.

Meanwhile, the politics of modern China, and the comparison of the 1960s with today (the late 1980s/ early 1990s), is a recurring issue in Tsui Hark's cinema.

---

11 In the train sequence, Tony Leung makes sure he consumes every single grain of rain in the hand-outs of food (even to the point of prising a single rice grain out of a crack in a table).

# 12

## *THE KILLER*

## *Diexie Shuangxiong*

The credits of *The Killer* (1989) tell us all we need to know:

TSUI HARK PRESENTS
A JOHN WOO FILM
STARRING CHOW YUN-FAT

Add to that a fantastic supporting cast, a brilliant technical crew, and some of the best action choreographers in the business (including Tony Ching Siu-tung and Yuen Cheung-yan), and you have one of the quintessential products of Hong Kong action cinema.

*The Killer* (*Dip Huet Seung Hung* in Cantonese, *Die Xue Shuang Xiong* in Mandarin = *Bloodshed Brothers*, 1989), was produced by Film Workshop/ Golden Princess/ Magnum, written by John Woo, produced by Tsui Hark, Peter Pau and Wong Wing-hang were DPs, the action was directed by Tony Ching Siu-tung, Alan Chui Chung San, Lau Chi Ho and Yuen Cheung-yan (with car stunts by Bruce Law),[12] music by Lowell Lo, editor: Kung-Wing Fan, music editor: David Wu Tai-wai, art dir. by Man-Wah Luk, costumes: Shirley Chan, sound fx: Siu-Lung Ching, hair by Benny Chow, make-up by Yu Lai Cheng and Yvonne Yen, and in charge of production was Claudie Chung Jan. Box office: HK $18.25m. Released: July 6, 1989. 105 mins.

Chow Yun-fat, Danny Lee Sau-yin, Paul Chu (Chu Kong), Kenneth Tsang, Sally Yeh Tse-man, Shing Fui-on, Lam Chung, Wing-Cho Yip, Ricky Yi Faan-wai, Barry Wong Ping-yiu, Fan Wei-yee, Alan Ng, Tommy Wong, and Parkman Wong Pak-man starred (many were Tsui Hark regulars).

Over the fall-out of Woo and Tsui on *The Killer*, Jasmine Chow (Chow Yun-fat's wife), explained that Tsui decided that he wasn't getting the recognition he thought he was due when *The Killer* started to receive

---

12 If there are car or motorbike stunts in a Hong Kong picture in the 1980s onwards, it's usually Bruce Law and his team.

plaudits. So Tsui argued with Woo over the ownership of the movie.

Tsui Hark said he didn't know exactly why he fell out with John Woo: when Woo received an award for *The Killer* and no one told Tsui, that rankled (and 'a lot of the people around him just got hostile', Tsui recalled).

❀

*The Killer* stars Chow Yun-Fat (never better) in a bold, brash, lush, baroque action thriller with religious and operatic overtones. A favourite with film critics (for all the obvious reasons – the religious themes, the brotherhood theme,[13] the masculinity-in-crisis theme, etc), *The Killer* is also preposterous and over-cooked, and in many sections is as dumb (but fun) as a *James Bond* movie. (Episodes of the movie, you have to admit, are really adolescent or even childish – men running around going bang-bang! with guns).

The dramatic components of *The Killer* are clichéd, routine:[14] the cold, distant, implacable and impossibly cool assassin Jeff, a.k.a. John a.k.a. Ah Jong (no ties, no family, an outsider and loner), a professional brilliant at his job (but his icy exterior hides a warm heart). Jenny, the woman (Sally Yeh, playing a nightclub singer) he maims by accident (blinding her),[15] and falls for and protects. The one last job the killer promises to do before he retires to the coast (and to pay for Jenny's eye operation). His target, the powerful crime boss Tony Wong (Wing-cho Yip), and his nephew Hoi (or Johnny, played by Shing Fui-on), who comes after him with hordes of henchmen. The unconventional cop Inspector Li Ying (Danny Lee Sau-yin) who gradually befriends the killer and fights beside him against Boss Wong and his crew. And finally the killer's faithful friend, the go-between, a retired, former hit man, Sidney Fung (Paul Chu Kong).

*The Killer* presents a series of brotherly relationships: Ah Jong and Fung, Ah Jong and Li, and Li and cop buddy Chang (Kenneth Tsang). Inevitably for a John Woo-helmed picture, each of these brotherhoods overshadows the heterosexual liaison between Ah Jong and Jenny. Tsui Hark was partly responsible for bumping up the significance of the romance, though Woo was clearly not particularly enchanted by it. He prefers to stage scenes of men smouldering with dramatic conflict over issues such as loyalty to each other, and devotion to their profession (whether it's the police force or the crime syndicate. It's not the outfit, legal or illegal, that counts, so much as the loyalty towards it).

So *The Killer* is another of John Woo's explorations of the notions of brotherhood, of honour, of loyalty. You can see *The Killer* and similar crime movies as a contemporary-set version of portraying the *jiangzhu*, the 'martial arts world', in which the code of honour, of chivalry, of brother-hood, prevails. The code of living honourably is invoked in the *jiangzhu*.

*The Killer* obviously appropriates and reworks elements of North American and French thrillers, including the gangster thrillers directed by

---

13 The narcissism of gangsters is present and correct in *The Killer* (such as Ah Jong with his scarves), tho' Inspector Li seems dandyish in his striped linen suits.
14 John Woo recalled that the story was based on a *yakuza* picture of the 1960s starring Ken Takakura.
15 One wonders if that motif came from doing gun stunts, where blanks can be dangerous.

Martin Scorsese and Jean-Pierre Melville (in particular *Le Samourai*).[16] And it's also drawing on the cowboy genre, where men are real men, where disputes are conducted with blammy gun-fights and yelled insults, and where women are always on the sidelines. One critic claimed that *The Killer* was an amalgam of Martin Scorsese, Stanley Kubrick, Sergei Eisenstein, Alfred Hitchcock, Don Siegel, Robert Aldrich, Francis Coppola, David Lean, Jean-Pierre Melville, Akira Kurosawa, Sergio Leone, Chang Cheh and Masaki Kobayashi.[17] Maybe. (John Woo happily renders his influences obvious, turning them into elaborate *hommages*). Actually, if you view *The Killer* as a Hong Kong movie, and as a Hong Kong action movie, it explains/ resolves everything.

❂

Altho' *The Killer* is usually set within the context of the cinema of John Woo (so it's 'John Woo did this' and 'John Woo did that'), you can also see it as a Tsui Hark picture. Among Tsui's influences are the casting of Sally Yeh Tse-man, for example (Yeh was a favourite actress of his in the 1980s – she's in the Tsui-produced films *I Love Maria, Diary of a Big Man* and *The Laser Man*, and Tsui's own favourite film of his as director, *Peking Opera Blues.* Yeh also sang the theme song of *The Killer*). There were Tsui regulars in the crew (such as Peter Pau, David Wu, Patrick Yip, Lowell Lo, Benny Chow, James Wong Jim, Patrick Leung, and Tony Ching Siu-tung). The Dragon Boat Race, a piece of traditional, Chinese culture, is likely a Tsui suggestion. It's possible that portraying Ah Jong and Sally as having a romantic relationship came from Tsui – Woo often holds back from man-woman romance, preferring to concentrate on the brotherhood theme.

And yet, *The Killer* can also be regarded as a 'Chow Yun-fat film': altho' both Tsui and Woo appear regularly in front of the camera in cameos, they are not (as they would admit!), superstar performers like Chow.

There's only one Chow Yun-fat, and altho' there are other action stars, in the West as well as in the East, who could've played this role, Chow makes it his own. When we see Ah Jong acting tenderly towards the little girl who's caught in the crossfire on the beach, we buy it, even tho' it's ridiculously over-wrought. (This is a typical piece of Hong Kong Movie Cheese, and Woo-ian OTT melodrama – putting a cute moppet in the midst of a ferocious fire-fight is the kind of over-cooked drama that D.W. Griffith shamelessly exploited in film after film. That the injured kid echoes Jenny in the opening scene is delightfully simplistic thematic plotting).

Altho' Chow Yun-fat and Danny Lee Sau-yin rightly receive most of the plaudits for the acting (they had already worked together several times before), Paul Chu-kong is superb as Chow's Triad cohort, suggesting, as with Chow and Lee, levels of suffering and angst beneath the surface (this movie features plenty of images of men brooding, and looking off into the distance. Sometimes the images resemble pop videos – even more so when Sally Yeh's songs drift over the top in the musical montages). And the supporting cast is excellent, too – from Kenneth Tsang's long-

16 John Woo's admiration for *Le Samouraï* is well-known: he has mined it on several occasions.
17 T. Williams, in Y. Tasker, 2002, 407.

suffering cop sidekick to Inspector Li, to Shing Fui-on chewing the scenery as the mob boss Johnny Wong (Woo encourages Shing to go way over-the-top – plenty of action movie directors relish the opportunity to encourage out-size performances from the actors playing their villains). And not forgetting a huge number of henchmen and stunt guys, who're blown to bits by either Chow or Lee.

The cast of *The Killer* seems to include everybody who was in Hong Kong at the time – there are many familiar faces in the background characters. If you watch Hong Kong movies from the 80s and 90s, you will see them. (Often they're playing henchmen who get shot up by either Chow or Lee).

❀

Ultimately, *The Killer* is a Hong Kong action movie: for anybody who's seen more'n a few Cantonese flicks, everything in *The Killer* is familiar – the super-cool action hero, the hysterical melodrama, the inter-departmental rivalries in the police force, the political pressure from above (transmitted through the police chiefs), the wayward cop, the reformed villain, the men-being-men and male friendship themes, and of course the wild stunts and blammy fire-fights.

*The Killer* isn't a one-off masterpiece that exists in a space of its own (like, say, *Vampyr* (1932) or *Sunrise* (1927)), it's very much a part of the Hong Kong tradition of cinema, from its genre (it's one of a gazillion police thrillers), to its so-familiar settings (the harbour, downtown, the nightclub, the car lot, Causeway Bay, Stanley Beach, Horizon Drive – even the church).

However, it *is* true that filmmakers such as Tsui Hark and John Woo can elevate thrillers and gangster flicks way above the run-of-the-mill Hong Kong pic.

The dime-store melodrama is shameless in *The Killer*: this is a movie where the cop and the killer face off against each other right next to a team of doctors desperately trying to bring a girl back to life! Talk about over-done! But that, of course, is why we love Hong Kong cinema! (The thinking seems to be: we've done this shoot-out scene before, why don't we add some extra elements to wrench the audience's heart and nerves even further?). Holding pistols pointed each other is reprised several times – in front of Jenny in her apartment, for instance, or lying on the floor of the church in the finale.

And this is a movie where the super-cool anti-hero enters a nightclub in slow motion – this's *before* he's shown us that he can single-handedly (single-gunnedly) take on a mobster and his henchmen, *before* we've seen him strut his stuff, and *before* he's established as a chilly, cool performer.

And that's why you cast Chow Yun-fat, a man who can walk into a nightclub (or thru a church) in slow motion and pull it off. So that, before he does anything, or says anything, or *is* anything, he's <u>Chow Yun-fat</u>!

❀

As an action film, *The Killer* doesn't disappoint: boat chases, car chases, car lot bust-ups, rooftop chases, tram chases, explosions, and some of the best shoot-outs ever put on celluloid (Bruce Law was a contributor, overseeing the car stunts). John Woo never uses one bullet where two hundred will do.[18] Only *Hard-Boiled* (1992), another Woo-directed extravaganza, employs more bullet hits, squibs and fake blood, more stunts and more slow motion (tho' other films of this period come to mind – like *Full Contact,* an astonishing, incendiary Ringo Lam-directed actioner from 1992 which also starred Chow Yun-fat).

*The Killer* also has religious motifs a-plenty (a favourite of John Woo's, who's a practising Catholic): the killer holes up in a rural church (thousands of candles, stained glass, a statue of the Virgin Mary and white doves), which is the site of the final, Alamo showdown.

> I spent a lot of money to make the perfect Virgin Mary statue, when it is shot to pieces, truth is destroyed by evil, and with it the spirit of chivalry displayed by ancient warriors. (2000, 66)

For some, John Woo's incorporation of Christian icons, such as an exploding statue of the Madonna,[19] is pretentious and over-egged. For others, such as Martin Scorsese, it's part of Woo's exploration of the theme of guilt, vengeance and (Christian) redemption. (Over-wrought? Woo doesn't care! Over-wrought, over-cooked and over-the-top is what he does for a living! If you want meek, humble, timid, delicate storytelling, look elsewhere!).

❁

The first act of *The Killer* climaxes with the assassination of the Triad politico at the Dragon Boat Race. Before that, we've seen Ah Jong performing multiple cold-blooded shootings, plus Danny Lee's Inspector Li Ying having his own adventures (including a superb downtown tram chase. This is part of the introduction of Lee's character, at the ten-minute mark: an unconventional but righteous policeman, Li goes undercover during the hand-over of weapons merchandize with some local hoods. It all goes wrong, inevitably, and Li is discovered, which cues another massive fire-fight followed by a chase on foot and tram. Mirroring Ah Jong's predicament of a bystander (Jenny) being injured by gun-play, a woman expires from a heart attack just as Li nails the gangleader on the tram. This part of *The Killer* features wonderful, atmospheric photography on the streets of downtown Hong Kong at night. No green screens here, and no boring city in Canada standing in for Hong Kong. It's the real Hong Kong, and the actors are really there, doing it all).

But after the act one climax, at the Dragon Boat Race, the 1989 film continues into a lengthy boat chase, followed by a fire-fight on a beach, followed by a car chase, followed by a face-off in a hospital – so it's really a continuous action sequence in the manner of a *James Bond* or *Indiana*

---

18 There's the warrior code in *The Killer* of saving one last bullet – for yourself or your victim. Yes – but how can you count when you're firing 100s of rounds from a pistol that holds six bullets?!
19 19 Music editor David Wu Tai-wai put in Georg Frideric Handel's *Messiah* in this scene. Wu recalled how he attended Mass with his wife and got the idea. When he showed the scene to Woo, taking out all of the sounds and putting in the *Messiah*, Woo's jaw hit the floor.

*Jones* or *Die Hard* movie, where one whammo, as producer Joel Silver calls them, is topped by another. (And of course, like James Bond, Ah Jong escapes at the end).

The first act of *The Killer* closes, then, with the face-off at gun-point which brings Inspector Li and Ah Jong face-to-face in the hospital in a spectacular manner (a favourite location in Hong Kong action movies, a setting purpose-built for shoot-outs in labyrinthine corridors, for chases thru operating theatres, for stunts in stair-wells or elevators, and not forgetting the mandatory leaping out of windows. Add to that characters disguised as doctors, the inevitable romance when the heroine patches up the hero, and – if you want to see them –  hospitals have the grand themes of Life and Death).

❀

The second and third acts of *The Killer* don't sag, tho' there are, admittedly, rather too many scenes of slo-mo photography of Ah Jong looking introspective (and ultra-cool), and of Inspector Li following suit (using the facial expressions that Oliver Reed called 'Moody Three'). Acts 2 and 3 of *The Killer* are bolstered dramatically by complications with the Triad gangs, with Sidney Fung's boss Johnny Wong, and with the order going out to get rid of Ah Jong ('kill him!' yells Wong as he hurries into his car in the parking lot). This is very familiar Hong Kong, action movie territory – about men being men, saving 'face', maintaining their pride/ dignity, and adhering to the quasi-chivalrous codes of gangsterdom. All of the gangster genre clichés are duly trotted out, but the sprightliness of the filmmaking, and the charisma of the lead actors, maintains interest (because there's no getting around the fact that we have seen this movie 100,000 times before).

The 2nd and 3rd acts of *The Killer* are also kept peppy by some action scenes – an attempt on Ah Jong's life at his apartment (where he blows away everybody with another gun fitted with unlimited ammo – where can we buy a gun like that?!); a car chase in a multi-level car lot (when Ah Jong messes up a bid to nobble Johnny Wong – the first time, apart from blinding Jenny, that we see him get it very wrong); an attempted collaring of Ah Jong at the airport (with Hitchcockian cat-and-mouse games); and another car lot shoot-out (this time involving Fung and Wong's heavies, with Chang getting shot. It's the same car lot as the first bust-up, but this time there's an abrupt cut to a rural highway, as the doggedly determined Chang, severly wounded, persists in performing his police duties, tailing the bad guys. Chang expires just after telling his boss the address of Ah Jong).

Another brilliantly inventive scene in *The Killer* has Ah Jong and cop Li Ying going literally head-to-head when Li ambushes Ah Jong at Jenny's apartment and they play the whole scene moving around the rooms with their guns pointed at each other's heads and hearts, while Jenny, unsuspecting, makes them tea. It's rightly played with a comical touch – because it's an absurd scenario; it's the farce version of a John Woo Mexican stand-off (one can spot the influence of Tsui Hark here). Anyhoo, no way are Inspector Li or Ah Jong going to open fire with Jenny right between them (not after she's been blinded once!). There's some amusing actorly bits of business – such as Jenny clutching Ah Jong and just missing the fact that he's holding a pistol at his new 'football friend' who's just dropped by, Inspector Li. These gags take *The Killer* into the farcical territory that Woo had explored in cheesy family fare such as *Run, Tiger Run* (1985). However, *The Killer* pulls back from the over-the-top jokes of *Run, Tiger Run.*

✿

The flipside of loyalty is betrayal: *The Killer* presents several instances of one-time brothers betraying each other, such as Sidney Fung and Ah Jong. This occurs in act two, in a scorching scene where Fung visits Ah Jong, with the hit-man confronting his colleague about his collusion in the attempt to kill him after the Dragon Boat Race festival. Both Chow Yun-fat and Paul Chu are brilliant in this scene which includes, in the usual heightened-hysterical manner of John Woo's cinema, guns being held at faces (and fired – but Ah Jong took the bullets out of his gun).

No one can miss the physical, even erotic intimacy of these scenes, where masculinity-in-crisis is aligned with gun-play. This is John Woo's version of soap opera melodrama, where the hysterical histrionics of television soap opera acting are played out with guns pointing at heads or backs.

Sidney Fung gets his own big fight scene in *The Killer*, when, with the stubborn, suicidal diligence of a Triad elder sticking to the old, chivalrous codes, he gets to shoot up Johnny Wong and his mob (demanding the money for Ah Jong! What a loyal friend!). It's yet another one-man-in-a-nest-of-vipers scene, a one-man-army scene. Somehow, Wong and Fung both survive, even tho' they're perforated with bullets (there are plenty of suspend-your-disbelief-now moments, including hostage scenarios and gun-in-mouth scenarios. The flair for physical acting, for blocking scenes, for how people can interact within the confines of a small room, is striking: the filmmaking really comes alive when a bunch of very hostile people are crammed into a little space, armed to the teeth). And then Fung, the schmuck, leads the hoods to the church, because he wants to deliver the $$$$ to Ah Jong! Ouch! Thereby damning himself, Ah Jong and many others in the subsequent fire-fight (Ah Jong puts Fung out of his misery, with a heroic bullet to the head, after Fung pleads that he doesn't want to die like a dog at the hands of the Triads).

The philosophy of the 1989 movie is delivered in an impressive piece of parallel action. Editor Kung-Wing Fan is brilliant here, cutting between Sidney Fung's frustrating and very painful attempts to secure the money owed to Ah Jong from Johnny Wong and his heavies with Inspector Li and Ah Jong smoking and shooting the breeze beside a pool (this comes after Li has tended Ah Jong's wound – a role usually taken up by the girlfriend-of-the-hero or the female sidekick in action movies).

Thus, Li Ying and Ah Jong discuss the issues of ethics and honour while Sidney Fung is being beaten about by Johnny Wong's henchmen. However, it's not parallel cutting for irony, but to illustrate the ethical debate of Ah Jong and Li, and to demonstrate that notions of loyalty and honour are worth fighting for, and to show that the cost of upholding such out-dated concepts in the modern age can be high. Fung puts his life on the line to maintain honour and loyalty.

❀

The fourth act of *The Killer* starts by bringing together Inspector Li and Ah Jong at his fancy Horizon Drive digs where, once again, Johnny Wong's henchmen try to kill him. The result? Yet another over-the-top, non-stop fire-fight with an endless supply of bullets. No matter how many stunt guys you throw against Chow Yun-fat and Danny Lee, they are shot to pieces (however, Ah Jong is injured here – but by Li, not Johnny Wong's sadly expendable heavies). And the Woo-ian face-off is reprised – to make it even sillier, we have Jenny taking up a gun, so it's a three-way gun scene.

By this time, Inspector Li has found being a cop even more irksome (he's thrown off the case by his angry boss, and his buddy Chang dies), and that Ah Jong's sense of honour and ethics seems more appealing.

The finale of *The Killer* is the expected blammy, bang-bang ending, with men being men, and women're relegated to crawling around on the floor, wailing helplessly. Yes, if you're a *real man* in a John Woo movie, you get to (1) die heroically, (2) survive heroically (if you're lucky), or (3) expire in a hail of bullets (if you're a henchman).

Stunt choreographers Tony Ching Siu-tung, Yuen Cheung-yan *et al* invent all manner of ways of firing a gun and people dying: Ah Jong slides backwards on a chair, dives onto the ground and slides, leaps over seats, while the henchmen crash through windows, against walls, through balustrades, from balconies, onto candles, are blown up by gas/ fuel, in slow motion, and riddled with bullet hits. Cars burn, smoke blows, and the sound of the wind is mixed high (so the patch of ground in front of the church resembles a dust-blown desert out of a Spaghetti Western). To step away from the usual wardrobe of men in suits (a cliché of all gangster flicks which *The Killer* has already used), the henchmen are clad in white overalls.

Let's forget the flaws in the screenwriting and construction of the finale of *The Killer* (like how Sidney Fung leads the mob straight to the church! *Duh!*), and focus on the marvellous stunts orchestrated by Tony Ching Siu-tung, Alan Chui Chung San, Lau Chi Ho and Yuen Cheung-yan and their teams, on the hyper-melodramatic interactions between the leads (teary, sweaty, over-heated, grimacing, wild-eyed), on the lovely cinematography (by Peter Pau and Wong Wing-hang) which captures our heroes diving left, right and centre in glowing light, and on the preposterousness of the whole enterprise ('Woo at his most hysterically excessive', noted Stephen Teo [178]).

In case you've forgotten scenes that ran by your eyes 20 or 30 minutes earlier (the film assumes you're an idiot suffering from memory loss), *The Killer* reprises many oh-so poignant moments from the newly-formed brotherhood of Ah Jong and Inspector Li. We cut, for instance, from the fire-fight in the church to the cute male bonding during the tending-a-wound scene at the lake, between Ah Jong and Li. So touching! So bittersweet! Ah, just when Li discovers a new buddy, he loses him!

Because, of course, at the end of *The Killer*, Chow Yun-fat's assassin Ah Jong dies, pin-cushioned with bullets (from Triad boss Johnny Wong, among others). It's the heroic immolation foreshadowed earlier, in a conversation between Ah Jong and Inspector Li. But, with bitter irony, Ah Jong's blinded by a bullet in the final confrontation with Wong. One of the (many) memorable images in this extraordinary film has Ah Jong and Jenny crawling across the ground looking for each other, both blinded, with the burning church behind them (is this a reference to the finale of *Duel In the Sun* (1946), another over-cooked, gun-and-passion melodrama?). They miss each other, and Ah Jong expires. Li shoots Wong in revenge, after the cops arrive, when Wong is pathetically pleading for protection from the police force. (Jenny, however, isn't given a proper final note or line in *The Killer* – the focus is on Li, who collapses in despair to the dirt, muttering Ah Jong's nickname, Shrimp Head).

❂

*The Killer* was criticized for its portrayal of the female character played by Sally Yeh Tse-man. Lisa Morton derides *The Killer* for its shallow, insensitive, 'callous treatment' of women:

> Woo seems incapable of creating a female character who is even remotely interesting or believable… *The Killer* marks a new low even for him… it's unforgivable that Woo simply never bothers to resolve her character… (LM, 163)

But according to John Woo in a 2007 interview, actress Sally Yeh let the film down by not offering enough of her schedule, forcing him to rewrite the story and focus more on the two men:

> I did try to make strong female characters in the past, but somehow, it never worked out. For example, when I was shooting *The Killer*, the original concept was a triangular love story, and the female character was supposed to be very strong, very brave and very smart, even though she's blind. But the actress didn't concentrate on this movie, and she gave limited time to shoot. So that forced me to change the script…

Once again, let's remind ourselves that the director doesn't do everything in a movie. Tsui Hark was producer, for instance (and he makes his presence felt on every project he produces), and other important talents influenced *The Killer* (scheduling is the producer's responsibility, not the director's, for instance). Also, John Woo *doesn't* write all of his movies – but in the case of *The Killer*, yes he did write the script (with assistance from Tsui).

Stephen Teo remarked that

the sum total of balletic violence and poetic meditations of killer and cop as they size each other up in almost transcendental terms, gives the impression that *The Killer* is more about sentiment and feeling. (177)

Paul Fonoroff wasn't convinced by *The Killer*:

It's all very pretty and very phoney. *The Killer* seems to say that it is perfectly all right to commit murder as long as you hate truly evil people and act kindly to women and children caught in your cross-fire. (34)

Paul Fonoroff is one of the most unpleasable of Hong Kong film critics – very few films are enshrined by the Fonster. But Fonoroff is certainly right to call *The Killer* phoney. It is remarkably, even alarmingly cheesy and fake.

It's truly preposterous and cartoonish, too, and it's scary how many film critics take it all straight, accepting instantly the received view that John Woo's cinema is seriously tackling issues of brotherhood, friendship between men, loyalty and honour. Or life and death.

Is it because the filmmaking is so accomplished in its portrayals of over-the-top action? (There's no denying that this is amazing filmmaking). Is it because the film seems to really 'mean' it, is so earnest? (The film takes itself seriously). Is it because the actors are trying so hard to sell it all? (Even though the performances are also cheesily exaggerated at times). Is it because the accumulation of film criticism about John Woo's cinema over the years has persuaded all of us to view these movies straight and seriously? (When they are also ridiculous).

Film critics who adore the filmic output of John Woo have answers for this, too:

– it's not ridiculous, it's 'operatic';[20]
– it's not violent and gory, it's a 'gun ballet';
– it's not homoerotic, it's about brotherhood.

John Woo himself was happy with *The Killer* – it's one of the films of his own that he liked.

---

20 But many operas have idiotic plots.

# 13

# *THE TERRACOTTA WARRIOR*

# *Chin Yung*

The Terracotta Warrior (*Chin Yung/ Gu Gam Daai Zin/ Yon Qing* in Cantonese, a.k.a. *Fight and Love With a Terracotta Warrior*, 1990) is a top-of-the-line, Chinese action-adventure movie with a romance and time travel theme, based on the novel by Lillian Lee. It was headed up by three of the greatest directors of action in world cinema: Tony Ching Siu-tung, Zhang Yimou and Tsui Hark. Art & Talent Group Inc. produced; Pik Wah Lee scripted; exec. producer: Kam Kwok-Leung; the producers were Tsui Hark, Zhu Mu and Hon Pau-chu; Peter Pau and Lee San-yip were DPs; Marco Mak Chi-sin edited; art dirs.: Kenneth Yee Chung-man[21] and Lau Man-Hung; costumes by Bruce Yu Ka-On; make-up: Man Yun-Ling; hair: Peng Yen-Lien; dialogue ed. by Pei-Ru Chang; sound ed.: Leung Ka-Lun; special fx by Siu-Lung Ching; music by Romeo Diaz, James Wong Jim and Joseph Koo; and Ching was of course action director (along with Bobby Woo Chi-lung, Andy Ma, Jack Gao, Lau Chi-Ho, with stunts by Jinghua Zhang). Category II. Released Apl 12, 1990. 106 mins. (145 mins).

In the cast were Zhang Yimou, Gong Li, Yu Rongguang, Wu Tian Ming, Cheung Jun Ying, Luk Shu Ming and Chiu Chi Gong. (The movie was remade by Jackie Chan and Stanley Tong in 2005 as *The Myth*).

Lilian Lee Bik-dut (b. 1959) is a Chinese novelist best-known for *Farewell My Concubine*; her fiction has provided the basis for several projects from Tsui Hark, including *Green Snake* and *A Terracotta Warrior*. Other Lee books have been adapted, including *Reincarnation of the Golden Lotus*, *Temptation of a Monk*, *Red and Black*, *Sheng Si Qiao* and *Tales From the Dark*.

In *The Terracotta Warrior*, Zhang Yimou stars as the First Emperor's (Lu Shuming) bodyguard, General Mong Tianfang, who has a forbidden love affair with one of the Boss Man's concubines, Dong'er, played by Gong Li. Zhang is impressive as the strong, silent type, who holds a flame

---

21 Tony Ching worked with Yee Chung-man many times, as has Tsui Hark – *Kung Fu Dunk, The Curse of the Golden Flower, An Empress and the Warriors, Jade Dynasty*, etc.

that never goes out for the concubine Dong'er. (Zhang is not so accomplished as the comical touches, where the fish out of water aspect of time travel is explored. There, in the 2005 remake, Jackie Chan wins). And Li is as appealing as ever, with her open features that seem purpose-built for cinema. Li is one of those actresses who lets all of her emotions flash across her face: she is perfect to play doomed lovers who look forlorn and weep at the slightest provocation. (One of Li's techniques, which she seems to employ in every role, is quivering with sadness and bursting into tears).

Meanwhile, Yu Rongguang plays the nefarious Bai Yunfei, a playboy type and actor who, underneath that sophisticated exterior, is a nasty piece of work. All three actors form an appealing central cast in *The Terracotta Warrior*.

✳

*The Terracotta Warrior* portrays, once again, that mythical China, that Ancient China, that China of the *jiangzhu*, the martial arts world, that never existed – but that *should've* existed – and if it did exist, it would look like *this*!

*The Terracotta Warrior* is thoroughly *Chinese* – it is a film made in China, set in China, and all about China and Chinese history. But the form draws heavily on Western and Hollywood models.

*The Terracotta Warrior* is proudly Chinese: it portrays a famous part of Chinese history, and takes in several famous settings, including the Great Wall itself (much later, Zhang Yimou directed a movie entitled *The Great Wall* in 2016).

This is grand, operatic filmmaking, with gutsy, sometimes hysterical forms of performance (and not only from the actors: the music, the sound effects, the visuals, the costumes – they're all bold).

The cinematography in *The Terracotta Warrior* – by Peter Pau and Lee San-yip – is absolutely spectacular. This is one of Tony Ching's finest-looking films, embodying his goal of maximum romanticism. The film has everything, photographically, including one of Hong Kong's cinema's great specialities – ravishing nighttime imagery. Nobody else can photograph night scenes like Chinese technicians. In addition, *The Terracotta Warrior* boasts sunsets and dawns, crystal-clear noonday scenes, and all sorts of fires, candlelight and natural light.

*The Terracotta Warrior* is a masterclass in cinematography. It's a riot of textures – of rain, of smoke, of floating leaves, of flickering flames. The interior of the Imperial Palace, for example, is exquisitely lit with diffuse light through hanging white scrims, coupled with light arcing through windows and plenty of smoke.

The costumes in *The Terracotta Warrior* were by Tsui Hark's regular costumier, Bruce Yu Ka-On, with make-up by Man Yun-Ling and hair by Peng Yen-Lien. *The Terracotta Warrior* is a handsome-looking production all-round, with the hair, make-up and costumes being especially fine (the crew clearly enjoyed coming up with exciting wardrobe ideas for Gong Li in her 1930s incarnation – heavy on the dyed fake fur and extravagant hats).

Musically, *The Terracotta Warrior* was written by Romeo Diaz, James Wong Jim and Joseph Koo – between them, they seem to have scored every Hong Kong movie of the 1980s-2000s. So we're in good hands. *Very* expert hands. If you hire James Wong Jim to compose your soundtrack, you won't have to worry about it – it'll be just fine. Together, Wong, Diaz and Koo provide the expected traditional, Chinese instrumentation and musical cues, as befitting a romance set partly in Ancient China. They'll bring the movie up to date with electronic and synthesized sounds (but less appealing, I think, compared to the traditional, Chinese orchestration). But there's no doubt that Wong, Diaz and Koo contribute immensely to the big emotional moments in *The Terracotta Warrior*, when the operatic film-making requires operatic music.

✳

The first act of *The Terracotta Warrior* illustrates a love affair out of Chinese mythology – the soldier and the courtesan, with the Emperor as the third main character, the patriarch, the authority who embodies the law (and the reasons why the lovers can't be together).

The romance is very conventional, but the clichés are delivered with such panache, we go along with it. Both Ching and Tsui (and Zhang) have returned to this sort of traditional, romantic scenery many times. Partly because it works, and because it's perhaps the central narrative element of cinema (and because they're softies at heart).

The first act of *The Terracotta Warrior* climaxes with the death of the lovers, in a spectacular fashion: Dong'er is burnt alive, while General Mong is buried alive under clay (he's the terracotta warrior of the title). The second act of *The Terracotta Warrior* cuts to the 1930s in China, to the glamorous world of movies and archaeological digs (with more than a few nods to the *Indiana Jones* series). The 1930s setting would appeal to Tsui Hark – it's the era of one of his great films of a few years earlier, *Shanghai Blues*.

The first act of *The Terracotta Warrior* is a mini-epic of its own, featuring the grand setting of the ancient capital of China, courtly intrigue, a cast of thousands, plenty of swordplay and action, romance, gorgeous costumes, impeccable make-up, and luscious lighting (the visuals in *The Terracotta Warrior*, as usual in a film helmed by Tony Ching Siu-tung, are outstanding). *The Terracotta Warrior* has got the back-lighting, the drifting, Autumnal leaves, the slow motion, the billowing smoke at night, the flickering firelight, the candles and lamps, the hangings a-fluttering, and plenty of rain scenes – all of the textures of Chinese, historical movies. (Once again, Chinese cinema demonstrates that it is the finest when it comes to staging historical extravaganzas, despite fierce competition from Western cinema, such as that of France).

In 36 or so minutes (it's a long first act), *The Terracotta Warrior* squeezes in grand processions, horse fights, an assassination attempt on the Emperor, a hunting scene, a budding romance (and love scene), a suicide bid, the induction of the concubines into the court, lyrical interludes, sword practice, political shenanigans behind the throne, and a grand dual death scene.

And, in typical style for a movie directed by Tony Ching Siu-tung, *The Terracotta Warrior* opens very big, with vistas of a huge, Imperial scheme, Ching's version of the building of the Pyramids or the Great Wall (the hauling of enormous artworks with ropes and wooden trolleys was used again as the opener for *Dr Wai* in 1996). This is followed by a royal hunt sequence, where the Emperor is attacked by an assassin – which means, of course, a ton of swordplay and daredevil horse-riding. The equestrian games and the royal hunt allow for plenty of action, of the acrobatic kind (including many horse falls for the stuntmen), plus some images of soldiers and riders out of Akira Kurosawa.

An important scene is seemingly modest, dramatically: Dong'er taps some bowls filled with rainwater to make musical sounds, while nearby General Mong practices his swordplay, with classic Tony Ching moves (in a courtyard filled with floating, Autumn leaves, a fundamental form of Chingian, poetic cinema. Electric fans, needless to say, are blowing on set throughout this movie).

The scene is a musical montage: it cuts between the two characters, using music (and editing) as the link: both Tony Ching and Zhang Yimou would return to this form of filmmaking several times – most notably in their collaboration in 2002's *Hero*. The music and the sounds that connect the characters are enhanced by the editing by Marco Mak Chi-sin: the film fuses the lovers together even when they're apart. (And it's typical, too, that the music begins simple and diegetic – we hear the sounds of Dong'er tapping the bowls – but then it becomes more orchestrated, with other instruments joining in).

✳

After such an inspired opening act, the second act of *The Terracotta Warrior*, set in the 1930s,[22] is a little less riveting in a few areas. For example, Gong Li's modern-day character Zhu Lili is allowed to squeal and over-act too much.

The second act brings Mr Brown and Bai Yunfei into play: Bai is a handsome playboy and actor who's cheesy and attractive on the outside, but the shiny, suave exterior hides the villain underneath. Bai reveals his true colours in a scene at an archaeological dig, where his disappointment with progress is expressed by beating up one of his underlings, and then stabbing him. This is where the clumsy goof Zhu Lili stumbles into the scene, and seems to have witnessed the murder (or maybe not).

Anyway, Bai Yunfei and his crew dealing with Zhu Lili leads to the big action sequence which ultimately brings General Mong the terracotta warrior back to life. The action scene is stuffed with visual effects (including models and explosions), and is centred around a plane flight. Up in the air, Bai is planning to bump off Zhu Lili, but by accident she shoots the pistol, damaging the plane, which crashes (after Bai has bailed out).

---

22 The shift from the ancient world to the Thirties is indicated with a shot of a propellor-powered plane landing. The image offers a striking contrast to the epic romance of the first act, and also depicts the new-fangled technology of flight.

Following many preposterous bits of business, the plane falls into the underground chamber where the terracotta warrior Mong Tianfang was sealed in mud. The film is now in rollercoaster mode, with one scene hurtling into the next – Mong and Zhu Lili encountering each other, Mong fighting Bai's henchmen, Bai and Mong duelling, etc.

A charming aspect of *The Terracotta Warrior* is the evocation of how filmmaking was done in the Thirties in China, complete with makeshift snow and rain (from watering cans on ladders above the actors. Things haven't changed much). Pik Wah Lee wrote the film, but these scenes were likely the suggestion of Tsui Hark – he is very fond of the mechanics of movie-making and theatre, and enjoys putting them on screen. General Mong has to deal with bewildering modern technology – cars, electric lamps, medicine, cameras, radio, steam engines, etc.

✳

The uneven second act is soon forgotten, because the third act of *The Terracotta Warrior* ramps up to the expected mayhem, swordplay, explosions and outrageous stunts. Fights on trains, inside planes, snakepit scenarios with walls closing in, colossal explosions – *The Terracotta Warrior* compacts a hundred years of action-adventure movies into 25 minutes.

Some of the gags in the climax of *The Terracotta Warrior* are distinctly Tsui Harkian: the heroes escaping ancient booby traps (*à la Indiana Jones*); the raising of the terracotta army from underground up to ground level; and the use of the plane (crashing into the temple and statuary).

The finale employs miniature photography extensively (courtesy of Cinefex Workshop), in order to capture the wild stunts of planes careening through the terracotta army, and the whole compound levitating to the surface.

This is bold, confident filmmaking, at once quaint and old-fashioned (reminiscent of, say, an Irving Allen disaster movie of the 1960s or 1970s), but filmed with a feeling for texture, light and atmosphere that shlocky adventure films seldom attain. The biggest scene is undoubtedly where the whole terracotta army, plus statues and a staircase, rises.

Tony Ching and Tsui Hark would return to this sort of grandiose finale several times (in the *Chinese Ghost Story* films, for instance). It's kitchen sink time – throw in everything you've got.

There are many memorable beats in the finale of *The Terracotta Warrior*. General Mong on horseback, sword drawn, facing the approaching plane; several sword versus gun duels; Mong mowing down henchmen on the train, etc.

✳

Narratively, all plays out as expected – the villain meets his come-uppance, the heroes escape, but with a bittersweet outcome: Zhu Lili expires (cue an emotional death scene, filmed in trembling close-ups, with Zhu Lili dying in General Mong's arms). Mong climbs free of the wreckage of the collapsed resting-place of the terracotta army, but we cut to a coda, set in the present day. This was filmed at the real museum in Xian in

Shaanxi province. Now Gong Li plays a student visiting the museum with a coachload of tourists. And working on cleaning the famous statues is none other than Mong, now in a modern guise. (Thus, not only is Dong'er/ Zhu Lili reborn in the form of the student, Mong continues, too. It's a cute, upbeat ending, which leads into the customary montage of highpoints from the film, accompanied by a pretty ballad sung by Sally Yeh and composed by Joseph Koo, with lyrics by James Wong Jim).

# 14

# *NEW DRAGON GATE INN*

## *San Lung Moon Haak Jaan*

INTRO.

This is orgasmically, transcendentally fantastic filmmaking! This is an ecstatic movie! A movie so good you can't believe it! *Dragon Inn* (Raymond Lee Wai-man, 1992, in Mandarin: *Xin Long Menm Ke Zhan*, a.k.a. *New Dragon Gate Inn*) is a super-charged, 100% masterpiece of *wuxia pian*. This movie takes its place among the Top Ten of martial arts movies, alongside *Hero* (2002), *Enter the Dragon* (1973), *Crouching Tiger, Hidden Dragon* (2000) and *Once Upon a Time In China* (1991). For the finale alone, it's going to be a favourite with thousands of action fans.

*New Dragon Gate Inn* was produced by Film Workshop and Seasonal Films, and distributed thru Golden Harvest. The script was by Tsui Hark, Charcoal Tan and Hiu Wing. Tsui and Ng See-yuen were the producers. The music was by Philip Chan and Chow Gam-wing; editing by Poon Hung; the DPs were Arthur Wong and Tom Lau Moon-tong; action directors: Tony Ching Siu-tung, Cheng Yiu-sing, Wing Cho, Xiong Xin-xin and Yuen Bun; art direction: Chiu Gwok-San, Yee-Fung Chung, Chi-Hing Leung and William Chang Suk-Ping; sound (Cantonese): Angie Lam; first A.D.: Wing-Chiu Cheng; costumes by Poon Kwok-Wah and Ching Tin-Giu; make-up by Poon Man-Wa and Man Yun-Ling; hair by Siu-Mui Chau and Ho Yau Chun Heung; and vfx by Cinefex Workshop. The team are all regulars in the Tsui Hark Circus, making *New Dragon Gate Inn* very much a Tsui-led movie. Box office: HK $21 million. Released: Aug 27, 1992. 103 minutes.

This is a platinum movie, a masterwork of entertainment. The pacing is lively, the energy created is formidable and irresistible, the staging is enormously imaginative, the technical aspects are superb, the characters are fascinating, the story is compelling (with an unusual structure), the music (by Chan and Chow) is superb, the costumes and design are stellar, the locations (the Chinese desert) are lavish, and the tone is spot-on (with just enough comedy and romance to offer a change of pace from the thrills, suspense and action). Yes, *New Dragon Gate Inn* is another movie in which Tsui Hark and the filmmakers have thrown in *everything*.

Thirty-plus years after it was made, *New Dragon Gate Inn* still impresses as one of the greatest action movies in the history of cinema. Seeing it in a theatre in Beijing, Shanghai or Hong Kong in 1992 must've been extraordinary.

The level of energy and vitality on display in *New Dragon Gate Inn* is absolutely thrilling: everybody is working at the top of their game. Maybe the shift from Hong Kong to the deserts of Dunhuang in Northwest China for the exteriors freed everyone in the production team up, because they were *white-hot* when they produced this movie! (altho' most 'o the picture was filmed back on sets in Hong Kong).

*New Dragon Gate Inn* is a remake, as everyone knows. But it's a remake of a movie that's very highly regarded: *Dragon Gate Inn* (1967) was one of King Hu's big successes, critically as well as theatrically.23 So Raymond Lee, Tsui Hark and Ng See-yuen were taking on an acknowledged hit movie. (That could be problematic for some viewers, who dislike remakes of masterpieces. Remake a minor movie, sure, but not a 100% masterwork).

In the defence of the movie, critics have pointed out that the 1992 version adds many new ingredients, reworks the original considerably, and is a new approach to the material.

Similarly, Tsui Hark insisted that his version of the *Dragon Gate Inn* mythology (of 2012) wasn't a remake of the 1992 movie. Tsui said rather than a remake, the new *Dragon Gate Inn* was a kind of sequel to the King Hu movie.24 A wise remark, because the 1992 movie deserves a place on the list of the top ten action movies made in China (or perhaps anywhere). Anyhoo, this all means that the 1967 *Dragon Gate Inn* made a huge impression on the young Tsui, for him to later rework it *twice*.

❊

It's worth noting that the international cut of *New Dragon Gate Inn* is *not* the version the filmmakers preferred. Tsui Hark explained that the movie was meant to be 80-85 minutes (like many Hong Kong movies), but for the laserdisc release (which was used for later DVD and video releases), the distributors added more scenes: they used master and cover shots of horse-riding, which weren't intended to be included. They added a voiceover. They re-dubbed the movie. And they changed the music. (The voiceover, for instance, explains about the Dong Chang and the historical context of the story – well, no Chinese audience needs a lecture about oppressive regimes! Meanwhile, there are too many horse-riding shots, which unbalances the pace of the narrative, extending the first act too much).

---

23 *Dragon Gate Inn* was King Hu's first big success. It was his first film made in Taiwan.
24 A sequel to *Dragon Gate Inn* had been considered, Tsui Hark recalled, soon after the 1992 movie, but due to conflicting schedules and other commitments, it didn't happen.

THE CAST.

Among the many, many marvellous elements in *New Dragon Gate Inn* is the incredible cast: *New Dragon Gate Inn* features pretty much every actor then working in Chinese movies. Many of the performers, for instance, also appeared in the *Once Upon a Time In China* movies, in *Tai Chi Master, Iron Monkey, The Blade, Police Story*, etc. The cast of *New Dragon Gate Inn* is a roll-call of your favourites from the period: Maggie Cheung Man-yuk, Brigitte Lin Ching-hsia,[25] Tony Leung Ka-Fai, Donnie Yen, Lau Shun, Yuen Bun, Elvis Tsui, Yuen Cheung-yan, Yen Shi-kwan, Xiong Xin-xin, Ngai Chung-wai and Lawrence Ng.

Everybody's here, and they're having a great time entertaining us with another old timer's tale from the *jianghzu*. (Except for one notable absence: Jet Li in the tailor-made role of the hero Zhao Huaian.[26] But he did essay the part in the remake of 2012, helmed by Tsui Hark). Brigitte Lin injured her eye[27] (deflecting arrows in a stunt at the Dunhuang location), and returned to a Hong Kong hospital. A double was used to film Lin's scenes (handily, Lin's warrior character is covered up with a scarf over her/ his face).

THE SCRIPT.

Scripts are routinely derided in Western critics' evaluation of Hong Kong movies – as if every North American movie has screenplays that exhibit the quality of *King Lear*. Yes, right! Every Summer, Hollywood releases twenty *King Lears*, fifteen *Hamlets* and ten damn *Othellos*!

But *New Dragon Gate Inn* has a fine script (by Tsui Hark, Charcoal Tan (co-writer of *Once Upon a Time In China 2* and *3*), and Hiu Wing) – and, yes, it's superior to most N. American, popcorn movies. For example, it orchestrates an enormous cast, and gives all of the principals things to achieve and do. It provides proper introductions for the main protagonists. It elegantly (and quickly) sets up the relationships between the charas. There is plenty of detail in the screenplay, too – the foreshadowing of the storm in the dialogue (and songs) of Jade, for example (and the character of Zhao Huaian is built up, too, b4 we meet him).

Tracking the action and the plot reveals just how carefully *New Dragon Gate Inn* is worked out. The movie not only delivers all of the expected scenes, and sequences of scenes, for a *wuxia pian*, it includes 100s of details and minor gags. And the camera is right in there, capturing it all. (For instance, to add to the already stuffed plotting, there's a wedding night, a drinking competition, cannibalism, bits of business with wine which might be poisoned, etc). The film is also crammed with minor details which embellish the characters and their relationships, plus some recurring elements (such as the flute, the tunnels, and cannibalism).

*New Dragon Gate Inn* is unusual structurally: it doesn't have a single

25 The characters of Brigitte Lin and Maggie Cheung were originally played in the 1967 *Dragon Gate Inn* by Polly Ling-feng and Cheng Pei-pei.
26 The remake of *Dragon Gate Inn* had been set up by Jet Li and his manager Jim Choi, with Michelle Yeoh to co-star, and filming to start in Beijing. However, when Choi was murdered, the production was scrapped, and the rival *Dragon Gate Inn* went ahead.
27 Tsui Hark recalled that he met Lin at the airport, on her way back to Hong Kong, feeling sorry for herself.

protagonist, for a start; the narrative focus shifts from character to character. Sometimes it follows the mysterious Swordswoman Yuan Mo-ya, and then her lover, Zhao Huaian. Sometimes we are with the two child hostages, and sometimes with the Chief Eunuch Cao. For much of the time, the script concentrates on Jade, mistress of the inn. For the creation of this character alone, the script of *New Dragon Gate Inn* is marvellous.

TECHNICAL ASPECTS.

Altho' there is sometimes confusion about who actually directed some movies which were produced by Tsui Hark but ostensibly helmed by someone else, much of *New Dragon Gate Inn* was directed by the credited director, Raymond Lee Wai-man (Li Hui Min – he also co-directed *The Swordsman* and co-directed *The Swordsman 3,* and co-produced *Iron Monkey, The Magic Crane, The Swordsman 3,* and *Wicked City* in this period). No doubt Tsui had his input on many areas of the production, and we know that Tsui is the kind of hands-on producer who can't stand back(!).

According to Tsui Hark, however, about 80% of *New Dragon Gate Inn* was filmed by him – partly because they were under the gun with schedules, and thus split the filming into two units (Raymond Lee in Dunhuang and Tsui in Hong Kong):

> ...for *Dragon Inn*, I was actually involved in the shooting. I shot something like 80 percent of the movie because we were in the situation of having to meet the talent's schedules. We were caught in a tight schedule on location in Dunhuang.

Numerous aspects of *New Dragon Gate Inn* bear Tsui Hark's imprint, from the comedy (the cannibalism gags are pure Tsui – from *We're Going To Eat You*), to the remarkable characterization of Maggie Cheung Man-yuk as Jade. (You can see Tsui's influence all over the studio-bound scenes, filmed in Hong Kong).

The Dragon Gate Inn itself has a delightful border town atmosphere, where anything goes (very similar to a frontier town in a Western).[28] Bandits, bad food (don't eat the meat!), wine, and everybody is glaring at everybody else. There's an earthy, somewhat sleazy air to the place, so that it resembles one of those border towns[29] in a Sam Peckinpah Western movie. And with Jade in charge, anything is possible!

The Dragon Gate Inn itself is sited improbably in the deep desert – so deep and so remote there isn't anything nearby for miles. And no roads, either (if the inn is situated on a trading route, there isn't much of a road or even a trail!). But that is the whole point, of course: this is a place so far from anywhere that anything goes (including cannibalism!).

The production design – by Chiu Gwok-San, Yee-Fung Chung, Chi-Hing Leung and William Chang Suk-Ping – is marvellous, filling the inn with rich textures and details. The cinematography (from Arthur Wong and Tom

---

28 *Dragon Gate Inn* has been called a riff on *Casablanca.*
29 The movie makes a big deal out of crossing a border.

Lau Moon-tong) lights the inn set every which way (once again, the night photography in a Hong Kong movie is especially fine: on top of everything else, *New Dragon Gate Inn* is a very *beautiful* movie. The photography, for instance, exploits the desert locations to maximum effect – it was worth every cent going out there).[30]

The inn has an intricate plan, comprising a large dining hall, upper balconies, pillars, basement kitchens, shadowy bedrooms, and secret tunnels. The action explores every part of the building over the course of the picture (including using the pillars and roof supports for staging the fights).

Many of the night exteriors are not filmed in the desert, however (where lighting large areas at night is a massive undertaking): it's that all-purpose spot in the New Territories, a patch of ground filled with smoke which many movies in the 1980s and 1990s used.

The outstanding score for *New Dragon Gate Inn* is a traditional Chinese piece, by Philip Chan and Chow Gam-wing,[31] featuring the sort of classical, Chinese music you might hear in the old Shaw Brothers movies. Pounding percussion, squealing woodwind, and jagged strings occur throughout. There's also a moment for lyrical flute music (played by Yuan Mo-ya to call her lover Zhao Huaian across the desert sands on his camels).

Later, a short but illuminating beat shows Yuan Mo-ya holding the flute, and closing her eyes; Zhao Huaian see her doing that, and closes his, too. it's a kind of romance-as-meditation scene. *New Dragon Gate Inn* is filled with subtle evocations of love, as well as the Jade-led, bawdy kind. (Yes, let's not forget that Jade sings several ribald songs, about red and white candles, and she's introduced (as is the Dragon Gate Inn itself) with a song about a girl in the desert who loves men).

And while we're raving about *New Dragon Gate Inn* from a technical point-of-view, let's not forget an oft-overlooked aspect of filmmaking: costume design. All of the *wuxia pian* and *kung fu* pictures of the Chinese New Wave are wild costume extravaganzas, offering a fantasy vision of Ancient China. *New Dragon Gate Inn* is no exception: Poon Kwok-Wah and Ching Tin-Giu orchestrate ornate costumes for Cao and the Dong Chang faction, with his officers in different, single colours (green, blue, red), and the crack warriors all in black, with wide-brimmed hats. Talking about hats – Brigitte Lin and her cohorts sport very wide straw hats (to protect against the sun – you see them everywhere in movies of this kind). The heroes're clad in sleek, black outfits,with white scarves and shirts (but all garments in *kung fu* and *wuxia pian* movies have to be loose enough for the actors and stunt teams to execute those all-important twirls and kicks).

In fact, the *sight* of clothes rippling in the high breeze is part of the effect of a Chinese action picture, and the *sound* of clothing flapping is also mixed high. Indeed, *kung fu* movies often use clothing as a weapon

---

30 You can see, too, that it was a tough shoot at times – stuntmen are performing difficult gags on hard, stony ground.
31 'It's probably the finest non-James Wong-composed score in all of Tsui Hark's films' (Lisa Morton, 95).

(outer garments dipped in water are employed as spears, for instance). And *New Dragon Gate Inn* includes an outrageous scene where the two heroines are undressing each other in the middle of a fight.

### THE CHARACTERS.

With formidable competition from a host of very strong performers, the actor who steals *New Dragon Gate Inn* is Maggie Cheung Man-yuk. She is a revelation in this 1992 movie. She plays the mistress of the Dragon Gate Inn, Jade, with a fiery, impish, sexy energy. Cheung's Jade is one of those super-kinetic characters who simply can't keep still; Cheung rises to the challenge of delivering a sassy, young woman who's so bursting with energy, she's leaping on top of tables, flying down from the upper balcony, slinking around the inn like a snake, flirting with every customer, and flashing those camera-melting eyes (Cheung is *very* beautiful in this movie).

It's a *tour-de-force* of *physical* performance. It's not a performance that's in the script – most of it has been created on the set, in the interactions with other actors, in the way that Maggie Cheung has been directed by Raymond Lee, Tsui Hark (and Tony Ching Siu-tung *et al*), and in the lively approach to the filmmaking. Name any of the famous spikey, independent, no-nonsense women in North American Westerns (Joan Crawford in *Johnny Guitar*32 (1954) comes to mind), and Cheung is their equal (I mean, you don't really believe that Joan Crawford could wield a gun, but you sure can buy that Maggie Cheung can kick ass!).

There's a delight in bawdy, sexy scenes, too, in *New Dragon Gate Inn,* with Jade being introduced fooling around with a sweaty client upstairs in her chambers at the inn (until he's dispatched with Jade's weapon of choice – throwing stars). Again, the staging is incredibly physical, with the actors rarely at rest (Jade displays her ingenuity in running rings around men, as they grapple on the bed). The corpse is promptly thrown down a chute to the kitchen (via one of many secret tunnels in the inn), where the cook starts to prepare the meat for the buns (another (tasty) slice of cannibalism33 – from *We're Going To Eat You* and *A Chinese Ghost Story 2*).

Downstairs, in the dining hall, Jade is flirting with every guy, including the General of the authorities, played by Elvis Tsui (they have a history). She's lifted onto tables, she spins around to evade lecherous advances, and as soon as Yuan Mo-ya enters the building, she is immediately intrigued. The characterzation of Jade foregrounds sex – there are many jokes about flutes and candles, for instance.

Watching Maggie Cheung take the movie into outer space with her performance is mesmerizing. Within the first act alone, Cheung has horsed around with a guy, then killed him, tussled in a near-naked lesbian dance

---

32 Stephen Teo has also compared *Dragon Inn* with *Johnny Guitar*, with its world of lone gunfighters, outlaws, lady bosses, and remote inns.
33 A later gag, seen as shadows on a wall, is pure Tsui Hark: Ngai the cook (Xiong Xin-xin) slices off the skin from a corpse hanging from a hook, while he merrily sings a Daki song (which's handily translated for us by Siu-chuen). And when the cook cuts up a roasted goat at lightning speed, it's a funny gag, but it also plays into the finale, when Ngai turns out to be a cool fighter.

with Brigitte Lin, flirted with the General (whom she's had a relationship with), encountered the hero while rolled up in a banner, had jealous fits, and even been the butt of jokes about menstruation in a circle of guys. Few actresses do so much in so short a time.

Meanwhile, Brigitte Lin plays Yuan Mo-ya as another of her cross-dressing warriors. Her Mo-ya is also mysterious (another Lin speciality), yet also with powerful feelings underneath that cool, enigmatic exterior. The erotic interplay between Yuan Mo-ya and Zhao Huaian is beautifully evoked, and the depths of Mo-ya's emotions are comically but also tenderly portrayed in the scene where she gets very drunk when her man joins Jade in her chambers.

If you like seeing sexy women being sexy, the scene in *New Dragon Gate Inn* that gives the two beautiful stars Brigitte Lin and Maggie Cheung a chance to shine is the one.[34] Unlike any comparable scene in any movie made in the West, the scene upstairs in Yuan Mo-ya's room combines a fight with aerial acrobatics, a catty face-off between two super-bitches, and a romantically-oriented interplay of bodies, movement and nudity with the lesbian subtext brought out into the open. As they fly around the room, yanking off each other's clothing (with Mo-ya always besting Jade – Jade is stripped piece by piece by Mo-ya, ending up nude), they admire each other's bodies (while the camera frames the actresses so that the jiggly bits're always cleverly obscured).

Altho' this scene is 'fan service' – undressing the two attractive, female stars (in the true, exploitation fashion in Hong Kong cinema) – it does have a dramatic component: the romantic rivalry between the two (Jade is miffed when any man ignores her, and Yuan Mo-ya does so as soon as 'he' enters the inn). So Jade wants to discover Mo-ya's identity. And anything in *New Dragon Gate Inn* is done physically, with movement – hence the undressing dance.

And even that isn't the end of it – because Jade ends up on the roof of the inn nearly naked. And just as Zhao Huaian is approaching across the desert on his camels (her response? Only to start singing!). So how does she find some clothes? Only by diving off the roof into the night, spinning thru the air, grabbing the Dragon Gate Inn's banner, and wrapping it around her body as she spins to the ground (a remarkable piece of invention, a touch of *Cleopatra*). So she greets Zhao dressed in a flag (a couple of guys're in the background in these scenes, ogling her partially-nude body – that's pure Tsui Hark!). Jade is simply one of those girls who finds herself in such sticky situations all the time (and she's also one of those women who can talk their out of it, while retaining their dignity). And right away, she's flirting with Zhao.

SEX AND PLEASURE.

Sexy! *New Dragon Gate Inn* puts together two beautiful stars – Tony Leung Ka-Fai and Maggie Cheung – and gives them a wedding night scene (the wedding sequence is pure Tsui Hark – especially in the way that it

34 The 'film's most famous scene... an astonishing scene, one as charged with eroticism as action' (Lisa Morton, 93).

instantly complicates the romantic triangle with Yuan Mo-ya). Jade is in heaven – dolling herself up (and somehow finding rolls of red cloth and red lanterns to decorate the inn).

Swept up to Jade's chambers in Zhao Huaian's arms, the couple perform an erotically-charged tussle of body-on-body that's played for comedy as well as thrills. Because much of the scene is a fight! After all, what is a love scene in an action movie going to be, but a fight! Jade wants Zhao, but Zhao only wants to know where the secret tunnel[35] is to lead his crew out of the Dragon Gate Inn in one piece. The bawdy dialogue (Jade tells Zhao that her tunnel is right there, and it's easy to find, as she grapples him on top of her on the table – she's dying for his candle to light her tunnel), is only part of the delight of this over-the-top honeymoon sequence. (Meanwhile, Yuan Mo-ya is drowning her sorrows with wine with the boys during a drinking competition, imagining that her lover Zhao really is falling for the slinky, sexy vixen Jade – she spotted Jade fiddling with the flute she gave Zhao, which Zhao also notices; much to Zhao's irritation, Jade snitched the flute, and dared him to get it back). When an erotic triangle is played with this amount of pizzazz, from a trio of incredible performers, you can't help but be won over.

There's a bawdy running gag about candles (the sort of gag that William Shakespeare couldn't resist – the Bard, bless him, was very fond of phallic jokes), candles and weiners and lighting the fire (meanwhile, the love object that's passed between Zhao Huaian and Yuan Mo-ya is a flute! Which Mo-ya puts to her pretty lips and plays, sending Zhao into paroxysms of delight!).

But even without that raunchy dialogue and phallic symbolism, *New Dragon Gate Inn* is a supremely *sexual* movie: just look at how many times bodies are tussling or grappling each other or spinning around each other or flying thru the air. There is an ecstatic freedom to the movement of the body in this hyper-kinetic *wuxia pian*.

This also applies to many *kung fu* and *wuxia* movies – they are often sexier and way more sensual than pornography. The emphasis on textures, on atmospheres, on clothing, on bodies, on bodies in contact and in motion, lends Chinese action movies a highly charged eroticism. It's the pleasures of a musical movie and a dance movie combined with exaggerated melodrama, passions running on ten, and an imaginative, operatic approach to filmmaking.

You can see where Chinese action movies are coming from, and where they are headed (pleasure – entertainment – show business), and you can't help but surrendering. The energy or *chi* flowing thru the movies is so high, so colourful, it makes many other movies seem like catatonic patients dying on a hospital bed in a lonely, suburban town. By comparison with a Chinese action movie, many another picture appears like someone in a coma.

Many of the details in the erotic triangle in the middle act of *New Dragon Gate Inn* are very Tsui Harkian – we've seen these looks of longing

---

35 The tunnel is discovered by Zhao later – it's the one in, where else?, the bed.

and jealousy before in films such as *Shanghai Blues* and *Peking Opera Blues*. Indeed, this part of *New Dragon Gate Inn* is like *Peking Opera Blues* in the desert.

Tsui Hark is never happier than when he's got some of his favourite actors and actresses on a single, large, multi-level set, divided into groups, where the characters have social obligations that tussle with unspoken desires, where their sense of duty to the group (plus their political affiliations) is at odds with their personal dreams and impulses.

ACTION.

With Tony Ching Siu-tung, Cheng Yiu-sing, Wing Cho, Xin Xin Xiong and Yuen Bun overseeing the action, *New Dragon Gate Inn* is a *tour-de-force* of imaginative action scenes. Like many a *wuxia pian* and *kung fu* movie, *New Dragon Gate Inn* frontloads the picture with a series of visceral encounters, many featuring terrific horse riding stunts and falls (filmed in the Chinese desert at Dunhuang). That is a mere prelude, however, to the key action sequence in act one, where Cao Shaoqin and his army ambush our heroes rescuing the hostage children.

Altho' it is very much a Hong Kong action picture, *New Dragon Gate Inn* was filmed in Mandarin and in Mainland China, in the deserts of Dunhuang. The locations alone are worth the price of the ticket – landscapes so impressive, you can point the camera in any direction and come up with gold. No computer-assisted imagery here, no blue screens or green screens – you can't beat being out in the real desert under the burning sun and riding across stones and sand. And, like all of Tsui Hark's historical movies, there is fire, smoke, rain, wind and lightning blowing and crackling throughout the picture.

One of the marks of genius of Hong Kong stunt teams is their uncanny, almost miraculous ability to mix actors who aren't martial artists with stunt doubles. In your average action movie in the West, it's easy as pie to see where the joins are, where the doubles replace the actors. In Hong Kong action cinema, the staging, choreography, camera angles and editing make it seamless.

Maggie Cheung, Brigitte Lin and Tony Leung are not martial artists (tho' they have appeared in many action movies), but Tony Ching Siu-tung, Cheng Yiu-sing, Wing Cho, Xiong Xin-xin and Yuen Bun and the stunt teams make them look like the *kung fu* masters they are supposed to be.

A LOOK AT EACH ACT.

In many respects *New Dragon Gate Inn* is an 'Eastern Western', a replaying of the North American cowboy genre within an Oriental, *jiangzhu* context (plus some King Hu, some Hong Kong action, and 'a distinctly Tsui Hark spin').[36] The movie opens with very lengthy scenes of horses and riders in spectacular landscapes (more shots than the filmmakers intended – added by the distributors). The voiceover explains the set-up: the Imperial regime of Cao Shaoqin and Dong Chang (= East Factory/ East

---

36 Lisa Morton, 92.

Wing/ East Agents/ Gestapo) is capturing and punishing anybody who steps in their way. Loading the front of the movie with hugely impressive production value scenes, the filmmakers create the world of *New Dragon Gate Inn:* a ruthless Imperial regime in the more remote, dustier, tougher regions of the Ming Dynasty.

There are many scenes of Imperial majesty and power for some ten minutes – soldiers on horseback carrying banners, Cao Shaoqin seated on a throne, with his minions arranged below him, and many deaths as the Dong Chang try out their new weaponry (including a 'phoenix arrow' that can fly around corners, a very Tsui Harkian gag).

The prologue of *New Dragon Gate Inn* is all about the villains: the training exercises of the élite, ninja-esque Black Flag squad, who practise their bow and arrow techniques on live (condemned) prisoners on horseback; the excessive torture of Defense Minister Yang Yu-xuan (Yen Shi Kwan); and, presiding over it all, the effete Chief Eunuch Cao Shaoqin[37] (played with vulpine relish by Donnie Yen, cast against type). In his eagerness to quash all opposition to his regime, Cao lets the children of Yang go free, using them as bait so that he can crush all those who aid the hostages in one fell swoop.

Evoking a corrupt regime is pretty much mandatory in *kung fu* and swordplay movies, in any era of cinema. So that when we are eventually introduced to our heroes (after quite some time – the main titles of *New Dragon Gate Inn* don't appear until some 8 minutes into the movie), we have a very good idea of what they're up against, and how anyone who opposes the totalitarian regime will be punished severely (thus also typing our heroes as social rebels). Of course, some critics linked the oppressive and violent regime of Cao Shaoqin and Dong Chang to the People's Republic of China's government (and the vicious political suppression embodied in the Tiananmen Square massacre).

The first act of *New Dragon Gate Inn* depicts the Dong Chang regime in the first half, building up to the rescue and the ambush in the middle of the act. In the second half, we're introduced to the Dragon Gate Inn itself (with a song, suitably, from Jade as the first thing we hear, about a girl in the desert who loves men). The first act climaxes with the arrival by camel of Zhao Huaian – a superb introduction for the hero (so now all of the pieces are in place).

❀

Riveting, compelling, thrilling, enchanting, yearning – *New Dragon Gate Inn* has everything, and *then some*. The second act often sags in an action movie, doesn't it?, for good reasons (try writing an action movie script, and you'll soon discover all of the reasons!).[38] But not in *New*

37 In Chinese cinema, eunuchs have exchanged their male 'essence' for supernatural power (eunuchs are typically ambitious, political characters, part of the Imperial court). There are jokes about Cao's eunuch status in the 1967 *Dragon Gate Inn*, which the 1992 movie doesn't use.

38 In fact, if you wanted to develop your enjoyment and appreciation of cinema and television (which, in the West, you might spend 4 hours a day on average watching), I'd recommend writing a script and having a go at editing. Working out the structure of a movie on paper will tell you plenty about how difficult it is, and cutting some scenes together will show you how many tricks and sleights of hand are involved in everything you've ever seen in film and TV.

*Dragon Gate Inn:* it has enough complexly entangled sexual desire, honour, ambition, greed, beauty, magic, scares, twists, buffoonery, and action for ten movies. There are ninja-swift dartings to and fro, around and on top of the Dragon Gate Inn;[39] there's a fierce rainstorm; there's a wine drinking contest (with no one wanting to lose face);[40] there's a fantastic bout of sex and comedy in the wedding night scene; and everybody is so jumpy they're clutching their swords and leaping up at the slightest slights.

Because everyone is pretending to be someone else, and the stakes are high (arrest or maybe instant execution), nerves are at a jangly pitch.[41] Each group is jostling for position, while Jade attempts to keep the peace (and stop them destroying her inn!). Jade's flaring temper is incredible to see, as she flings wine at people,[42] berates the Dong Chang officials for creating a mess, and yells at everybody (except Zhao Huaian, of course).

The second act of *New Dragon Gate Inn* is filled with short but delightful two-hander scenes: Jade and Zhao, Jade and Cha, Zhao and Cha, Zhao and Yuan Mo-ya. Each scene is performed and cut at a sprightly pace, and staged with very dynamic movements. Some are romantic scenes (Jade and Zhao, Zhao and Mo-Ya), some are combative scenes between opposing sides (Cha and Zhao), and some are political manœuvring scenes (Jade and Cha, Cha and Zhao).

Cha and his Dong Chang cronies appear in the midst of the storm, posing as merchants, but they're really after Zhao Huaian and his rebels. There are many scenes where characters jostle for position, pretending to laugh good-naturedly, while under the tables they're getting ready to throw darts.

The second act climaxes with a series of short but intense action scenes, inside the bedrooms of the Dragon Gate Inn: Zhao Huaian and Cha (fighting under and over a roofbeam); Zhao and Siu-chuen (whom he immobilizes at a pressure point); Cha and Jade (she rumbles him, he tries to enlist her aid in snaring Zhao & co.); and Zhao and Yuan Mo-ya (they share a moment of meditation amidst memories and flute music).

This really is perfect filmmaking: a great cast, colourful, rounded characters, a fascinating scenario, an exotic setting, beautiful music, and building suspense. The shifting positions in the endless cat-and-mouse manœuvres are deftly tracked, as each group tries to gain the upper hand, without knowing what quite the others are up to. And Jade, who seems to be everywhere, tries to keep on top of it all.

The audience has already seen several action scenes, and it knows that more are coming up – but the 1992 movie teases the audience by leading up to a smackdown, then edging away from it. For example, in the dining hall, Zhao Huaian berates Cha and the oppressive regime of the Emperor, and it seems as if the film is going to dive into another massive brawl. Tables are smashed with fists in ferocious anger, eyes glare at each

---

39 Including two of the Dong Chang guys getting frazzled by lightning – they turn up next morning as breakfast!
40 The rebels cleverly water down their wine.
41 There are many scenes where characters, desperate not to reveal their identity, pretend to act cool and casual.
42 But she happily accepts several bribes, slipping them into her cleavage.

other, and impish Jade flits between the opposing sides, sprinkling water on the faces, trying to cool everyone down.

The arrival of the General and his boys, still looking for the wanted rebels Zhao Huaian and co., complicates the middle act once more. Here the Dong Chang are out-foxed, when Yuan Mo-ya secretly shows the General their authorized, Imperial papers (pretending to be Dong Chang, working undercover).

The tension mounts and mounts in the middle act of *New Dragon Gate Inn* (using the three-act model), with editor Poon Hung controlling the pacing and the delights with supreme judgement. Incredibly, *everyone* gets their moment to shine (incredible partly because they are so many characters), and, also incredibly, the movie is clever and skilful enough to take a breather from the shenanigans inside the Dragon Gate Inn. So there's a lyrical interlude framed against the sunset outside when Zhao Huaian wonders when all of this is going to be over (not for a few more hours, I hope!), and even the child hostages enjoy a moment of relaxation on the roof of the inn (that scene is beautifully empty of action and incident: the kids eat fruit, and look at the moon, and they talk about their mom. That's all. And in an action movie thrill-ride, it's marvellous to be able to stop the headlong rush like that for something pretty inconsequential. However, let's not forget, too, that the two moppets are what is at stake in *New Dragon Gate Inn*).

❀

As *New Dragon Gate Inn* moves towards its finale, the suspense keeps mounting: there are multiple events taking place simultaneously (such as the drinking contest continuing downstairs, and Jade and Zhao Huaian tussling upstairs), with the 1992 movie cutting repeatedly to Chief Eunuch Cao approaching on horseback with his army of expert warriors in black (we know that Donnie Yen as Cao Shaoqin has yet to reveal his true colours and go into battle. You don't cast Yen in an action movie and not have him go to work! So the audience knows that the fight is coming up).

It builds and builds – like foreplay not even the gods could resist (!) – until it explodes. You are waiting for it to happen, and the filmmakers tease us by having the impatient Ho Fu smash his cup of wine on the floor in frustration, and everybody draws their swords, but then, no, they settle down again.

One of the heroes (Ho Fu) and the chief villain (Cha) begin the smackdown, and then it's all swords drawn and a full-on brawl and sword fight. Inside the inn, there are numerous action beats to delight the audience: Yuan Mo-ya swirling like a dervish, the Dong Chang crew tussling with everyone, and even Jade leaps into the fray. Especially satisfying is to see Jade have a moment to shine when she demolishes the evil, smug Cha: first, she duels with Cha's chief lieutenant, Siu-chuen, pushing him back until he's squished gorily between some mill wheels. Then (this is pure Tsui Hark!), she takes a bucket of blood that drips from the corpse, scurries over the dining hall, and throws it in Cha's face, yelling at him to eat his own blood. Then she runs him through with a sword.

Blood and guts this vicious is seldom seen in Western movies perpetrated by female stars – and with such venom (thus the Dong Chang are dealt with).

Yuan Mo-ya tells Ho Fu and Iron to flee with the kids in their baskets – but they run into a hail of arrows from some of the Dong Chang out-riders, arriving at night.[43] The death of Jin and Ho (crouched over the kids, to protect them), as with the death of Cha and his crew, indicates that the stakes are so much higher now (with about fifteen minutes still to run).

Without a doubt, the finale of *New Dragon Gate Inn* is one of the greatest action scenes ever filmed. Action directors Tony Ching Siu-tung, Cheng Yiu-sing, Wing Cho, Xiong Xin-xin and Yuen Bun and the stunt team go absolutely nuts with spins, kicks, leaps, acrobatics, thrusts, swipes, punches, and every possible combination of sword-on-sword action imaginable. Even by Hong Kong film standards, the finale of *New Dragon Gate Inn* is simply tremendous. It's as if nothing could hold back the filmmakers, nothing could get in their way, and nothing could stop them from delivering this sensational mix of action, comedy and thrills.

It really is beautiful to witness, and awe-inspiring, too: you can see how *on fire* the filmmakers were in this period of cinema in China (there's a similar energy running thru most of the Chinese action movies of the early 1990s). The giant bust-up in the Dragon Gate Inn would be enough for many a movie (it's like watching a summary of thousands of Shaw Brothers movies!), but that's only *part* of the climax of this mind-boggingly wonderful movie!

Because Chief Eunuch Cao and the villains are hurtling towards the Dragon Gate Inn across the desert on horseback in clouds of dust. The attack begins with a remarkable sequence of arrows shot into the inn, as the horsemen encircle the building.[44] Horse riders storm into the inn (and onto the roof). Yuan Mo-ya goes into overdrive as the spinning, magical swordswoman who decapitates two villains while zipping thru the air, flying on a red banner (coming to the aid of Jade, who's taken on the riders and been thrown to the floor).

The editing of *New Dragon Gate Inn* (by Poon Hung) is blisteringly good, the staging is fabulously imaginative, and the visceral thrill is profound – to see Maggie Cheung and Brigitte Lin going supernova with their anger and battle frenzy is simply amazing (and yet the movie even has time for Jade to rescue the flute and hand it back to Yuan Mo-ya. *New Dragon Gate Inn* is full of poignant moments like that).

When the heroes try to break away from the inn during the Dong Chang assault, making a bid for freedom, they are cut down. Characters that we seem to have spent a long time with (and grown to like) are expiring all over the place, made into human pin-cushions by the arrows.

But even this is not the end of the finale of *New Dragon Gate Inn* – the incendiary action keeps on coming! And the filmmakers aren't out of imagination and playfulness and wit yet! Because we still haven't had the long-expected clash between the chief villain (Chief Eunuch Cao) and the

43 This is probably the scene where Brigitte Lin injured her eye.
44 Cao signals the attack by just lifting his finger.

surviving heroes: Jade, Zhao Huaian and Yuan Mo-ya. (Cao is alerted to the presence of the heroes when the red scarf of one of the kids blows free in the high wind. As soon as it falls, Cao leaps out of his wagon and onto the back of a horse, in hot pursuit).

The four-way sword fight that tops the finale of *New Dragon Gate Inn* is like no sword fight in *any* Western movie (before 1992 – or since!), and like few in Hong Kong cinema, for its ferocity, its invention, its daring, its audacity and its flair ('one of the greatest in the martial arts cinema', reckoned Lisa Morton [LM, 95]).

You can see the stamp of action choreographer Tony Ching Siu-tung all over this majestic piece of cinema (Ching would use very similar techniques in movies like *Hero, A Chinese Ghost Story, The Curse of the Golden Flower* and *House of Flying Daggers*).[45] Ching gets his combatants into the air, and spinning and kicking, with his team's unsurpassed use of wires (it's as if there is simply *nothing* that Ching and his team can't do!). The fight contains literally 100s of beats and moves, which flash by with the speed of a slashing blade, yet the staging and the editing keeps the movements clear and readable.

The setting certainly helps plenty: here's a Hong Kong *wuxia pian* that leaves behind the forest and the bamboo and the stony land of the New Territories (or the village back-lot sets), for the bright, merciless light and choking dust of the desert.[46] The implacable violence of the desert is employed throughout *New Dragon Gate Inn* (the characters can't leave during the storm, for instance), and pays off again when a dust storm buries the remaining characters in sand. In one incredible shot (of many shots in this exhilarating sequence), the camera is tracking laterally across a stony slope while the combatants duel, tumble and run, barely seen in the clouds of dust.

That Yuan Mo-ya is mortally wounded by Cao Shaoqin and sinks to her death in quicksand adds an extra level of desperation and tragedy to the finale, partly because Mo-ya is played by one of the stars, Brigitte Lin (in this movie, only three people survive: Jade, Zhao Huaian and Ngai the cook. But the movie makes sure that the children had been led far away by Ngai).

Meanwhile, the element of sorcery in fighting techniques that Cao Shaoqin possesses is just enough to be scary without going overboard. But he is matched, unexpectedly, by the Daki character, Ngai (played by Xiong Xin-xin), still clinging to his beloved meat cleaver (!). It's a real crowd-pleaser that Ngai is able to slice away Cao's leg and his arm to the bone and to burrow underground (seen in other movies of the time, like Jacky Cheung's character Autumn in *A Chinese Ghost Story 2*). But it still takes all three of the remaining heroes to dispatch Cao (he manages to

45 The final swordplay scenes feature many of Ching's flourishes, such as swords drawing energy lines on the ground, and swordsman descending in the air directly above their victim.
46 You can be sure that the performers found this a tough sequence to shoot – bone-hard stones to land on, dust and dirt, and that very hot sun. Also, many actors filmed other movies at the same time – but there's no chance of that in the Gobi desert far from a studio. Which perhaps meant that even more time and energy was focussed on this single movie than usual.

wound all of them pretty badly). Zhao deals the killing blow with a smaller sword cleverly buried inside his blade (shoved into Cao's neck).

And the *dénouement* of *New Dragon Gate Inn* is perfect: brief but poignant. First, the aftermath of the ferocious battle, with the combatants recovering on the desert floor, to the sounds of the flute music (which evokes Yuan Mo-ya – we see a C.U. of the flute on the sand, the only thing left of Mo-ya).

Second, Zhao Huaian opts to leave the desert (on his camels, with the children), and Jade and Ngai later decide to join him – by burning down the Dragon Gate Inn. Out comes the wine, doused on the walls, and the building is torched with satisfaction by Jade. Cut to the wide, high angle shot of the inn in flames, with Jade and Ngai on horseback riding off to catch up Zhao (accompanied by a plangent piece of ethnic music).

Thus ends one of the greatest movies ever made.

The Killer (1989).

The Terracotta Warrior (1989).

New Dragon Gate Inn (1992).
(This page and over).

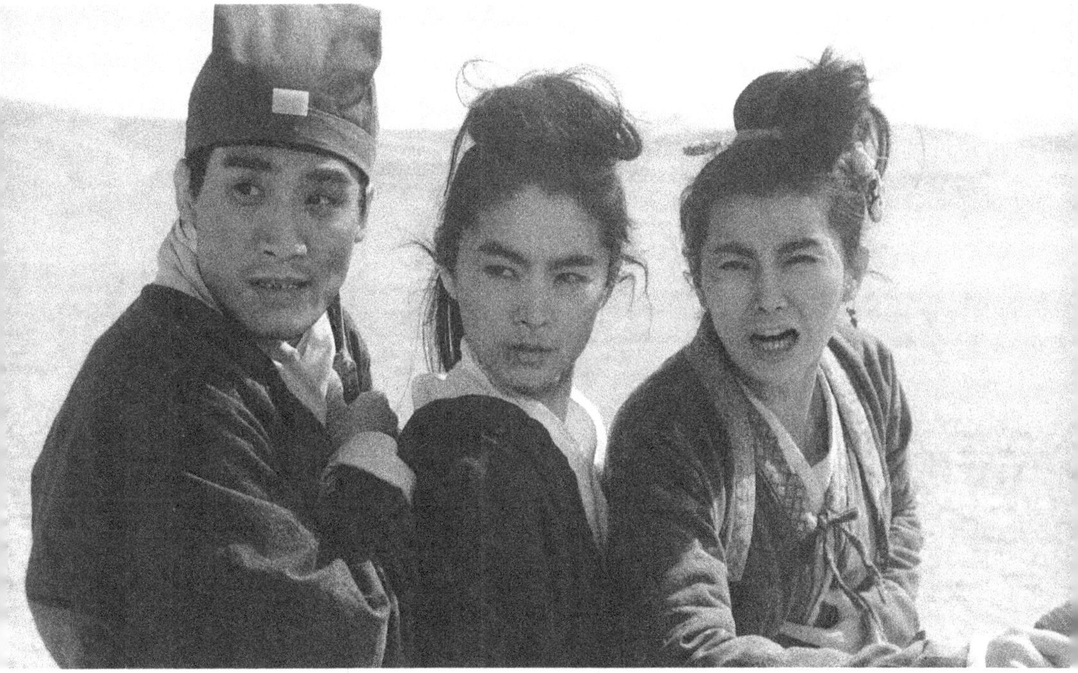

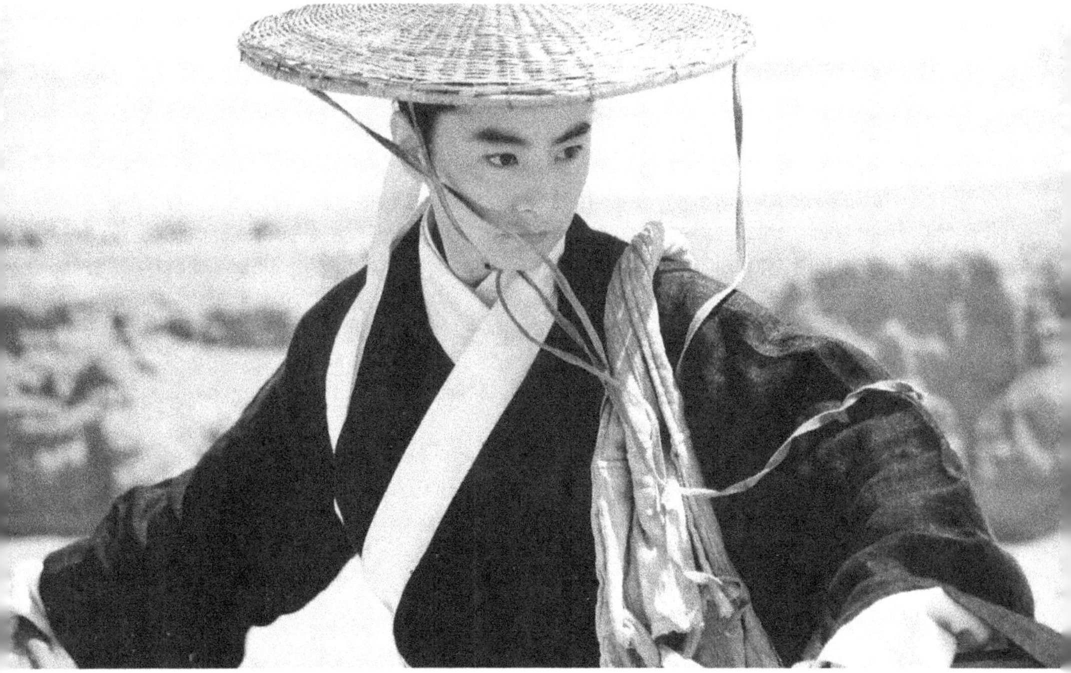

# 15

# *THE WICKED CITY*

## *Yao Sau Do Si*

*The Wicked City* (*Yao Sau Do Si*, 1992), was directed by Peter Mak Tai-kit, and produced by Tsui Hark, Raymond Lee and Marco Mak Chi-sin. Tsui and Roy Szeto Chuk-hon scripted. Yiu-Sing Cheung and Chris Kin-sang Lee were action directors, Kiyoko Ogino and Richard Yuen composed the music, costumes by Chris Wong, art. dir. by Eddie Ma, Kwong-Hung Chan and Wai-Keung Lau were DPs, special fx by Justo D. Cascante, and Marco Mak Chi-sin was editor. It starred Leon Lai Ming, Jacky Cheung Hak-yow, Michelle Reiss, Yuen Woo-ping, Carman Lee, Roy Cheung and Tatsuya Nakadai (Tsui was able to cast Japanese actor Tatsuya Nakadai in *Wicked City* – he had appeared in one of Tsui's favourite films, *Yojimbo*). Released: Nov 20, 1992. 87 mins.

    *The Wicked City* was a live-action version of the Japanese *animé* (1987), a fantasy horror outing with some sci-fi elements. *The Wicked City* was a superb run at reproducing the look and pace of a *manga* in live-action. *The Wicked City* looks forward to Tsui Hark-produced movies such as *Black Mask*: every shot has elaborate, look-at-me lighting, is tilted off the horizontal, selects an unusual camera angle (if a scene contains a standard shot at eye-level, it rapidly replaces that with an unusual angle), and smoke billows all over downtown Hong Kong. Saturated blues, plenty of backlighting, smoke, mist, fog, rain – textures of all kinds (*The Wicked City* is true cinematographer's movie).[1] Costume, make-up, hair, props, art direction, production design – *The Wicked City* has the comicbook look down pat.

    The Tsui Hark-produced *Wicked City* used some of the hallmarks of his movies, such as visual effects, a comicbook look, rapid editing, a relentless pace, powerful women, romance, intense action scenes, smoke and mist in every shot, etc. Tsui also makes his presence felt in one of the key roles of a producer: casting (many in the cast had appeared in Tsui's

---

[1] And, once again, the way that Hong Kong DPs light and photograph night scenes is remarkable (there are many in *The Wicked City*).

movies).

Once again, the *dynamism* of the performance style pops out of the screen in *The Wicked City*: this is not a movie where actors stand about stiffly and deliver dialogue! They are twisting, leaping, crouching, contorting.

Critics noted the nods to *Alien Nation, Blade Runner, Ghostbusters* and other Japanese *anime* such as *The Legend of the Overfiend* in *The Wicked City*,2 tho' this was very much a Hong Kong movie, with its own take on fantasy and horror.3

*The Wicked City* also happily mixes genres, in the grand but casual, Hong Kong cinematic manner: thus, altho' the horror/ fantasy/ science fiction elements pop out first (they're impossible to miss!), there is plenty of melodrama and romance (the sub-plot of Taki and his ex-girlfriend Windy, for instance); there is comedy; and there is the thriller/ urban genre (instead of hunting down gangsters, it's rapters, but the anti-rapter squad are sharp-suited guys, as in Hong Kong's staple genre, the thriller/ gangster flick).

Not as explicit sexually as the Japanese animated version (tho' Michelle Reiss plays many scenes topless), but the live-action *The Wicked City* makes up for that with hyper-kinetic visual effects mixed in with super-dynamic action. Nine years on from *Zu: Warriors From the Magic Mountain*, the visual effects arm of Film Workshop was really getting into its stride. The comicbook approached to visual effects of *The Wicked City* was very much in the Western/ Hollywood manner – from the early 1990s era, one might cite *The Mask, Ghostbusters 2,* and *The Crow.* In terms of visual effects and practical effects, *The Wicked City* has got the lot: men in suits (well, *every* monster in movies is a guy in a suit!), animatronics, partial bodies, special make-up, miniatures, fire, smoke, squibs, explosions, lots of opticals, different film speeds, super-impositions, and some early digital animation.

❁

*The Wicked City* opens with a tourist shot of Tokyo, Japan (a nod to the *anime* and *manga*), and cuts to downtown Hong Kong, the famous glittering lights view of the 'scrapers at the harbour. Plus some jumbo jets careening overhead (Hong Kong's airport was famously very near the city, and jets often appear in Hong Kong movies).

A city of the future, then, the great city of the Orient, the in-between colony (neither 'British' nor Chinese), a city over-run with rapters – monsters in human form (monsters which burst out of humans, an *anime* staple). No need for a political/ ideological gloss, then, from critics – *The Wicked City* contains it, foregrounds it – it's alien/ monsters and humans, it's us and them, it's Chinese and everyone else, Chinese and foreigners (*gweilo* – aliens). 4

Taki (Leon Li) and Ken Kai (Jacky Cheung) are agents working for the

2 Later you could add *Men In Black*.
3 'Aspects of sci-fi, horror, action, suspense, melodrama, and special effects combine to create this cinematic chow mein', as Stokes and Hoover put it (264).
4 But crrritics have of course seen analogies in *The Wicked City* – like, *duh*, the rapters're Mainland Chinese people.

Anti-Rapter Bureau in Hong Kong: it's a simple battle against monsters story, then. Yes. The complications to the plot-mix include several part-rapter charas, including Ken Kai, Taki's ex, Windy (Michelle Reiss), the squad's boss Sergeant Kayama (Yuen Woo-ping), Daishu (Tatsuya Nakadai), the 150 year-old tyro, and his out-of-control son Shudo (Roy Cheung), who's spreading a drug called Happiness.

*The Wicked City* ends with typically OTT action scenes, involving flying motorcycles, people falling from skyscrapers, people flying, goop smothering a car, exploding cars, a duel on the engine of a jumbo jet (where Shudo meets his demise), climaxing with the jet landing atop the Bank of China building.

Narratively and dramatically, the ending of *The Wicked City* plays out as you'd expect (tho' with more deaths than usual – Ken Kai and Daishu expire, as well as the villain, Shudo). And the ex-lovers remain exes, going their separate ways.

*THE WICKED CITY*: THE *ANIMÉ*

Tsui Hark produced the live-action version (1992) of the Japanese animation *Wicked City* (1987, a.k.a. *Demon Beast City/ Supernatural Beast City/ Monster City*). *Wicked City* is a horror/ fantasy thriller of the *Legend of the Overfiend* kind. It's demons/ monsters making mischief in the human world, with the heroes hunting down demons. Yoshiaki Kawajiri directed for Madhouse, and Kisei Cho scripted from Hideyuki Kikuchi's[5] novel (design was by Kawajiri and Kazuo Oga, one of the great designers of *animé*). The evocation of the contemporary city in *Wicked City* is the classic one of *animé* of the 1980s-2010s: hotels, airports, freeways, bars and cars. *Wicked City* is an *animé* version of a futuristic *film noir* – it has the cool, grizzled male heroes who smoke, it has slinky, sarcastic *femme fatales*, it has the German Expressionist lighting (complete with oceans of fog and back-light), it has the nighttime settings, it has shoot-outs and guns and it has the erotic encounters in hotel rooms. (So it's easy to see why it would appeal to Hong Kong filmmakers).

Style-wise, *Wicked City* features the blue and red lighting and colours[6] that director Yoshiaki Kawajiri is known for (Kawajiri (b. 1950) went on to helm the incredible *Ninja Scroll* series, *Demon City Shinjuku*, *Cyber City Oedo 808*, *Midnight Eye Goku* and *Vampire Hunter*, among others. Kawajiri also worked on *Future Boy Conan* (for Hayao Miyazaki), *Cleopatra* (for Osamu Tezuka), *Harmageddon* and *Dagger of Kamui* (both for Rintaro).

The hero, Taki, takes a woman to bed who turns into a monster halfway thru the lovemaking. She becomes a spider-woman, pinning Taki

5 Hideyuki Kikuchi also wrote *Darkside Blues*, *Vampire Hunter D* and *Demon City Shinjuku*.
6 Well, blues and reds are *very* Eighties (they crop up in *animé* such as *Appleseed* and *Dominion: Tank Police*.

in a deadly, praying mantis-like embrace. And between her legs is a gaping, toothed vagina. *Euuww!* (There's no need for a Freudian analysis, as Philip Brophy pointed out in *100 Anime*, because *Wicked City* is, like *Urotsukidoji*, its own psychoanalysis, its own theorizing: the scene is simply 'a thrilling depiction of what it would be like to have sex with a woman who suddenly turns into a sexy spidery monster' [2005, 245]).

*Wicked City* certainly contains plenty of arresting visuals and set-pieces. The filmmakers battle against the constraints of the budget, and in some areas the quality of the animation is lacking – but the team make up for the limitations with some inventive designs and dynamic stag-ing. And the action set-pieces deliver in terms of grotesquerie and thrills.

The first big action sequence in *Wicked City* is stunningly conceived: a fight between the hero Taki and a couple of demons on an airport runway, right underneath jumbo jets screaming just feet overhead.

Among the many men vs. monster set-pieces in *Wicked City*, the finale is a fitting spectacle. Set in a church (yet again with Christian iconography in a Japanese movie), the three charas battle the Chief Villain. One of the most memorable images has long, nasty, red tentacles exploding from inside a state of the Virgin Mary (not a scene you're likely to see in a Western animation any time soon!).

As Brian Camp noted in *Anime Classics*, *Wicked City* 'stands out as an atmosperic and imaginative thriller that managed to fuse film noir, sci-fi, horror, crime movies, and sex thrillers in ways that live-action films have yet to match' (396). Several elements from *Wicked City* pop up in later works from Tsui Hark – red tentacles, spider-women and demon hunters.

# 16

# *IRON MONKEY*

## *Siu Nin Wong Fei-hung*
## *Ji Tit Ma Lau*

INTRO.

*Iron Monkey* (1993, dir. Yuen Woo-ping; Mandarin: *Shiàonián Huáng Feihóng Zhi Tie Maliú = The Young Wong Fei-hung: Iron Monkey*) is a superlative slice of Hong Kong *kung fu* hokum focussing on the father of Wong Fei-hung. Clearly cashing in on the *kung fu* cycle of the early Nineties which had been launched with such magnificence by *Once Upon a Time In China* (and also as a kind of spin-off[7] to the *Once Upon a Time In China* films from the same producer – our man, Tsui Hark), *Iron Monkey* features two Robin Hood/ Zorro-style doctors,[8] Dr Yang (Yu Rongguang) and Wong Fei-ying (Donnie Yen),[9] Wong Fei-hung's father. The young Wong Fei-hung also appears (played by a young girl, martial artist Tsang Sze-man/ Angie Tsang), and Jean Wang[10] plays a rescued prostitute, Miss Ho (a.k.a. Miss Orchid). Also in the cast were James Wong Jim (wonderful), Yuen Shun Yee, Lee Fai, Mandy Chan Chi-man, Hsiao Ho, and Yen Shi Kwan.

Iron Monkey was produced by Film Workshop/ Paragon Films/ Longshong Pictures/ Golden Harvest; it was co-written by Tang Pik-yin, Tan Cheung, Tsui Hark and Lau Tai-mok; DP: Chi-Wai Tam; action directors: Yuen Woo-ping, Yuen Cheung-yan, Yuen Shun-yee and Kuk Hin-chiu; music by Gam-Wing Chow, Johnny Njo and Wai Lap Wu; editing

---

7 *Iron Monkey* can be regarded as prequel to the *Once Upon a Time In China* series: Tsang Sze-man is cast as the young Wong clearly to resemble Jet Li.
8 We see Dr Yang as Iron Monkey in very much the Robin Hood and Zorro mold, who steals from the rich to give to the poor and the needy (glimpsed in a series of vivid vignettes halfway thru act one), and Wong Kei-ying, who comes to befriend Dr Yang, when his identity is disclosed in the third act.
9 In *Heroes Among Heroes*, a.k.a. *Wong Fei Hung and Beggar So* (1993), Donnie Yen played Beggar So to Wong Gok's Wong Fei-hung.
10 Jean Wang (b. 1970), a former model from Taiwan, was a favourite with Tsui Hark's productions at this time, appearing in three of the *Once Upon a Time In China* movies, plus *The Swordsman 2* and *An Dou*. Later, Wang acted mainly in television. In *Iron Monkey*, in one of her first action roles, she is, unusually for a Tsui-produced script, the only significant female presence.

by Chi Wai Chan, Angie Lam, and Marco Mak Chi-sin; prod. des. and art dir. by Ringo Cheung; costumes by Bo-Ling Ng; sound recorder: Shao Lung Chou; and sound editor: Gam-Wing Chow. Tsui Hark oversaw post-production of *Iron Monkey*, which reveals his input in the editing, the sound mix, the music, etc. Released: Sept 3, 1993.[11]

*Iron Monkey* was a re-make of *Iron Monkey* (Chen Kuan-tai, 1977), starring Chen Kuan-tai, Kam Kong, Wilson Tong and Chi Kuan-chun. And there was a sequel, *Iron Monkey 2,* prod. by William Lan Tin-hung and Lee Shin for Gold Rush, wr. by Lee Man-choi and dir. by Chiu Lo-kong. Yuen Woo-ping was action dir. Donnie Yen, Wu Ma, Billy Chow, Yuan Wen-qing and Chang Jian-li headed up the cast.

YUEN WOO-PING.

Yuen Woo-ping (b. 1945 – Yuen Huopin in Mandarin) is part of a famous family of Yuens, the 'Yuen Clan': Yuen Cheung-yan (who was the action director for *Charlie's Angels,* 2000), Sunny Yuen, known for playing villains, Brandy Yuen, a martial artist, Yuen Yat Chor, and their father, Simon Yuen, a.k.a. Yuen Siu-tin (Yuen senior was a Peking Opera teacher, a stunt director on the original Wong Fei-hung movies, and an actor (Yuen junior appeared in some of the Wong Fei-hung films). Yuen appears as the *sifu* in *Drunken Master* and *Snake In the Eagle's Shadow,* for instance, both directed by his son, Yuen Woo-ping).

Yuen Woo-ping achieved fame in the West when he worked as the action director on the *Matrix* movies (which were of course heavily influenced by Hong Kong action cinema, as well as Japanese *anime*). Yuen is an extraordinary director with an impressive list of credits as director that includes *Iron Monkey, Tai Chi Master* and *Wing Chun.* He was also the action choreographer for *Crouching Tiger, Hidden Dragon* and the Wong Fei-hung cash-in, *Last Hero In China.* As well as an incredible facility for staging action (with wirework a speciality), Yuen adds a lot of humour to his direction, reminding us that martial arts cinema is always partly putting on a show.

With Yuen Woo-ping at the helm, at the very least *Iron Monkey* is going to be a crackingly good action movie.[12] It is! – and Yuen adds in his customary eccentric sense of humour, which keeps the whole movie skipping along as lightly as a ninja racing along the rooftops at night (some of the comedy clearly stems from the Tsui Hark – having a real monkey being brought in by the police as they try to round up Iron Monkey is very Tsui-ian).

Yu Rongguang and Lee Fai recalled that Yuen Woo-ping was very strict about how *kung fu* was put on screen: moves had to look clear and powerful, and action would be repeated until it was right. Making *Iron*

---

11 The release was delayed by the additional shooting. Commentators reckon the picture might've fared better at the b.o. if it had been released as planned. *Iron Monkey* was filmed during a hot Summer.
12 Yuen is in his element in *Iron Monkey,* Lisa Morton noted, 'and several of the film's fights are justifiably famous in martial arts film circles' (LM, 199).

*Monkey* was exhausting,[13] Yu said,[14] and Lee cried several times. Not only did everything have to look great and convincing (and emotional), Yuen liked to shoot lengthy takes sometimes, a departure from the usual approach of filming stunts and fights in very short shots. It meant that the actors had to remember many moves. (And Yuen liked to use the principal actors where possible). Yuen would also keep filming takes until he was satisfied the shot was the best it could be.

▶

THE STORY.

*Iron Monkey* is pure gold entertainment, a great night at the movies. The casting is strong, the five leads are appealing, the production values are sumptuous, the story is delightfully old-fashioned and conventional, and the humour is pitched at a level crude and knockabout at times, but staying this side of 'PG-13' (altho' the violence against women – and children – later in the picture would put it into the 'R' category in the West).

You can't help but be won over by a movie like *Iron Monkey*. It's undemanding fare, and gorgeously achieved. Technically, *Iron Monkey* is rich – it creates town life in the late 19th entury with some delightful vignettes (starving kids, over-worked kids, noodle stalls, merchants, inns and restaurants), and an acute feeling for texture (plenty of rain scenes, lovely golden afternoon light, and of course always with the smoke in every scene).

The production values and cinematography (by Chi-Wai Tam;) of *Iron Monkey* are very fine: largely filmed in the studio and on standing backlot sets, this is a very handsome show. Warm hues predominate, with even daytime scenes having a golden glow about them.

*Iron Monkey* is, like all of the *kung fu* cycle *circa* 1991-94, a fantasy of Ye Olde China, a Chocolate Box China... (And, like the Wild West in American Westerns or Sherwood Forest in British *Robin Hood* films, it never existed. But it *should've*!). Yet, altho' it seems like a Ye Olde China that's been concocted for marketing to a global audience, the primary audience would be local: Hong Kong. *Iron Monkey* is made for a first-run audience watching the movie in Hong Kong's Central or Kowloon.

Some of the humour's directed against the authorities: in *Iron Monkey,* as in many *kung fu* and martial arts flicks, the authorities are corrupt (when will we get the leaders we deserve? is one of the complaints of the characters. Critics will automatically seize upon such comments as critiques of the People's Republic of China, but such sentiments could apply for any era from the past ten thousand years). So the chief constable of the local police, Master Fox (Yuen Shun-yi), is a bumbling fool, and the local magistrate Cheng (James Wong Jim) is only concerned with hanging onto his money like a miser, and maintaining his harem of nine mistresses (there's an amusing scene where Cheng is horsing around under the covers at night with a bevy of beauties, and later taking a bath).

---

13 Many of the performers affirmed that safety was a key issue on a Yuen Woo-ping movie. But you can also see that filmmaking this rough and ready will likely lead to bruises at the very least. And while safety is an issue, many Western producers would think again about putting their stars into the midst of an intense fire sequence coupled with wires and height.
14 Yu injured his legs during production, and needed assistance from wires.

*Iron Monkey* is one of the lesser-known of the *kung fu* movies of the early Nineties cycle, being over-shadowed by the many *Swordsmans*, *Fong Sai-yuks* and *Once Upon a Time In Chinas*. It deserves more recognition, simply as an action movie, and also as a delightfully energetic reworking of the enduring Wong Fei-hung mythology (it fared better when it was released in the U.S.A. in Oct, 2001 by Miramax).15 You can imagine local audiences in Hong Kong lapping up *Iron Monkey* and its comicbook approach to late 19th century, Chinese legends (with, thankfully, the colonial/ political elements put to one side. After all, you don't need to have political-ideological-philosophical-social issues rammed into your eyeballs every time you visit a cinema in Victoria or Central (have you ever had the Communist Party Manifesto jammed into your eye sockets? It hurts!). Other movies and other filmmakers can do that! Not every movie has to be an arty Wong Kair-wai film!).

The storytelling in *Iron Monkey* is traditional – or that's how it seems at first. In fact, it's more layered and complex than that. There is an elaborate flashback, for instance, filmed in black-and-white, which delineates, in a remarkably deft shorthand manner, how Miss Orchid was saved from a life of prostitution by Dr Yang (after her baby dies in childbirth).

The flashback is initiated by Miss Orchid singing a lullaby to the young Wong Fei-hung, recovering from an illness caught in jail. There is also a sweet scene where Dr Yang is answering Orchid's song with his own, in the courtyard of Po Chi Lam (and that's all we need to see to evoke their tender, affectionate relationship. No kissing or dialogue is required). If we think of Yuen Woo-ping as the master of action choreography (which he is!), we often forget that he is, like all of the great Hong Kong directors, a master storyteller. *Iron Monkey* knows, for example, when to slow down and explore the characters a little, and when to have smaller, intimate scenes (like the two-hander between Yang and Orchid, over food. The script is a lot richer than many a Shaw Brothers actioner).

There is time for comedic episodes (some were added by Tsui Hark), such as when Yang and Orchid impersonate Imperial officials visiting Governor Cheng and Master Fox and intimidate them. (James Wong Jim, one of the most talented people in Hong Kong cinema, and a key collaborator with Tsui Hark, is terrific as the foolish, selfish and dim-witted Cheng).

*Iron Monkey* is a movie which includes plenty of moods and tones – the form of the action comedy in Hong Kong cinema is flexible enough to include all sorts of bits of business, from lyrical musical interludes to slapstick comedy, from dramatic flashbacks to romantic scenes. (Reminding us that the *form* of Hong Kong cinema is open enough to include many genres and styles within a single movie – and sometimes it seems as if all of Hong Kong's film output moves towards the state of

15 For the 2001 release, the movie was re-cut, re-dubbed, cleaned up, with new sound mixes and new fx (from MetroLight Studios and Pixel Magic). The re-editing of *Iron Monkey* included attempts to make the movie more palatable to a Western audience – taking out comedy in the midst of action scenes, rewriting the subtitles, reducing the political elements, cutting back on the violence, adding more 'realistic' sound effects, and using a different music track (courtesy of James L. Venable).

musical cinema).

The father-son relationship is sweetly played in *Iron Monkey* – these are two of the most famous characters in all of Chinese cinema. Donnie Yen plays Wong Fei-ying as a stern, upright but kind-hearted man, keen to offer a noble example to his offspring (there isn't much mention of Mrs Wong). Tsang Sze-man as Fei-hung, meanwhile, is charming and agile when needed (it was Tsang's first movie; she was playing ten, tho' she said she was about 14 at the time. Her mom was on set every day. Everybody on the set pampered her, she recalled).

▶

Apparently, in his role as *über*-producer. Tsui Hark thought there wasn't enough comedy in *Iron Monkey,* so he ordered some additional shoots (this has occurred with other productions that Tsui has produced). I wonder if the playful fights over food or the cooking scenes or the scene where Iron Monkey impersonates the Governor were among those added by Tsui. Tsui always keeps an eager eye on the *balance* of elements in a movie: all-out action is great, but Tsui always includes other ingredients.

Food, cooking and hunger are prominent motifs in *Iron Monkey:* Wong Fei-ying and Wong Fei-hung are poor, and desperate for food (to the point where Fei-ying sneakily snatches up some food fallen on the ground). When Iron Monkey and Fei-ying find sanctuary with some friendly villagers towards the end of the 1993 movie, they are given some rice in bowls; but they realize that no one else is eating in the crowd around them (the villagers have sacrificed their own food for the two doctors). There are cooking scenes (which manage to include extravagant *kung fu* moves), and a number of shared dinners (including one where the two doctors disagree over whether the recovering Fei-hung should be allowed to eat roast duck, and there's a fight with chopsticks).

Again and again in the *kung fu* and swordplay movies of the early 1990s, altho' Western critics go on and on about the run-up to the 1997 Handover, there's actually a far greater emphasis on issues such as the *body* – on the body in motion and action, of course, but also the body when it's wounded and needs healing, the body when it's hungry and needs feeding, the body when it's working, and the body and sex.

The *sensuality* and *texture* and *physicality* of the *wuxia pian* and historical movies of the early 1990s (and in all of the *wuxia pian* since then), is often a much, much more palpable element than global or local politics.

▶

But *Iron Monkey* is course also a *major* action movie – it's a Yuen Woo-ping movie, after all! – and in that respect, it's hugely satisfying (the real *sifu* in this movie is of course director and actionmeister Yuen Woo-ping). By the time the first act's over in *Iron Monkey*, we've seen four or five action scenes, and action's also been employed in many other smaller scenes (such as the outstanding dreamy sequence where Dr Yang and Miss Orchid collect some paper blown around by the breeze in the clinic, a scene which demonstrates their martial arts prowess as well as evoking their romantic relationship.[16] Why bother with a conventional love scene, when you can have the actors flying around the room in slow motion, smiling at each other? Yes, Liz Taylor and Montgomery Clift didn't do that – but they would've if they could!).

Meanwhile, most of the second half of *Iron Monkey* is non-stop action, enough to satisfy even the hungriest of action movie groupies. Everybody gets to show off their skills as fighting machines. Li'l Wong Fei-hung gets to wield the trademark umbrella in a street brawl. Later, the movie has Wong swinging a pole *wushu*-style against the four fake Shaolin monks and the psychotic White Eagle (and rescuing Miss Orchid in the process – a reversal of the scene earlier, where Miss Orchid saved Wong). Cue the music of 'Under the General's Orders'! (The *wushu* set-pieces seem to consciously allude to the young Jet Li's martial arts style in his Mainland China competitions).

Another fight involving Wong Fei-hung has the little tyke taking on some (younger) street punks after demonstrating his *wushu* moves to some admiring kids. Like a monkey, Wong is everywhere, inventively besting his opponents (tables are flung and smashed regularly). The question of how a child of about ten can take on adults in a brutal fight is answered thus: he's Wong Fei-hung! You have to remember that Fei-hung is a young Robin Hood – he always has to win!

Shaolin heavies turn up from time to time to create havoc (in one scene, they're dressed as Japanese ninja). But they are no match for Dr Yang, or Wong senior – or Miss Orchid. The mid-film night scene where Iron Monkey takes on the four agents is just one of many wonderful action episodes in *Iron Monkey*.

Miss Orchid also has her own marvellously acrobatic fight scene with the Shaolin heavies in Po Chi Lam (in its use of small tables to leap on and to kick at the assailants, it's reminiscent of the action style that Yuen Woo-ping and his boys choreographed for Michelle Yeoh in *Tai Chi Master*, made around the same time as *Iron Monkey*). The preamble to the fight has the four shameless 'monks' pushing poor Orchid around and cackling and drooling over her: again, Chinese filmmakers advance the threat and violence against women much farther than their Western counterparts: the men hit Orchid repeatedly, shove her to the floor, slap her several times, and keep their feet on her body to hold her down. Then they rip off her clothes – which's the cue for Wong Fei-hung to leap to her rescue from the upper balcony (wielding the trademark pole).

However, most screen time in *Iron Monkey* is given over to the multiple smackdowns between Iron Monkey, Wong Fei-ying and the Imperial official, Hin Hung (played with sneering, cackling glee by Yam Sai-kwoon). Hung is a villain with several vicious martial arts techniques, including the King Kong[17] Palm (meanwhile, the heroes possess chains, the Hung Gar style and of course the shadowless kick. As the fights

16 There are other romantic scenes, such as when Miss Orchid and Iron Monkey meet on the roofs at night in the rain, when they're clad in their black, ninja outfits. They walk home in the rain, under an umbrella, arm-in-arm.
17 Is the name – King Kong – another Tsui-ism?

progress, they announce the techniques they're employing, like giving a running sports commentary for the audience). Hung has a couple of vicious henchmen – Disfigured Swordsman (Hsiao Ho) and White Eagle (Lee Fai).[18]

The first heroes vs. villain fight in *Iron Monkey* begins in the courtroom (where Hin Hung is lounging about in the judge's chair and being fed tender morsels by a hooker), and hurries out onto the roofs. The combatants are all over the place, performing 100s of intricate moves, poses and martial arts styles. It's breathtaking – especially to see Iron Monkey and Wong Fei-ying working together to defeat Hung. In the event, they are both severely wounded by the King Kong Palm of Hung.

Returning to Po Chi Lam clinic to recover (which doesn't take too long),[19] the conflicts resume again. Like many of the *kung fu* flicks of the early Nineties period, wooden logs play a key role, as well as fire (*lots* of fire! The scene culminates in the recreation of a raging inferno below the logs, and a full-body burn for the villain). There's a beat where Iron Monkey and Wong senior, working together, balance on a log atop a pole, like a seesaw – a nod, perhaps, to the famous finale of *Once Upon a Time In China* with its wobbly ladders (which, as Tsui Hark related, the stunt teams couldn't get to work, so Tsui brought in Yuen Woo-ping and his stunt team – these are people who can seemingly do anything in cinema).

What can the filmmakers do that hasn't been seen before? (at least for a few months!), they might have asked themselves. How about an intense, three-way martial arts duel fought twelve feet in the air, on the top of wooden poles? Yes – and to make things *really* damn difficult, how about there's a fire raging below?! Oh, and let's shoot it at night! (Difficult for the characters, but nigh on impossible for the filmmakers and the actors – you can see that this must've been absolute misery to film.[20] And it could've been achieved in only one place on Earth: Hong Kong! Indeed – Yu Rongguang said it took 15-20 days just to film this one scene! And it's only five minutes on screen!).

Miss Orchid gets her moment to shine, too – while the boys take on Hin Hung as a double act, she fights with White Eagle, trumping the guy by flicking a ball bearing into his eye – thru his sword (a great, gruesome touch).[21]

---

18 Lee Fai is a regular stunt double in Tsui Hark's movies (doubling for Maggie Cheung in *Dragon Gate Inn*, for instance) – but here, Tsui decided to have her made up in a ugly fashion, and to play a guy. Lee was trained in Peking Opera performance (in Hong Kong), and later taught martial and Tai Chi (as well as entering competitions).
19 The healing sequence, which includes acupuncture and bleeding the patient, also involves taking a revolting potion of poisons (which we don't see). In his films as a director, including the *Wong Fei-hung* series, Tsui Hark never misses an opportunity to display traditional, Chinese arts.
20 For instance, the fire had to be put out and re-set numerous times.
21 The music of Ennio Morricone from the *Fistful of Dollars* series is inserted at this point – that's a Tsui Hark idea.

# 17

# *THE MAGIC CRANE*

# *San Sin Hok Za*

*The Magic Crane* (*Xin Xian He Shen Zhen*, dir. Benny Chan, 1993), starred Anita Mui Yim-fong, Tony Leung Chiu-wai, Rosamund Kwan, Lawrence Ng, Norman Chu, Jay Lau Gam-Ling, Vindy Chan Wai-Yee, Lau Shun and Damian Lau. Tsui Hark and Jobic Chui Daat-Choh co-wrote the script, based on Wolong Sheng's (Long-Sheng Wo's) book *Xian He Shen Zhen*. Long Shong Pictures and Film Workshop produced; Tsui Hark was producer; Ringo Cheung Sek-Wah was art dir.; Tung Hon-Wan and Chan Kok-Hong did the make-up; the DPs were Tony Miu King-Fai, Tom Lau Moon-Tong and Ko Chiu-Lam; Lau Chi-hoi was action director (8 assistant action directors are credited); costumes by Pat Tang Yu-Hiu, Chan Sau-Ming and Chiu Gwok-San; hair by Lee Chi-Din and Lee Lin-Dai; music by Jonathon Wong Bong;[22] C.Y. Kong was music producer; Siu-Lung Ching was sound effects editor; Marco Mak Chi-cin edited. Released: Aug 19, 1993. 96 mins.

Once again, in critical summaries, Tsui Hark's name overshadows that of the other filmmakers. Benny Chan was the director (this was one of his first films as director). Tsui's contribution included production and co-scripting; *The Magic Crane* was also a Film Workshop production, and many in the team were Tsui regulars.

At this moment in Tsui Hark's career, any director accepting the job of director with Tsui as producer (plus his company) would realize that the gorilla in the room would dominate the affair.

*The Magic Crane* is usually critically dismissed as a *Swordsman* clone, an attempt at concocting another visual effects-heavy, starry, martial arts fantasy movie, which's let down by the story and the formulaic, factory-based approach. (Well, that applies to 99% of movies – they're all factory-made, they feature stars to bring in audiences, they have familiar stories, they're usually adaptations of existing material, etc).

---

22 The theme songs (composed by Ta Chiang Wu, Mark Lui and James Wong Jim) were sung by Anita Mui, Jacky Cheung and Winnie Hsin.

In *The Magic Crane* we are back in the martial arts world again, the *jiangzhu* of movies of the era such as *The Swordsman* and *New Dragon Gate Inn* (there are numerous affinities between *The Magic Crane* and the *Swordsman* series). So the background story is of warring schools, clans, communities, special martial arts books, with the martial artists caught in the middle.

The cast is stellar, with three big Hong Kong stars (Mui, Kwan and Leung). There are three main protagonists in *The Magic Crane*:

• Anita Mui Yim-fong's[23] warrior Pak Wan-Fai, who rides a large crane;

• Tony Leung as another of his hapless, well-meaning figures, Ma Kwun-Mo (our audience identification guy);

• and Rosamund Kwan's imperious warrior Butterfly Lam, queen of her clan.

Of the three central characters, Ma Kwun-Mo is designed as the most accessible, even though he's not a regular guy – he's a topnotch martial artist. Butterfly Lam is the chip-on-the-shoulder character, who's looking for payback (her characterization is reminiscent of the warrior queens in *The Swordsman 2* and *3* – and not only Asia the Invincible).

The Crane Girl, however, Pak Wan-Fai, is kept at a distance. Her other-worldly characterization is of a pure, innocent woman who has somehow remained above and beyond the rough-and-ready world of martial arts. (Pak insists that she has never spent much time with men; much is made of a moment when Ma turns his head by accident and seems to kiss Pak. The gentle comedy contrasts with the coarse 'fan service' of the portrayal of Lady Jade Flute, the nudity and the 'Cheerful Drugs').

But while many critics bemoaned the hackneyed story and characters, and pointed out that it made only HK $8 million in local territory, that wasn't entirely what *The Magic Crane* was about, or why it was enjoyable.

*The Magic Crane* was another action-based fantasy adventure spiced with plenty of comedy, a combination of the martial arts genre, the fantasy/ visual effects genre, and the goofy, Hong Kong comedy. The comical tone is set by Tony Leung's Ma Kwun-Mo (and his banter with his *sifu*, played by Kelvin Wong-siu) – it's high spirited adventure movie-making, not be taken seriously, a movie as pure entertainment.

*The Magic Crane* is *not* an epic martial arts movie, and it's not a serious drama – it's a mix of wistful and mysterious Chinese mythology, outrageous special effects which includes fights with giant monsters, and *Indiana Jones*-style adventure.

We've got a giant crane bird that the heroes ride about on, a tortoise the size of a football field, a swarm of poisonous bats (a call-back to the sort of horror in *Black Mask*), and villains wielding giant bells as weapons.

So, no, *The Magic Crane* doesn't make 'sense', but neither do most of the blockbuster movies released in the West each Summer and over the vacations if you stop and think about the story.

The weapons that the two sisterly rivals employ in *The Magic Crane*

23 The movie exploits Anita Mui's magnetism several times (when she plays the magic flute, for instance, there are big close-ups of her famous puckered lips).

are musical: Pak Wan-Fai is armed with a magical flute, and Butterfly Lam has a lute. It's certainly striking to see the girls going into battle wielding musical instruments instead of swords, guns, knives, spears, whips, etc. The action choreographers, for instance, turn Butterfly Lam into a Peking Opera acrobat, as she spins and leaps while holding her lute.

Lau Shun delivers another of his over-the-top magical figures in *The Magic Crane*, this time playing a blind, crippled martial arts warrior (from the Tai-kok Temple), in a truly out-there scene in a cave. Yat Yeung-Tze is thrown into the cave by the heroes, and discovers that the reverend of Tai-kok is not someone you want to get too close to. After much intense action with chains and grappling bodies, Yat Yeung-Tze emerges with extra powers (which he uses in the finale).

*The Magic Crane* is a new low in the feminism of Tsui Hark's cinema, however: despite featuring two strong warrior-women, there is some shameless pandering to the lowest common denominator with scenes where a young woman called Lady Jade Flute disrobes repeatedly, parading in front of crowds. Jay Lau as Lady Jade Flute gamely plays up the nudity, tho' it's fairly demeaning (it's more like the trashy genre cinema that Hong Kong releases each year). And later, there are drugs dispensed by Yat Yeung-Tze which fill Lady Jade Flute with the urge to make love. Worse yet, Lady Jade is a prominent victim, expiring (tho' charas such as Lam Hoi-ping come back to life).

❧

In true Tsui Hark style, before 30 minutes have passed, the 1993 movie has already staged an attack by poisonous bats, two rescues by Pak Wan-Fai and her giant bird, and several bust-ups between rival clans at an inn (where the screen is teeming with flaying swordsmen).[24]

There's barely any time to breathe in the pacing of *The Magic Crane* – it's cut by Tsui Hark's regular axe-man, Marco Mak Chi-sin, and that means a frantic pace (*The Magic Crane* might benefit from 5-10 minutes more character-based material in the first act, because the characters aren't quite there. In comparable flicks such as *The Swordsman* and *A Chinese Ghost Story*, there are more character-led scenes,

Forget about slowing down – *The Magic Crane* doesn't have a draggy middle act (it's in three acts – running to 96 minutes). Oh no, it races from one scene of flailing swords to another. The action directors (Lau Chi-hoi *et al*) seem to be aiming to win the prize for Most Actors On Wires In One Scene (usually held by Tony Ching Siu-tung, closely tied with Yuen Bun and Yuen Woo-ping). Oh yes, we've got stunt guys on wires all over the place in the inn, where the rival clans are bickering and fighting (as they wait for a cure to the poisoning from another rival clan).

In an inventive departure from the usual MacGuffin in an action movie, the thing everybody is fighting over is… the gall bladder of a giant, fiery tortoise! (Surely this is one of Tsui Hark's eccentric additions?!) Because the warriors are clambering over each other to grab this object (about the size of a baseketball, it pulses with life). It's played comically, with the

24 In *The Magic Crane*, characters don't use doors – they smash thru the roof, thru the floor, and thru many windows and walls (so many times, it's a recurring gag).

tortoise gall bladder too hot to handle, so it's being thrown about like a beach ball, as each clan attempts to snaffle it for themselves. (However, there *is* the conventional MacGuffin of a *wuxia pian* here – the special martial arts book or scroll).

The emotional/ psychological complications in act two include the arrival of Lam Hoi-ping, who's Butterfly Lam's father (he's played by Norman Chu Shiu-keung, who was the cop hero of *We're Going To Eat You*); Buttefly Lam and Pak Wan-Fai are thus sisters (sort of), whose relationship has turned very sour (the mother is once again absent – this is yet another narrative about father complex girls).

*The Magic Crane* ends with the absolutely mandatory Big Action Scene (or rather, in the Hong Kong tradition, several Big Action Scenes). Butterfly Lam fights Pak Wan-Fai, Pak Wan-Fai fights Butterfly Lam, Lam Hoi-ping returns from death to fight Yat Yeung-Tze, and Yat Yeung-Tze fights them all.

As the theme of the women's magical weaponry in *The Magic Crane* has been musicial instruments, what does Yat Yeung-Tze bring to the party? Only a giant bell (the size of a Buick, which he holds effortlessly above his head). When he whacks it (which's often), it damages opponents internally, with its sound. So Pak with her flute and Lam with her lute fire back sounds.

Tsui Hark is right – China does have exotic mythologies which provide rich material for movies. One thing's for sure, no Western/ North American action movie would have the heroes armed with a lute and a flute and the villain with a bell! Unless it's a comedy. Which *The Magic Crane* is. But it's also drawing on Chinese culture thru and thru – this is a thoroughly *Chinese* movie (even tho' it employs Western/ North American elements).

And the villain is nobbled in a musical manner, too – high up in the air, Pak Wan-fai shoves her flute into Yat Yeung-Tze's torso and plays it. It blows him up – literally – so he eventually explodes into pieces.

But wait a minute, surely Crane Girl Anita Mui Yim-fong hasn't been killed, in this sacrifical act to waste the villain? Apparently, no: we don't see her after the explosion, but the other heroes discuss the possibility that she's not dead. Because, after all, Lam Hoi-ping has waltzed back into the film after seemingly expiring (and he was given a death scene, too). So, no, you can't kill off Anita Mui!

And in true Tsui Hark style, how does *The Magic Crane* end? Only with our heroes on horseback and in motion in the wilderness (just how many Tsui films of this period close).

# 18

# *BURNING PARADISE*

# *Huo Shao Hong Lian Si*

*Burning Paradise* (1994, *Huo Shao Hong Lian Si*, a.k.a. *The Rape of the/ The Destruction of the Red Lotus Temple*) was written by Nam Yin and Wong Wan-choi, prod. by Tsui Hark and Benzheng Yu, dir. by Ringo Lam Ling-tung, art dir. by Ranxin Qu, action dir. by Chris Lee King-sang, the DP was Gao Ziyi, music by Chun-hung, and D.L.O. Film Productions/ Golden Harvest/ Silver Medal Productions produced. Willie Chi Tian-sheng, Carman Lee, Wong Kam-long, Yang Sheng, and Lee Tien-san appeared. Released: Mch 26, 1994.[25] 100 mins.

So we're back with yet another version of the Red Lotus Temple (or monastery) tale in Chinese mythology, with the destruction of the Shaolin Temple, the capture of Shaolin monks, and the heroes Fong Sai-yuk (winningly played by newcomer Willie Chi) and Hung Hei-kwuen (Yang Sheng) fighting back. (The story's been told many times in cinema and television, and Hung and Fong have been played by all sorts of actors over the years. For an audience in the colony, this would be very familiar material).

Every single aspect of the narrative of *Burning Paradise* is conventional: heroes are heroes, villains are venal, and women are princesses to be rescued (*Burning Paradise* adds the traditional bickering between Fong Sai-yuk and Dou Dou which masks their attraction; meanwhile, Hung Hei-kwuen is not left out, and has a sort of relationship with Brooke (Chun Lam), one of the villain's underlings). Indeed, the storytelling is so conventional, some critics (and fans) would've preferred it if Ringo Lam had stayed with contemporary thrillers with a potentially political edge, like the *On Fire* series.

Tsui Hark as producer seems to have been thinking of his upcoming production of *The Blade* which has the same sort of earthy, grim, bloody feel. This is the cruel underbelly of the *jiangzhu*, where sudden death never seems very far away.

---

25 The box office in Canton was poor – $1.8m gross.

*Burning Paradise* contains some crude humour, too – as one would expect from a Tsui Hark-produced film which takes a much earthier approach to the swordplay genre.

▶

Once again, it's the Imperial forces who play the bad guys – Qing troops in black and red, and the super-villain is the customary aged Qing (Manchu) official.

The super-villain of *Burning Paradise*, Elder Kung (played with scene-chewing relish by Wong Kam-long), is a thoroughly nasty piece of work – cruel, creepy, ugly, selfish, decadent and fatally, murderously bored. He is the sort of guy who, when interrupted in the bedroom in the middle of seducing the captured heroine, races towards the hapless underling who's dared enter the chamber and decapitates her. And then he arrogantly brandishes the severed head while pontificating on his evil schemes.

In a truly bizarre piece of business, Elder Kung is also a frustrated artist! He's Jackson Pollock as Fu Manchu, the super-villain as a New York action painter. Thus, during a dialogue scene with the heroes, Kung is also painting (the heroes, understandably, can't make head or tail of this). Kung is the sort of artist who, when he wants a blood-red colour, will cut one of his victims to drip out some *real* blood. Even more inventive, Kung deploys his brushes and pigment as weapons in the finale, turning drops of paint flung at Fong and Hung into bullets.

▶

The opening sequence of *Burning Paradise* features the mandatory Big Action Scene – it's a rip-roaring blast of rapidfire action, swordplay, gory gags,[26] tumbling and horseback stunts, set in the dusty desert (the terrain of *New Dragon Gate Inn* and *The Blade* ). As Fong Sai-yuk, Willie Chi performs numerous Peking Opera acrobatics – why scramble inelegantly across the desert floor when you can tumble and somersault like an actor making his entrance on stage?

Following the sunlit opening sequence (which also introduces the main female character, Dou Dou, played by Carman Lee), *Burning Paradise* dives into the darkness and horror of the Red Lotus Temple, a very elaborate set which's almost the star of the show (courtesy of art director Ranxin Qu). It draws on many classic examples from the action-adventure genre – every cheesy, historical picture of the 1960s, for instance, or the Indian temple in *Indiana Jones and the Temple of Doom* which housed the Kali cult. The temple is a labyrinth of multiple levels, fire pits, walkways, drawbridges, ropes, and more booby traps and hidden weapons than a *Dungeons and Dragons* game (stakes, flying darts, trapdoors, poisoned gas, etc).

Fire is one of the signature motifs here (as always in Hong Kong cinema, and director Ringo Lam Ling-tung is very fond of it – his best-known films are the *On Fire* series) – it seems to be burning everywhere, giving the interior scenes a hallucinatory, flickering atmosphere, and suggesting that an apocalypse is about to be unleashed at any moment,

---

26 Limbs're sliced off, and a horse is decapitated.

and is barely being suppressed. (Hong Kong action movies might not have budgets big enough for intricate visual effects to match Hollywood, but there's always money for gasoline). And outside, the Red Lotus Temple has victims hung upside-down on poles, buried in the ground, and a pile of skulls.

▶

So, *Burning Paradise* ends exactly as you expect, with plenty of fights, a colossal smackdown between Hung Hei-kwuen and Fong Sai-yuk and Elder Kung, the heroes managing to flee, and the mandatory explosions which destory the Red Lotus Temple.

Or, put it another way: the fights simply continue, as they have done throughout acts one and two of *Burning Paradise*. But they get bigger and wilder. We know that Ringo Lam is fond of fire in his movies, and that Hong Kong filmmakers never let a chance to set fire to something go by, but *Burning Paradise* is pretty over-the-top even by Hong Kong action cinema standards. The crew must've carried cigarette lighters, matches, gas bottles, petrol cannisters and flame-throwers all the time).

▶

Is *Burning Paradise* a scorching political critique of contemporary China? Is it a hyper-intelligent deconstruction of modern life in Asia? Is it a postmodern philosophical disquisition on the precariousness of being alive in nineteen ninety-four?

No.

It's actually a very old-fashioned movie, despite its raw energy and is revitalizing of the *wuxia pian* genre in 1994's Hong Kong. Old-fashioned to the point where the characterizations are paper-thin and archaic, and the narrative structure is gloriously simplistic. The *delivery* of that simplicity is fiendishly complicated, however, mechanically and cinematically. (Indeed, as Ringo Lam remarked of *Full Contact*, he wanted to avoid political commentary – this seems to have been the case with *Burning Paradise*, too).

# 19

# DR WAI IN "THE SCRIPTURE WITH NO WORDS"

## Yale: Mo Him Wong

*Dr Wai In "The Scripture With No Words"* (*Yale: Mo Him Wong*, a.k.a. *Mao Xian Wang*, 1996) is an action-adventure comedy starring Jet Li and directed by Tony Ching Siu-tung. Produced by Tsai Mu-ho, Wong Sing-ping and Charles Heung Wah-keung for Win's Entertainment and Eastern Production; exec. producer: Tiffany Chen Ming-Ying; wr. by Lam Wai-Lun, Roy Szeto Cheuk-hon and Sandy Shaw Lai-King; DPs: Tom Lau Moon-tong and Edmond Fung Yuen-man; music by Frankie Chan; ed. by Marco Mak Chi-sin and Angie Lam; art dirs.: Jason Mok, Kenneth Yee Chung-man and Fu Tak-Lam; hair by Chau Siu-Mui; costumes by Mok Kwan-kit, William Fung Kwun-Man and Chan Gai-Dung; make-up: Man Yun-Ling and Xu Qiu-Wen; and action dirs.: Tony Ching and Ma Yuk-shing. Released: Mch 14, 1996. 87/ 91 mins.

The teaming of Ching Siu-tung and Jet Li as actor and director has produced some of the finest moments in recent, Chinese cinema – *Hero, The Warlords, The Swordsman 2, The Emperor and the White Snake*, etc (Ching brings the best out of Li, and Li inspires Ching to ever-greater filmic heights). *Dr Wai* features terrific support from Rosamund Kwan, Takeshi Kaneshiro, Charlie Yeung, Ngai Sing, Billy Chow and Law Kar-ying.

The production of *Dr Wai* was set back by a fire[27] which ruined film sets (that cost HK $10 million – a lot of money in the Hong Kong film industry). *Dr Wai* globe-trots – from the desert in Xian to Shanghai to the Great Wall of China (some of the film was shot in and around Beijing).

A higher budget outing than your average Hong Kong picture, you can see the Hong Kong dollars being burnt up on the screen as a railroad engine careens thru a crowded downtown area (and thru the facades of several buildings), sending stunt guys flying in all directions; as a prehistoric, mechanical Golden Ox out of Homer's *Odyssey* goes haywire

---

27 It's scary just how many fires occur in every film production centre on Earth, even today.

(in the prologue); and later buildings are collapsing; characters smash through brick walls, and so on.

A historical adventure set in the 1930s in Shanghai, during the Japanese Occupation, *Dr Wai* doesn't labour its political elements, because they are already shining in neon (particularly when *Dr Wai* was released a year before the 1997 Hand-over). An oppressive regime – no, *two* oppressive regimes are here! – Japan and Mainland China! And quite a bit of time is spent with a newspaper that's struggling to keeping on reporting the news in the face of aggressive social and political forces, a commentary upon governments suppressing the media. The newspaper is run by an editor called the Headmaster, played by Hong Kong veteran Law Kar-ying. (And during the finale, a vision of the future is shown to the heroes, in the form of newsreel footage of the fall of Japan in WWII and the atomic bombs. To put those serious issues into a goofy action-adventure yarn is unusual).

However, Chinese cinema, and Hong Kong cinema, has mined the political conflicts between China and Japan many, many times. You can bet that ever since the 1930s the issue has appeared in several films every year. It is a very familiar political background, which can be evoked instantly in a shorthand manner. The audience knows exactly where they are. (And, like all explosive situations or war zones, you can plump your characters down in the midst of it all and generate instant drama).

Dr Wai is portrayed as the superhero-ish, all-round adventurer of a million movie serials – he can ride horses (and leap from them), he can wisecrack, he can flirt with women, and he can beat up henchmen like it's nothing. And nothing is ever seriously in jeopardy because, as with those million adventure movies, we know that the hero will always prevail. But we go along for the ride.

It works also because of the casting – the role was clearly written by Roy Szeto Cheuk-hon, Lam Wai-Lun and Sandy Shaw Lai-King knowing that Jet Li would be playing Dr Wai and Chow Si-Kit in the present day. Similarly, the romantic subplots work because they are built around the sort of characters that Rosamund Kwan plays (in particular opposite Li, as in the *Once Upon a Time In China* series).

*Dr Wai In "The Scripture With No Words"* is a counterpart (and a kind of sequel) to *The Terracotta Warrior,* which Tony Ching Siu-tung directed in 1989: both are comical adventures in the Hollywood Hokum style, which travel between the past and the present (tho' the present day in *The Terracotta Warrior* is the Thirties, and here we go back from the present – 1996 – to the Thirties. And back even further, to set up the MacGuffin, the magical box).

*Dr Wai In "The Scripture With No Words"* shamelessly steals from the *Indiana Jones* series,[28] just as *The Terracotta Warrior* had done (and Jackie Chan did in his *Armor of God* films): Dr Wai is an archæologist adventurer who's charged with finding a magical box from ancient times (the box leads to the scripture). So there's a comical sidekick, a *femme*

---

28 And from Dr Wisley Wei by Ni Kuang.

*fatale* among the Japanese, outrageous action set-pieces, and our hero's pitted against numerous henchmen as he fights for the Right and the Good.

*Dr Wai In "The Scripture With No Words"* is more Hong Kong hokum, delivered with a breezy touch which makes the Hollywood action movie counterparts look like rusty tanks mired in mud. So light, so fast! – *Dr Wai* hurtles along like the out-of-control steam engine in one of its very expensive set-pieces.

And the wonder of *Dr Wai* is of course Jet Li – and Li as directed by the amazing Tony Ching Siu-tung, a director who never lets mere physical laws hold back his performers or his movies. If Ching wants to place an actor *right up there*, he doesn't let anything or anyone stop him doing it! And Li moves with the grace of Gene Kelly or Fred Astaire at their very best. The man is a cinematic dream, a man who exudes more charisma and charm than a whole army of wannabe stars.

Dr Wai is a counterpoint to Wong Fei-hung in the Jet Li cinematic canon of the Nineties era – again, he's clad in white and pale colours (and one of the only guys wearing a hat, so you can spot him anywhere). At one point, he uses an umbrella as a weapon, as he does in the *Once Upon a Time In China* series.

Once again Jet Li has a flirtatious relationship with Rosamund Kwan, his co-star in the *Once Upon a Time In China* series (and other movies, such as *The Swordsman 2*). In the present day, Kwan is Chow Si-Kit's wife in the process of a fractious divorce with Chow; in the past, Kwan plays a formidable Japanese agent, Cammy.

And the teaming of Jet Li with the gorgeous Takeshi Kaneshiro as his comical sidekick Shing is a winner – Kaneshiro gamely goofs it up for the camera (stepping away from his familiar serious dramatic roles,[29] or his soap operaish parts). The 1996 movie contains two flirtatious relationships – between Dr Wai and Cammy, and between Shing and Yan-yan.

One of the delights of *Dr Wai In "The Scripture With No Words"* is seeing familiar Hong Kong stars cutting loose a little – Rosamund Kwan, under-rated by some Western critics as pretty and pert but merely adequate as an actress, gets to play a woman who conducts dodgy laboratory experiments on men! This includes the sight of Kwan playing Madame Cammy as a dominatrix in black wielding a whip. (Kwan is more game for trying new things than critics giver her credit for. Look at her in *Assassins* (Bill Chung Siu-hung, 1993), for instance. And any actress is going to jump at the chance to fling a whip about, clad in clingy black dress like a 1930s Catwoman, and perform martial arts stunts that run rings around the guys).

Another scene where actors let their hair down – literally – has Messers Kaneshiro and Li dragging up as two of mobster Hung Sing's many concubines. They're in glitzy drag so that they can perform another staple of the action-adventure genre – the comical heist (to snaffle a document from the Japanese Embassy in Shanghai during a high-class

---

29 Is this the same Takeshi Kaneshiro who smoulders so impressively in *The House of Flying Daggers?* It's hard to believe!

function). The Embassy party gives us the ritzy setting for a picture set in Shanghai in the 1930s.

The scene where Dr Wai and Cammy are in a near-clinch in the office with the safe in the Embassy seems especially Tsui Harkian in its evocation of crossdressing – a man in drag is almost-about-to seduce a woman. (It's funny also because it draws on the characters that Kwan and Li have played together. Earlier, Kaneshiro and Li deflect the amorous attentions of two guys).

※

Once again, Tony Ching Siu-tung demonstrates his mastery of visual effects in *Dr Wai In "The Scripture With No Words"*. Indeed, he may be the finest film director of visual effects in Hong Kong, even including Tsui Hark. Models, optical effects, digital animation, special make-up, and 100s of practical effects, *Dr Wai* is virtually a whole history of visual effects filmmaking.[30] Exploding buildings, collapsing walls, a sword duel with giant, flaming swords – *Dr Wai* has got the lot. Jet Li fights Sumo wrestlers (!), grapples a giant rat, parachutes out of a crashing plane with Rosamund Kwan, and dispatches henchmen by the score.

There are rivals after the godly box, as in the usual treasure seeking plot – such as the gangster Hung Sing (a.k.a. Hung Hung Sing Sing, played by Colin Chou). The heroes have several tussles with Hung Sing – the finest one climaxes act two, and features Dr Wai using wire in the ninja fashion fired from fountain pens (because he's an author, right? And the pen is mightier than the sword). In a warehouse setting, the participants smash into piles of iron pipes, scaffolding and the mandatory ingredient of any Hong Kong action scene: large glass windows. Dr Wai gallops into the fray on a horse and carriage, and Hung Sing uses a huge steel pulley to smash it to pieces and knock out the horse.

This is one of the great duels in Jet Li's film career – it's played in the comical action style, but that doesn't make it less impressive on a physical and practical level. The King of Adventurers tops every move or gadget that Hung Sing produces – a rifle, a pistol, etc. In a send-up of *Once Upon a Time In China*, Dr Wai fires the spines of an umbrella at Hung, piercing him like a pin cushion. Dr Wai doesn't finish off Hung (he escapes), but he does save the newspaper editor, the Headmaster.

Another action sequence in act two of *Dr Wai* sees a bunch of heavies storming the newspaper offices to beat up the Headmaster and threaten the operation (the Headmaster turns out to be a martial artist as well as a journalist fighting for free speech). Charlie Yeung – very cute in bunches and overalls – receives her finest moment in *Dr Wai* when she takes on the hoods out in the street.[31] Tiny and skinny she may be, but with Tony Ching directing the film, Yeung can be portrayed as kicking ass (including with several kicks). Yeung is good – but Jet Li is better, entering the fray and demonstrating once again why he's such a wonderful action movie star.

30 Thomas Weisser enthused: 'the most impressive collection of special effects ever amassed for one movie' (58).
31 Dr Wai comes up the idea of having everybody carrying fake boxes, and splitting up outside, to put the heavies off the scent.

Yet another action scene – which tops act two – sees the King of Adventurers taking on Sumo wrestlers, of all things. It seems to be a case of the writers answering the question: who *hasn't* Jet Li battled yet in a movie? (There is a connection, albeit tenuous – some of the villainous forces in *Dr Wai* are Japanese).

While Shing wisely hides during the fights (in the role of the cowardly sidekick), Dr Wai dispatches the Sumo wrestlers. And before that, he tackles the famous 'Chinjas', Tony Ching's version of Japanese ninjas. It's not a Ching movie without a bunch of stunt guys dressed in black, Japanese *shinobi* outfits: here, Dr Wai employs sneaky moves of the *James Bond* sort: frying the ninjas with electricity as they're connected by metal chains to a wire fence, for example (the same wire fence that Dr Wai had used to deflect their throwing stars).

✳

One half of the final act of *Dr Wai* takes place in a plane flying towards the Great Wall of China. Many of the gags in the aircraft are self-consciously old-fashioned – this might be a Bob Hope and Bing Crosby *Road To…* movie from the 1940s. Hung Sing is by now the all-purpose villain, exploding into the scene from the floor of the plane, and continuing into the temple finale. Plus we have that very dangerous box, and explosives, too, and people switching sides – so there are plenty of ingredients for the writers to use to keep the adventure bubbling along. The plane has to crash, and our heroes have to bail out – this is an *Indiana Jones* type of movie. The budget of *Dr Wai* was high enough to film real aerial footage and freefall images not often seen in Hong Kong cinema.

In the second half of the finale of *Dr Wai* – in the usual setting of the Big Set (statues, a temple, sand, flickering torches) – there are four heroes – Jet Li, Rosamund Kwan, Takeshi Kaneshiro and Charlie Yeung. They make an appealing group, and you look at them and think, wait a minute, it's two guys and two women! It's nearly always several guys and one woman in the finale of any action-adventure flick (if the female chara is included at all, or she's a hostage to be rescued).

Hung Sing returns to create mayhem in the underground temple, battling each of the heroes in a series of farcical fights as they struggle to keep hold of the magical box. The to-ing and fro-ing is rapid and complicated: every part of the set is used for bits of comical business.

The flaming swords duel is a marvellous combination of practical effects and optical animation: the swords flail like whips, scorching the ground, and sending out sparks when they clash. The magic box performs plenty of work in the finale, too: it's opened several times and transforms the characters into æthereal forms, including being composed of little, steel balls (these are early versions of computer-aided effects).

*Dr Wai* is funny, too. Our heroes ask to see the future from a wise sage who materializes when the box and the scripture are re-united; they look on a wedding scene: when Shing asks to see his finest achievement in the future, it's the same scene (much to Yan-yan's dismay). Meanwhile, Dr Wai carries the romantic subplot – the estrangement from his wife,

Monica (so that the stories in the past and the present day scenes continue to mingle).

✳

The 1996 movie for some versions included additional footage overseen by Tsui Hark and Gordon Chan.32 The scenes created a framing story set in the present day, with Jet Li as Chow Si-Kit, a writer, and his sidekicks. Tsui's influence on *Dr Wai In "The Scripture With No Words"* is obvious, from the look, the pace and the visual fx to the casting and the story (Tsui has explored the same era several times). The movie featured some of the same crew that work regularly with Tsui.

And yet, the reception/ perception of *Dr Wai In "The Scripture With No Words"* in the West has been hampered by poor print quality, and an English dub which doesn't always clarify the time-jumping plot. *Dr Wai In "The Scripture With No Words"* deserves to be better known as a nimble, funny and occasionally spectacular outing. (Unfortunately, shoddy prints with bad audio harm the impact of too many Hong Kong movies. They look like they were tossed away after they'd been used for a month in the theatres, and somebody picked up the film cans from the garbage. These sorts of pics really do need vivid, sharp prints and bright, clear sound).

*Dr Wai In "The Scripture With No Words"* is a time travel movie, a movie with two time zones, and a movie with real sections and fictional sections (in the Cantonese version). The gimmick that ties it together is that the hero, Chow Si-Kit, is a writer, and the movie portrays his stories. So we are cutting back and forth between the 'real' present day and the fictional past. In the present tense, as well as writing his novel, Chow is struggling with the divorce of his wife Monica Kwan (Rosamund Kwan). In the past, multiple stories are related: the main one is the quest/ chase narrative of the magical scripture and the special box.

A third time travel layer in *Dr Wai* involves the back-story of the Pandora's Box: it's part of a ferocious battle sequence featuring the Salt Gang with swords, guns and horses (their descendants in the Thirties are searching for the box). In the flashback, the box is opened and all Hell breaks loose (white light bursts out, as always, and the warriors are frazzled. It's another Ark of the Covenant-style sequence from *Raiders of the Lost Ark*).

Knitting the skittering narrative structure together in *Dr Wai* are several voiceovers, and the actors playing dual roles, in the manner of *The Wizard of Oz*. So Chow Si-Kit the writer also plays Dr Wai, the King of Adventurers, in the past. His assistant, Shing (Takeshi Kaneshiro) appears as the goofball Shing, his other assistant, the punky Yvonne (Charlie Yeung), is Yan-yan, and Monica, Chow's soon-to-be-ex-wife (Rosamund Kwan), is also Madame Cammy, a Japanese agent.

It sounds complicated because it *is* complicated, but the 1996 movie delivers the narrative structure in a light-hearted, comical-adventurous (and comicbook) manner. Once the film has cut back and forth a couple of times, the narrative structure is easy to follow. (Several movies more

---

32 Some say it was for the Hong Kong version, others for the international version.

recently have approached fantasy and writing in the same way, with the reality and the fantasy intermingling, and commenting upon each other).

As the story progresses in *Dr Wai*, the characters change according to input from Chow Si-Kit: Cammy, for instance, starts the movie as a Japanese agent dominatrix but becomes more genteel towards the end, dressing in a traditional *kimono*. (Both Shing and Yvonne have been adjusting the story while Chow is away or asleep; Chow also alters their take on the plot when he sees what they've written. And while Chow is in hospital, and Monica visits him, she rewrites the ending of his story).

The framing story receives a happy ending, with the estranged husband and wife agreeing not to sign the divorce papers. They appear in the final shot, on the streets of downtown Hong Kong.

Dithering about in the present day is a trifling matter of little significance – as Chow Si-kit gets writer's block and can't think of any new plots, and battles with his dissatisfied wife Monica.

The 1930s action-adventure parts of *Dr Wai* are far more compelling than the present-day scenes: the comical antics of Chow, Shing and Yvonne in the newspaper office, and the angry encounters between Chow and his wife Monica, are over-shadowed by the 1930s sections. The editing between the two time zones is slick – *Dr Wai* was cut by the two finest editors in Chinese cinema – Marco Mak Chi-sin and Angie Lam, but the modern-day scenes are just too routine, and they don't exploit the potential of the four actors (Li, Kwan, Kaneshiro and Yeung). And the addition of voiceovers to explain things as we hop between now and then isn't necessary.

But this might be because framing stories in general are seldom as gripping as the main story, as in two Tim Burton pics, *Edward Scissorhands* (1991) and *Alice In Wonderland* (2010). Not every movie can be *The Wizard of Oz*, where the framing story is essential.

　　✳

As usual with over-the-top, Hong Kong comicbook movies, the usual critics didn't go for it, and the usual critics enjoyed it (you know who they are – is it worth quoting them again?). So the grumpy critics complained about the lack of story, the paper-thin characters, the adolescent tone, etc, and the positive critics enjoyed the self-conscious hokum, the vivid photography, and the visual effects.

*Dr Wai In "The Scripture With No Words"* is not a movie to resist or to fight, as with a Hollywood musical movie, or forerunners like *Romancing the Stone* and *Indiana Jones*. You're wasting your time.

For fans of Hong Kong action cinema, there is plenty to enjoy here – not least in seeing Jet Li in a non-serious role (except perhaps in the angry divorce scenes with Rosamund Kwan). Li, as his portrayal of Wong Fei-hung showed, is a very appealing action hero. And when he sends himself up (as in his Wong Jing-directed films), it's even better.

# 20

# *SHANGHAI GRAND*

# *Xin Shanghai Tan*

*Shanghai Grand* (Cantonese: *San Seong Hoi Taan*, 1996) was prod. by Win's Entertainment and Film Workshop; co-written by Sandy Shaw Lai-King, Matthew Chow Hoi-kwong and Poon Man-kit; dir. Poon Man-kit; prod.: Tiffany Chen and Tsui Hark; ed: Marco Mak Chi-sin; art dir.: Bruce Yu Ka-on; music: Wu Wai-lap and Raymond Wong;[33] and DP: Poon Hang-sang. Released: July 13, 1996. 96 mins.

*Shanghai Grand* starred Andy Lau Tak-wah, Leslie Cheung Kwok-wing, Ning Jing, Wu Hsing-kuo, Amanda Lee, Jung Woo-sung, Almen Wong Pui-ha, Chan Kin-yat, Jung Woo-sung, Lee Kin-yan, Tse Liu-shut, Yip Chun and Lau Shun. It was filmed in Shanghai, on the Old Shanghai set at the Shanghai Film Studios.

A period gangster tale, set in the 1930s, just prior to the Sino-Japanese War, it was based on the TV series *The Bund* of 1980 (where Chow Yun-fat had played the Leslie Cheung role of Hui Man-keung, the Taiwanese spy).

Any film starring Andy Lau *and* Leslie Cheung is going to be watchable (just one of them is plenty already). They are both amazing, as always. Lau – 35 at the time – manages to play a youth on the make who's around 19 or 20. Meanwhile, Cheung is timeless, ageless, matchless.

*Shanghai Grand* 'displays Tsui's talent as a producer to the fullest and finest effect', noted Lisa Morton (LM, 208). Definitely – this is a big production for a Chinese movie, recreating Shanghai of the 1930s with a keen eye for detail. The streets teem with extras, period cars, trucks, trams, markets, cinemas, and tenements. And the film called for a host of character actors to fulfil the roles of gangsters lower down the pecking order in the Triads. A huge production like this requires the producers – Tsui Hark and Tiffany Chen – to keep on top of a big cast and challenging scenes.

&.

---

33 Andy Lau sang the insert songs and the theme songs (rather than Leslie Chueng).

*Shanghai Grand* establishes itself as a rough-and-ready and scarily violent movie from the opening sequence, which wrongfoots the audience by being set at sea, at night, and in a storm. The star, Leslie Cheung Kwok-wing, is introduced as one of a bunch of captives being menaced by a very nasty Chinese bruiser (Yiu's assassin) played by Almen Wong Pui-ha (she was Madame M. in *Naked Weapon*).

In subsequent scenes, the violence of the Triad world is graphically portrayed – torture with axes and nails hammered into pieces of wood are just the beginning (in the climax of act one). It's as if the movie, being Category IIA rated, is keen to show what the television drama of 1980 wasn't allowed to show.

So this is Ye Olde China, where the struggle to survive in the Big, Bad City is uppermost; everyone is jostling for a better deal (or even just a decent meal). *Shanghau Grand's* story charts the progress of two young men (played by Leslie Cheung and Andy Lau) as they navigate the cruel, uncaring world of modern China. They begin as underlings in the world of organized crime (where they are rudely and aggressively belittled by their superiors), and fight to establish themselves.

The first act of *Shanghai Grand* charts the tussles of Ting Lik (Andy Lau) and Hui Man-keung (Leslie Cheung) with the Triad outfits in Shanghai, building up to an intense face-off with one of the Mr Bigs in town, Brother Wing of the Axe Gang (this is after Ting has set about Shorty Chiu in a quarrel over Fung Ching-ching (Ning Jing), daughter of Triad boss Fung King-yiu). [34] The action is fast and furious in the climax of act 1 of *Shanghai Grand*, with Ting and Hui managing to kill Brother Wing and his henchmen (the dependable Stephen Tung Wai was action choreographer).

The rise to power follows in act two of *Shanghai Grand*, with Ting Lik becoming a boss of his own criminal outfit. Act two climaxes with an enormous fire-fight with Hui Man-keung taking on 10,000 henchmen, while having to protect Ching-ching from the crossfire. In *Shanghai Grand*, Leslie Cheung seems to be continually harrassed by heavies with guns.

*Shanghai Grand* closes with several fire-fights and tussles. The most over-the-top one sees Ting Lik being trapped by the *femme fatale* Yiu's assassin (Almen Wong), and chained to a bed. The S/M play is enhanced when the assassin produces a giant snake to take care of Ting (typing her as a *femme fatale* out of mythology, a snake-woman). But then, this is a Hong Kong action movie, so death by snake is not unusual: thus, Andy Lau is being squeezed by the boa constrictor until he wrestles himself free, and sets it on the *femme fatale*.

Crime doesn't pay – in this movie, anyway. So both Ting and Hui have to die – in two big action sequences. Both deaths are heroic – Ting is riddled with bullets next to his limo and expires in a crucifixion pose. Hui sinks into the Big Sleep in a getaway car, thinking back to his life with his brother-in-arms, Ting.

---

34 There's a romantic sub-plot in *Shanghai Grand*, with Ting hankering after Boss Fung's daughter Fung Ching-ching (caught between the two, Ching-ching is partly the cause of everything going wrong).

# 21

# *BLACK MASK*

## *Hak Hap*

*Black Mask* (Daniel Lee Yan-kong,[35] 1996, *Hei Xia* in Mandarin = *Black Hero*) was a superhero movie starring Jet Li, produced by Tsui Hark and action directed by Yuen Woo-ping and Deon Lam Dik-on. The story was by Lee Tat Chi and Pang Chi Ming. The script was by Teddy Chan, Ann Hui, Tsui Hark and Joe Ma. Tony Cheung was DP. Music was by Teddy Robin Kwan.[36] Editing by Cheung Ka-Fai. Make-up and costumes by Fung Kwan-man and Kwan Mei-bo. Art dir. by Eddie Ma Poon-chiu and Bil Lui. Produced by Film Workshop/ Tommy Boy/ Win's Entertainment. Box office: HK $13,286,788 and U.S. $12,504,289. Released: Nov 9, 1996. 102 mins (89 mins in the U.S.A.).

In the cast were Jet Li, Damian Lau Ching-wan, Karen Mok, Xiong Xin-xin, Françoise Yip, Moses Chan, Patrick Lung, Anthony Wong Chau-sang, Russ Price and Winston Ellis (a superb cast). And they're given names from Hong Kong cinema (Tsui, Shek, Szeto, etc). Altho' Tsui Hark is one of four writers on *Black Mask* (the others were Teddy Chan, Joe Ma and, intriguingly, director Ann Hui), his influence can be discerned in many places (such as casting, action, visuals, prominent female charas, and the gender reversals).

*Black Mask* was adapted from the 1992 comic by Li Chi-Tak: this was a *manhua,* a term for *manga*-style comics which employ Japanese comicbook forms but are produced in China (they're called *manhwa* in Korea, and 'international *manga*' or 'global *manga*' for other territories).

*Black Mask* was considered strong enough as a commercial proposition to have several dubs and versions, including a British one. As usual, different territories used different sound mixes (the North American version added a hip-hop score, for instance), with the Taiwanese print containing scenes that weren't in any other print.

Among superhero movies, and *manga*-ish movies, *Black Mask* is very

35 Daniel Lee (b. 1960) started out as an art director. He later directed big Chinese movies such as *The Climbers, Dragon Blade, 14 Blades, Time Raiders* and *Three Kingdoms.*
36 In the Cantonese cut, not in the international cut (where it was hip-hop music).

fine indeed. It's suitably ridiculous in its concept and story, delightfully wild in its visuals and its action, and features a strong, appealing cast. The visual style is an entertaining cinematic approximation of a 'comicbook' style, in the manner of Western flicks like *Dick Tracy* (1990), *The Crow* (1994) and *Batman* (1989). Meanwhile, Oriental pictures such as *City Hunter* (1993) and *The Wicked City* (1992),[37] which Tsui Hark produced, are forerunners of *Black Mask* (and also based on Japanese comics).

There's a fervid, restless, even apocalyptic intensity to *Black Mask*, a reflection perhaps of the unease in Hong Kong pre-Handover (that's the right-on, intellectual, left-liberal interpretation). Or maybe the filmmakers just enjoyed conjuring flashy, blue-hued, off-kilter camerawork, wobbly, back-lit close-ups of Chinese actors glaring at each other, wild wire-work stunts, and a score comprising twangy guitar.

*Black Mask* is one of those comicbook adaptations where every set seems to have water dripping in front of the camera lens (because it looks cool, right?) – even characters who're making tons of money can't afford to repair their roofs. It's the TV commercial and MTV pop promo approach – backlighting, smoke, rain, shiny surfaces, plastic, concrete, PVC, long lenses, all of those glossy, ad-man visual devices which film critics continue to insist on dubbing 'stylish' (a term devoid of value).

*Black Mask* has affinities of mood and approach with trashy thrillers such as *Naked Killer* (1992)[38] – guns, cars, cops, gangsters, and bondage gear. In fact, you could intercut parts of *Black Mask* with *Naked Killer* or many sleazy Hong Kong thrillers and it would fit seamlessly (but that's true of 99% of the movies made in Hong Kong!). Because, in spite of its sci-fi concepts, its computers, its superhero elements and its comicboook visuals, *Black Mask* is still a thriller involving crime lords and cops set in contemporary Hong Kong.

❂

The character of Tsui Chik fits Jet Li like a glove (Li has the uncanny ability to slip into every one of his roles seamlessly, yet of course he always remains 'Jet Li', and we are always conscious of looking at superstar 'Jet Li' in every single one of his performances. The same thing occurs with actors like Marlon Brando and Orson Welles. However, Li isn't one of those stars who always seem to play the same sort of character, with a paper-thin acting range (like Robert Redford or John Wayne). Tsui Chik in *Black Mask* is utterly different from Wong Fei-hung or Fong Sai-yuk, for instance!).

Black Mask is not Wong Fei-hung – there's no question that Black

---

37 *Black Mask* is a kind of follow-up to *The Wicked City* (it's conceived in similar over-the-top, cartoony colours).
38 From its fab title to its beyond-camp approach to weary old crime/ triller clichés and scenarios, *Naked Killer* is a hoot. *Naked Killer* boasts a terrific, up-for-it cast (Chingmy Yau Suk-ching, Carrie Ng Kar-lai, Simon Yam Tat-wah, Sugawara Madoka, Kelly Yiu and Johnny Lo Hwei-kong), who deliver with just the right amount of bitchy seriousness and mock drama.
Like *Black Mask*, *Naked Killer* is paper-thin, has no more meaning than a plastic cup, and is gloriously, gleefully violent. And it goes much further than Tsui Hark's evocations of wild women: *Naked Killer* understands that a really furious woman wreaking her revenge on guys, beating them up, kicking them in the balls (and stabbing their balls), smashing her fists into their faces, piercing them with a pair of scissors, and tearing off their bits, is very funny. Especially when the person doing that is the super-babe Chingmy Yau!

Mask is going to wield a gun! Fighting off assailants with an umbrella just wouldn't cut it here! Indeed, the body count in *Black Mask* is very high (and gory), as henchmen are blasted away (and stabbed, and blown up) with alarming regularity.

❁

So Tsui Chik is a kick-ass action hero who's undergone one of those shadowy government/ military (Nazi-like) experiments to make him impervious to pain (that he's a superhuman warrior is a given – he's played by Jet Li!). Tsui was part of the 701 Squad, an elite, S.W.A.T.-style assassination team (tho' for which nation isn't stated).[39] But he's going straight now, having left the 701 Squad (following the prologue): now he's a librarian! (The later flashback explains that Tsui escaped the 701 Squad, also rescuing Yeuk-lan. The rest were hunted down by their creators. No, don't ask why Tsui has managed to elude them).

We see this back-story in *Black Mask* in the black-and-white preamble (which features routine laboratory and experiment scenery, with big close-ups of injections, and the victim reacting with howls of agony[40]); the credits and prologue are different in the international versions (the Cantonese version includes a voiceover from Tsui Chik which explains more; the narration in the international cuts emphasizes different elements). So, yes, it *is* pretty hokey – but no more'n *every single superhero movie you've ever seen!* Name me a superhero movie with a premise that *isn't* childishly dumb! (Even the term, 'superhero', means god-like heroism).

After all, why would anybody dress up in a silly Bat costume to fight crime? Director Tim Burton, producer Jon Peters *et al* wrestled with that in 1989, for the *Batman* movie, and didn't crack it (their solution – he's mad! schizo! – isn't convincing. Later *Bat*-flicks didn't satisfactorily solve it, either).

So *Black Mask* doesn't make sense in many places – but that's no different from most (all?) superhero movies. And there are parts where a Western audience might require a little more help with the story. For instance: what do the villains want?[41] But all you need to know to enjoy *Black Mask* is villains = crime/ drugs/ money/ 701 Squad; the heroes = fighting crime/ ex-701 Squad. With Jet Li in the middle. Sort of.

Next, we see Tsui Chik going into action as Black Mask in an outstanding set-piece of pounding action, hundreds of stunts and gags, wirework, explosions, machine guns, vehicles, blood, and fire. Yes, and there's even a tank letting loose at the hero (in what appears to be an underground car lot!).[42] As if we needed reminding that we are watching a Tsui Hark/ Yuen-Woo-ping/ Jet Li/ Daniel Lee action movie. (Black Mask is essentially a Japanese ninja, down to his black costume, his bottomless

39 Lisa Morton complained that we don't know much about the 701 Squad, or Tsui Chik, or where they're based, or who's fighting in the opening scene (212).
40 Because no secret laboratory experiment can be tranquil and painless.
41 There's a lot of busying about with computers and discs in the villains' watery den, and evocations of cyber-theft, but it isn't wholly clear. (The jokes about CDs and VCDs being used as weapons are fun – Hong Kong being famous for its rampant video piracy). The background plot, anyway, involves drug syndicates, making money, and revenge for the 701 Squad.
42 The climax of act one looks like it was filmed in the same set, re-dressed.

bag of tricks and weaponry, and his acrobatics and flight. When Black Mask enters a fight, he does so in grand style, and he's shooting at henchmen sliding along a cable, wielding a machine gun. The ninja element is of course yet another that's tailor-made for the Nipponese *animé* market).

Following the explosive opening sequence, *Black Mask* shifts to that most thrilling of all settings in the contemporary, capitalist world: the library! Tsui Chik's double life as a librarian is perfectly nerdish: but you can see Tsui Hark's influence once again, because Tsui is observed thru the eyes of a woman (Tracy – Karen Mok), and in an eroticized manner. This is classic Tsui Hark: so that the guys who gather around Tracy[43] suggest that she might look for a boyfriend nearby (Tracy has hysterics when she's dumped by a guy she hasn't even met yet!). So Tracy contemplates Tsui, finding him too passive, too wimpy, and too geeky for her.

Tsui Hark loves to make a beautiful human being like Jet Li the object of women's affection: it's a running gag thru the *Once Upon a Time In China* series and the *Swordsman* series, for example. That *Black Mask* turns the hero into a sex object in the first ten minutes is typical of Tsui's gender reversal politics.

❀

*Black Mask* was filmed in a cartoony style that looked to Japanese *manga* and *animé* (deep passions for Tsui Hark), as much as North American superhero movies (and the look of science fiction like *Blade Runner. The Green Hornet* is also a reference – Bruce Lee played the Hornet's sidekick Kato in the A.B.C. TV series, 1966). Chinese action movies are very popular in Japan (it's one of Jackie Chan's primary markets). The *manhua* comic by Li Chi-Tak was likely influenced by Chinese action movies as well as taking the form of Japanese *manga* (so the cross-pollenation of cultural influences is considerable).

You can almost see the speech bubbles and the sound effects from a *manga* in *Black Mask*: BAAAAM! KYAAH! KLANG! Bright colours like the colour panels at the front of a *manga* (walls or screens that glow bright red behind the actors in silhouette, for instance), punchy editing (editing like a punch in the face), and off-kilter camera angles *à la* the *Batman* TV show (but, hell, *every* Hong Kong action movie shoots off the horizontal! No camera operator looks thru the eyepiece of a 35mm camera on a Hong Kong picture and gets out a spirit level and agonizes whether the bottom of the frame is perfectly horizontal or not! Besides, everyone's too busy on a Hong Kong set to notice!).

*Black Mask* contains many of the classic ingredients of a superhero franchise, including: (1) the split personality/ role of the superhero: by day he's a mild-mannered librarian! By night he's a gun-totin' ninja! (2) an on-off companion, Tracy; (3) a buddy who doesn't know his secret (cop Shek – Lau Ching-wan); (4) disguises; (5) shadowy government experiments; (6) fearsome villains (Commander Hung Kuk – Patrick Lung Kong); and of course (7) the Big Bad City.

---

43 Her co-workers have slunk in from another movie – a cheesy, romantic comedy, perhaps.

Yes, and the background story in *Black Mask* is about the wars among drug lords in Hong Kong (hell, where have we heard that one before!). Someone is bumping off all of the drug bosses, one by one, in scenes of over-the-top violence and bloodshed (with ridiculous ingredients, like spraying acid from sprinklers that pop up from the floor.[44] Well, hell, this *is* a superhero movie!). And, this being the mid-Nineties, there's also quite a bit of narrative complication involving computers and hacking and the like (tho' nothing that would give *Ghost In the Shell* anything to worry about). Trouble is, computers are dead boring, unless you shift into virtual reality territory, or can think up something as compelling as futuristic thrillers like Masamune Shirow's extraordinary *Ghost In the Shell manga.*

❖

*Black Mask* adds a John Wooian buddy-brothers element to the proceedings, with Tsui Chik's friend, jaded, weary super-cop Inspector Shek (Damian Lau Ching-wan). And, true to the Wooian formula of brotherhood among 'men's men', there is much antagonism between the two, with the usual glaring at each other from inches away (with trembling, sweaty faces).[45] Later, Shek, furious with Tsui over the deaths of his fellow cops, his brothers-in-arms, fights Tsui in a graveyard (of course Tsui bests him, and in the finale ends up rescuing him).

Also in the manic dim sum mix of *Black Mask* is the eye candy of Françoise Yip[46] playing Tsui Chik's former girlfriend Yeuk-lan (we see him saving her from falling to her death in a cheesy, black-and-white flashback). However, when they greet there's no kissing on the cheek, let alone the mouth. Oh no! This is a Jet Li movie! Li does *not* do pecks on the cheek, and certainly does not smooch heroines into submission! So they hug, brother-sister fashion (the S/M and sex is reserved for *femme fatale* Feuk-lan when she's hanging out with the villains). These are middle-act scenes (*Black Mask* is constructed in 3 acts), where back-story is typically inserted. Later in the 1996 movie, Tsui hooks up with the ditzy, child-like (and rather irritating) fellow-librarian Tracy.

The attempts at light-hearted sections in *Black Mask*, some of them built around the kooky behaviour of Tracy (played a little self-consciously by Karen Mok), as she tries to bring a bit of sunshine into the perpetually solemn mood of Tsui Chik, aren't wholly successful (they cook, play video games, etc, while Tracy had been kidnapped by Tsui).[47] These are the elements, as we know, that don't always translate so well overseas (which, with comedy being absolutely primary in Hong Kong cinema, and a major genre, is such a pity).

---

44 How long did it take the villains to install and test those sprinklers?! It's the sort of bonkers concept that looks great, plays great, but doesn't make a lick of sense if you think about it! Ah, but it does deliver a variation on ye olde crime bosses-meeting-in-a-warehouse scene.
45 Indeed, Lisa Morton suggests that both Tsui and Shek may be gay – they don't have girlfriends, and the only flirtation is between Shek and Tsui (LM, 212). Yet Yeuk-lan is definitely portrayed as Tsui's former lover, and Tracy flirts with Tsui.
46 Françoise Yip arrived on the Hong Kong film scene in *Infatuation* (1995) and *Wild* (1996), where she played sexy, out-of-control women.
47 Tsui Chik is a somewhat uncaring hero – he manhandles Tracy roughly, injects her to put her out, and even chains her up for her own safety, while he goes out to battle the bad guys. *Black Mask* is not the finest instance of Tsui Hark's feminism on screen.

This being one of Hong Kong's contemporary action thrillers, the violence in *Black Mask seems* to take on a tougher, rougher edge. Why is it that aggression and conflict *seems* more extreme when it's set in (something like) the present day? Because those *kung fu* movies based in the past are also astonishingly violent! (Is it because audiences can imagine the violence happening to them, that there is less 'distance' between the audience and the acts on screen in something contemporary?).

The filmmakers also include a sadomasochistic motif which seems tailor-made for the Japanese movie market: Tsui Chik's former girlfriend Yeuk-lan is strung up in the air in bondage gear and a coloured wig. (In Japanese *ecchi manga*, this sort of scene is not uncommon. Usually before or after a gang rape scene). Not only that, there's a macabre sex-and-death sequence *à la In the Realm of the Senses*: Yeuk-lan is taken by one of the drug lords, King Kau (played by veteran Hong Kong star Anthony Wong Chau-sang, a fearless actor who'll try anything, and doesn't care how stupid[48] he looks)[49] on a table, right in the middle of a slambang action scene, where Black Mask is hareing around the joint wasting heavies by the dozen (the equivalent in a North American movie would be Princess Leia fooling around with Boba Fett while Luke Skywalker wastes the stormtroopers).

As if this isn't pervy enough, the filmmakers also deliver another item for the Japanese *mondo/ trasho* cinema fans: Yeuk-lan takes a shaving razor out of her *bouche*[50] and slices up the drug lord so he collapses (like a scene from the famous *Lady Snowblood manga* ).

Sex *and* violence! Or rather: sex *and* action *and* violence! And superheroics! It's all fantastically over-the-top, and totally throwaway, utterly disposable like a half-eaten pot of chicken noodles.

On the down side, for a director/ producer who's expressed his wishes to exalt the role of women in his movies, the treatment of Françoise Yip's Feuk-lan – trussed up in S/M gear then schtupped – is probably his lowest point.

*Black Mask* does deliver some gruesome scenes as the filmmakers explore new ways of dispatching henchmen and victims. In one nasty sequence, bodies are hung up in black plastic bags on a rail (like film costumes being stored!), and blood drips out of them onto the lens of the camera as it takes a worm's-eye-view shot. (These corpses are, apparently, King Kau's relatives! That is, if we believe what the very unhinged Kau tells Shek!).

❧

*Black Mask* is jammed with action: the first act (of three acts)

48 Wong sports an incredible costume of shorts and, of all things, a clear, plastic smock.
49 The amazing Anthony Wong also appeared in *Time and Tide*. Lisa Morton called Wong 'arguably the best character actor in the world today'. Certainly, you watch an Anthony Wong performance wondering what the hell he's going to try next.
    Anthony Wong has played psychos regularly (in, for, *Taxi Hunter* and *Retribution Sight Unseen*), a necrophiliac Public Security officer (in *Daughter of Darkness*), a raging queen (in *Lamb Killer*), a cannibal (in *The Untold Story*), and a sadistic spouse in *Love To Kill*). If you want a very scary weirdo, an actor who'll try anything, and doesn't care how ugly he looks, Anthony Wong is your man!
50 A call-back to a gag in *We're Going To Eat You.*

contains the opening teaser; the crime lord warehouse slaugther; and it climaxes with a wild battle at King Kau's place. Act two includes the flashbacks to Tsui Chik and Yeuk-lan and the replay[51] of that scene in the present tense (when Yeuk-lan's ordered to kill Tsui); a scene with Tsui and Tracy in her car being attacked; an enormous battle in a hospital with an unkillable member of the 701 Squad; and the climax of act two – the scaffolding fight. Act three is of course the Big Finish, culminating in the hero vs. villain smackdown.

The hospital action scene (a favourite locale for Hong Kong action movies) is one of the craziest: it's edited by Cheung Ka-Fai like a pinball game, with Inspector Shek getting to shine, and it closes with the mandatory Big Explosion. Yeuk-lan gets tto show off in her own action sequence, duking it out with Shek. Once again, Hong Kong cinema features a woman kicking ass with a ferocity unknown in Western cinema. And once again the blend of stunt doubles with the lead actress (Françoise Yip) is seamless.

The sequence where Commander Hung and his henchmen immobilize and truss up Tracy's car is delightfully inventive (and seems to have been copied wholesale in one of the *Captain America* movies). The scene would be sufficient for many an action movie, but it's only one section of a lengthy bust-up in the back alleys at night between Black Mask and Hung's boys.

In between the numerous action sequences, Inspector Shek and Tsui Chik meet at the police station, talk, contemplate the sunset, and develop their uneasy alliance. And Chik tuts and sighs at Tracy's antics as he keeps her under lock and key (and chain) in his funky industrial digs on the waterside. (Black Mask's identity is maintained in front of Shek and Tracy until about halfway thru the picture).

❱

The rest of *Black Mask* plays out pretty much how you'd expect. The story is, inevitably, fairly routine and formulaic. But, remember folks, a Hong Kong action movie is 30% story and 70% action, as Chow Yun-fat noted. You want 'story'? Go rent *Dr Zhivago* or *Wuthering Heights*! You didn't come here for 'story' and 'characters' and 'themes' and 'issues' and 'philosophy' and hyper-theoretical-psychological-political commentary, now, did you? No! – you came here to see Big Explosions, Daredevil Stunts, Cool Gadgets, and People Beating Up Each Other!

So the bizarre super-villain Commander Hung looms larger as *Black Mask* unfolds, orchestrating the usual Super-Villain Scheme (to control all drug supplies in Asia, or something like that). With his long, straggly hair, tinted round glasses, and Christian paraphernalia (such as crosses and, curiously, a postcard depicting Sandro Botticelli's *Pietà*), Hung (Patrick Lung-kong) is wholly a Japanese *manga* heavy – a cross between John Lennon and a drug addict (there are loads of charas like this in *animé* and *manga*. The Christian symbols type Hung as exotic and foreign – just as Christianity was exotic and foreign to Europe and North America at some

---

51 It's replayed again, in the scaffolding fight.

time. I mean, Christianity is an imported desert religion from 2,000 years ago in the Middle East).

Meanwhile Black Mask is teaming up with Inspector Shek and klutzy Tracy, and fending off assassins in the form of unfeeling super-soldiers.

In *Black Mask*, the filmmakers are blowing stuff up every 2.578 minutes, the stunt team are delivering high impact fight choreography (with 7.915 kicks, 15.600312 punches and 4.56184 blocks per minute), and the soundtrack (by Teddy Robin Kwan) includes retro twangy guitar sounds à la John Barry's timeless *James Bond* scores of the Sixties.

One of the great fights in the second half of *Black Mask* occurs way up in the scaffolding and pipes of a very tall building (it looks like it was a nightmare to shoot, logistically. But Yuen Woo-ping and his stunt team seem to relish a challenge! And of course, one of the hallmarks of the Yuen action style is acrobatics at scary heights). Yeuk-lan arrives as the *femme fatale* super-bitch ordered by He Who Must Be Obeyed (Hung) to kill Tsui Chik.[52] In the event, even tho' she smashes Tsui about a lot, and has him hanging off the building, holding on for dear life (while Tracy tries to save him), Yeuk-lan relents (here the (reprised) flashback where Tsui saved her pays off). But that's not good enough for super-villain Commander Hung (who pops up form nowhere, nearby), and he kills his assassin with a sniper rifle (a pointless murder – just to show who's boss, I guess. And, no, don't ask why Hung doesn't kill Black Mask first, when he's got the opportunity, and deal with Yeuk-lan later. Indeed, this part of *Black Mask* doesn't wholly make sense, story-wise).[53] The scene culminates with another of Tsui Hark's favourite action movie devices – the rapid cable descent (movies like the 1990s *Batman* cycle had popularized giant cable stunts, but it took the Chinese action teams to raise them to the next level. And in films such as *Time and Tide*, the cable descents are astonishing).

The finale of *Black Mask* takes place in the usual spot for any action movie – the villain's lair (a *James Bond*-ish network of tunnels, drains and water – because, yes, it's *below* police headquarters! And nobody in the HQ noticed people hurrying out for noodles at all hours).[54] Fire, water, smoke, explosions, bombs, wirework, motorcycles, super-guns, kickboxing, *kung fu*, empty-handed combat – the finale has the lot, including the expected punchy-kicky duel between the hero and the villain (Patrick Lung as Commander Hung does well with martial arts considering he's a twisted, old coot). There's a riff on the martial arts staple of wet rope – wet, electrical cables (which of course emit sparks).

And, in true Hong Kong tradition, the duel in *Black Mask* goes on much longer than a Western equivalent (partly because it doesn't cut away to parallel scenes). Where a Western movie would pause for witty quips, or

---

52 In a silly moment, Tracy climbs *up* the tower, instead of finding a way to escape *down*, so she can flee. This was reprised in the *Black Mask* sequel (where it's just as dumb).
53 For instance, Tracy, a timid librarian, suddenly becomes a tough sidekick who can raid a hospital for blood and transfuse it into Tsui Chik; and when he's recovered, she keeps pace with Tsui.
54 Water, yes – the villains' lair is stuffed with electrical equipment, and ranks of computers, but there's water everywhere in it! Looks great (gotta have those liquid reflections on the walls, right?), but not health and safety, not good!

other characters hurrying in to help (or watch), the duel only pauses for breath, then it carries on.

Both Commander Hung and Black Mask get beaten around considerably in the final smackdown, which is a brutal affair. It all plays out as expected (the chief henchmen's nobbled (using the laser guns), the villain's killed, Black Mask saves his chum Inspector Shek (he's the princess with a bomb attached), stuff blows up, and afterwards there's a short *dénoue-ment* at a harbour with the three principals.

Wicked City (1992).

The Magic Crane (1993).

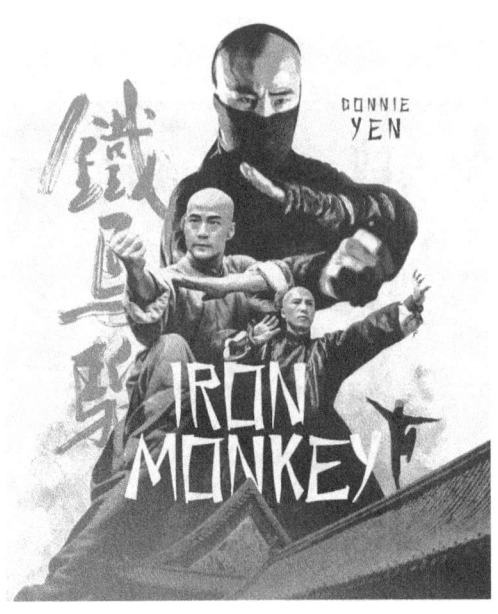

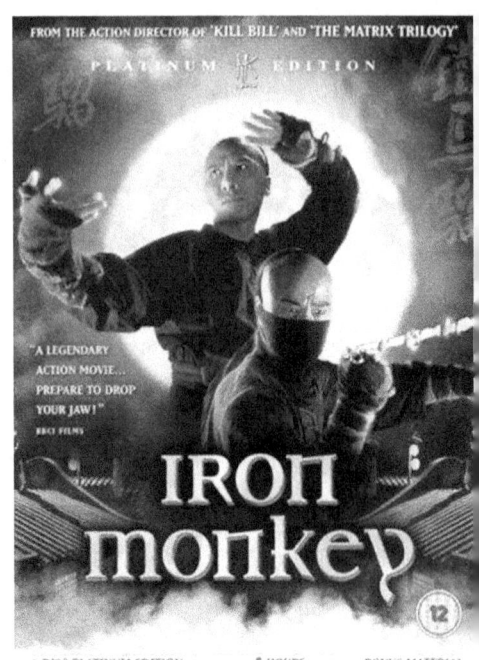

Iron Monkey (1993).

2 DISC PLATINUM EDITION includes over 5 HOURS of amazing BONUS MATERIAL

Dr Wai (1996).

Black Mask
(1996).

# 22

# THE ERA OF VAMPIRES/
# TSUI HARK'S VAMPIRE HUNTERS

## Qian Nián Jiang Shi Wáng

*Vampire Hunters* (*Qian Nian Jiang Shi Wang,* a.k.a. *The Era of Vampires,* dir. Wellson Chin Sing-wai, 2002) was marketed in the Western world as *Tsui Hark's Vampire Hunters*. Altho' it was directed by Chin, *Vampire Hunters* certainly had Tsui's imprint on it (he was the producer and has the writing credit); Film Workshop/ Hark & Co./ Fortissimo Films produced the movie. It seems that if Tsui is involved in a movie, his name overshadows everyone else's (even including big stars); besides, Tsui regulars were among the crew.

*Vampire Hunters* didn't have big stars (the cast included Ken Chang, Michael Chow, Danny Chan, Lam Suet, Horace Kee, Anya Wu and Yu Rongguang, with Ji Chun-hua as the *sifu*. *Vampire Hunters,* a late addition to the *kung fu* and historical cycle of the early 1990s, was lit by Joe Chan Kwong-hung, Sunny Tsang Tat-sze, and Herman Yau Lai-to, with music by J.M. Morgan, editing by Marco Mak Chi-sin, make-up by Maggie Choy Yin-ching and Carmen Man Lai-yee, action direction by Tony Tam Jan-dung, and visual effects by Koan Hui-on and Cinefex Workshop. Released in the U.S.A.: May, 23, 2003. 112 mins.

As pure entertainment, *Vampire Hunters* is pure delight. Leave your brain in the Dodge Viper, turn up with some popcorn and soda, and just enjoy a bunch of filmmakers going all-out to entertain you. The sheer energy of Hong Kong cinema wins you over. It's impossible to resist. They want you to have a good time – and you do! I'd rather watch a movie like *Vampire Hunters* than 99.99% of Western cinema's output.

*Vampire Hunters* is a fantasy horror picture in the manner of *The Bride With White Hair* and *A Chinese Ghost Story* (in some respects, it's a direct sequel to either franchise). Gore, horror, swordplay, black humour, visual effects, special make-up, night scenes filled with swirling smoke, flickering torches and ghostly figures, all set in the familiar world of *jiangzhu* (which Chinese cinema has been mining for 80 or more years).

Plus plenty of the ancient and mediæval Chinese lore, legend and superstition which Tsui Hark loves to ladle into his movies (sometimes a Tsui Hark movie comes across as in part an anthropological study, as Tsui and the writers explore the thousand-and-one wonders of Chinese mythology and folklore. If there's an obscure slice of myth or legend or a bizarre superstitition that has cinematic possibilities, Tsui will embrace it in his films. He must collect wacky stories of yore, and pore over old books of Chinese lore, folk tales and anthropology).

*Vampire Hunters* has got the lot, folklore-wise, with the ringing of bells, the burning of incense, the rituals in the Buddhist temple at the altar, the hopping corpses, the zombies, and a stunning King of Vampires as the chief villain.

The vampire hunters of the title are the usual Buddhist monks of many a Chinese fantasy movie: there's a *sifu* (Master of Invincible Weapons) and four disciples (named Swift Sabre, Deadly Dagger, Killer Hand and Shadowless Kick).[1] For much of the time, *Vampire Hunters* is in a team format, following the adventures of the four monks. The hunters aren't differentiated much, tho' one of them does form a romantic attachment with the female lead, Sasa (Anya Wu), the daughter of Master of Invincible Weapons.[2] The *sifu* appears in the opening action sequence, then disappears for a time, leaving the four less-than-formidable monks to take centre stage.

As well as monks hunting down nasty zombies and vampires, *Vampire Hunters* also contains a treasure seeking plot and clan rivalry (no fantasy adventure or historical horror movie would be complete with such elements). The bars of gold are of course cursed.[3]

*Vampire Hunters* looks, as most fantasy movies from Hong Kong do, ravishing: the 2002 movie is a throwaway piece of popcorn entertainment, assuredly, yet it contains intricate lighting effects worthy of a David Lean or Merchant-Irvoy picture (indeed, you could say that even an average Hong Kong movie has more complex and more inventive lighting than most Western pictures, including, yes, the masterworks of Lean and Merchant-Ivory).

*Vampire Hunters* is a night picture, as horror movies and vampire movies tend to be (well, in Hong Kong cinema they are): the day scenes are photographed with a deliberately flat and unengaging light. But the night scenes pop out of the screen with vibrantly red lanterns, flaming torches, numerous, billowing explosions, and thick, swirling smoke. Out of that chaotic night in the *jiangzhu, anything* could emerge. Chinese fantasy movies turn night into a magical place of infinite possibilities. It's part of the sensuality of Chinese cinema, the sexiness of texture, atmosphere and Gothika. In a Western movie, we *know* what's out there; in a Chinese movie, *anything* could be out there – spinning, hopping, flying ghouls, a

1 There's a joke about their fancy names when they turn up as workers – the boss gives them working class names like Kung and Choi.
2 Another Tsui Hark staple has the monks spying on Sasa taking a bath, a scene much exploited in the *Chinese Ghost Story* pictures.
3 A guy dies from a snake lurking in the chest of gold.

slithering 100-foot tongue, or monsters in the sand that grab you as you walk by. In its range of monsters and nasty critters, Chinese horror cinema far out-does its Western counterparts.

As for action, *Vampire Hunters* has a series of thrilling set-pieces: a vampire attack on a gang of robbers at night; the vampire hunters trying to control a crazed vampire in the opening teaser; multiple duels with spears and swords; a vicious smackdown with the gang leader; a duel between the leader and the Taoist priest; chases thru night forests with vampires and horses; and a ninja vs. monk face-off on the rooftops.

There are plenty of duels for action fans, including some outstanding swordplay and wirework featuring Yu Rongguang, best-known as Iron Monkey (in the wonderful 1993 movie *Iron Monkey*, also produced by Tsui Hark). Sure, *Vampire Hunters* isn't placed in the elevated catgegory of Hong Kong action movies by crrritics, alongside *The Bride With White Hair* or *Project A, Part 2*, but it really rocks when it gets going (which's often – there are *no* lulls in this 1,000 miles-an-hour movie).

And when it comes to depicting age-old clichés like vampires, *Vampire Hunters* makes pretty much *every* Western attempt seem lame and bloodless by comparison. Because Hong Kong filmmakers are *so good* at depicting *physical* action (well, they're the finest in the world, without a doubt, in live-action), they can portray the *physical* and *sensual* aspects of vampirism to an astonishing, visceral degree. So the King Vampire in *Vampire Hunters* is a fabulously effective movie ghoul with fearsomely cold and withering bad breath, an ability to suck out the essence of its victims thru the eyes and mouth, a method of capturing victims by freezing them and drawing them in, a penchant for travelling underground at speed, an ability to leap and fly, and an indestructible form. It grabs horses from underneath the ground and drags them into a grave. The vampire hunters hack it in half, and behead it, and it rebirths itself. The *sifu*'s magical sword splits it down the middle, and its torso opens to reveal a grotesque head being born.

All of this occurs in the finale of *Vampire Hunters*, where the gags are coming thick and fast, in one of those stops-all-out final acts set at night outdoors (in a lightning storm, of course!), that Hong Kong filmmakers make one of their specialities. The finale throws in every trick and technique from the entire history of cinema, including a vast battery of special effects and practical effects, not to mention visual effects created in post-production. Narratively, it is straightforward – a team of hunters try to bring down an unstoppable monster. But how that scenario is dramatized and visualized is remarkable, the filmmaking is so inventive. As a thrill ride, this is one of the best in recent Hong Kong movies.

The score of *Vampire Hunters* by J.M. Morgan is superb, fully exploring the possibilities for suspense and atmosphere. And the soundtrack has been given a state of the art treatment by the sound team,[4] paintingdrawing on the hi-tech sound design of Western movies. Gone is the single wind sound effect and a couple of rolls of thunder of

---

4 Martin Chappell and Les McKenzie were re-recording mixers, with flley work by Yu Ka-luk.

your typical Hong Kong *wuxia pian*: *Vampire Hunters* boasts low rumbles, whooshes, and every variety of sound effect for nasty goop, cracking bones, and rotting flesh slurping open to reveal decayed organs.

As a visual effects movie, *Vampire Hunters* is, like many of Tsui Hark's movies, a feast. Every possible trick and gimmick has been employed by the filmmakers, including digital effects. Like many Hong Kong movies, *Vampire Hunters* revels in the art and craft of movie-making, to the point where it is a film school: *everything* is here (and then some!).

And not only is *Vampire Hunters* a textbook of filmmaking techniques, it is also a movie about the *joy* of filmmaking. Again, as with many Hong Kong movies, the pleasure (and hard work) that the filmmakers experienced as they produced the picture oozes out of every frame (even tho' this movie has fewer laughs than similar fare from Hong Kong).5

This is not to be under-estimated: it is certainly a vital ingredient of Hong Kong cinema that the fun of making movies (and the silliness of the enterprise) is part of the package. After all, it's a bunch of highly talented people who're delivering ridiculous stories about vampires, zombies and flying monks. (And this is also what disappoints the viewer about many movies in the Western world – the weariness and cynicism of the filmmakers, and how they haven't got the energy anymore to really deliver a story, even if it's riddled with clichés. Hong Kong cinema knows how to make clichés *really* work).

It shouldn't matter to the audience if a movie took two weeks to shoot (*Vivre Sa Vie*, 1962) or years (*Apocalypse Now*, 1979), or if a movie was enjoyable to make (*Spirited Away*, 2001) or absolute hell (*Cleopatra*, 1963). Usually it doesn't matter. But audiences do sometimes pick up on how much enjoyment the performers and the crews are having.

You pick up on the scary levels of *anger* in the movies of Ingmar Bergman and Jean-Luc Godard, for instance. They're masterpieces, but, *whoa*, look at the rage bellowing off the screen in *Weekend* or *Persona*! (Hell, Godard and Bergman sure were *furious* with, well, *everything* and *everybody* in the Sixties!).

But quite a few Western movies don't seem to give a hoot whether you – the audience – are enjoying yourself or not. They are either up their own heinie, or so self-absorbed with their own self-importance and self-righteousness, or they're so jaded and worn out. They're just machines, churned out for money.

Well, yes, Hong Kong movies are also sausage-meated out seeking the all-important HK $$$$$. But, maybe because the city and its 7 million-strong audience is small, maybe because everybody knows everybody else, there's a genuine attempt at *entertaining* audiences.

---

5 There are fun moments, tho', like when Sasa, part-way to becoming a vampire, has a croaky voice.

# 23

# *XANDA*

# *Sanda*

*Xanda* (*Sanda,* 2004) was directed by Tsui Hark's regular editor, Marco Mak Chi-sin (born Non 6, 1951), prod. by Film Workshop/ Fortissimo Film/ Hark & Co./ Shenzhen Film Enterprise, executive prods. were: Satoru Iseki, Nansun Shi Nan-sheng and Le Qun Song, prod. by Tsui Hark, line prods. were: Kenny Chan and Yuan Nong, wr. by Kai-Cheung Chung, Derick Lau, Ask Lee, Xiao-Long Lin and Tsui, action dirs. were Kau Chim Man, Cheung Man, Kou Zhan-Wen and Ma Zhong Xuan, music: Tommy Wai, DPs: Sunny Tsang Tat Sze, Mak Hoi-Man and Herman Yau, editing: Liu Shun-Xiang, Marco Mak Chi-sin and Anglie Lam On-yee, prod. des.: Oliver Wong, sound: Felix Sze Ming Chung, and costumes: Cheung Man. In the cast were: Sang Wei Lin, Zhao Zi Long, Teng Jun, Ni Jing Yang, Li Tie and Zhang Hong Jun. Released Feb 19, 2004. 85/ 91 mins.

*Five* writers! *Four* producers! – but *Xanda* turns out to be a very traditional and old-fashioned yarn. Sure, it's given a hi-tech gloss, but this is a very conventional movie. As to why it took *five writers* to produce what is a very formulaic and straightforward film script is a mystery: it's a screenplay that any half-decent film student could produce.

The contemporary tone of the movie is courtesy primarily to the very flashy editing by Marco Mak Chi-sin, Angie Lam On-yee and Liu Shun-Xiang. Two of those editors – Mak and Lam – are among the finest in the world. They have cut many masterpieces of Asian cinema. As editors of action, they have no peers in Western cinema.

However, you'd have to admit that Marco Mak Chi-sin, Angie Lam On-yee and Liu Shun-Xiang have indulged themselves tremendously in *Xanda*, turning the 2004 production into a giant, colourful Editing Festival, a Carnival of Editors, where every form of film editing and every editorial gimmick is given their own stall, their own festival float, their own fireworks display. Speed ramping, step-motion, jump cuts, smash cuts, cuts on sound, and every sort of dissolve – they're all here (and that's in the first six minutes!).

Yes – forget the fighting and the martial arts – *Xanda* delivers editing as *kung fu*, editing as swordplay, where magical swords slice through celluloid or pixels and bytes with the joy of itself.

The other technical aspects of *Xanda* are impressive – cinematography, music, sound effects, lighting, costumes, production design, hair, make-up, etc – but, as every film editor knows, all of that is mere stuff for the editor to use. As film editors often note, the production can spend millions of dollars and months of effort on shooting, on travelling to locations, on costumes and props, on building extravagant sets, on stunts and all the rest, but *all of that* ultimately runs through the editing suite, through the fingers and hands of one guy and their editorial assistant.

As to the action scenes of the Xanda sport, of course they are splendidly staged and filmed. Tho' why filmmakers keep referencing *Raging Bull* every time anybody steps into a boxing ring is perplexing. Why does every portrayal of a boxing match or similar sport in movies have to use slow motion and bits of sweat flying about?

As to the story, *Xanda* trundles out the old chestnut of the boy Zhang Guo Qiang (Sang Wei-lin) from the sticks who comes to the Big City and has adventures. He meets new people (some appealing, some indifferent, some blunt, some violent, some corrupt), encounters a tough *dojo* (where they teach the sport of Xanda), which is run by a tough coach (Zhang Hong-Jun), of course, and learns about the wicked ways of the world. The subplot is – guess what?! – romance. (*Xanda* is set in the People's Republic of China, in Shenzhen).

This is an updated version of an olde martiale arts yarn of yore, where a kid enters a martial arts competition in order to raise $$$$ for his friend who was injured in a fight (he even has a sweetheart back home in the country whom he dreams about. She's cute and meek! She's in a wheelchair! Bite me!).[6] Change the costumes, and this might be a Shaw Brothers picture from 1976 or 1956. Why not? That's what all film industries do – recycle ye olde stories. New actors in old stories.

And *Xanda* ends exactly as formula dictates: pregnant girlfriend Ning leaves – and on the same night that Zhang Guo Qiang is fighting his major engagement. It's wholly artificial, and plays out exactly as expected. As does the sappy ending, with Ning and Qiang re-united on the bridge back in the sticks.

With a producer and a co-writing credit, Tsui Hark of course makes his presence felt in *Xanda*. The bumping up of the roles of the girlfriend back home, plus the young woman Liu Xiao Ning (Ni Jing Yang) that Qiang meets in Shenzhen seem typically Tsui-ian. Some shots are completely Tsui-ish – fish in close-up in a tank, and charas looking at each other thru the fish tank.

Also, *Xanda* possesses some of the tone and attitude of Tsui's contemporary-set films (there's a desperation-to-be-cool here, as found in

---

6 Later, a character prates about loss and fear with a mean-spirited venom.

Tsui's recent modern movies, like *Time and Tide* and *All These Women*, as if *Xanda* is all too conscious of trying to appeal to a youth audience. The aching to be young, hip and trendy always feels false to me. Filmmakers as good as Tsui Hark or Marco Mak don't need to pander to that).

# 24

# *SWORD MASTER*

## *San Shao Ye De Jian*

Tsui Hark has co-writer and producer credit on *Sword Master* (Cantonese: *San Shao Ye De Jian,* 2016): it is a swordplay movie set in the *jiangzhu*, Tsui's home-from-home. It might be another movie that Tsui considered directing. Chun Tin-Nam and Derek Yee Tung-sing co-wrote the screenplay from the novel *The Third Master's Sword* by Gu Long and the 1977 film *Death Duel.* It was produced by Film Unlimited Production/ Bona Entertainment/ Bona Film Group/ Wanda Film and Television Media. The producers were Peggy Lee Kam-man, Mandy Law Hiu-man, Don Yu Dong, Jeffrey Chan and Tsui Hark; Derek Yee Tung-sing directed. The action dirs. were Yuen Bun, Amy Lee Wai-choh and Dion Lam Dik-on. Music: Peter Kam. DPs: William Chan Wai-lin and Chan Chi-ying. Art dirs.: Silver Cheung Sai-wang, Fion Li Ching-Yu, Wu Zhen, Joel Chong Kwok-wing and Shi Bin. Vfx sup.: Luk Jung Sung-jin. Costumes: Stanley Cheung Sai-kit. Make-up: Kwan Lee-Na and Liu Yi. Hair: Lau Wai-hing and Liu Qui-ju. Editors: Derek Hui Wang-fu and Li Rui-liang. Sound: Guo Xiao-shi. Sound designers: Kinson Tsang King-cheung, George Lee Yiu-keung, Yiu Chun-hin and Lai Chi-hung. Category IIB. Released: Dec 2, 2016. 108 mins.

In the cast were Kenny Lin Geng-xin, Peter Ho Yun-tung, Jiang Yi-yan, Jian Meng-jie, Edward Gu, Norman Chu Siu-keung, Ku Kuan-chung, Jamie Lik Kim-ming, Pau Hei-ching, Tie Nan and Ma Jing-jing.

*Sword Master* was a remake of *Death Duel* (*San Shao Ye De Jian,* 1977), a Shaw Brothers movie which had starred Derek Yee Tung-sing, Ling Yun and Candice Yu in the three main roles. *Death Duel* was written and directed by Chor Yuen from Gong Lu's novel. Runme Shaw was the producer. *Death Duel* was released on July 7, 1977 and was 90 minutes long.

The cast of *Death Duel* includes many names that later became famous in Hong Kong cinema, including actors Yuen Wah, Ti Lung, Lo Lieh and Yuen Biao, director Corey Yuen, and composer and editor David

Chiang (who was a regular collaborator with Tsui Hark). And Norman Chu was in the original *Death Duel*, while in the 2016 remake he plays Hsieh's father and the clan leader.

Derek Yee Tung-sing (b. 1957) was an actor who'd been in everything (begining in 1977 with *Lady Exterminator, Jade Tiger* and *Death Duel*). He also worked as producer, writer and director. His directing credits included *Full Throttle, Viva Erotica, The Lunatics, Lost In Time, One Nite In Mongkok, Shinjuku Incident* and *The Great Magician.*

▶

At the heart of *Sword Master* is a story of two would-be brothers, or twins, the nihilistic sword master Yen Shisan (Ho) and the son of Hsieh clan and now drifter Hsieh Shao-feng (Lin). Both are portraits of people that don't fit in, that are doomed in some way by their pasts and their origins (or they are running away from them). Swordsman Yen embodies a bleak, pessimistic view of life. The film explores each character first before bringing them together.

The third main character in *Sword Master* is the prostitute Chiu Ti, known as the 'Princess' (and 'Sweetie'). Winningly played by Jian Yi-yan (another of the tiny, skinny young women in Chinese cinema), the 'Princess' pals up with the drifter Hsieh (their companionship is at first awkward and suspicious, but later the 'Princess' comes to recognize Hsieh as her protector. Hsieh, blind drunk, staggers into the brothel one time and ends up staying there when he can't pay).

With Tsui Hark regular Yuen Bun heading up the action choreography team, *Sword Master* is bound to feature outstanding action sequences. The movie doesn't hang about: swordsmen are going at it furiously from a minute into the 2016 picture. From that point onwards, there is enough action to satisfy the most ravenous action fan.

Of course, this being a *wuxia pian,* there are magical swords, ancient clans, bustling villages, crusty travellers in the *jiangzhu*, and some fantasy elements. And as this is a Category IIB movie, there are gloomier, grittier sides to the piece – like how Swordsman Yen holes up in a graveyard (albeit one art directed like a setting from *The Wizard of Oz*, complete with trees in full, white blossom). The bordello contrasts beautiful, young women with gruesome punters. The village bustles with life (and cute, young kids), but everyone's living in poverty.

▶

*Sword Master* opens with scenes of Swordsman Yen which are given the full, Chinese Gothic treatment: straggly wigs, painted faces, glowering looks, and a world evoked thru visual effects (gloomy skies, misty mountainscapes, wide rivers, etc). Swordsman Yen strides thru this Comicbook China as if the star of *The Crow* (Brandon Lee) was appearing in a *wuxia* picture. (*Sword Master* is a movie version of a Chinese comic, which are called *manwua* rather than *manga*).

Swordsman Yen is yet another depiction of the *ronin*, the lone, wandering swordsman, who's adrift in the dangerous, rough-and-tumble martial arts world. It's not easy being Swordsman Yen! He cuts up those who dare to challenge him (in the first scene), and does his best to distance himself from everybody (including his on-off sidekick).

*Sword Master* was part of the recent cycle of big budget *wuxia pian*, filled with visual effects, filmed in Mandarin on the Mainland, and in 3-D (it was based at the Hengdian World Studios).

*Sword Master* is a slick, entertaining movie, though it possesses a nastier, cruel side in its depictions of the relationships between some of the characters. Many scenes take place in a brothel, which's given an exaggerated, colourful appearance. This masks the barely-suppressed aggression and exploitation of the women by brutish men (in one scene, for instance, the 'Princess' is whipped by an impossible-to-please client).

The brothel madame, Madame Han, played by Tian Miao, steals this part of *Sword Master* – the movie is unusual, perhaps, in giving several roles to older women (the madame, the 'Princess's' mother, etc).

*Sword Master* takes an intriguing turn at the beginning of the third act with a dip into the past of Hsieh and Mu-Yung, where they are portrayed as teens and later lovers (cue gorgeous waterfall settings and drifting blossom). *Sword Master* becomes a different film here, stepping away from the brooding swordsmen for a while. The too-sweet, too-cute flashback sequence prepares the audience for the ferocity of the finale, when Mu-Yung transforms the scorn of a woman spurned into a murderous rage.

The finale of *Sword Master* brings together all of the cast for a mass battle at the HQ of the Hsieh Clan: the action is magnificent, varying between ferocious duels between two participants, and group battles. Yuen Bun, Amy Lee Wai-choh and Dion Lam Dik-on and the stunt team work to their fullest to deliver sensational action. Every part of the interior of the Hsieh compound is employed – characters burst thru the windows, thru the roof, leap on the chandeliers, the standing lamps, etc.

Hostilities begin in a suitably sinister manner as the Divine Might crew materialize from inside a poisonous fog on the lower approach to the Hsieh mansion. Claws on chains shoot out of the mist, grabbing victims and poisoning them. Hsieh's patriarch has his finest moments in *Sword Master* here, fending off the assailants single-handed (I mean, single-sworded). The battle formations that the Hsieh instantly move into are brilliantly achieved.

The finale of *Sword Master* includes the mandatory duels between the hero and the rivals – Hsieh Shao-feng takes on the jealous admirer Chu, and the jilted bride and now highly competent warrior Princess Mu-Yung Chiu-ti. This fight is especially inventive, with Mu-Yung performing numerous spins and lunges as she tries to land a hit on Hsieh. That Mu-Yung has loved him for so long and has been spurned and abandoned adds a passionate subtext to their duel. Mu-Yung is a figure of fury in a flowing white dress. There's no doubt that Mu-Yung is determined to kill Hsieh for his betrayals, and it's right that Hsieh, even tho' he's the greatest swordsman in the world, should find Mu-Yung a challenging opponent. Playing out the erotic triangle in the standard manner, it's actually ardent admirer Chu who stabs Mu-Yung not Hsieh (after she has mistakenly stabbed Chu in her blind fury). Chu in turn kills her just so she can't have Hsieh. In this movie, if a jealous, selfish lover can't have the one they want, no one else gets them, either. Mu-Yung expires in Hsieh's arms.

*Sword Master*'s climax has much pretty everything you could wish for. Yet the 2016 film is not over once it's played out: the Swordsman Yen and Hsieh plot is not resolved yet, so the two men stage a duel on top of a mountain (Swordsman Yen had sat out the smackdown between the two clans – watching from the sidelines. It's not his fight).

# 25

# *THE THOUSAND FACES OF DUNJIA*

# *Qimen Dunjia*

Now we come to a 2017 production entitled *The Thousand Faces of Dunjia* (a.k.a. *Qimen Dunjia* or *The Miracle Fighters*). Tsui Hark co-produced and co-scripted the movie (and co-edited it), and it was produced by Film Workshop (and many other companies). This, plus the presence of his ex-wife Nansun Shi Nan-sheng as fellow producer, suggests that *The Thousand Faces of Dunjia* might've been a movie that Tsui had planned to direct. (Do we need to point out that this is a Chinese subject with Chinese characters made in China by a Chinese crew and Chinese actors for a Chinese audience?).

*The Thousand Faces of Dunjia* was prod. by Wei Junzi, Huang Yonghui, Nansun Shi, Tsui Hark, Sham Tam, and Wayne Wei Jiang (plus seventeen executive producers/ co-presenters, including: Elaine Feng, Ziyan Huang, Allen Zhu, Peter Zheng, Zhao Zhang, Qi Lin, Yan Yun) for Vision Pictures/ Acme Image/ Beijing Jinhui/ Yinghau Entertainment/ Star Century Picture/ Film Can/ Heyi Pictures/ Film Workshop. A host of other companies were credited as co-producers, including: Beijing Three Stones Media/ Tianjin Mayan Media/ Shanghai Morejoy Entertainment and Flagship Entertainment. So many producers! So many production companies! Can't movies be made with one or two producers anymore, like the first *Star Wars*? Tsui scripted, and Yuen Woo-ping directed. Released: Dec 15, 2017. 113 mins.

In the cast were Da Peng (Chengpeng Dong), Aarif Rahman Lee, Ni Ni, Zhou Dongyu, Wu Bai, Ada Liu Yan, Tiger Xu Ming-hu, Yilong Zhang, Darren Leung, Haoyu Yang, Akbep, Lue Wei, Xiaoming Huang, Shan Peng Dang, Jianwei Liu, Binglei Li, Xing Yu, Xiangdon Xu, Fei Hu, Yang Yiwei, Xie Miao, Mo Tse and Sun Mingming.

Tsui Hark and Yuen Woo-ping had of course collaborated many times: Yuen had helped out Tsui on the *Once Upon a Time In China* movies, for example, and Tsui had produced one of Yuen's finest films, *Iron Monkey*. *The Thousand Faces of Dunjia* resembles *Black Mask 2* (2002) in parts, which Yuen action-directed (along with Yuen Bun) for Tsui – it featues the same sort of monster battles.

With two of the greatest directors of action in cinema leading the production, the action is bound to be excellent. And it is. They are aided by an enormous production team, including people who've worked with them for decades (Tsui Hark and Nansun Shi Nan-sheng have worked together for over 35 years, for example).

So here are back in the *jiangzhu*, a cinematic realm Tsui Hark and Yuen Woo-ping know very well (indeed, one would imagine that Tsui would live there if he could, maybe as one of the wise *sifu* who are expert swordsmen).

But this time it's a fantasy/ horror/ martial arts movie with thousands of post-production visual effects and computer-aided animation, in addition to the numerous practical effects, wire-work and in-camera effects that Hong Kong cinema employs in every single movie.

So it's monsters and transformations and martial arts duels delivered with the familiar scary-joky attitude that Chinese cinema can't help using.

*The Thousand Faces of Dunjia* is fun, fast, very silly, and very entertaining. It's a movie-movie, a movie that knows and celebrates that it's a movie, and has no pretences to be anything else.

So don't fight *The Thousand Faces of Dunjia* – you won't win! It's a movie to be enjoyed, that's all. There's no need to work against it, to wish it was 'better', to point out all the 'flaws'.

*The Thousand Faces of Dunjia* is also a movie without a substantial subtext or political agenda, unless you count the usual action-adventure genre themes of 'doing the right thing', 'being righteous'; protecting one's community' and 'saving the world'.

If this had been made in the early 1990s, Brigitte Lin would have played the tomboy swordswoman Metal Dragonfly, Jet Li would be the co-leader of the Wuyin Clan, and Maggie Cheung would've been the kooky Circle.

It's also a remake – of *The Miracle Fighters* (1982), which had also been helmed by Yuen Woo-ping. In the cast of the 1982 flick were Yuen Cheung Yan, Yuen Hsun Yee, Eddy Ko and Leung Kar Yan. A sequel followed (*The Miracle Fighters 2*) in 1983. The story is changed for the 2017 remake (the 1982 film featured a Manchu general in an Imperial court. But it featured many silly items such as 'a fighting stick figure, a barber/ beautician assassin in drag, flying drillbits, acrobatic cheerleader demons, killer midgets, and, of course, the triumphant return of Urn Man', as Jeff Yang put it (170).

Tsui Hark's motifs are everywhere in *The Thousand Faces of Dunjia* – ridiculous monsters and horror movie genre send-ups; simple-minded but well-meaning heroes; a bunch of warriors each given their own quirky outfits; group jokes; flashy, tomboyish swordswomen; fish; Peking Opera acrobatics; and of course his beloved disguises and transformations. For example, a beautiful courtesan in a brothel turns out to be an ugly woman underneath (and played by a guy in the crossdressing Peking Opera tradition) and the tiny, vulnerable, childish waif Xiao Yuan/ Circle metamorphoses into a giant phoenix bird.

Sections of *The Thousand Faces of Dunjia* shamelessly replay some of Tsui Hark's greatest hits in cinema – there's a stop-over in the middle of a sand-blown desert, for instance, recalling *New Dragon Gate Inn*. The group reactions to jokes among the warriors in the Wuyin Clan (which Tsui has been using since *We're Going To Eat You* in 1980).

Many gags in *The Thousand Faces of Dunjia* are staples of Yuen Woo-ping's cinema that he's been using for eons – rapid flying scenes with wires, flamboyant swordplay, and black humour from ugly character actors. With the addition of computer-aassisted animation, we have the familiar bits of business with tables (as in *Wing Chun*, 1994), but now the tables are not there, they're cartoons added later.

ॐ

The plot of *The Thousand Faces of Dunjia* combines the usual swordplay movie with a demon hunting plot – the Wuyin Clan of warriors are seeking out nasty aliens who threaten the beloved land of China. *The Thousand Faces of Dunjia* shares many affinities with *Journey To the West 2*, released earlier in the same year (2017), and with the second *Detective Dee* sequel, released the following year (even the opening credits are similar).

There are four main characters in *The Thousand Faces of Dunjia*:
- the swordswoman of the Wuyin Clan, Metal Dragonfly (Ni Ni);
- her counterpart, Zhuge Qingyun (Da Peng);
- Circle/ Xiao Yuan (Zhou Dongyu),  their new leader;
- and the policeman Dao Yichang (Aarif Lee). Pop star Wu Bai (from *Time and Tide*) appears as an elder swordsman, Big Brother/ Boss.

The two female leads steal the 2017 movie – Ni Ni as Wuyin swordswoman Metal Dragonfly and Zhou Dongyu as Xiao Yuan/ Circle, the new leader of the Clan. Ni Ni plays Dragonfly with the same cool, detached, all-business attitude reminiscent of Michelle Yeoh or Brigitte Lin (she poses like a guy, and smokes). Dragonfly's flirtatious relationship with Zhuge Qingyun is amusing, as is her jealousy over Circle's antics (likewise, Zhuge is irked when Dragonfly seems too familiar with the policeman Dao). Zhou Dongyu steals every scene she's in as the unlikely new leader of the Wuyin warriors. It's an entertaining turn from Zhou as a simple-minded, naïve kook who's all over Zhuge (hugging him). The fact that inside Circle is an enormous phoenix is unbelievable, but the Wuyin Clan have to go along with it – the blue-purple phoenix is the only thing that can go up against the monsters from outer space and win.

Structurally, *The Thousand Faces of Dunjia* follows the standard template of Hong Kong movies. For instance, the climax to act two mirrors the climax to act one (the aliens cutting loose). And the finale is of course a repeat of the same: battles with the henchmen of the aliens, followed by superhero duels between the aliens and the heroes' leader, Circle-as-phoenix.

The tender relationship between Circle/ Xiao Yuan and Constable Dao Yichang is one of the charming friendships-moving-into-possible-romance of Tsui Hark's cinema. There isn't a main romantic subplot in *The Thousand Faces of Dunjia,* but there are two minor quasi-romantic relationships – Circle and Dao and Dragonfly and Zhuge.

The Dao-Circle relationship is of two simple-minded, well-meaning but lost souls – both have been removed from their homes and their natural surroundings. They bond in their loneliness (a common feature of Tsui Hark's romantic plots). Circle's powers of rebirth are formidable – in between the action set-pieces in act three is a scene where Circle literally heals Dao's wounds – a missing leg and a chopped-off arm. Yes, Circle has the powers to bring things full circle, growing back Dao's limbs (and later Circle heals Dragonfly, who's been poisoned by Ghost, and Zhuge).

The Dragonfly-Zhuge relationship is the very familiar one in Chinese cinema of lovers who can't admit their love, or display it, or reciprocate it. This is all about the suppression of yearning in the face of duty, of working for the good of the community: it's society over individuality, duty over desire.

So the Dragonfly-Zhuge, relationship is depicted with the usual lingering looks, subtextual interplay, and a stern suppression of sexual feelings. So, instead of scenes of lovemaking, we have slapping – when Zhuge gets too fresh with her, Dragonfly slaps him (her jealousy over his relationship with Circle is one motive for more slapping). And he slaps her back occasionally.

Compared to simialr relationships in the *Swordsman* series and the *Chinese Ghost Story* series, there are no sex scenes in *The Thousand Faces of Dunjia*, or even stand-ins for sex scenes (the slapping scene is a humorous synecdoche, perhaps).

❧

The finale of *The Thousand Faces of Dunjia* begins with the third act (it's a long third act, as usual in Chinese and Hong Kong cinemas). There are moire disguises and reveals, including Big Boss facing off against himself (who is Ghost in disguise). There are the expected multiple duels, though the focus is on the four main characters (Dragonfly, Zhuge, Circle and Dao), rather than the group of Wuyin warriors (it's possible that more of the secondary duels were filmed but cut. It does seem odd that the group of Wuyin fighters have far less to do than expected).

The finale's action set-pieces run through hundreds of bits of business, combining wire-work (many of the duels take place in the air), numerous practical gags (like shattering and puppeteered props), with post-production animation. Zhuge, Dragonfly and Big Boss meet their match, and are defeated, leaving the stage clear for the arrival of Circle in her phoenix guise to take on the two demons from outer space.

*The Thousand Faces of Dunjia* thus hands over the storytelling to the animators in several companies in Asia (including Asymmetric V.F.X., Mofac and Terminal F.X.). So for several minutes of *The Thousand Faces of Dunjia* we are watching entirely animated scenes. A cartoon, in fact.

It's a monster battle, which Asian cinema of course absolutely adores. Phoenix triumphs with some clever moves (using the emeny's explosives against them, for instance).

To enhance the jeopardy, *The Thousand Faces of Dunjia* depicts Circle dying – in Constable Dao's arms (to make it even more melodramatic). Circle has healed Dao, which weakened her, and then Dragonfly. She is buried in an earth mound and given a funeral (again, there are many echoes of the *Chinese Ghost Story* films). But as she is half-phoenix, we know that she will be resurrected for the climax.

# 26

## *THE CLIMBERS*

## *Pan Den Zhe*

It's difficult to work out just what Tsui Hark did for the production of *The Climbers* (= *Paandangze* in Cantonese, 2019), because he shares a producer with an astonishihg number of executive producers, producers, line producers and planners. Well, *The Climbers* is a big production, but does it really need *that* many film producers? And *that* many film companies? (Maybe if you put in 10 *yuan* you received a producer's credit and a little red, Chinese flag?).

Thus, organizing the finance for *The Climbers* was an epic undertaking in itself, whether or not the movie got made: a bunch of people had to arrange the finance and legal contracts for all of those companies and all of those producers.

*The Climbers* was produced by a huge number of companies, too, headed up by Shanghai Film Group. They included Huayi Brothers Pictures, Shanghai Film Media Asia, Beijing Anrul Media, Gao Sheng Wealth Holding Group and many, many more (most were Beijing or Shanghai firms).

*The Climbers* was prod. by Tsui Hark, Susanna Tsang Pui-san, Ren Zhonglun, Yin Jianua, Huang Ji, and 27 presenters/ producers (and 6 assoc. prods., and 3 planners), A. Lai, Daniel Lee Wan-kong and Ying Shang scripted, and Daniel Lee directed (Tsui Hark had worked with Lee before – he produced *Black Mask*, which Lee helmed). DPs: Tony Cheun, Chow Chi-fai, Sunny Tsang, and Mike Lau; music: Henry Lai Wan-man; costumes: Debby Wong; art dirs.: Eddy Wong, Wenlong Zhu and Daniel Lee; editors: Jack Tang and Lin Li; executive vfx prod.: Eui Dong Park; and sound design by Phyllis Cheng and Peter Mullen. Released Sept 23, 2019. 2h 05m.

In the cast were Jacky Wu Jing, Zhang Ziyi, Zhang Yi, Boran Jing Boo-ran, Hu Ge, Wang Jing-chun and He Lin. Jackie Chan has a cameo. *The Climbers* was a big hit in China (with a box office gross of US $154 million).

The outdoor sequences were filmed in Tibet, with principal photography running from February to April, 2019.

The story of *The Climbers* is about the ascent of Mount Everest in 1960 and then again in the early 1970s. So it's a mountaineering film – and that means manly effort, team bonding, tough training, spectacular vistas and of course danger and accidents (no mountaineering movie depicts the team waltzing up to the summit like it's nothing, and ski-ing back down in time for cocktails).

But what *The Climbers* is *really* about is another Chiense propaganda outing. The movie states plainly that:

China is wonderful!

The Chinese people are amazing!

The people of the People's Republic of China can do anything!

But that's no doubt different to many a movie: an American war movie claims that the U.S.A. won the Second World War single-handed, for example. If it's a French WWII film, no, the French government didn't capitaulate to the Nazis, there was a Resistance!

It seems in the Chinese movie industry that any big budget production has to include (or has to be, in itself), Chinese propaganda, spreading the ideology and culture of the People's Republic of China. The bigger the budget gets of a movie, the louder the shouting about Wonderful China becomes (and the cheesier and stupider the script. This also applies to any big production. The more money there is at stake, everything inevitably becomes watered down, more melodramatic, and cheesier).

It's not only the climbing of Mount Everest (= *Qomolangma* in Tibetan, which means *Big, Scary, Very Dangerous Mountain*), and the nationalist pride, it's the surveying (and the height of the rock at the summit not the snowcap). Those issues are still being debated today.

Jacky Wu Jing heads up a cast of gnarly, macho guys (and some youngsters in bit parts) who attempt a second run at Mount Everest, because the first one (in 1960) failed to record the climb with photographic evidence (thus, the camera is all-important in this movie – something that filmmakers can relate to). Some of the characters (such as Fang Wuzhou) were based on real people (Fang, for example, died in 2015).

In this very contrived screenplay (by A. Lai, Daniel Lee and Ying Shang), two romantic interest subplots are very artificially inserted, to balance the all-male, so-manly slant of the film. Zhang Ziyi (playing a meteorologist) is brought in to provide some eye candy in a love-from-afar scenario with the main star, Jacky Wu Jing, and there's another romantic subplot (involving Li Guoliang and Hei Mudan).

So *The Climbers* is going to follow a very familiar storyline – you will be able to predict every part of the plot. And it will deliver pro-Chunese ideology and politics:

The Chinese discovered writing before anyone else!

The Chinese were the first on the Moon!

The Chinese colonized Mars first!

Or maybe the message of *The Climbers* is: do not under any

circumstances even think of climbing Mount Everest!

Technically, *The Climbers* is superb, with the expected incredible cinematography of the Himalayas, coupled with numerous visual effects shots to augment the many scenes staged in the studio (all mountaineering films recreate the mountains in the studio – except maybe the famous German silent movies, when that really is Leni Riefenstahl hopping around the Alpine peaks in *The Holy Mountain* (a.k.a. *Bergilme*, dir. Arnold Franck, 1926), one of the great silent, German mountain films). I wonder if Tsui Hark was asked to help with the production of the visual effects sequences for *The Climbers*, being an expert in the field.

One aspect of *The Climbers* is truly horrible: the score by Henry Lai Wan-man (Carol Kuswanto provided additional music). *The Climbers* is another movie which has been spotted to allow no more than 5 seconds to pass without some underscore. A new scene will start (the previous one having been jammed with music), and after five seconds without music, the darn score starts up again.

This isn't the fault of the composer, Henry Lai Wan-man, but of the film producers and editors. Actually, it's the *producers* who tend to oversee where and when the music plays in a movie (if the director is elsewhere, but even then producers often overrule directors). And someone among those 5,921 producers of *The Climbers* has asserted their authority (not at gun-point, we hope!) and ordered musical cues for 99% of the 125-minute running time.

In addition, the music by Henry Lai Wan-man is over-poweringly cheesy and melodramatic. In the romantic scenes, it's over-cooked orchestral strings (creating an oppressive, claustrophobic effect in *The Climbers'* first act, as it plays underneath the romantic scenes between Wu Jing and Zhang Ziyi, swamping everything – their performances, the dialogue, everything). And in the heroic scenes, it's brassy, orchestral sounds (as always for heroic deeds and manly scenes in movies). And the form of music that should be outlawed – tear-drop piano – is used underneath the poignant scenes (*why*? why is slow, Chopinesque piano-plinking the only type of frigging music that film producers today will accept for weepy scenes?).

▶

Action-wise, *The Climbers* delivered some impressive sequences, as we'd expect from a Chinese action team – for tumbles, acrobatics and wirework, Chinese cinema rules supreme (Alan Ng Wing-lum was action director). There's no doubt that *The Climbers* is very exciting in parts, and certainly captures the foolishness of climbing mountains and the numerous dangers (and also the exhilaration, the joy of being high above it all. I love mountains with a passion, and mountaineering movies. And there are moments when you're in the mountains which are absolutely ecstatic).

The first action scenes occurred in the first half of the first act of *The Climbers,* as the 1960 expedition to Mount Everest is hit by an enormous avalanche (mandatory in a mountaineering movie. Indeed, there's another avalanche later in the film. They occur every five minutes on Everest).

There's even a scene where the surviving three climbers perform a sort of Peking Opera stunt – clambering on each other's shoulders in order to get past a particuarly steep and difficult section of jagged rock.

The second action sequence spiced up the middle section of the 2019 production (it was part of the training and acclimatisation process). Not far from Mount Everest in the Himalayas (on the Tibetan side, of course), the young group of climbers (ledy by Captain Fang this time) encounters tricky crevasses and slippery snow and ice. Resourceful Fang employs a folding ladder to stop him and his colleague from plummeting into a crevasse, while the second romantic subplot couple (Li Guoliang – Boran Jing and Hei Mudan – Quiniciren) find themselves pinioned in another ice and rock trench.

However, some of the action in *The Climbers* is ridiculous. For example, instead of a sex/ love scene in act one, Wu Jing clambers over a factory like a monkey (*parkours*-style). He's a brilliant team leader and mountain climber, but an emotional cripple: he can't confess his love for Zhang Ziyi (which he attempts to do atop a factory silo). In the middle of the film, to keep up the slog thru the boring romantic subplot, Wu saves Zhang from a falling rock on Mount Everest by throwing himself between it and her. He ends up lying above Zhang, holding up the rock with steely effort, an unsubtle stand-in for sex.

Some of the action in other scenes in *The Climbers* is over-cooked – Chinese/ Hong Kong cinema can't resist going to town with action. The training exercise includes a mass panic and people falling into crevasses. Blown by the high gales on Everest, the team somehow lash themselves to foldable ladders, spending the night tied to a rock in their sleeping bags (don't try this at home).

▶

*The Climbers* ends with the expected spectacular victory, with the Chinese mountaineering team reaching the top of Mount Big, Scary, Very Dangerous Peak (though not without the usual set-backs of avalanches, crevasses, high winds and extreme cold).

And it's here that the endpoint of *The Climbers'* cheesy, routine romantic subplot is inserted in a shameless slice of over-done melodrama: Zhang Ziyi's meteorologist expires while she's talking on the radio to Captain Fang who's near the summit. Even compared to the over-cooked hysterics of Chinese cinema, this is over-the-top.

Jackie Chan pops up in the midst of the end credits to offer the last words (paying his respects to the climbers who died). It's always great to see Chan in anything – he can make the opening of an envelope fun.

FIVE HEROES  A COVEN OF VAMPIRES
A LOT OF BAD BLOOD

TSUI HARK'S
VAMPIRE
HUNTERS

The Era of Vampires (2002).

The Thousand
Faces of Dunjia
(2017).

The Climbers (2019)

# 27

# OTHER MOVIES PRODUCED BY TSUI HARK

*THE DIARY OF A BIG MAN*

*The Diary of a Big Man* (1988, *Daai jeung foo yat gei*, a.k.a. *Big Husband's Diary*), was a Chow Yun-fat comedy about a guy with multiple wives from Cinema City and Film Workshop, wr. by Ng Man-fai and Phillip Cheng, dir. by Chor Yuen, prod. by Tsui Hark, music by Romeo Diaz, James Wong Jim and David Wu Tai-wai, and DPs: Lee San-ip and Lam Wa-chiu. Released July 21, 1988. 89 mins.

In the cast were many Tsui Hark regulars, including: Sally Yeh Tse-man, Joey Wong Jo-yin, Waise Lee Chi-hung, Kent Cheng Jak-si, Carrie Ng Kar-lai, David Wu Tai-wai and Chu Yuan. According to Joey Wong, Tsui Hark directed the movie on video, and later invited Chor Yuen to direct it for theatrical release.

*GUNMEN*

*Gunmen* (1988, *Tian Huo Di Wang*) was a Cinema City/ Film Workshop production, wr. by Kam-Fai Law and Wang Fung Lip, dir. by Kirk Wong, prod. by Tsui Hark and Margaret Wong, music and editing by David Wu Tai-wai, ph. by Ardy Lam, art dir. by Yiu-Kwong Lee and Eddie Ma, costumes by Shirley Chan, and stunt co-ordinators: Hark-On Fung and Buddy Joe Hooker. Released: Oct 22, 1988. 87 mins.

In the cast were: Adam Cheng, Waise Lee, David Wu Tai-wai, Tony Ka-fai Leung, Mark Cheng, Carrie Ng Kar-lai and Elizabeth Lee. *Gunmen* was a period crime drama – set amongst the drug trade in the 1930s in Shanghai.

*THE LASER MAN*

Another Film Workshop comedy (co-prod. with S.J.M. and Peter Wang Films), *The Laser Man* (1988), wr. and dir. by Peter Wang Zheng-fang, exec. prod. by Sophie Lo and Tsui Hark, prod. by Peter Wang, DP: Ernest R. Dickerson, ed. by Grahame Weinbren, music by Marco Daring, casting by Judy Dennis, prod. des. by Lester Cohen and cost. by Barbara Weiss. Released: Sept 25, 1988. 92 mins.

In the cast were: Tony Leung Ka-fai, Sally Yeh, Marc Hayashi, Peter Wang, George Bartenieff, Joan Copeland, and David Chan.

*JUST HEROES*

*Just Heroes* (a.k.a. *Tragic Heroes*, *Yi Dan Qun Ying* in Cantonese, 1989) was produced by Magnum Films, prod. by Alan Ng and Tsui Hark, exec. prod. by Chang Cheh, wr. by Ni Kuang, Tommy Hau and Yiu Yau Hung, dir. by John Woo and Wu Ma, ed. by Choi Hung, music by Sherman Chow, DPs: Wai Ki Cho and Tung Lung Yee, and action dirs. were Lau Kar-wing and Yuen Bun. Released: Sept 14, 1989. 97 mins.

In the cast were: David Chiang Da-wei, Danny Lee Sau-yin, Chen Kuan-tai, Stephen Chow Sing-chi, Lo Lieh, Ti Lung, Cally Kwong Mei-wan, Wu Ma, Shing Fui-on, James Wong Jim, Bill Tung, Zhao Lei and Tien Niu. This crime drama from the two Woos – Woo and Wu – was made to raise money for Chang Cheh, and for the Hong Kong Directors' Union.

*OLD MASTER Q*

*Old Master Q* (2001) was dir. by Herman Yau Lai-to, wr. by Roy Szeto Cheuk-hon, Tsui Hark, Herman Yau and Man Choi-lee, exec. prod. by Charles Heung and Tsui Hark, music: Jan Hung Mak, DP: Puccini Yu, ed.: Ki-Hop Chan, and vfx supervisors: Eddy Wong and Victor Wong. Released: Apl 5, 2011. 102 mins.

In the cast were Nicholas Tse, Cecilia Cheung, Michael Wai-Man Chan, Alfred Cheung, Koon-Lan Law, and Emily Kwan.

*Old Master Q* was a live-action version of the long-running cartoon, film, TV series and comic series *Old Master Q* by Alfonso Wong (first published in 1962). *Old Master Q* exists in many forms – the live-action movie produced by Tsui Hark is just one of many.

## THE WARRIOR

*The Warrior* (a.k.a. *Wong Fei-hung: Brave Into the World,* 2006) was prod. by Yang Yong, dir. by Tiger Fu Yin and Chen Yue-Hu, script by Tiger Fu Yin, Chen Yue-Hu and Yang Yong, music: Peter Kam Pau Tat and James Wong Jim. Tsui Hark has art dir., presenter and co-script credits. Released: July 12, 2006. 88 mins.

*The Warrior* was a Wong Fei-hung adventure in animated form.

# FILMOGRAPHY

## MOVIES AS DIRECTOR

*The Butterfly Murders*, 1979
*We're Going To Eat You*, 1980
*Dangerous Encounters of the First Kind*, 1980
*All the Wrong Clues*, 1981
*Zu: Warriors From the Magic Mountain*, 1983
*Search For the Gods*, 1983
*Aces Go Places 3*, 1984
*Shanghai Blues*, 1984
*Working Class*, 1985
*Peking Opera Blues*, 1986
*Spirit Chaser Aisha*, 1986
*The Master*, 1989
*A Better Tomorrow 3*, 1989
*The Swordsman*, 1990
*Once Upon a Time in China*, 1991
*The Banquet*, 1991
*The Raid*, 1991
*Once Upon a Time in China 2*, 1992
*Twin Dragons*, 1992
*Once Upon a Time in China 3*, 1993
*Green Snake*, 1993
*Once Upon a Time in China 5*, 1994
*The Lovers*, 1994
*The Chinese Feast*, 1995
*Love In the Time of Twilight*, 1995
*The Blade*, 1995
*Tristar*, 1996
*Double Team*, 1997
*Knock Off*, 1998
*Time and Tide*, 2000
*The Legend of Zu*, 2001
*Black Mask 2: City of Masks*, 2002
*In The Blue*, 2005
*Seven Swords*, 2005
*The Warrior*, 2006
*Triangle*, 2007
*Missing*, 2008
*All About Women*, 2008
*Detective Dee and the Mystery of the Phantom Flame*, 2010
*The Flying Swords of Dragon Gate*, 2011

*Young Detective Dee: Rise of the Sea Dragon,* 2013
*Catching Monkey 3-D,* 2013
*The Taking of Tiger Mountain,* 2014
*Journey To the West: The Demons Strike Back,* 2017
*Detective Dee and the Four Heavenly Kings,* 2018
*The Battle At Lake Changjin,* 2021
*The Battle At Lake Changjin 2,* 2022
*The Legend of the Condor Heroes: The Great Hero,* 2025


MOVIES AS PRODUCER


*All the Wrong Spies,* 1983
*A Better Tomorrow,* 1986
*The Laser Man,* 1986
*A Chinese Ghost Story,* 1987
*A Better Tomorrow 2,* 1987
*The Big Heat,* 1988
*Gunmen,* 1988
*Diary of a Big Man,* 1988
*The King of Chess,* 1988/ 1992
*The Master,* 1989
*A Better Tomorrow 3,* 1989
*The Killer,* 1989
*Just Heroes,* 1989
*The Terracotta Warrior,* 1989
*The Swordsman,* 1990
*A Chinese Ghost Story 2,* 1990
*A Chinese Ghost Story 3,* 1991
*New Dragon Gate Inn,* 1992
*The Swordsman 2,* 1992
*The Wicked City,* 1992
*Once Upon a Time in China 2,* 1992
*Once Upon a Time in China 3,* 1993
*Green Snake,* 1993
*The Swordsman 3/ The East Is Red,* 1993
*Once Upon a Time in China 4,* 1993
*Once Upon a Time in China 5,* 1994
*The Lovers,* 1994
*Burning Paradise,* 1994
*The Chinese Feast,* 1995
*The Blade,* 1995
*Shanghai Grand,* 1996
*A Chinese Ghost Story: The Tsui Hark Animation,* 1997
*Once Upon a Time in China and America,* 1997
*Time and Tide,* 2000
*The Legend of Zu,* 2001
*Old Master Q,* 2001
*Tsui Hark's Vampire Hunters,* 2002
*Black Mask 2: City of Masks,* 2002
*Xanda,* 2004
*Seven Swords,* 2005
*Triangle,* 2006
*Missing,* 2008
*All About Women,* 2008

*Detective Dee and the Mystery of the Phantom Flame,* 2010
*The Flying Swords of Dragon Gate,* 2011
*Young Detective Dee: Rise of the Sea Dragon,* 2013
*Christmas Rose,* 2013
*The Taking of Tiger Mountain,* 2014
*Sword Master,* 2016
*The Thousand Faces of Dunjia,* 2017
*Journey To the West: The Demons Strike Back,* 2017
*Detective Dee and the Four Heavenly Kings,* 2018
*The Climbers,* 2019
*The Battle At Lake Changjin,* 2021
*The Battle At Lake Changjin 2,* 2022

# RECOMMENDED BOOKS AND WEBSITES

One of the finest general introductions to the history of Hong Kong cinema, and a great place to start, is *Hong Kong Cinema* (1997) by Stephen Teo. David Bordwell and Kristin Thompson are consistently excellent commentators on film, in books such as *Film History: An Introduction* (2010) and Bordwell's account of Hong Kong cinema, *Planet Hong Kong: Popular Cinema and the Art of Entertainment* (2000).

Bey Logan's *Hong Kong Action Cinema* (1995) is an entertaining introduction to the action side of Hong Kong cinema (with many valuable illustrations). *Kung-fu Cult Masters: From Bruce Lee To 'Crouching Tiger'* (2003) takes a more theoretical approach to the same subject.

For surveys of films, Jeff Yang's *Once Upon a Time In China* (2003) is superb, as is *Hong Kong Babylon* (1997) by F. Dannen & B. Long (this book also features many interviews with the key players in the Hong Kong industry). Lisa Morton's *The Cinema of Tsui Hark* (2001) is an important early study.

Jackie Chan has attracted many studies and biographies, including *Jackie Chan* by C. Gentry (1997), *The Essential Jackie Chan Sourcebook* by J. Rovin & K. Tracy (1997), and *Dying For Action: The Life and Times of Jackie Chan* by R. Witterstaetter (1997). And Chan's own memoirs: *I Am Jackie Chan* (1998) and *Never Grow Up* (2018).

Among critical essays, I would recommend *At Full Speed: Hong Kong Cinema In a Borderless World* (1998, edited by E.C.M. Yau) and *The Cinema of Hong Kong* (2002), edited by P. Fu & D. Desser.


WEBSITES

Hong Kong Movie Database
Love Hong Kong Film
Hong Kong Cinemagic
Film Workshop
Jet Li    jetli.com

# BIBLIOGRAPHY

## ON TSUI HARK

B. Accomando. "Army of Darkness: Hong Kong Director Tsui Hark Takes On the West", *Giant Robot*, 8, 1997

G. Hendrix. "Tsui Hark: Great Directors", *Senses of Cinema*, July, 2013

Howard Hampton. "Once Upon a Time In Hong Kong", *Film Comment*, 33, 1997

Hal Hinson. "*Peking Opera Blues*," *Washington Post*, Oct 14, 1988

D. Houx. "The Underrated Insanity of Tsui Hark and Jean-Claude van Damme's *Knock Off*', *Badass Digest*, 2014

A. Hwang. "The Irresistible: Hong Kong Movie *Once Upon a Time In China* Series", *Asian Cinema*, 10, 1, 1998

Y. Lee. "Artist Provocateur – On Tsui Hark", Hong Kong International Film Festival, 23, 1999

P. Macias. "Animerica Interview: Tsui Hark", *Animerica*, 7, 10

*The Making of A Chinese Ghost Story: The Tsui Hark Animation*, Hong Kong, 1997

L. Morton. *The Cinema of Tsui Hark*, McFarland, Jefferson, North Carolina, 2001

C. Reid. "Interview With Tsui Hark", *Film Quarterly*, 48, 3, 1995

S. Short. "Tsui Hark", interview, *Time*, CNN, 2000

Chuck Stephens. "Tsui Hark's Planet Hong Kong", *Village Voice*, May 1, 2001

S. Tan. "Ban(g)! Ban(g)! *Dangerous Encounter – 1st Kind*', *Asian Cinema*, 8, 1, 1996

Stephen Teo. "Tsui Hark: Filmography", *Senses of Cinema* 17, Nov, 2011

Tsui Hark. Interview, in F. Dannen, 1997

Ben Umstead. "An Interview With Tsui Hark", *Twitch*/ N.Y.A.F.F., 2011, July 11, 2011

## OTHERS

A. Abbas. *Hong Kong*, University of Minnoestoa Press, Minneapolis, 1997

J. Abert. *A Knight At the Movies: Medieval History On Film*, Routledge, London, 2003

G. Adair. *Vietnam on Film*, Proteus, New York, NY, 1981

—. *Hollywood's Vietnam*, Heinemann, London, 1989

R.C. Allen, ed. *Channels of Discourse: Television and Contemporary Criticism*, Methuen, London, 1987

R. Altman, ed. *Sound Theory, Sound Practice*, Routledge, London, 1992

—. *Film/ Genre*, British Film Institute, London, 1999

M. Anderegg, ed. *Inventing Vietnam*, Temple University Press, Philadelphia, PA, 1991

G. Andrew. *The Film Handbook*, Longman, London, 1989

—. *Stranger Than Paradise: Maverick Filmmakers In Recent American Cinema*, Prion, 1998

J. Arroyo. *Action/ Spectacle Cinema*, British Film Institute, London, 2000

A. Assister & A. Carol, eds. *Bad Girls and Dirty Pictures: The Challenge To Reclaim Feminism*, Pluto Press, London, 1993

A. Auster. *How the War Was Remembered: Hollywood and Vietnam*, Praeger, New York, NY, 1988

R. Baker & T. Russell. *The Essential Guide To Hong Kong Movies*, Eastern Heroes, London, 1994

—. *The Essential Guide To the Best of Eastern Heroes*, Eastern Heroes, London, 1995

—. *The Essential Guide To Deadly China Dolls*, Eastern Heroes, London, 1996

M. Barker, ed. *The Video Nasties: Freedom and Censorship In the Media*, Pluto Press, London, 1984

—. & J. Petley, eds. *Ill Effects: The Media/ Violence Debate*, Routledge, London, 1997

L. Bawden, ed. *The Oxford Companion To Film*, Oxford University Press, Oxford, 1976

J. Baxter. *George Lucas*, HarperCollins, London, 1999

J. Beck, ed. *Animation Art*, Flame Tree Publishing, London, 2004
M. Beja. *Film and Literature: An Introduction,* Longman, London, 1979
R. Bergan & R. Karney. *Bloomsbury Foreign Film Guide*, Bloomsbury, London, 1988
I. Bergman. *Talking With Ingmar Bergman*, Dallas, TX, 1983
—. *Bergman on Bergman, Interviews with Ingmar Bergman*, eds. S. Björkman, *et al,* tr. P. B. Austin, Touchstone, New York, NY, 1986
—. *The Magic Lantern: An Autobiography*, London, 1988
C. Berry. *Perspectives On Chinese Cinema*, B.F.I., London, 1991
P. Biskind. *Easy Riders, Raging Bulls: How the Sex 'n' Drugs 'n' Rock 'n' Roll Generation Saved Hollywood*, Bloomsbury, London, 1998
—. *Down and Dirty Pictures: Miramax, Sundance and the Rise of Independent Film*, Bloomsbury, London, 2004
M. Bliss. *Between the Bullets: The Spiritual Cinema of John Woo*, Scarecrow Press, Lanham, MD, 2002
A. Block & L. Wilson, eds. *George Lucas's Blockbusting*, HarperCollins, New York, 2010
D. Bordwell & K. Thompson. *Film Art: An Introduction*, McGraw-Hill Publishing Company, New York, NY, 1979
—. *et al. The Classical Hollywood Cinema: Film Style and Mode of Production To 1960*, Routledge, London, 1985
—. *Narration In the Fiction Film*, Routledge, London, 1988
—. *Making Meaning*, Harvard University Press, Cambridge, MA, 1989
—. & N. Caroll, eds. *Post-Theory: Reconstructing Film Studies*, University of Wisconsin Press, Madison, WI, 1996
—. *Planet Hong Kong: Popular Cinema and the Art of Entertainment,* Harvard University Press, 2000
—. "Aesthetics in Action: *Kungfu*, Gunplay and Cinematic Expressivity", in E. Yau, 2001
—. *The Way Hollywood Tells It*, University of California Press, Berkeley, CA, 2006
J. Bower, ed. *The Cinema of Japan and Korea*, Wallflower Press, London, 2004
D. Breskin. *Inner Voices: Filmmakers In Conversation*, Da Capo, New York, 1997
A. Britton *et al. American Nightmare: Essays On the Horror Film*, Toronto, 1979
A. Brown. *Directing Hong Kong: The Political Cinema of John Woo and Wong Kar-Wai*, Routledge/ Curzon, 2001
R. Brown. *Overtones and Undertones: Reading Film Music*, University of California Press, Berkeley, CA, 1994
N. Browne *et al*, eds. *New Chinese Cinema*, Cambridge University Press, 1994
S. Bukatman. *Terminal Identity: The Virtual Subject In Postmodern Science Fiction*, Duke University Press, Durham, NC, 1993
G. Burt. *The Art of Film Music*, Northeastern University Press, 1994
B. Camp & J. Davis. *Anime Classics*, Stone Bridge Press, CA, 2007
J. Campbell. *The Power of Myth*, with B. Moyers, ed. B.S. Flowers, Doubleday, New York, NY, 1988
J. Chan. *I Am Jackie Chan*, with Jeff Yang, Pan Books, 1998
—. *Never Grow Up*, Simon & Schuster, London, 2018
J. Charles. *The Hong Kong Filmography: 1977-1997*, McFarland, 2000
D. Chou. "*Once Upon a Time In China and America"*, *S.M.R. Home Theatre*, Nov, 1998.
R. Chu. "*Swordman II* and *The East Is Red"*, *Bright Lights*, 13, 1994
C. Chun-shu & Shelley Hsueh-lun Chang. *Redefining History: Ghosts, Spirits, and Human Society in Pu Sung-ling's World, 1640–1715*, University of Michigan Press, Ann Arbor, 1998
D. Chute & Cheng-Sim Lim, eds. *Heroic Grace: The Chinese Martial Arts Film*, University of California, Los Angeles, Film and Television Archive, 2003
P. Clark. *Chinese Cinema: Culture and Politics Since 1949*, Cambridge University Press, 1987
J. Clements & H. McCarthy, eds. *The Anime Encyclopedia*, Stone Bridge Press, Berkeley, CA, 2001/ 2007/ 2015
S. Cohan & I.R. Hark, eds. *Screening the Male: Exploring Masculinities In Hollywood Cinema*, Routledge, London, 1993
J. Collins *et al*, eds. *Film Theory Goes To the Movies*, Routledge, New York, NY, 1993
D.A. Cook. *A History of Narrative Film*, W.W. Norton, New York, NY, 1981, 1990, 1996
P. Cook, ed. *The Cinema Book*, British Film Institute, London, 1985/ 1999
S. Cornelius & I. Smith. *New Chinese Cinema*, Wallflower Press, London, 2002
J. Crist, ed. *Take 22: Moviemakers On Moviemaking*, Continuum, New York, NY, 1991
F. Dannen & B. Long. *Hong Kong Babylon*, Faber, London, 1997
G. Deleuze & F. Guattari. *Cinema 1: The Movement Image*, Athlone Press, London, 1989
—. *Cinema 2: The Time Image*, Athlone Press, London, 1989
C. Desjardins. *Outlaw Masters of Japanese Film*, I.B. Tauris, London, 2005
D. Desser. *Eros Plus Massacre: An Introduction to the Japanese New Wave Cinema*, Indiana University Press, Bloomington, IN, 1988
L. Dittmar & G. Michael. *From Hanoi To Hollywood*, Rutgers University Press, NJ, 1991
J. Donald, ed. *Fantasy and the Cinema*, British Film Institute, London, 1989

K.J. Donnelly, ed. *Film Music*, Edinburgh University Press, Edinburgh, 2001
C. Ducker & Stuart Cutler. *The H.K.S. Guide To Jet Li*, Hong Kong Superstars, London, 2000
M. Eagleton, ed. *Feminist Literary Theory: A Reader*, Blackwell, Oxford, 1986
—. ed. *Feminist Literary Criticism*, Longman, London, 1991
A. Easthope, ed. *Contemporary Film Theory*, Longman, London, 1993
P. Ettedgui. *Production Design & Art Direction*, RotoVision, 1999
D. Fairservice. *Film Editing*, Manchester University Press, Manchester, 2001
K. Fang. *John Woo's A Better Tomorrow, The New Hong Kong Cinema*, Hong Kong University Press, Hong Kong, 2004
C. Finch. *Special Effects*, Abbeville, 1984
J. Finler. *The Movie Director's Story*, Octopus Books, London, 1985
—. *The Hollywood Story*, Wallflower Press, London, 2003
C. Fleming. *High Concept: Don Simpson and the Hollywood Culture of Excess*, Bloomsbury, London, 1998
J. Fletcher & A. Benjamin, eds. *Abjection, Melancholia and Love: The Work of Julia Kristeva*, Routledge, London, 1990
K. Fowkes. *Giving Up the Ghost: Spirits, Ghosts and Angels In Mainstream Comedy Films*, Wayne State University Press, Detroit, MI, 1998
A. Frank. *Horror Films*, Hamlyn, London, 1977
—. *The Horror Film Handbook*, Barnes & Noble, 1982
K. French, ed. *Screen Violence*, Bloomsbury, London, 1996
P. Fu & D. Desser, eds. *The Cinema of Hong Kong*, Cambridge University Press, Cambridge, 2002
Lisa Funnell. *Warrior Women: Gender, Race, and the Transnational Chinese Action Star*, State University of New York Press, 2014
M. Gallagher. "Masculinity In Translation: Jackie Chan", *Velvet Light Trap*, 39, 1997
—. *Tony Leung Chiu-wai*, British Film Institute, 2018
L. Gamman & M. Marshment, eds. *The Female Gaze: Women as Viewers of Popular Culture*, Women's Press, London, 1988
J. Geiger & R. Rutsky, eds. *Film Analysis*, Norton & Company, New York, NY, 2005
K. Gelder & S. Thornton, eds. *The Subcultures Reader*, Routledge, London, 1997
—. ed. *The Horror Reader*, Routledge, London, 2000
J. Gelmis. *The Film Director as Superstar*, Penguin, London, 1974
C. Gentry. *Jackie Chan*, Taylor, Dallas, TX, 1997
Jean-Luc Godard. *Godard On Godard*, eds. J. Narobi & T. Milne, Da Capo, New York, NY, 1986
—. *Interviews*, ed. D. Sterritt, University of Mississippi Press, Jackson, 1998
L. Goldberg *et al*, eds. *Science Fiction Filmmaking In the 1980s*, McFarland, Jefferson, 1995
M. Goodwin & N. Wise. *On the Edge: The Life and Times of Francis Coppola*, William Morrow, New York, NY, 1989
B.K. Grant, ed. *Film Genre*, Scarecrow Press, Metuchen, NJ, 1977
—. ed. *Planks of Reason: Essays On the Horror Film*, Scarecrow Press, Metuchen, NJ, 1984
—. *Film Genre Reader II*, University of Texas Press, Austin, TX, 1995
—. ed. *The Dread of Difference: Gender and the Horror Film*, University of Texas Press, Austin, TX, 1996
E. Grosz. *Sexual Subversions*, Allen & Unwin, London, 1989
—. *Jacques Lacan: A Feminist Introduction*, Routledge, London, 1990
—. *Volatile Bodies*, Indiana University Press, Bloomington, IN, 1994
—. *Space, Time and Perversion*, Routledge, London, 1995
K. Hall. *John Woo: The Films*, McFarland & Co., Jefferson, N.C., 1999
L. Halliwell. *Halliwell's Filmgoer's Companion*, 7th edition, Granada, London, 1980
D. Hamamoto & S. Liu, eds. *Countervision: Asian-American Film Criticism*, Temple University Press, Philadelphia, PA, 2000
S. Hammond. *Hollywood East*, Contemporary Books, Lincoln, IL, 2000
P. Hardy, ed. *The Aurum Encyclopedia of Science Fiction*, Aurum, London, 1991
C. Heard. *Ten Thousand Bullets: The Cinematic Journey of John Woo*, Lone Eagle Publishing Co., L.A., 2000
S. & N. Hibbin. *The Official James Bond Movie Book*, Hamlyn, London, 1989
G. Hickenlooper. *Reel Conversations: Candid Interviews With Film's Foremost Directors and Critics*, Citadel, New York, NY, 1991
J. Hillier. *The New Hollywood*, Studio Vista, London, 1992
—. *American Independent Cinema: A Sight & Sound Reader*, British Film Institute, London, 2001
L.C. Hillstrom, ed. *International Dictionary of Films and Filmmakers: Directors*, St James Press, London, 1997
Sam Ho, ed. *The Swordsman and His Juang Hu: Tsui Hark and Hong Kong Film*, Hong Kong University Press, Hong Kong, 2002
Hong Kong Film Archive. *The Making of Martial Arts Films*, Hong Kong Provisional Urban Council, 1999
Hong Kong International Film Festival. *Hong Kong Panorama*, Leisure and Cultural Services

Department

Hong Kong International Film Festival. *Hong Kong New Wave: Twenty Years After*, Provisional Urban Council of Hong Kong, 1999

Hong Kong International Film Festival. *Hong Kong Cinema '79-'89*, Leisure and Cultural Services Department, 2000

D. Hudson. *Draculas, Vampires, and Other Undead Forms*, Rowman & Littlefield, 2009

D. Hughes. *Comic Book Movies*, Virgin, London, 2003

L. Hughes. *The Rough Guide To Gangster Movies*, Penguin, 2005

L. Hunt. "Once Upon a Time In China: Kung Fu From Bruce Lee To Jet Li", *Framework*, 40, 1999

—. *Kung-fu Cult Masters: From Bruce Lee To 'Crouching Tiger'*, Wallflower Press, London, 2003

J. Hunter. *Eros In Hell: Sex, Blood and Madness In Japanese Cinema*, Creation Books, London, 1998

J. Inverne. *Musicals*, Faber, London, 2009

L. Irigiaray. *The Irigaray Reader,* ed. M. Whitford, Blackwell, Oxford, 1991

S. Jackson & J. Jones, eds. *Contemporary Feminist Theories*, Edinburgh University Press, Edinburgh, 1998

S. Jaworzyn, ed. *Shock: The Essential Guide To Exploitation Cinema*, Titan Books, London, 1996

S. Jeffords. *Hard Bodies: Hollywood Masculinity In the Reagan Era*, Rutgers University Press, New Brunswick, NJ, 1994

E. Jeffreys & L. Edwards, eds. *Celebrity In China*, Hong Kong University Press, Hong Kong, 2010

K. Kalinak. *Settling the Score: Music and the Classical Hollywood Film*, University of Wisconsin Press, Madison, WI, 1992

B.F. Kawin. *Mindscreen: Bergman, Godard and First-Person Film*, Princeton University Press, Princeton, NJ, 1978

—. *How Movies Work*, Macmillan, New York, NY, 1987

P. Keough, ed. *Flesh and Blood: The National Society of Film Critics on Sex, Violence, and Censorship*, Mercury House, San Francisco, CA, 1995

M. Kinder. *Playing With Power In Movies*, University of California Press, Berkeley, CA, 1991

P. Kolker. *The Altering Eye: Contemporary International Cinema*, Oxford University Press, New York, NY, 1983

—. *A Cinema of Loneliness: Penn, Stone, Kubrick, Scorsese, Spielberg, Altman*, Oxford University Press, New York, NY, 2000

P. Kramer. *The Big Picture: Hollywood Cinema From Star Wars To Titanic*, British Film Institute, London, 2001

—. *The New Hollywood*, Wallflower Press, London, 2005

J. Kristeva. *About Chinese Women*, tr. A. Barrows, Marion Boyars, London, 1977

—. *Desire In Language: A Semiotic Approach To Literature and Art*, ed. L.S. Roudiez, tr. T. Gora *et al*, Blackwell 1982

—. *Powers of Horror: An Essay on Abjection*, tr. L.S. Roudiez, Columbia University Press, New York, NY, 1982

—. *Revolution In Poetic Language*, tr. M. Walker, Columbia University Press, New York, NY, 1984

—. *The Kristeva Reader*, ed. T. Moi, Blackwell, Oxford, 1986

—. *Tales of Love*, tr. L.S. Roudiez, Columbia University Press, New York, NY, 1987

—. *Black Sun: Depression and Melancholy*, tr. L.S. Roudiez, Columbia University Press, New York, NY, 1989

—. *Strangers To Ourselves*, tr. L.S. Roudiez, Harvester Wheatsheaf 1991

J. Kwok Wah Lau. "Imploding Genre, Gender and History: *Peking Opera Blues*", in J. Geiger, 2005

M. Lanning. *Vietnam At the Movies*, Fawcett Columbine, New York, NY, 1994

R. Lapsley & M. Westlake, eds. *Film Theory: An Introduction*, Manchester University Press, Manchester, 1988

Shing-hou Lau, ed. *A Study of the Hong Kong Martial Arts Film*, Hong Kong International Film Festival, 1980

—. *A Study of the Hong Kong Swordplay Film, 1945-80*, Hong Kong International Film Festival, 1981

Law Kar, ed. *Fifty Years of Elecric Shadows*, Hong Kong International Film Festival, 1997

M. Lee. *"Once Upon a Time In China"*, Criterion, 2021

J. Lent. *The Asian Film Industry*, Austin, TX, 1990

T. Leung Siu-hung. "Mastering Action", Hong Kong Cinemagic, March, 2006

E. Levy. *Cinema of Outsiders: The Rise of American Independent Film,* New York University Press, New York, NY, 1999

J. Lewis. *The Road To Romance and Ruin: Teen Films and Youth Culture*, Routledge, London, 1992

—. *Whom God Wishes To Destroy: Francis Coppola and the New Hollywood*, Duke

University Press, Durham, NC, 1995
—. ed. *New American Cinema*, Duke University Press, Durham, NC, 1998
—. *Hollywood v. Hard Core: How the Struggle Over Censorship Created the Modern Film Industry*, New York University Press, New York, NY, 2000
J. Leyda. ed. *Film Makers Speak: Voices of Film Experience*, Da Capo, New York, NY, 1977
V. LoBrutto. *Sound-On-Film*, Praeger, New York, NY, 1994
B. Logan. *Hong Kong Action Cinema*, Titan, London, 1995
S. Lu, ed. *Transnational Chinese Cinemas*, University of Hawaii Press, Honolulu, 1997
H. Ludi. *Movie Worlds: Production Design In Film*, Mengers, Stuttgart, 2000
B. McCabe. *The Rough Guide To Comedy Movies*, Rough Guides, London, 2005
R. Maltby. *Harmless Entertainment: Hollywood and the Ideology of Consensus*, Scarecrow Press, Metuchen, NJ, 1983
—. & I. Craven. *Hollywood Cinema: An Introduction*, Blackwell, Oxford, 1995
—. *Hollywood Cinema*, 2nd ed., Blackwell, Oxford, 2003
E. Marks & I. de Courtivron, eds. *New French Feminisms: an anthology*, Harvester Wheatsheaf, Hemel Hempstead, 1981
G. Mast *et al*, eds. *Film Theory and Criticism: Introductory Readings*, Oxford University Press, New York, NY, 1992a
—. & B Kawin. *A Short History of the Movies*, Macmillan, New York, NY, 1992b
C. Marx. *Jet Li*, Martial Arts Masters, Rosen Publishing Group, 2002
T.D. Matthews. *Censored*, Chatto & Windus, London, 1994
F. McConnell. *Storytelling and Mythmaking*, Oxford University Press, New York, NY, 1979
S.Y. McDougal. *Made Into Movies: From Literature To Film*, Holt, Rinehart and Winston, New York, NY, 1985
M. Medved. *Hollywood vs. America*, HarperCollins, London, 1992
R. Meyers. *Martial Arts Movies*, Citadel Press, NJ, 1985
—. *Great Martial Arts Movies*, Citadel Press, NJ, 2001
D. Millar. *Cinema Secrets: Special Effects*, Apple Press, 1990
T. Miller *et al*, eds. *Global Hollywood*, British Film Institute, London, 2001
T. Moi. *Sexual/ Textual Politics: Feminist Literary Theory*, Methuen, London, 1983
J. Monaco. *The New Wave: Truffaut, Godard, Chabrol, Rohmer, Rivette*, Oxford University Press, New York, NY, 1977
—. *American Film Now*, New American Library, London, 1979
—. *How To Read a Film*, Oxford University Press, Oxford, 1981
R. Murray. *Images In the Dark: An Encyclopedia of Gay and Lesbian Film and Video*, Titan Books, London, 1998
S. Neale. *Cinema and Technology*, Macmillan, London, 1985
—. & M. Smith, eds. *Contemporary Hollywood Cinema*, Routledge, London, 1998
—. *Genre and Contemporary Hollywood*, Routledge, London, 2002
J. Nelmes, ed. *An Introduction To Film Studies*, Routledge, London, 1996
D. Neumann, ed. *Film Architecture: From Metropolis To Blade Runner*, Prestel-Verlag, New York, NY, 1996
K. Newman. *Nightmare Movies*, Harmony, New York, NY, 1988
—. *Millennium Movies*, Titan Books, London, 1999
G. Nowell-Smith, ed. *The Oxford History of World Cinema*, Oxford University Press, Oxford, 1996
D. O'Brien. *Spooky Encounters: A Gwailo's Guide To Hong Kong Horror*, Headpress, 2004
T. Ohanian & M. Phillips. *Digital Filmmaking*, 2nd ed., Focal Press, Boston, MA, 2000
J. Orr. *Contemporary Cinema*, Edinburgh University Press, Edinburgh, 1998
B. Palmer *et al*. *The Encyclopedia of Martial Arts Movies*, Scarecrow Press, NJ, 1995
A. Paludan. *Chronicle of the Chinese Emperors*, Thames & Hudson, 1998
L. Pang. *Masculinities and Hong Kong Cinema*, Kent State University Press, 2005
D. Parkinson. *The Rough Guide To Film Musicals*, Penguin, London, 2007
J. Parish. *Jet Li: A Biography*, Thunder's Mouth Press, New York, 2002
F. Patten. *Watching Anime, Reading Manga*, Stone Bridge Press, CA, 2004
D. Peary & G. Peary, eds. *The American Animated Cartoon*, Dutton, New York, NY, 1980
—. *Cult Movies 2*, Vermilion, London, 1984
—. *Cult Movies 3*, Sigwick & Jackson, London, 1989
C. Penley, ed. *Feminism and Film Theory*, Routledge, London, 1988
D. Petrie. *Screening Europe: Image and Identity In Contemporary European Cinema*, British Film Institute, London, 1992
P. Phillips. *Understanding Film Texts*, British Film Institute, London, 2000
M. Pierson. *Special Effects*, Columbia University Press, New York, NY, 2002
L. Pietropaolo & A. Testaferri, eds. *Feminisms In the Cinema*, Indiana University Press, Bloomington, IN, 1995
D. Pollock. *Skywalking: The Life and Films of George Lucas*, Crown, New York, NY, 1983, 1990, 2000
M. Polly. *Bruce Lee*, Simon & Schuster, New York, 2018
S. Prince, ed. *Screening Violence*, Athlone Press, London, 2000
D. Prindle. *Risky Business: The Political Economy of Hollywood*, Westview, Boulder, CO,

1993

N. Proferes. *Film Directing Fundamentals*, Focal Press, Boston, MA, 2001

M. Pye & Lynda Myles. *The Movie Brats: How the Film Generation Took Over Hollywood*, Faber, London, 1979

T. Reeves. *The Worldwide Guide To Movie Locations*, Titan Books, London, 2003

P. Rice & P. Waugh, eds. *Modern Literary Theory: A Reader*, Arnold, London, 1992

D. Richie. *The Films of Akira Kurosawa*, University of California Press, Berkeley, CA, 1965

R. Rickitt. *Special Effects*, Aurum, London, 2006

B. Robb. *Screams and Nightmares*, Titan Books, London, 1998

J. Robertson. *The British Board of Film Censors*, Croom Helm, 1985

D. Robinson. *World Cinema*, Methuen, London, 1981

W.H. Rockett. *Devouring Whirlwind: Terror and Transcendence In the Cinema of Cruelty*, Greenwood Press, New York, NY, 1988

S. Rohdie. *The Passion of Pier Paolo Pasolini*, British Film Institute, London, 1995

J. Romney & A. Wootton, eds. *Celluloid Jukebox: Popular Music and the Movies Since the 50s*, British Film Institute, London, 1995

P. Rosen, ed. *Narrative, Apparatus, Ideology: A Film Theory Reader*, Columbia University Press, New York, NY, 1986

J. Rosenbaum. *Placing Movies*, University of California Press, Berkeley, CA, 1995

R. Rosenblum & R. Karen. *When the Shooting Stops... The Cutting Begins: A Film Editor's Story*, Da Capo Press, New York, NY, 1979

J. Ross. *The Incredibly Strange Film Book: An Alternative History of Cinema*, Simon and Schuster, 1993

*The Rough Guide To China*, Penguin, 2017

R. Roud. *Jean-Luc Godard*, Thames & Hudson, London, 1970

J. Rovin & K. Tracy. *The Essential Jackie Chan Sourcebook*, Pocket Books, New York, 1997

M. Rubin. *Thrillers*, Cambridge University Press, Cambridge, 1999

K. Russell. *A British Picture: An Autobiography*, Heinemann, London, 1989

V. Russo. *The Celluloid Closet: Homosexuality In the Movies*, Harper & Row, New York, NY, 1981

K. Sandler. *Reading the Rabbit: Explorations In Warner Bros. Animation*, Rutgers University Press, Brunswick, NJ, 1998

A. Sarris. *The American Cinema*, Dutton, New York, NY, 1968

T. Sato. *Currents In Japanese Cinema*, Kodansha, New York, 1982

D. Schaefer & L. Salvato, eds. *Masters of Light*, University of California Press, Berkeley, CA, 1984

T. Schatz. *Hollywood Genres,* Random House, New York, NY, 1981

—. *Old Hollywood/ New Hollywood*, UMI Research Press, Ann Arbor, MI, 1983

—. *The Genius of the System: Hollywood Filmmaking In the Studio Era*, Pantheon, New York, NY 1988

F. Schodt. *Inside the Robot Kingdom: Japan, Mechatronics and the Coming Robotopia*, Kodansha, Tokyo, 1988

—. *Manga! Manga! The World of Japanese Magazines*, Kodansha International, London, 1997

—. *Dreamland Japan: Writings On Modern Manga*, Stone Bridge Press, Berkeley, CA, 2002

P. Schrader. *Transcendental Style In Film: Ozu, Bresson, Dreyer*, Da Capo Press, 1972

A. Schroeder. *Tsui Hark's Zu: Warriors From the Magic Mountain*, Hong Kong University Press, Hong Kong, 2004

R. Schubart. *Super Bitches and Action Babes: The Female Hero In Popular Cinema, 1970-2006,* McFarland, 2007

M. Schumacher. *Francis Ford Coppola*, Bloomsbury, London, 2000

M. Scorsese. *Scorsese On Scorsese*, ed. D. Thompson & I. Christie, Faber, London, 1989, 1995

*Screen Reader I: Cinema/ Ideology/ Politics*, Society for Education in Film & TV, 1977

*Screen Reader II: Cinema and Semiotics*, British Film Institute, London, 1982

C. Sharrett, ed. *Crisis Cinema*, Maisonneuve Press, Washington, DC, 1993

—. *Mythologies of Violence In Postmodern Media*, Wayne State University Press, 1999

M. Shiel & T. Fitzmaurice, eds. *Screenng the City*, Verso, London, 2003

D. Shipman. *The Story of Cinema*, Hodder & Stoughton, London, 1984

T. Shone. *Blockbuster: How the Jaws and Jedi Generation Turned Hollywood Into a Boom-Town*, Scribner, London, 2005

E. Showalter, ed. *The New Feminist Criticism,* Virago, London, 1986

E. Siciliano. *Pasolini: A Biography*, Bloomsbury, London, 1987

L. Sider *et al*, eds. *Soundscapes: The School of Sound Lectures 1998-2001*, Wallflower Press, London, 2003

M. Singer. *A History of the American Avant-Garde Cinema*, American Federation of the Arts, New York, NY, 1976

P. Adams Sitney, ed. *The Film Culture Reader*, Praeger, New York, NY, 1970

—. ed. *The Avant-Garde Film: A Reader of Theory and Criticism*, New York University Press,

New York, NY, 1978

—. *Visionary Film: The American Avant-Garde, 1943-1978*, 2nd ed., Oxford University Press, New York, NY, 1979

G. Smith. *Epic Films*, McFarland, Jefferson, NC, 1991

J. Smith. *Looking Away: Hollywood and Vietnam*, Scribner's, New York, NY, 1975

T.G. Smith. *Industrial Light and Magic: The Art of Special Effects*, Columbus Books, 1986

E. Smoodin. *Animating Culture: Hollywood Cartoons From the Sound Era*, Roundhouse, 1993

—. ed. *Disney Discourse: Producing the Magic Kingdom*, Routledge, London, 1994

V. Sobchack. *The Limits of Infinity: The American Science Fiction Film*, A.S. Barnes, New York, NY, 1980

—. *Screening Space: The American Science Fiction Film*, Ungar, New York, NY, 1987/ 1993

J. Squire, ed. *The Movie Business Book*, Fireside, New York, NY, 1992

J. Staiger. *Interpreting Films*, Princeton University Press, Princeton, NJ, 1992

—. *Perverse Spectators: The Practices of Film Reception,* New York University Press, New York, NY, 2000

N. Stair. *Michelle Yeoh,* Rosen Publishing Group, 2001

B. Steene. *Ingmar Bergman*, Twayne, Boston, MA, 1968

L. Stern. *The Scorsese Connection*, British Film Institute, London, 1995

D. Sterritt. *The Films of Jean-Luc Godard*, Cambridge University Press, Cambridge, 1999

G. Stewart. *Between Film and Screen: Modernism's Photo Synthesis*, University of Chicago Press, Chicago, IL, 1999

M. Stokes & R. Maltby, eds. *Identifying Hollywood Audiences*, British Film Institute, London, 1999

J. Storey, ed. *Cultural Theory and Popular Culture*, Harvester Wheatsheaf, Hemel Hempstead, 1994

J.M. Straczynski. *The Complete Book of Scriptwriting*, Titan Books, London, 1997

J. Stringer. "Problems With the Treatment of Hong Kong Cinema As Camp", *Asian Cinema*, 8, 2, 1996

—. ed. *Movie Blockbusters*, Routledge, London, 2003

C. Sylvester, ed. *The Penguin Book of Hollywood*, Penguin, London, 1999

K. Tam & W. Dissanayake. *New Chinese Cinema*, Oxford University Press, Hong Kong, 1998

A. Tarkovsky. *Sculpting In Time: Reflections On the Cinema*, tr. K. Hunter-Blair, Faber, London, 1989

C. Tashiro. *Pretty Pictures: Production Design and the History Film,* University of Texas Press, 1998

Y. Tasker. *Spectacular Bodies: Gender, Genre and the Action Cinema*, Routledge, London, 1993

R. Taylor *et al*, eds. *The B.F.I. Companion To Eastern European and Russian Cinema*, British Film Institute, London, 2000

S. Teo. *Hong Kong Cinema*, British Film Institute, London, 1997

—. "Tsui Hark", in C. Yau, 1998

B. Thomas. *Video Hound's Dragon: Asian Action and Cult Flicks*, Visible Ink Press, 2003

K. Thompson & D. Bordwell. *Film History: An Introduction*, McGraw-Hill, New York, NY, 1994/ 2010

—. *Storytelling In the New Hollywood*, Harvard University Press, Cambridge, MA, 1999

D. Thomson. *A Biographical Dictionary of Film,* Deutsch, London, 1995

S. Thrower, ed. *Eyeball: Compendium: Sex and Horror, Art and Exploitation*, F.A.B. Press, Godalming, Surrey, 2003

C. Tohill & P. Tombs. *Immoral Tales: Sex and Horror Cinema In Europe 1956-1984*, Titan Books, London, 1995

J. Trevelyan. *What the Censor Saw*, Michael Joseph, London, 1973

A.D. Vacche. *Cinema and Painting*, Athlone Press, London, 1996

K. Van Gunden. *Fantasy Films*, McFarland, Jefferson, NC 1989

—. *Postmodern Auteurs: Coppola, Lucas, De Palma, Spielberg and Scorsese*, McFarland, Jefferson, NC 1991

M.C. Vaz. *From Star Wars To Indiana Jones*, Chronicle, San Francisco, CA, 1994

—. & P.R. Duignan. *Industrial Light & Magic*, Virgin, London, 1996

G. Vincendeau, ed. *Encyclopedia of European Cinema*, British Film Institute, London, 1995

—. ed. *Film/ Literature/ Heritage: A Sight & Sound Reader*, British Film Institute, London, 2001

P. Virillio. *War and Cinema*, Verso, London, 1992

D. Vivier & T. Podvin. "Through the Lens of Arthur Wong", Hong Kong Cinemagic, Jan 2005

H. Vogel. *Entertainment Industry Economics*, Cambridge University Press, Cambridge, 1995

C. Vogler. *The Writer's Journey: Mythic Structure For Storytellers and Screenwriters*, Pan, London, 1998

J. Wasko. *Movies and Money*, Ablex, NJ, 1982

—. *Hollywood In the Information Age*, Polity Press, Cambridge, 1994

E. Weiss. & J. Belton, eds. *Film Sound: Theory and Practice*, Columbia University Press,

New York, NY, 1989

T. Weisser. *Asian Cult Cinema*, Boulveard Books, New York, NY, 1997

O. Welles. *This is Orson Welles*, HarperCollins, London, 1992

P. Wells. *Understanding Animation*, Routledge, London, 1998

D. West. *Chasing Dragons: An Introduction To the Martial Arts Film*, I.B. Tauris, London, 2006

L. Williams, ed. *Viewing Positions: Ways of Seeing Film*, Rutgers University Press, New Brunswick, NJ, 1995

T. Williams. "To Live and Die In Hong Kong", *Cineaction*, 36, 1995

—. "Kwan Tak-hing and the New Generation", *Asian Cinema*, 10, 1, 1998

—. "Space, Place and Spectacle: the Crisis Cinema of John Woo", in P. Fu, 2002

R. Witterstaetter. *Dying For Action: The Life and Times of Jackie Chan*, Warner Books, New York, 1997

M. Wolf. *The Entertainment Economy*, Penguin, London, 1999

P. Wollen: *Signs and Meaning In the Cinema*, Secker & Warburg, London, 1972

J. Woo. Interview, in J. Arroyo, 2000

—. *Interviews; Conversations With Filmmakers Series*, ed. R. Elder, University Press of Mississippi, 2005

M. Wood. *Cine East: Hong Kong Cinema Through the Looking Glass*, F.A.B. Press, 1998

R. Wood. *Hollywood From Vietnam To Reagan... and Beyond*, Columbia University Press, New York, NY, 2003

T. Woods. *Beginning Postmodernism*, Manchester University Press, Manchester, 1999

J. Wyatt. *High Concept: Movies and Marketing In Hollywood*, University of Texas Press, Austin, TX, 1994

J. Yang *et al. Eastern Standard Time: A Guide To Asian Influence On American Culture*, Houghton Mifflin, Boston, MA, 1997

—. *Once Upon a Time In China*, Atria Books, New York, NY, 2003

E.C.M. Yau, ed. *At Full Speed: Hong Kong Cinema In a Borderless World*, University of Minnesota Press, Minneapolis, MN, 1998

Z. Yimou. *Zhang Yimou: Interviews, Conversations With Filmmakers Series*, ed. F. Gateward, University Press of Mississippi, 2001

Judith T. Zeitlin. *Historian of the Strange: Pu Songling and the Chinese Classical Tale*, Stanford University Press, Stanford, CA, 1993

Y. Zhang & X. Zhiwei, eds. *Encyclopedia of Chinese Film*, Routledge, 1998

J. Zipes. *The Enchanted Screen: The Unknown History of Fairy-tale Films*, Routledge, New York, NY, 2011

S. Zizek. *Enjoy Your Symptom Jacques Lacan In Hollywood and Out*, Routledge, New York, NY, 1992

—. *The Fright of Real Tears: The Uses and Misuses of Lacan In Film Theory*, British Film Institute, London, 1999

JEREMY ROBINSON has published poetry, fiction, and studies of J.R.R. Tolkien, Samuel Beckett, Thomas Hardy, André Gide and D.H. Lawrence. Robinson has edited poetry books by Novalis, Ursula Le Guin, Friedrich Hölderlin, Francesco Petrarch, Dante Alighieri, Arseny Tarkovsky, and Rainer Maria Rilke.

Books on film and animation include: *The Akira Book* • *The Art of Katsuhiro Otomo* • *The Art of Masamune Shirow* • *The Ghost In the Shell Book* • *Fullmetal Alchemist* • *Cowboy Bebop: The Anime and Movie* • *The Cinema of Hayao Miyazaki* • *Hayao Miyazaki: Pocket Guide* • *Princess Mononoke: Pocket Movie Guide* • *Spirited Away: Pocket Movie Guide* • *Blade Runner and the Cinema of Philip K. Dick* • *Blade Runner: Pocket Movie Guide* • *The Cinema of Donald Cammell* • *Performance: Donald Cammell: Nic Roeg: Pocket Movie Guide* • *Pasolini: Il Cinema di Poesia/ The Cinema of Poetry* • *Salo: Pocket Movie Guide* • *The Trilogy of Life Movies: Pocket Movie Guide* • *The Gospel According To Matthew: Pocket Movie Guide* • *The Ecstatic Cinema of Tony Ching Siu-tung* • *Tsui Hark: The Dragon Master of Chinese Cinema* • *The Swordsman: Pocket Movie Guide* • *A Chinese Ghost Story: Pocket Movie Guide* • *Ken Russell: England's Great Visionary Film Director and Music Lover* • *Tommy: Ken Russell: The Who: Pocket Movie Guide* • *Women In Love: Ken Russell: D.H. Lawrence: Pocket Movie Guide* • *The Devils: Ken Russell: Pocket Movie Guide* • *Walerian Borowczyk: Cinema of Erotic Dreams* • *The Beast: Pocket Movie Guide* • *The Lord of the Rings Movies* • *The Fellowship of the Ring: Pocket Movie Guide* • *The Two Towers: Pocket Movie Guide* • *The Return of the King: Pocket Movie Guide* • *Jean-Luc Godard: The Passion of Cinema* • *The Sacred Cinema of Andrei Tarkovsky* • *Andrei Tarkovsky: Pocket Guide*.

'It's amazing for me to see my work treated with such passion and respect. There is nothing resembling it in the U.S. in relation to my work.'
(Andrea Dworkin)

'This model monograph – it is an exemplary job, and I'm very proud that he has accorded me a couple of mentions… The subject matter of his book is beautifully organised and dead on beam.'
(Lawrence Durrell, on *The Light Eternal: A Study of J.M.W. Turner*)

'Jeremy Robinson's poetry is certainly jammed with ideas, and I find it very interesting for that reason. It's certainly a strong imprint of his personality.'
(Colin Wilson)

'*Sex-Magic-Poetry-Cornwall* is a very rich essay... It is a very good piece… vastly stimulating and insightful.'
(Peter Redgrove)

# CRESCENT MOON PUBLISHING

web: www.crmoon.com e-mail: cresmopub@yahoo.co.uk

## ARTS, PAINTING, SCULPTURE

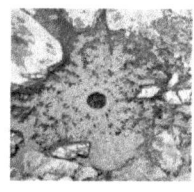

The Art of Andy Goldsworthy
Andy Goldsworthy: Touching Nature
Andy Goldsworthy in Close-Up
Andy Goldsworthy: Pocket Guide
Andy Goldsworthy In America
Land Art: A Complete Guide
The Art of Richard Long
Richard Long: Pocket Guide
Land Art In the UK
Land Art in Close-Up
Land Art In the U.S.A.
Land Art: Pocket Guide
Installation Art in Close-Up
Minimal Art and Artists In the 1960s and After
Colourfield Painting
Land Art DVD, TV documentary
Andy Goldsworthy DVD, TV documentary
The Erotic Object: Sexuality in Sculpture From Prehistory to the Present Day
Sex in Art: Pornography and Pleasure in Painting and Sculpture
Postwar Art
Sacred Gardens: The Garden in Myth, Religion and Art
Glorification: Religious Abstraction in Renaissance and 20th Century Art
Early Netherlandish Painting
Leonardo da Vinci
Piero della Francesca
Giovanni Bellini
Fra Angelico: Art and Religion in the Renaissance
Mark Rothko: The Art of Transcendence
Frank Stella: American Abstract Artist
Jasper Johns
Brice Marden
Alison Wilding: The Embrace of Sculpture
Vincent van Gogh: Visionary Landscapes
Eric Gill: Nuptials of God
Constantin Brancusi: Sculpting the Essence of Things
Max Beckmann
Caravaggio
Gustave Moreau
Egon Schiele: Sex and Death In Purple Stockings
Delizioso Fotografico Fervore: Works In Process 1
Sacro Cuore: Works In Process 2
The Light Eternal: J.M.W. Turner
The Madonna Glorified: Karen Arthurs

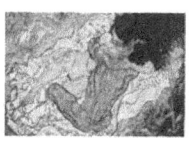

# LITERATURE

J.R.R. Tolkien: The Books, The Films, The Whole Cultural Phenomenon
J.R.R. Tolkien: Pocket Guide
Tolkien's Heroic Quest
The *Earthsea* Books of Ursula Le Guin
Beauties, Beasts and Enchantment: Classic French Fairy Tales
German Popular Stories by the Brothers Grimm
Philip Pullman and *His Dark Materials*
Sexing Hardy: Thomas Hardy and Feminism
Thomas Hardy's *Tess of the d'Urbervilles*
Thomas Hardy's *Jude the Obscure*
Thomas Hardy: The Tragic Novels
Love and Tragedy: Thomas Hardy
The Poetry of Landscape in Hardy
Wessex Revisited: Thomas Hardy and John Cowper Powys
Wolfgang Iser: Essays and Interviews
Petrarch, Dante and the Troubadours
Maurice Sendak and the Art of Children's Book Illustration
Andrea Dworkin
Cixous, Irigaray, Kristeva: The *Jouissance* of French Feminism
Julia Kristeva: Art, Love, Melancholy, Philosophy, Semiotics and Psychoanalysis
Hélène Cixous I Love You: The *Jouissance* of Writing
Luce Irigaray: Lips, Kissing, and the Politics of Sexual Difference
Peter Redgrove: Here Comes the Flood
Peter Redgrove: Sex-Magic-Poetry-Cornwall
Lawrence Durrell: Between Love and Death, East and West
Love, Culture & Poetry: Lawrence Durrell
Cavafy: Anatomy of a Soul
German Romantic Poetry: Goethe, Novalis, Heine, Hölderlin
Feminism and Shakespeare
Shakespeare: Love, Poetry & Magic
The Passion of D.H. Lawrence
D.H. Lawrence: Symbolic Landscapes
D.H. Lawrence: Infinite Sensual Violence
Rimbaud: Arthur Rimbaud and the Magic of Poetry
The Ecstasies of John Cowper Powys
Sensualism and Mythology: The Wessex Novels of John Cowper Powys
Amorous Life: John Cowper Powys and the Manifestation of Affectivity (H.W. Fawkner)
Postmodern Powys: New Essays on John Cowper Powys (Joe Boulter)
Rethinking Powys: Critical Essays on John Cowper Powys
Paul Bowles & Bernardo Bertolucci
Rainer Maria Rilke
Joseph Conrad: *Heart of Darkness*
In the Dim Void: Samuel Beckett
Samuel Beckett Goes into the Silence
André Gide: Fiction and Fervour
Jackie Collins and the Blockbuster Novel
Blinded By Her Light: The Love-Poetry of Robert Graves
The Passion of Colours: Travels In Mediterranean Lands
Poetic Forms

## POETRY

Ursula Le Guin: Walking In Cornwall
Peter Redgrove: Here Comes The Flood
Peter Redgrove: Sex-Magic-Poetry-Cornwall
Dante: Selections From the Vita Nuova
Petrarch, Dante and the Troubadours
William Shakespeare: Sonnets
William Shakespeare: Complete Poems
Blinded By Her Light: The Love-Poetry of Robert Graves
Emily Dickinson: Selected Poems
Emily Brontë: Poems
Thomas Hardy: Selected Poems
Percy Bysshe Shelley: Poems
John Keats: Selected Poems
Joh n Keats: Poems of 1820
D.H. Lawrence: Selected Poems
Edmund Spenser: Poems
Edmund Spenser: Amoretti
John Donne: Poems
Henry Vaughan: Poems
Sir Thomas Wyatt: Poems
Robert Herrick: Selected Poems
Rilke: Space, Essence and Angels in the Poetry of Rainer Maria Rilke
Rainer Maria Rilke: Selected Poems
Friedrich Hölderlin: Selected Poems
Arseny Tarkovsky: Selected Poems
Arthur Rimbaud: Selected Poems
Arthur Rimbaud: A Season in Hell
Arthur Rimbaud and the Magic of Poetry
Novalis: Hymns To the Night
German Romantic Poetry
Paul Verlaine: Selected Poems
Elizaethan Sonnet Cycles
D.J. Enright: By-Blows
Jeremy Reed: Brigitte's Blue Heart
Jeremy Reed: Claudia Schiffer's Red Shoes
Gorgeous Little Orpheus
Radiance: New Poems
Crescent Moon Book of Nature Poetry
Crescent Moon Book of Love Poetry
Crescent Moon Book of Mystical Poetry
Crescent Moon Book of Elizabethan Love Poetry
Crescent Moon Book of Metaphysical Poetry
Crescent Moon Book of Romantic Poetry
Pagan America: New American Poetry

# MEDIA, CINEMA, FEMINISM and CULTURAL STUDIES

J.R.R. Tolkien: The Books, The Films, The Whole Cultural Phenomenon
J.R.R. Tolkien: Pocket Guide
The *Lord of the Rings* Movies: Pocket Guide
The Cinema of Hayao Miyazaki
Hayao Miyazaki: *Princess Mononoke*: Pocket Movie Guide
Hayao Miyazaki: *Spirited Away*: Pocket Movie Guide
Tim Burton : Hallowe'en For Hollywood
Ken Russell
Ken Russell: *Tommy*: Pocket Movie Guide
The Ghost Dance: The Origins of Religion
The Peyote Cult
Cixous, Irigaray, Kristeva: The *Jouissance* of French Feminism
Julia Kristeva: Art, Love, Melancholy, Philosophy, Semiotics and Psychoanalysis
Luce Irigaray: Lips, Kissing, and the Politics of Sexual Difference
Hélene Cixous I Love You: The *Jouissance* of Writing
Andrea Dworkin
'Cosmo Woman': The World of Women's Magazines
Women in Pop Music
HomeGround: The Kate Bush Anthology
Discovering the Goddess (Geoffrey Ashe)
The Poetry of Cinema
The Sacred Cinema of Andrei Tarkovsky
Andrei Tarkovsky: Pocket Guide
Andrei Tarkovsky: *Mirror*: Pocket Movie Guide
Andrei Tarkovsky: *The Sacrifice*: Pocket Movie Guide
Walerian Borowczyk: Cinema of Erotic Dreams
Jean-Luc Godard: The Passion of Cinema
Jean-Luc Godard: *Hail Mary*: Pocket Movie Guide
Jean-Luc Godard: *Contempt*: Pocket Movie Guide
Jean-Luc Godard: *Pierrot le Fou*: Pocket Movie Guide
John Hughes and Eighties Cinema
*Ferris Bueller's Day Off*: Pocket Movie Guide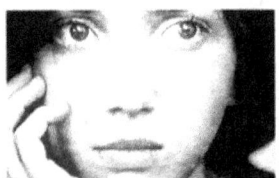
Jean-Luc Godard: Pocket Guide
The Cinema of Richard Linklater
Liv Tyler: Star In Ascendance
*Blade Runner* and the Films of Philip K. Dick
Paul Bowles and Bernardo Bertolucci
Media Hell: Radio, TV and the Press
An Open Letter to the BBC
Detonation Britain: Nuclear War in the UK
Feminism and Shakespeare
Wild Zones: Pornography, Art and Feminism
Sex in Art: Pornography and Pleasure in Painting and Sculpture
Sexing Hardy: Thomas Hardy and Feminism

CRESCENT MOON PUBLISHING
P.O. Box 1312, Maidstone, Kent, ME14 5XU, Great Britain. www.crmoon.com

cresmopub@yahoo.co.uk   www.crescentmoon.org.uk

www.ingramcontent.com/pod-product-compliance
Lightning Source LLC
Chambersburg PA
CBHW071246220526
45468CB00001B/15

\* 9 7 8 1 8 6 1 7 1 1 8 3 0 \*